McClane's
GAME FISH OF
NORTH AMERICA

McClane's
GAME FISH OF NORTH AMERICA

By

A. J. McCLANE

and

KEITH GARDNER

Paintings by FRANCIS WATKINS

Designed by

GARY GRETTER

BONANZA BOOKS
New York

This 1989 edition is published by Bonanza Books,
distributed by Crown Publishers, Inc., 225 Park
Avenue South, New York, New York 10003,
by arrangement with Times Books, a division
of Random House, Inc.

Printed and Bound in the United States of America

Library of Congress Cataloging-in-Publication Data

McClane, A. J. (Albert Jules), 1922-
   [Game fish of North America]
   McClane's game fish of North America / by
A. J. McClane and Keith Gardner.
   Reprint. Originally published: New York, N.Y. :
Times Books.
  c1984.
   Bibliography: p.
   Includes index
   1. Fishing—North America.   2. Fishes—
North America.
  I. Gardner, Keith, 1930– . II. Title.
  III. Title: Game and fish of North America.
  [SH462.M26 1989]
  799.1′097—dc20   89-1012
                               CIP

ISBN 0-517-68852-2

h g f e d c b a

CONTENTS

INTRODUCTION   vii

ATLANTIC SALMON   2

LANDLOCKED SALMON   16

BROOK TROUT   24

BROWN TROUT   36

RAINBOW TROUT   54

STEELHEAD   74

CUTTHROAT TROUT   94

ARCTIC GRAYLING   104

ARCTIC CHAR   114

LAKE TROUT   122

PACIFIC SALMON   130

NORTHERN PIKE and WHITEFISH   148

WALLEYE   158

MUSKELLUNGE   168

SMALLMOUTH BASS   180

LARGEMOUTH BASS   194

CONTENTS

BONEFISH   208

TARPON   222

PERMIT and OTHER JACKS   232

BARRACUDA   240

SHARKS   248

RED DRUM   258

BLUEFISH   266

SPOTTED SEATROUT and WEAKFISH   278

STRIPED BASS   288

SHAD   304

BLUE MARLIN, SWORDFISH and WHITE MARLIN   314

STRIPED MARLIN and BLACK MARLIN   332

SAILFISH and DOLPHIN   342

TUNA and MACKEREL   354

ACKNOWLEDGMENTS and CREDITS   366

BIBLIOGRAPHY   368

INDEX   370

INTRODUCTION

When President George Washington caused the first lighthouse to be built at Montauk Point, New York, on January 2, 1776, it was only a glimmer in the darkness of the New World, and the fact that it still beckons safe passage is now a nautical commonplace. But it also sheds light on one of the greatest sport-fishing ports in North America, a mere 100 miles from midtown Manhattan. On a day when the sea is singing its siren song, echoing to the repetitive leaps of a white marlin, hammering out showers of wet sparks in an electric charge of fury, making the transition from Times Square to Montauk is like visiting another planet. But how can we mention Montauk without also mentioning Hatteras, Destin, Palm Beach, Key West, Walker's Cay, Chub Cay, Cozumel, Cabo San Lucas, *ad infinitum.*

However you measure it, North America offers the greatest sport fishing in the world. No other continent has the incomparable variety of game fish, from polar to tropical species in habitats that range from torrential mountain streams to the vast current systems that flow through the western Atlantic and eastern Pacific. There are wonderful—indeed, unique—angling experiences to be enjoyed on other continents, and I have sampled the best of them, but nowhere else do we find so diverse a fauna—from Arctic char in the barren lands to bonefish on the great sand flats—than in North America, and all of it is accessible to the average traveler.

According to the last National Survey of Fishing (U.S. Fish and Wildlife Service) and a similar study made by the Canadian Government, some 60 million citizens enjoy approximately 900 million recreational days with rod-and-reel at a cost in excess of 70 billion dollars. This makes fishing our number one participation sport. Foreign visitors will have no difficulty in arranging a fishing trip, as there are more camps and resorts catering to the sportsman here than anywhere else in the world. Wilderness float trips, pack trips by horse or foot, big-game angling, stream trout fishing, surf fishing, houseboat cruises and numerous other adventures are within easy reach of any port of entry.

Describing all the angling locations on our continent in a volume of any size would be a feat comparable to carving Izaak Walton's 350 editions of *The Compleat Angler* on a pinhead. We have divided this book into thirty chapters, each covering a major game fish, including in some sections associate species either taxonomically related or unrelated just as they appear when you are actually fishing. It would be difficult to conceive of *not* catching dolphin in the same areas where sailfish are found, for example, or to cast to that trophy permit in waters where other carangids are absent.

In addition, fifty authors contributed their expertise to the geographic sections of this book. Their observations on specific locations are invaluable, as most of these writers, in addition to being skilled anglers, actually live in the regions they describe.

Although the Bahamas are not by any stretch of the imagination a titular part of North America, this sweep of island-dotted sea was pivotal in the development of saltwater angling and is so convenient to our coast and so heavily trafficked by stateside boats that their omission would leave an unbrushed corner in the continental picture. Thus, we have piscatorially adopted that Commonwealth.

I have written or edited several angling reference books and learned much in the process. A distillation of *McClane's Game Fish of North America* represents over a thousand years of collective angling experience, which is a unique dimension in Walton's art.

A J McClane

McClane's
GAME FISH OF
NORTH AMERICA

ATLANTIC SALMON

Salmo salar

One reason for fishing Atlantic salmon is to test your skill against what is potentially the largest fish that can be taken on a fly in fresh water. It is not likely that a weight comparable to the record 79 pounds, 2 ounces (beached on the Norwegian side of the Tana River in 1928) will ever surface again. But the remote possibility of a 60-pound fish still exists, and salmon of half this size are fairly common.

Back in the river after a long and mysterious journey in the ocean's depths, Walton's "king amongst gamefish" comes home in a royal dress of glittering mail to finish the long crusade to its natal stones. A spring or summer fish, it is full of violent energy. After years of escaping from otters, seals, mink, ospreys, nets, gigs, snares, traps and all the predatory fishes of the sea, a salmon returns to its familiar currents physiologically reprogrammed for life in fresh water. Troglodyte man painted its likeness on the walls of caves and carved its image in stone and bone, as though saying "this is what a fish should look like," even though their Cro-Magnon kitchen middens were full of cod and pike bones.

By the mid-twentieth century *Salmo salar* was a nearly extinct species in the United States. The history of its decline brought about by the Industrial Revolution is best described in Anthony Netboy's monumental work *The Atlantic Salmon— A Vanishing Species?* (Houghton Mifflin, New York, 1968). Although the salmon is once again beginning to prosper under various restoration programs in New England, its long-term survival is still in doubt. Ever since the late 1960s, a vast fleet of commercial fishermen using sophisticated electronic gear have been gill-netting the salmon's feeding grounds off Greenland and the Faroe and Lofoton islands, where the world's genetically different stocks converge. At the same time, river habitat is being destroyed by the sulfur and nitrogen oxides vented from modern industrial

Salmon fishing in the rivers of the Gaspé Peninsula is without peer. Once a playground of royalty, today, the Matapedia (above) is one of many classic waters available to the tourist angler.

ATLANTIC SALMON

plants burning fossil fuels. These oxides circulate with the great air masses that form our weather systems and, when moistened by vapor, shower down in the form of acid rain or snow, souring biosystems in which few aquatic organisms will grow. And with the spiraling cost of salmon in the marketplace, poaching has spread like a virus throughout the salmon's kingdom.

Elitists believe that angling will not survive without the incentive of aristocratic salmon clubs to assume the responsibility of preserving individual rivers, but clubs are dwindling in number and one gets the feeling that we are watching the *Titanic* sink under the wealthiest imaginable auspices.

As an angling journalist, I am often asked where the best salmon fishing can be found. After almost four decades of throwing Jock Scotts from Spain to Labrador, I have concluded that cost plays a factor; salmon fishing is expensive. Its cost is only exceeded by marlin fishing in Australia. Aside from the hobgoblins that frequently possess Salar's soul, there will be droughts and floods and other unpredictable phenomena that can leave one fishless on the classic waters of the world. If I were departing tomorrow, my destination would be Canada, on Quebec's Gaspé Peninsula, or one of the rivers on the north shore of the St. Lawrence, or even cold and foggy Labrador. Here, the price can be reasonable as compared to most European rivers. Even Iceland, which was a bargain basement fishery when I first went there in 1956, now requires Fort Knox as a personal piggy bank, and, despite a brilliant oligarchy of river managers, nobody can guarantee success.

Salmon fishing in North America differs from Europe in a variety of ways. With a few Quebec exceptions, Canadian rivers, as well as those in Maine, are restricted to fly-fishing only—natural or preserved baits, or metal lures of any kind, are prohibited. Another distinction is the type of tackle used. Among European anglers, the double-handed fly rod, in excess of 12 feet, is by far the most popular tool. However, shorter, single-handed rods of 8½ to 9½ feet are dominant in North America, and even lightweight 7½- to 8-foot graphite and boron rods are effectively fished in low water. If there is a standard for rivers of the western Atlantic, it would appear to be a 9-foot rod, calibered for a No. 8 or 9 line. In many North American rivers, the salmon come readily to a dry fly, even in the subarctic latitudes of Labrador. The theories advanced for their reluctance to surface rise in European streams[1] are legion. The ultimate difference, and I don't feel this is a

personal prejudice, is that salmon in North American rivers, particularly those taken in the Maritime provinces, are more consistently acrobatic when hooked. During my over three decades of salmon fishing on both sides of the Atlantic, I have never found European fish that provided the wild aerial displays that are common to Canadian streams. Undeniably, the length of time a salmon spends in the river, water temperature, current velocity, sexual maturation and genetic race affect an individual performance, but even a "black" or spent salmon (legally taken in some New Brunswick rivers) can justify their patronym *salar*, the "leaper." A bright Canadian fish of 18 to 28 pounds has no peer. I have taken salmon of all sizes, including several over 40 pounds in Norwegian fjords where the fish were only 6 or 8 miles from the sea, and seldom caught one that jumped and even then, never repetitively.

When salmon enter a river they are not seeking food. The fish occasionally roll or leap over the surface, but are not rising to insects, so the traditional concepts of fly-fishing have no value. There is no viable hatch to match and, therefore, it may take an hour or more to get a fish interested in the fly. This can become an Olympian test of endurance. On rare occasions, they will strike almost recklessly, a response that R. V. Righyni explained in his book, *Salmon Taking Times* (MacDonald, London, 1965), which cites the fluctuations of atmospheric pressure and the amount of dissolved oxygen in the water as the causes. Essentially, salmon fishing is a game of repetitive casting, until a fly of a given size and shape, worked at just the right depth and speed, is accepted. That master salmon angler, Lee Wulff, who has devoted half a century to this occult art, summed it up in his penultimate book, *The Atlantic Salmon* (Nick Lyons Books, New York, 1983):

> Neither this book nor any written word can describe exactly how a salmon fly should look nor how it should move to lure a salmon. To do this is no more possible than to describe adequately the taste of a particular apple or the shape of a cloud. Words will not do it but experience will so condition a fisherman that he can look at a fly as it is fished, either his own or that of another angler, and know that it is "right" for the fish. Lacking experience in judging the speed and drift of the wet fly, an angler could do worse than to study closely the fly of a competent angler and imitate him as well as possible, until he has some real experience of his own to go by.

Undeniably, there is an element of luck

DISTRIBUTION

---

[1] Atlantic salmon are taken occasionally on the dry fly in Great Britain, notably on Scotland's Spey River.

Angling author Art Lee takes a nice salmon on Richard's Pool in the Matapedia. Although double-handed rods are still used to some extent in Canada and almost exclusively in Europe, the light, single-handed fly rod is more popular in North America.

involved, but there is also a method of shuffling through the fly box that obviates the chance factor. The trick is to present different silhouettes, deep or shallow, floating high or low, or skimming the surface. Like some whimsical Nero, a big salmon may spend two or three weeks in a pool critically reviewing the flies of a hundred anglers before rising in a solid take. Even on days when they are coming to a "hot" pattern, repetitive casting to a visible fish, or at least in a known lie, is the basic tenet. There may be refusal rises, but if the fish shows any interest at all, it can be caught on the next cast, or on a different fly about 50 percent of the time.

Salmon Fishing in Practice

In North America, salmon fishing begins in May at the southern latitude of Maine's Penobscot River and starts as late as July in the Ungava Bay region of Nouvelle Quebec. As a rule, the rivers will be high and the currents strong. The tactical concept, particularly on big waters like the Moise, Matapedia, Restigouche and Grand Cascapedia, is to use flies in No. 2/0 and 3/0, often with double hooks to get them down deep. As the season progresses and the water warms, you can use smaller flies (No. 4 or 6 wet patterns) fished close to the surface. Most anglers agree that the distinction between fishing on the bottom and at the top occurs when the water temperature reaches 48°F to 50°F. If the river becomes very warm, then trout-sized flies in No. 10, 12 and even 14, fished wet or dry, are often productive. Autumn is an uncertain season; you may have to continue with summer methods if the river is low, but if cold fall rains have raised the level, then larger sunk patterns should be your choice. Of course, what is cold, what is warm, or high or low, is all relative, as subarctic rivers can be frigid even in summer and at low level torrential enough to

Dry-Fly-Fishing for Salmon

Fishing with the dry fly is strictly a North American technique. Although the fish have been caught on floating patterns in European waters, the chances of success are remote. On Icelandic rivers, dry flies tend to frighten rather than attract. However, in Maine and Canada the method is often extremely effective, especially late in the season. As a rule, dry-fly-fishing is considered most productive when our rivers warm to over 60°F (15.6°C) but temperature is probably less of an influence than the fact that water levels are usually low in summer. Therefore, the salmon are concentrated in smaller areas, which can be fished more effectively. The dry fly works just as well in cold Labrador rivers during low water periods.

For salmon, the dry fly is usually cast slightly upstream and across the current (as opposed to quartering downstream with the wet fly) and allowed to drift dead on the surface. If a fish has already been located at a downstream position, you can angle the cast down or even directly downstream to make short drifts on a slack line—this limits the length of the float. Drag is no problem; in fact, after the float is completed, a slowly dragging dry fly or one that is twitched over the

surface will sometimes provoke slashing rises.

It is important to follow the fly visually because a salmon will often make not one, but several false rises to a dry, bumping it with a closed mouth or balancing it on the end of its snout like a seal playing with a rubber ball or sinking it with its head or tail. If the angler strikes at these false rises (and on occasion a big one may come up a half dozen times), the fish will be put down. Obviously, a salmon must take the fly in its mouth before it can be hooked, but playful passes are not recognized by inexperienced anglers and can be misread even by veterans. Fortunately, most salmon will take the fly in a swift rush, especially in turbulent waters.

Some of the popular North American dry-fly patterns are the White Wulff, Royal Wulff, Irresistible, Bomber, Brown Bivisible, Muddler, Black Skater and MacIntosh. Atlantic salmon can be caught on very small dry flies (No. 14 and even 16), however, this requires a delicate tippet and an expert's skill. The popular sizes range from No. 4 to 12.

handle tugboat traffic. The rule I rely on is visual: Select the size fly that swims at the same speed as the current. A small, lightly dressed pattern will always swing around quicker than a large one in any given stream velocity. You must control its speed and depth to get a good presentation, and there's a considerable difference between water resistance on a fly of half an inch in length and one 3 inches long.

The usual procedure is to cast a wet fly across and downstream, at about a 45-degree angle. The line should fall as straight as possible to bring the fly under immediate tension, then form a slight belly so the current will swing the fly broadside over the salmon. If the cast falls slack, the fly may just sit there until an arc forms in the line, which suddenly drags the feathers over the fish at an exaggerated speed. It's important to keep the fly from lagging behind the line as it swings around in the current. A slack cast can be mended by rolling or lifting the line clear of the surface in an upstream direction, without disturbing the swim of

the fly; but this maneuver will frighten the fish if executed poorly.

The experienced angler fishes with his eyes as well as his hands. In slow water, for example, it may be necessary to lift the rod and strip line to put the fly under tension and keep it moving at the correct speed. Conversely, fast currents may require lowering the rod to play out a few yards of line to decrease it. What you want to avoid is accelerating drag, which ends with the fly whipping around out of control. At the end of the drift, the usual procedure is to retrieve the fly in short jerks and pauses. If this doesn't produce a strike, increase the fly's return speed on each playback. Occasionally, when working over fish that have been in the river for some weeks, a very fast retrieve will trigger solid strikes, especially in slow currents. In any event, if a salmon indicates some interest by moving toward the fly, no matter how brief, the fish will probably take if you duplicate that cast without altering its angle or length. If the fish doesn't respond after a reasonable period, rest the lie for 10 or 15 minutes before trying a different pattern or fly size. Bear in mind that while a No. 6 Butterfly may have achieved instant success in the pool above, as you progress downstream into new water, possibly into faster or staler currents, it may require a No. 10 in the same pattern to maintain a controlled drift.

Equally important to fishing technique is the knowledge that can only be acquired through a local guide or by long experience on a particular river. There is no universal rule concerning the visible characteristics of water that create a lie—it exists in many forms. The resting site (or lie) is a result of river hydraulics, which in various places allows the salmon to hold in the current with an economy of effort where it can remain almost motionless for long periods in its upstream journey. The water must also be at an optimum temperature with enough movement to supply adequate dissolved oxygen. In very hot weather, for example, a logical place to find salmon is near the mouth of a cold tributary stream. However, the lie may be nothing more than a slight depression below a log cribbing, the bulkhead of a bridge, a minor channel off the main current, a string of boulders in midstream, or just a projection of grassy bank. These are a few that come to mind—places where there is a change of flow, usually where a weak current and a strong current converge. As other fish move upstream, they follow exactly the same paths. These lies never remain vacant for very long, for even if a salmon is caught, or the fish continue traveling, a

Progressive Casting

Whether fishing with the wet fly, or dry fly, progressive casting is the key to catching salmon. Beginning with short casts, the angler lets his fly drift over known, or unseen lies, letting it swing downstream before retrieving and repeating the cast. If a fish doesn't show, the next series of casts should be lengthened a few feet, and then extended on subsequent casts until all the likely spots are covered. If a salmon flashes or moves near the fly, that particular cast should be repeated at exactly the same angle and distance. When one area is covered, the angler wades to the next drop and repeats the same casting pattern. While wading in shallow water, salmon can be approached much more closely than trout, so be alert even when making very short casts. Salmon only panic when the angler approaches from deep water, seemingly threatening their escape.

new tenant or even a school will choose the identical position to rest. Casting blind is seldom productive without that all-important local knowledge of where the fish will hold. Quite often, half a mile or more of river may be consistently fishless in that salmon, finding no suitable lie, pass through quickly on their migration. And as water levels drop from high to low during the season, the exact location used by the fish may change and indeed even be abandoned in feeble currents. Few Americans, except those who live in coastal Maine, have the opportunity to observe a salmon river's metamorphosis day by day, since most of us are limited to perhaps two weeks for a trip. Frequently, weather conditions are "abnormal" and the lies that produced last year are not holding fish now; the salmon may pause, but not long enough to be "taking" fish as they hurry along on their journey.

Salmon Fishing in the United States

The first record of an Atlantic salmon caught on the fly in North America was that of British Colonel John Enys, on the Saranac River, New York, in 1787. In Colonial times, salmon thrived in all the Ontario and Champlain tributaries that drained into the St. Lawrence River. The salmon's southernmost distribution extended as far as the Connecticut River, which was the most productive fishery on our continent, despite the fact that both the Hudson and Delaware rivers had sporadic small runs (these were returns from plantings made in the early eighteenth century).

The proliferation of dams and pollution during the next century gradually destroyed our salmon habitats to the point that angling for the species became almost nonexistent. The state of Maine began a restoration program in 1948 to reestablish the fishery, and today there are similar projects under way throughout New England, which offer some hope, optimistic though it may be, that more Americans will know the joys of catching this noble game fish before the end of the next decade. It is expected that by 1986, when the last fish ladder is in place at Wilder, Vermont, salmon fishing will again exist in the 407-mile length of the Connecticut River. There is no question that the angling will never be what it once was—a game played in lonely places, with only a vagrant moose for an audience.

At present, Maine is the only state with fishable

Salmon Flies

Hair-wing salmon flies evolved in North America during the 1930s. Lacking the exotic ingredients for tying traditional British feather-wing patterns (which may require as many as twenty-four different materials in the Jock Scott, and exotica such as macaw, amherst pheasant, bustard and chatterer feathers), the frugal, but innovative, flytiers of Maine and the Maritimes simplified their patterns and began using native materials such as bear, moose, deer, skunk and squirrel hair. This resulted in *a whole new genre of highly effective salmon flies such as the Rat series. Although simplified hair-wing versions of traditional patterns (some date back to England in 1725) such as the Silver Doctor, Dusty Miller, Jock Scott and Black Dose lack the beauty of the originals, they are still effective.*

Popular Atlantic salmon flies tied by the Orvis Company, Manchester, Vermont.

populations of Atlantic salmon. There are eight rivers officially designated as salmon fisheries: the Penobscot, Narraguagus, Machias, East Machias, Dennys, Pleasant, Union and Sheepscot. These are public waters where an angler may wait two hours or more to take his turn at popular sites, such as the Cable Pool on the Narraguagus or the Line Pool on the Machias. Although a carnival atmosphere prevails, about 3,000 salmon were caught in 1982. Maine once had thirty-five salmon rivers, so restoration of the total resource is a long-term project. The deep and swift-flowing Penobscot is the state's most productive river today, and there is every indication that it will again become a major fishery.

Salmon Fishing in Canada

There are some 400 salmon rivers in eastern Canada, the greatest resource of its kind in the world, and more and more are being liberalized or open to public fishing in Quebec, which began disbanding private club waters in the 1970s. The term "public" fishing is, of course, used in a qualified sense. On the eleven rivers now available in Quebec's Gaspé Peninsula, fishing permits are offered on a daily fee basis at either non-reserved or reserved locations. The non-reserved permits can be had at a very modest fee. They will for

Carl Tillmans with a 20-pound Moise salmon taken on a 9-foot fly rod with a No. 8 weight-forward line, which is typical tackle on North American rivers. However, early in the season, when heavy currents prevail and big 2/0 or 3/0 flies are needed, a 9½- to 10½-foot rod with No. 10 sinking-tip line is more suitable.

example, allow you to fish eighty-three pools on the Matane River, or forty-one pools on the fabled Matapedia. In addition, you will need a Quebec salmon fishing license. Naturally, non-reserved waters are crowded at times, especially in the holiday month of July. However, for the serious angler, as opposed to the casual tourist, reserved waters are preferable. The reserved permits are generally on more productive pools in rivers such as the Cascapedia, Patapedia, Dartmouth, York and St. Jean. The number of anglers allowed on these reserved sections is limited, which greatly reduces the fishing pressure. Reserved beats are more costly, but the higher rates will include a guide and canoe, and on some rivers, meals and lodging. For information, you can contact the Department of Leisure, Hunting and Fishing, 150 Boulevard St. Cyrille Est., Quebec G1R 4Y1.

In an easily accessible province like New Brunswick, there are numerous camps offering accommodations and fishing. There are twenty-five camps on the Miramichi River alone. As in Europe, there are also clubs and associations that own or lease stretches of river that offer angling on a rental basis, even on prime waters such as the Restigouche or Miramichi. And there are public waters in the Maritimes, especially in Nova Scotia and Newfoundland, that require nothing more than a valid license. Canada also has salmon camps that can only be reached by aircraft in the subarctic reaches of Quebec and Labrador that provide first-class angling at a package price. Many outfitters advertise in the classified sections of the major American outdoor magazines, but the most comprehensive listing can be obtained by joining the Atlantic Salmon Association (1434 St. Catherine Street West, Suite 109, Montreal, Quebec H3G 1R4). It would be impossible to describe all the salmon rivers in Canada, but a sampler of some of its outstanding waters follows.

Restigouche River

The Restigouche is, without question, one of North America's major salmon rivers in both size and importance. It gathers its waters in two provinces—the lower St. Lawrence region of Quebec, as well as the entire northern portion of New Brunswick. This watershed is so extensive that the Restigouche boasts eight recognized salmon rivers among its tributaries, including well-known waters such as the Patapedia, the Kedgwikck and the Upsalquich. Even the famous Matapedia River is technically a tributary of the Restigouche.

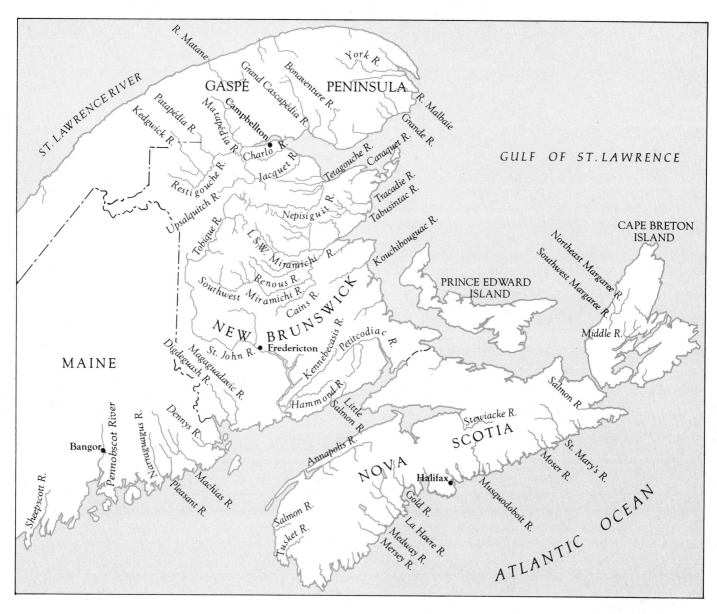

As in the case with other major rivers flowing into the Baie des Chaleurs, Restigouche River fish are big. The average size is approximately 20 pounds, and the chances of killing salmon in the 35- to 40-pound class are excellent during the first half of the three-month season, which closes at the end of August. The first run of salmon usually enters the Restigouche after the first week of June, and consists mostly of large, multiple spawners. To call it a run is an understatement—it's more like an invasion. Within twenty-four hours after the first fish is caught in the tidal pools, every bit of holding water as far as 50 miles upstream yields salmon.

The prime time on the Restigouche is June 15th to July 15th in normal years, but during this period the water is generally murky, so anglers use forward-taper sinking lines or sinking tips to get the flies down to the salmon. No. 1/0 flies are commonly used with 20-pound-test leaders, and the Rat series are among the most popular dressings (especially the Rusty Rat, Silver Rat and Black Rat). During the first half of the season, the pools on the Restigouche are unrecognizable, and

most fishing is done on what appears to be nothing more than just a flat stretch of water. As a matter of fact, salmon seem to rest virtually anywhere in the world until the water drops. All fishing on the Restigouche is done from Gaspé riverboats, where the guides simply hold the boats within easy casting distance of known lies. During low water conditions after mid-July, the fish retire to recognized holding pools such as Brandy Brook and Matapedia Pool. The latter is also known as Millionaire's Pool, and as many as 2,000 salmon have been counted in it at one time. When the water clears in July, most anglers revert to No. 4, 6 and 8 double hooks, and 10- to 12-pound leader. The Rat patterns are still productive, but the Orange Blossom, Silver Doctor and Green Highlander are also necessary additions to the fly box. Grilse, or one-sea-winter fish, generally show up after July 10th and in August, a fresh run of first-time spawners in the 8- to 16-pound range come in.

The tidal pools of the Restigouche are controlled by the Quebec government, which charges a daily access fee. The remainder of the

Maine and the Maritimes

Presently, Maine has the only self-sustaining runs of fishable salmon populations, dominated by those of the Penobscot River. The quality of angling to the north and east encompasses some of the world's most productive rivers, such as the Restigouche, the Grand Cascapedia and the Miramichi. New Brunswick and the Gaspé attract a great number of tourist fishermen and accommodations can be found on or near all the major rivers.

river, largely in New Brunswick, is split between some twenty-five private clubs with exclusive fishing rights (Crown reserve water and freehold water). Many of the clubs make unbooked water available to nonmembers, but the waiting list is often long for the best beats. A few of the clubs advertise in fishing magazines.

Grand Cascapedia

The Grand Cascapedia is considered one of the four best Atlantic salmon rivers in the world. Buffered against social changes by private clubs until 1982, salmon fishing on this river is a sport with well-defined norms of good sportsmanship. It is a big river, originating deep in the Chic Choc Mountains and flowing halfway across Quebec's Gaspé Peninsula to empty into the Baie des Chaleurs. In its lower sections, the Cascapedia slips over shallow gravel beds and numerous sand bars; in its upper reaches are deep, dark water pools carved out of bedrock.

Grand Cascapedia fish are big. The yearly average range is between 20 and 24 pounds, with a number of salmon over 40 pounds killed every season. The record salmon was a 55-pound fish, taken in 1939. Salmon equally large are seen in shallow water pools every year, though none have been tempted by a fly since.

An early run of big salmon enter the Grand Cascapedia during the spate water of May, and they move quickly into headwater sanctuaries. The first fishable run, also consisting of large multiple spawners, shows up around June 10th to provide good fishing in the Englehardt Home Pool

and Middle Camp 424. Within the week, Big John, Home Pool at Three Island, Berry Mountain Pool and Parson's Pool produce fish.

Prime time for the Cascapedia is the last week of June and the first few days of July. Water levels are high and all fishing must be done from 26-foot Gaspé riverboats with heavy equipment and big flies. Rods are necessarily 9½ to 10½ feet long in order to cast the big No. 2/0 and 3/0 double-hook flies. Standard leader is 25-pound-test, and any less than 200 yards of backing is considered inadequate for catching these 30- to 40-pound salmon in heavy water. Featherwing dressings of the Durham Ranger and Lady Amherst are productive patterns; the Dusty Miller and Yellow Canary are also popular. As the water clears and the levels drop in July, anglers go to smaller sizes of the same patterns, in addition to the Night Hawk, Blue Charm, Cascapedia Special and Kinsey Special. The most important elements appear to be Jungle Cock eyes and red lacquer on the heads. Big brown deer hair Bombers and Wulffs are popular dry flies.

The Cascapedia is a changeable river after mid-July. A prolonged dry spell can reduce it to a wan specter of its former flow; but rain in the headwaters can swell the river overnight. The better pools upstream (Forks, Brush Pile, Murdock, Big Joanathan and Jam Rapids) can be fished by wading, though anglers must be aware of water level fluctuations at all times.

In 1982, the Société Cascapedia took over management of the river with a mandate to develop the sport fishery. The organization consists of the Maria Indian band at the mouth,

Quebec's North Shore

The classic rivers of Quebec's north shore of the St. Lawrence offer a wide range of river size and type. Sparsely settled, particularly east of Sept-Iles, some rivers can only be reached by plane or boat in the summer months. Large multiple spawners are most common in the Moise and decrease in abundance with a decrease in river size. Anticosti Island produces mostly small fish but the landscape is idyllic.

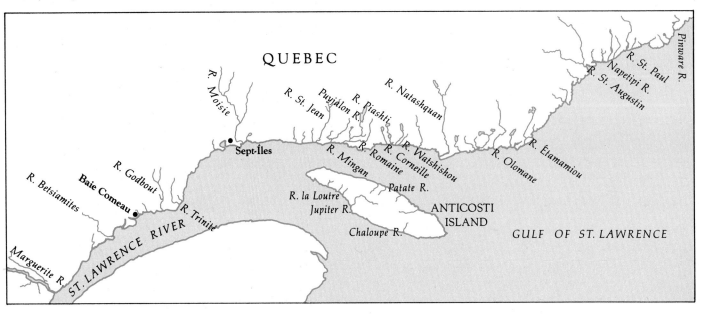

the municipalities along its banks and the property owners. Daily fishing by wading, as well as from a boat with a guide, is available through the management group. Campgrounds with facilities are located at the mouth of the Cascapedia. Fishing privileges and accommodations can also be found at Horse Island camp and other outfitters' camps along the river.

Matapedia River

With its headwaters almost within sight of the St. Lawrence, the Matapedia River flows about 60 miles across the Gaspé Peninsula to join the Restigouche at the western tip of the Baie des Chaleurs. The Matapedia is among Quebec's most famous and productive salmon rivers with an annual catch of about 2,000 salmon, most of these over 20 pounds.

Accessibility is another reason for its popularity—more than three-quarters of the Matapedia is controlled by the provincial government, which offers water that can be fished for the price of a daily pass, and some choice water that must be reserved in advance. The latter, known as the Glenn Emma-MacDonnell Sector, with twenty marked pools, is limited to ten rods a day (with a maximum of two rods per party for four days at a time), and these must be booked early in January. Three fishing clubs also hold leases on the river. The Matapedia is a wide, running river and in the lower half, the pools can only be fished properly from boats, especially in high water during the first three or four weeks of the season. From roughly the village of Heppel through to the top pools, wading is possible once the spring spate settles down.

The first run of big fish enters the Matapedia during the third week of May, before the season opens June 1st. Most of these big, multiple spawners head straight up into the headwater sanctuaries, but a few stragglers provide some fishing as soon as the season opens. Contrary to logical progression, the best fishing during the first part of June is in the upper pools, rather than the lower. A ten-day lull takes place on the Matapedia during mid-June, but at the end of the third week, a heavy run of salmon enters the river. These fish are in the 16- to 25-pound range, with the occasional 40-pounder among them. Local guides recommend fairly heavy tackle, with 20-pound-test leaders. Favored fly patterns are the Lady Amherst, Green Highlander, Cosseboom and Silver Rat, dressed on No. 2/0 double hooks during murky water. As the water clears, the Rusty Rat becomes more productive.

Lawlor Rock and Home Pool on the Tobique Salmon Club's lease are among the most productive early in the season. Mann's Pool and Home Pool at the Cold Spring Camp also produce

Hand tailing a salmon on the La Loutre River is but a small part of the angling experience. Canadian rivers in their primitive beauty offer a wealth of enjoyment "far from the madding crowd."

ATLANTIC SALMON

salmon regularly. In the Glenn Emma-MacDonnell Sector, upper and lower, McNeill's and Edgar's are among the best. Beyond that sector, the best pools are the Covered Bridge Pool at Routhierville, upper and lower Adam's at St. Florence and the Salmon Hole at Heppel.

Fishing becomes difficult toward mid-July, even though there are more fish in the river. Flies, such as the Silver Rat, Rusty Rat, Green Highlander, the Blue Rat and the Blue Charm featherwing (dressed on No. 4, 6 and 8 hooks), are favored. Dry flies like the Bomber and White Wulff are effective. Though there are generally no strong runs of salmon on the Matapedia during the second half of the season, fish come in regularly right through to the end of August—mostly first-year spawners in the 14- to 16-pound range. Grilse (roughly one third of the fish registered on the Matapedia every summer) become a nuisance after the first week of July.

Most salmon anglers who fish the government-run waters congregate at either the Restigouche Hotel in the town of Matapedia, or at the Auberge de la Montagne in Routhierville, halfway up the river.

The three private clubs—Cold Spring Camp,

Rivers of The North

The wilderness region of Labrador and New Quebec offers superb salmon fishing in swift, bouldery streams. Most of these waters are reached by air via Fort Chimo or Goose Bay. This is hilly, often foggy country, where lichens and mosses carpet vast coniferous forests. There are fly-in camps on every major river and while the salmon may not reach sizes comparable to those of the Gaspé, they are abundant. Large brook trout and Arctic char are common to this region, providing a variety of sport.

Tobique Salmon Club and the Restigouche Salmon Club—control some 12 miles of the Matapedia. In the past, they have sold available time not booked by members, and have now become more like outfitters. Though daily fees include meals, accommodations, guides and boats, they are still expensive.

Moisie River

The 220-mile long Moisie is considered the north Canadian coast's most beautiful river. From its headwaters, deep in the Quebec wilderness, it flows through a steep-sloped valley to the St. Lawrence, 15 miles east of Sept Iles; at its mouth, the river is almost half a mile wide. Moisie salmon are big and plentiful. The annual catch amounts to some 1,200 fish, averaging about 16 pounds, but fish in excess of 35 pounds are caught each season. When commercial fishing was still permitted in the estuary, 60-pound salmon were occasionally taken in the nets. The present rod-and-reel record is 45 pounds, 2 ounces.

Most big salmon are caught in the public sector at the mouth of the river in early June. (This is tidal water with no clearly defined pools.) Anglers are permitted to fish with spinning or trolling tackle in Sector B of the Moisie, located downstream from the Highway 138 bridge. Above the bridge, in Sector A, only flies are permitted. Moisie River salmon normally enter the river immediately after the spring spate subsides, usually around June 7th, and the fishing remains good to the end of the month. However, the spring runoff is a deciding factor; even though salmon may appear in the estuary as early as May 19th, they will not ascend the river during high water conditions. The portion of the Moisie from the end of Sector A to the mouth of the Joseph River, a tributary stream located about 30 miles upriver, is controlled by private clubs with exclusive fishing rights. Prime time is the month of June. One of the best salmon pools in the world—the Ouapetec Pool—is located in this stretch.

The Upper Moisie Fishing Club, an outfitter's lodge, is located upstream and has accommodations for visiting anglers. Though a few fish reach this sector earlier, the best fishing starts around July 7th. Pointe Pool, located just above base camp, is a good producer, and while Kachapahun Pool, also near the camp, is a difficult pool to fish properly, it holds some big salmon. Coapoacho Pool, located some 90 miles inland, has become an excellent pool since the construction of the fishway at the Falls. Observers

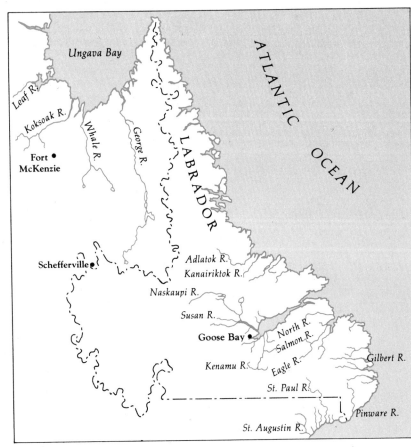

say that at the height of the season, there are often more than 1,000 salmon in this pool. The construction of the fishway has opened an additional 40 miles of virgin salmon water, most of it open to the public.

Since the Moisie is a big river, most fishing is done from boats by necessity. In early season, sinking lines are favored, but as water levels drop, floating lines come into use. Ten-foot graphite rods are ideal, and 150 yards of 20-pound Dacron backing is the absolute minimum. Since the water is heavily tannin stained, leaders can be fairly heavy—up to 20-pound-test tippet, depending on the size fly used—and between 9 and 16 feet long. Throughout June, the salmon are tempted with No. 2/0 double-hook patterns, such as the Black Dose and Lady Amherst. Beyond the tidal waters, early season anglers start with No. 4 double hooks and gradually drop to sizes 6, 8 and 10 by the end of June. The Olin Black-and-Gold and Bates' Killer account for more salmon than any other dressing. Next in order of preference are the Akroyd, the Moonlight and the Rat series. In the upper waters, dry flies dressed on No. 12, 14 and 16 hooks are effective.

Sectors A and B in the tidal waters are open to all anglers on an unlimited basis and are accessible by road. Food and lodging are available in nearby Sept Iles. The next 30 miles or so are private water, accessible for the most part only by invitation. However, seven of the Moisie Salmon Club's better pools have been made available to members of the Association de Protection de la Rivière Moisie. Club and outfitter waters, along with the open sector above the fishway, are accessible only by float plane.

York River

The York rises in the highlands of the Gaspé's north shore and brawls its way 70 miles to Gaspé Bay at the tip of the peninsula. At one time, most of its fishable waters were the preserve of sporting royalty, but during the 1970s the Quebec government disbanded private clubs on the York. Today, all but 10 miles of the river are open to the public.

The public sector of the York is part of a ZEC (an acronym for the French term "controlled exploitation zone"), which is managed by the Société de Gestion des Rivières York et Dartmouth (P.O. Box 1446, Gaspé, Quebec, GOC 1RO). Daily passes and season memberships are available, but some sectors of the river have a restricted number of rods per day and advance reservations are necessary. One private club maintains riparian rights on the lower 10 miles where fishing is restricted to club members and their guests. The Ash Inn, more commonly known as Baker's Hotel, has a small beat below

The broad and turbulent George River in New Quebec is fished mainly by wading or from shore. Camps here are accessible only by air. Despite its remote location, the river is very popular. Inuit (Eskimo) guides make skilled companions on the George. Salmon are seldom large but an abundance of 8- to 12-pound fish provides memorable sport.

the club and fishing is available to patrons of the inn. For reservations, write to the establishment (P.O. Box 160, Gaspé Sud, Quebec, COC 1RO). Anglers fishing the ZEC waters can find excellent accommodations at one of the many hotels and motels in the town of Gaspé, especially during the prime period. Campgrounds with facilities are also available nearby.

The first run of fish enters the York around June 10th in normal years, but it takes them four or five days to reach the public ZEC waters where the best fishing usually occurs between June 20th and the beginning of July. At this time, the fish are bright and strong and the water conditions excellent. In July, the water starts to drop dramatically and warm-weather fishing conditions prevail. In spite of this, a good angler who knows salmon will consistently take fish right through to the end of August when the season closes. Key Pool is tops on the entire ZEC water, producing salmon from the time the fish enter the river to the season closing. Grand Fork is another good pool, the Mississippi is worthwhile and the Mountaineer is also productive. All major pools are well marked along the road. Lesser pools usually have

Public Rivers in Newfoundland

There are 135 salmon rivers on the island portion of the province (30 more in mainland Labrador) open to public fishing. Although most are heavily fished, the island offers considerable sport to about 20,000 licensed anglers, with a catch dominated by grilse. Camps are found on all major rivers.

maintained trails leading to them.

At almost any point along the York, a good caster can put his fly on the opposite bank with a double-haul, yet this stream produces a modest number of salmon that exceed 30 pounds. The average weighs 12 to 14 pounds.

Standard equipment, consisting of a 9-foot graphite rod, loaded with a No. 8- or 10-weight line, 150 yards of Dacron backing and a 9-foot tapered leader of 12-pound-test monofilament is adequate. Sinking tip lines will often produce results when the salmon are reluctant to rise to a surface fly. Favorite fly patterns on the York are the Rusty Rat, Silver Rat and Blue Charm—double hooks during high water and singles later. In June, most anglers use No. 4 flies, but as the season progresses they drop to 6, 8 and 10. A favorite local wet fly is the Major Briggs made with a tip of oval silver tinsel, a golden pheasant tail, a body of peacock herl and a black-and-white hair wing.

George River

Ever since 1956, when a tent camp was established on the George River, anglers have been flying north to enjoy the raw beauty of Inuit country and often some of the best angling in New Quebec. Rising along the Quebec-Labrador border, the George wanders north for some 250 miles, gathering strength with every tributary, to empty into Ungava Bay. The only settlement is at its mouth—an Inuit village called George River Settlement by the natives and Port Nouveau Quebec on recent maps.

The major run of salmon enters the George River during the last week of July, and often covers 20 to 25 miles a day, reaching the middle camps by early August. Once the first run has entered fresh water, the George quickly fills with fish. Despite the remoteness of this river, it accounted for roughly 10 percent of Quebec's total annual catch in normal years. These salmon average in the 8- to 10-pound class, though the chances of taking salmon between 12 and 15 pounds are good. The upper limit appears to be about 25 pounds.

As productive as it is, the George is a difficult river to fish properly. The current is strong and the boulder-strewn shallows too dangerous to permit wading in most places. Fishing is done from outcroppings or boulders close to shore. Boats are used principally for transportation. Few pools, as we know them, exist on the George. The river is basically flat and featureless, and the salmon seek

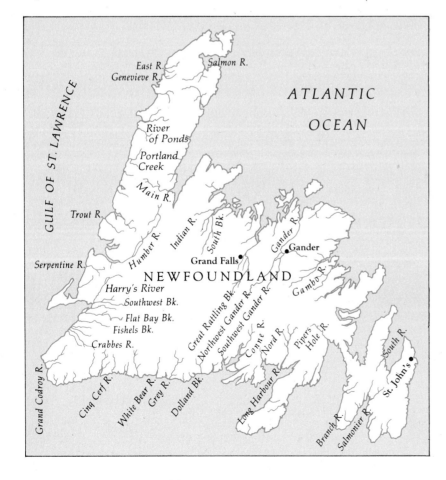

areas where the current flow is to their liking. Changes in water levels can alter this flow enough to change the salmon lies from one day to the next.

The first real holding water on the George is at Helen's Falls, where anglers can find some of the best salmon fishing. The pool at the base of the falls virtually always holds salmon eager to take a fly. Naturally, with the fishing as good as it is, Helen's Falls Fishing Camp is booked solid from year to year. The camp is one of five outfitters catering to salmon anglers on the George River, and there is another on the Depas River, a major tributary. All camps provide lodging, meals, guides and boats as part of their package.

The most effective fly patterns on the George are either black or green in color, or a combination of both, such as the Black Bear Green Butt. No. 4 and 6 hooks are most suitable, including double hooks to provide weight in the more turbulent pools.

There are three other salmon river systems in the Ungava region: the Leaf, Koksoak and the Whale. In common with the George, these are reached by bush plane from Fort Chimo. Canada's northernmost salmon camp is on the Delay River, a tributary to the Koksoak.

Miramichi River

The 450-mile long Miramichi River meanders northeast through New Brunswick to the St. Lawrence River and is one of the most popular and productive waters in Canada. In years past, the river system, which includes the Main Southeast Branch, Little Southwest Branch and the Northwest Branch, has produced up to 25,000 salmon—one of the most viable fisheries in the world.[2] Grilse of 3 to 5 pounds (one-year sea fish) once totally dominated the catch, but there have been an increasing number of large salmon caught since the 1970s in the 18- to 30-pound class.

The first runs of salmon enter the Miramichi about June 15th, and with sufficient summer rain, continue to arrive through mid-July. Hot August weather generally brings a low-water period and the fishing conditions are difficult. With cooling September temperatures and rising water levels, bright, late-run fish arrive. This is often one of the best periods of the season, which closes on October 15th. Three of the Miramichi tributaries, the swift flowing Renous, the ledgy Dungarvon and the tannin-stained Cains, produce good summer fishing, but the latter is best known as an autumn river. The Cains is slow flowing and particularly suited to the dry fly.

The Miramichi is one of the few Canadian streams from which black salmon (kelts) are legally taken. The survival ratio of post-spawners returning to the sea is low in this river and consequently, fish that have overwintered are a negative factor in maintaining the stock. Although no longer silver in color, or prime in flesh, these salmon are active when hooked and provide sport for many anglers. The black salmon season begins right after spring thaw (about April 15th).

Popular fly patterns on the Miramichi include the Buck Bug, Cosseboom (green and silver), Butterfly, Conrad, Black Dose, Hairy Mary and the Rat series in No. 4 to 12 sizes during normal water conditions. Larger flies in the 0 sizes are effective in high, spring water for the black salmon.

[2] During the four-year period from 1979 to 1982 the reported angling catch varied from 17,493 to 18,990, a reflection of world decline, but still a very substantial number.

15

LANDLOCKED SALMON

Salmo salar

T hat polished cleric the Reverend
Henry Van Dyke, author of
Fisherman's Luck (Charles Scribner's
Sons, 1899), offered this paean to the landlocked
salmon:

> *Thou art not to be measured by quantity but by
> quality, and thy five pounds of pure vigour will
> outweigh a score of pounds of flesh less vitalized by
> spirit. Thou feedest on the flies of the air, and thy
> food is transformed into an aerial passion for flight,
> as thou springest across the pool, vaulting toward
> the sky. Thine eyes have grown large and keen by
> peering through the foam, and the feathered hook
> that can deceive thee must be deftly tied and
> delicately cast. Thy tail and fins, by ceaseless
> contact with the rapids, have broadened and
> strengthened, so that they can flash thy slender body
> like a living arrow up the fall. As Launcelot among
> the knights, so art thou among the fish, the plain
> armoured hero, the sun-burnt champion of the
> water folk.*

I doubt if the fish ever gets sunburned, as the
weather always seems to be pouring rain or
generating a heavy fog whenever I venture into
landlock country, but the good Reverend caught
the spiritual values of a fish "begat by the old
salmon of the sea."

In the Montagnais Indian language, the
landlocked salmon is known as *winanishe*—or
ouinaniche, according to the old French spelling,
now *ouananiche* or literally "little brother of the
salmon." The etymology traced to the Cree root
wan means "to lose or mistake" and in the allied
tongue of the Ojibway *waninishka* is to "go around
by a circuitous route." *Ishe* is an Indian
diminutive, so what we really have collectively is a
"little lost brother of the salmon," which is
perhaps more descriptive of the fish than our name
landlocked; while some populations are physically
isolated with no access to the sea, others could
readily migrate to a marine environment, yet for

A landlocked salmon comes to the fly on Maine's west branch of the Penobscot River. Only mystique and angling technique separate this non-migratory form of Salmo salar *from the anadromous Atlantic salmon.*

17

LANDLOCKED SALMON

evolutionary reasons they remain in fresh water. Quebec biologists Gaétan Hayeur and Gilles Shooner discovered a population of "estuarine" Atlantic salmon in the Koksoak and its tributaries, the Caniapiscau[1] and Mélèzes rivers (1978). Although dominantly a watershed of sea-run fish, an estimated 32 percent do not migrate seaward during maturation and a significant number remain in fresh water, or move down to the Koksoak estuary between repeated spawnings. The biologists suggest that this may be an adaptation to severe environmental conditions (the Koksoak drainage is the northernmost limit of *salar* in North America), which were geographically more widespread in the postglacial epoch. There is no taxonomic difference between a sea-run salmon and a landlocked salmon; the latter does not achieve the great weights of an ocean migrant; however, in some modern fisheries "little brother" attains very substantial sizes (individual fish often exceed the stream average for anadromous salmon). Although the landlocked salmon is not recognized by the International Game Fish Association, nor the American Fisheries Society, as a species distinct from the Atlantic salmon (*Salmo salar*), in the angler's mind it is a totally different quarry with a mystique, tradition and life history entirely its own.

DISTRIBUTION

The landlocked salmon was first described at Sebago Lake in Maine (it was not native to all the state's waters, even absent from famed Moosehead Lake, where it was introduced in 1896) and given the subspecific scientific name *Salmo salar sebago*, while the ouananiche held the trinominal *Salmo salar ouananiche*. However, any distinction in shape and coloration (some Labrador and Quebec populations are longer and darker in color) is due to environmental conditions after countless thousands of years of isolation in diverse habitats. Many large landlocked salmon (10 to 20 pounds) were caught before the turn of the century in Moosehead, Rangely and Fish River lakes, culminating in a 22½-pound fish taken at Sebago Lake in 1907. The exceptional sizes of these early-day fish may be due to a more abundant food supply, or rapid growth due to stocking in new environments, or even the presence of sea-run salmon in watersheds that were not blocked by dams at the time. Although Quebec's *winanishe* were often reported in comparable sizes, Dr. Leroy M. Yale (*The Land of the Winanishe*, Charles

Scribner's Sons, 1897) made this observation:

> In railway and hotel prospectuses, the winanishe weighs from 5 to 14 pounds. In Lake St. John and the Grande Décharge, the average is two and a half; 4-pounders are large, and not too plentiful, while 6-pounders are scarce.
>
> Now and then solitary fish of great size are seen, old habitants dating from "les premières années" when "ça en bouillait, Monsieur, des grosses comme des carcajous" (it just boiled, sir, with ones as big as wild cats), but they are intensely wary and carefully guarded by the demon of ill luck. In Maine today, most landlocked salmon taken by anglers run from 1½ to 4½ pounds (14 to 22 inches in length). The larger fish are usually seven years old, which, with rare exceptions, is their terminal age in Maine waters. In those years when food is abundant (smelt populations fluctuate), these fish may reach 6 to 10 pounds. Remote Quebec watersheds such as the Kaniapiskau River and some eastern United States lakes such as New York's Lake George and Lake Champlain presently produce fish in the 10- to 18-pound range, which is clearly in the "big brother" class.

Historically, landlocked salmon were introduced from Maine to nearly every state in the Union beginning as early as 1874—as far south as South Carolina and as far west as California. Virtually all of these transplants were unsuccessful except in New Hampshire, Vermont and New York. In Canada, as in Maine, the fish occurred naturally in Labrador, Newfoundland, Quebec, New Brunswick, Nova Scotia and in both Lake Ontario and Lake Champlain. Although many foreign introductions were attempted, the only fishery established outside of North America was in Argentina, where landlocked salmon thrived in several watersheds, fattening on a diet of freshwater crabs and crayfish. Probably the most productive river was the Traful, flowing from Lake Traful to the Estancia Primavera, certainly one of the most beautiful waters I have ever fished with numerous 8- to 12-pound salmon. There is a photo in Leander McCormick's book *Fishing Round the World* (Charles Scribner's Sons, New York, 1937) of Guy Dawson holding a 25-pound "Sebago" (the Argentinian stock came from Maine's Sebago Lake) taken from the Traful in the early 1930s. There are disparate native landlocked salmon populations such as the so-called Saimma salmon, endemic to Finland and Russia, and the Gullspang salmon found in Sweden. Compared to a silvery Maine landlock, the Saimma strain, at least those few I have caught, is unusual in being sparsely

[1]Alternate spelling on different maps: "Kaniapiskau." Camp uses the K (probably phonetic Cree Indian).

spotted and having a mauve and yellow coloration. The Gullspang strain, experimentally stocked in Lake Michigan, reportedly attains weights up to 60 pounds, and although several fish exceeding 30 pounds were caught by trollers near Ludington during the 1981 season, there have been no returns since. The present record for landlocked salmon (Atlantic salmon line-class record for 20-pound-test) is 32 pounds taken near Ludington in July 1981.

Landlocked salmon occur in more than 200 lakes and streams in Maine. The most productive of these are Eagle, Square, Long and St. Froid lakes in Aroostook County; Schoodic, Love and West Grand lakes in Washington County; Sebago Lake in Cumberland County; Moosehead Lake in Piscataquis County and Rangley Lake in Franklin County. Both East Grand Lake and Spednic Lake, which share the border with New Brunswick, are excellent salmon fisheries and have produced fish up to 10 pounds in recent seasons. Outstanding streams include the Moose River, Magalloway, Rapid River, Fish River, Crooked River, Cold Stream, Kennebago River and the West Branch of the Penobscot. Although turbulent Grand Lake Stream is a relatively short (3 miles) thoroughfare between West Grand Lake and Big Lake, it produces numerous small landlocks to the dry fly.

Elsewhere in the United States, New Hampshire's Lake Winnepesaukee and the Androscoggin, Upper Connecticut and Merrymeeting rivers provide modest salmon fishing. Vermont's Lake Memphremagog and Lake Champlain (shared by New York and its tributary streams: the Saranac and Bouquet rivers) are especially productive. Lake Champlain with its tremendous food supply produces faster-growing salmon than Maine, with three year olds at 21 inches, exceeding 3 pounds in weight; evidently this population has a longer life span as some ten-year-old fish have been reported. Lake Ontario, which supported salmon since ancient times (they became extinct between 1880 and 1900 when its major spawning tributaries, the Oswego and Salmon rivers, were dammed and polluted by a then thriving lumber industry), has enjoyed a renaissance through restocking. The present New York record is an 18-pound landlocked salmon from the Oswego River taken in 1978. Lake George is also producing very large salmon.

Unlike the sea-run Atlantic salmon, which does not feed when it enters fresh water in its pre-spawning period, the landlocked salmon is a feeding fish throughout the year. Consequently, angling technique and tackle, with the exception of trolling, are similar to the methods used for trout. Although smelt is the dominant food item, some lakes are lacking. Even when present, the landlocked salmon is an opportunist, consuming other foods of cyclic abundance. An emergence of mayflies or caddis can trigger a wonderful rise, but in addition, wind-blown terrestrials such as flying ants, beetles, grasshoppers, moths and bees often create great moments for the dry fly on surface-cruising salmon.

While fishing with my old friend Stanley Leen last July on Maine's Junior Lake, we arrived on an evening when a tremendous Green Drake hatch took place. Before dark, we caught and released thirty-three landlocked salmon on floating

---

How to Tell Brown Trout from Salmon

In waters inhabited by both brown trout and landlocked salmon (Salmo salar) an identification problem does, on rare occasions, occur due to their similarity in shape and sometimes color. Both species can be very silvery and darkly spotted (especially in lake environments), or brown in coloration with dark and even red spots. This 9-pound, 3-ounce male landlocked salmon greatly resembles a brown trout and has the kype or cartilaginous protuberance extending from the lower jaw which is typical of large salmonids close to spawning. Color is not always a reliable means of distinguishing between the two species in the field. However, three characters that help in identification are the teeth, tail shape and the color of the adipose fin.

The vomerine teeth found on the roof of the mouth are the most useful character; in the brown trout these teeth are strongly developed and form a double zigzag row, while in the salmon, they are poorly developed in a single row or may be absent entirely, as the salmon's vomerine teeth are deciduous and can be broken off.

The tail of a large brown trout is square to fan-shaped, while that of the salmon is slightly forked or nearly square in older fish. The adipose fin (the small fleshy fin located between the tail and dorsal fin) is spotted or fringed with red or orange on the brown trout, but is slate gray to olive, and never spotted on the salmon.

imitations. The action was so sustained, in a short period of time, that we often had double hookups. True, these were mostly small, 12- to 16-inch fish, with a few to 20 inches, but against our light rods they had springs in their tails. With a band of vocal loons in calling attendance and fish madly jumping over water that had turned crimson and gold in a setting sun, it was like watching an ancient tribal fire dance.

The Cycle of the Season

Landlocked salmon fishing begins in the early spring as soon as the ice cover has fractured and melted on northern lakes. That clarion call "ice-out," which usually comes in late April at Maine latitudes, arouses a holiday spirit among New England anglers. For a brief period, the open water is almost a uniform 40°F at all depths, but it quickly warms into the 45- to 55-degree range— the point at which salmon begin a feeding orgy, raiding the shoals and shoreline and the mouths of brooks in search of smelt.

There is no water temperature barrier to inhibit the salmon from feeding freely at the surface or in

Fly Rod Trolling for Landlocks

Springtime trolling for landlocked salmon with the fly rod is usually done with two or three anglers in the boat. It is advantageous in either case that the rods be widely separated and the flies fished at different distances, not only to prevent tangling, but to provide greater water coverage. Although streamer flies are generally trolled 30 to 60 feet behind the boat, landlocks are often attracted to an outboard's wake and may be caught close to the stern. Long fly rods (8½ to 9 feet) help to keep the lines separated, especially when the boat is maneuvering in turns. A sinking tip line, or intermediate sinker is preferable, so the flies troll 2 or 3 feet under the surface. The fish feed in small schools and on a good day, double and even triple hookups occur. Once a salmon is taken, the boat's position should be noted in relation to shore sightings and the same area trolled again, or until the action ceases.

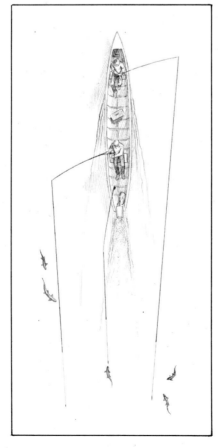

very shallow water. By far, the most popular method of fishing at this time is with a trolled streamer fly. Trolling at a brisk pace covers more area and landlocked salmon prefer a fly that moves quickly. They not only show no fear of a running outboard motor, but will often strike a lure back in the prop wash.

Depending on the weather, good fishing may continue into June, or if cool and rainy days prevail, the sport can excel even in July. When surface temperatures warm to about 65°F, the salmon remain in deeper water where trolling with spoons, spinners and natural baits is the most effective method. New England weather is notoriously contrary however, and good sport with the fly rod may continue into the summer period. This is especially true on waters that provide big mayfly hatches. August is usually a dead month except for trollers working very deep with lead-core, wire lines or even downriggers. However, as the water begins to cool again in September, salmon revert to their springtime pattern of surface and shallow-water feeding, concentrating near tributary streams or the outlets of lakes preparatory to spawning. Trolling for landlocked salmon is done from a variety of craft, but the standard in Maine is a 20-foot-square stern canoe or Grand Laker. This is the most stable design in strong winds and the choice of guides throughout the state.

Lake Memphremagog

Though fully two thirds of its 33-mile length is in Quebec Province, Vermonters consider Lake Memphremagog their state's second largest body of water. Like Champlain, its larger international sister to the west, Memphremagog lies in north-south orientation, boasts excellent sport fishing for big rainbow and brown trout as well as laker trout, smallmouth bass, walleyes and a variety of panfish. The glamour species here is the landlocked salmon.

Memphremagog salmon fishing rivaled that in Maine during the early 1900s, but tributary damming, erratic water flows and a combination of the usual diminishing effects of blossoming civilization began a decline in the fishery, especially obvious during the middle 1950s. Stocking programs begun in 1973, coupled with improved water quality, have sparked a marked turnaround.

Though numbers of larger fish are fewer than in the lake's heyday, enough salmon in the 5- to 8-pound class are consistently taken to bring in

Maine's West Grand Lake is a good producer of small landlocks, beginning in May and into early summer. Although a 4- or 5-pound fish is exceptional here, anglers are often rewarded with fast dry-fly fishing during the evening mayfly hatches.

anglers from some distance. Fish from 1½ to 3 pounds can be expected regularly and each year specimens cracking the 10-pound mark are reported in closed angling circles.

Fishing follows the usual pattern from top water activity after ice-out, to deep water during warm weather, then back to top water action by September. The lake's physiology creates distinct migratory patterns and it is vital to understand lake makeup and seasonal shifts for consistent success.

The southern end is shallow, the deepest spot being just 45 feet. Here, however, the lake's three major tributaries enter. Two of them, the Barton and Black, flow into South Bay, while the Clyde River enters the main lake at the town of Newport a couple of miles farther north. Some salmon are taken early at the mouth of the former tributaries, but it is the Clyde River mouth that provides the greater action. Ice-out occurs from late April into early May. A brief two-week period in May provides productive, though unaesthetic fly-fishing in the Clyde above Gardner Park, Newport. Locals fish the bridge at the Clyde's mouth after ice-out, while many visitors and residents alike turn to boats for the traditional trolling.

Though salmon can be taken by casting flies or spinning lures from a boat close to the Newport dock, trolling accounts for most of the fish. It is the quick-paced troll typical to the sport that is most successful. Traditional New England salmon streamer patterns dressed both on single and double hooks are still successfully used here. Barnes Special, Black Ghost, Nine-Three and Memphremagog Smelt (which originated in this country) are popular, but many other patterns work well. Mooselook Wobblers and Seneca Sidewinder spoons have been traditional favorites though the newer high-speed trolling spoons are producing excellent results for those who

experiment. Westport Wobbler and Flutter Chuck are examples.

Trollers work the Newport Harbor area south to north along both the western and eastern shores, then between Black and Bell islands and on up to the international border slicing through Province Island. In most years this area produces until sometime in June. After ice-out on the Quebec side, fish are taken near the town of Austin, in and around Sargeants Bay, MacPherson Bay and off many points.

As the weather warms, salmon move from U.S. waters to congregate on the Owl's Head Mountain drop-off. A Quebec license is needed. Here the bottom drops from 20 to 260 feet. Further north is

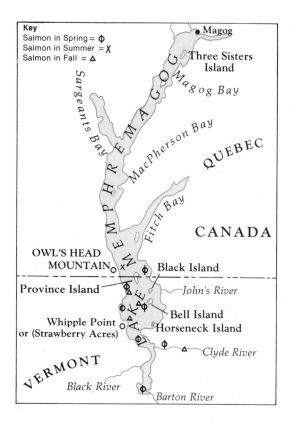

One of the most accessible resort areas in the northeast, Lake Memphremagog straddles the Vermont and Quebec border. In the summer season the best fishing is found in the deeper locations on the Canadian side, where a Quebec license is needed.

LANDLOCKED SALMON

a trench over 350 feet. While the salmon gorge on rainbow smelt at the mountain drop-off, anglers anchor and still-fish with dead smelt or nightcrawlers—unglamorous but highly productive. Heavy concentrations of anchored boats preclude trolling, but those who troll or cast

The Kaniapiskau River (also spelled Caniapiscau) is one of the most popular locations for large landlocked salmon in Canada today. The river camps can only be reached by float plane.

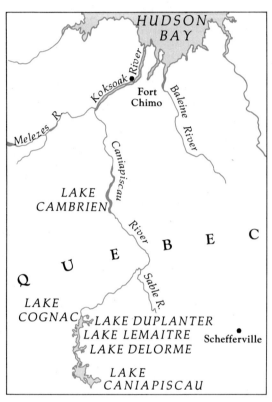

Historically one of the most famous landlocked salmon waters in Canada, Lac-St-Jean does not yield the large fish of bygone days, yet it remains one of the most consistent producers of 2- to 6-pound fish.

early and late in the day along the nearby west shore frequently take nice salmon (or rainbows).

Downrigger trolling can be effective during summer, but few try it once salmon leave the mountain drop-off. Fall sees a reverse of the previous fish movements. In September, around Bell and Black islands as well as other points on the U.S. side, salmon begin feeding actively near the surface and may be taken casting flies or hard lures. Small, smelt-imitative patterns or small, silver Hopkins spoons are effective. An electric motor is the ticket for stalking porpoising salmon to within casting distance. Later in the month salmon run as far as the power dam on the Clyde. Many big fish are taken, but it is shoulder-to-shoulder fishing at a spawning river bottleneck.

Much opportunity exists for variations on techniques—especially in spring. There is good potential for taking more fish by casting when properly positioned to intercept fish.

Lake charts are available from Canadian Hydrographic Service, Chart Distribution, Department of Energy, Mines and Resources, Box 8080, Ottawa, Canada K1A 0E9. Information is available from Newport Aqua Sports Haven, Farrants Point, Newport, VT 05855; telephone (802) 334-5911; and Information Division, Vermont Fish & Game Department, Montpelier, VT 05602; telephone (802) 828-3371.

Kaniapiskau River

Like extended fingers, the Kaniapiskau River reaches deep into the remote land shared by both Quebec and Labrador some 600 miles from its mouth at Ungava Bay. Hydroelectric development has diverted some of its water toward James Bay to the west and consequently affected the fish populations in the lower waters, but the upper portion of the river continues to flow free as it has since the last Ice Age. In its headwaters, the Kaniapiskau is a big river with long stretches of rapid and stunningly beautiful falls. The river is crystal clear and anglers can frequently see salmon as well as brook trout of 3 to 4 pounds swimming right under the boat. This is, without question, one of North America's prime landlocked salmon waters. While the majority of the fish run from 3 to 6 pounds, landlocked salmon up to 14 pounds are caught regularly. Whatever the size, the fish are abundant and full of fight.

The fishing usually starts between June 5th and June 12th when the current opens leads above falls and rapids. At this time the salmon hang right on the lip of the falls where they readily take lures such as the 5-inch, jointed Rapalas in either gold or silver. After ice-out in mid-June the best fishing is at the base of falls and rapids—especially in areas where the falls open into a small lake.

Until receding water levels force the fish into fast water pools at the end of June, most landlocked salmon are caught by high-speed trolling with Rapalas and silver spoons. Some salmon remain in these areas all summer long, but after the beginning of July the most productive fishing is found in the pools of the river. In fact, the fishing is so good that Jack Artwood at Kaniapiskau River Camps allows only fly-fishing on the river itself, so that the salmon can be released unharmed. Best flies are the Grey Ghost and Green Ghost tied tandem to produce a fly about 4 inches long. Proficient fly-fishermen can cast from shore using floating lines. Those not used to laying out distance can troll using a sinking line.

Accommodations at the Kaniapiskau River Camps consist of comfortable, heated cabins with log interiors. All services—meals, boats and guides—are provided. The camps are located at sites where the river flows into a lake to provide maximum esthetics. Accessibility is via regular jet service to Labrador City and then 65 miles northwest by chartered float plane. Details on the camps are available by writing to Kaniapiskau River Fishing Camps, 703 Lakeside Drive, Labrador City, Labrador, Canada, A2V 1B9; telephone (709) 944-7459.

Lac-St-Jean

Lac-St-Jean forms the headwaters of the Saguenay River. Its abundant population of landlocked salmon offers exciting and productive fishing in both lake and river, depending on the time of the year. At first ice-out in early to mid-May the major schools can be found at the southeast corner of the lake, somewhere near the village of St-Gédéon. As a matter of fact, landlocked salmon can be caught even before ice-out by fishing the half-mile lead of open water at the mouth of the Metabetchouan River near the village of Desbiens. Soon after ice-out, the schools of salmon generally start their slow exodus along the eastern shore of the 120-mile-wide lake basin. By late May the best fishing is close to shore between Desbiens and Chambord and by mid-June, the fish are concentrated at Pointe-de-la-Traverse and the mouth of the Ouiatchuan River. From there the fishing swings rapidly towards Roverbal and the mouth of the Chamouchouane River, which they

eventually enter by mid-July. Once in the Chamouchouane, the best fishing takes place in the pools below Chute-à-l'Ours and Chute-à-Michel.

Streamer flies such as the Grey Ghost, Mickey Finn, Magog Smelt and Muddler Minnow will also take Lac-St-Jean salmon, but casting is not nearly as productive as trolling unless the fish are on a feeding spree. In the Chamouchouane, a few anglers use wet flies such as Jack Scott, Silver Doctor, Cow Dung, Parmachene Belle, Scarlet Ibis and Seth Green with some degree of success, but fishing with live bait produces the most salmon by far. The rig usually consists of several nightcrawlers on a snelled hook attached some 2 feet above a bell sinker heavy enough to hold the current. Most fishing is done from shore near the base of the falls. Lac-St-Jean salmon are usually in the 2- to 6-pound range, though larger fish are caught on occasion.

Anglers fishing Lac-St-Jean can rent boats and motors from either Alonzo Tremblay (Club Ouananiche, P.O. Box 5, Chambord, Quebec, Canada; telephone [418] 342-6628) or Gilles Trudel (Camping Rocher Percé, Chambord, Quebec, Canada, G0W 1G0; telephone [418] 342-6459). Both have housekeeping cabins and guides available, though anglers can also stay in nearby motels. Those who wish to bring their own boats should remember that this lake can turn treacherous from one moment to the next and anything less than a 14-footer with a 10-horsepower motor is inadequate. Launching facilities can be found near all villages.

Tandem-hook streamer flies are designed for salmon trolling and have two single hooks connected by a fine, flexible wire. Most of these patterns are imitative or fancifully suggest that slender forage fish, the smelt, with a 3- to 6-inch-long body. Normal hook shank lengths cannot effectively position a single hook in a trolling fly as landlocked salmon often strike laterally at the tail of an evasive smelt or at its head to cripple it before swallowing it. Trolling streamers are also tied in a similar fashion but with more durable hair wings for Pacific salmon, where the slender-bodied eulachon (candlefish) is a common forage species. The following patterns, however, are New England in origin and are old favorites for the landlock: (left, top to bottom) Grey Ghost, Supervisor, Pink Lady, Green Ghost, Red and White and Green King; (right, top to bottom) Queen Bee, Mickey Finn, Parma Belle, Barnes Special, Nine-Three and Black Ghost.

BROOK
TROUT

Salvelinus fontinalis

The youthful voice of Rider Hollow Stream is just a faint echo now, and the blossoming of its rhododendron is hazier than the memory of the boy who hid in its tunnels. Born in a mountain spring so frigid that it would numb my lips to drink it, the little stream tumbled over mossy rocks creating pools of liquid crystal where brook trout dwelled. Seen now, balanced on crimson fins in a purling current, the brook trout arouses the nostalgia one feels for days when the secrets of angling were contained in a Prince Albert tobacco tin full of dew worms. As a game fish, *Salvelinus fontinalis* (the generic is an ancient name for char and *fontinalis* means living in cold springs) is not a stellar acrobat like the high-flying rainbow trout, nor is it frustratingly wary and strong as the brown trout.

The brook trout is native only to the eastern portion of North America from the Saskatchewan River to Labrador and from the Maritime Provinces southward along the Appalachians to Georgia, and west to Iowa. However, big brook trout, fish of 5 pounds or more, are only common in Labrador and Quebec, and in the Hudson Bay drainage of Ontario in big rivers like the Sutton, Albany, Winisk and its tributaries the Asheweig and Croal, and in Manitoba's Gods River and South Knife. Brook trout have been widely transplanted to our western United States but here, they seldom reach trophy sizes. There are exceptions, notably Henry's Lake in Idaho, where growing conditions are favorable; however, these brook trout survive chiefly in cold headwater streams, isolated beaver ponds and high-altitude lakes where a short growing season and marginal food supplies produce dense populations of small fish averaging 6 to 8 inches in length. Compared to Maine, for example, with its mostly fertile 2,365 squaretail ponds and 32,732 miles of stream designated as brook trout habitat, there is only minimal angling opportunity for large fish west of the Mississippi. But the cutthroat trout, native to

Hunting sculpins is virtually a team sport for brook trout in northern lakes and rivers. The sculpin or "muddler minnow," a choice food that hides under rocks, is the subject of many famous fly patterns.

25

BROOK TROUT

DISTRIBUTION

the Rocky Mountains, and absent from eastern waters, is an admirable substitute for *fontinalis* from an angling standpoint, attaining large sizes and often occupying a niche exclusive of the competitive brown and rainbow trout.

The brook trout is easily distinguished from other salmonids by a unique pattern of dark wavy lines or vermaculations on its olive-colored back and dorsal fin, and the red spots surrounded by pale blue halos on its flanks. The belly will vary from pearly white on an immature fish, coloring to orange with age, often becoming red. In Nature's sense of continuity, the lower fins are peach to crimson with a median stripe of black and a white anterior edge. The caudal fin of young brook trout is slightly forked, but becomes almost square with maturity and thus the name "squaretail" is widely used by anglers. Some populations are darker in color than others, depending on the habitat and dominant food supply, but as Henry David Thoreau observed "they glisten like the fairest flowers." Sea-run brook trout differ in coloration

in being an overall greenish-blue dorsally, with silvery sides showing a few pink spots, and a white belly. In some lackluster estuaries the salter may look like it has been swimming in laundry bleach; even the silver tarnishes. However, those bright colors are regained within two weeks after returning to the river.

Anadromous populations of brook trout are often incorrectly called "sea trout," a term internationally applicable to the anadromous brown trout. There is no taxonomic difference between the salter and its non-migratory form. Presumably a certain percentage of any population will enter a marine environment from coastal streams, especially in the Maritime Provinces of Canada. The seaward migration takes place after spawning in late October to early December, and the trout return to fresh water in late May and June, or in August

---

Strains of Brook Trout and Their Management

Strains refer to local populations or stocks of a species that are genetically distinct in appearance, behavior or other attributes and adapted for life in a particular environment. Adaptation to local conditions is a concept applying to living things in general that can affect survival and well-being when an organism is transplanted from its natural home. Success of the transplant depends on the closeness of the environmental match or on the organism's ability to adapt to new conditions. Only comparatively recently has the importance of strains been given adequate attention in fishery management.

Trout and salmon adaptability has also been altered by husbandry practices within the artificial environment of a "fish hatchery." Salmonids are genetically plastic. Relatively few generations of intentional or inadvertent selection can produce strains preeminently suited for life in the fish culturist's pool, but not so able to cope with rigors encountered in lakes, rivers and oceans. Many data have accumulated showing that differences between strains have important implications in management.

Domesticated inbred strains of brook trout stocked in several Adirondack Mountain (New York) ponds clearly and consistently showed far poorer performance than wild counterparts.

Domesticated and one or more wild strains of trout were hatched and reared in the same cultural environment, then released simultaneously as fall fingerlings in the same water. Inventories were conducted on the number and size of the trout remaining at successive six-month intervals throughout the natural life span of the wild strain, about five years for these particular native stocks. Most of the domestic trout "disappeared" after the second year of life. The great disparity in survival resulted in wild strains producing an average of six times more fish flesh over their life span than did the domestic strain.

Between-strain differences in fishing success may also be demonstrated. In a small 5-acre pond, 50 percent to 65 percent of the domestic-strain brook trout were caught in each of three succeeding fishing seasons compared with 10 percent to 25 percent of a wild Adirondack strain also in the pond. Both cohorts had been stocked as fall fingerlings. Wet flies fished near the surface were the predominant angling method used; other tactics might have produced less contrasting or different results. Orientation toward surface feeding or preference for more shallow-water habitat could be explanations for the greater capture rate of the domestic strain. In another study when fingerlings of two wild and a

domestic strain were transferred from rearing quarters into a column of water 2 feet deep, the wild fish immediately sounded to a resting position on the bottom, while domestics swam near the surface.

Domestic strains of trout readily become conditioned by artificial feeding and wallow and slurp near the surface when food is offered. Under similiar circumstances, wild trout hold at or on the bottom of the tank, rise swiftly to take individual food particles, swirl and return to the bottom. Some wild strains are noticeably more flighty and do not feed well when disturbed. Wild brook trout grow more slowly on artificial rations than domestic, even when external disturbances are minimized through the use of automated feeders.

Wildness per se in a strain does not assure superior performance, at least when releases are made outside native waters. Eggs were obtained from two Canadian populations of brook trout from adjacent watersheds in the southeast corner of James Bay, Quebec: Assinica Lake on the Broadback River and the Temiscamie River, part of the Rupert River system and a complex of large lakes. Obvious differences in color are apparent between the two Canadian populations. Temiscamie trout exhibit a prominent array of large spots, especially conspicuous in breeding males, but also

and September, depending on latitude. This is not an extensive journey, such as that of shad or salmon, but is confined to estuaries and shore areas where for several months the fish travel in small schools gobbling amphipods, sand launce, silversides and other saltwater foods. Anadromous brook trout are most common in Hudson Bay, James Bay, Ungava Bay and around the Atlantic shores of Newfoundland and Quebec. In the early 1800s, salters provided great sport throughout New England and as far south as Long Island, New York. However, there are no outstanding fisheries in this southern portion of their range today. Salters gain weight in their coastal feeding, but unlike the brown and rainbow trout, they never achieve great size. For example, the 4- and 5- pound brook trout found in many Hudson Bay tributaries invariably have some history of migration, but the maximum weights are not comparable to resident populations in a fertile lacustrine environment.

In wilderness waters, the brook trout is without guile. In rivers and lakes that are seldom fished, the squaretail will come easily to the fly. This gullibility is frequently emphasized as characteristic of the species, but it's illusory in the broad picture. There are numerous accessible brook trout waters in the Adirondacks and New England, which receive constant, if not heavy fishing pressure that requires skilled angling to realize even modest success. In civilized places, *fontinalis* can be both shy and selective. I have taken 4- to 7- pound brook trout in remote Quebec lakes to the point of almost indifference, only to be frustrated by a 10-inch fish steadily rising to mayflies in a Maine pond. But undeniably, gullibility played a key role in the brook trout's history, as there was a time when returning a fish to the water was considered a kind of piscatorial aberration.

In the genesis of American trout fishing, the post-Civil War period saw a tremendous growth in the number of people astream, and until the brown trout (introduced from Germany in 1883)

obvious in females and juveniles. Assinica trout have fewer spots, especially red ones, and these are small and pale in color. The latter strain tends to mature later in life, usually at two and three years of age, while Temiscamie trout mature a year earlier. Both Assinica and Temiscamie strains of brook trout attain a large size for brook trout, commonly over 5 pounds, and a long life expectancy of six to ten or more years.

The Canadian strains were established in foster waters in the Adirondacks and these populations provided a source of eggs for additional experiments. Introduced Temiscamie-strain trout generally showed better survival than Assinica. When crosses were made between the Assinica or Temiscamie strain and an inbred domestic brook trout, nearly twice as many Temiscamie hybrids showed up in subsequent samples in several planted lakes of the southwestern Adirondacks, but recoveries were in about equal numbers in some northern lakes. Such differential performance is not now readily explainable, but apparently the two strains are unequally adaptable to transplantation in some Adirondack waters. Both crosses showed hybrid vigor in growth, attaining a greater size than either parent when all were stocked in the same lake.

In the previous example, survival and age at maturity have obvious practical implications, while color intensity and pattern have aesthetic value. In agriculture, and experimentally in the biological sciences, strain differences or combinations in the form of hybrid or selected varieties have great value for special purposes or for increasing production. Fishery science is only beginning to exploit genetics as a tool of management. There is a wide variation of intraspecific characteristics throughout the natural range of a species, but it is impractical within any present concept to describe them all or to identify and interpret the total array of differences. What is important is retaining enough variation so that full genetic expression for adaptability and manipulation is preserved for management.

BROOK TROUT

became widely established at the turn of the century, our native brook trout was the singular quarry of eastern anglers. By buckboard, carriage and a spreading network of railroads, vacationists flocked to the ponds and streams of Maine, New York, Pennsylvania and Michigan where trout were in abundant supply. Unfortunately, *fontinalis* was easily seduced with worms and brightly colored wet flies and, lacking a conservation ethic, baskets of a hundred fish of all sizes per angler per day were displayed on hotel lawns for the admiration of ladies in crinoline skirts and bodices. My grandfather William McClane, who was an engineer on the Long Island Railroad, and fished its streams in the 1870s, once told me of a catch of nearly 600 trout, each weighing from 3 to 6 *ounces*, taken by two anglers and sold to a Manhattan restaurant. Even fingerling were fair game. Considering the relatively small size of its waters, it was inevitable that New York's streams would be rapidly depleted.

With new railroads tracking into the heartland of Catskill watersheds, the pressure shifted to the Beaverkill, Esopus and Neversink, then the

Adirondacks (advertised as "now populous with inns"), the Poconos, then as far north as the mighty Nipigon River in Ontario, where giant brook trout dwelled. In an essay on Nipigon fishing (1896), A. R. MacDonough lamented,

> Americans on either side of the border concern themselves little about coming generations. Yet, interest, if not duty, should prompt them to take some care that this superb river shall not lose its preeminence as the finest trouting water of the world. It is no longer possible, as it was reported to be twenty-five years ago, to take in one day a barrel of trout averaging four pounds, nor will the angler now fill his basket within sight of Red Rock Landing.

The fact that the world's record brook trout of 14¼ pounds was caught as late as 1916 is testimony to its once tremendous productivity.

As early as 1864, visionary fish culturist Seth Green built a hatchery near Mumford, New York, and began raising brook trout to supplement the declining wild stocks. Green started the process of domestication—breeding fish that would accept an artificial diet, yet resist diseases and the stress of crowding. The very qualities needed for survival in the wild had to be sacrificed for tamed hatchery life. Initially, Green's brook trout often jumped out of troughs and raceways when approached at feeding time; a suicidal act under the circumstances, but a synaptic reaction to escape. A skill they soon lost. Succeeding generations of Mumford fish evolved into amenable boarders on a diet of ground meats instead of mayflies; however, when planted in the wild, these domesticated trout were unable to compete with native fish for resting and feeding sites, and their potential life span had been genetically abbreviated. Today, in many eastern upland streams brook trout seldom survive longer than three years with a climax size of about 12 inches. Statistically, for every 10,000 fry that emerge from the egg, only 200 will achieve age three, and about 25 will reach age four. During the halcyon era of squaretail fishing in Maine, from the 1880s to the 1920s, five- to seven-year-old brook trout weighing 3 to 5 pounds were not uncommon. Obviously, this wild genetic stock has survived, as the state continues to produce occasional trophy fish. At Pierce Pond in Somerset County, camp owner Gary Cobb records the number of squaretails weighing 3 pounds or

Favorite Flies

In the trophy brook trout waters of northern Manitoba, Quebec and Labrador, dry-fly-fishing is extremely effective during July and August when profuse hatches of stoneflies, caddis and mayflies occur. During a warm summer these emergences can be spectacular over the open water of lakes as well as on the rivers. Durable floating patterns tied on No. 10 and 12 hooks such as the Irresistible, Goofus Bug, White Wulff and Goddard Caddis are eminently practical as large brook trout have strong jaws and sharp teeth. I have caught Labrador fish of over 6 pounds on clipped deer hair bass bugs. However, at these latitudes most of the surface activity is in the late afternoon and evening hours when water temperatures are peaking. In cold weather, and generally during the morning hours, deeply fished wet flies, nymphs and streamers are essential. The standard bearer in squaretail country is the Muddler Minnow designed by Don Gapen, who ran a fishing camp on the Nipigon River, Ontario, during the 1940s. This streamer pattern, a revolutionary fly design, imitates the sculpin (Cottidae), a common forage fish in all northern waters and highly esteemed by brook trout. Gapen caught a 10 pound, 4 ounce squaretail on the

Muddler in the Nipigon (July 14, 1951) and since that time fly patterns with broad, flat heads, similar to the natural sculpin, have multiplied a thousand-fold. Other favorites for big brook trout are the Multi-Color Marabou, Black and White Marabou, Marabou Leech, Gray Ghost, Gray Matuka, Brown Woolly Worm and that perennial favorite the Royal Coachman streamer. These should be tied on No. 2 to 6 hooks.

more, and over 60 appeared on the 1982 log. In Canada, there are even longer-lived brook trout populations such as the Assinica strain (see page 26), which attains an age of ten years or more, and weights of 9 to 11 pounds. However, our native trout lives in a delicate balance everywhere because of habitat destruction and overfishing. Foam-flecked rivers running through forests where the logger's ax has never echoed do offer fabulous sport, yet any of these could be wiped out tomorrow. In the vast wilderness of Labrador, for example, there are probably no more than half a dozen watersheds with populations of large brook trout. One of the most popular today is the Minipi River with its Northern Labrador Camps.

Few anglers in modern history have ever experienced the discovery of a pristine brook trout fishery, a place that has never been visited except by a few Indians and trappers. Lee Wulff, who pioneered many eastern Canadian rivers, described his first journey to the Minipi basin, which, fortunately, has survived the mindless destruction that has been endemic to delicately balanced fisheries throughout the North country. It is, indeed, an event worth recording.

Minipi River

My world in the summer of 1957 was a beautiful world; the endless evergreen forests, the marshes and the muskeg stretched away in one direction to the bright blue arms of the sea and the other to the mountain peaks far in the interior. I flew low over the lakes in the basin below, and could see here and there the spreading circles that showed where a trout had risen. Picking a lake near the center of the chain, I settled into an easy glide and headed for a point close to shore near the outlet. I taxied to shore, tied up the plane and, already wader clad, I moved out into the smooth flow where it quickened above the white water spilling to the next lake. There were mayflies hatching, big green drakes, and the trout were rising to them. I put on a Gray Wulff and drifted it gently over a slick. The response was immediate—a head and tail rise with a high back and big dorsal fin showing. The line tightened and I was fast to my first Minipi trout. The big male fought well but in due time came to my waiting hand. I judged him to be 6 pounds or a little better, and soon he was packed in moss for the trip back to Goose Bay. Then I went back to fishing.

That spot gave me more than a dozen similar brook trout ranging from 4 to 6 pounds, all of which I released before I lifted off that lake up to

the next one in the chain—a lake that later came to be named Ann Marie. Again I fished at the outlet. The mayfly hatch was over. This time I offered a big red and yellow streamer and, again, the trout were eager to respond. They were there in unbelievable numbers. None were smaller than 4 pounds. I saved one of the bigger fish. Back at Goose Bay that evening she weighed 7½ pounds.

The Minipi waters are peat-stained to a medium brown, the color of lightly brewed tea. Looking into them at close range I could see a great deal of insect life, scuds and the nymphs of mayflies, and stone flies and the cases of caddis. Northern Pike are there too. They usually frequent the lakes, but often they will take a streamer in the fast water these trout like best. On several occasions I had

In many rivers both east and west, the brook trout is in competition with other species and is not the dominant catch. Here on the upper Green River in Wyoming, rainbow trout are more common; however, brook trout up to 1½ pounds are taken with some frequency, especially along cutbanks and where springs enter the stream.

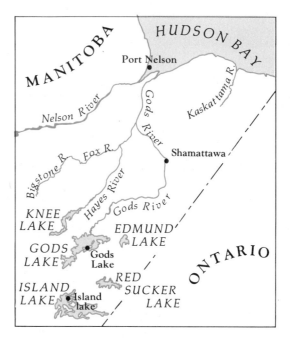

One of the best brook trout waters in northern Canada is Manitoba's Gods River, which flows into Hudson Bay. Reached by air about 370 miles northeast of Winnipeg, this huge, fast-flowing stream produces 3- to 5-pound trout with some frequency. The watershed is also noted for pike, lake trout and whitefish. There are comfortable lodges on Gods Lake and River.

BROOK TROUT

pike hit one of the trout I was playing and give it up to me only when it was deeply slashed and had to be killed.

Many of the Minipi lakes are shallow and the mayflies and other insects thrive in those shallow areas. However, after the big spring hatches in the lakes, the trout tend to concentrate at the inlets or "thoroughfares" between the lakes for the summer and early fall. They favor the deep waters, I believe, only when winter covers the lakes with ice and the greater depth may offer greater comfort and safety.

Nowhere else in Labrador did I find a trout area

The Brook Trout and Daniel Webster

The world-record brook trout was caught in 1916 by Dr. William J. Cook in the Nipigon River of Ontario. Perhaps it was prophetic that another fish of exactly the same weight was spiritually captured by Senator Daniel Webster in 1832. Webster's fish, immortalized in a Currier & Ives lithograph, with its dimensions traced and then carved into a weathervane for New York's Brookhaven Presbyterian Church, is a charming legend, but factually confused. It is said that the Senator got up during a sermon and hastened to the stream, where he hooked the great trout while a gathering congregation cheered or chorused hallelujahs. Invocation from the Scriptures may have been part of Webster's technique, but where did he catch the fish? In one version, it was the Nissequoque River and by another, more logical account, it was Carmans River — one on the north and the other on the south shore of Long Island. The size of the weathervane was also deliberately

exaggerated by its artisan for better visibility. And while both streams have access to salt water, an environment where brown and rainbow trout grow to record sizes, the anadromous brook trout seldom attains a weight of more than 5 pounds, even after debauching in the bounty of the sea. Although Webster's fish was entered into our Congressional Record many years later, it appears to be a myth based on an amusing incident — exactly what we'll never know.

In 1961, the church was moved to nearby Bellport, where both the original weathervane and Currier & Ives version of the faithful black slave, Apaius Enos, netting Webster's trout (as he captionally exclaims, "We hab you now, sar!") can be seen at the Bellport Historical Society Museum. Evidently, the lithographers were realistic, as what "we hab" in the print is about 3 pounds.

to equal the Minipi basins. The upper waters of the Eagle River system had brook trout that sometimes grew as large, and at places they seemed to be more plentiful, but nowhere else was the average weight as high and the fish as deep and strong.

The following year I flew in to Minipi again to set up a temporary camp and make a movie with Dick Wolff of Garcia. We spent a week in the basin. Our fish averaged nearly 5 pounds and we caught hundreds of them. Only one of them weighed less than 4 pounds, and we guessed that one at 2½ pounds.

Where were the little ones? They were in the small pockets and shallows. As in all natural situations where a prolific species is not heavily preyed upon, it is made up of mature individuals. They are the strongest and most efficient. They will maintain a maximum total weight for the food of the stream. The smaller, growing trout require more food per pound than their parents. Only when the big fish grow old and weaken or die can the younger ones move in and take over the good feeding areas.

Labrador's trout resources were soon in danger. Once the seaplanes made the waters available, the pressure was inordinately heavy. The fish concentrated at the inlets and outlets of the lakes were unsophisticated and easily caught. Whole lakes were quickly devastated. The daily limit was fifteen fish per angler, no license required. A family fishing over a weekend could legally take home hundreds of pounds of fine brook trout. Sometimes they were fed to the sled dogs that had to be maintained over the summer.

I brought together Bob Albee, sportsman, and Ray Cooper, a guide who had opened a fishing camp. We developed a program to preserve those fantastic trout. The camp rules were catch-and-release, with one trophy fish to take home. Those regulations worked (and spread slowly to other camps). The big breeding stock, which was eliminated in so many other northern waters with the advent of roads or seaplanes, is still relatively intact in the basin. Fishing there next season can still bring an angler a brook trout as big as 8 or 9 pounds. There are 5-pounders in quantity. They're all wiser and harder to catch now because of the catch-and-release program, but they, the mayflies and all the other aquatic insects are still there to create a brook trout fisherman's version of heaven. For information and reservations contact Jack E. Cooper Minipi Camps, P.O. Box 340, Happy Valley, Labrador, Canada A0P 1E0; telephone (709) 896-2891.

Eagle Lake

During the 1950s, Dew Line air force personnel at Goose Bay in Labrador, looking for unusual fishing, set out to explore the headwaters of the Eagle River to the southeast. They found a brook trout paradise. Every lake they sampled contained fish in abundance, and one out of five produced trophy trout. Fortunately, this territory is in the middle of an inhospitable area—often referred to as "The Land God Gave to Cain." Buffered from the encroachment of civilization by bogs, black flies, often foggy weather and a taiga wilderness of black spruce forest and lichen-strewn tundra, it can only be reached by float plane or helicopter from Goose Bay.

Igloo Lake has become the pivotal location of the Eagle River headwaters due to the fact that it has the only commercial camp, plus the consistency of its remarkable fishing. Virtually every party who has visited Igloo has returned with 7- and 8-pound brook trout and the conviction that when the world record is broken it will be a fish from this region. To maintain the quality of these waters only one big fish may be killed, although a legal limit of smaller fish from specified, nearby lake and streams can be kept for food.

Fly-fishing is the principal and popular method, but spinning is allowed provided all treble hook lures are replaced with single hooks. Streamer flies and large wet flies, particularly bulky dressings such as the Burlap, or Fledermaus, are generally effective. Although Igloo is a shallow lake many regulars use sinking or sinking-tip lines in the belief that big brook trout seldom exert themselves and it is often necessary to drop the lure down to a tempting level. However, the action with dry flies can be phenomenal at times using any large hair-wing, or hair-bodied pattern like the Bomber, and even clipped-hair bass bugs. Igloo Lake fish consider such morsels a mere appetizer.

Accommodations at Igloo consist of spartan plywood-construction cabins. The camp provides guides, boats and motors as well as meals. Accessibility is via regularly scheduled airlines to Goose Bay, Labrador, and then by chartered float plane for about one hour to camp. For information and reservations contact: Goose Bay Outfitters, P.O. Box 171, Happy Valley, Labrador, Canada AOP 1EO; telephone (709) 896-2423.

Mistassini Watershed

This watershed drains the heartland of Quebec

from Mistassini Provincial Park. Countless rivers flow in all directions to fill huge Lake Mistassini and eventually funnel into James Bay, via the Rupert River. Its remoteness in over 5,000 square miles of wilderness protects a genetic strain of big trout and the region consistently produces fish ranging from 3 to 8 pounds. Lake Mistassini itself provides good angling, although here, it's unusual to catch fish exceeding 4 pounds except during June and early July, when large trout congregate among the islands where Lake Mistassini empties into the Rupert River. The better fishing begins in August, extending into the first two weeks of September in the three major rivers that flow into the lake from the northeast—the Cheno, Toqueco and the Papas—and at the same time, the Temiskamie River, which flows into nearby Lake Albanel. The Papas is considered the most productive for 6- to 8-pound brook trout.

The Eagle River watershed is one of the top brook trout spots in eastern Canada. Fish of 7 and 8 pounds are not uncommon at Igloo Lake. The chance of a squaretail in double-digit size is excellent. This is a remote fly-in location with only one commercial camp reached from Goose Bay.

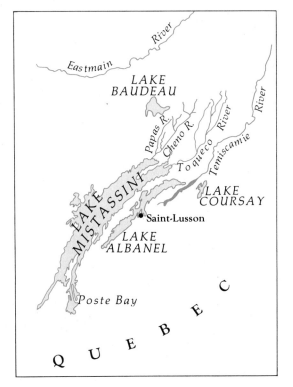

The Temiskamie strain of large brook trout thrives in Mistassini Provincial Park, a 5,000-square-mile wilderness region. A few trout exceeding 10 pounds have been caught here in recent years. The Papas is highly rated for 6- to 8-pound fish, but the Cheno, Toqueco and Temiskamie are also excellent.

BROOK TROUT

Streamer flies, especially the Muddler Minnow, are generally the most productive lures. However, dry-fly-fishing is often effective using the same technique followed for Atlantic salmon; the angler covers the pool by casting diagonally across current and letting the fly sweep around before picking up and casting a foot or so further in progressive arcs (see page 214). Spinning tackle is permitted in the Cheno and Ioqueco rivers. Wobbling spoons and spinners in the one-fourth- to one-half-ounce sizes are recommended. There is no regulation in effect regarding treble hooks, but single hooks make releasing easier and are less injurious to the trout. Spinning is a more popular method in the lakes where northern pike, walleye, smallmouth bass and lake trout offer a variety of angling.

The only accommodations at the river outpost camps consist of tents, and anglers must bring their own sleeping bags. Guides prepare the meals. The main camp at Vieux Poste on Lake Mistassini offers comfortable log cabins with outdoor plumbing. Mistassini is accessible by scheduled Nordair flights from Montreal to Chibougamau and then by chartered float plane to Vieux Poste (about a one-hour flight). Visitors can also drive to Chibougamau and fly to Vieux Poste. The camps on the Papas, Cheno, Toqueco and Temiskamie are reached by float plane from the main camp. All four rivers are serviced by the Mistassini Lake Outfitting Camps (P.O. Box 157, Chibougamau, Quebec, Canada G8P 2K6; telephone [418] 748-3171), which is operated by the Cree Indian Band of Mistassini.

Baxter State Park

It's common wisdom among anglers that native brook trout fisheries in this country have undergone a steady decline since the middle of the nineteenth century. Wild brook trout, after all, are creatures of clear and cold wilderness waters, and fishing has declined with habitat. More than thirty years ago, Bob Elliot wrote in *The Eastern Brook Trout* that northern Maine would be the last refuge of that species in America. That sober prediction has become increasingly true, especially as acid rain continues to devastate the fabled brook trout waters of New York's Adirondack Mountains to the west. It is that devastation, however, that in some ways protects the fishing in northeastern Maine, because the Adirondacks seem to act as a figurative buffer in being the first mountain range confronting the northeasterly flow of pollutant-laden air. Because of that geographic buffer and because so many of its waters are remote—unreachable even by float plane because of their small size—the brook trout waters of northern Maine offer anglers a chance to fish a hundred years back in time for wild brook trout in a true wilderness setting. It is without question the best region for public brook trout fishing in America, and my favorite spot within it is Baxter State Park in northcentral Maine.

Best reached by driving the Maine Turnpike northeast to Millinocket, Baxter Park has become increasingly crowded thanks to the backpacking boom of the past two decades. In order to preserve the wilderness experience offered by the park, its administration now limits the number of people in the park at one time through a reservation system. Camping is permitted only at designated sites, and these sites, which at many locations along the park's 75-mile trail system are limited to a *single* site (often a lean-to), are themselves designed to enhance a solitary, wilderness experience. As the park becomes increasingly popular, reservations are an absolute must and should be made early in the year. Happily, most backpackers don't seem to

---

Trout Stuffed with Crabmeat

Purists will agree that pan-fried trout cooked at streamside is a culinary superlative, assuming, of course, that the chef has mastered this basic skill. To achieve a crisp skin without burning, the trick is, of course, to use a heat-tolerant oil (such as peanut) for browning the flour- or cornmeal-dusted fish, then sprinkling them with hot, melted sweet butter just before serving. But for a candlelit dinner presentation at home, and equally memorable for your guests, is crabmeat-stuffed trout, a delectable contrast in textures and flavors that is really simple to prepare. Fresh (pasteurized) blue crabmeat can be found in virtually all convenience stores.

4 trout, 12 ounces each, kited
   and boned
3 stale rolls
1 cup milk
1 whole egg
1 extra egg yolk
1/3 cup chopped raw bacon
1/3 cup chopped onion
8 ounces lump crabmeat
1 tablespoon minced parsley
1 teaspoon dried tarragon
juice of ½ lemon
½ teaspoon Worcestershire
   sauce
dash of Tabasco

salt and pepper,
melted butter
paprika

First prepare the stuffing: Soak the rolls in milk; squeeze dry and add eggs. Sauté the bacon and onion until the onion is limp and amber in color but not brown. Add the crabmeat and sauté for 5 minutes. Add to bread mixture and then stir in remaining ingredients except the trout, melted butter and paprika. Add salt and pepper to taste. Spread stuffing inside each trout and fold over the halves. Oil the baking pan to prevent the fish skin from sticking and brush the top of each trout with melted butter. Bake in a 400-degree oven for about 15 to 18 minutes, or until the skin is brown and crisp. Sprinkle generously with paprika during the last few minutes of cooking. Makes four servings.

The Appalachian strain of brook trout common to many eastern upland streams seldom exceeds 12 inches in length, yet it is dear to the heart of the fly fisher. The red-spotted brookie thrives in cold, unpolluted water, and the joy of fishing it is due less to the challenge than to the wilderness experience it represents.

fish. Both information and reservations can be obtained by mail only from the Baxter State Park Reservation Clerk, 64 Balsam Drive, Millinocket, Maine 04462. A nominal fee is charged for campsite use.

The best starting point is Roaring Brook Campground, located in the park's southeastern corner and reached by road from Millinocket. Roads to the park, by the way, are generally good gravel and are private, being owned and maintained by area paper companies. Public use is permitted, and you will pass through periodic paper company checkpoints where you'll be asked to report your destination and expected length of stay. Drive carefully: The lumber trucks are big, and the roads are narrow.

After an overnight at Roaring Brook, where there are numerous campsites, hike north for about 7 miles to Russell Pond. It's a fairly gentle hike and the trail is well marked. You might be tempted to fish Wassataquoik Stream near the trail crossing en route, but the fishing at Russell and environs is much better. In addition to campsites, there's a ranger's cabin at Russell where canoes are available for hire, which will simplify your fishing considerably. Brook trout up to a foot are fairly common here, and 2- to 3-pound fish are a genuine possibility. Use a canoe to cruise some distance off the shoreline, and cast small dry or

For the camper and backpacker, Maine's Baxter State Park offers a great wilderness experience. It is not a region of large trout (although 2 to 3 pounders are a real possibility), but it is the best region for public brook trout fishing in America. Camping is permitted at designated sites along the 75-mile trail system.

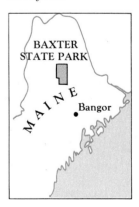

BROOK TROUT

A mayfly hatch on Anne Marie Lake in the Minipi watershed brings large brook trout to the surface. Trophy fish of over 6 pounds are common due to the catch-and-release policy in effect. Fish of double-digit sizes have been caught here in recent seasons.

wet flies toward shore. Numerous moose frequent this pond both early and late in the day, and watching them will cause many a missed strike.

There's a variety of other fishing in the immediate vicinity, and the most productive I've found has been in Turner Deadwater, which is a short distance from Russell and on the trail to Wassataquoik Lake. Here Turner Brook spreads out as a long, slow-flowing flat dotted with stumps and boulders and with marshy edges. Leave the trail and hike upstream along either edge, casting toward the center. Keep an eye out for moose (they're common here) and count on getting your feet wet. The fishing's worth the effort.

From Russell, you have a couple of choices. Hike north, if you like, to Pogy Pond, where there's another campsite. Pogy is relatively shallow and fishes best early in the season. Nearby Weed Pond is reputed to have both larger fish and faster fishing, but getting there means bushwhacking in and out in a day, and I've never bothered. From Pogy, you can head north to camp at Branch Ponds, where the fishing, while still good, also has some road access and isn't as good as that in the park interior.

Alternatively, from Russell you can hike up into Wassataquoik Lake, at which the park administration maintains a primitive four-person

cabin and a canoe for public use (again, by reservation only). Wassataquoik is deeper than most ponds in the park, and the shoreline drops quickly into deep water. Fish the inlet and outlet, plus the tributary mouth below Green Falls. Most of the fish here seem to be what some locals call "racers," slim, dark brook trout of 7 to 9 inches. This lake is unusual in that it still (as of 1983) has a remnant population of blueback trout, a small, deep-dwelling form of landlocked char. You'll share this lake with both loons and moose. From here, it's a short hike up to Little Wassataquoik Lake, where there's also a campsite and better fishing in its shallower water.

On the western side of the park, there is sometimes good fishing for large brook trout in Nesowadnehunk Lake (locally pronounced "solderhunk"), but it's big water with road access, and it's fished hard. I've always been happier fishing Nesowadnehunk Stream, which is designated as fly-fishing-only water and looks as if it belongs in a picture book from the 1800s. It's generally easy wading on a gravel bottom. It also gets lots of pressure, especially in the immediate vicinity of the Nesowadnehunk camping area, which is the park's western entrance. The farther away from the road you follow the stream, the better the fishing.

Tackle for fishing this area should be adapted to both backpacking and the special needs of pond fishing from shore. An ultralight spinning outfit and a collection of small spoons and spinners is easy to pack. For fly-fishing, a 4-piece, 9-foot graphite fly rod for a 6-weight line is ideal. The length will be a substantial advantage in canoe fishing or when making long roll casts when the shoreline prohibits a backcast. You should also carry a full complement of lines on spare spools: floating, intermediate, slow-sinking and fast-sinking to cover possible contingencies. It's satisfying to know that brook trout in this part of the world will still take a Royal Coachman wet fly with abandon. You can count on doing well with either a Royal Wulff or an Adams dry in No. 12 to 18, but you'll also want some caddis dries in the same sizes, plus a few No. 20 to 24 midges. Some Muddlers, Mickey Finns and Black Ghosts will do in the streamer department, and you should also have a representative selection of nymphs, especially an assortment of Gold-Ribbed Hare's Ears. If you're fishing in the fall, don't go without a good assortment of flying ant dry-fly patterns in both black and brown.

The best fishing is certainly in June and September. Although Maine's trout season opens in April, ice and snow usually keep Baxter's fishing closed until mid-May. The statewide 5-trout limit applies to Baxter, and live fish may not be used as bait within park waters. Under current regulations, brooks and some small ponds are closed after August 15. Check the rulebook supplied with your Maine fishing license, which is required in the park for both residents and non-residents. Licenses are obtainable in Millinocket on your way in. Be forewarned that Maine's blackflies in June are as horrendous as the fishing is good. Newer insect repellents with high concentrations of DEET are effective here.

This has been no more than a sampling of some park waters, and much of the fun in fishing there lies on a trail not yet taken to a pond or brook not yet fished.

BROWN TROUT

Salmo trutta

In 1809 Sir George Cayley, "the father of aerodynamics," was looking at a brown trout, and what he saw led him to coin a new word, a word that he was then uniquely capable of conceiving (though thanks to him it is now common to us all): "streamlined."

Sir George was not a naif who believed trout were born square and eroded individually into their form, but that the *species* had through aeons been shaped by flowing water, and had *evolved* to allow the stream to slip sleekly by. But Sir George's intellect was focused on the physics of flying rather than the biology of changing. Minimalizing resistance to environmental stress he could fully understand; that every living thing is geomorphically dynamic took five more decades and Charles Darwin (and A. R. Wallace) to perceive.

This fish's form has shaped the modern world, and the literature of the English-speaking peoples would be unthinkable without its presence. It shares with birds and deer the distinction of being the wild beasts we most delight in. Real values never come cheap; humanity has spent enormous treasure on brown trout. Consider only what expenditures Europeans suffered to ensure that their expelled colonials should continue to enjoy the motherland's native trout.

Shipments of Atlantic salmon eggs were begun in 1852 to Australia and repeated in 1858 and 1860. These were failures, but from them Englishmen learned that if they loaded enough ice to maintain salmonid eggs at a temperature of 33° to 35°F, brooding could be maintained for more than 150 days. In 1864, a fresh batch of 90,000 salmon eggs was dispatched with approximately 1,500 eggs from River Itchen brown trout, included at the insistence of a few devotees such as Francis Francis, the most popular fishing writer of the time and author of the wonderful *A Book on Angling.* Aboard the clipper *Norfolk* in a specially built house that held 30 tons of ice, a few of these

Of European origin, the brown trout, in its many strains and subspecies, has been a favorite game and food fish since prehistoric times. It has become ubiquitous in North America, and rivals the rainbow trout in popularity with fly-fishermen.

BROWN TROUT

eggs survived a January-to-April voyage in 1864. The hatched salmon disappeared, but the trout became brood stock for the great New Zealand and Tasmanian fisheries—and the technique for transporting brown trout eggs was established. Subsequent shipments went to Africa and India, and then, in 1880, the American angler, writer and fish culturist Fred Mather went to an International Fisheries Exposition in Berlin, where he met the president of the Deutscher Fischerei Verein, the Baron Lucius von Behr. The pair became friends, fished brown trout together in Black Forest streams, and von Behr promised Mather a gift of eggs, 80,000 of which arrived in New York in February 1883, aboard the liner *Werra.* Mather brooded part of the shipment at the Long Island hatchery he operated for New York State and sent some on to two other hatcheries, including one at Northville, Michigan, which stocked the resultant fry in the Pere Marquette River, the first brown trout stream in North America and still a notable fishery. Von Behr sent more of his golden, red-speckled Continental fish, and these were shortly mingling with black-spotted Loch Leven trout from the Howietoun hatchery in Scotland. In the next sixteen years they were stocked in thirty-eight states and territories.

The citizens of Newfoundland had sense enough to acquire Loch Levens in 1886, Quebec took some New York stock in 1890, and the fish marched across Canada. Only the Yukon, Northwest Territories and Prince Edward Island have not yet introduced them.

DISTRIBUTION

This is LeTort Spring Creek, the showpiece of Pennsylvania limestone trout fishing streams. Slow, weed-filled water allows the trout ample time to be critical of both fly and presentation.

Not everyone applauded. Deforestation and its resultant warming of watersheds drove the pretty little char called brook trout into headwaters, leaving the major fluminae to the brown, but the European was much more difficult to catch than the char, and angler complaints that began in the 1880s have not entirely ceased today, although nowadays it is principally eastern Canadians with their excellent brook trout fishing who still slang the brown trout. The Americans have long since accommodated to them, and hordes of western Canadians invade the Yellowstone area each summer for its outstanding brown trout fishing.

The fish instituted a revolution in trout tackle and techniques that continues to this day. From downstream, wet-fly-fishermen with bright attractor flies, the European-Americans became upstream, dry-fly and nymph fishermen with imitative flies. The long, weepy rod that is ideal for roll casting a leash of wet flies and keeping them properly sodden evolved in the micrometer-worn hands of American artisans into a crisp-tip, dry-fly rod that desiccates hackles with darting false casts and delivers the fly with delicate exactitude. Brown trout and dry fly arrived in the New World almost simultaneously and wrought profound changes in the sport of trout fishing because of the brown trout's formidable gifts as a quarry that likes to feed on the surface drift but likes not to be caught.

If Sir George Cayley had looked at his trout living in a current he might have gone on to discover the influence of stream hydraulics on the conduct of fluvial brown trout, as did Dr. Robert Bachman, in a monumental study begun in 1977. A Naval Academy graduate retired after twenty years of active duty who wanted a second career in trout ecology, Bachman erected an 18-foot observation tower on a protected stretch of Pennsylvania's Spruce Creek and over the

succeeding five years spent thousands of hours in a burlap-draped blind with polarized binoculars and a microcomputer into which he punched brown trout behavioral data. Bachman found he could identify individual trout by idiosyncratic spot patterns on their flanks directly below the dorsal fin (fish Number 31 was dubbed "Beethoven" because he had three spots followed by an unspotted space and then a final spot).

His study fish would typically enter the pool as young-of-the-year 3-inchers and after a brief familiarization tour one would adopt a rock as its home, rest its chin on the leading edge of that rock, and proceed to feed on the surface and underwater drift. The rock would be selected to provide a cushion of disturbed water so little swimming energetics were required to maintain position. The fish would continue to use this identical rock throughout its lifetime, returning to it after its upstream spawning migration in the fall and defending its territory from the encroachments of other fish. Some trout would adopt fast-water positions and some slow, some deep water and some shallow. In the slow tail of

his study, pool cruising was common, but the fish in current positions would seldom move far for food, confining themselves to quick darts left or right or to the surface for items in the drift. They would feed incessantly throughout the day.

"I've seen adult trout feed up to 300 times an hour in shallow water at 2:00 P.M. in bright sunlight on the hottest day in August," Bachman says. He is not talking about concentrated feeding during a hatch of insects, but just the normal activity of a brown trout sampling the benthic drift. "Fish take a particular site in the stream and wait for food to come to them. They don't swim around looking for food. Fish know the spots in the stream where they can expend the least amount of energy while waiting for food. I call these spots 'seats in the restaurant'—the more seats, the more trout. The fish stay in these spots whether a lot of food drifts by or whether pickings are lean."

Bachman's study trout were stream bred and protected from angling (save for a single instance of poaching), tagging, fin clipping, electro-shocking, etc., until near the conclusion of his

BROWN TROUT

study when he electroshocked some fish for examination.

In one experiment, Bachman sent a colleague approximately 100 feet downstream of the nearest study fish with instructions to wade across. The man had scarcely entered the water when the near fish bolted toward a holt, panicking others into joining him (the protective sanctuary is used by a number of fish in common). Bachman's trout could consistently see an approaching angler long before he was in casting distance of them, and fish with a shallow-water feeding spot were the first to take cover. They were also likely to be mature trout rather than juveniles.

At age five, and approximately 11 inches long, these Spruce Creek entomophagic trout achieved their maximum growth. A few mature fish evidently become piscivorous, and these develop into legendary monsters: salmon-sized, night-prowling trout.

Another experiment, introducing 170 hatchery trout amidst his 200 stream-bred fish, produced violent territorial fights and within six weeks four fifths of the hatchery stock had been driven away, but some of the dominant wild fish that engaged in many battles exhausted themselves and also disappeared from the population. Only two of the hatchery trout overwintered and were part of the population next spring.

Bachman's observations of wild brown trout behavior ironically correspond with the conventional wisdom of this fish. *They take best at dawn, dusk and at night,* because that is when they have the greatest difficulty seeing anglers and inspecting their flies. *Only fingerlings are in shallow water,* because adult shallow-water fish have already run to cover before an angler arrives. *They are found in shaded, protected places,* because approaching anglers frighten them away from their feeding stations. *Mature trout are a deep-water fish,* because those are the only ones that are still on their feeding station as we approach—they can't see terrestrial creatures as well as those with shallow stations (Bachman's poachers, incidentally, took a few of his deep-water fish with minnows).

The Spruce Creek study fish would run for cover at the approach of a man, even run for cover if a mallard sat down. Obviously such extraordinary wariness is not true of the trout that continue rising while an angler in plain sight goes through the ritual of changing flies and making presentations until he catches it or puts it down. Such public characters are either stocked fish that associate man with food or wild trout that have become familiar with anglers because of their near-constant presence. Under conditions of heavy angling pressure a fish cannot remain in its sanctuary on pain of starving.

These Spruce Creek brown trout took less than 15 percent of their food from the bottom, so unless an insect entered the benthic drift by rising off bottom or by falling into the creek, it was largely protected from trout.

The implications of Bachman's researches will occupy biologists and anglers for decades, but they are not confined to brown trout. Bachman began his studies at the instigation of Dr. Robert Butler, who observed similar behavior of brook trout, brown trout and cutthroat in Sagehen Creek in the Cascade Range of northern California.

Brown trout vision is one of the most remarkable among fishes. Both their *cone* or daytime color vision and their *rod* or nighttime black-and-white vision are superior to ours (except in resolving power, our fovea have five times as many cones as trout), but, in addition, their retinas have two foveae or areas of finest distinctions, and their egg-shaped lenses are capable of focusing *simultaneously* on both a distant and near subject. It is as if each eye were *at the same time* a microscope and a telescope.

And yet a blind brown trout can continue to feed, that is to thoroughly perceive its environment, through its lateral line system, which receives low-frequency vibrations. These can be water washing off a submerged rock, the footfall of an angler walking the bank, even something as infinitesimal as an insect lighting on the water's surface.

Brown trout can also smell like a thousand bloodhounds thanks to nares unconnected to the throat. Each of the two nostrils is a connected pair lined with cilia that keep a flow of water passing in one and out the other.

Entomophagic brown trout have been studied by biologists in considerable detail. Dr. Paul Needham, in a classic 1938 investigation done on an upstate New York stream, examined stomach contents of brown trout between 5 and 12 inches (average of 8) and concluded that 80 percent of the diet was mayflies, mostly nymphs, 10 percent caddis and 10 percent a potpourri of miscellaneous food items. In Lake Michigan, where brown trout prosper and grow to scarcely credible dimensions, the herring called alewife (*Alosa pseudoharengus*) is a favored prey. In Flaming Gorge Reservoir, an impoundment of the Green River astride the Utah-Wyoming border, rainbow trout are preferred, and brown trout in excess of 20 pounds are taken with large trolling plugs painted to resemble a rainbow trout (whose actual use as bait is prohibited). Diet, therefore, is that of a generalized predator willing to accept what is available.

If a brown trout becomes piscivorous, it can grow to thrilling dimensions in North America. They have been caught in excess of 33 pounds in both Flaming Gorge and the White River of Arkansas. Divers who have probed plunge pools below dams on the Missouri River system in Montana swear 40-pound brown trout are there. (Argentina has produced them to almost 36 pounds, and fisheries biologists monitoring spawning runs in a handful of Bavarian lakes have actually weighed brown trout to 55 pounds. A fabled German innkeeper named Stoffelmeier, during the period 1930 to 1946, took twenty-four trout weighing between 55 pounds and 68 pounds, 5 ounces. These fish were trolled up with huge spoons leading from a winch mounted directly on the boat, not a rod-and-reel catch. Austro-Bavarian *Seeforellen* are evidently a strain with inherently greater growth potential than plain *Salmo trutta*.)

Yet the art of fly-fishing, in all its glorious ramifications, was developed to take brown trout that will be measured in inches and ounces rather than yardage and pounds.

Brown trout in North America are a fall-spawning fish, and this is the angler's opportunity to take big lacustrine specimens by fly-fishing tributary rivers. They will also spawn along lake shorelines if no tributaries are present. The run will take place from September to December, but is most commonly an October to November occurrence. Diminishing light, falling temperature and rising waters are triggering agents. A raw, gray day in October's chill is the time to seek outsized fish in streams above a brown trout lake. Often they will be accompanied by rainbow or cutthroat trout gleaning spilt eggs. Preparatory to laying 600 to 3,000 eggs (depending on size of the fish), the female cuts the usual salmonid redd with her tail in the stream's bottom gravel while a hook-jawed male guards the redd area from a post slightly downstream. This annual distortion of the male

Note how this male brown trout is peering to see the gross stone-fly imitation in his mouth.

face, called a kype, makes his mouth a better weapon and running a fly or lure past a flamboyantly brilliant spawning male on the redd is tantamount to rattling a watchdog's chain. The endocrinal secretions that prepare them for these nuptials do nothing whatsoever for their table qualities, so killing a spawner is pointless unless you have a taste for mounting fish with grotesquely distorted faces.

Incubation is largely governed by temperature. The lovely and historically important Beaverkill River in New York's Catskill Mountains, which is annually the destination of pilgrimages by thousands of brown trout fly-fishermen from all over the world, is an absolutely miserable environment for trout eggs through the winter, featuring temperatures in the low 30s, and anchor ice at least part of the time. Beaverkill trout eggs may require more than five months in the gravel.

Considering how cavalierly most fish breed, the salmonids are comparatively solicitous and a high percentage of eggs succeed in becoming free-swimming fry, which unfortunately is the undoing of more than 90 percent of them. As they come out of the gravel they are considered just another food form by sculpins, fallfish, darters, dace, kingfishers, herons and mature trout. Those that escape the first-year holocaust are decimated times five in each succeeding year, and the average life expectancy is only three years. That will be a foot-long trout, which is also about the limit of reliance on an insect diet. The few survivors who go to four or five years will be 17 to 20 inches, and unless the stream is extraordinarily fecund of insects (like the Bow River of Alberta), they will be fanged cannibals devouring anything with fins that is small enough to swallow. In environments both richer and more protective than freestone streams (such as alkaline lakes), brown trout may last a half dozen or even a dozen years. The longevity record is eighteen years.

When much of Oklahoma's topsoil blew away to California in the 1930s, fisheries biologists

BROWN TROUT

began to consider whether agriculture and industrialism were having an effect on trout, principally browns and rainbows. This was a black moment in the careers of hatchery personnel. They had, for half a century, indulged a typically American approach to manifestly declining trout populations: Develop rapid-growth stock in hatcheries and plant them on demand. Frank Mather, the pioneer American fish culturist, inaugurated an era of fisheries management à la the County Agent who advises farmers. Now biologists began investigating the trout's environment and found it to be unhealthy. Funds were diverted to "stream improvement structures," that is, fisheries management advanced from the agricultural stage to industrialism. Afield in rubber boots they repaired the ravages of rapacious farming with check dams, single-wing deflectors, riprap, straight log dams, deflectors, barrier dams, V dams and willow weeping everywhere. Their finest discovery was the barbed wire fence that denies access to stream banks (especially effective with cows).

One of the first of these earnest souls who tried to undo the messy works of man and tidy up those of God was that staunch capitalist and devoted brown trout fisherman Edward Ringwood Hewitt, author of *A Trout and Salmon Fisherman for Seventy-Five Years* (Scribner's, New York, 1950), which title understates his actual longevity in the sport. Hewitt's Big Bend water on the upper Neversink received, at his inspiration, a series of dams I have

never seen duplicated elsewhere, even though they marvelously concentrate trout, as well as aerate the water. John Atherton described them well in *The Fly and the Fish* (The Macmillan Co., New York, 1951).

These low dams made fine holding pools out of otherwise unproductive riffles and flats. They were built two logs high, and faced on the upstream side with heavy planks running from the top of the dam to the stream bed at a long angle. The falling water dug holes back under these dams, making fine hides, and there were always big trout in them for us to try to lure out.

Big Bend is still a haunt of brown trout fishermen. One of them is the late Robert Deindorfer, author of *The Incompleat Angler, Fishing Izaak Walton's Favorite Rivers* (E.P. Dutton, New York, 1977). Deindorfer was concentrating one evening on a foot-long brown trout, a fish that had trouble accepting his fly, when from under the nearest specimen of those "fine hides" "A Thing" with .50 caliber rose moles emerged, swallowed the target fish whole and returned underneath the cedar planking. After that Deindorfer took to stalking the small, placid (and rather silty) Neversink with tarpon tackle.

The sheer expense of stream improvement limits its application to public waters, but I would still like to process every state and federal fisheries biologist in North America through a day's inspection of Hewitt's Neversink. With a chain saw and a pair of husky teenagers you can accomplish small miracles of habitat improvement. Barbed wire and willows help, too, and meadow streams, in addition to protection from livestock, can benefit from long-stem fescues that sag over the stream bank in summer and form a cool, shaded tunnel for edge-oriented trout. Most of the trout I have persuaded to come out from undercut banks have been large (meaning elderly) specimens.

Cheaper than stream improvement, and increasingly the focus of fisheries biologists, is management of the brown trout's primary predator. The biologists have become concerned with controlling the conduct of fishermen because organized fishermen have demanded it. At first, restrictions on equipment were tried. These began eight centuries ago in Scotland with regulations limiting the use of nets. The most recent is for fly-fishing only or single-hook lure only. The rationale for artificials only is that trout tend to swiftly swallow a baited hook and consequent mortalities are high.

The classic water on the Beaverkill River begins at Junction Pool where it flows to Barnharts, Hendricksons, Wagontracks, Mountain Pool, Painter's Bend and other historic locations. Designated no-kill sections have helped to maintain quality angling.

This brings us to the nub. Isn't the idea of catching the fish to kill and eat it? In Europe it largely still is, but the North American system of open waters, publicly available, has produced a doctrine of limited kill so that more anglers can enjoy catching (and releasing) their trout. Barbless single-hook artificial lures make for easy releasing. This management of the fishery by managing the fishermen was begun in 1934 when Governor Gifford Pinchot of Pennsylvania established "Fishermen's Paradise" on Spring Creek at the encouragement of his son-in-law, Edward Ringwood Hewitt. It was most succinctly expressed by Lee Wulff, the innovative angler, filmmaker, casting instructor, fly tier and author of *The Atlantic Salmon* (Winchester Press, Piscataway, New Jersey, 1983), a hallmark text, when he said, "A trout is too valuable to be used only once." This insight swept North American fishery departments with the force of revelation. The resultant no-kill waters are now thronged with anglers all season long, many of them fly-fishermen. The rationale for a closed season to protect the trout at least part of the year (generally coincident with the spawn) disappears in no-kill waters. Nowadays you can find some hardy souls on the Beaverkill no-kill in mid-winter.

Fishing for brown trout peaks in temperatures between 56° and 65°F and pH values between 6.8 and 7.8. Over much of their range, July and August are going to be uncomfortably hot for the fish, driving them into nocturnality and to spring heads. Of recent years, I have taken to wearing a small electronic temperature gauge on my wader belt with the probe wire strapped to one leg with rubber bands and the thermistor tip located at ankle height. If the display indicates 81°F or higher I cannot be fishing for brown trout because they are dead; at 44°F their metabolism is too slowed for effective angling; but a spring at the customary groundwater temperature of 50°F will make its surroundings highly attractive to the trout. Bankside springs in summer will reveal themselves by the presence of mint, but only repetitive (and tedious) sampling with a mercury thermometer or constant readout from the electronic gauge can reveal subaquatic springs, unless you are given to wet wading. When every trout for 600 yards is at the head of one small pool memorable feats can occur. My record is eight acceptances to thirteen dry-fly presentations on the Esopus, casting straight upstream into the lowest reading I could find on a hot day in August.

Night fishing is an acquired taste, but it and the spawning run are practically the only means by

Susan McClane's guide has netted her brown trout during a float of the Madison River in Montana. In the boat is tackle manufacturer Bing McClellan, whose specialty is ingenious soft-plastic lures.

which Legendary Monsters will be taken from rivers. On sultry summer nights the drill is to take rod in one hand, tip pointing behind you, and a powerful flashlight in the other, and walk the stream bank. Do not leave the beam on a seen trout; that will move him. Take it right on past him, turn it off, move to a good casting position and try him with a large dark wet fly. At night you can get away with a tippet that would be unacceptable to the fish by day.

Father Walton (in *The Compleat Angler*) thought brown trout at their peak of palatability after the leafy month of May:

> . . . *especially he loves the may-flie; and these make the trout bold and lusty and he is usually fatter and better meat at the end of the month than at any other time of the year.*

For his waters he was undoubtedly right, but in North America we are blessed with a plentitude of crustaceans that make for a red-fleshed, delicious fish, a trout being basically no better in your diet than his own was. I have had 6-inch *fontinalis*, a species and size renowned as breakfast fare, from barren Rocky Mountain lakes that had flesh the color and flavor of wet cotton, but a brown trout done as *truite à bleu* after a lifetime of three years eating *Mysis*, *Gammarus* and cressbugs would be fit for champagne, or a vintage Meursault, or an *auslese* Moselle served ice cold in chilled stemware. All the trout recipes of *haute cuisine* were inspired by this fish. Smoked I prefer them to salmon, but in North America it is better to cook them. There is a nematode loose in some western American trout streams that can use trout and mammals as vectors in its complicated life. Cooking destroys it. In mammals it migrates from the digestive system to the brain.

The panoply of flies that North Americans have devised to beguile brown trout are one of the glories of the sport, but the Quill Gordons produced now by all the best tiers look nothing like the shaggy, back-winged, undivided-winged,

43

BROWN TROUT

long-bodied, large flies of that pattern tied by Mr. Gordon and in the collection of the Anglers' Club of New York. I still prefer them as Elsie Darbee tied them for me before her death, but Mr. Gordon obviously did not have in mind the imitation of *Epeorus pleuralis* as hatchmakers claim, and which besides has a yellow belly on the river he mainly fished. Since you can read elsewhere how the Hendrickson and the Light Cahill got their names, permit me to tell you what cannot be read elsewhere: Some years ago the state of Wyoming conducted an experimental fishery on one small trout stream. Access could be strictly controlled and accurate catch records maintained. Aside from confirming the conventional wisdom that most fishermen are rotten at it and a few deadly, they discovered that the least effective

Field Identification of Sea Trout vs. Atlantic Salmon

Sea trout or anadromous brown trout closely resemble Atlantic salmon and may be confused in the area where their range overlaps from Maine to Newfoundland (including Nova Scotia). There are three reliable characteristics in identification: (1) the vomerine teeth on the roof of the mouth occur in a double zigzag row in the sea trout, and in a single row in the sometimes toothless salmon; (2) the adipose fin of the sea trout is usually colored with red or orange, but on the salmon it is always an overall slate gray to olive; (3) the caudal fin or tail of the adult sea trout is square to fan shaped, while that of the salmon is concave to almost square. The comparative length of the maxillary is often cited as reliable, but this is not always valid.

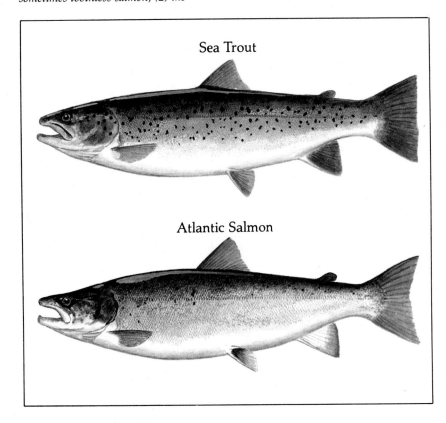

Sea Trout

Atlantic Salmon

pattern you can tie on the end of your leader is the Royal Coachman.

On the Beaverkill, the Adams is now the most popular pattern because word has gone out that it is favored by Ed Van Put, New York's Senior Fisheries Technician for the area and a wizard angler. During Edward Ringwood Hewitt's almost endless lifetime fishing the Beaverkill, his favorite fly was the Brown Bivisible. The latest *wunderkind* pattern is the McMurray Ant, a clever concept in which two little blobs of balsa lacquered black or red and strung on a short length of monofilament are lashed to the hook and a hackle wound on between them. This is approaching parlously to bass bugs, which have taken many a fine brown trout later reported as a dry-fly catch. I predict a long popularity for the McMurray Ant because its indefinite flotation leaves it out there where the trout can exercise their willingness to jump to false conclusions. I haven't even given up on the Royal Coachman yet, especially dry in sizes from No. 18 down, and wet as a steelhead attractor.

The cult of the twitched fly was inaugurated in North America with publication of Leonard M. Wright Jr.'s *Fishing the Dry Fly as a Living Insect* (E.P. Dutton, New York, 1972), and in the United Kingdom through the writings of the late Oliver Kite, who called the practice the "induced take." In the hands of devotees, Wright's Fluttering Caddis pattern has left not just the "sudden inch" he recommended, but yard-long grooves in water that had heretofore known only drag-free dead drifting (save for that old reprobate Hewitt and his skater patterns, which nobody fished because roosters don't grow hackles large enough to tie them). Nonetheless drag-free is desirable most of the time; I have even watched Wright fishing drag-free and adamantly upstream. The George Harvey system of tapering leaders so the points fall in S curves is a wonderful aid to drag-free floats as is wading directly upstream and throwing a straight line so that your line, leader and fly are all in exactly the same current.

Sea Trout

European anglers cherish sea trout, the anadromous version of brown trout, second only to Atlantic salmon, and pay stiff fees for the privilege of fishing for them. In North America, they are a long-ignored fish that is just beginning to receive the attention of biologists and anglers. They are found in Newfoundland, Nova Scotia, Maine, New Hampshire, Massachusetts,

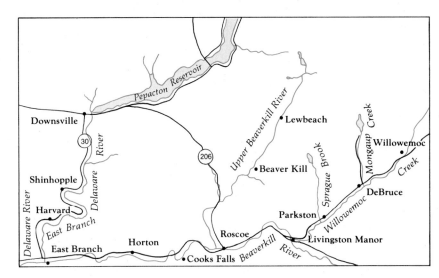

Connecticut and in at least one New York State stream. They are also part of the mix of anadromous salmonids that run into the Smith River in northern California (renowned for its big chinook salmon, which respond well to fly-fishing with leadcore shooting heads from tiny skiffs the size of coracles), where the locals whack them sharply with a blunt instrument and say, "That's a funny looking steelhead."

These are not genetically distinctive sea trout in North America, but simply the common brown trout with a *Wanderjahr* of saltwater existence, or in many cases only a few months. Maine, New Hampshire and Massachusetts are deliberately fostering them by stocking brooks that have an undammed exit to the sea and insufficient freshwater capacity for the head of fish.

The Newfoundland monsters include a pair taken from a *barachois* (Canadian French for lagoon) named Lower Pond, which lacks inspiration, at a locale named Witless Bay. In 1960, Lower Pond produced a 27-pound, 10-ounce sea trout taken on a No. 10 brown fly. In 1962, a fish of 28 pounds, 8 ounces took a worm bait. These fish are evidently of Newfoundland's Loch Leven stock from the last century. Loch Leven trout in Loch Leven now average about 1½ pounds each, which would not even make a suitable meal for a 28-pounder. That the 27-pounder was taken on such a small, drab fly probably indicates crustacean feeding.

The Nova Scotian sea trout populate many streams, with the Annis, Cornwallis and Guysborough arguably the best. Visitors have little competition, since Nova Scotians prefer angling for Atlantic salmon.

Maine has recorded some remarkable growth rates for their fish. Sea trout (or rather, would-be sea trout) stocked in May at less than 6 inches and 3 ounces were 15-inch pounders to 17-inch, 2-pounders in October. Stream-resident browns could be expected to add 1 or 2 inches in a comparable period.

Sea trout flies are normally in the No. 6 to 10 range, imitative of crustaceans or small baitfish. Slender little silver streamers and our old friend the Muddler Minnow are preferred by many. In Europe, night fishing is passionately pursued. Americans tend to favor the low end of an ebb tide when fish can be expected to concentrate in pools—during the spawning run in late fall. A summer fishery in estuaries and salt ponds is beginning to be practiced. When a run of spawners or egg-gleaners come into an Atlantic salmon river the doctrine is that sea trout will

occupy the tails of pools because they hold in slower water than salmon.

A very attractive fishery can probably be developed in North America for this interesting creature once selective breeding of returned fish develops a more anadromously determined strain. This is necessary because European sea trout (and salmon) have diseases endemic in their populations unknown on this side of the Atlantic and to obtain sea trout brood stock that can be certified as non-carriers is tantamount to impossible. There *are* some European sea trout loose in Connecticut streams, relics of a stocking program from more than two decades ago, but that state now concentrates its funds available for anadromous fish on the magnificent multi-state and federal attempts to restore Atlantic salmon to the Connecticut River system.

Actually, sea trout fresh in the river are the easiest of brown trout to take, especially after dark, but to choose any form of brown trout will never be easy. It is not supposed to be easy; it is supposed to be fascinating.

Each fall when ocean temperatures around Long Island fall enough to allow them to come up from the depths, a few Legendary Brutes slip into the island's heavily hammered trout streams to spawn. The few that are caught become newspaper celebrities and are guaranteed taxidermy.

The Beaverkill

The Beaverkill has long been New York's most famous trout stream. Located in the southern Catskills, it is near New York City and its surrounding populations. This proximity, and a pioneer railroad which promoted the stream and its fishing, hastened the Beaverkill's notoriety. As early as 1876, at a time when General George Armstrong Custer and his Seventh Cavalry were riding to meet the Sioux at Little Big Horn, trout fishermen from the New York City area were regularly boarding passenger trains to and from Livingston Manor to fish the famed Beaverkill.

Murdochs on the Beaverkill was a favorite.

Every trout fisherman should pilgrimage to the Beaverkill watershed. The famous pools are downstream from Roscoe, but don't overlook the Willowemoc.

BROWN TROUT

Other boardinghouses and resorts in the area catered to these early anglers, and catches of native brook trout were plentiful. In those days a fisherman was considered a "sportsman" even if he killed in excess of 100 trout in a single day, as long as he accomplished the feat with a hook-and-line.

With increased fishing pressure and no limits, the Beaverkill's trout populations soon began to dwindle. No limits soon gave way to no trout. The railroad, not wishing to lose passengers, began replenishing the stream with brook trout. In 1878 alone, the New York-Oswego Midland, whose tracks paralleled the banks of the stream, stocked 1,500,000 trout in the Beaverkill and surrounding waters!

Brook trout gave way to browns, as the

Keith Gardner casts into the shade for brown trout on the east branch of New York's Delaware River. In summer, this water would fish best at night.

Beaverkill was one of the first American streams to be stocked with these European imports. This act was to be the river's salvation, for the brown was a little more difficult to catch and could inhabit miles of the Beaverkill's lower reaches which warmed too much for native brook trout. By the late 1880s browns were well established and had considerably increased the trout holding water of the river.

The Beaverkill flows out of the Catskill forest preserve and runs in an east-west direction, approximately 45 miles past the hamlets of Lew Beach, Roscoe, Cooks Falls, Horton and Peakville, before joining the East Branch of the Delaware River. It is the only major tributary of the Delaware that is free of dams.

Even though it flows freely without interruption from natural or man-made barriers, the Beaverkill

is commonly referred to as if it were two different rivers: the upper Beaverkill and the lower Beaverkill. This separation of the river is justified for a variety of reasons, one of which is that the river doubles in size after being joined by the Willowemoc Creek at Junction Pool near Roscoe. Another reason for this distinction is that the water downstream of this point is entirely open to public fishing, while the upper stream is mostly posted and private. Water temperatures are yet another reason, since they also differ between the two sections. The lower river is so large and wide that even the tallest trees do not adequately shade it. Temperatures each year rise into the 80s for short periods in mid-summer, and trout survival often depends on finding spring holes and cooler tributary mouths. The upper Beaverkill is well shaded with mature hardwoods and hemlocks, and is supplied by many cooler tributaries and spring runs that keep temperatures down, rarely rising above those preferred by trout.

Because of water temperatures, fish populations also vary between the two river sections. Native brook trout inhabit the entire upper Beaverkill, but are rarely caught downstream of Junction Pool. The majority of trout, brooks and browns caught on the upper water are wild fish (born in the stream), while the lower river has only a small population of wild trout, and is dependent on stocked fish. However, almost all of the large browns taken in the lower Beaverkill are wild fish. Rainbows are rare in both sections, with all the larger trout of this species being stocked by the private fishing clubs.

The upper Beaverkill flows through a lightly inhabited valley where the stream, valley floor or bottomland is privately owned and divided into large estates devoted to trout fishing and trout fishing clubs. The only public fishing on the upper river is at the headwaters on State forest land, 1.9 miles at the State campsite at Beaverkill, and the 2.5 miles immediately upstream of Junction Pool.

In its earlier days, the upper Beaverkill, with its populations of brook trout, attracted anglers. As the fishing pressure increased, so did the practice of posting. When it appeared that the public may not have a place to fish, the New York Conservation Department began purchasing fishing easements (in 1936) from Junction Pool downstream. These permanent rights allow fishermen to walk the stream along its banks for the sole purpose of fishing. Today there are 14 miles of public water on the Beaverkill.

The lower river flows through a narrow, rocky, mountainous valley. The surrounding hillsides are

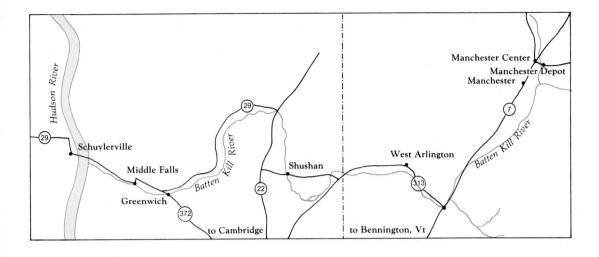

Of all the most reputable American brown trout streams, none is more difficult than the Battenkill in Vermont, but in summer the trout respond to a Tricorythodes *hatch that occurs virtually every day.*

heavily wooded and steep, and whitetail deer are plentiful. Deer hunting camps are numerous along the dirt roads and trails that wind up the hollows of Beaverkill tributaries. The lower river is very accessible from Old Route 17, which parallels much of the stream's right bank, and from the modern four-lane Route 17 that not only parallels the river, but crosses back and forth in several locations, giving even greater access.

From Junction Pool downstream for the next 4 miles are the most famous pools in angling literature: Barnhardts, Hendricksons, Cairns and Wagontracks to name a few. One of the two popular no-kill stretches is also in this section, beginning 1 mile below Junction Pool and running downstream 2.5 miles. The other is at the tiny hamlet of Horton and is 1.8 miles in length. This water is well posted with signs marking the boundaries and informing anglers that all trout must be returned, that artificial lures only are to be used and that the season is year-'round.

In the 1930s, the Beaverkill had a reputation for having good numbers of 1- and 2-pound brown trout in the lower river. That fishing exists today in the no-kill water. These sections are by far the most popular with fly-fishermen. Brown trout in the 12- to 15-inch size range are common, as are catches of twenty or more trout in a day's fishing. With an abundant food supply consisting of large populations of minnows and a rich assortment of aquatic insects, trout growth is excellent and occasionally produces a truly big brown.

The lower Beaverkill produces all the major mayfly hatches that dry-fly-fishermen are fond of. The hatches, lots of rising trout and a wide river with plenty of room for a backcast make it easy to understand why so many travel great distances to fish here.

A drive along the Beaverkill today will show the railroad that followed the stream and popularized its early fishing fell on hard times and has long been abandoned. Not so the Beaverkill—it is as popular as ever! Now cars line its banks, and it is not unusual to count a dozen parked at a favorite pool.

The Beaverkill has a large following of trout fishermen who fish its waters regularly throughout the season. As in the late 1890s, many still come from the New York City area, but a check of license plates along the river will also reveal that today's anglers come from all over the United States. These fishermen defend and maintain a river they love, an angling tradition and a trout fishery they are proud of.

Catch the Hendrickson hatch during the first week of May and you will understand why this legendary river continues to be a valuable part of American trout fishing.

For information contact the New York State Dept. of Environmental Conservation, Albany, NY 12233; telephone (415) 421-6554.

The Battenkill

As a trout stream, its wide reputation depends as much on the surrounding scenery as it does on the fishing, which is often difficult. The Battenkill starts as a series of small, mountain tributaries in southwestern Vermont. The dominant feature here is Equinox Mountain with Manchester Village at its base, a popular resort area since the 1850s. Most of the initial tributaries come together in Manchester, from which the river flows for about 20 miles into New York and, eventually, the Hudson. There is an additional 15 miles of good trout water after the state line, but downstream from Greenwich, New York, the river grows and warms to a point at which trout fishing is marginal at best.

Between Manchester and Arlington, the river has a gentle gradient, which means long, flat runs with relatively few riffle areas in between. Few riffles mean the hatches aren't very diverse. Predictable among them, however, are Hendricksons (usually around mid-May), Sulphurs (*E. dorothea,* an evening hatch in early to mid-June), and *Tricorythodes* mayflies in the mornings from mid-July until early October. The latter hatch offers the most consistent fishing and, often, the largest fish. Access in this stretch is from either Route 7-A or from River Road, and is perhaps best accomplished by walking up or downstream at bridge crossings between these two roads. Almost all of this section is not posted in any way. There are both wild brook trout and wild browns in this water; no stocking is done, and fish populations hold up well in the face of heavy pressure. The lack of consistent, heavy insect hatches and the slow clear water makes fishing difficult, and the most skilled anglers are content with a few fish in a day's outing here.

From Arlington along Route 313 west to the state line, the river's gradient steepens and it assumes the riffle/pool configuration typical of other eastern trout streams. Insect hatches in this section are both more diverse and more prolific. In addition to those previously mentioned, anglers may encounter a variety of caddisflies, some stoneflies, Blue Quills (*Paraleptophlebia* mayflies in early season), and a variety of Blue-Winged Olives (*Baetis* mayflies of several species at various times of the year). The river in this section, about 10 miles, is 60 to 70 feet wide and easily waded, which makes it picture-book water for a dry-fly man. The water is typically clear and remains cold through the summer even as the level drops, thanks to substantial springs both in the tributaries and in the river bottom itself. Fish here typically hold close to both banks where there's optimum cover, and the regulars do best by carefully wading the middle and fishing into the bank. The wild browns in this stretch are both spooky and educated. Small fly patterns and fine, long leaders are the rule of thumb.

From the New York State line downstream 4.4 miles to the Eagleville covered bridge (where apple pie à la mode is reputed to have been invented), there is a special-regulations section: artificials only, with a limit of three fish over 10 inches. All of the trout in this section are wild also, and the type of fishing generally matches the Arlington water, although the current regulations appear to be breeding a brown trout race that never exceeds 9½ inches long.

From Eagleville along Route 29 to Greenwich, New York, the river grows and also becomes gradually warmer. Pools are larger and deeper, and some stocking does take place. This water (about 10 miles) holds some very large browns that come rarely to either fly or bait. Anglers here also contend with a growing population of chubs that are ever ready to drown a carefully presented dry fly. The average size of trout taken on the fly in this section is larger than found farther upstream, however, which, during a good hatch, makes this stretch worth the aggravation.

In spite of its difficulty, the Battenkill continues to attract large numbers of anglers. Both the Orvis Company, which has manufactured fishing tackle since 1856 in Manchester, and The American Museum of Fly Fishing are located near the Vermont water, as is an extraordinary number of fine restaurants, motels and gift-shopping centers. If a humiliation astream here is to be suffered, it may at least be suffered in style.

For information contact the New York State Dept. of Environmental Conservation, Albany, NY 12233; telephone (415) 421-6554.

The LeTort and the Cumberland Valley

In some cases it is the stream that makes the angler; in others it is the angler who makes the stream. In the case of the LeTort, it is definitely the former.

The deep, placid, food-rich water with its sophisticated fish create a demanding situation. Successful fishing is contingent upon the combination of a good approach, proper execution and worthy imitation. The most skittish fish are those off to the side in shallow water. The most exacting feeders are those sipping minutiae. The most complicated to land are the better ones that run downstream, then settle under the submerged, overhanging elodea.

This little piece of unstocked eastern water features a brown trout bloodline that is a combination of Loch Leven and German fish. No two are marked the same and there is wide variation in both color and spotting.

The different feeding patterns challenge the angler to do his best. There is dainty daytime sipping of terrestrial insects, ants and jassids in particular, in spring, summer and fall. Dog days are grasshopper and Japanese beetle time. In the winter after spawning, there is rooting for sow bugs and scuds, which creates an exacting situation.

The flowage from two outcroppings of limestone springs passes through commercial cress beds, then past a large quarry and under Interstate Route 81. Between this, and the streets and houses of Carlisle, are beautiful open meadows and a man-made spawning area. This area is governed by special catch-and-release regulations featuring fly-fishing. It is the area that visitors seek out and it is the stretch that has made fly-fishing history, and by this time is steeped in tradition. Many anglers have made a pilgrimage to fish the LeTort.

Initiated by the Court is a short juvenile section, then the stream flows through the heart of

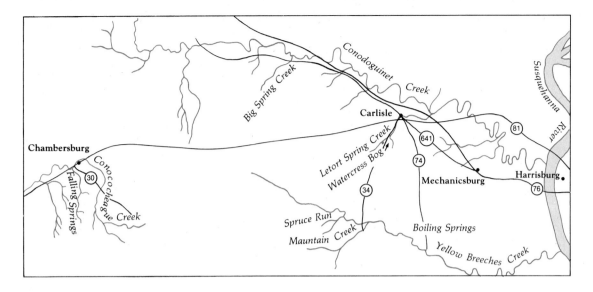

LeTort Spring Creek is in the center of the Pennsylvania limestone country, where cold springs of alkaline water grow large stocks of wild trout. This is the U.S. equivalent of the chalk streams of southern England.

town and the United States War College and then by the Cumberland County Home and Dickinson College intramural sports field. The volume is larger here having picked up the flow from several stronger springs.

Downstream from this point are four miles of potentially great but polluted water. Reclamation, however, is under way, for the construction of a new complete disposal plant is in progress. The topography and landscape here remind one of a picture of the River Itchen in Hampshire, England, probably the most famous trout stream on earth.

In the vicinity are the strongest springs north of Florida, and they form their own spring creeks. A great headquarters is Allenberry Inn, along the Yellow Breeches Creek. Within walking and fishing distance is massive Boiling Springs, with its 7-acre crystal pond and fish-productive outlet into a regulated section of the Breeches. Twelve miles to the west is Big Spring, second in volume to Boiling Springs, the greatest in Pennsylvania. Thirty-three miles south on Interstate Route 81 is Falling Springs, which flows through Chambersburg to join the Conococheague, a freestone trout stream. The first named are a part of the Susquehanna River watershed, the latter two the Potomac.

This group of local springs and resultant streams should be considered by the angler as a unit. Most visiting fishermen move about during the course of a day, the current fly hatch being a determining factor.

August is discouraging on many mountain freestone streams due to low warm water and few, if any, aquatic insects. This is not the case with the limestoners of the Cumberland Valley. A fisherman can enjoy the cream of it; that is, encounter many rising trout in the course of a day's fishing. At a comfortable hour in the morning there is a massive emergence of a tiny mayfly of the caenis family on Falling Springs and Big Spring. Trycorythodes is unique among mayflies in that it emerges, molts, mates and

returns between 8:00 and 11:00 A.M. Trout take them exceedingly well, tipping and sipping as fast as they can. Even though the fly is tiny, usually being imitated by ties on No. 22 or 24 hooks, large trout make the most of it along with the smaller ones. Falling Springs is one of the few streams in Pennsylvania that has a native population of rainbow trout. Once the hatch is over and the insects have drifted by, it is time to leave the stream, for there won't be any feeding until the next morning.

After lunch it is time to look for sippers of small landborn insects and slurpers of beetles and grasshoppers on the LeTort. Along with worthy imitations of these two, try an imitation cricket, a great local favorite fly.

Come late evening, things happen on the Yellow Breeches below the outlet of Boiling Springs. There will be the emergence of the duns and the fall of the spinner of a white fly of fair size. A common imitation of *Ephoron leukon* is an all-white fly tied spent on a long shank No. 16 hook. You may see more surface feeding fish this day in August than you have seen all season long up to that time.

The LeTort more than most other trout streams has made a place in American fly-fishing history. Fortunately for this writer, he has been a witness to much of it.

Vincent Marinaro for a few years took at least part of his precious vacation on the LeTort, spending nights in my fishing hut. We had been experiencing frustration with our feeble attempt to cope with those dainty surface feeders that numbered about thirty in the meadow. One evening after my work I met him there and found him to be full of himself. He told me he had the problem solved, and he let it be known that he would show me how to hook these fish.

He had tied a fly to be opaque instead of translucent and at the same time one that is flush floating in the surface tension instead of high riding on its toes. He named it "Jassid" because it imitated the small leafhoppers, which, he advised, are known as jassids. This new style of tie caught fish for both of us that evening and soon became indispensable. Joe Brooks used it on the LeTort, then wrote about it and later reported that it was an effective fly for him on the Itchen.

Then there was that hot summer day when Ernie Schweibert and I were not doing as well as we thought we should with our artificial hoppers. Too many of those LeTort trout, which took the real thing, passed up his Joe's Hopper, and my gold brick, a "fore-and-aft" hackle fly on a long-shank hook. The next day he advised that he had something new in a hopper imitation, which he had concocted the previous night at the motel, and he gave me one for testing. They were without hackles, something unheard of up to that time for a dry-fly tie. The yellow body was realistic

Henryville on the Brodheads watershed is one of the historic place names in American trout fishing. Many presidents have fished there, but the water can be difficult.

looking, having been made of a new material that would not soak up the water—nylon. The wing was bucktail with two turkey feathers to simulate legs. The hair wing, being multi-tubular, would have to float the body and the hook. I did not think the fly would float, but it did. It fooled fish considerably better than our old imitations. That was the genesis and maiden flight for the fly now listed in the catalogs as the LeTort Hopper.

Eddie Shenk, premier fly-fisherman and fly tier of Carlisle, started to do well with a smaller all-black version, which came to be known as the LeTort Cricket.

The presence of flying ants is not as predictable as the timetable for the various aquatic hatches, but some years they are on our waters about August 10th and again in early October and late

spring. Trout seem to relish ants above all else no matter whether they are the big ones or the little ones, the dark ones or the light ones. It appears that some of the fish that surface feed on them do not feed up top on anything else the year-'round.

My teenage daughter had a sorrel pony, which she took to the shows and races, penned up in the meadow corral. This one had a beautiful amber plume. At an opportune time one of us would slip in and cut off a few hairs from that tail. In tying the Cinnamon Ant, the strand of hair was used as the tying thread. A back end of body was built up, the narrowest of hackle was tied in the wasp waist, after which the front end was built up and tied off. At first this fly was named after its benefactor, Flamette, but later as its use and reputation spread, it came to be known in the fly-fishing fraternity as the Cinnamon Ant.

To meet the challenge of the demanding LeTort, it is important for her anglers to be observant and innovative; and that is the indirect reason why the stream has taken a place in American fly-fishing history and tradition. There are those who think of it as a shrine, and there are those who say, "If you can catch them there, you can catch them anywhere." And, too, some fishermen are not geared for it.

The Brodheads Creek

The Brodheads Creek courses beneath the blue-green ridges of northeastern Pennsylvania's Pocono Mountains. Named for a family of colonial settlers, the scenic stream is history haunted. In Revolutionary War days it watered General Sullivan's troops and horses. And in the late nineteenth and early twentieth centuries the Brodheads was one of the meccas for eastern fly anglers, immortalized by Ernest Schweibert in his classic story, "Homage to Henryville."

The Brodheads is formed by the convergence of some small streams in the vicinity of the hamlet of Canadensis in Monroe County. It meanders south in gentle riffles and brandy-tinted glides for roughly 10 miles to Stroudsburg and to its confluence with the Delaware, approximately 3 to 4 miles distant.

The Paradise—known to old-timers as the Paradise Branch of the Brodheads—rises near the village of Swiftwater, flowing east for about 5 miles to its junction with the main stream at Henryville.

Both the Paradise stretch and the main stream from Canadensis to Analomink (just above Stroudsburg) are virtually all private water and are

The gray cliffs stretch of Montana's Madison River is not heavily fished, has large brown trout, needs a good float guide to handle some rough water and is a likely place to meet a rattlesnake.

posted accordingly. The 5 miles from Analomink to the Delaware is open to public fishing throughout the Pennsylvania trout season which lasts from mid-April to Labor Day, except when extended seasons are in force. In 1983, the Brodheads was open for trout fishing through February with the creel limit set at three fish. Six is the limit during the regular season.

Throughout most of its course the main stream averages roughly 50 feet in width. It is easily accessible from Route 447, which parallels it. After the flood of 1955 the open water, below Analomink, was channelized. Some siltation has resulted—a situation abetted by the relative dearth of bankside vegetation. Nonetheless, the Pennsylvania Fish Commission reports natural reproduction of trout in this area. Above Analomink, in the more heavily wooded private stretches, ideal stream conditions promote excellent spawning. Even so, private water is heavily stocked, as is the public stretch, by the Fish Commission. The result is a heavy head of trout (many very large ones), in the open water

from Analomink to the Delaware.

Since there are no lure restrictions in this area, it is crowded from mid-April to mid- or late May when traffic lessens appreciably. Then water is usually clear and lower. These factors are most conducive to fly-fishing, and some devotees of the long rod come from great distances to sample the fabled Brodheads. While there are brook and rainbow trout throughout the Brodheads, brown trout are preponderant.

Fly life is prevalent but not so profuse as I found it on the Brodheads thirty years ago. Some anglers and biologists blame use of insecticides and the channelization through Stroudsburg as the reasons. Still, there are pronounced hatches of Quill Gordon and Hendrickson mayflies throughout the watershed in early season. In late May and into June there are hatches of Light Cahills and Sulphurs, particularly during evenings. Caddisflies are common on the Brodheads throughout the season. A well-known imitation of the Caddis is The Henryville dry fly. Stoneflies abound throughout spring and summer.

BROWN TROUT

At the turn of August-September, motels in the town of Ennis begin to fill with brown trout anglers who want the best of the Madison experience.

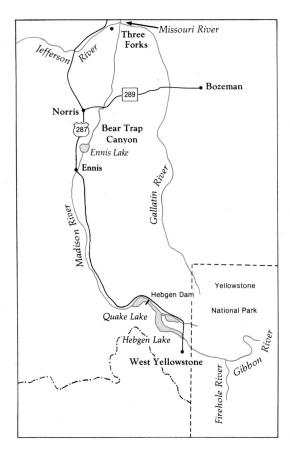

The Madison River begins in Yellowstone Park with the confluence of the Firehole and the meandering Gibbon rivers.
It is singular for an absence of pools and has been described as "one long riffle."

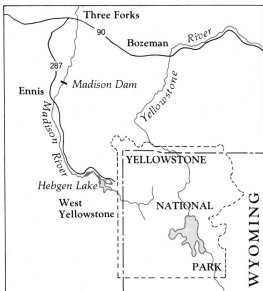

In July a small black stonefly emerges. For years I've matched it with a Black Bivisible dry fly (No. 14 or 16). It has been very effective, probably because it represents ants and beetles as well. In the low, clear water of late summer and fall more realistic terrestrial insects are great favorites.

Accommodations vary (motels, tourist homes and campgrounds) and are plentiful throughout the Pocono region. The area can be reached from major eastern population centers within two to three hours. Information can be obtained from: The Pocono Mountain Vacation Bureau, 1004 Main Street, Stroudsburg, PA 18360; telephone (717) 421-5791.

The Madison River

The Madison River probably is Montana's best-known and most popular, blue-ribbon trout stream. It also is likely the state's hardest fished stream. Fishermen come not only from all over America to fish the Madison, but from around the world as well.

The river's popularity is well deserved. It offers hundreds of miles of premier fishing for brown and rainbow trout, American grayling (in certain sections only) and mountain whitefish. Although it does not produce the huge trout so often taken in other western rivers, the Madison provides fast fishing for trout of average size, and also gives up fish of 4 to 5 pounds with some regularity. Brown trout seem to outnumber rainbows by about 2 to 1, although the rainbow population appears to be increasing in recent seasons.

Fully 95 percent of the Madison flows through southwest Montana's Madison Valley, but the river originates in the Wyoming portion of Yellowstone National Park. It flows northwesterly into Montana's Hebgen Lake, then through Earthquake Lake (formed in 1959 when an earthquake dumped a mountain into the river, burying alive nearly thirty people in a riverside campground, and temporarily damming the river). From Quake Lake the river continues northward, closely paralleling US Route 287, past the towns of Cameron and Ennis, and pours into Ennis Lake, formed by a power dam (Madison Dam), some 15 miles downriver from Ennis. From the Madison Dam the river boils through Beartrap Canyon—a miles-long stretch stiff with large fish, but fishable with difficulty and danger only from rubber rafts or on foot. Below the Beartrap the Madison flattens out and rolls on to its junction with the Missouri River near Three Forks, Montana.

The Madison is a large stream with varying

character. It has been called "one continuous riffle" by anglers less than enthused over it, but the river is readable by fishermen who know it well. The Madison in Yellowstone Park is perhaps the best dry-fly water. Here there are long stretches of air-clear, flat runs, with trout holding alongside and beneath streamers of yellow-green weed, and along the banks draped with lodgepole pines and other logs.

Below Earthquake Lake, the Madison is an unattractive, bulldozed stream. The Army Corps of Engineers ripped the river apart (necessarily) following the 1959 earthquake, but despite the appearance of that stretch of water, it provides some of the Madison's best fishing. The angler who simply wants fish, and cares little about a river's esthetic qualities, will enjoy that part of the Madison.

Montana no longer stocks trout in the Madison following surveys that proved stocking disrupted native populations and did not improve the fishing. Since stocking was halted about five years ago, the native population of brown and rainbow trout has skyrocketed, and the quality of the fishing has greatly improved.

June and early July are very popular times for Madison River fishing. This is when the fabled stonefly ("salmon" fly) hatch occurs, but later, through the summer and early fall, good fishing comes with caddis and flying ant hatches, and in late August and September—when grasshoppers fill the meadows—the fishing can be extraordinary.

The Madison is wadable in all sections except Beartrap Canyon, but it is famous as a float stream. Guides with MacKenzie River and other "float boats" are available in Ennis, Cameron, Bozeman and other river area towns.

R A I N B O W
T R O U T

Oncorhynchus mykiss*

The Salmonidae family contains over sixty species and thousands of races and strains, approximately half of which must be variations of our friend from out of the Golden West, the black-spotted trout with ruddy fasciae on its flanks—the rainbow, or do you prefer Kamloops, or perhaps steelhead, or redband trout, or. . . ? Studies have been made to determine its, or rather *their*, relationship to the cutthroat trout, the California golden trout, the Kern River golden trout subspecies, the Gila trout, the Apache trout, the Rio Truchas trout of Mexico and the Mexican golden trout. Based on what must have been a really tedious series of morphological measurements and meristic counts, the computer decided all of the above had shared characteristics, although some are cousins and some kissing cousins. I have caught strongly colored rainbows in Babine Lake, British Columbia, that also had throats as rubicund as a Seville orange, and caught from California's Kern River, high in the Sierra Nevada, silvery rainbows with a rose fillet on their sides, whose snow-white bellies were thickly dusted with gold.

William B. Willers, biologist and trout fisherman, succinctly poses the core question: "Where rainbows have been introduced into inland waters containing native populations of cutthroats, hybridization nearly always occurs. Nevertheless, the view that they constitute separate and valid species is virtually universal among biologists." How true, but an unwillingness to hybridize is the single most important criterion for species status. Perhaps these black-spotted fish from steep western watersheds have a non-Linnaean logic of their own: "Don't ask me what I am today, I may change my mind tomorrow."

The native southern range was from the vicinity of Ciudad Durango in Mexico's Sierra Madre

The native southern range was from the vicinity of Ciudad Durango in Mexico's Sierra Madre

*Scientific name revised, 1989. Pacific drainage trout genus are no longer of the name *Salmo*.

A Pacific watershed fish that has been transplanted worldwide, rainbows are entomophagic with a preference for subaquatic forms, such as nymphs and larvae, but they also take floating fare. They are free risers to a greater extent than brown trout.

RAINBOW TROUT

Orientale. That is almost as far south as Mazatlan, but of course they are confined to mountain streams at low latitudes. Rainbows were a western-slope-of-the-Rockies fish, except for a pair of incursions over the Continental Divide, in the headwaters of British Columbia's Peace River, and in Alberta's Athabasca River. In Soviet Asia they are found as far south as Kamchatka Peninsula.

DISTRIBUTION

That was the natural range. The fish is now found in all the provinces of Canada except the Northwest Territories; in all the states of the United States except Florida, Mississippi and Louisiana,[1] and in all continents except Antarctica (they have been stocked in France's Kerguelen Islands south of the Indian Ocean opposite Antarctica, but haven't made it ashore yet). Here we have a leading candidate for the blue riband: the world's most popular game fish. In the enormous pool of its genetic diversity, you may almost specify the trout of your dreams, and somewhere there is, or can be, the exact rainbow for you.

Dr. Lauren R. Donaldson, long head of the College of Ocean and Fishery Sciences of the University of Washington in Seattle, wanted the piscine equivalent of a battery chicken, and he got it. The college had begun selective breeding of rainbows in 1932. In the beginning, the fish became sexually mature at age four, weighing 1½ pounds, and the hens would contain 400 to 500 eggs. More recently, this hatchery population has produced 1½-pound bucks at age one. The females now mature in their second year, weigh 10 pounds, and yield 10,000 eggs on their first spawning. "We like to think our results compare with the poultrymen's development of the broad-breasted turkey," says Dr. Donaldson. Fast-growing fish are essential to the increasing commercial market. The Danish brands of packaged frozen rainbow (Denmark's second largest industry) that have been available for years, principally in Europe and North America, now have competition from Finland, Norway, Great Britain, Italy, France, Japan, Australia and the United States. The Italians are marketing approximately 21,000 tons of rainbow trout per annum nowadays. United States production, mostly centered in the Snake River valley in southern Idaho, runs about 13,000 tons, part of this destined to stock angling waters.

Though essentially a spring-spawning fish, some rainbow populations have been discovered that spawn as early as November or as late as August. In hatchery operations, by selective breeding and photoperiod manipulation, races of rainbows have now been achieved that spawn in each month of the year. For commercial production this is a priceless asset; it means new product is maturing constantly. By transporting Idaho hatchery rainbows conditioned to fall spawning into warm (62°F) California waters, spawning *twice* a year has even been achieved. "Of all the salmonids the rainbow trout exhibit the greatest genetic diversity," says Dr. Donaldson. It is precisely this plasticity that makes commercial hatchery production, sea ranching and sea farming of rainbow trout the booming growth industry it is. Fishing rights on the high seas are now subject to increasing regulation as a hungry human population disputes the distribution of what was once thought to be inexhaustible resources. Humanity needs a new chicken, a chicken with fins. We are witnessing the development of one in our own lifetime.

Rainbows can be completely mature at 4 inches in some headwater creeks, but a 52½-pound specimen was netted from a British Columbian lake. This is larger than any steelhead yet reported, the largest to date being a full 10 pounds lighter than that freshwater fish. Growth of lacustrine rainbows can be spectacular if they are stocked in lakes with good populations of kokanee. Lake Pend Oreille, Idaho, had that precondition when Kamloops rainbow fingerlings were stocked in 1942. In four years some had reached 25 pounds; in five years the lake record of 37 pounds was set. The freshwater sockeye is now the subject of a new stocking program at Pend Oreille. Idaho biologists anticipate the lake will return to its former productivity.

Stream rainbows will seldom exceed 1 foot. The researches of Dr. Robert Bachman and others indicate that in typical trout streams the nutritive value of an insect diet allows growth beyond 12 inches only in rare individuals. Trout that have developed beyond 14 inches are almost certainly already embarked on a career of eating little fish. This probably happens more often with rainbows than with other trout, because from the beginning of hatchery operations some steelhead were inadvertently mixed into the gene pool. Meat-eating stream fish go where the meat is—downstream into rivers, lakes and oceans. If it is a cold lake full of kokanee, you get giant trout in very few years. If it is a cool lake full of stunted,

[1]Dr. Robert J. Behnke, the outstanding American salmonid biologist, has made population studies of eastern Oregon redband trout in desert streams with water temperatures an incredible 83°F, so there is yet hope those three states can join the bandwagon.

ravenous pike you are going to lose the wandering steelhead/rainbow, while the rainbow/steelhead that remains in the creek also remains small on an insect diet. So extensive has rainbow stocking been in the United States that in all likelihood the only purebred strains remaining are in western headwater creeks with natural barriers to prevent incursions by hatchery stock or their offspring. In the name of goodness and mercy, *do not* take your Vibert box full of hatchery rainbow eggs into unsullied water. Every pure strain from this enormously diverse species that we can identify and isolate, the better. Different races can vary in temperature tolerance, resistance to specific diseases, growth potential, piscivorous inclinations, wanderlust and many other qualities that must now be specifically bred for in that genetic mishmash, the hatchery-product rainbow, a creature that will yield almost any quality you want because it has almost everything conceivable.

Spawning rainbows can often be identified by high color: The rose flanks become a scarlet band. Males develop a kyped face, hooked and ugly. This they wield in dominance fights, biting at each other to determine who has the honor of being the primary spawner with a given henfish. She digs her redd by lying on her side and flipping her tail vigorously upward. This momentarily releases the hydraulic pressure of the current and the unpressurized gravel leaps free of the streambed and is carried a short distance downstream. She and the dominant male then spawn, but subdominant bucks and even male parr will join in, and she will cover the redd by digging upstream exactly as she did on the redd itself. This continues until she is spawned out.

Hatching is dependent on water temperature, but should occur within four to seven weeks. The alevin stay put for as long as a week, absorbing most of their egg sac. Siltation is a danger to both egg and alevin. Unsound forestry and farming practices that muddy spawning creeks can result in trout suffocated in the redd/womb. The hen has picked her reddsite for good underground seepage, but this must be maintained until the hatch. Once they are out of the gravel, rainbow alevins wait fifteen days or so before taking food. Planktonic crustacea is first, and then insects at all stages of their development. If fly-fishing had not previously been developed for brown trout and

salmon, it would have to be invented for rainbow trout.

The spawn usually occurs in water of 50° to 60°F, which also is the temperature range for maximum growth of rainbows. Survival for a repeat spawn varies from as low as only 5 percent to as much as 57 percent. Individuals have been know to spawn successfully on five successive years. The best survival rates are with young henfish. Males and elderly females are more likely to give up the ghost after providing for their succession. Sexual maturation can be as young as

Slack in the flanks, this rainbow is spawned out and is properly being returned to the water. The scene is southwest Alaska, where catches of 100 trout a day have been recorded.

age one or as late as age six. If that six-year-old, first-spawner lives in a lake full of kokanees, it will be the catch of a lifetime—a double-digit giant.

In addition to insects, crustaceans, fish and eggs escaped during salmon spawning, rainbow trout eat canned maize, marshmallows, earthworms and pork rind. The construction of large impoundments on southern rivers with cold-water discharges from the base of tall dams produced some tailwater trout fisheries on streams that had formerly been noted for their catfish. A

RAINBOW TROUT

catfisherman, the son of generations of catfishermen, tends to be conservative in his angling techniques, and unlikely to take seriously the concept that small artificial insects would interest fish. Introduce such a gentleman to fish raised to catchable size on pellets made of dry fish meal, grain meals, vegetable protein meals and assorted nutrients, and the gentleman will almost certainly conclude that if catfish will take canned corn, marshmallows and their ilk, trout will too. He is absolutely correct. I have shared a johnboat with gentlemen who confounded the southern heat by going shirtless underneath their faded denim bib coveralls and were amazingly dexterous as they flipped a cube of cheesebait concealing their hook into the river, then flipped out a trout. They also skinned their trout just as catfishermen are wont to do, dusted them in cornmeal and fried them in hot lard, with hush puppies, of course.

Casting for a rainbow in the swift waters of a nameless southwestern Alaska stream.

I t is well to remember, when dry-fly-fishing the Beaverkill or Henry's Fork of the Snake, that in all likelihood you could catch more trout with almost any substance that smelled as if it had a high-protein content. Trout fishermen may be capable of self-delusion concerning the art of angling, but rainbow trout are remarkably like channel catfish—omnivores who will try to eat anything, especially if it seems to have an animal basis. I have generally found that cheese is more effective than marshmallows. The killer bait is a combination of nightcrawler and marshmallow. The earthy bouquet of live animal protein brings them in, then the taste of sugar unhinges their reason.

If you are a largemouth bass fisherman rather than a catfish sportsman, try angling for rainbows with the black jig-and-eel pork rind lure that is commonly used for winter bass fishing. This is particularly effective in water of dubious quality where the presence of leeches is indisputable.

Regardless of how large minnowing trout may grow, they continue to be susceptible to the fly, both insect and artificial. I have seen rainbows that could not be less than 10 pounds sipping minute mayflies as avidly as a child with popcorn.

Lake rainbows have a much larger volume of food forms available, as a rule, and have no current to breast. Their growth rates usually exceed those of stream fish by multiples. They can grow to many pounds on a wholly insectivorous diet, or on crustaceans such as *Gammarus* or *Mysis*.

Kamloops introduced into some fishless lakes swarming with *Gammarus* ballooned to 14 pounds in only three years! The conveyor-belt simplicity of stream feeding is a great convenience to trout, but as we have seen, a diet of single insects limits growth. The lake fish can munch whole windrows of them, as well as such intermediaries as kokanee, tadpoles and frogs, and lacustrine predatory insects. In British Columbia, the traveling sedge, a big caddisfly that experiences the greatest difficulty launching itself from the water, is in some watersheds a dietary mainstay of shockingly large rainbows. I have raised 4-pound trout up through 9 feet of water to take a Sofa Pillow brought across the surface with the palsied-hand retrieve and a fast stripping-in of line.

Rainbows prefer water between 44° and 75°F, and they continue putting on weight in the range from 40° to 70°. At only 2 or 3 ounces they

become euryhaline, or capable of tolerating a wide range of salinity. The desert redband trout that Dr. Behnke discovered were *feeding* at 83°F, and every year tons of rainbows are taken by ice fishermen. This is an unusually adaptive fish. At Dauphin Island, near Mobile, Alabama, rainbows have been cage cultured in Gulf of Mexico waters. The essential criterion is water below 70° for a 120-day growing season. What they do *not* like, and ill tolerate, is gentle-gradient moving water. There are few acceptable rainbow river fisheries on the eastern seaboard because the watersheds are insufficiently steep. Their need is for excellent oxygenation in the redd, and the precipitous Pacific Coast rivers have this in abundance. Once successfully hatched, their adaptable natures allow at least some races of them to permeate most temperate aquatic environments. Many if not most stream and lake rainbows have a life

expectancy of only three or four years, but Great Lakes fish seem to last six to eight years, and some wild Alaskan strains reportedly can reach twelve years. If that latter age can be attained in southerly waters, fish culturists will (undoubtedly) want to introduce *them* into the hatchery-product gene pool. There is little point now to object if someone wants to throw one more fish into what is already a bouillabaisse.

If the same intensity of selective breeding that has gone into producing the chicken with fins were applied to making a rainbow more tolerant of low oxygenation in the redd, a trout of lazy rivers might be possible. I know lots of lazy rivers with very large populations of minnows and rough fish. A twelve-year-old rainbow in such a milieu would be the stuff of dreams.

That 52½-pound British Columbia rainbow was a Kamloops of the Gerrard strain, the same strain

RAINBOW TROUT

that was used to stock Lake Pend Oreille. They are characteristically slow to mature, and do not make a spawning run until they are six or seven years old. Even without a support base of kokanees, trout that long-lived should provide capital sport. Gerrard is on the Lardeau River, a tributary of Kootenay Lake, whose reputation as an excellent fishery for large trout remains undiminished by time.

My first rainbow was a 7-inch trout taken from the North Fork of the Stanislaus River in California's Sierra Nevada range in 1941. He fought much more than a 13-inch brown trout caught the same day. The tackle to which they succumbed was a bankside willow pole cut with my Boy Scout knife, 2 yards of 9-pound-test braided black silk casting line, a small gold-plated hook and a single salmon egg. It was most curious to see the obvious black line running out into a river full of golden sand (iron pyrites, alas; the gold was long gone) and pale rock. Both trout evidently considered it some marvelous new discovery of where to find those delicious red eggs.

The entire panoply of freshwater tackle is used to fish for rainbow trout, and since that willow-pole fish I believe I have personally used just about everything except dynamite. The troll catches I have made in the Great Lakes using downriggers and otter boards (now called sideplaners) were entertaining because downrigger trolling rods are long and limber, intended to whip upward and set the hook when a fish takes. A long rod (8 feet or more) always seems more enjoyable to me whether spinning, bait casting or fly casting.

Rainbows in rivulets are for ultralight spinning and 3-, 4- and 5-weight fly tackle. Distance casting for steelhead, or for lake rainbows rising at a distance, calls for 8-, 9- and 10-weight rods and lines. In all cases I would want a 9-foot boron rod, and even longer in graphite. Under the spell of Lee Wulff, I fished with midge rods for years, but now reserve them for tunnel streams with a low overstory. In such short rods, bamboo still has its charms because the weight of the wood makes for a slower casting cycle than modern synthetics.

Since entomophagic stream trout are seldom going to be longer than a foot, they are scarcely going to require backing on a fly reel. But remember, rainbows nowadays (who are not true wild trout) may be making a spawning run out of downstream lakes at strange times of year. Every now and then, casting a small fly to a little sipping rise, a fish of unexpected avoirdupois will take.

Pools are for brown trout; look for rainbows in faster water. I like to fish down riffles with big

stoneflies because stoneflies need the aeration that riffles provide. Fishing *up* riffles is frequently impossible because water speed is too fast to permit stripping-in fly line to maintain contact with the fly. You can fish upstream effectively by switching to ultralight spinning tackle with a weighted stonefly or a small jig. The spinning reel will retrieve fast enough unless you are in one of the torrents of spring. Do not ignore a riffle because it seems to be only an inch or two of water over monotonous gravel without shelter for the trout. Rainbows will go into such water whenever they want stoneflies, and *some* fish want a stonefly every hour of the clock.

In much of the United States, fly-fishing for rainbow trout is still done over hatchery fish, who have much experience of human beings as creatures who bring food, but little experience of insects. I would fish an active, skittering dry fly, or an upswimming nymph à la Leisenring or Charles E. Brooks, with more confidence over stocked rainbows than any other fish. Bear in mind when selecting flies for these trout that 85 percent of all known species of animal life are insects, and a trout that doesn't keep sipping away at what the drift brings him is shortly going to be hungry.

As you will see in Eric Peper's admirable report on the incredibly difficult wild rainbows of Henry's Fork of the Snake River in Idaho, they are not incredibly difficult, despite their press. There *are* some difficult rainbows, however. It is not solely brown trout that can try men's souls. When some of us who fish the Beaverkill's brown trout want a lesson in *hard* fishing, we go downstream to the Delaware River and fish its red-sided trout. The Delaware is the eastern seaboard's premier rainbow fishery in terms of head of trout, size of trout and size of hatches. I believe they are overfed by magnificent populations of fly life, but I have gone fishless on the Delaware during no-hatches as well as heavy hatches, and I have watched some warrantedly famous fishermen casting with elegant precision to rising Delaware rainbows, futilely.

Dr. Charles M. Mottley, a fisheries biologist from Cornell University, conducted a study of the meristics of Kamloops trout in British Columbia in the late 1930s. Until the early 1930s, fisheries biologists considered that one indicator of species differentiation was the count of scales along a fish's lateral line. Mottley determined that scale count varied with water temperature. By incubating a mountain Kamloops trout egg at the lower temperatures found at sea level, he could bring its scale count down to that of a steelhead egg, and vice versa. The observable difference between two subspecies, races or strains of rainbow could be eliminated in one generation. Mottley's work became a classic of ichthyology. It made his reputation, and attracted the attention of Roderick L. Haig-Brown, who made Mottley's studies a keystone of his most famous book, *The Western Angler* (Morrow, New York, 1939), which remains in print to this day.

For a few decades, Mottley's work with rainbows papered over a philosophical split that is probably intrinsic to the study of natural history, that between "lumpers" and "splitters"; between those biologists who want the category of species to be broad, inclusive and simple, and those who want it to be restrictive and sophisticated. The splitters reigned before Mottley. They are back again, but now they have gone inside the cell. They can make differentiations on the basis of the chromosomes of two genotypes, even the amino acid sequence of a molecule.

Rainbows were the species used in a series of experiments in learning. A red-tipped trigger that would release food pellets when struck was mounted beneath the surface of an aquarium. The pellets were released from a station separate from the trigger. The trout hit the trigger 50 times on the first day; within 10 days they were up to 250 per day, and sustained at that level. They had rationalized their conduct to the point of approaching the trigger from an angle that allowed them to nudge it and glide directly to the pellet station. Some old trigger hands were then removed and hand fed for three months. When returned to the aquarium they resumed triggering immediately.

Lauren Donaldson believes the evolution of salmonids is henceforth in the hands of humanity. His own work was a powerful impetus to farming and ranching them, but in addition to developing strains that produce maximum poundage per unit of food, such attributes as disease resistance through habitat preference can be sought for. Tensleep rainbows, from the hatchery by that name in Wyoming, have been introduced into East Canyon Reservoir in Utah because their deep-water preference avoids contact with the disfiguring anchor worm that infects surface-feeding trout in the reservoir.

The warm-water rainbow is being actively sought by Texas Parks and Wildlife biologists, whose hatchery stock is often subject to low, hot water during dry summers. In addition to the redbands discovered by Behnke, they are experimenting with trout from the Firehole River in Yellowstone National Park.

Man and rainbow have come a long way together, and will share the future also. NASA released a study for a large, self-sufficient space colony in 1977. The animals they calculated should be taken aboard two by two (or more) were chickens, rabbits, goats, cattle and trout. I know in my bones which trout it is going to be.

The Namekagon River

Northern Wisconsin means muskies to most anglers—Tiger Cat Flowage, the Chippewa Flowage, and a host of lakes that harbor this sought-after fighter. A few will think of the storied Bois Brule, a lovely river that feeds Lake Superior, and annually sees excellent spawning runs of both brown and rainbow trout. Another fishery exists in northern Wisconsin though; one that has the potential to satisfy the desires of almost any angler.

The Namekagon River originates at Namekagon Lake in Bayfield County, then wends its way more than 60 miles through Sawyer, Washburn and Burnett counties to where it meets the St. Croix River at Riverside, Wisconsin

Wisconsin's Namekagon River, upstream from Hayward, is an outstanding fishery curiously lacking in national reputation.

(about 30 miles south of Duluth, Minnesota). The Namekagon was, in 1967, included with the St. Croix in the National Wild and Scenic Rivers Act, so its character and surroundings should, in the future, be much as they are today.

The Namekagon has always been popular for canoeing throughout its length, and, in fact, this is one of the more effective ways to fish it. As a result of this popularity, the visiting angler will find many locations for camping, ranging from rustic riverside sites to fully equipped locations with swimming pools, motor-home hookups and the like.

RAINBOW TROUT

There are really two sections to the Namekagon. The upper river, 20 miles from Hayward, Wisconsin, upstream to Namekagon Lake, is trout water. The lower river provides fine fishing for smallmouth, walleyes, northern pike and muskellunge, not to mention a variety of panfish.

The upper river is easily fished by wading. Most of the lower section can be more comfortably fished with a canoe or small boat. The excellent fishing in the lower section is regularly enjoyed, while the trout fishing upstream receives relatively little attention after the traditional mid-May opening day. In fact, a recent survey showed that 60 percent of total fishing pressure took place in the month of May on the upper river, even though the trout season in Wisconsin runs through September.

Midwestern trout fishermen are missing a good bet! The Namekagon's upper 20 miles are a rich and productive fishery. From Namekagon Lake downstream to Cable the river is 8 miles of rapid, woodland stream with few road crossings. Native brook trout are still present in this upper stretch. From Cable downstream to Hayward, the river is quite wide with a combination of pools and riffles and many alder-lined, undercut banks. Brown trout, both wild and stocked, and rainbows predominate in this 12-mile stretch.

The fisherman benefits from the presence of three lakes (or "flowage," as they are called here) in the upper 20 miles. These serve to stabilize the river's flow, minimizing high-water periods, and act as collecting basins, providing nutrients to the waters downstream. Depending upon the time of the year, the fact that the flowages warm the waters downstream may be either benefit or detriment. In early season, for example, a fly hatch may have ended in the section near Hayward and just be starting near Cable.

The Namekagon has a rich and varied population of trout food forms. Among mayflies, the more popular fishing hatches are the Hendrickson (*Ephemerella subvaria*), the brown drake (*Ephemera simulans*), the giant Michigan mayfly (*Hexagenia limbata*), the white fly (*Ephoron leukon*) and the tiny black and white *Tricorythodes*. Because of Wisconsin's May opener, the Hendrickson hatch may occur, in a warm spring, too early for anglers to enjoy it. Normal emergence is around the first week of May. The brown drake appears early in June, *limbata* in late June, and the white fly and *Tricorythodes* in mid- to late July. Lesser hatches that can provide exceptional fishing include the *Stenonemas* (March brown, Gray Fox and Cahill) along with the large, yellow *Potamanthus distinctus* mayfly. A second large brown drake hatch, *Hexagenia atrocaudata*, which occurs on mid-July evenings, has also provided some outstanding fishing.

The Namekagon has a wide variety of caddis hatches along with large populations of stoneflies, including the huge *Pteronarcys* genus. The best dry-fly-fishing, however, will be to the prolific mayfly hatches, and the best fishing to these hatches is in the evenings from late May through mid-July.

The populations of mayflies, caddisflies and stoneflies in the Namekagon are supplemented by large quantities of dragonflies, dobsonflies, freshwater shrimp and staggering numbers of crayfish, as well as sculpins and shiners. This underwater cornucopia keeps larger fish well hidden and feeding subsurface during the day, except in the presence of a very large insect hatch. The huge amounts of food available in the river grow some large, healthy fish as well. A recent electrofishing survey yielded an 11-pound brown trout. A 16-inch fish, showing the full benefit of his environment, may easily exceed 2 pounds.

For many years the upper Namekagon was maligned by anglers in the region because, day-in and day-out, the average fish caught would be on the order of 9 inches long. Recently, enlightened management practices, including fall stocking and stocking throughout the length of the river rather than only at bridge sites, have allowed greater holdover populations and more growth opportunity, resulting in a larger average size of caught fish. Careful anglers can now expect to hook a good percentage of fish 12 inches or longer. In addition, beginning with the 1983 season, no fish between 10 and 16 inches may be kept within a 6.6-mile stretch near the town of Seeley. The new legislation preserves the prime breeding stock and provides better sport for the angler.

The upper Namekagon is easy to wade. The few deep holes that exist are easy to spot, so late evening fishing here is not the threat that it is on some other rivers. For dedicated fly-fishermen there are no local fly shops to guide you to the prevailing hatch, so a bit of homework with a good reference book would be worthwhile. The hints offered here are by no means all-inclusive.

Daytime fishing is best accomplished with nymphs; the most productive being a hellgrammite

One of the most elegant forms of camouflage to be found in nature is the rainbow's glory. This one is about to be returned to the river—the Green River, which winds through Utah, Colorado and Wyoming.

imitation, as it mimics both the *Pteronarcys* stonefly and the larva of the dobsonfly. A good dragonfly nymph is a close second choice. You will see fish rising during the day, but these will be either small trout or chubs in most cases. A large streamer fished deep and carefully under banks and in slow deep pools will often produce.

Often in the summer, an angler will fish the Namekagon by day, and swear that it is a barren river. He will return as the trees begin to shade the water and stare with disbelief as the water begins to boil with the rises of fish he would not have thought could be sheltered in the stream. It may require several visits before you see a "superfeed" and you may have to catch a major hatch or spinner fall, but once experienced, you'll be a Namekagon devotee for life. There are *big* fish here that would do a river anywhere proud. They are not dumb, and they do not come easy, but trying for them is a pleasant effort in this beautiful spot.

It seems safe to assume that Namekagon trout fishing will continue to improve. The Wild and Scenic River Act prohibits new construction along the river's banks, and the U. S. Park Service is attempting to create a 500-foot "green belt" along both banks, which will help in controlling erosion and in maintaining cooler water temperatures.

There are several access points in the upper 20 miles of river via both county roads and US Route 63, which parallels much of the river. The most popular access point is in the village of Seeley, as it is extremely pleasant water to fish. However,

the angler's chances for large fish are probably better further downstream in the 4½ miles of river above Hayward and below the small lake called Phipps Flowage.

While there is some trout fishing just below the dam in Hayward, the lower river is best known for warm-water species, principally smallmouth bass. This is pleasant fishing, largely in wilderness settings, much of it in fast-moving water. Successful anglers use small spinning lures and rubber jigs or fish hellgramites, either live or imitations. Fly-fishing with nymphs is another effective method, and smallmouth often rise to the same hatches as the trout do upstream.

There are northern pike throughout the river, including the upper section where more than one late evening trout angler has thought he had a record brown hooked on his slow-fished streamer fly. Favorite spots for northern pike along the length of the river are the slower moving stretches found just upstream of the flowages. Walleyed pike are prevalent in the lower river also along with panfish.

The Trego Flowage, a roughly 6-mile-long widening of the river below the village of Trego, has an excellent and not too widely known muskellunge population. In fact, from Trego downstream, the river is populated with these monster game fish, and the casual angler can be surprised when his tackle is suddenly either broken or stripped. The majority of fishermen in this area of the country believe that lakes are the home of the revered muskellunge, and they do not bother fishing rivers for this species. While muskellunge never provide the easiest fishing, the Namekagon offers the visiting angler a chance to show the locals a new trick. As everywhere, suckers are a favorite bait.

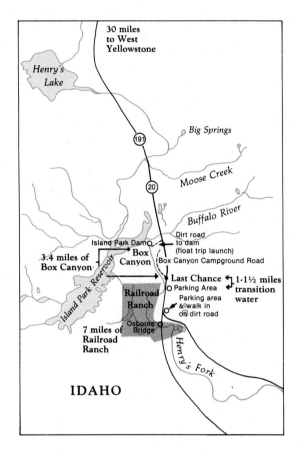

Henry's Fork of the Snake River in Idaho is a giant chalk stream filled with rainbow trout and frequent hatches of insects. For dry-fly-fishing it is probably incomparable.

From Trego downstream, much of the river is away from roads, and it is a virtual necessity to fish from either canoe or small boat. There are few white water stretches here to speak of, and the floating fisherman can enjoy a near wilderness experience. Game is plentiful, and fall anglers often plan for a mixed bag of fish and upland game. The lower Namekagon, fished from a canoe, allows the visitor to see northern Wisconsin in both the manner and the condition that the early fur traders and loggers saw it. The last 15 to 20 miles of the river before it enters the St. Croix at Riverside, Wisconsin, is wild country, and fishing is quite good for bass, northern pike and muskellunge.

For the visiting angler without a canoe, several outfitters along the length of the river offer equipment rentals and pickups from pre-agreed locations. Because the area is a popular vacation region, accommodations are well distributed and range from adequate to luxury. Easiest access to the area from the south is via US Route 53 or US Route 63 to Trego, then US Route 63 upriver from Trego to Cable. The river flows from the east into Cable, and driving West on Bayfield County Road M will take you to the headwaters at Namekagon Lake.

The later in the summer one visits the river, the more the references above to "canoe or small boat" should say, "canoe only." Lower water conditions of late summer will mean that only a canoe will clear bottom in some sections, and even then a wrong decision on current may mean a short walk to deeper water. At any time, however, the Namekagon is a beautiful river that will reward the careful angler.

Henry's Fork of the Snake

The Henry's Fork, also called the North Fork of the Snake on some maps, offers some of the finest trout fishing in the United States. The river flows through extreme southeastern Idaho, just to the west of Yellowstone and Grand Teton National parks. The river is the product of the outlet of Henry's Lake, a notable fishery in its own right, and the Big Springs of the Henry's Fork. These source waters flow into the Island Park Reservoir, which was created in the late 1960s to irrigate the many farms in the lower valley. The U.S. Forest Service controls the flow from the dam to ensure stable water levels in the river.

The most productive portion of the Henry's

Fork, and the most important to the visiting angler, is the upper 10 to 12 miles from Island Park dam downstream through Harriman State Park, which is better known to anglers as the Railroad Ranch. The ranch includes about 7 miles of stream. It was built by the Harriman family during the construction of the Union Pacific Railroad. The family deeded the ranch to the state of Idaho several years ago, and it has been managed as a park since then.

Island Park dam is about 30 miles south of the west entrance to Yellowstone Park. US Route 191, which turns south out of West Yellowstone, parallels the Henry's Fork until it crosses the river at Osborne Bridge near the downstream end of Railroad Ranch. The river only runs near the road for approximately a mile in the town of Last Chance, Idaho. Other access to the river is on foot, either from Box Canyon Campground on the upper few miles, or from parking lots located at the upper and middle portions of the ranch and at Osborne Bridge. All of this section of the river may be fished only with single, barbless-hook, artificial lures, and the Railroad Ranch stretch is restricted to artificial flies only.

The Henry's Fork is primarily a rainbow trout fishery, and it contains some brook trout. Rocky Mountain whitefish are found throughout the river. There is no stocking in the upper section of the river, and spawning takes place throughout

this mileage. The Idaho Fish and Game Department estimates that there are 6,000 to 7,000 trout over 10 inches per mile of stream. The rainbows in the Henry's Fork are known to grow as large as 8 pounds.

The upper Henry's Fork is really two rivers in one, the Box Canyon and the Railroad Ranch. The upper 3.4 miles is a rough and tumble stretch flowing through a pine-capped canyon. This is the Box Canyon. The river ranges from 60 to 120 feet wide here, and it is fast flowing and boulder strewn. It is in the canyon that one has the best chance to hook a trophy fish. Many rainbows from 10 to 15 pounds are taken in the Box Canyon each year. Except for the major stonefly hatches in the canyon each June, the fishing here is primarily with big stonefly nymphs and streamers, or with spinning lures.

Below Box Canyon, the river widens to 100 yards and more. There is about 1½ miles of "transition" water where the river calms itself from the rush down the canyon before entering the slow, meandering flow through the ranch. Here both dry-fly tactics, deep nymphs and streamer fishing may be productive. While the Box Canyon may intimidate the would-be wader, the stretch through the transition water welcomes him. The transition water is very pleasant to fish, and it is much more forgiving than the challenging flats encountered on the ranch.

RAINBOW TROUT

The ranch water is a meadow stream, placid and easily wadeable. In the early season, its gravel bottom is clearly seen, but as the season goes on the weed growth builds, until by early autumn, its currents are choked with a rich growth of grass and mosses. Because of the dense weed growth, this is primarily dry-fly and floating nymph water, and it provides as severe a test of the angler's skill as may be found.

The Henry's Fork provides good fishing for the entire season. Because its flow is controlled by the outflow from Island Park dam, the Henry's Fork is not subjected to heavy runoff from snowmelt or storms, as are other Rocky Mountain rivers. The combined influences of the dam outlet and the Big Springs maintain water temperatures at ideal levels. The management of the dam has recently been taken over by the U.S. Forest Service from the Idaho Fish and Game Department. Their policies have differed on water releases, but the only effect has been a slight variation in the hatching cycles of some of the aquatic insects. Fishing has not been affected at all. The general season for fishing in Idaho begins at the end of May and extends until late November; however, there are local exceptions to this, and the visiting angler should check a complete statement of regulations before fishing.

Cataloging the insect life of the Henry's Fork is a major task because the river is an "insect factory." Ideal conditions exist for all varieties of trout stream insects, and the fly one fishes at a given time will be dictated by the part of the stream being fished. In June, for example, the Box Canyon will be playing host to the giant western stonefly or salmonfly, *Pteronarcys californica*, while the meadow sections of the river have major hatches of *Ephemerella infrequens*, a light olive mayfly, called the pale morning dun.

Generally speaking, the Box Canyon has only two hatches of significance to the dry-fly angler. These are the *Pteronarcys* stonefly, which hatches in mid-June, and the *Acroneuria*, or golden stonefly, which follows in late June. These two hatches offer an excellent opportunity to hook a very large trout on a dry fly; however, while fishing and particularly wading the Box Canyon in June, water temperatures represent a challenge that is not for the faint of heart. This is heavy water, and one must be prepared to follow a big fish should it decide to head downriver.

Imitations for the *Pteronarcys* adult include the Sofa Pillow and Bird's Stonefly, or any of the many popular salmonfly imitations in No. 4 and 6. The *Acroneuria* adult is imitated by similar

"Trude-style" patterns with golden yellow bodies in No. 8.

Following the two major stonefly hatches, the Box Canyon is fished most productively with weighted stonefly nymphs and weighted streamers. The best patterns will be imitations of the big *Pteronarcys* nymphs, which should be black, heavy, and tied on No. 4 and 6 streamer hooks. The attrition on nymphs is considerable, because if you fish these flies properly, you will leave many of them on the bottom of the river. Streamer patterns may be either imitators or attractors, but imitations of either the sculpin or the golden dace will probably produce most consistently. All patterns should be tied with plenty of weight to get down among the pockets of the heavy current of "The Box."

A substantial rod is needed to fish Box Canyon effectively, along with a reel with a good drag and plenty of backing. I recommend an 8½-foot or longer rod that handles an 8-weight line. The water is not so deep that a sinking line is needed, but you may want a sink tip in addition to a floater, specifically for swimming streamer patterns just a bit deeper. If you plan on landing your fish, don't go any lighter than 0X on your tippet, even during hatches. This is very swift current, and the flies are big. Generally, even the biggest fish will not be gut shy.

Leaving the Box Canyon is like entering a different world. The high stone walls give way to an open landscape and the rushing current smooths to a gentler flow. You enter the dry-fly angler's Nirvana. Beginning with the pale morning dun mentioned earlier, the hatches extend for the entire season, overlapping each other and, in some cases, repeating. In the Railroad Ranch section, the fishing is always to rising trout; first, because they are there, and second, because the heavy weed growth makes subsurface fishing a fruitless task in most cases. Some experts will attempt to lure the big rainbows from the weeds with well-presented leech or sculpin imitations, but this is not necessary when there are rising fish.

The pale morning dun (*Ephemerella infrequens*) generally begins hatching in the first week of June and will continue until near the end of June. The hatch normally appears near 11:00 A.M. and lasts until about 3:00 P.M. The best imitations are tied in No. 18, and they have bright olive (almost chartreuse) bodies and pale gray wings. My personal favorites are thorax-style flies with a single turkey feather clump for a wing and very sparse dun hackle. For this hatch, and for all mayfly hatches mentioned, it is wise to have both imitations of the dun and of the floating nymph when fishing the Henry's Fork. As a general rule, the floating nymph imitations should be the same size as the dun and they should have a slightly darker body color and a buoyant, grey wing pad.

Following the pale morning dun emergence, about mid-June, *Baetis parvus* emerges. This tiny (No. 20) mayfly appears in the late afternoon, complementing nicely the end of the *infrequens* emergence. Often, when both hatches are dense, you will not even have to change flies as the trout do not seem to care whether the imitation is No. 18 or 20. In fact, the body color of *Baetis* is slightly darker with a brownish tint, and as *infrequens* ends and *Baetis* begins, the trout will show a marked preference for floating nymphs of *Baetis*.

As June blends into July, the insect activity on the Henry's Fork becomes almost unimaginable. Mornings will have spinner falls of the pale morning dun (brown body, clear wing, No. 16 or 18), and *Baetis* (brown thorax, white body, clear wing, No. 20), along with emergence of the Western green drake, *Ephemerella grandis*. Evenings will yield a variety of caddisfly hatches along with the brown drake, *Ephemera simulans*, on the lower, slower, silt-bottomed stretches of the Railroad Ranch. *Baetis* spinners will appear in the evenings as well.

The hatch of the Western green drake brings an almost carnival atmosphere to the Henry's Fork. Anglers arrive from all over the United States and, in fact, the world, to experience the sight of big rainbows rising to the large (No. 10) green-bodied mayflies, and, of course, they are filled with the hope of tangling with just one of those trout. In recent years, because of the crowds, the "drake hatch" has become more spectacle than fishing experience, and its attraction is an oddity because this hatch is less reliable and less productive than most that the river has to offer.

By mid-July, the stonefly and green drake festivals are over, the crowds are thinner, and the weather is delightful. The river has entered what I call "the olive season." Olive mayflies abound, beginning with the small Western green drake, *Ephemerella flavilinea*, and continuing to *Ephemerella inermis*, then a reappearance (or possibly continuance) of *E. infrequens*, and yet another appearance of *Baetis parvus*, followed by *Pseudocloeon edmundsi*. The practical angler can imitate all of these insects with a single pattern tied in a variety of sizes. Dun and floating nymph imitations should have bright olive bodies and grey wings (or wing pads, for nymphs). In the order in which they were named above, the sizes of these mayflies are: 14, 18, 16, 20 and 24. Personally, I don't like fishing No. 24's, and I have found a 22 to be quite adequate.

The *flavilinea* olive generally stops hatching by the end of July. The other olive mayflies are in evidence to some degree until early September, with the smaller species being prevalent later in the season.

During August and September, terrestrial insects add to the picnic with grasshoppers, beetles and flying ants tempting the big rainbows from their bankside lies. Important, too, for the bank feeders is the tiny (No. 22) black-bodied, white-winged *Tricorythodes* mayfly spinner. These tiny flies appear near 8:00 A.M., and their mating flight lasts about an hour and a half. During this period, many large fish will take up feeding stations close to the banks to sip in the little spinners. During this hatch, and others on the Henry's Fork, it is wise to take into account the effect that the wind will have in distributing the insects. In a gentle wind, often the lee bank will be barren of insects (and fish), while the windward bank is filled with activity. A strong wind, on the other hand, may make the lee bank the more attractive for both fish and flies.

Another August spinner fall of importance to the angler is *Callibaetis nigritus*. These mayflies descend in massive swarms in the calm, pond-like waters in the middle of the Railroad Ranch, creating feeding orgies between 9:00 A.M. and 11:00 A.M. Imitations are tied on No. 14 hooks with grayish-tan bodies and black-and-white speckled wings.

With the preponderance of insects available to the fish of the Henry's Fork and the ideal feeding conditions they enjoy, the fishing can be very difficult. To be successful, the angler must call upon all of his experience and adapt his technique to the conditions the river presents. If he can do this well, he will join those who say the Henry's Fork offers "the greatest dry-fly-fishing in the world."

In addition to knowing the flies that are likely to be on the water at a given time, the angler must also *observe*. He must note what stage of the insect the fish are taking: dun, nymph or spinner. This can be determined by the rise form. The axiom of the Henry's Fork is "Look for the big heads." If you can see the head, the fish is probably taking duns;

RAINBOW TROUT

if you see only a big bulge, try a nymph. If the bulge (or head) isn't big, chances are the fish is not worth your best effort...but there are exceptions!

Accommodations near the Henry's Fork range from hotels to campgrounds, which may be found at numerous locations along US Route 191 from West Yellowstone to Ashton, Idaho. Well-equipped fly shops can be found in West Yellowstone and in Last Chance, Idaho, right on the Henry's Fork. For one's first trip to this river, a float trip is recommended, not only to see and experience the river, but also to see where the fishermen tend to congregate. Often, 10 additional minutes of walking on your next trip will grant you solitude and many rising fish to work over at your leisure.

Future prospects for the Henry's Fork are excellent. Today, the fishing there is better than ever, and wise and well-enforced regulations promise continued good fishing in the future. While the river gets a lot of fishing pressure, it is a big river, and it can sustain the pressure provided that the laws protecting both its flow and its breeding stock are enforced—and they are. The Henry's Fork is patrolled almost daily by officers of the Idaho Fish and Game Department in kayaks. There is every reason to believe that the Henry's Fork will continue to provide one of North America's richest angling experiences.

Bow River

Understanding the Bow River downstream from Calgary, Alberta, is a full-time occupation. The Bow is automatically associated with great trout fishing and, at this point, I suppose that is the only constant fact of the river.

The Bow is an alpine stream, a freestone river, which originates at the Bow Glacier in Banff Park.

Inadequate sewage treatment by the boomtown of Calgary has so enriched the Bow River that its rainbow trout fishing has become world famous.

From its origin, it falls and tumbles west through canyons on its way to the prairie. At Calgary the river suddenly changes from a fast-falling alpine river to a flat, easy-rolling prairie stream. By nature, the Bow should harbor Dolly Varden, Rocky Mountain whitefish and cutthroat. The cutthroat and Dolly Varden have managed to hang on by a thread, but the whitefish remain in vast numbers and today represent the highest population of any single species in the river.

In 1905, a fisheries wagon, bound for a trout stocking in Banff, broke an axle and the attendants decided to put the load of rainbows in the Bow rather than let them die. That was the beginning of the rainbow fishery that has made the Bow a legend.

A freestone river is by nature somewhat sterile. It does not contain the limestone or alkaline base required to promote the growth of plant life, which in turn harbors insect life. Without the insects the trout have limited food available and thus the typical freestone river has only limited fish populations. To compound the problems of sustaining large numbers of large fish in a freestone river, there is, in the case of the Bow, the scouring each spring as melting snow drains into the river. This sudden flush cleans the river bottom and leaves it even more void of insects and plant life. This annual event combined with low water levels that prevail during the winter in mountain streams would naturally leave the Bow River as a mediocre sport fishery.

Now, enter a city of 500,000-plus population, which straddles the Bow at the head of its transformation to a prairie stream. The city dumps vast amounts of nitrogen and phosphates into the river and artificially enriches the river. Plant life suddenly flourishes and insects abound in spite of nature's design. Trout abound now and reach unnaturally large proportions for a freestone stream. It is a paradoxical situation. It is a man-made fishery that would otherwise never have occurred.

Reservoirs and weirs have slowed the flow of the river and made possible the governing of the flow. Scouring is not as severe below the dams. The insects and plant life manage to endure the spring flush of water and the Bow continues to survive as a major sport fishing attraction to residents and nonresidents alike. The river is hailed by outdoor writers and fishing editors from all over the world as the finest sport fishery of its type on earth. The local fisherman reads the rave reviews and plans to make a trip to this magnificent river. When he arrives he may or may not catch fish even though

he did exactly what the wizard who wrote the
article said would work. Herein lies the problem
with the Bow River.

A. J. McClane in *Sports Afield* wrote of dry-fly-
fishing beyond his wildest dreams. The next
season fishermen from all over North America
flocked to the river with dainty dry-fly tackle in
hand and could not find a rising fish. This has
nothing to do with the *credibility* of fishing
journalists. It has to do with the everchanging
nature of the river itself. When McClane fished
the Bow, the river had received little runoff for
three consecutive springs. There was low water
and the plants and insects were at a peak density as
a result of no spring flush. Mayflies and caddisflies
rose above the river in clouds; even seagulls
collected in large flocks to dine on insects. There
were literally schools of trout too big to measure in
inches, nodding and feeding on the surface. The
sight was enough to stop the hearts of fly-
fishermen. The fishing was spectacular. It was the
finest dry-fly-fishing in all the world at that time.

A year later when all the dry-fly enthusiasts
arrived, the river had undergone a heavy spring
flush and a major portion of the insect population
had been dislodged and washed away. Areas where
fishing had been prevalent the year before were
physically changed as the hydraulic force of the
water brought silt beds to what had previously
been rocky stretches of the river. The fish had
moved and it was a different game. The dry-fly

activity was sparse and only a fraction of what it
had been the previous year. Fishermen left the
river disgruntled. What was all the fuss about?

Well, fishing will be fishing and there will be
good days and bad, but if we take a common-sense
look at the river that was never meant to be, we
will find a basic approach that will consistently
catch fish and other methods that might be treated
as a bonus under certain conditions. Fishermen
who travel to this fine river should know these
basics and then they will stand less chance of
disappointment and a greater chance of success.

Consider the Bow River as a freestone river,
which just happens to have a fine population of
large carnivorous rainbow and brown trout.
Depend little on insects, but rather streamer
patterns, which represent baitfish or perhaps
leeches. Yes, the Bow abounds with leeches,
which the trout feed on quite regularly.
Unfortunately, the increasing population of the
leeches in the river mark the deterioration of the
water quality. Be that as it may, the leeches are
there and the fish eat them. These streamer
patterns; which might include dace patterns,
marabou daces, muddlers, etc., may be fished deep
with a sinking line or they may be fished near the
surface on a floating line. In any case the majority
of the time the trout will take the streamers as they
are swept downstream of the fisherman and as the
retrieve or stripping motion begins. In many
stretches the trout are almost always along the

RAINBOW TROUT

banks, and in other stretches, especially where the river shows no particular dominant current, trout may be anywhere from bank to bank.

Should there be dry-fly activity on the Bow, it will fall into one of three major classifications: caddisflies, mayflies and midges. Caddisflies will be dominant and they usually are at their strongest in the evening. Strong hatches may be so dense that breathing without inhaling them becomes a problem. I have experienced such hatches and take a bandanna along to cover my face like a bank robber. Breathing is easier. A caddis or sedge imitation fished on the surface and danced along against the current will get strikes when the fish happen to look that way. There is probably no hatch more exciting on the Bow River, which inspires slashing and thrashing by the trout, than the last 15 minutes of daylight on a July evening when caddisflies are swarming. There is also probably no more frustrating fishing either. The flies are so thick that the trout feed in a frenzy and dart here and there with no apparent pattern in mind. Your imitation is simply one in a million. It is exciting just the same and well worth the frustration involved.

Mayflies may hatch right in midday and through the evening on the Bow and the hatches may appear as a single insect drifting along the current every two minutes, or as hundreds and thousands of insects drifting and hopping and dancing, trying to get airborne. The trout respond to a major mayfly hatch in a much more gentlemanly manner than they do to caddis hatches. They tend to lie in their own feeding lanes and gently nod a black nose out of the surface with a delicate slurp and then retire to their position in the current. Numbers of fish may range from a single trout to as many as fifty or more working a hatch.

When the trout are seriously taking mayflies the fishing is wonderful. The fisherman must above all things be accurate. A reasonable imitation of the mayfly will be taken without reservation if it is placed exactly above the fish's feeding lane. If the fly drifts precisely over his nose, the odds are that it will disappear into his waiting jaws. If it is two inches to one side or the other of his nose, chances are more likely that he will not respond. Fishing to a specific trout of 18 to 24 inches, and watching his response to the fly, is a fabulous experience.

It should be mentioned that the reputation of the Bow River of late has attracted many fishermen who honestly believe that to catch fish one must merely be present. Nothing could be further from the truth. While Bow River trout may not be the most selective feeding fish in the world, they still require pinpoint casting ability. Many disappointed fishermen have only themselves to blame for fishless days. If you can't deliver the goods, do not expect the fish to commit suicide.

August through October is the time for trico fishing. These are tiny midges that hatch in swarms and appear to the uneducated eye as gnats hovering above the water. Trout of all sizes respond to the trico hatches, which may occur morning or evening. No. 18 and smaller hooks are the ticket, usually tied with black bodies and white spent wings. This method of dry-fly-fishing requires the most delicate tackle and touch possible, and when a big fish is hooked the likelihood of landing him is slim. This type of fishing is demanding and the rewards are few in terms of landed fish, but the challenge is there. A 3- or 4-pound rainbow or brown caught on the surface on a No. 22 fly is worth a lot of broken leaders and straightened hooks.

All the dry-fly-fishing described heretofore represents the ultimate that the fisherman might expect, and more often than not the river will lend itself to wet-fly and streamer fishing. Keeping in tune with the level of spring runoff will certainly help the fisherman know what type of fishing to expect in a given season. The more runoff, the less surface activity, as a rule.

The Bow River usually suffers in August from an overaccumulation of plant life, which chokes up many stretches and makes fishing impossible. During this period there is less fishable water and the fisherman will find weedless streamers and dry flies his best bet. The fish are still there, but getting at them is more difficult, as is landing them when they have a convenient weed bank in which to dive.

September usually marks the dying and dislodging of plant life, and then casting is even more difficult. Floating weeds are everywhere, and again weedless streamers are excellent. In back eddies there may be trico and mayfly hatches that can be reached without the obstruction of weeds.

Thus far I have failed to mention nymph fishing in the Bow. There are good numbers of stonefly nymphs in the river and various methods of fishing them will work well before the plant life obstructs casting. This usually means late June and July. Many fishermen have inquired about the possibilities of a major stonefly hatch on the Bow River in anticipation of hatches comparable to the great salmonfly hatches on Montana rivers. Though the stoneflies do rarely hatch en masse, my experience has been that such hatches occur in the dark. The greatest hatch I ever witnessed was

70

just at dark on a July evening amidst a tremendous caddis swarm. I was dazzled by the plopping of huge stoneflies hitting the water all around me. I had waited for years for this night and I quickly tied on a Sofa Pillow and waited for the water to boil. The large stoneflies swam like small boats through the slashing of jaws, but the trout were preoccupied with caddis, and to my knowledge, not one stonefly was taken. The stonefly nymph is the phase of the creature the trout readily accept and one might grow old and gray waiting to catch a trout on a stonefly hatch on the Bow.

Today the Bow River is receiving more phosphorus and nitrogen than it can handle. The plant life in the river is surging in response to the overenrichment and the result is the slowing of the current, which in turn lessens the natural oxygenation of the water. The slower current allows the water to get warmer than it should, which also depletes the oxygen. The loss of flow and oxygen resulting from the massive growths of plant life now threaten the river with potentially devastating fishkills. New treatment plants are promised for the future, which will regulate the flow of artificial enrichment into the river. The question is whether the river will survive until the treatment is implemented.

The amazing fishery in the Bow River is one of coincidence. It was never designed to be as fine as it is. Now that man has created this unique opportunity it will be interesting to see whether he is capable or concerned enough to maintain the finest fishing resource of its kind.

You can book the river by writing the Bow River Company, P.O. Box 57, Okotoks, Alberta, Canada T0L 1T0; telephone (403) 938-3259.

Lake Taneycomo Trout

Lake Taneycomo in southwestern Missouri was originally part of the White River. White River means trout fishing. Taneycomo, made by damming the river between Table Rock Lake and Bull Shoals, is one of the most productive trout waters in the Midwest. Being floatable and wadeable as well, it is a prime attraction for anglers.

The lake is a long, narrow body with many access spots and trout docks along its length. The town of Branson, Missouri, sits right on its banks. Fall and winter fishing are the best; however, since it is a highly planted lake, one can catch a limit of trout most days of the year. Besides planted rainbow, there are now some brown trout getting into the 10-pound class. Many rainbows are taken

each year in the 6- to 10-pound range. A state hatchery at its headwaters assures Taneycomo a constant supply of fighting trout.

The most productive area for larger trout in the late season is right below the dam, where one can wade from a public fishing site. A constant supply of cold water, drawn from the bottom of Table Rock Lake, helps keep the trout in prime condition. This water, always in the 40°F range, rolls over gravel and sandbars into deep holes and makes ideal trout habitat. The cool water plus the bottom makeup of Taneycomo support a large

Lake Taneycomo has been noted for rainbows, but a stock of large brown trout is increasingly evident, though they are not caught in rainbow numbers.

population of freshwater shrimp. These nutritious morsels allow the trout to grow faster than normal. Since Taneycomo is set in hilly Ozark Mountain country, the steep banks and quick runoffs wash down a multitude of other food on which the trout thrive.

The dam at Table Rock controls the water level of Taneycomo. Unfortunately, trout fishermen never know when power will be generated causing subsequent rushes of water, so it is a very changeable body of water, with a rise of 4 to 5 feet possible at any time. Boat fishing is best when the water is running. Fishermen can run upstream with their motors, then drift leisurely down using live bait such as nightcrawlers, spawn or small wobbling spoons or plugs.

For the fly-rod angler, bank fishing when the water is barely moving can be productive. Light, one thirty-second to one-eighth jigs are the ticket. Most fly-fishermen attach floats to their lines to keep the jigs and flies riding just over the bottom. By line watching and keeping a sharp eye on the brightly colored float, the slightest hit of a trout can be detected.

Taneycomo is truly one of the top trout fishing waters in the Midwest. Bull Shoals and Table Rock are nearby with bass fishing, and a visitor can have the best of both sports during his vacation.

For information contact the Branson Chamber of Commerce, Box 220, Branson, MO 65616.

Rainbow Fishing in Alaska

Alaska has the world's best trophy rainbow fishing, and every year thousands of anglers make the long trip there to tangle with rainbows that range from 3 to 15 pounds. These are not stocked fish. They grow slowly, and they've made their living the hard way; so catching them is not as simple as it may seem. Because these fish are slow-growing, Alaska has declared the Lake Iliamna drainage a trophy fish area. Here you can enjoy catching rainbows but you may not keep them to eat or hang on the wall. In other parts of the state most camps will either urge you to release all trout or make a flat rule that you do. They recognize that it simply is not a good idea to kill big rainbows that took years to produce.

Helicopters are also forbidden to use as search vehicles. There are many out-of-the-way streams and lakes that hold superb rainbows. The concept is that some of these places should be made deliberately inaccessible, or at best, man should have to work hard if he wants to fish them.

The best rainbow fishing in Alaska lies in the Bristol Bay region, which is roughly the size of Ohio. It contains the state's largest lake (Iliamna),

In the Bristol Bay watershed of Alaska, there is a concentration of what are probably the finest rainbow trout lakes and rivers in the world, but even lesser Alaskan rainbow fishing would be considered extraordinary elsewhere.

which holds 1,000 square miles of water. Lake Clark is not far and it is Alaska's sixth largest lake, with 110 square miles of surface. The Iliamna drainage holds the very best of the rainbow fishing. Almost any river that drains into this huge lake holds some rainbows, and the big Copper River is perhaps the best of them all. It is so good that to many Lower Forty anglers the Copper is better known than rivers in states near their homes.

The country southwest of Lake Iliamna is remote and wild, accessible only by float plane. The Wood River/Tikchick wilderness area includes many lakes and rivers that contain rainbows. A number of lakes are connected to the Wood River, and camps such as Bristol Bay Lodge, Golden Horn Lodge and Tikchick Narrows Lodge can fly their clients to nearby streams that annually produce many large rainbows. The tundra also holds a number of smaller lakes scattered about that hold rainbows up to 6 or 8 pounds. Many of these streams furnish dry-fly-fishing for smaller trout all through the summer.

However, to obtain the best trophy rainbow fishing, the angler must fish these two regions at specific times. So many salmon of the same size as the big rainbows, and many larger than, move into these rivers during their spawning run, causing the rainbows to leave the rivers for deep-water sanctuaries. If there is not too much snowmelt in June and as late as the first week of July, before the salmon start moving in, the trophy rainbow fishing can be excellent. The big rainbows are in the river and have not been intimidated by the salmon. And, once the salmon arrive, the huge number of eggs they lay furnish a prime food source for the rainbows.

Rainbows are opportunistic and will eat smaller trout or anything they can find. The Alaskan rivers are surprisingly devoid of food. There are very few nymphs under the rocks and in fifteen trips I have made to the state, I cannot recall seeing a crayfish, but they do have sculpins. These, I believe, furnish the major food source for the larger rainbows for most of the year. In many rivers the sculpins are the conventional brown color, but in many cases the sculpins are greenish or olive in color. It is wise to carry sculpin patterns in all these colors. These larger rainbows want a huge offering, and the sculpin flies should be dressed on extra long shank hooks from No. 1 to 4/0. Sculpins have no swim bladder and remain constantly on the bottom. The flies should be heavily weighted and they should be fished by crawling them over the river floor.

ALASKA

•Anchorage

Tikchik Lakes

Wood River Lakes

Lake Iliamna

GULF OF ALASKA

BRISTOL BAY

A wild rainbow from Babine Lake, British Columbia. They frequently hybridize with cutthroat, producing unusually handsome offspring.

Another type of fly that is deadly on rainbows (and all the salmons) is one that has a basic fluorescent salmon-colored body with some flash. One of the most prized patterns is easy to tie. Using a No. 2 to 1/0 hook tie in a short white tail of marabou or soft bucktail, cover the hook shank with a full body of fluorescent-dyed, salmon-colored chenille, then add a collar in hula skirt fashion at the eye of the fly of Mylar that is about one-sixty-fourth inch wide. When this fly is retrieved in an up-and-down fashion the Mylar skirt opens and closes, causing a flutter motion that flashes like a wobbling spoon. Another pattern that no angler should be without in Alaska is the double egg pattern, sometimes called Babine. It is tied on a No. 2 to 1/0 hook and is simply two round salmon egg imitations made with chenille, with two wraps of soft, white hackle between the egg forms. Both of the patterns described should be tied weighted and unweighted. I often tie a mono weed guard on the weighted patterns, so that I can keep the eggs in contact with the bottom and not get hung.

For the person who is seriously seeking a trophy rainbow and wants everything in his favor, he should consider fishing the two mentioned areas from mid-September through October. The salmon have left, most of the eggs are gone, and the rainbows are moving back into the shallow rivers. The fish are feeding up for the long winter siege and this brief period furnishes the very best of this sport.

If the angler prefers spinning or plug casting gear, he will want to use Glo-Bugs or spoons and spinners that work right on the bottom. The key to catching big bows with this tackle is to keep the lures near the bottom. The Pixie Spoon in the one-half- to three-quarter-ounce size that carries a salmon-colored, plastic insert in the middle of the spoon is considered by many guides to be the single best salmon and rainbow lure ever! It can be purchased in many tackle stores in Alaska and most camps in the Bristol Bay region carry them.

Rods for fishing these big rainbows have to be slightly on the stiff side. Fly-fishing requires throwing weighted flies on sinking lines, and an 8-weight is about right. Always carry sink tip, and sinking and floating lines, for you will have to adjust to specific fishing situations. For spinning and plug tackle I suggest a rod that throws three-eighth- to three-fourth-ounce lures. Reels should have good drags—these fish can make long runs.

Most of the rainbow fishing is done by wading, so insulated chest-high waders are recommended. I also carry hand warmers and wool gloves with only the fingers cut from the glove which are necessary for me to work the tackle. Dress warmly and always take raingear. But, if you're willing to fish Bristol Bay in the fall, you will catch the biggest rainbows of your life.

For information, contact the Alaska Sport-fishing Lodge Association, 500 Wall Street #401, Seattle, WA 98121; telephone 1-800-352-2003.

S T E E L H E A D

*Oncorhynchus mykiss**

In the marginal stillwater of California's Eel River, a rainbow trout parr scarcely out of the alevin stage and not yet 2 inches long took shelter from the storming current and the bigger trout with rubicund flanks that would cheerfully eat it if it dared venture into deeper water. Overhead on the surface stood a tiny mayfly with glassine wings, an insect that would measure a quarter inch long, setae included. The parr nipped one of the fly's six legs and pulled it underwater. The insect jerked its leg back and replanted it on the rubbery surface. When the parr grabbed another leg, the insect retrieved it and took wing in exasperation. Watching such a first encounter one may deduce that rainbow trout have an instinct for surface feeding, but experience is required before the practice is mastered. This fish has a theoretical growth potential to nearly 50 pounds (the current IGFA record is a 42-pound, 2-ounce Alaskan fish caught in 1970), and when it returns to its natal stream after one to four years of marine life in the North Pacific, it *remembers*. To cast one of Roderick Haig-Brown's Steelhead Bee patterns, tied on a No. 10 hook, onto the smooth-running river surface and then see a trout as long as one's leg rise and make the intercept is an apogean angling experience.

Steelhead are a polyanadromous[1] form of rainbow trout. Biologists who specialize in

---

[1]Steelhead and sea-run cutthroat are potentially multiple spawners, unlike mature Pacific salmon, all of whom die after the spawn; in fact most steelhead do too. Survival is limited to approximately 5 to 15 percent, varying with the river, or rather with the race, for each steelhead river has a unique strain evolved for its peculiar conditions. Haphazard stocking has damaged some of these gene pools.

---

*Scientific name revised, 1989. Pacific drainage trout genus are no longer of the name *Salmo*.

Steelhead are the anadromous form of rainbow trout, with a weight capability approaching 50 pounds. From south of San Francisco to Alaska, they are a cult fish. Successful Great Lakes' plantings have generated enormous tourism.

STEELHEAD

anadromous fish divide their subjects' lives into freshwater/saltwater histories expressed in the fashion of 1/1 for one year as parr-and-river-smolt and one year as a prespawning ocean fish.[2] This fellow would be a grilse (called a "half-pounder" in West Coast steelhead parlance) weighing 1 to 3 pounds. They feed more in freshwater than larger and older fish and make delightful trout-rod sport. Steelhead rarely top seven years of age, and this brute could be expressed as either 3/4 or 4/3.

Duration of stream residency has little to do with eventual size, and multiple spawning doesn't either. Consumption of body fats during the spawning run just about equals last year's ocean-feeding profit, so the steelhead that makes three spawns in its lifetime will weigh about what it did immediately before the first spawn. The size of steelhead, which is the reason to fish for them rather than for resident rainbows, is almost wholly dependent on the number of years of prespawning ocean residency. The fish that smolts and goes off for four continuous years of marine feeding will weigh 20 to 35 pounds on its first and last spawn.

This was probably the life history of Karl Mausser's 33-pound buck, the largest fly-caught steelhead to date, taken in October 1962, from the Kispiox River in the Skeena watershed of northern British Columbia. I met Mausser on the river sixteen years later, still trying to top his own record.

S ome steelhead do not feed in streams, some eat a lot. A young summer fish with many months before his spawning will eat, but an elderly winter fish already far gone in the physiological changes that accompany ripening gonads, which include virtual atrophication of parts of the alimentary canal, will live off stored fat. All of them will pick up salmon eggs, evidently a profound instinct, but as a matter of fact salmon cut efficient redds and anglers may well contribute more eggs to the stream environment than salmon do. And even "nonfeeding" mature steelhead will reenact the feeding rituals of youth, rising to insignificant insects and their imitations, intercepting a nymph no bigger than one of the spots on their steely flanks (as well as the feeding of their immediate ocean past, rushing and biting a spoon that flashes like a eulachon).

This fish becomes a sporting quarry when it comes inland to spawn, and though most spawning is accomplished in March through May,

The Grand Banks cod-fishing dory has found a second home on western rivers, where its high ends provide reserve buoyancy on white-water stretches between placid runs, such as these steelhead anglers are enjoying.

DISTRIBUTION

when the Pacific Northwest is perpetually cold and rainsoaked, the fish will at some point in their range be entering the rivers every month of the year, including mid-summer, when the rivers that have summer runs provide the most prized steelhead fishing of all.

The female selects a redd site by sensing for percolation, or interstitial flow through the gravel. The eggs need both protection and oxygenation, which can almost be defined as cold, since warm water is inferior to cold in oxygen retention. By turning on her side and making powerful upsweeps of her tail, the reddsite gravel is freed from the bottom and swept downstream. Depending on her size, this continues until she has made an excavation from 1 to 6 feet in diameter and a few inches to a foot deep. The senior male of the spawning menage will mate with her. He will

[2] In actual practice some smoltification occurs after only months in the stream, and many ocean-residence periods are months rather than a year or more, so a 1/1 fish may be eighteen months or less, rather than two years.

76

typically be the largest and most heavily kyped of her entourage. Junior males will probably have lost some scales from their sides where he has repulsed them, and their ranks might include sexually mature parr who may dart in at the moment she and her mate are gaping and expressing eggs and milt, and add their own milt to the mix.

The natural order obviously intends that steelhead eggs shall receive thorough fertilization and a diverse genetic mix. She will drop no more than a fifth of her eggs at a time, moving immediately upstream of the redd and making another, whose displaced gravel will cover the previously fertilized eggs. Assuming she is an 8-pounder, these will number 3,500 to 4,200 according to one authority. Another prefers 1,000 eggs per pound of hen. Females are believed to return downstream forthwith, reabsorbing a dozen

or two eggs that never got out. Males, though, go looking for another female if they have any unspent milt, and generally remain streambound longer. This is believed to contribute to their much higher mortality. These spawning steelhead are dark, the hens olivaceous and the bucks ruddy. After spawning they turn pale grey and begin dropping downstream. Years ago these were known as "spawners," which struck me as illogical since they manifestly had finished that activity; or "kelts" and "slinks" by anglers who were acquainted with the Atlantic salmon literature. Now they are "runbacks."

Because most fish merely broadcast eggs and milt, we are justified in calling steelhead comparatively solicitous parents, but it is largely wasted effort. One Canadian study of 100 spawners along 350 meters of creek estimated

STEELHEAD

Hatchery Fish

There are far more steelhead being taken out of many Pacific Coast rivers today than they can naturally produce. Releasing hatchery smolts into streams so they will imprint and return has caused problems, though. In years past, fisheries managers often stocked without regard to genetic reality: hatchery steelhead from 7-pounds-at-spawning stock returned to their imprinted river and went to a redd with wild native fish that were 15-pounds-at-spawning. The resultant crossbreeds were seldom as large as the wild fish and they and their hatchery parents drew the ire of anglers who had made a pilgrimage to a special river renowned for producing trophies. The hatchery fish were also wandering. They evidently imprint much less than native fish and were turning up in rivers they were not intended for. A reaction to this was inevitable. The new doctrine is to respect the genetic integrity of each river's stock. The California Gene Resource Conservation Program says:

While hatchery production of salmonids has been somewhat successful in compensating for declines in natural production, hatchery programs are no longer viewed as an adequate or "best" means of meeting fishery demands. Evidence from Oregon indicates that hatchery releases may yield diminishing returns from the ocean fishery. Even more importantly, hatchery practices may have already contributed to losses and changes in the genetic diversity important to fishery stability and productivity . . . Genetic and behavioral data now available strongly suggest that stocks spawning in different seasons in particular stretches of water on specific streams are genetically distinct. These stocks demonstrate an important degree of genetic adaptation to local conditions.

An innovative biologist working with a Trout Unlimited chapter that had a pet river produced the simple solution that would have avoided the problem in the first place. Jeff Cederholm of the Washington Department of Natural Resources and his club instituted a program of using broodstock taken from their river, trucked to a hatchery, their offspring raised there and returned to rearing ponds on the stream for imprinting prior to smoltification. They got vastly enhanced runs with the fin-clipped hatchery stock as large and wild as the non-clipped stream breeders. They also began stocking barren tributaries with excess wild eggs in Whitlock-Vibert boxes.

These enhancement programs, which are widespread in Washington and Oregon, began more than forty years ago as mandated by law to replace fisheries damaged or destroyed by the series of huge dams that were built on the Columbia River system. With further habitat deterioration, enhancement has been extended. The U.S. Supreme Court's affirmation that treaty Mongol-Americans have a right to 50 percent of the harvestable case area fish, and that they may sell them commercially, has made the tribes to a great extent economically dependent on maintaining a healthy, and a large, stock of salmon and steelhead. Enhancement looks to be the way of the future, but one trusts it can be managed with greater genetic sophistication in the future. For instance, to know what constitutes the 100 percent that treaty tribesmen may harvest 50 percent of is going to call for fish and game departments to acquire knowledge they have henceforth blundered along without. Through judicial fiat the tribes have also acquired the right to have their fish protected from environmental degradation. That is going to provide some tort actions that conservationist European-Americans will join in gleefully. The steelhead, in fact, has become an inadvertent instigator of social innovations that should improve the quality of angling far from the Pacific Northwest.

production at 300,000 fry. In other words, 3,000 die for every survivor. Egg to alevin requires gravel time of twenty days at 60°F, fifty days at 50°F, and eighty days at 40°F. Depending on whom you listen to, alevin absorb their yolk sac and become fry in three days to three weeks, whereupon they exit the gravel in hours or only after another two weeks of tortuous wiggling. Survival to fry can be as much as 80 percent under good conditions, but 35 percent is probably closer to average. Suffocation through siltation is a primary reason for these crib deaths.

Once the swim-up has been accomplished and the fry find the calm shallows, serious predation begins by senior parr, sculpin, cutthroat, Dolly Varden, young salmon, mergansers, kingfishers, loons, great blue herons and even the dipper or water ouzel. There is no help for parr except size, and so they eat, sliding gradually into deeper water as they put on weight, adopting a territory and defending it from others. They will do this for less than one to four years prior to smoltification. Those that remain in the stream for two or three years, which the majority do, acquire a new enemy when they reach a length that can be stretched to make them a catchable, legal trout.

Some recent discoveries with smolting coho salmon can probably be extended to steelhead with fair accuracy. The triggering hormone that turns the barred parr into a slender silver smolt is thyroxin, and the secretion of thyroxin is lunar stimulated. Within two days of a new moon thyroxin levels peak, the fish turns silver and the migration begins, traveling mostly at night close to shore, as do salmon smolts, by the light of the moon. A tidewater period of unknown days or weeks is presumed while adjusting to oceanic salinity. I suspect that is a brief adjustment. One winter day when an upstream rainfall put enough head of water into one of the little rivers north of San Francisco to raise the lagoon to flood stage and broach the barrier beach, I watched returning adult steelhead that were being angled for by surfcasters surge forward as the first runnel of river ran across the beach, swimming with their backs out of water and their bellies in the wet sand, rather like giant grunion coming in to mate. (The steelhead had their noses pressed against the surfside sand, smelling the freshwater seepage.) They had been to sea for months or years and didn't waste a second on osmoregulation.

Some high-seas catches of tagged fish by Japanese research vessels tell us most of what we know of steelhead in the ocean. They are a top-of-the-water-column, or epipelagic, predator with a taste for squid, fish and amphipods taken within 30 or 40 feet of the surface. That is where planktonic-feeding smelts and herring would be because phytoplankton needs sun to bloom. Along with chinooks and coho, sockeyes and pinks, they wander offshore and northerly, following surface isobars of approximately 50°F. This takes them to the southern edge of the Aleutian chain until the fall chill pushes them southerly and easterly. They are not a school fish in the Pacific (or the river either). Indeed, one of the functions of anadromy is to reunite scattered breeding partners. Whatever they are eating out there is fat because stream rainbow trout are not a particularly juicy fish, but returning steelhead and onchorynchid salmon are self-basting at the cookfire.

Steelhead rivers circle the north Pacific basin. On the Asian shore they are found south to the 38th parallel, which puts them into Korea, Manchuria and Siberia. In the eastern Pacific they have been recorded to the Tijuana River, which debouches into the Pacific near San Ysidro, California, but quickly turns south into Mexico. There are some rainbow trout streams on the rugged and inaccessible west coast of Baja California Norte that might bear investigation. Southern California streams have been abstracted to the extent that even estivorous fish would have difficulty surviving, but the San Lorenzo River, which enters the sea at the resort town of Santa Cruz south of San Francisco, has a lagoon open year-'round and an annual run of winter steelhead. I once took a sea-liced 7-pound hen from a San Lorenzo pool no larger than a Hollywood bathtub. Fishing spate rivers, such as Papermill Creek, north of San Francisco, and the San Lorenzo, can only be done by local residents who follow one or two days after a winter rainstorm has pulled a run in. Traveling anglers need target rivers long enough either to hold more than one run at a time (at some point along their length) or to keep them in the river for weeks or months. Steelhead spawners can get in and out of short coastal rivers in less than a week. I have caught runbacks while the river was still rising.

By the 1890s, sport angling for steelhead began to appear in the eastern press. Correspondents, in the pages of *Forest and Stream*, quibbled publicly over the identification of steelhead as salmon or trout, over whether it would respond to the gentleman's fly or required the vulgarian's spoon.[3]

Steelhead were perceived by the Gentry, or those who aspired to be, as a Pacific equivalent of Atlanic salmon, as a fish that would take a fly, unlike the onchorynchid salmons, considered more fit to be canned than angled over. These distinctions persist in the American social fabric. Blue-collar countryfolk kill hordes of steelhead parr for the table, while conservation organizations of elitist fly-fishermen petition to have the fish protected for sporting purposes only.

Making steelhead congruent with Atlantic salmon is an incomplete process that may require another decade or two, but we can date its beginning to the publication in 1928 of Zane Grey's *Tales of Fresh-Water Fishing* (A.S. Barnes & Co., Cranbury, N.J., 1971), which contained tales of his exploits with the steelhead of Oregon's Rogue River. Grey achieved for steelhead what Father Walton did for angling and what Peter Benchley did for the great white shark: mass identity, a necessary precursor of status. Grey dearly loved the fish and the Rogue and established a camp there in the early 1920s, which he frequented for many years until the North Umpqua captured his affections. On the latter river it was his practice to send a guide out early in the morning to occupy the best casting position on a favorite riffle. The man did not disturb the fish and his presence prevented others from doing so, save for the occasional importunate angler who would simply receive a cash bonus to move on. Grey liked uncrowded steelheading.

The fly-fishing practiced by Grey and his friends has always been a minority form of steelhead angling. American fishermen have preferred bait-and lure-casting tackle for more than a century now, since the development of quadruple-multiplying bait-casting reels by Kentucky watchmakers who intended them to be used casting minnows and frogs for black bass. The steelhead fisherman, with his cluster of salmon eggs held down to the bottom by a pencil sinker (which seldom snags), applied the bait-casting reel, and more recently the European spinning reel, to his purposes, but found the single-handed 6-foot bass rod, and even the 7-foot spinning rod inadequate. Controlling the drift of a lure or bait calls for a two-handed 7½- to 9- or 10-foot rod with a sensitive tip, because the fish do not attack eggs, they merely intercept them. "Bite" detection is critical when bait fishing for steelhead.

[3]Rudyard Kipling caught what he thought were quinnat salmon (chinooks) on spoon in 1889 while fishing the Clackamas River in Washington, but these were actually runback steelhead that had failed to respond to his flies. Sorting out the several species of Pacific salmon, and differentiating them from steelhead trout, took a bit of time.

STEELHEAD

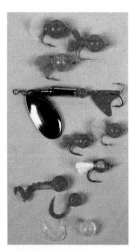

Steelhead lures of recent years have been following the bass fishing trend to soft plastics, but instead of plastic worms, the inspiration is salmon eggs, the colors normally brightly fluorescent. Such lures are held down with pencil lead sinkers (which seldom snag). For off-colored water, spinners and spoons remain popular and can be deadly. The doctrine is that steelhead lures must be fished completely on the bottom—but every now and then the occasional dry-fly fisherman messes up the doctrine.

Drift Fishing

This is the traditional non-fly-fisherman's steelhead technique. The classic bait is a cluster of salmon eggs wrapped in red mesh, which allows the eggs to gradually leach their flavor into the current. Recently ghost shrimp have become popular, and steelhead have been caught with the ubiquitous nightcrawler as well as canned corn and marshmallows, two popular grocery store trout baits. Lures are also used in drift fishing: spoons, spinners, the steelhead bobber and plugs. This is bank or anchored boat casting with a *drifting* bait, not fishing from a boat.

Drift fishing uses a three-way swivel with pencil lead off one eye (often inserted in a short length of rubber surgical tubing wired to the eye), and casting line and leader knotted on the other two eyes. You cast across and up, engage the reel and feel the lead *tick* bottom. On a successful cast you should feel at least three *ticks*. Beginning with excessive lead and trimming as dictated by current speed and depth are usual. To keep the egg cluster, or yarn fly, off bottom, a fluorescent bobber is strung on the leader next to the hook. The dedicated drifter will have a lash-up of eggs, yarn and bobber all working for him.

Plugs for drift fishing used to be the buoyant, banana-shaped Flatfish with its tight wiggle that makes the rod tip throb, and they are still popular, but a quarter century has seen the rise of bulbous fluorescent red, orange, chartreuse, etc., bobber lures that both imitate an egg cluster and can be embellished with one. The Cherry Bobber was the first of these. They may or may not be topped by a spinner blade, and the rage of the last few years has been one with rubber propeller blades, a spinning bobber dubbed the Spin-N-Glo.

Pulling Plugs

Also called running plugs, this is *harling,* so popular with Norwegian *kleppers,* midwestern American walleye fishermen, etc. It is simply drifting downstream while checking your progress by rowing upstream. This lets your plugs or lures precede you. The boat can be swung to place the plugs in what seems the most advantageous currents. In fact, since it is a downstream variation on trolling, the fishing is actually performed by the oarsman. It is consequently popular with professional guides, who know from sad experience that the less angling done by their clients the more successful they will be. The plug-pulling angler gets to strike his fish and reel it in.

For tourists who want to catch steelhead, that is enough. Some plug-pullers on Oregon's Rogue River have a clever technique for fly-fishing-only water. Instead of running plugs they run flies—which is precisely what Norwegian *kleppers* do on Atlantic salmon rivers.

Plunking

Bobbers and banana plugs are favorites for a companionable form of steelhead angling called plunking. This is simply soaking bait with the line taut to a heavy sinker, and the bait is a lure activated by the current. With a Spin-N-Glo decorated with an egg cluster *whirring* away near the bottom, a driftwood fire and congenial associates, the plunker sits on a camp chair, enjoys his beverage and probably has a bell on his sand-spiked rod to advise him of a fish.

The Art of the Single Egg

This art requires a few split shot to carry out a single salmon egg with a small gold hook embedded in it (gold so as not to discolor the translucent egg with a dark hook). Four- or 6-pound monofilament line is tied directly to the hook. The rod should be a soft-actioned fly rod, a wet fly rod, mounted with spinning guides. Since a spinning reel offers too much friction for the light shot and egg, the line is stored on a fly reel and the casting portion pulled off into a stripping basket worn around the waist. The game is absolutely worthless unless your egg is on bottom and free-drifting back toward you in the vigorous current of typical steelhead holding water. One does not see or feel a strike so much as one perceives a tremor, but steelhead and salmon have virtually a compulsion to pick up eggs, for whatever reason, and the master of single-egging can take a fearsome number of fish on a light line.

The Floating Bobber

The "vigorous current of typical steelhead holding water" may be not so much what steelhead want to hold in but what anglers prefer to fish because it simplifies their problems, and encourages trout to make hasty decisions. The Canadians have long made extensive use of the fishing float, or bobber, that we all grew up using for panfish. Once trial and error has determined how deep the water, and the float adjusted to put a bait near bottom, prolonged fishing in quiet backwaters, eddies and deep, slow pools is possible. An Englishman adept at such fluvial, coarse-fishing practices as stret-pegging and long-trotting could quite likely make a demon steelhead drift fisherman, since detecting pickups is *the* problem when drifting. Very long rods should be used for float fishing so the line can lead directly from rod tip to the bobber.

Noodle Rods

This brings us to the revolution in steelhead rods brought about by a retired Michigan teacher named Dick Swan, a cheerful enthusiast who believes rods as tall as a giraffe and long leaders of 2-pound-test monofilament are perfectly mated to double-digit steelhead in a strong current. He and his acolytes catch *lots* of fish, and their tackle and techniques are so functionally efficient that they may be the wave of the future. Noodle rods are so-called in pursuit of the axiom "limp as a wet noodle." They were initially dubbed "bike" rods because some early models were crafted of the whip antennae night bicyclers use to carry metallized fluorescent pennants to warn motorists. Swan's concept is elegantly simple: 4-pound-test monofilament leaders are many times more effective than 8-pound, and 2-pound-test more effective than 4-pound. His problem, of course, was how to maintain a hookup with 2-pound-test when the quarry is not a diminutive sprat but a large, very disturbed game fish.

The answer is an utterly wishy-washy rod, a dozen or more feet long, which is allowed to bend into a deep C shape when flexed by a fish. The angler actually points the rod shaft backwards over his shoulder, and the fish bends the tip forward. This configuration absorbs most stresses, and if the spinning reel's drag is not inordinately uneven, a prolonged fish fight may follow. Noodle rod devotees concede their technique results in more breakoffs than proceed from stouter tackle, but insist they enjoy many more hookups. Swan has taken chinooks to 28 pounds on 2-pound-test, and a steelhead of 13 pounds, 5 ounces. To complement the light leaders, thin-wire No. 12 and 14 bait hooks are used. Noodle rod fishermen favor closed-face spinning reels and 6- or 8-pound-test line leading to the customary swivel with attachment for a pencil-lead sinker.

Fly-Fishing

The mechanics of fly-fishing must be built into one's synapses rather than purchased at a tackle

Some favorite West Coast steelhead flies from Buz's Fly and Tackle Shop in Visalia, California. These are typical California-Oregon patterns with heavy dressings and much tinsel. Their sizes will run No. 2-8. In Washington and British Columbia, larger hooks and sparser, less gaudy dressings are favored.

shop, so eventually serious steelhead fishermen take it up to enhance their enjoyment of the sport. A fly-caught fish is simply more entertaining than one taken any other way, especially if you tied the fly yourself.

Before sinking fly lines arrived we left our silk or nylon lines ungreased and hoped the current would submerge them. When Ashaway brought out a braided weight-forward line of Dacron, a material with a specific gravity slightly heavier than water, it was greeted by steelhead fishermen with sellout enthusiasm. The breakthrough was brought about by the Sunset Line & Twine Company's introduction in 1953 of a semi-metallic sinking fly line, and to an even greater extent by Scientific Anglers' 1954 production of Wet Cel lines, a superior article that preceded a whole generation of ever-faster sinking lines, culminating (if it has) in fly lines with a core of lead wire, and lines with powdered lead in their PVC coating.

When lines floated or could only be coaxed into a shallow sink, we used long leaders tipped with flies such as C. Jim Pray's Optic series, which featured a brass ball head pinched on the hook, then lacquered black and painted with two large round eyes. Also popular were Peter J. Schwab's series of bucktails with copper wire bodies. Casting in a crosswind one December day on the Russian River, I put a large Red Optic into my ear (and you would be amazed at how much blood you can get out of a pierced ear). For the last thirty years the winter steelheader has been fishing fly lines that plummet to the bottom, and increasingly short leaders to prevent his fly from billowing upward. Except in Washington, some devoted

STEELHEAD

acolytes of Roderick Haig-Brown are preaching floating double-tapers, long leaders and really big flies for winter steelhead. Bill McMillan's Winter Hope pattern is available commercially in sizes from 2/0 to 6/0. That is big, and it makes better sense to put weight in the hook rather than wrapped around it.

Haig-Brown, an Anglo-Canadian literary stylist whose long shelf of fishing-book titles contains much writing on steelhead, came to believe that "...dry-fly-fishing, under summer and fall conditions, is the most effective fly-fishing method, as well as the most attractive." His most famous pattern is the Steelhead Bee, a dry fly with divided fox squirrel wings tied far forward. The pattern is intended to be fished as a skater, that is, drawn across the surface, and the wings are cocked forward to prevent a nose dive. You can actually rock it from hackle tips to wing tips and back again, which is so engrossing that the rise of a fish is often a brutal shock. I have seen stale steelhead come up out of 8 feet of green water to take the floating fly during almost-freezing fall cold snaps, conditions so unpropitious that even putting on a dry fly was an act of daring, so it may be that Haig-Brown, normally quite diffident about his fishing and not given to outspoken *dicta*, was the pioneer who led us out of decades of bottom-scratching.

The vastly experienced steelhead angler, writer and artist Russell Chatham, is an outspoken traditionalist of the sunk line, advocating a 10-weight shooting head on a 9-foot rod and a selection of flies that satisfy four criteria: large, small, bright and dark. I would prefer another half foot on that rod, and would even more prefer that it was a 14-foot, two-handed English salmon rod. I have two of those and it is amazing how simple distance casting becomes with them, haul and double-haul forgotten. The salmon rod functions easily in overhead casting, picking up and carrying an enormous length of line, and it excels with the rolling Spey cast.

Chatham believes "... it is simply a matter of the fish biting or not, depending upon moods in no way connected with the pattern of fly." There is one way you can influence those moods in steelhead and all other fishes: by repetitively showing them the same fly or lure you bore them. After fruitlessly working down a run with a large orange wet fly I would go back up with a dark dry fly. Over and over, with fish as different as trout and blue runners, I have seen the introduction of a new lure reawaken interest. When fishing under crowded conditions, I want to know what those ahead of me are using so I can do *otherwise*, and

when a team of friends are working the same water they should vary both their flies and their approaches—sunk fly, greased line, dry fly, etc.

An orange fly to suggest salmon eggs is a steelhead cliché that often works, but I have watched a lot of steelhead that didn't twitch a muscle when an orange fly went past. A new fad for purple flies is developing remarkable momentum.

Considering that I have to span the continent to fish for steelhead, at an expense of time and money that would give me excellent fishing for Atlantic salmon near at hand, and yet I have continued to do so, and become morose if a year passes without them figuring in my sporting life, the conclusion is inescapable that I have imprinted on steelhead rivers.

Olympic Peninsula Steelhead

The rivers of Washington's Olympic Peninsula course through the great rain forest valleys. They have Indian names which describe today's reservation lands: Quinault, Queets, Hoh and the Quillayute system. On these ancestral fishing grounds near tidewater, native Americans net trout and salmon for commercial sale. The upstream sport fishermen find the fish ascending for their spawning beds in Olympic National Park. This often acrimonious division of our game fish resources has such deep-seated cultural origins that it continues to plague efforts at proper management.

The Quinault is the peninsula river that flows from high country sources to the sea. The water below Lake Quinault can be fished only with a reservation guide. A national park road parallels the upper river, while its headwaters meander with various trails. There are summer-run steelhead here for the backpacker. The winter Quinault runs clearer than any anadromous river I know. When storms have caramelized neighboring watersheds, it is still running green. Snow brings drought, and the river becomes liquid air and gossamer lines are needed for its 10-pound steelhead.

The Queets is often so white with glacial melt that extra-large, bright lures are required. Sadly, few steelhead pass beyond the gillnets at the river's mouth.

The lower Hoh, below the Highway 101 bridge, offers very long drifts bordered by lovely sandbars. This is an exceedingly popular one-day float that ends at the take-out opposite the tiny Hoh Indian

Reservation. If limited to one river for winter fly-fishing, do not hesitate to choose the Hoh.

Forks is a small lumber community and the headquarters for steelheading in the peninsula. A number of secondary roads provide access points to the Calawah, Bogachiel and Soleduck—all tributaries of the Quillayute. When the winter rains come, each of these rivers "go out" and swing back into shape with a unique style and timetable. Fish move on the clearing water. Sections go cold on the single hot river. The great steelhead may come anytime, but as winter progresses the average weight increases until it is over 10 pounds by season's end. The two-year ocean steelhead represents at least half the total. There are few jacks or "half-pounders"—steelhead under 3 pounds. The three-year ocean fish may weigh 20 pounds. The steelhead spending four years at sea is rare and represents the ultimate size potential.

The Olympic Peninsula's winter stream fishing provides the visiting angler with a better opportunity at taking a trophy steelhead (16 pounds or better) than any other area in the United States. If a guide is hired (Forks Guide Association), the odds are dramatically increased. Fishing from February 15th to March 15th can give those odds an extra boost. Each year or so a steelhead over 30 pounds is caught from one of these half dozen rivers. The Indian gillnet fishery has reported steelhead of similar size.

The favored steelheading outfit if drift fishing bait or bobbers consists of a rod 8 to 9 feet long and a bait-casting reel filled with at least 100 yards of 10- to 17-pound-test line. Spinning outfits are popular, too, especially with spoons and spinners. I have often used an 8-foot spinning rod and 10-pound-test line to cast one-half-ounce spoons.

The fly-fisherman will cast an 8- to 10-weight outfit with fast sinking lines. The fly pattern is less important than its construction. The dressing should be sparse; a tinsel body or lead underbody is needed. The reel must have plenty of backing and have a dependable drag.

Klamath River

The Klamath River is the earliest of California's nearly two dozen steelhead rivers. The first steelheads, generally half-pounders that can run as large as 2½ and 3 pounds, will move through the lower river up as far as the mouth of the Trinity River, the major tributary to the Klamath, where they hold in the mouths of the cooler-flowing feeder creeks. The runs get heavier through August and they are prime during September and

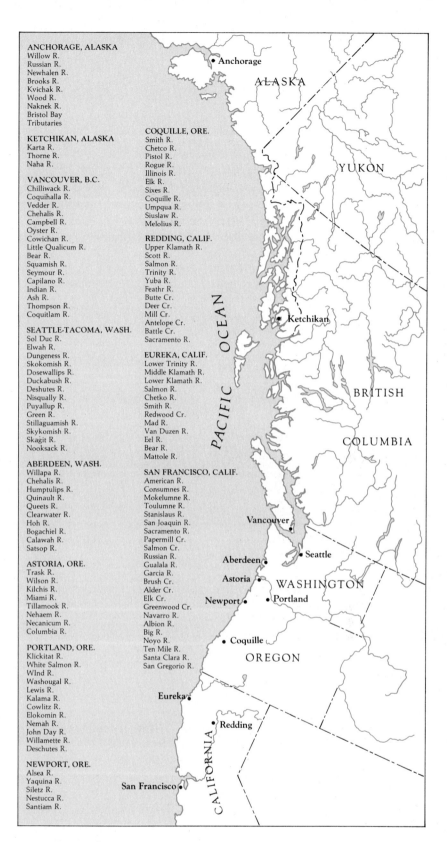

For the flying steelhead fisherman, a selection of streams that can be readily reached out of major West Coast cities and towns.

STEELHEAD

October in the area near the Salmon and Scott rivers. The much larger winter steelhead (over 12 pounds) are not fished heavily by either visiting or local anglers. However, there are fish available most years through the following March and fishing quality depends more on the state of the weather than the availability of fish.

The Klamath is actually three different streams. This is a matter of location, access and the kind of terrain the river runs through. The lower 40 miles of the river, up to Cappell Creek and Johnson's,

The Klamath River in northern California is famous for a race of small steelhead that are ready risers. It is also a beautiful stream and has productive tributaries, such as the Trinity River.

run through a modestly steep canyon where access is very difficult, except for anglers equipped with a jet-powered boat. The jets have blossomed on the lower river and now there is plenty of angling pressure.

From Johnson's to nearby Orleans, the river runs through a steep canyon and there is a road right along the bank. However, the river is generally very difficult to get to and the country is so rocky that it is difficult to fish the river except for a few spots. Access can be total to anglers who hire a guide with a float boat or those who use rafts. Each year rafting in this and other sections of the river has become more popular for fishermen and even dedicated fly-fishermen have found this the best way to fish the river between Orleans and the mouth of the Trinity at Weitchpec.

The section of the Klamath from just below Orleans to the base of Iron Gate Dam is the part that is world famous for the excellence of the summer (actually fall) steelhead fishing. The river here is about 90 percent accessible because it runs through National Forest lands. There are almost endless spots where fly-fishing can be done with relative ease. This has attracted fly-fishermen from all over the world and some special techniques have been developed in recent years to exploit the heavy runs of steelhead, especially the half-pounders.

There is always the common fly-fishing equipment, which generally consists of 9-foot rods with 6- to 10-pound-test. Virtually 100 percent of the experienced anglers use fast-sinking lines for the Klamath, though a few will be seen with sink tips and slow-sinking fly lines and shooting tapers. The shooting heads have become the basic line of many anglers. It is often necessary to make long casts of up to 100 feet in order to quarter the better lies on the river. A shooting head does this much better than other lines and quick-sinking features allow the line to sink down in the often heavy currents.

Almost all of the spin fishermen who currently fish the Klamath have switched from lures to flies. This is a relatively recent development and the technique has been worked out in the past decade. The fishermen use a plastic bubble, not to be confused with a fishing float. The better bubbles can be injected with water or other substances in order to make them heavier for distance casting or to make them sink slowly. It has been discovered by Klamath anglers that often the bigger and more desirable steelhead will decide to hold in fairly shallow water. Deep-worked flies, baits or lures will not produce as well as those that ride a foot or so below the surface. Just as often, the steelhead will become perverse and start hitting only flies or lures that are bounced along bottom. The angler with the proper bubble can take advantage of the conditions he finds.

There are currently no favorite lures for the Klamath. Probably every season everything ever created to attract trout will be used by some Klamath River fishermen. But two flies, the Silver Hilton and the Brindle Bug, come as close as possible to a universal offering for steelhead in this river. The Hilton has a black body, generally wrapped with a silver, oval tinsel; body material is chenille; wing and hackle are grizzly, as is the tail. The Bug has a brindle-colored body of chenille and a brown hackle and tail. These two flies (from No. 8 through 2) take the bulk of the steelhead currently extracted from the Klamath.

The uppermost section of the Klamath deserves a special comment or two. This is an area that actually runs through a desert (unlike the rest of the river, which runs through a rain forest). Local anglers call it the "banana belt" because the weather is so different from that found in the rest of the rivers in California. Knowing about this belt can save a trip for a visiting angler. If the weather is bad, as it usually is after the yearly rains start to fall (mid-November or early December), the visitor should head for the area near Iron Gate Dam, the upper limit of the steelhead runs. Fishing, of course, can be good, bad or indifferent, depending on other conditions, but water in the upper river is relatively cool because it comes from deep within two reservoirs—Copco, as well as Iron Gate—and if it is clear anywhere in the river this is the spot where it is clearest and where it clears fastest.

The Klamath also has a couple of major tributary rivers. Besides the Trinity, there are the Salmon and the Scott rivers. If a trip is ruined by poor water conditions in the more famous Klamath, these other rivers (fairly major flows in their own right) can provide fishing action that could not be found in the parent stream. They are all accessible to visiting anglers.

Chinook salmon arrive on approximately the same schedule as do steelhead, but fishing for them ends in November each season. They are seriously fished in the lower 40 miles of the river by hordes of anglers, with the peak months being August and September. In this part of the river they are still in prime condition, but they begin to decline rapidly because the water in the Klamath is relatively warm when the first salmon arrive.

As far up as Johnson's the river can be fished mostly only from a jet boat. The best spots to find salmon are at the mouths of cooler feeder streams. This is also where the most salmon will be found as they proceed upstream, with pods of them gathering near the rivers and creeks. Except for key spots, such as the mouth of the Trinity, Salmon, Scott and Shasta rivers, the salmon will be found only as incidental targets for other than Indian net fishermen. In the last decade, Indian netting has been a very controversial part of the Klamath River fishing scene, but it is limited primarily to salmon fishing and does not yet affect steelhead fishing.

For information contact the Redwood Empire Association, Spear Street Towers, Suite 1001, Market Plaza, San Francisco, CA 94105; telephone (517) 373-1195.

Thanks to Michigan's innovative stocking program, all of these trout streams now have steelhead and Pacific salmon runs.

Michigan's "Big Three"

An avid steelhead fisherman can fly or drive thousands of miles in hot pursuit of this premier fighter, but if his destination does not include Michigan's St. Joe River, Grand River (and tributaries) or the Big Manistee River in March, April or November, he is missing the opportunity for steelhead action that can boggle one's mind. Although this Midwest fishery is not blessed with stocks of wild trout as found on the West Coast, rest assured, there is no difference in the fighting ability of these distant relatives. In lieu of wild strains of steelheads, Michigan's Department of Natural Resources conducts a vigorous steelhead hatchery program. This program provides annual plants of almost 1,000,000 fingerlings and smolts in these three river systems alone.

Early March snowmelt encourages large runs of fish to enter the southernmost St. Joe River. As the murky waters recede, anglers employ three methods of hooking steelhead:

Drift fishing (bottom-bouncing bait) is the traditional method for the few wading anglers that congregate at the Barrien Springs Dam. This method is also used by boat fishermen, as they anchor out from their favorite run and cast their favorite bait-spawn bags to the top of the drift.

STEELHEAD

Spawn bags contain either steelhead eggs (eight to ten to a bag), or salmon eggs (three to four to a bag), tied up in different colors of nylon mesh material. The bag is tied off with thin wire or nylon thread and hangs from the bend of a hook by just a few strands of the strong material. A steelheader must have a basic color selection of red, orange, hot pink and chartreuse spawn bags in order to ensure fishing action.

The "drop-back" method of fishing is a St. Joe River original. The boat is anchored directly above a favorite deep run. Tadpollys or Flatfish are tied to the leader coming off the three-way swivel

Freshwater Steelhead

The successful establishment of coho and chinook runs in rivers tributary to the Great Lakes was followed shortly by steelhead stockings that have been highly popular with Midwestern anglers. Dick Swan, for instance, is a Michigan resident who developed his noodle rods for fishing the Pere Marquette, Betsie, Manistee and other local streams whose very clear water called for refined techniques. Michigan annually releases about 1,000,000 steelhead smolts in various rivers so they will imprint on the individual stream's distinctive bouquet before dropping down to Lake Michigan for one to four years of "ocean" life. Comparatively insignificant predation produces a return of 20 to 25 percent of stocked freshwater steelhead, whereas 9 to as little as 3 percent of Pacific steelhead return as adults. Great Lakes steelhead average the same 8 pounds that is customary on the Pacific Coast. The Ontario provincial record is a 29-pounder, and Michigan's record is a fish of 26 pounds.

Among other states with freshwater steelhead programs, the most adven-

turous to date is New York, whose Finger Lakes are deep, cold and well-populated with smelt. Lake Ontario steelhead running into New York's Salmon River have been taken in excess of 20 pounds, and there are both spring and fall runs. This stock was obtained from Washington State. Freshwater steelhead can presently be fished in Michigan, Wisconsin, Ontario, Indiana, New York and Pennsylvania. They can be stocked wherever there are trout streams tributary to a cold water (or a two-tier) reservoir. Because they economically impact neighboring communities in a highly favorable fashion, we are going to be seeing many more freshwater steelhead.

(spawn bags can also be fished this way). The lure is worked through the run by releasing a few feet of line at regular intervals. This drops the plug back down through the run, antagonizing fish as it moves.

"Hot-Shottin" is a recent West Coast method that has already found its way into Michigan. West Coast drift boats are rowed against the current to hold the wobbling plugs in the drift (same as the drop-back method). The boat is moved very slowly downstream, working the plugs ("pulling plugs") in the current. The St. Joe is fast becoming more popular for this method of fishing than other Michigan rivers. This is due to its longer runs that are free from logs and other snags. Baits, including Flatfish, Tadpollys, Hot-n-Tots, Bagley Minnow, as well as the Hot Shot, are all successful fish catchers when used with this new method. The St. Joe River is a boat fisherman's dream!

The Grand River has to be the most unique steelhead river in the nation. Its 160-mile long currents begin near the state capitol of Lansing and flow through the heart of Michigan's second largest city—Grand Rapids. Recently installed fish ladders ensure the arrival of migrating steelhead to the steps of the capitol. As politics will have it, the Grand River system has already received a plant of over 1,000,000 fish in one year. It's average annual plant of young steelhead exceeds 500,000.

Sixth Street Dam (spillway) in downtown Grand Rapids is the hot steelhead site. Spring runoff waters offer boaters unbelievable action. It is possible to battle thirty to forty fish in one day at this time. In the fall, the low water allows waders to work the entire breadth of the wide stream. For those desiring more eye-appealing steelhead environs, the many tributaries will fill the bill. The most popular fishing method on the Grand is drifting spawn bags or high-visibility, colored Burl's Nuggets (plastic spawn). There are a few waders who prefer to toss spinners. This group, however, makes its own spinners because of the rough bottom found at Sixth Street Dam. Solo waders should use a wading staff at this site. Two or more can wade together using the buddy system.

Michigan's older, most famous steelhead river, the Big Manistee River, is still a blue-ribbon steelhead stream. The most popular fishing site on this river is at Tippy Dam, near Wellston, Michigan. The site attracts hundreds of drift fishermen in mid-April and November. Spawn bags, Nuggets and wigglers (mayfly nymph) are the choice baits, however, the Spring Wiggler fly pattern is gaining popularity among spin fishermen. Like spawn bags and Nuggets, the Spring Wiggler should be tied in various colored bodies.

One other method of fishing is very popular at Tippy just below the cofferdam. Bobber (float) fishing for steelheads was "born" at this site and continues to be the only method used below the cofferdam. The same drift baits are used with the bobber. The bobber is rigged for steelhead much the same as for bluegills. The lead weight (split shot) is attached below the bobber to where it just clears the rocky bottom. The baited hook is 18 to 24 inches below the weight. Since steelhead generally just "mouth" such baits, it is necessary to respond to the slightest movement of the bobber with the rod.

Boat fishing is very popular in the lower river, with spawn bags as the most popular bait. Deep holes, strewn with logs, offer the boaters a real challenge. These shorter runs and the amount of snags have discouraged some "hot-shotters" from fishing on the Big Manistee.

The most revolutionary method of steelhead fishing found among these crowded sites is the noodle rod technique. Long leaders of 2- and 4-pound-test, serving the popular baits on No. 14 and 12 hooks, with rods up to 15 feet are used. These long whips are designed to cushion the light monofilament. When doubled over into the configuration of the big C, maximum pressure is applied to the fish, while protecting the line from parting. The fine diameter leader delivers the bait to the spooky fish in a less threatening manner and generates far more fishing action than was ever imagined possible. The rod and properly adjusted reel drag then offer a sport fishing experience.

For information contact the Michigan Travel Bureau, Michigan Dept. of Commerce, Box 30226, Lansing, MI 48909.

Oregon's Deschutes River

The Deschutes River was first discovered by white men when Lewis and Clark made their expedition into the West. A few years later the river was tagged with its name by Hudson's Bay trappers, "River of the Falls." Although the river's source is far away to the south in the Oregon Cascade range, it is only the lower 100 miles that hold steelhead. Once they ranged over a larger area of the river, but the construction of hydroelectric dams just above the community of Warm Springs stopped all upriver migration. This 100-mile area

The Deschutes River is a tributary of the Columbia that can be fished out of Portland or the Seattle-Tacoma area. Note the lady is garbed for typical Pacific Northwest weather—cold and wet.

can, however, provide some of the finest steelhead angling available.

There are three groups of steelhead available for the angler in the Deschutes and three areas in which to fish. The three types of fish are wild Deschutes steelhead, hatchery-raised Deschutes steelhead, and a mixed group of wild and hatchery non-Deschutes steelhead that stray into the river on their way to upper Columbia River tributaries. Studies done by the Oregon Department of Fish and Wildlife show that these non-Deschutes strays usually confine themselves to the lower 15 or 20 miles of the river.

The first area of the river where steelhead are found is Warm Springs to Maupin, the section farthest south and the upriver limit for steelhead. There are but few access points along this section, and the most popular way to fish is by either drift boat or raft float trip. Current regulations prohibit fishing from any floating device; boats can be used only for transportation. Boaters are also required to purchase a river-use permit.

In the second section, from Maupin to Macks Canyon, a road parallels the east bank of the river for about 26 miles. The BLM controls a large portion of this area, and many campsites have been established for the angler who wishes to fish from the bank. At Maupin, motels, restaurants and stores are available. The Oasis Resort (Box 146, Maupin, OR 97037; telephone (503) 395-2611) has been a Deschutes River institution since the 1920s or 1930s and is a fine place to book a guide or to get up-to-the-minute information. Information about guided trips can also be obtained from the Oregon Guides and Packers

STEELHEAD

Association (Box 3797, Portland, OR 97208).

The third area of the Deschutes is the 25-mile section from Macks Canyon to the mouth of the river. Here again there is little access, and most of the fishing is done by using either drift boats, rafts or power boats to transport the angler to favored fishing spots. Guides for this area can also be contacted through the Oregon Guides and Packers. Motel, restaurant and store accommodations can be found at both The Dalles and at Biggs Junction on Interstate 84. The state of Oregon also maintains a campers' park at the mouth of the river. From this point one can hike along the river bank. It was in this area of the Deschutes that in 1946 a world-record, fly-caught steelhead was taken. The fish was 28 pounds and, while it may have been a true Deschutes River fish, speculation is that it was probably a stray destined for an upper Columbia River tributary.

Fishing is limited to artificial lures and flies, and only hatchery steelhead with a well-healed clipped fin may be kept.

Spinners and wobbling spoons are two very popular lures used by spin and level wind casters. Brand names such as the Steelie, Spinner Bug, Rooster Tail and Mepps are among the favorites. Other steelhead lures like the Lil' Corkie, Glo-Go and Spin-N-Glo also work well when drifted near the bottom.

Each season (which for steelhead is basically from July through October) the Deschutes becomes more popular as a fly-fishing river. This river, probably more than any other, offers the best chance to hook steelhead on the widest variety of fly-fishing techniques. Whether an angler wants to work a fast-sinking shooting head and large wet fly, or a midge rod and a dry fly, the chances are excellent that he will hook a steelhead. The most popular and probably most successful method is to cast a floating line at a slight downstream angle, mend the line to get a natural drift. Fly outfits in the 6- to 10-weight category are all adequate for Deschutes steelhead. The heavier outfits may be an advantage during windy periods. They also can bring a fish to beach more quickly to facilitate the speedier release of wild fish. Along with the heavier rods, stronger leader tippets may confidently be used on the Deschutes. Tippets of 10 to 12 pounds generally work well since the water is seldom what could be called "gin clear." These heavier tippets help to bring the final dogged moments of the fight to a faster end, helping to prevent undue stress on fish that will be released. Don't think that a strong tippet and heavy rod will diminish the fight of

This dark female steelhead is from the Morice River in northern British Columbia. She took a dry fly from a run that did not appear promising.

these fish. Once they have made up their mind to go, there is little that can stop them. Fly patterns that have become standard on the Deschutes are the Skunk, Deschutes Demon, Max Canyon, Juicy Bug and Del Cooper. Generally they are tied on No. 8 to 2 hooks.

Regardless of the choice of tackle that one prefers, the Deschutes is a beautiful river with superb fish that demand the utmost respect from anglers.

For information contact the Oregon Chamber of Commerce, 101 Transportation Building, Salem, OR 97310.

The Washougal River

A small river by northwest standards, the Washougal flows into the north bank of the Columbia River 14 miles east of Vancouver, Washington. Draining a low range of hills swept by repetitive forest burns prior to World War II, this river is subject to radical extremes in flow with winter floods common and trickling summer lows the norm.

Without the stabilizing mountain snowpack or lake-fed source common to many Northwest rivers, the Washougal's angling conditions are frequently frustrating during the peak hatchery runs of winter steelhead that occur in December and January as well as during the peak hatchery returns of summer steelhead that arrive from late June through July. However, when water flows are optimum, the Washougal has a nice variety of pools, glides, pockets and riffles that can provide good angling on the hatchery returns using either flies or conventional drift tackle.

It is noteworthy that the Washougal River is perhaps better known for its Skamania stock of hatchery-bred, summer-run steelhead than for its actual angling. The Skamania Hatchery, built on the canyon-cooled North or West Fork of this river in 1956, provided the first really successful program for rearing and selection of delicate summer-run steelhead in hatchery confinement. However, growing numbers of both anglers and fishery biologists on the West Coast have begun to seriously question the overall impacts of that seeming success due to the negative impacts now

identified as having occurred to the wild stocks of steelhead that must cohabit with the drastically altered genetic composition of the hatchery stocks. This is true of many hatchery steelhead and salmon programs in the Northwest, but it is especially worrisome with the Skamania stock of fish as they have been so widely dispersed outside their native range, including over twenty river systems in Washington, several in Oregon, a few in California, one in Idaho, and with eggs sent as far as the Midwest and even internationally.

The wild runs of summer steelhead enter the Washougal from March through early June with more arriving in September and October, while winter runs of wild steelhead enter from November through early December and again in March and April. Although water flows are often more favorable for angling during these intervals, the depleted wild runs of both winter and summer steelhead are quite small populations. Good angling is most uncertain on these wild runs and catch-and-release is a commendable ethic.

Both fly- and conventional drift fishing are popular on the Washougal. During the winter

STEELHEAD

(November to April) drift fishermen use 8- to 10-foot rods ranging from light to heavy action depending on varying water flows. Both spin reels and bait-casting reels are employed using lines from 8- to 20-pound-test to meet water conditions. The favored bait is boraxed roe, although worms and sand shrimp are also good. The better lures are Oakies, Corkies, Glo-Gos, Spin-N-Glos, and varied wobblers and spinners. All are effective.

Winter fly-fishermen on the Washougal have proven that the floating line can be used to good effect when combined with large flies on No. 2/0 to 6/0 hooks, or on No. 2 to 1 extra-stout wired hooks, without resorting to lead. Supple 9½- to 11-foot fly rods carrying 8- to 10-weight lines are popular with the floating lines and big hooks. Reliable fly patterns are the Winter's Hope, General Practitioner, Washougal Olive, Silver and Black, Silver and Orange, Paint Brush and Stone Nymph. Early and late in the winter, if water temperatures reach the mid-40s, some winter steelhead are even being taken on the surface with riffle-hitched flies.

In the summer, drift fishermen use 7½- to 8½-foot rods of light to medium action with 4- to 10-pound-test lines on either spin- or bait-casting reels. Boraxed roe is still popular, although crawfish tails, worms and sand shrimp are also used. The same lures as mentioned for winter use are popular and effective.

Fly-fishermen on the Washougal use primarily a floating line with rods from 8 to 9½ feet and lines from 6- to 8-weight during the summer-run period (March to October). Popular fly patterns include the Muddler, Steelhead Caddis, Greased Liner, Dragonfly, Stone Nymph, Teeny Nymph, Steelhead Bee, October Caddis, Washougal Olive, General Practitioner and Brad's Brat. Surface fishing has proven very effective here, as on many other rivers for summer steelhead, if water temperatures range from the upper 40s to the mid-60s.

The angling on the Washougal River is limited to 12 to 13 miles of water (the sport fishing deadline being Salmon Falls Bridge), and much of that water lies within residential ownership that provides very little public access. There are three public fishing sites at mid-river and two city parks on the lower river where fishing pressure is often condensed. Crowding is a problem during hatchery return peaks. Hatchery summer-run fish that average 10 pounds are the main attraction, with the rare steelhead to 20 pounds. Receiving only slightly less attention are the winter runs

averaging 2 to 3 pounds less per fish. Tackle is available locally at a sport shop in the town of Camas and at a riverside grocery on the upper river.

For information contact the Washington Travel Development, Dept. of Commerce, 101 General Administration Building, Olympia, WA 98504.

The Babine

The source of the Babine River is Babine Lake, 75 miles by gravel road northeast of Smithers, British Columbia. The river leaves the lake at ancient Fort Babine, ancestral home of the Carrier Indians. Babine is French for "pendulous lip" so named because in the past Carrier women wore bone plugs called labrets in their lower lip, which distended them far beyond normal shape.

The river flows north for only one mile from Babine to Nilkitkwa Lake, a shallow, 3-mile-long pond choked with grass and dotted with muskrat nests. Smokehouse Island, where the Indians cure their salmon, is located at the head of the lake. Off Smokehouse Bar, in June and July, large Kamloops rainbow trout forage on sockeye salmon fry, and can be taken on streamer patterns such as a No. 6 Black-Nosed Dace. Here too, in late September, coho (silver) salmon may be found massed as they await their time to spawn in the river downstream from the fort. No. 4 green or orange, silver-bodied Comet patterns fished on shooting taper fly lines score well. These waters are limited to fly-fishing only.

The Canadian government maintains a salmon counting wier where the Babine leaves Nilkitkwa Lake. Downstream from here the river takes on new character as it winds and riffles through a primeval forest of spruce and fir. The gravel bars are lined with cottonwood turned so brilliantly golden by the first frosts that they seem to shine with their own inner light. The Babine steelhead run is not large; estimated at from 1,500 to 3,000 fish consisting of four- to five-year-olds who have spent two to three years in fresh water and two years at sea. The vast majority are first-time spawners. Trophy steelhead in the 20- to 30-pound class are predominantly males, though females to 22 pounds have been recorded. Males in excess of 40 pounds have been captured by Indian nets.

Babine steelhead, classified as summer-run fish, enter the Skeena River system from the Pacific in July and August but must ascend nearly 200 miles to the mouth of the Babine, and then another 68 miles to the Babine's headwaters. They reach the fishing waters in September and October. By this time they have developed the crimson-sided appearance of large rainbow trout, a pre-nuptial coloration. Spawning takes place in the spring.

Virtually all the fishing on the Babine is limited to a 13-mile stretch below the wier at Nilkitkwa. There is public access at the wier and for about a mile downstream. Beyond this point jet boats are needed. Two fine lodges serve the river and offer jet boat guiding and accommodations. The lower river runs through a crashing and treacherous gorge. There are no roads.

Nine-foot fly rods, fishing 8- to 10-weight, fast-sinking shooting tapers or high-density, sink-tip fly lines work best. Rim-controlled, single-action fly reels capable of holding a fly line plus plenty of backing are a must. During high water conditions short lengths of lead-core fly line are sometimes added to the end to help get it down. Short leaders of 4 to 8 feet tapered to 10-pound points are preferred. Some anglers twist lead wire around leader barrel knots for added sink. Flies can be weighted or unweighted according to preference.

Fluorescent patterns dressed from No. 1/0 to 6 are popular. The famous Babine Special as well as the Polar Shrimp, Flaming Betty and Skykomish Sunrise tied with fluorescent chenille work well. Dark patterns such as the Green-Butted Skunk, Dark Montreal, McClouds Ugly, Black Matuka and Boss produce fish when all others fail. Flies should be fished with as little drag as possible.

Lure fishermen are successful using standard 9-foot, double-handed, steelhead-type casting rods equipped with either level-wind or spinning reels with ample line capacity and a smooth, dependable drag system. Wobbling spoons and drift-type, imitation-egg-cluster lures produce well. Bait is not allowed.

Felt-soled waders are a must. Some prefer aluminum-cleated sandals as well. Bring warm clothes and raingear.

The Babine shares honors with other equally famous British Columbian rivers—all part of the Skeena River drainage. The remote Sustut; the Maurice and Bulkley near Smithers; the Lakelse and Copper near Terrace; and the world famous Kispiox out of Hazelton all produce giant steelhead. Most of these rivers have recently been classified as "Special River" by the British Columbian Fish and Wildlife Branch with reduced limits in force and special licenses required.

For information contact the Ministry of Tourism of British Columbia, 1117 Wall St., Victoria, BC, Canada V8W 272; telephone (604) 387-1642.

Bundled against the New York State cold, this angler has a Lake Ontario steelhead making a run up the Salmon River.

The Dean River

The Dean River is isolated and remote, 325 air miles north up British Columbia's rugged coastline from Vancouver. It was named by exploring Captain James Vancouver in 1793 for his friend Dean James King of Ireland. The river supports one of North America's largest natural summer steelhead runs.

The Dean flows 140 miles northwest from its source high in the Chilcoltin Plateau, through the rough Coastal Mountains, to find the Pacific at the head of one of Canada's most magnificent fjords, the Dean Channel. Its upper reaches have chalk stream qualities wandering through high mountain meadows, and offering excellent spring and early-summer fishing for medium-sized rainbows. Lodges at Nimpo and Anahim Lakes service this area and are accessible off the Bella Coola highway. From this point to the mouth is

STEELHEAD

roadless wilderness. Two excellent small lodges and a yacht operation serve the river, offering transportation to the best fishing waters.

Anadromous fish utilize the lower 50 miles of the river, with fishing allowed as far as Kalone Creek, 24 miles upstream from the mouth.

Dean River steelhead are very aggressive, and under low-water conditions may be taken on dry- and riffle-hitched flies, and with greased line. No. 6 Bucktail Caddis, Humpies, Royal Wulffs and dark Bivisibles fished upstream, and No. 6 Black Crickets riffle-hitched and fished downstream and across in the tail-outs all work well, especially over fresh-run, eager fish. The Golden and Silver Demon, Princeton, Thor, Cummings and similar patterns fished damp by swimming the fly downstream and across on a greased line will consistently produce during these periods as well.

The Dean's level fluctuates a great deal during the steelhead run. During high water periods, fish move well to fluorescent patterns such as the Babine Special and the Bella Coola Bombshell, or dark patterns such as the Boss, Skunk, Black Matuka and Silver Hilton dressed on No. 2 and 4 hooks fished on high-density, sink tip lines. Shooting tapers also have their place under these conditions. Nine-foot fly rods carrying 8- or 9-weight lines are the most popular. Single-action reels with good drags or rim control plus ample backing capacity are a must.

A great portion of the Dean has been designated fly-fishing only; however, conventional tackle is allowed from the Sakumtha River downstream to the mouth. Standard double-handed, steelhead-type casting rigs (see Babine) are used successfully.

The valley of the lower Dean River is a wonder. Five-thousand-foot, cloud-piercing peaks capped with snow rise suddenly from the wooded valley floor. Waterfalls tumble from this high escarpment. Eagles soar, mountain goats watch curiously from the misty crags while the valley is the home of the wolf, the black bear and the grizzly.

Chinook salmon run the river in June and July. This is primarily a lure fishery because the river is usually high and off-color most of this period. Spoons and drift-type lures are used.

Though steelhead may be found in the Dean River throughout the entire year, very heavy runs of ocean-bright fish occur from mid-July through September. The steelhead population consists primarily of maiden fish having spent two and three years in fresh water and then two winters and three summers in the ocean. Repeat spawners account for only 7 percent of the run. Though fish in excess of 30 pounds have been reported, males in the 19- to 25-pound class make up the bulk of the trophy fish taken annually. The average Dean River male steelhead weighs 15½ pounds, the average female 11 pounds (Survey of the 1981 Dean River Steelhead Fishery; G.A. George).

The lower Dean is accessible only by airplane or boat. There is an overgrown yet usable gravel airstrip at Kimsquit, the deserted logging station at the river mouth, offering very limited access on the first 2 miles of river. Upstream from here, the river rushes through the Dean Falls, a rugged one-half-mile-long canyon. Trails and an old logging road lead a short distance above the falls.

Felt-soled waders are a must and there are places

Special rowing rigs for inflatables make them a preferred craft with many guides on western rivers, especially those with dangerous white-water stretches.

where aluminum-cleated sandals are of great help. Weather is changeable and can range from the mid-40s to the mid-90s during the summer months. It rains and mists frequently.

A "Special River" license is required to fish the Dean. Reduced limits are in force and the release of fish encouraged.

For information contact the Ministry of Tourism of British Columbia, 1117 Wall St., Victoria, BC, Canada; telephone (604) 387-1642.

CUTTHROAT TROUT

*Oncorhynchus clarki**

My remedy for world weariness is to visit a land where the flowers are scarlet and the trout are gold and the lodge pole pines march straight up the mountains. To see a wild river splash and dance down granite stairs, scattering bright drops that fizz out in an iridescent veil, to hear the bugling of a bull elk and to smell bacon sputtering over a wood fire is a modern day anachronism. The Rocky Mountain region is obviously no longer the wilderness it was when Lewis and Clark made their passage in 1805, yet it remains one of the most sparsely settled areas in America. If you draw a circle with a 200-mile radius from West Yellowstone, it would encompass most of the classic trout fishing in the United States. Within this circle flow all size waters, from infant brooks to great torrents that roar through remote canyons, and at the very heart of it is 3,400-square-mile Yellowstone Park with over 800 miles of blue ribbon trout streams, and the redoubt of *Oncorhynchus clarki*, the cutthroat trout.

One of the great North American experiences, particularly for visitors from foreign countries who are outdoors-oriented, is a trip to Yellowstone Park. I don't recommend the family summer vacation months when hundreds of thousands of people create traffic jams comparable to a foggy night on the New Jersey Turnpike. Any chance to gawk at smelly geysers, vagrant bears, nearsighted moose and bands of bison on a tilted landscape is a wilderness attraction without peer. But by mid-September the tourist flow becomes a trickle and you get the feeling that my wife expressed as we stood on a rock-strewn summit facing the Beartooth Range: "We are the only people in the world." Quite apart from this unaccustomed sense of freedom, the best of all angling begins in September and runs through the first powdery snows (which disappear quickly) into the blushing days of autumn. Several factors conspire to make the fall a golden period. For one thing, water

*Scientific name revised, 1989. Pacific drainage trout genus are no longer of the name *Salmo*.

Caught in the surface film, a grasshopper is about to fall victim to a cutthroat trout. The least wary of all trout, the cutthroat, in its many subspecies, is a fragile resource of our western waters.

CUTTHROAT TROUT

levels of the major rivers, which are swollen by snow runoff during the warm days of summer, drop to a "normal" flow, which in terms of fly-fishing is the ideal situation of low, clear pools and sparkling riffles. On great rivers like the Snake, Madison or Yellowstone, which can knock a man off his feet during the summer months, it's possible to wade and cast over stretches that were almost immune to fishing by the regular vacationer. Insect pests have long gone, and the air invigorates like an Alsatian wine. I remember sitting on the bank of Slough Creek eating a sandwich while watching the antics of a moose family on the other bank. In the pool between us, the water was dimpled by forty or fifty cutthroat trout. There were so many fish feeding simultaneously that their winking rises appeared like rain splattering the surface.

Slough Creek is a place of unsurpassed beauty. Unlike many trout streams in Yellowstone Park, which are paralleled by roads, the alpine reaches of this stream require an hour's hike initially up a steep grade, which is enough to discourage the casual angler. You could drive to the campground and fish the easily accessible lower 5 miles, but upstream in that section known as First Meadows, and somewhat beyond in the Second Meadows (both of which are reached from a trail off the entrance road), are more miles of crystalline meandering water surrounded by towering mountain peaks. The river's source is in the Beartooths near Grasshopper Glacier and it flows into the Lamar River, a Yellowstone tributary. Slough Creek is a no-kill stream that supports an abundance of 14- to 20-inch cutthroat trout, a marvelous place to cast dry flies with a very light rod. On my last trip into the Meadows, with Tom McNally of the *Chicago Tribune,* we caught and released about thirty trout each, with a number of them exceeding 20 inches. However, it's not the quality of the angling that is so compelling as the feeling, I suppose, of being transposed to a valley that was chronologically bypassed. The sight of a Slough Creek cutthroat rising to catch a grasshopper provides continuity, although it does not explain the countless grasshoppers visible in the frozen wall of the glacier, victims of some strange phenomenon in the last millennium, or the near distinction of the cutthroat in the past century.

Few modern anglers realize that 100 years ago, the only trout found in the vast area extending from east of the Sierras in California through Montana and south to northern Mexico (with very few exceptions) was the cutthroat. All of our western rivers famous today for rainbow and brown

trout fishing such as the Madison, Big Hole, Jefferson, Platte, Gunnison, Clark Fork, Henry's Fork, Green, New Fork, ad infinitum were inhabited solely by cutthroat trout. In an historical sense, this transition is similar to the decline of our native brook trout in the eastern United States. Both are very vulnerable to angling, the cutthroat even more so than the brook trout, mutually unable to compete with other species and they were almost mindlessly killed in years past, not only by sport but also commercial fishermen. Until shortly after the turn of the century, tons of huge Lahontan cutthroat were purveyed in San Francisco markets for 25 to 50 cents a pound. In addition, the cutthroat is so closely related to the rainbow trout that the two species readily hybridize in inland waters, frequently producing fertile offspring; as a result, many pristine populations have been eliminated. Admittedly, the rainbow cutthroat hybrid is a superior game fish, consistently acrobatic, which the cutthroat is not, but on the other hand certain virtues are sacrificed.

It is difficult to describe a typical cutthroat trout except in a very general way as there are fifteen recognized subspecies in addition to hybrids and while they are all beautiful fish, the differences in coloration and even game qualities run to extremes. They all have in common a "cut," a patch of orange or red on the membrane of the throat, which they wear like a tribal mark. Some populations are brightly colored with large dark spots, others more somber in dress with very fine black pepper spotting but, as a rule, the most handsome are mature males, especially those that enjoy a dominantly crustacean diet. And while the gaily colored cutthroat in Yellowstone River is hardly a dynamic game fish, I have taken almost monochromatic silvery cutthroat in high mountain lakes of the Wind River system that were comparable to landlocked salmon in their spirited play. The leading authority today on native western trouts is Dr. Robert J. Behnke of Colorado State University, and his observations that follow, on the various cutthroat subspecies, reveal an unparalleled complexity in *Salmo clarki.*

Cutthroat Trout Subspecies

The cutthroat trout is an example of a highly variable (polytypic) species. Many parts (subspecies) make up the whole (species). Each of the subspecies, and even local populations within

a subspecies, exhibit their own peculiarities in life history and specialties that reflect evolutionary adaptations to different environments. These different life histories of the various forms specialized to life in small brooks, large rivers, lakes and the sea, their different food habits, migration patterns and appearance make it virtually impossible to accurately characterize the species as a whole except in the most general manner. Exceptions to all descriptive statements can be found. For example, it is generally true that, in respect to environmental disturbances, the cutthroat trout is like the canary in the mine—it is the first species to be eliminated. Most of the remnant populations of the interior subspecies are now largely restricted to the uppermost, coldest, headwater tributaries. Brook, brown and rainbow trout now dominate most of the original range of the interior subspecies. Certain subspecies, however, such as the cutthroat native to the Humboldt River, Nevada, and to the Bear River in Wyoming, evolved in rivers of semi-desert regions and they acquired adaptations to harsh and greatly fluctuating environments. Today these "desert adapted" cutthroat trout can be found thriving in highly unlikely habitat; small streams subjected to tremendous variation in flow, turbidity and temperature—to 80°F in the summer. In these areas, the hardy brown trout is found restricted to the colder, clearer, more stable

tributaries. The great diversity found in the numerous specialized forms of cutthroat trout is a natural resource that holds great promise for modern fisheries management.

Along the Pacific Coast, the coastal subspecies occurs from the Eel River, northern California, to Gore Point on the Kenai Peninsula, Alaska (Prince William Sound). The coastal cutthroat does not occur far from the sea, typically within 100 miles of the coast. East of the Cascade Range a number of subspecies occur. The numerous subspecies of interior cutthroat trout can be grouped into two major evolutionary lines—the "westslope" cutthroat trout, *Oncorhynchus clarki lewisi*, native to the upper Columbia River basin and to the South Saskatchewan River basin of Montana and Alberta, and to the headwaters of the Missouri River, downstream to the Great Falls of the Missouri (where Lewis and Clark first encountered this fish, hence the scientific name *O. clarki lewisi*); and the "Yellowstone" cutthroat trout, *Oncorhynchus clarki bouvieri*, whose evolutionary history is associated with the Snake River division of the Columbia basin. The Yellowstone cutthroat trout crossed the Continental Divide from the upper Snake River several thousand years ago after the glacial ice melted from the Yellowstone Plateau, to become established in Yellowstone Lake and the Yellowstone River downstream to the Tongue River, Wyoming. All other interior

Floating the upper Snake River in Grand Teton National Park for cutthroats is popular among tourist anglers. There are many guides available for this trip through some of the most spectacular of western landscapes.

CUTTHROAT TROUT

subspecies of cutthroat trout are derived from an ancestor of the Yellowstone cutthroat.

During glacial epochs distribution of cutthroat trout throughout the now arid West was facilitated by periods of cooler, wetter climate. From about 10,000 to 50,000 years ago a series of great lakes filled the present desert basins of the West (collectively called the Great Basin). Lake Bonneville of Utah, of which Great Salt Lake is a remnant, attained a size comparable to present Lake Michigan, and Lake Lahontan, Nevada, covered an area similar in size to Lake Erie; Pyramid Lake represents the relic waters of Lake Lahontan. Giant cutthroat trout were the top predator fish in these ancient lakes and they persisted in Pyramid Lake until 1938 when spawning runs were blocked in the Truckee River (the present cutthroat trout of Pyramid Lake are derived from other sources and stocked from hatcheries). This long evolutionary history as a large predator in ancient Lake Lahontan made the Lahontan cutthroat trout of Pyramid Lake the largest of all cutthroat trout.

During the glacial periods, the ancestral cutthroat trout dispersed into the Colorado River drainage and, from there, crossed the Continental Divide to gain access to the Rio Grande and to the headwaters of the South Platte and Arkansas river basins of Colorado and subsequently evolved into the present subspecies. The southernmost known native distribution of cutthroat trout occurs in southcentral New Mexico, in streams draining to the Pecos River from Sierra Blanca Peak (Rio Grande cutthroat), although unverified nineteenth century reports mention cutthroat

trout in Texas and Mexico. An examination of the distribution and divergences in the cutthroat trout species indicates that the cutthroat was in North America, penetrated inland and diverged into three major evolutionary lines (coastal, westslope and Yellowstone subspecies) before any member of the rainbow trout species was on the scene. This is interpreted by the fact that only cutthroat trout are native to the upper Columbia River basin above the major falls that form a barrier to fish migration. The westslope cutthroat is the native trout above the major barrier falls on the Kootenai, Pend Oreille and Spokane rivers. The Yellowstone cutthroat is the native trout above Shoshone Falls on the Snake River. The cutthroat trout must have achieved this distribution before the impassable falls were created by geological events, blocking access to the later invading rainbow trout. After the invasion of rainbow trout, cutthroat trout were essentially eliminated in the Columbia basin from the areas below the barrier falls westward to the Cascade Mountains. The introduction of rainbow trout (and brown and brook trout) by man during the past 100 years into areas where they were not native has had the same impact; the native cutthroat typically soon disappears after the establishment of non-native trout.

Cutthroat trout are spring spawners. Spawning is typically initiated when water temperatures rise to about 45°F. This may occur as early as January and February in Pacific Coast streams under a moderate climatic regime or as late as July in cold, high elevation waters. As with most trout species, cutthroat trout spawn in streams, the female constructs a redd in a gravel area with good percolation ensuring adequate oxygen to the developing eggs. There are examples where cutthroat trout successfully spawn in lakes lacking suitable inlet or outlet streams. This is possible if the lake has a gravel bar subjected to upwelling of well-oxygenated water. The eggs hatch in about thirty days when water temperatures average about 52°F. Colder temperatures prolong the incubation period and warmer temperatures accelerate development, but temperatures above 55°F cause high mortality and abnormalities.

Growth rate is highly variable in different environments and depends on abundance, accessibility, and size of the food organisms, length of growing season with optimum

Montana's Slough Creek is one of the prettiest cutthroat streams in the Rockies. The upper reaches of the river at First and Second Meadows require at least an hour's hike to reach but are worth the effort. This is a no-kill stream with an abundance of 14- to 20-inch trout.

temperatures (from 50° to 65°F) and degree of competition from other fish species. In very small streams cutthroat trout may spawn at two years of age at 5 or 6 inches in size, have a maximum life span of only three or four years and rarely exceed a maximum size of 7 or 8 inches. Sea-run cutthroat, lake-adapted populations and populations in larger streams may live for seven to ten years. In high elevation lakes with extremely cold water and a short growing season, cutthroat trout may live fifteen to twenty years or more.

Sea-run cutthroat typically migrate to bays and estuaries in their third or fourth year of life where they intensively feed and grow for a few months before returning to overwinter in fresh water. The major life history difference between sea-run cutthroat trout and sea-run rainbow trout (steelhead) is that the cutthroat spend only a few months each year in the marine environment and stay in bays and estuaries not far from the shore, never migrating into the open ocean, whereas steelhead, after smolting and migrating, typically spend eighteen to thirty months in the ocean, often more than 1,000 miles from the coast, before sexually maturing and returning to their home rivers to spawn. Because of the relatively short time spent in the sea during their life, the sea-run cutthroat trout rarely exceeds 4 pounds. In lakes with forage fishes, cutthroat trout may be highly predaceous and attain a size of 12 pounds or more. In several studies of lakes with both rainbow trout and cutthroat trout, the cutthroat is, typically, more predaceous than the rainbow and reaches a larger maximum size. The largest of all cutthroat trout is the Lahontan cutthroat trout, a highly specialized predator. The official world record cutthroat trout came from Pyramid Lake, Nevada, and weighed 41 pounds, but unverified reports from the Indian tribal fishery of Pyramid Lake during the early part of this century gave maximum weights of the native cutthroat trout to 60 pounds and more. The cutthroat trout of Bear Lake, Utah-Idaho, a lake in the Bonneville desert basin, has been recorded to 19 pounds in recent years. Rainbow cutthroat hybrids may exhibit rapid growth and great size. Hybrid specimens to 30 pounds have been caught in Ashley Lake, Montana.

The cutthroat trout is more vulnerable to being caught by anglers than any other species of trout. Cutthroat exhibit a general lack of wariness and can be readily caught on a wide variety of flies, lures and baits. An exception may be found in high elevation lakes where only a single species of a tiny invertebrate food organism may dominate

the food supply and the cutthroat becomes conditioned to feed on this one organism. In this situation, they may ignore all else. In studies on cutthroat trout it has been demonstrated that light fishing pressure of only a relatively few hours per surface acre per year can overexploit the population (50 percent or more of the catchable

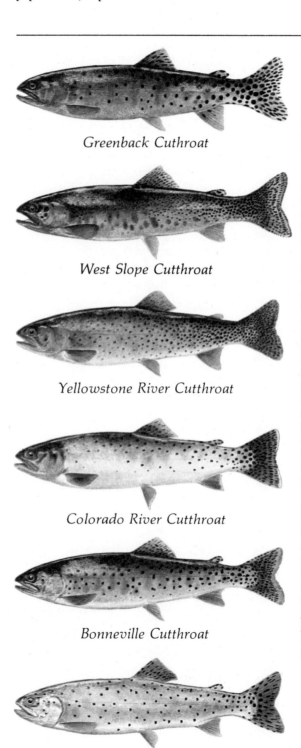

Greenback Cuthroat

West Slope Cutthroat

Yellowstone River Cutthroat

Colorado River Cutthroat

Bonneville Cutthroat

Lahontan Cutthroat

Subspecies of Cutthroat

Each of the fifteen recognized subspecies has its own common name, such as coastal cutthroat trout, Lahontan cutthroat trout, west slope cutthroat trout, greenback cutthroat trout, Rio Grande cutthroat trout, etc. The cutthroat trout is closely related to the rainbow trout.

Besides the cutthroat mark, cutthroat trout differ from rainbow trout by the presence of basibranchial (hyoid) teeth in their throat between the gill arches. Cutthroat trout typically have longer heads and jaws than rainbow trout and, particularly among the inland subspecies, cutthroat trout can be readily distinguished from rainbow trout by their much larger spots and brighter coloration. The west slope, Colorado River, Rio Grande and greenback subspecies may be exceptionally colored with bright crimson, gold and orange colors. The intensity of coloration, however, is dependent on age, sex and diet. The most intense colors are found on mature males feeding on crustaceans rich in carotenoid pigments.

CUTTHROAT TROUT

Countless beautiful lakes are found in the alpine reaches of the Jim Bridger Wilderness of Wyoming. This area, accessible only by backpacking or horse (there are outfitters in Pinedale), produces cutthroat trout as well as cutthroat and golden and cutthroat and rainbow hybrids.

size fish are caught). This susceptibility to angling puts the cutthroat trout at a severe disadvantage when coexisting with other trout species, especially brown trout. A stream near Taos, New Mexico, was sampled by electrofishing (fish are stunned with electrical current) in 1966 when the stream was on private land and not open to public fishing. A test section of the stream held 420 cutthroat trout and 37 brown trout. Two years later, after the stream was opened to public fishing, the test section yielded 37 cutthroat trout and 137 brown trout. With two years of fishing pressure the cutthroat trout population declined by 93 percent and the brown trout population increased by 270 percent. Obviously, proper management of cutthroat trout requires consideration of special protective regulations to prevent overexploitation. Because of its vulnerability to angling, the cutthroat trout is the species that yields the most outstanding results from special regulation (regulations designed to recycle all or most of the catch). In Idaho, cutthroat trout populations increased in abundance from six to thirteen times in streams under special regulations. In the Yellowstone River, below Yellowstone Lake, where all trout must be released after catching, it is now estimated that the average cutthroat trout in the population is caught and released seven times during the fishing season to support a total annual catch (and release) of about 500 pounds of trout per surface acre of river, or a catch of 10,000 pounds per mile of river—probably the finest natural trout fishery in the world in relation to total catch per unit area

and average size of fish in the catch (14 to 18 inches). These results cannot be duplicated with any other species of trout.

The coastal subspecies of cutthroat trout still inhabits its original range but has been reduced in abundance due to watershed degradation from logging and livestock grazing and angling overexploitation. The interior subspecies of cutthroat have suffered catastrophic declines. Some subspecies are extinct and some are currently protected by the Endangered Species Act. The greatest concentration of interior cutthroat trout presently occurs in Yellowstone Lake and River in Yellowstone Park and on the other side of the Continental Divide in the upper Snake River drainage of Yellowstone and Teton National parks. Other pockets where fairly substantial numbers of native cutthroat trout still hold on are the upper Salmon and St. Joe rivers of Idaho; Henry's Lake, Idaho; Flathead Lake, Montana; and the upper Flathead River drainage in Glacier National Park.

Pyramid Lake

When the footloose Captain John Fremont first viewed the strikingly blue waters of a sprawling desert lake in 1843, high spires of rock resembled pictures he had seen of the Egyptian pyramid of Cheops so he named this remnant of the once gigantic Lahontan Sea, Pyramid Lake. Today this Nevada lake—located about 35 miles northeast of Reno's neon-spangled streets—attracts trout fishermen from all sections of our country. It's the only water I know of where cutthroat trout of 10 pounds and heavier are caught every year. Located on the Paiute Indian Reservation, this holdover from the Pleistocene period is renowned for the big Lahontan trout it once yielded including the rod-and-reel record 41-pounder taken by John Skimmerhorn in 1925—a record that will most likely never fall. However, in scattered Sagebrush State museums old yellow-edged photos show wagons heaped with tiers of huge trout from Pyramid, some surely large enough to top Skimmerhorn's record catch by 10 or even 20 pounds.

But Lahontan cutthroats fell upon hard times. Commercial fishing took its toll when big spawners were vulnerable as they ascended the Truckee River. In an early irrigation project, the Derby Dam was constructed across the Truckee River shortly after the turn of this century. Water was diverted to Lahontan Reservoir to irrigate rich farmlands in the Fallon area under an enterprise known as the Newlands Project. The effect on Pyramid was disastrous. Within a few years the shrinking lake's shoreline dropped 100 feet and no one knows how many outsized cutthroats expired in hot, unscreened irrigation ditches. For years the Indians bitterly fought with the government over increased river flow. Eventually bars of silt built up at the river's mouth further impeding spawning runs in the only river that enters the lake.

By the 1930s the big Lahontan trout were in real trouble and the original strain was believed extinct prior to 1950. Some biologists felt the receding lake had become too alkaline to support trout, but stocking other strains from waters along the California-Nevada border and Idaho once again built up populations. By the early 1970s, 10-pounders were again showing up in catches with a few fish topping 20 pounds. A 23-pound, 8-ounce heavyweight set a modern record in 1977, and a 24-pound, 10-ounce cutthroat rainbow hybrid set a record for these fish in 1976.

Trouble struck again in the 1970s, when the dreaded "whirling disease" hit several of the lake's hatcheries substantially reducing stocking programs. In 1955, a hatchery capable of producing 1,000,000 young annually was completed in the foothills near Sutcliffe on the west side of the lake. Also completed were innovative mesh holding pens where cutthroats could become acclimatized in Pyramid's highly alkaline waters before their final release. Restorative programs are now being planned under supervision of the United States Department of Fish and Wildlife Service along with the Nevada Fish and Game Department and Pyramid Lake Indian Tribal Council.

Though some cutthroats are caught year-'round, October through mid-April are the top months. Most anglers work from the lake's west side, which is bordered by a paved road with numerous access points. There are a store, motel and fine launching ramps at Sutcliffe. There are also a large campground and launching ramp 10 miles farther north at Warrior's Point. (Visiting anglers must possess special Indian fishing permits. These may be picked up at Sutcliffe or by writing to Pyramid Lake Tribal Council, P. O. Box 256, Nixon, NV 89424.)

Pyramid boasts a 72-mile shoreline made up of alkali-whitened washes, runty sage, hot springs and jagged formations of tufa rock. Operated as a trophy-fish lake, the daily limit is two trout not less than 19 inches in length. Thus an 18-inch trout, which would be a substantial catch just about anywhere, is merely an undersized

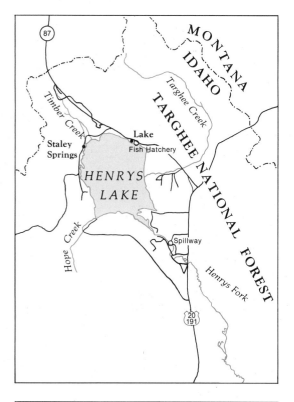

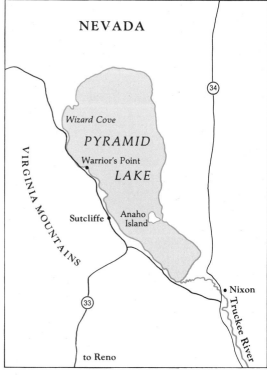

Henrys Lake is one of the most outstanding trout fisheries in the West. In addition to native cutthroat, this more than 6,000-acre weed-bottomed reservoir produces rainbows and some large brook trout. It is mannaged as a trophy-only fishery. The trout population is supplemented by spawn taking and rearing at the lake's hatchery.

An hour's drive north of nightlife-oriented Reno, Pyramid Lake offers very exciting daytime pleasures with its often fabulous cutthroat trout fishing. The peak period here is from October through April; some of the largest fish are caught during the winter season. The town of Sutcliffe is a pivotal location for angling necessities, including Paiute Indian fishing permits.

CUTTHROAT TROUT

No angling career is complete without at least one visit to Yellowstone Park. Famed for its Yellowstone cutthroat, a distinct subspecies, the park and its environs offer many miles of streams accessible to the motorist, hiker and backpacker.

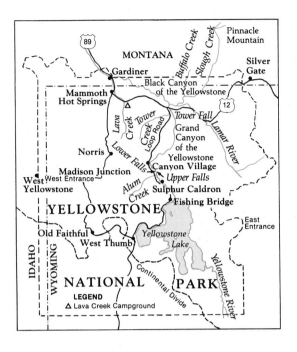

throwback at Pyramid. The use of live or natural bait is illegal for non-Indian anglers. The favorite trolling rig on this big lake is a quarter-ounce sliding sinker threaded on the end of 8- or 10-pound-test monofilament. A swivel cinched to the end of the line holds the sinker in place. A 3- to 5-foot leader is secured to the opposite end of the swivel and your choice of lures tied to the leader. Two artificials take the vast majority of Pyramid cutthroats. A medium-sized, black-spotted, grayish-green Flatfish is the local favorite, bearing in mind that cutthroats forage deep down in the depths, and lures that fail to tiptoe along the bottom rarely score. Another popular lure is the one-quarter-ounce Tor-p-do Wobbling Spoon trolled along the bottom without additional weight. A variety of color combinations work. The Dardevle and Kastmaster spoons are also successful at times. Most of the trout taken by

Twenty-mile-long (62,000 acres) Bear Lake, straddling the Utah and Idaho border, is one of the top producers of 5- to 10-pound cutthroats in the U.S. today. Although fish can be taken throughout the year, spring and winter are the peak seasons. Deep trolling with spoons is the most effective method on Bear Lake.

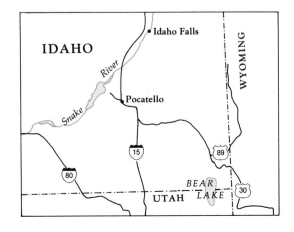

trollers are caught close to the banks.

Seldom does a winter or early spring day pass when a contingent of fly casters aren't braving the lake's icy waters. A No. 4, 6 or 8 Black Woolly Worm is the most popular fly on Pyramid. However, Gray, Brown, Green and even White Woolly Worms produce big cutthroats when fished near the bottom. Experienced casters favor sinking shooting heads to get the fly down deep, and as quickly as possible. When casting from the bank the object is to work the fly over drop-offs, as the trout wait along these shelves to ambush cui-ui minnows (a species of sucker unique to Pyramid Lake). The lake can become very rough and, often, the choppier it gets the better the shore fishing.

Yellowstone River

The upper Yellowstone River is a stream of great contrasts. One of the most accessible locations, Buffalo Ford, where you can virtually park your car on the river bank, is too heavily trafficked for the dyed-in-the-wool fly-fisher, yet it produces an amazing number of 14- to 16-inch cutthroat trout, some of which are probably caught and released on an almost daily basis. Yet, there are stretches like the Yellowstone headwaters above the 30-mile-long lake that can only be reached by canoe (no power boats are allowed), or by a rugged hike into primitive country. The headwaters is essentially a many-channeled meadow stream harboring small trout, but with an abundance of wildlife in attendance. The river flows north into the South East Arm of 139-square-mile Yellowstone Lake. While the cutthroat here do not attain the great sizes of those found in Pyramid Lake, bear in mind that the Yellowstone cutthroat is a distinct subspecies (*Oncorhynchus clarki bouvieri*) and a willing fly taker.

One mile below the lake's outlet at Fishing Bridge and extending for 6 miles to Sulphur Caldron is the most accessible portion of the upper Yellowstone. This no-kill stretch holds a tremendous population of cutthroat with the occasional fish in the 20-inch class. From Sulphur Caldron to Alum Creek (a tributary) the Yellowstone is a wildlife sanctuary closed to fishing, but open to the nature lover who wants to view the peregrinations of elk, moose, buffalo, mule deer, bear and antelope. Downstream from Alum Creek below Yellowstone Falls is the Grand Canyon of the Yellowstone, which is strictly for aspiring alpinists. I only made that descent once, in younger days, and can hardly recommend it for

the casual angler. The confining cliffs are nearly vertical drops of over 1,000 feet and the quality of the fishing below is not significantly better than the run above Sulphur Caldron. By choice, I would continue driving on the Loop Road to beyond its intersection with the Silver Gate (Cooke City) Road and hike into Black Canyon.

The Black Canyon section more or less parallels the road on the north and it requires a hike of 1 to 4 miles to reach the river, depending on your access point. The walking is easy but inasmuch as it requires some effort, the Black Canyon is not much visited and it offers, in my opinion, the best cutthroat angling on the Yellowstone. If you hike in, by all means take a compass and a map, as the river meanders. For first-timers, a good trail can be found east of Lava Creek Campgrounds near the junction of Old Tower Falls Road. Black Canyon can be visited in one day but ideally, I would plan to overnight with the minimal sleeping bag and suitable foodstuffs. There is about 20 miles of river to fish. The Canyon stretch ends at the town of Gardiner, Montana, which is really the end of pristine cutthroat water on the Yellowstone; from here downstream, below Emigrant, rainbow and brown trout become dominant fisheries, maintaining an excellence that is world renown.

If you plan to do any camping in the park, be certain to check on any necessary permits at the entry gates. For fishing maps, topographical maps, angling advice, tackle and guide services visit Bud

Lilly's Tackle Shop in West Yellowstone, or telephone (406) 646-7801. Bear in mind that fishing regulations change periodically, as the park's rivers are subject to an ongoing management program.

The cutthroat is the trout most vulnerable to angling. In the no-kill section of Yellowstone River, it is estimated that the average cutthroat is caught and released seven times during the fishing season.

ARCTIC
GRAYLING

Thymallus arcticus

The enormous rock mass engulfs more than half of Canada and much of the northeastern and northcentral United States. A low slab of ancient granite and gneiss, basalt and greenstone encompassing 2,146,000 square miles, it is the largest of Earth's eleven Precambrian shields, each one a continental nucleus afloat on the magma. No life forms save the most primitive plants are fossilized in Precambrian formations, for these are rocks from the earliest geological era, igneous and metamorphosed mineral mixtures that solidified as much as 3,740,000,000 years ago (on a scale that assumes planetary genesis at 4,600,000,000 years). The surface of Earth is a crust of frozen stone, some of which has degraded into soil, some into vivification. The Canadian Shield's center is a 470,000-square-mile mediterranean sea called Hudson's Bay, but, being drowned under the brackish bay, represents only a fraction of the Shield's inundation. Lakes and muskeg together are estimated to cover half of the Shield, lakes alone a quarter, and everywhere they are connected by an incessant running of becks, creeks, gills, rills, streams and rivers full of fish.

The people in this country are Mongols with folk names such as Inuit and Cree, Dogrib and Chipewyan. Most of them are quite friendly to Euro-Americans, but their dogs are not. Do not pet the yellow-eyed dogs or even go near them unless you carry a dog whip or a loaded firearm. In winter, the Mongols use these dogs to travel far from snowmobile trails in pursuit of game, or to follow trap lines. If a snowmobile breaks down in the back country you have a serious problem, perhaps one insoluble in this life. If a dog dies there will be five dogs left to take you home, and the six of you can eat the dead dog.

The fish in this country are as specialized for cold as the squat Mongols, whose epicanthic eye folds protect their tear ducts from temperatures that average − 20°F in January and can reach

Because of a paucity of milt and eggs, the male Arctic grayling must assure close proximity during the spawning act by embracing his mate with his large dorsal. These salmonids of far northern streams are willing biters of small lures.

ARCTIC GRAYLING

down to −70°. One fish, the Arctic grayling, also has a unique eye and exhibits conduct that indicates it does not see this world as do most fishes, or as you and I, though fish and human eyes are much alike. The Arctic grayling's pupil is pear-shaped with the point forward. It can see minute surface insects through 10 or 12 feet of water, yet after rising to one, often must try repetitively before capturing it. In fact, Arctic grayling appear to be advanced presbyopes, with an almost hawk-like distance vision but in need of reading glasses.

Thymallus arcticus ranges from the western shore of Hudson's Bay across the continent and penetrates the Asian mainland west to the Kara and Ob rivers of Siberia and south to the upper Yalu, the Sino-Korean border river. The southern limit now of natural stocks is to the headwaters of the Missouri River drainage in Yellowstone. Though they were once in tributaries to Lakes Superior, Michigan and Huron, those populations were extinguished by human agency: drastic watershed degradation through clear-cutting, abetted by gross commercial overfishing.

Stocked populations exist at high altitudes in many U.S. western states. Alpine lakes with insufficient oxygen for the maintenance of trout can often support grayling, whose O_2 requirements are quite low, as one would expect of a fish evolved to spend nine months a year under ice. (Water averages only one-thirtieth the oxygen content of air, and fishkills from oxygen depletion are common.) The southern breed, generally referred to as the Montana grayling, has healthy populations in the Madison River, the upper Beaverhead and Big Hole, and in headwater lakes of the Gibbon River within Yellowstone National Park. In comparison with grayling of the Arctic watershed, the Montana strain suffers from a short life, which restricts its size, and a congenitally small dorsal. Inexperienced anglers often mistake them for whitefish.

Grayling are a recent addition to the Canadian Shield's biota, because everything is a recent addition to the Shield. It is raw rock from the beginning because the Pleistocene glaciations denuded and mammilated it, then polished it with embedded grit. The ice caps left Canadian erratics (solitary boulders deposited by melting) as far south as Missouri. The latest retreat began 20,000 years ago and a brief reversal occurred 6,000 years ago.

This is the charm of the country: smoothed rock knolls that have not had time to weather since they were bared and buffed, hollows mantled with glacial till and loess, a boreal conifer forest or taiga

DISTRIBUTION

to the south and tundra over permafrost to the north. In summer there is enough daylight to fish until midnight. This is the Arctic grayling's heartland, where they prosper as nowhere else.

When seeking large specimens of any fish it is crucial to locate their heartland. Marginal populations at the limits of the species' thermal tolerance are unlikely to have the steadily ticking metabolism that produces fat, elderly fish. The Montana grayling, for instance, begins its reproductive life at two and dies at age four or five. A 2-pounder is huge. In the Arctic watershed most grayling do not even sexually mature until their fourth year and are often still prospering at age twelve. A handful reach fourteen.

The Mongols in their many tongues call them "little blue fish" and net them for dog food, declining to eat grayling themselves as long as lake trout or whitefish are available. The *voyageurs*, adopting the native name, dubbed them *poisson bleu* even though their mother tongue already had *ombre* (shadow) available.

The flesh of Arctic grayling is firm and white, but so delicately flavored that palates inured to common fare will find them insipid. Taste one that has come from the same cookfire as whitefish or lake trout and you will understand the Mongols' preference. They are commonly fried with potatoes as part of the ubiquitous shore lunch, an institution in the north country for which they are ill-suited. Poached and properly sauced they carry the sauce well. Smoked they are ambrosial, but what fish isn't?

Some Canadian and Alaskan populations may spawn every other year, a few every third year. The eggs hatch after eleven to twenty-one days as compared to three months for fall-spawning trout. They mate immediately after ice-out in streams, and the remarkable color variation within a population indicates which is spawning this year—females and non-spawning males are dowdy while spawning males have brilliant blues, purples and lilac shades, with golden or brassy sheens and dorsals dotted with almost fluorescent blue spots.

The female excavates no redd, but lies alongside the male and both undergo the customary salmonid quivering and gaping while he expresses milt and she ejects a mean of 6,500 to 9,700 eggs. During reproduction the male positions himself next to the female and, leaning toward her, folds his dorsal fin over her back to be perfectly oriented

during the brief seconds when eggs and milt are expelled. This conduct is unique among known species of fish. The male has the largest dorsal and it is longest aft, where it reaches to or beyond his adipose fin. The female's smaller fin is longest in front. Another unusual (but not unique) use of fins by grayling is their custom of propping themselves on the stream bottom by spreading their pectorals.

Unlike trout they are a gregarious fish, and a school viewed at the bottom of a deep, clear, swift pool is reminiscent of a fighter squadron ready to scramble. Look closely and you will see the biggest fish in the van where they have first choice from the benthic drift. By fishing only the heads of pools and runs you can selectively angle for the largest. The middle of the school will be a same-sized, younger year-class, and the rear will be juveniles. Schooling by year-class is of course common among fishes, especially the immature; multiple-year-class schooling with rank based on territorial dominance by alpha males is unheard of except among grayling. The Thymallidae are unique or unusual in at least three respects: vision, mating and schooling. They warrant much closer examination than biologists have given them, but since the genus is insufficiently fecund to support commercial fishing it will always be among the last to receive study funding.

One additive study claims that virtually the entire diet of Arctic grayling is composed of insects and cites in support monographs published in 1938, 1964, 1970 and 1973. Another specifies terrestrial insects as of primary importance, and a third selects invertebrate crustaceans such as *Mysis* and *Gammarus*. Crustaceans will no doubt be important to baby grayling—described by one observer as "two eyeballs on a thread"—who begin feeding on the local zooplankton the third day after hatching and doubtless continue as both they and the zooplankton mature, but terrestrial insects will be only briefly available at the height of summer. Since each study introduces a new, and different, grayling, perhaps we should accept them all and even look for more.

The Arctic grayling I have dressed had teeth on both jaws, the palatines, the tongue and on the head of the vomer—which sounds like wretched excess for capturing insects and scuds. It is quite difficult for a salmonid to grow much beyond 2 pounds on an invertebrate diet. However, large grayling become carnivorous with maturity, while retaining invertebrates as a support diet.

Convinced of the general truth of this I once devoted a week in the Great Slave Lake area—a watershed permeated with coregonids of many

This is a typical grayling with appropriate tackle. They are a small stream and lake fish, and no one has yet caught a 6-pounder.

species—to fishing only silvery minnow imitations for grayling. The experiment consistently produced larger specimens than I have taken before and each one slain contained at least one small coregonid. A cisco or a juvenile whitefish makes an excellent buffer between zooplankton and adult grayling.

The stomachs of Arctic grayling have yielded wasps and bees, lemmings and beetles, grasshoppers and fish eggs, but much if not most of their diet seems to come from on top. Scott and Crossman's *Freshwater Fishes of Canada* (Department of Environment, Fisheries Research Board of Canada, Ottawa, Ontario, Bulletin 184, 1973) rightly notes "their habit of testing almost

Arctic grayling country is invariably beautiful. The fish will hold in riffles, runs and pools. In lakes, they cruise shorelines. This angler is fishing a southwestern Alaska stream.

everything on the surface of the water." Nevertheless, the experience of almost all of us who annually go to the Canadian Shield for sport is that you can seldom go wrong with a small dark dry fly. The experience of Europeans with their species of grayling, *T. thymallus*, is that the creatures are so remarkably educable that in alpine Central Europe they are cherished beyond trout. Even the lowland British race, which becomes prime only in winter when insect hatches are past, receives in fall the respectful presentation of imitative patterns. Unfortunately we will probably

never learn if Arctic grayling can become *selective* (in the jargon of fly-fishermen) because the Black Gnat syndrome is rooted in reality. I have at hand a list of thirteen predominate Shield aquatic insects. It includes mayflies, caddisflies, stoneflies and chironomids. They are uniformly black, gray or dark brown. They range in size from No. 12 to 22, but most are No. 14. I suppose you could tie some of your Arctic grayling No. 14 Black Gnat dry flies upwinged, downwinged and spentwinged for variety, but a simple hackled pattern will suffice.

One memorably cold September morning on a Shield river I massaged silicone fly line dressing into a No. 20 Black Ant dry fly that was just two whorls of dubbing spun on the hook. On a 5X tippet I took thirteen grayling in thirteen casts, all in the 15- to 18-inch range, and was unexpectedly taken (and broken) by the alpha male of the pool on my fourteenth cast. (Unexpectedly, because the big fish normally come first with this species.) Surface insect activity is greatly reduced by mid-September and it is possible that the big male, well in excess of 20 inches, was looking for small whitefish or grayling. It is also possible that he had been caught a few times since the local fishing lodge opened for its season.

P romptly release grayling you are not going to eat or have mounted as a trophy—and as a matter of fact, don't try to have one mounted, the colors are too evanescent and the dorsal too delicate for the art of taxidermy to convincingly represent. Grayling trophies are best preserved by photography.

This fish feeds utterly unlike trout, or any other fluvial species I have watched. Their preference is strongly for pools or, at very least, for deep runs with strong standing waves indicative of boulders that buffer the current; I have seldom caught an Arctic grayling in a riffle, possibly because in thin water I have always fished them with drag-free floating flies or nymphs. Charles F. Waterman reports that riffles in a Yukon stream were unproductive until he induced gross drag, the sort that leaves a V wake. Advice from that particular source is always to be cherished.

In the pool, ranked in their dominance hierarchy, they seem not to dart from side to side for items in the drift as do trout, but to rise and fall as if on an elevator. I cannot recall an instance of an Arctic grayling giving off Skues "little brown wink underwater," the tell-tale of a nymphing trout as it twists and turns to intercept.

The rise to surface flies is not preceded by taking a feeding station high in the water column as do trout, but by coming all the way up from the bottom of the pool and going all the way back down again. One could speculate that Arctic grayling have such a brief annual experience of water with a liquid surface that they never learn to feed efficiently off the top. One shouldn't do so; the European grayling, who have as much surface experience as trout, still come up from the bottom (as do seatrout, brown trout of anadromous inclinations, despite a history of river feeding as parr). Swimmingly done it would be ruinously wasteful of calories, but they accomplish it by tilting their pectorals and aquaplaning up by force of current, necessarily dropping downstream as they do so. The insect is taken, often only after many attempts, and then they aquaplane back to the bottom. Since this rise may have come up through 10 or 15 feet of water, the fish will be yards aft of his position when he regains the bottom, but he can easily move forward to his territory in the multi-directional burble of frictionally interrupted bottom laminate (without friction between stream layers moving at different speeds, and friction with the streambed itself, rivers could theoretically accelerate until they were traveling more than 1,000 miles per hour).

Father Walton promulgated the false doctrine that grayling have tender mouths and must be played with a delicate hand. Grayling, European as well as Arctic, have small terminal mouths, square-shaped when open, with tough, rubbery lips, the lower pale or white. Indeed, getting Arctic grayling off barbed hooks can be a messy affair best avoided by flattening barbs.

There is one peculiarity of Arctic grayling I have seen reported only once, in an obscure Canadian book: The graceful, lovely creatures are seemingly made of solid rock or cast iron. They will still squirm and wriggle while clasped in a grip that would squash trout. The flesh that is so delicately textured when cooked that its myotomes separate under the fork is incredibly rigid alive. With a barbless or flattened hook it is possible to leave them in the water and twitch it out with longnose pliers or a Mayo-Hegar needle holder, sold in tackle shops under the name "forceps."

In the taking of "this dainty fish," Izaak Walton has it exactly right:

First note that he grows not to the bigness of a Trout; for the biggest of them do not usually exceed

Flying in is the normal transportation to grayling country. This float plane is at Frontier Fishing Lodge on Great Slave Lake. The adjacent Stark River is enormously productive of Arctic grayling.

eighteen inches. He lives in such rivers as the Trout does; and is usually taken with the same baits as the Trout is, and after the same manner; for he will bite both at the minnow, or worm, or fly, though he bites not often at the minnow, and is very gamesome at the fly; and much simpler, and therefore bolder than a Trout; for he will rise twenty times at a fly, if you miss him, and yet rise again.

I would begin counting Arctic grayling as a trophy at 19 inches fork length and about 3 pounds, although a fat one that size could top 3½. The present record, taken in 1967, was a fraction of an inch short of 30 inches and 1 ounce short of 6 pounds. That came from the Katseyedie River at Great Bear Lake in the Northwest Territories. Grayling are therefore the most diminutive of the salmonid game fishes. You must turn to commercial food fish such as ciscoes and bloaters to find smaller members of the Salmonidae family. Such a fish is ideally taken on light fly-fishing and ultralight spinning tackle, but there is a complication or two worth discussion.

Floating fly lines will of course suffice for dry-fly-fishing, but trophy seekers who want to fish streamers or bucktails will find it nearly impossible to get to the bottom of the often deep pools in fast current without resorting to high-speed sinking lines or even lead-core. With 30 or more feet of line that weighs perhaps 550 grains attached to him, the grayling will find it nearly impossible to jump. He will erect his dorsal and try to otterboard his way across current from you, but he is much

ARCTIC GRAYLING

like a kite with too much tail. The fly tackle to take trophy fish has minimized the experience as sport. My fishing for salmonids has been almost wholly with fly for the past forty years, but I am driven to conclude that ultralight spinning tackle is less destructive of sport when a small fish must be sought on bottom in fast current. Weighted spinners, spoons or lead-head jigs in one-eighth-ounce size, fished upstream on 2-pound-test monofilament line, will find bottom in anything short of a torrent. Retrieve should be slightly faster than the current speed to maintain contact with the lure and detect strikes. It helps to immerse the rod tip slightly. I would begin fishing minnow imitations with something silvery-white to represent a small whitefish, then switch to a dark lure to represent baby grayling.

Locating Arctic grayling is customarily the guide's responsibility, but if he is napping or you are out on your own remember their gregariousness means quite a bit of water will be vacant because they are schooled elsewhere. Fishing the water in a

The Ugashik River has traditionally produced the largest Alaskan grayling. There are rumors of monsters (if you can call a 5- or 6-pound fish a monster) off St. Lawrence Island in the Bering Sea, but no one has brought in the proof.

is to disembark and wade when you locate a school.

Lacustrine grayling in my experience are the largest, although my first grayling came from a lake in Saskatchewan and measured a noble 4 inches. They are also difficult to locate without an experienced local guide. Canadian biologists who have made gillnet sets to sample lake populations report grayling appear only in the top 10 feet. I have had best results walking graveled lake shorelines during the evening looking for rises. If these prove to be grayling of a fishable size, well and good. If they are quite small coregonids, switch to a streamer fly; large grayling and lake trout will also be patrolling the lake shore looking for concentrations of what *they* want to catch, which is small fish intent upon insects.

The largest hatches on most Shield lakes will come in August, often quite late at night or infamously early in the morning! When an entire bay, silver in the crepuscular light, is ringed with rises a cast dry fly might produce 3 pounds of grayling, 5 of lake whitefish (a formidable battler), or 15 of lake trout (at high latitudes an absolute *terror*). For this reason grayling fly tackle should feature a reel with much more backing than you would normally use for such small fish.

The monotonously dusky hue of Shield insects, and the avidity with which Arctic grayling surface feed during their brief annual access to the surface, does not mean that pitching a dark fly on the water guarantees fish. That remarkable distance vision can clearly see tippets, and is less disturbed by fine than coarse. A real or artificial insect is one thing, an insect-on-a-string is another. My first thought when the bite stops is to find fresh fish, but experiments in going fine have generally been productive. During my week-long experience fishing tiny, curlytailed plastic jigs for grayling, I switched back and forth between spools of 2-pound-test monofilament and 4-pound-test. With the former, fish could be hooked almost at will but often not held, with the latter vice-versa.

Any fish, even such determined creatures as grayling, can be hammered into staleness. In the case where there is plenty of water but few anglers, as in the American West, we change fish. In crowded eastern waters we stand our ground and change flies. In the Canadian Shield we move on to another variety of fishing, taking advantage of the large number of game fish species available. One typically begins fly-fishing or spinning for grayling shortly after a breakfast of English proportions, moves on to trolling or casting spoons for lake trout until sufficient for lunch have been

grayling river can be more famine than feast.

Active gulls probably mean a hatch is in progress, and grayling will be feeding under them. A monocular or binoculars can help when searching for rises. Because they school and because selective fishing for the biggest means working only the heads of pools, float fishing from a drifting boat is ideal for Arctic grayling. The drill

Map showing Alaska with labeled locations including Fairbanks, Anchorage, King Salmon, Katmai Nat'l Monument, Ugashik Lakes, Pilot Point, Ugashik River, Kodiak Island, Bristol Bay, Alaska Peninsula, and a Legend indicating Airports.

caught, perhaps divides the afternoon between spoon casting for pike and fly-fishing or spinning for lake whitefish, and then returns to grayling after dinner.

An inexplicable grayling migration up the Stark River that enters Great Slave Lake astounded me one afternoon. A parade of thousands of small grayling, 4 feet from shore, the column perhaps eight fish abreast, rout step, passing upstream. They continued for many minutes. Each fish was no longer than my hand. The dozen-plus grayling monographs in my library include such arcana as unpublished theses and microfiches, but not a word on mass migration of juveniles.

There are occasional rumors from the Canadian Shield, from Norway and from Finland of 7-pound grayling, but no one has yet produced the fish. Every Cree, Chipewyan or Dogrib who has netted one of more than 3 pounds for me has grunted his pleasure and called it "big blue fish." Considering the volume of fish they gillnet every year their judgment must be definitive. My own library contains a record of the largest grayling ever reported. It is within a copy of Francis M. Walbran's 1895 volume, *Grayling and How to Catch Them* (The Angler Co., Ltd., Scarborough, Britain). Walbran was a correspondent of *The Field* and a great lover of winter grayling fishing. The flyleaf of my copy bears the inscription "D.J.W. Edwardes, Rhyd-y-goise, Carmarthenshire, 1900." On the verso, in the same hand, is written:

1928 N. TEST
Oct. 2nd   14 grayling (8 = 10½ lbs)
Oct. 3rd   4 grayling, best 1½ lbs
Oct. 4th   10 grayling (kept 3 = 4½ lbs)
Oct. 5th   4 grayling (kept 2 = 2¾ lbs)
Oct. 8th   8 grayling (kept 1 = 6 lbs)

Walbran took a 3-pound, 10-ounce grayling from the Test on a worm, according to F.N. Halford, and in 1904 that was tied by a fly-caught grayling. These are simply enormous fish for the United Kingdom. The possibility that Mr. Edwardes actually *weighed* a 6-pounder on October 8, 1928, is minuscule, incredible, impossible. And yet. . . .

Ugashik Lakes

The Ugashik Lake area has long been famous for producing the largest grayling in Alaska. The state record of 4 pounds, 6 ounces was caught from Ugashik narrows. The narrows is a three-quarter-mile length of water connecting Upper and Lower Ugashik lakes. The lakes are on the Alaskan Peninsula, southwest of the town of King Salmon—a 45-minute float plane flight via Peninsula Airlines. Ten miles northwest of the narrows by boat is Pilot Point, located on the Bering Sea. Upper Ugashik is approximately 23 miles long; Lower Ugashik about 9 miles long. A short section of river runs out to the Bering Sea at Pilot Point. The narrows wind in a serpentine course around many small islands then into a lagoon that flows into the lower lake.

The narrows can be fished by wading, but a boat is advantageous when fishing the mouth of the lagoon, and to change locations quickly if wind rises. Wind from the Bering Sea is a problem. The area is largely flat, but there are some bluffs at the upper narrows that can be reached by boat and provide enough lee to make casting possible.

Arctic grayling is the principal fish here, but anglers can also expect to catch large Arctic char, Dolly Varden and lake trout. Rainbow trout do not enter Ugashik Lake. Sockeye salmon arrive at Pilot Point by the end of July, and by the middle of August they congregate at the narrows. Coho will start by mid-September and pass through the narrows into tributary streams by October. But grayling are the real Ugashik trophy because at any time of the season, weather permitting, one can consistently catch these beautiful game fish. The average weight will be around 3 pounds, with an occasional larger fish—but a record catch could come on the next cast.

The major reason Ugashik grayling attain trophy proportions is diet. Alaskan biologists are now studying the variety of isopod, a freshwater crustacean that is abundant in the Ugashik area, but which has not yet been identified to species. This aquatic sow bug is the grayling's main food. The crustaceans *average* 1½ inches in length! They are thick in the narrows and in large underwater springs on the southwest side of the upper lake. These crystal-clear springs, which I discovered quite by accident, attract large grayling. I spent three days fishing this area. On many releases the grayling stomachs would actually rattle, so gorged were they with isopods. More than 3,000 species of Isopoda have been identified to date—fresh water, marine and terrestrial. The Ugashik variety is obviously nutritious.

A variety of equipment can be successfully used for grayling, but it should be light. Most anglers take 8- to 10-weight rods to Alaska because of the big fish often encountered. However, a 3-pound grayling provides little sport on heavy tackle, but

ARCTIC GRAYLING

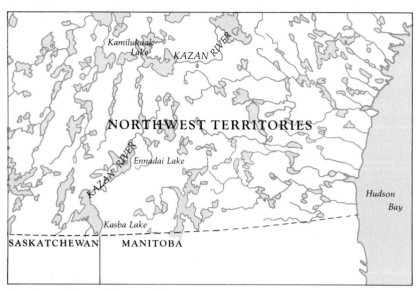

The Kazan River in the vicinity of Kasba Lake has been the trophy grayling hot spot of Canada in recent years.

on 4- or 5-weight rods they are a spectacular quarry. Bring both floating and sinking fly lines. Whether fly-fishing or spinning, 4-pound-test is more than adequate as either line or tippet material.

Because of the grayling's inferior mouth, it is best to use small spinning lures on the order of Mepps, Roostertail and Panther Martin. Small wobbling spoons such as Dardevles can also be effective, and the midget F-2 and F-3 Flatfish in black, frog and scale finishes.

The most effective flies can depend on time of year. Imitations of salmon eggs would be appropriate when sockeye and coho are in the narrows. A wise choice anytime would be isopod and sculpin patterns. Caddis, mayfly and chironomids are also available to the grayling. For floating patterns I would definitely have a supply of Adams, Light Cahill, Humpy and any of the Wulff ties. The grayling's preference for the color black will help with your choice of nymphs, streamers and leeches, as long as they are not too large. If all your standard patterns are tied on No. 10 and 12 hooks, including dry flies, they should be effective. The fish are such free feeders in the narrows and over the springs that one could use a dry fly, streamer or nymph on successive casts and probably catch grayling on each one.

One of my favorite flies other than the isopod patterns is a No. 10, 3X-long, Black Marabou Leech with a slight amount of weight in it. But the top flies of all were the isopod patterns we tied on the spot ourselves. Just a few turns of lead wire, a thick tan or olive-brown chenille body, then palmered Woolly Worm-fashion with a brown hackle on 3X-long No. 4 to 12 hooks.

Jim Meyers' Ugashik Lake Lodge at the south end of the narrows accommodates twelve anglers and has a season from mid-June through September. Runs of all five North American species of Pacific salmon pass through, including chinooks to 70 pounds. Pike of 20 to 30 pounds are also available locally. One of Meyers' grayling anglers took a fish all the way back to Arkansas before weighing it at 5 pounds, 2 ounces. He saw another angler break off on a fish that appeared to be an 8- to 8½-pound carp until it displayed its grayling dorsal. The address is Wonders of Alaska, Inc., Ugashik Lake Lodge, P.O. Box 1906, Vancouver, WA 98668; telephone (800) 426-2650. In Alaska they are Ugashik Lake Lodge, P.O. Box 253, King Salmon, AK 96613.

Kazan River

The Kazan River in the Northwest Territories of Canada is one of the world's premier Arctic grayling streams. The Kazan is located 340 miles south of the Arctic Circle and 50 miles north of the junction of the N.W.T., Manitoba and Saskatchewan. It is fed by the chill waters of Kasba Lake, which rarely get warmer than 45°F. After running for over 100 miles it flows through lakes with names such as Ennadai, Kamilukuak and Yathkyed en route to Hudson Bay. On most rivers or lakes a 2-pound grayling is an admirable catch—on the Kazan 3-pounders are common. Leon Chandler, an expert New York fly-fisherman, caught a grayling of over 5 pounds. Naturally there are campfire tales of even larger grayling being hooked on this river, and Kazan regulars feel it's only a matter of time until the present 5-pound, 15-ounce world record is broken here.

The way to fish this river is to book into Doug Hill's Kasba Lake Lodge, the only camp on this 1,000-square-mile lake. A half hour float plane flight puts you on the Kazan. Peculiar to this part of the world is the terrain, which is ribbed with ancient eskers. These are the tailings of crushed rock and sand left by glaciers millennia ago. Bush pilots use them as their silent compass, for eskers always run north and south. The Kazan passes through a triangle of eskers, thus it widens and slows its pace to accommodate float plane landings. The camp provides boats, motors and skilled guides who take guests from the lake into the fast waters of the Kazan. Fishing their way up river, anglers will find almost any rapids productive. However, there is one large set, about thirty-five minutes from the float plane dock, that spreads across the entire 60-yard width of the river. This is where the brutes are usually found.

Arctic grayling can be taken effectively on ultralight spinning, spin-casting and fly-fishing tackle. Spinning and spin-casting rods should be 5½-feet long and designed to cast with 4- to 6-pound-test monofilament lines. Spinning reels should have smooth drags and a spool capacity of at least 100 yards of line. Big grayling running with the swift Kazan current can swiftly strip a reel. Occasionally anglers have to chase a hooked fish down river by boat. The most effective lures on the Kazan have been the Super Vibrax and Mepps spinners in No. 0, 1 and 2 sizes, silver or copper color. Also, small spoons weighing one-eighth ounce to one-quarter ounce are popular. Single hooks are a requirement on the Kazan. Doug Hill supplies them to his guests at no cost. The singles, particularly with the barb removed, make it easier to release the fish. It is permissible to keep a trophy fish for mounting or small ones for a shore lunch. However, conservation is stressed to preserve the unusually high quality of this angling.

Fly-fishing on the Kazan is superb. Ideally, the rod should be 7½-feet long, designed for a 7-weight floating, double-tapered line. Leaders should be as long as the rod and tapered down to 3X. Dry flies in dark or subdued colors such as the Black Gnat and Adams tied on No. 12 to 16 hooks are best, but don't hesitate to try nymphs or wet flies such as the Gold-Ribbed Hare's Ear, Black Gnat or Coachman if the grayling aren't coming to the top.

The Kazan River can be fished in three ways: on foot with waders along the shore, from dry rocks in mid-stream or from an anchored boat. In mid-stream, where the current is strongest, spinning gear is most effective. The technique is to cast spinners and small spoons slightly upstream into the white water and maneuver the lure past protruding boulders. Big grayling often hold in the calm pockets behind the rocks. While you are in mid-stream, never pass up the deep pools below rapids. These pools are often like aquariums; you can see schools of grayling at the bottom. Huge lake trout sometimes haunt these deep holes, feeding on grayling. It is not uncommon for a grayling to be lost to a 30-pound-plus trout in the middle of a fight. The Kazan's shallow shorelines are readily fished with the fly since the current is slower, permitting long drifts with floating patterns. The grayling gather here because the wind blows insects out of shoreline bushes. However, because of slippery rocks due to algal

The small, white-lipped terminal mouth of grayling is rubbery. Flattened barbs make hook removal much easier.

growths it is recommended to use waders with felt soles.

Weather dictates the Kazan grayling season. Even though, into July, there will probably still be ice flows on the lake, the season generally runs from late June through August. The fly-fishing gets better as the season progresses; August is the premier month. The reason: more insects. Unfortunately these mosquitoes and black flies can be bothersome. It's essential to carry plenty of repellent and head nets.

For booking the lodge, write or call Doug Hill, Box 96, Parksville, B.C., Canada V0R 2S0; telephone (604) 248-3572. The lodge radio-phone for in-season booking is X0W 254 via Selkirk, Manitoba.

ARCTIC CHAR

Salvelinus alpinus

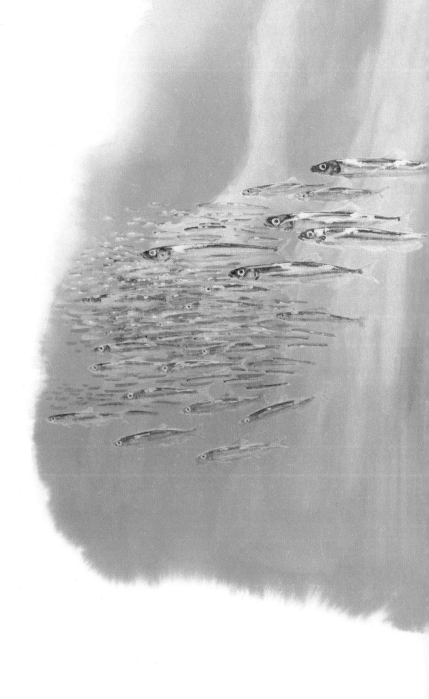

According to precipitation, the Arctic is a vast desert, greater than the Sahara, Gobi and Mojave combined, yet there are lakes, streams and soggy tundra everywhere. Even in the two months that are not winter, it is bitter cold and frost occurs. Everything that lives in it is specialized to withstand cold and if you go there you will genuinely suffer unless you adapt too. You must take care not to get wet away from a source of fire, not to fall down amidst sled dogs, not to round a bend of the stream and meet a grizzly or a polar bear far from your boat and rifle. It is not good country for the unwary or unlucky, but the people may be the finest on Earth. The quarry for anglers is anadromous Arctic char. North America is blessed with anadromous salmonids but devotees of Atlantic salmon and Pacific steelhead who have not yet experienced sea-run Arctic char have denied themselves a revelation: This may be quite literally the strongest fish that swims. It is unquestionably the strongest salmonid.

It is also the most economical fish in the world to angle for. Char live far from the great temperate-zone cities where most of us live and work, so costly and time-consuming parlays of three or four airlines and charter services are necessary to reach the Arctic north of Canada and Alaska, but once there each hookup gives you at least three distinct fish fights. Each time you think you have the fish whipped, off he goes again— triple the sport at no additional expense. The exception will break your tackle or spool you early on. I once asked the premier American conservation author, George Reiger, to keep me company on a char trip 400 miles inside the Arctic Circle. At 6 feet, 4 inches and considerably more than 200 pounds, Reiger is imposing when delivering keynote addresses at conventions devoted to protecting fish and wildlife from the many outrages civilization inflicts upon them. His métier as an angler is gross saltwater brutes, and

Arctic char live amidst icebergs, belugas, Inuit fishermen and vast schools of smelt, whose oily flesh makes the char, in turn, as richly nutritious as any fish that swims. Only their remoteness inhibits their popularity.

115

ARCTIC CHAR

his experience with tuna and jacks, the most brutish of all, is vast.

"Tell me what these char are like," he said.

"Imagine amberjacks in a strong river current and you have it," I said.

Amberjacks, if you fish them with sufficiently stout tackle, will pull boats around backwards. Two days later Reiger ran past me chasing his first Arctic char. For the remainder of that week, to paraphrase V. Nabokov, he ran past me, I ran past him, we ran past us. More often than not we trudged back upstream disconsolate at another loss. It was amazing that a mere 10-pound char could get into a 10-knot current and spool 250 yards of 20-pound-test line. It was appalling that the same size fish could swim upstream *into* that current and be completely unstoppable, unturnable, uncontrollable.

Anadromy does wonderful things to salmonids (except brook trout, the little *fontinalis* achieves neither particular size nor vigor in saltwater), but it is crucial to Arctic char. Wholly freshwater populations are customarily parr-marked small fish even when elderly. McCart ("A Review of the Systematics and Ecology of Arctic Char, *Salvelinus alpinus*, in the Western Arctic," McCart, P.J., *Can. Tech. Rep. Fish. Aquat. Sci.* 935: vii plus 89 p., 1980) defines four major life history types: *lake resident* (including spawning), *isolated stream resident* located above impassable falls, *anadromous* fish that spawn and overwinter in streams that provide perennial groundwater, and *residual* fish, which are small males that mature without making a seaward journey despite their association with anadromous populations. Only sea-feeding populations are of real interest to anglers.

These fish will average 5 to 7 pounds but they have been taken on rod-and-reel to more than 32 pounds. A Russian fish from Novaya Zemyla weighed 34 pounds. On my latest char trip I saw net-caught specimens to 25 pounds, though our party failed to top 15 pounds on spoon and fly. More important than size is freshness. The West Coast cult of bright steelhead would better be applied to Arctic char, for stale steelhead and Atlantic salmon can still exhibit considerable force of character, but the gross morphological changes that distort char advanced in their spawning run evidently sap their strength as well. The fish with sea lice on him is the one you want. I would not care to fish them so much as 30 miles

upriver; I would much prefer to be within the smell of the sea.

In fact, they can be fished in salt water itself. The Inuit who net them each summer know their migration routes well and these have been confirmed through studies undertaken by Fisheries and Oceans Canada. During their brief, voracious summer feeding and growing season in salt water, char confine themselves almost wholly to a narrow longshore corridor. The most densely populated salt water will be points of land off mainland shores out to 100 yards. Further offshore, off islands, inside bays in areas of high salinity are less favored. The Inuit run their gillnets from a brackish shoreline out. Trolling or casting the same water will produce char early in the saltwater season. Since they will work quite close to shore in shallow water, a high point for spotting fish can be helpful. They will be in isolated schools and, without the encumbrance of stream rocks and river currents, can be fished on quite fine tackle. I have never done this because casting rivers is so much more interesting than any form of slackwater fishing, and only rivers have that marvelous fish-concentrating device: a waterfall. But any angler who yearns for light-tackle records under the International Game Fish Association's sporting specifications might consider fishing saltwater char early in the season before spawning runs have fully developed.[1]

Arctic char season for anadromous fish begins late down in the southern limit of their range, in Labrador and Nouvelle Quebec. "Late" is September most years, and I have found even mid-September early in the Ungava Bay area near the mouth of Hudson's Bay. As you go north the runs begin earlier. At the top of Baffin Island, 400 miles inside the Arctic Circle (66° 30'N), fishing the saltchuck at Koluktoo Bay begins about the first of August, then by mid-August it is time to move inside the river and fish the run. Some years snow will begin before September.

This species is the most northerly of freshwater fish and makes its diet basically from anything animal that can be caught and swallowed. A small char will enter salt water and proceed to feed on capelin, sculpin, seasnails, lumpfish, sand lance, various invertebrates and Arctic cod. The anadromous fish do most of their feeding in two or three months of saltwater life, but both sea-run and dwarf freshwater char feed heavily on chironomid larvae (midges) and caddisflies in fresh water. Spawning fish that transit lakes have been observed with their forehead out of water and mouth agape as they swam through enormous

DISTRIBUTION

[1] In a personal communication, A.H. Kristofferson, fishery management biologist with Fisheries and Oceans Canada, reports that recent research fails to disclose any overwintering in salt water by Arctic char populations east of the Mackenzie River. He further notes that anadromous fish that are going to spawn in a given year do *not* go to sea that summer prior to the fall spawn, but remain in fresh water throughout the summer. The upstream migration in these populations is not a spawning run, therefore, but a return to fresh water of nonspawning fish after a summer of sea feeding. There is some variation from this extraordinary conduct, but it is believed to be incidental. Obviously this is a species of remarkable plasticity.

windrows of chironomids. Fly-fishing with light trout tackle for char that weigh many pounds is possible under such circumstances. I have taken char at Finger Lakes in northern Quebec with stomachs that resembled stuffed sausage casings, so utterly packed were they with Diptera larvae. The caddis, incidentally, is a large gray insect when winged and possibly is circumpolar like Arctic char. It is ubiquitous in the rivers of Iceland, and in the great inland seas of Canada's Northwest Territories (Great Slave and Great Bear lakes) one can cast gray caddis imitations to rising fish by the midnight sun. If these insects are different species or genera, then convergent evolution in the polar north favors gray Trichoptera.

Predation on Arctic char is performed (as noted) by themselves, by seals and by man. Loons and terns doubtless harvest juveniles. The great dolphins called killer whales may take some adults, but they are interested in narwhals (the cetacean with the wonderful twisted ivory unicorn tusk), belugas (the white whale) and seals. Netsmen can do terrible damage to a spawning run. Healthy stocks were found in the Sylvia Grinnell River at Frobisher Bay, Baffin Island, in 1955, but on my two trips in the early 1980s, en route north through Frobisher Bay, angling was out of the question: Monofilament gillnets were shortstopping so many fish it was worth conversation if one had taken a char by hook-and-line *last* year, much less this. Overexploitation ruined this fishery in a single decade.

In various Inuit dialects this fish is *irkaluk, ekaluk, eqaluk*—which means "fish." They have specific terms for juveniles and adults, males and females (freshwater char are *ivitaruk*, for instance) and of course for other species of fish, but Arctic char are so central to Inuit survival their name is synonymous with the order of Pisces itself.

The Inuit eat this fish as they traditionally eat all their meat— raw. The Cree doubtless intended their name for the Inuit, *eskimos* ("eaters of raw meat"), to be derogatory because the Cree were not on the friendliest terms with the Inuit in times past. Cooking destroys vitamins that can only be replaced by vegetables or fruits. The Inuit cannot get a crop out of the ground during their fleeting summer. If you intend to dwell among the Inuit and hope to avoid scurvy you would be well advised to do as they and take your fish as *sashimi* and your caribou and seal as steak tartare. I do not

Hal Janssen with an Arctic char from Alaska's Ugashik watershed, a prolific fishery that demands a variety of tackle to properly fish it.

have to advise you to eat the fat first. When you are up there you will eat fat with alacrity. You will spoon Crisco out of the can, and smack your lips. Frozen char brought home to the temperate zone can be prepared in any fashion recommended for salmon or trout. Think of char flesh as a superior form of salmon and you will be guided to correct methods: poached, as gravlax, smoked over fruitwood or hickory, etc. My most memorable meal of char came out of a No. 10 tin can. Elisa Pewatoaluk's grandfather set up a snagging operation one afternoon across the Robertson River from where I was fly-fishing. His tackle consisted of a 10/0 treble hook, the shank thickly wrapped with heavy lead wire, and a coil of 100-pound-test monofilament. With a brief bolo-twirl he would send this formidable engine across and a bit upstream, then as it was swept downcurrent his left hand would jerk it in a yard at a time, taking hold immediately behind where his right hand held the line. I managed to put four double-digit

ARCTIC CHAR

char on the bank with a No. 5/0 Winter's Hope steelhead fly while he did a bit more than 20, and considered myself very fortunate to do so. A brace of his sons, and Elisa, studied the technique and attempted to emulate him but lacked his manifest virtuosity. They poached one chunked fish in a can of river water on a portable gasoline camp stove and we ate its juicy, rich, orange flesh with our fingers.

Reproduction

There is a guppy found off the west coast of Florida that lives an existence so solitary that when mating time arrives it is equipped with both male

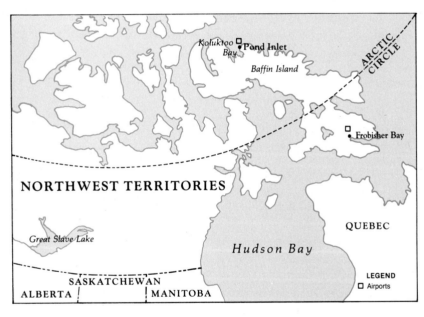

Four hundred miles inside the Arctic Circle, the Robertson River debouches into Koluktoo Bay, a char fishery where you can watch the first winter snows creep down the mountain in August, day by day.

and female sex products. If two of them meet they undertake the kissing that makes guppies so popular with home aquarists, then alternately chase each other until they decide to mate. At that instant the catcher extrudes milt and the catchee extrudes ova. If they never meet the lone guppy mates with itself. This is hermaphroditic sexual reproduction, not parthenogenesis, which has been noted among some insects, worms and crustaceans. Parthenogenesis requires reproduction without fertilization by spermatozoa. Most creatures solve this problem by continuing association of suitable breeding partners, called schooling, and/or by migration to a mating site. This is the way of anadromous Arctic char. Aerial surveys indicate they spawn only in sizable streams; Kristofferson also notes some evidence of lake spawning by both anadromous and

nonanadromous Arctic char, although the isolating mechanism is ill understood, thus maintaining a geological separation from *lake resident* as well as *isolated stream resident* populations. They select quiet pools close to springheads, groundwater sources that will remain ice-free during truly brutal winters. Males develop hooked, or kyped, lower jaws and use them to defend territories. Both sexes become ventrally scarlet and males may turn partially black, especially on the anal, caudal and dorsal fins. While the male fights off rivals the female cuts a redd, then they spawn, often with small residual males rushing in to take part, as do the sexually mature parr of Atlantic salmon and many trout species. In addition, both male and female will probably spawn with more than one partner. This practice, plus that of satellite spawners, ensures a well-mixed gene pool. Her eggs are large and need to be. They will be laid down in fall and not hatch until, probably, next April and the fry will stay in the gravel until mid-July ice-out.

Female anadromous char seldom spawn every year and at any rate don't mature until age four through thirteen (far northern populations), males a bit younger. The fish can live a reported forty years although they will probably achieve maximum growth by age twenty. Even with spawning every other year, or every third year, there will be opportunity for many progeny in such a life. Elderly fish have been taken displaying full secondary sexual characteristics and even bearing eggs. They do not go into small streams for their spawn or for over-wintering. If char in the past attempted that they probably fell prey to the polar bears, or even wolves (wolves have been observed fishing spawning runs of various species).

Tackle for Arctic Char

Tackle, flies and lures for fishing anadromous char are determined by enormous natural forces such as permafrost. It is thought the Arctic earth froze during the last ice age, the Pleistocene. In places this is more than 1,000 feet deep, but subpermafrost springs pierce it and remain open due to their continuous flow of thermally stable water. In summer the top few inches to a yard thaws. This is the *active layer*. The summer rains are confined to this thin soil and quickly saturate it and run off into rivers. Spates swell in a matter of hours and can fall almost visibly. When water is high, swift and colored, heavy spoons on plugging or spinning tackle are called for. It may require lead-core shooting heads and gaudy No. 5/0 flies to get down to the chars' level with something they can see as it is swept past in the torrent. Two days later light spinners and small flies on wet-tip lines may suffice.

There are two points to remember when tackling up for anadromous char: They will all or most of the time be on the bottom in swift current, and they are going to make unbelievable inroads into your tackle supply. Pack at least three times the lures and terminal tackle you think necessary and take spare lines and reels. One afternoon I had fish deprive me of two lead-core fly lines, almost a dozen 1-ounce spoons and the totality of my composure.

Select spoons on the basis of density (to give a good sink rate) and bright fluorescent color, preferably at the warm end of the spectrum. There is a French-made, cast-brass spoon with thick metal and fluorescent orange-red plastic insert that is widely available in North America. Experienced char fishers dote on it for heavy water. Heavy spinners in both brass and nickel finishes will offer a change of pace. Showing the same lure repetitively to fish that have grown bored with it is a waste of time.

Fresh char will take any fly you can put in front of them. This will often necessitate enormous hooks and lead-weighted fly lines. Before a char trip I mail-order from Pacific Coast fly shops the lines and flies developed for winter steelhead. These are perfect for char. Char have well-developed dentition and you can expect an occasional biteoff when fishing monofilament leaders. Refrain from steel leaders or heavy saltwater shock tippets. They will reduce strikes, always.

Saltwater rods, though, are fine gear for char. A fly rod for light tarpon fishing, 9 or 10 feet and swinging at least a 10-weight fly line, will keep you in control of a 550-grain, lead-core shooting head. When trapped by an obstruction and unable to follow a fish I have found 250 yards of backing inadequate, but probably a half mile of line would have been insufficient too.

A plug-casting or spinning rod should be selected on its merit as a fish-fighting implement. Precise or delicate presentation is not likely to be the issue. I like a 6-foot graphite designed for deep-jigging in southern salt water. With a spool full of 20-pound-test monofilament this is considered adequate for grouper, permit and school tarpon. It has won a few char arguments but some large bright fish have run away from it.

A char fight on spoon or spinner begins with a positive take, often some violent head shaking and

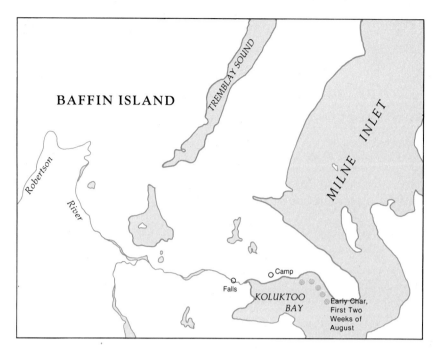

then a run. If the first run is not serious be patient, the second will be. On a fly the fish will jump one or two times during his serious runs. You may not see these because you will be concerned about your footing as you run too. If you win the steeplechase your gillie should have a long-handled net big enough for a 30-pounder.

Fresh from the sea it will have green-gray shoulders shading gradually into a white belly, and the flanks will carry large pale spots, often salmon-pink. Trout always have a light background and dark spots, chars the reverse.

Dolly Varden and Bull Trout

Salvelinus alpinus is believed to be the genotype from which a variety of other chars evolved. The Arctic char is so close to Dolly Varden (*S. malma*) in appearance that integrating is suspected in some watersheds. Indeed whole populations of char are classified as Dolly Varden by one biologist and Arctic char by another. Behnke (1972) refers to *S. alpinus* as "a species complex," and "a polymorphous species."

In a study of char head and cranial skeleton characteristics published in 1978 by Dr. Ted Cavender, most Dolly Varden of the contiguous U.S. states and southern Canada were reclassified as bull trout (*S. confluentus*) and most Alaskan and northern Canadian populations as Dolly Varden. The biologists now believe few Dolly Varden char exceed 6 or 7 pounds. This means the large char of the Rocky Mountains that we have been calling Dolly Varden are now bull trout, including the 32-pounder from Lake Pend Oreille, Idaho, that became the all-tackle record in 1949. Since only trained taxonomists can differentiate Dolly Varden from bull trout, and that only after

Saltwater char fishing at Koluktoo Bay can be light-tackle casting and trolling, but once the fish move into the Robertson River, stout line or leaders are needed. The river is swift and the fish are sea-bright and strong.

119

dissection, record applications to the International Game Fish Association will henceforth have to be particularly specific about the locale of capture.

In June, spawning runs of big bulls depart high-country impoundments into their feeder streams. This fishing is exactly as that for Arctic char—equipment, techniques, lures—but you are in American motel culture rather than among Inuit sealers and caribou hunters.

Eastern Relicts

Blueback trout were *Salvelinus oquassa* but have been reclassified into *alpinus*. They were widespread in Maine's Rangely Lakes, one of which is Oquossoc Lake. Human rapacity reduced them to near extinction by 1904. They are a deep water, plankton feeder for most of the year, but on their fall spawning runs they become readily available and the farmers and lumberjacks of nineteenth-century Maine took them with dipnets, gigs and everything else that would suffice. The small fish (9 or 10 inches) were slaughtered in such volume they were even on the market as fertilizer and commercial livestock food.

Blueback have survived, but barely. They can be found in headwater ponds of the St. John, Penobscot and Red rivers. The biggest come from the Red River watershed ponds of Black, Deboullie, Garden and Pushineer. By day they can be taken with small jigs 30 to 50 feet deep—if you can locate them, alternately slow-troll very small spinners at those depths. But in late June and early July they come up at night to feed on aquatic and terrestrial insects and provide dry-fly-fishing.

Sunapee trout (*Salvelinus aureolus*) are now considered an *alpinus* relict like bluebacks and Marston trout. They were first identified in Sunapee Lake, New Hampshire, but have been transplanted. Floods Pond in Maine is thought to have the only pure strain. Elsewhere they hybridize with brook and lake trout. They are very deep in summer, but are sometimes taken in winter by pickerel fishermen. This pretty little char often has butter-yellow lower flanks, making it precisely the sort of fish to take a photograph of if you happen to catch one when pickerel fishing in Maine or New Hampshire in winter.

Quebec Red Trout

The so-called Quebec red trout is a colorful relict of the Arctic char. Populations were once found in numerous waters throughout the Province, but its range has been severely reduced over the past few decades and today it occurs in comparatively few deep, cold lakes of the Quebec north shore. Lac des Sables and Lac Paradis continue to produce good fishing for this form of char due to the rigid control exerted by the outfitter (Club Lacs des Sables et Paradis, P.O. Box 22, Petites Bergeronnes, Quebec, Canada G0T 1G0) whose lease covers both lakes as well as several smaller brook trout lakes in the surrounding hills. Located just an hour's drive beyond Tadoussac and the spectacular Saguenay fjord, these club waters offer the most productive red trout fishing accessible by road today. Housekeeping cabins, boats and motors are available at the club, but advance reservations are suggested since accommodations are limited, especially in early summer. The territory is accessible by car with only a 10-mile ride over maintained bush road from the blacktop to camp.

Although described in historical as well as contemporary literature with a maximum size of 2 pounds, red trout of 4 pounds or more are caught annually in Lac des Sables where the record is a few ounces over 9 pounds. However, the fish of 1½ to 3 pounds most often appear in the angler's creel. Lac des Sables (which also supports a brook trout fishery) holds the largest char, and Lac Paradis has the greatest number. Paradis is only accessible by boat and a short 10-minute portage. Immediately after ice-out in mid-May the char can be found gorging themselves on the smelt run. During this period they can be taken by casting spinners, wobbling spoons, floating Rapalas and streamer flies in shallow water. As the weather warms the char quickly retreat to the depths and by the beginning of July are found at the 50-foot level. Slow trolling or deep jigging with small spoons is the most effective method then.

Robertson River

Fishing the Robertson River's Jacuzzi Pool before it boils beyond the Rock of Despair and tumbles into Baffin Island's Koluktoo Bay reminds me of John Taintor Foote's *The Diver Takes to Pinochle*. In that story, two anglers hear of a fabulous lake and stream in northern Maine where they will catch beautiful brook trout on every cast. Off they go, only to find the camp full of fishermen playing pinochle. Figuring the lake's charms were exaggerated or that they missed all the action, the two anglers half-heartedly cast and find that, indeed, they unfailingly catch doubles of beautiful

The PBY, or Canso in Canadian parlance, has in recent years been known to ferry Arctic char anglers into some Canadian camps in the northeast. This was a World War II-vintage sub spotter. Fans of antique aircraft should go to the Arctic or the tropics.

brook trout. So spectacular is the fishing, so guaranteed the results, that the two friends are soon at the pinochle board with the other guests!

The Robertson River in late August is not quite that guaranteed. I can recall making at least seven casts during a three-day outing there without hooking an Arctic char, but the fishing is spectacular enough that I spent many long minutes resting my tired right wrist and contemplating the roaring water with the knowledge that as soon as I stepped back to the edge of the Jacuzzi Pool, I was slated for yet another bulldog-stubborn, 15-minute fight from the most powerful fish I have ever caught in fresh water.

However, if world-record seeking isn't your cup of tea, I doubt anyone could become so bored at Koluktoo Bay that he would take up pinochle. The Inuit are generous and fascinating people, and they are happy to have you share their daily events — whether they be a caribou hunt or a dinner of ringed seal ribs in barbecue sauce. In addition, purple sandpipers and golden plovers decorate your campsite, and glaucous gulls and Arctic foxes will tidy up the gills and guts of the char you decide to pack out. In short, the only thing Koluktoo Bay has in common with John Taintor Foote's mythical spa in Maine is that you will catch fish, cast after cast after cast.

Getting there is easy, it only seems to take forever. You'll inevitably have an overnight layover in the forlorn, but curiously fascinating town of Frobisher Bay near the Sylvia Grinnell River, which used to be as noted for record-sized Arctic char as the Robertson River is today (before the netters overfished the Sylvia Grinnell).

You can try to parlay the Air Canada, Nordair and Bradley Air Service flights all on your own, but it is easier to let Viking Adventures, Unit 151, 1915 Denmar Road, Rickering, Ontario, Canada L1V 3E1; telephone (416) 683-6119, handle all arrangements for you, including your hotel in Frobisher Bay and your staging stay at Pond Inlet on the northern end of Baffin Island. The accommodations at Robertson River are very basic, consisting of wood frame, heated tents with sleeping bags. The camp is 400 miles inside the Arctic Circle so the weather requires warm wool clothing. Except for the Inuit game delicacies and char, canned food is staple.

The Robertson is too deep and turbulent for wading. Casting from the bank with spinning or bait-casting tackle calibered for 12- to 20-pound-test lines (minimum 225 yards) is the routine. Wobbling spoons in the one-half- to 2-ounce weights are most effective as the lure must sink fast in the swift current. Fly-fishing is viable with high-density sinking, or lead core lines. Robertson River char run from 10 to 20 pounds, but larger fish are every day possible. The season at this latitude is limited to six weeks, from mid-July until the end of August.

LAKE
TROUT

Salvelinus namaycush

Whenever somebody mentions lake trout, it brings to mind a day when the sky was wooled with clouds and a rain was sweeping across the North Country, in a place so barren that only the tough dwarf spruce and mosses could cling to the wind cleft rocks. I caught a lake trout that morning as long as the canoe paddle, a frost green monster of well over 40 pounds that came ponderously from the depths. Each time Billy Gray Eagle hoisted another one quivering in his great landing net, and I signaled once again to release the fish, my Dogrib friend sat down laughing. It must have been the pinnacle of Dogrib comedy to see a man pull a fish out of water, only to look at it, pat it on the head and put it back again. But to me, *Salvelinus namaycush* is a numerical achievement on the one hand, for nature endowed it with a long life span — and a numerical challenge on the other. Although the rod-caught record from Great Bear Lake stands at 65 pounds, it is still a ghost of the 102-pound lake trout gill-netted by commercial fishermen in Lake Athabasca, Saskatchewan, in 1961. Ironically, this fish was a "rawner," or sexually immature (though aged by Canadian biologists between twenty and twenty-six years), and had it survived its alloted two score years, it would undoubtedly resemble a small blimp.

Among the salmonides this enormous char is third only to taimen and chinook salmon in potential weight. It is customarily taken in the United States and southern Canada as part of the summer troll fishery on large lakes where it is so marginally game that angling for it can be categorized more as subsistence fishing than sport. Seek it in its northern heartland and you will be fortunate to land 50 percent of those hooked. Lake trout from a lake or river with a surface temperature of approximately 50°F and hooked while using light tackle are one of angling's great experiences: a running, twirling, dervish of a fight.

The large gray char called "lake trout" is designed for dark skies and bone-chilling water. The fish are vigorous in the far north and sluggish in the temperate south (in areas of the U.S.). Only Arctic char go farther north in North American fresh water.

LAKE TROUT

Lake trout have strange eyes. This fish as a mature animal with a double-digit weight can feed on *individual* cladoceran components of the zooplankton, which is comparable to a man singling out one egg in a bowl of caviar. Virtually all tiny fish can do this, of course, but the faculty is uncommon to say the least in gross specimens (we are not talking about filter feeding or about engulfing a mass of phytoplankton for its small component of zooplankters). Those keen eyes are so sensitive that hatchery lake trout fry must be kept indoors under gloomy illumination or they develop cataracts.

As with Arctic char, Dolly Varden and bull trout (whose existence as separate species is arguable), lake trout are remarkable for the plasticity of their taxon. The ruined, but now recovering, Great Lakes fishery[1] for them contained two subspecies, an extremely fat and oily char called the siscowet, inedible unless smoked, and the "humper," a fish intermediate in fat content between siscowet and lake trout. Lake Superior siscowets ran as high as 88.8 percent fat content by dry weight. Within the species, strains with distinctive markings have been noted. The Great Lakes fish were originally red-finned, although that population has been reduced to a few localities in Lake Superior. The species is a fall spawner, although "fall" can be from mid-August to January at some places in the range. Lake Superior siscowets spawn in June. The color of its flesh can vary from white to scarlet, its quality from exquisite to regurgitative. One attribute that seems universal throughout the strains is a dislike for salt water, but it will tolerate salinities up to about 12 percent, and the Finns have established a population in the brackish north Baltic Sea. Oceanic salt water commonly has a salinity of 35 percent and the lethal limits for lake trout are 20 to 27 percent depending on the age of the fish.

Lake trout are the quarry of ice fishermen, downrigger trollers, spoon casters, fly-fishermen, gill-netters, seine-netters, sea lampreys, larger lake trout, and a variety of parasitic protozoans, trematodes and nematodes. They cohabit the same lake as pike without either becoming the subject of the other's predation thanks to vastly different habitat preferences—clear rocky water for trout and weedy shallows for pike. Lake trout are a coldwater stenotherm with a preference for 50°F or a bit more. Sixty degrees is getting too warm for them, although they will enter water in the 60s to feed, especially at night, and that would be a very hungry fish looking for minnows, shiners, sculpin and the like. At 75°F, the ideal

temperature for largemouth bass, the lake trout dies. One may then angle for lake trout with casting tackle as long as there is cold water on top, in the spring and fall in the southern range, and through summer in alpine lakes and in high latitudes. Only Arctic char occupy more northerly fresh waters. Lake trout sites have been found on Baffin, Victoria, King William, Southampton and Banks islands in the Arctic, and how a saltwater-intolerant species made the migration remains mysterious. It is hypothesized that they make ocean passages in a fresh or brackish boundary of meltwater under the ice.

One other criteria than cold water is required for fishing them with light tackle—gloom. A high mountain lake warmed by the sun is best fished in the crepuscular hours. A better prospect is an expedition to the Northwest Territories, where the weather can be trusted to turn resident European-Americans to that hue charmingly dubbed fish-belly white. Murky clouds, an icy drizzle and a dim sun are ideal. Trolling spoons just under the surface one morning on Great Slave Lake my partner and I hooked seventeen lake trout in 3½ hours, a fish approximately every 12½ minutes. In actual practice, strikes came as soon as scudding cloud cover obscured the sun and stopped immediately in sunshine. This was in Christie Bay in the eastern arm of Great Slave, where the lake's depth plummets to 2,000 feet and a fish has no problem modulating his light environment. Probably the popularity of lake trout with ice fishermen can be attributed to their shallow ranging under the photoscreen of ice. The unofficial depth records are 1,315 feet for a trout taken from Lake Tahoe on the California-Nevada border, and 1,400 for a Great Bear Lake specimen in the Northwest Territories. No one has information on what the fish were doing at such depths, but presumably they were following a food form by senses other than sight, since even their extraordinarily sensitive eyes are unlikely to be able to see below 750 feet.

At various times and places at least fifteen scientific and thirty-five common names have been used as synonyms for lake trout. In New England it is still often a togue. Among the Quebecois it is *touladi*. In the western United States, mackinaw is fairly common. Many Canadians prefer gray trout. There is a strong movement among fisheries biologists who

DISTRIBUTION

[1]Commercially overfished, they were then subject to new predation from sea lampreys, which reduced the stock to commercial extinction in some lakes. The Great Lakes sport fishery is now maintained by stocking, and evidence of natural spawning is rare. Some biologists attribute this to a return by mature fish to where the hatchery truck dropped them as juveniles—which is apt to be a boat launch ramp.

specialize in chars to call it a lake char. My own preference is for gray char, but in this book we follow the dictates of the Committee on Names of Fishes of the American Fisheries Society.

Like all chars, lake trout have dark dorsal skins with pale spots, just the reverse of trouts. My impression is that big lakes produce a paler fish than small ones. From glacial *etangs* in Nouvelle Quebec I have caught dark brown fish with paired and anal fins white-edged and orange-red, almost like brook trout. There is no mistaking a lake trout because its deeply forked tail is unique among adult salmonids. A square tail (as the one word "squaretail," a common synonym for brook trout) is an adaptation for mobility and low-end acceleration, just what a stream resident needs to intercept current-borne food forms. A forked tail is hydrodynamically superior for speed (see the marlins and tunas for examples) and is what you need if you are going to run down prey in the open ocean or in lakes (baby salmonines invariably have deeply lunate tails to help them run for their lives). Evidently Robinson Jeffers' question:

> *What but the wolf's tooth whittled so fine*
> *The fleet limbs of the antelope?*
> *What but fear winged the birds, and hunger*
> *Jeweled with such eyes the great goshawk's head?*

can be applied to the propellors of fish.[2] The dorsal fin of lake trout is mounted farther aft than other trouts, and the head is a larger component of the body than with most, occupying 20 to 28 percent of total length. There are teeth on everything inside the mouth—palatines, tongue, jaws, etc.— except on the shaft of the vomer, and these are not stubby little teeth for mashing insects. I have been laid open to the bone by more species of fish than I care to recall and I treat double-digit lake trout with more respect than I do pike and barracuda, and only slightly less carefully than bluefish and sharks.

Supposedly there is sexual dimorphism in lake trout to the extent of males possessing a longer, more pointed snout than females, as is usual with the trouts and salmons. This may be true, but if you want to accurately sex them examine the gonads. Ovaries are triangular in cross-section and testes round. The males that are spawning in a given year (intermittent spawning is common, and far northern populations may spawn only every third year) develop iridescent dark bands during the actual spawn itself, but this would be a phenomenon observable only by scuba divers who dive at night in late fall in cold northern or alpine lakes.

At approximately 35 or 40 pounds, lake trout begin to develop a most unsightly puffiness about the head, accompanied by ventral swelling and the general appearance of obesity. These of course are precisely the fish that custom calls "trophies"

Lake trout hooked deep often arrive at the surface rolled up in the leader in the same fashion as billfish. Hooked shallow, they will pivot around the hook point but seldom wrap up in it.

[2]A 1928 study of 1,347 Tweed sea trout found their lunate (or falcate) tails had squared off by an average fork length of 20 inches, and the posterior margin actually rounded at 27 inches.

PACIFIC SALMON

Oncorhynchus

In comparison with dinosaurs and mastodons, fish are infrequent in the fossil record. One that squeezed through the crack of chance was discovered a few years ago in Oregon (two sites, and another two in California). His name is *Smilodonichthys rastrosus*, or sabre-toothed salmon. The specimen paleontologists whisked clean of sandstone from the Torrential Beds deposit has been dated to 4,500,000 to 5,000,000 years BP (Before Present). The skeletal structure is akin to the oncorhynchid salmons, and the fish was sympatric in both space and time with chinooks and coho, but it was anomalous in three respects: There were two 6-inch breeding teeth jutting horizontally out of the upper jaw, rather like ivory mustaches; there was a very high number of gill rakers, as is common with plankton-straining fish; and the size has been estimated at up to 8 feet long with a weight of as much as 400 pounds.

Since the sabre-tooth didn't make it down the gamut of time, we are left with chinooks (*Oncorhynchus tshawytscha*) as the giant of salmonids. (There are *reports* of taimen [*Hucho taimen*] in Siberia that exceed 150 pounds.) A commercially netted Alaskan fish was 126 pounds and 4 feet, 10 inches long. The latest angling record is a 1977, 93-pounder that supplanted a 1959, 92-pounder. As a practical matter, a 60-pound chinook would be the trophy of a lifetime, and the average hook-and-line fish is under 20 pounds.

The popular name derives from a tribe of head-flattening Mongol-Americans who lived on the lower Columbia River (and subsisted largely on salmon). The generic name for the oncorhynchids means "hooked snout," and the chinook's specific name is vernacular for the fish in the Kamchatka Peninsula of the Soviet Union.

This cosmopolitan animal ranges naturally from California to northern Hokkaido and has been transplanted all over the United States (including Georgia, Louisiana and Mississippi!) and into at

Chinook and other Pacific salmon are subject to predation by seals, sea lions, killer whales and, above all, man, but their enormous fecundity ensures that millions survive to propagate one of the world's great sport and food sources.

PACIFIC SALMON

least twenty-four foreign countries. It has taken hold only on South Island, New Zealand, and in the U.S.-Canadian Great Lakes, where with coho, it constitutes a major new sport fishery that has become crucial to the tourism industries of adjacent states and provinces.

They also wander of their own volition. Sizable runs have been found off Newport Beach, south of Los Angeles, and a yard-long, 19-pounder in 1982 descended the St. Lawrence River to the vicinity of Montreal.

Chinook are *almost* unique among the Pacific

salmons in that they come in two colors: Most of them have red flesh, but as much as 30 percent of some populations have white (also a rare occurrence with cohos). This natural oddity is deplored by fishmongers because housewives like their salmon red. (And they get it, too; white chinook plus red dye plus brine and hot smoke make kippered salmon. Red chinook mildly cured with salt and sugar is lox.)

Red or pink flesh in fish is due to a diet high in carotenoids, a component of exoskeletal creatures, such as krill, shrimp and crabs (and for that

DISTRIBUTION

This southwestern Alaskan male coho has an advanced kype or snout distortion, used in breeding fights with other coho males. Like all Pacific salmon, he will die after spawning.

matter, insects; I have caught white-meated brook trout, customarily a red-fleshed fish, in high-altitude Rocky Mountain watersheds deficient in Class Insecta). Should we infer that white-fleshed chinooks are the result of a largely piscine diet? It is difficult to imagine a North Pacific predatory fish *not* eating the pelagic crustacea in which the region abounds. If white flesh is genetically determined, we have a mystery: How does the fish avoid absorption of carotenoids?

Diet, of course, is extremely diverse throughout the range. In the Pacific Northwest, oily herrings,

eulachon, smelts and anchovies are taken. Among lacustrine populations, various shads are popular and the shad-like alewife, an Atlantic species that invaded the Great Lakes via the Welland Canal,⸰ proved to be a bonanza for chinooks and coho when they were introduced. Before the salmon were stocked, alewives constituted 90 percent of the lakes' fish biomass. Great Lakes salmon trollers now use their electronics to locate alewife schools and immediately are marking salmon either beneath or amidst them. An alewife diet makes an inferior food fish, by the way. Chinooks are not above cannibalism. They have been taken far up tributaries of the Columbia River with their bellies full of salmon smolts.

The great British biologist J.B.S. Haldane drolly observed, "Like an operatic hero, the Pacific salmon dies after mating." The sole known exception is chinooks. In a New Hampshire freshwater population, precocious males who spawned ancillary to the primary spawning couple have been known to survive up to five months. Some spawned-out year-old parr have smolted, gone to sea and successfully returned. This bears further investigation. The means by which precocious parr avoided the rapid post-spawn deterioration of adult salmon may offer insight into the aging process.

Chinook spawning runs are quite complicated. In some rivers they may occur every month of the year, and each run will represent a race destined for one particular tributary or one portion of the main river. The river is located by scent after one to six years at sea. A great deal of prose and film has been spent celebrating the ability of anadromous fish to sniff their way home, but, in fact, even a highly specialized sight hunter such as we are can detect 10,000-odd combinations of the seven basic odors.

Big fish make king-size nests. The female of the pair of chinook breeders may dig her redd a foot deep and 12 feet long. The location can be anywhere from just above high tide to 2,000 miles up some superflumina like the Yukon River. Spawning can take place from July to November, and the eggs hatch in seven to twelve weeks. The alevin-parr-smolt process can be concluded in a few months in some rivers or prolonged for two years in others. Unlike coho, freshwater chinook juveniles do not seem to eat fish. They are entomophages, or at least purebred chinook are:

PACIFIC SALMON

There is evidence for some natural hybridization between chinook and coho, and heaven only knows what diet the breed prefers. In the United States there are 380-odd streams in which chinook spawn, not counting tributaries of the Yukon and Kuskokwim rivers, which is not counting a lot.

Commercial exploitation of chinook salmon is as old as the coastal Mongol-Americans, who traded dried, pulverized and smoked fish to inland tribes (without damage to the resource), but commercial canning of chinook salmon was in operation in California by 1864, and though habitat degradation (principally in the form of dams) has reduced the stock in its southern range, there is scarcely anyone alive who hasn't eaten oncorhynchid salmon. You pay top price for red chinook, which nowadays is largely sold as fresh, frozen or smoked troll-caught fish. Gillnetted salmon have deteriorated a bit by the time the nets are hauled, and will likely be canned. Drop-offs

Great Lakes Salmon Migrations

Salmon in the Great Lakes is one of the greatest "fish stories" in the history of angling. Pacific Coast anadromous salmon were first introduced into Bear Creek, a tributary of the Manistee River, which flows into Lake Michigan at Manistee, Michigan, in 1966. The little smolts migrated downstream and into Lake Michigan, where they fed heavily on abundant alewives and quickly grew to sizes exceeding 20 pounds. By 1968, a fishing explosion occurred on Lake Michigan and its tributaries, as anglers all around the lake began catching silver-bright, red-fleshed, good-eating coho or "silver" salmon weighing from 3 pounds to 20 pounds or more.

So successful was the Michigan Department of Natural Resource's original introduction of cohos into Lake Michigan, that Michigan's DNR then introduced salmon to feeder streams of Lakes Superior and Huron. Other states bordering the Great Lakes followed suit, so that today Lakes Erie and Ontario also hold salmon.

However, none of the other Great Lakes now have salmon fishing comparable to that of Lake Michigan. The major reason for this, according to fishery biologists, is that the other great lakes do not provide an environment as suitable to coho and chinook salmon as does Lake Michigan. For example, Lake Superior is far colder on the average than is Lake Michigan, and salmon introduced to Superior feeder streams and rivers do not prosper as do salmon stocked in Lake Michigan tributaries.

Lake Michigan's salmon fishing in a normal season begins in late March and April, shortly after ice leaves the shoreline shallows of the big lake. Most of Lake Michigan's salmon winter in the lower third of the lake, and, as the water begins to warm in early spring, they move into the extreme lower Illinois and Indiana portions of the lake. This is shoal water and, since it warms faster than more northerly areas of Lake Michigan, alewives and smelt converge on the lake's southern shallows—and they are followed by foraging cohos and chinook. Thus the first productive salmon fishing of every season is in the lower part of the Lake Michigan area, ranging from Waukegan, Illinois, on the northwest side to about South Haven on the northeast side.

As the weather warms, both coho and chinook salmon move northward along both coasts of Lake Michigan, and through June and July the best fishing usually is from about Milwaukee to Kewaunee on the west coast, and from around South Haven to Ludington on the east coast. By late August, the salmon start grouping off the mouths of their natal rivers, which they will mount to spawn in the period from the end of August through October. All of this, however, is generalization because there are varying strains of salmon in each of the Great Lakes, different year classes, and weather and water conditions always affect the movements of Great Lakes salmon.

Coho Salmon

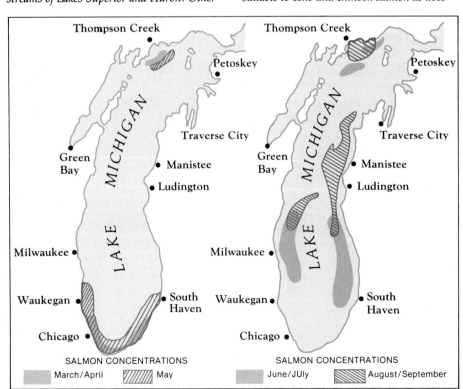

SALMON CONCENTRATIONS
March/April   May

SALMON CONCENTRATIONS
June/JUly   August/September

from gillnets are estimated at 40 percent! Nevertheless, the market demand is such that poaching is rife. In 1981, the National Marine Fisheries Service estimated that, in addition to the enormous legal catch, approximately 40,000 fall chinook on the Columbia River managed to "disappear" between Bonneville and McNary dams.

Thanks to hatchery fish and channel-bred enhancement of the wild spawn, we now have more salmon loose in the North Pacific than fifty years ago. In 1977, Oregon alone released 35,800,000 fall chinook, 16,800,000 summer chinook and 1,600,000 spring chinook. The Soviet Union has twenty-two Pacific salmon hatcheries and intends to augment them with another fifty-two. The plan is for production of 10,000,000 chinooks (among 2,000,000,000 total salmon fry) for 1985, 30,000,000 chinooks by 1990 and 50,000,000 chinooks by the year 2000. In Alaska, commercial landings of all salmon are now achieving new records, thanks to enhancement, surpassing even the glory years of the 1930s. Alaska salmon record-keeping goes back to 1884, but no one ever heard of such things as an escapement on the Nushagak River in 1980 of 141,000 chinook brood fish.

Angling for chinooks was formerly a troll fishery, period, in salt water, using the local pelagic baitfish, ranging from sardines in California to candlefish farther north. Such are the marvels of a shortened workweek, and a human population with disposable time and income to investigate and experiment, that now the sahib (or memsahib) can take his chinooks casting lures, or even fly-fishing in fresh water. Yet, probably 90 percent of sport-caught chinooks are still taken on the troll, and there are new developments that make the practice more interesting than formerly. The downrigger, which is becoming universal in salmon trolling, permits the use of much lighter tackle than the poker-stiff rods and heavy lines we used to fish in the days of *sinker releases*. This was a spring-loaded, brass plunger between line and leader that would release a heavy lead sinker when a salmon struck. This was better sport than reeling in a chinook with a 5-pound sinker still attached to the line, but the necessary rods would have been better matched against giant tuna.

Another blessing is the wide deployment of electronic Fathometers during the last two

decades. No one dreamed, when we fished blind, that there could be so *many* game fish disinterested in a sporting fling. Now, at least, when the markers of fish appear on your graph, you can adjust the downrigger cannonball's depth to present your bait at the correct level, for chinook are not inclined to run up and down the water column chasing bait (except for morning and evening ventures to the surface).

To get an even better insight into chinook conduct than sonar can produce, a professional engineer and passionate amateur fisherman named Charlie White rigged an underwater television camera in his trolling array and filmed the fish *in situ*. His conclusions, some of them heretical, were that large salmon are selective for large bait; that bait and lures dipped in thick bilge oil were more attractive than adjacent clean lures (!); that dozens of failed attempts to take a lure occur before some salmon finally succeeds; that a very long leader should separate a bait or lure from any flasher in order to mitigate erratic lure motion (this means the usual yard-or-less of leader with an 8-inch rubber snubber should be retired from the salmon fleet); that spinners make both herring and flies more attractive; and that when on the feed chinooks prefer a swiftly rotating herring over a slow roller, but when not on the feed they still prefer the fast rotation, but at a slower trolling speed.

Since all of us who have trolled with graph-paper sonars have remarked on the paucity of *eaters* compared to *lookers*, perhaps this failure of fish to hook themselves indicates insufficient motivation. More widespread use of the spinner-and-fly combination may be in order, as well as larger lures, and perhaps disconnecting any flashers from the tackle train, and using them as blind attractors attached to the cannonball. After all, more than one saltwater captain has chromed his propellers to gain flash. White's insistence that big chinook are devotees of a mouthful is echoed by Canadian fish and game department experiments, which add further that big spoons are almost *twice* as effective as big plugs.

Great Lakes fishermen of recent years have developed a doctrine of downrigger fishing with paper-thin "flutter" spoons used for fast trolling, which for chinooks is deemed to be 3 to 3½ miles per hour. The rationale for fast trolling is twain: It shortens the time between fish (though not

A major river, such as the Columbia, will have Pacific salmon runs somewhere along its length throughout the year. These are peaks for the lower Columbia runs only.

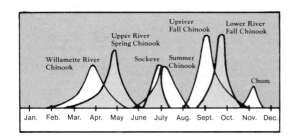

necessarily between bites), and if the salmon displayed on your electronics are cohos, you are moving at the "right" speed for that species, just about double the inchmeal pace one normally trolls for chinooks.

In addition to the troll fleet of amateurs there are a few thousand professionals still at work, though seining and gillnetting are more cost effective. A professional salmon troller differs from an amateur largely in the size of his tackle: He may have forty or fifty lures strung out along stainless steel cable to depths of 50 fathoms, with his 35-pound cannonballs virtually scratching the backs of the halibuts. But they will probably be the same lures used by amateurs, and some professionals prefer to use open skiffs and angling tackle. Out of respect for the strength of chinooks (as well as their market value), plugs designed for them normally come with a pierced head through

which a section of chafe-proof bead chain rides. Attached to the top is your leader and to the bottom is a heavy treble hook followed by another strung on an 80-pound-test trailer of braided Dacron line. This allows the plug freedom to fibrillate unencumbered by the weight of hooks and hook hangers, and when a salmon takes, the buoyant lure slides up the line. With this scheme a break off, when snagged, also returns the lure body to you.

Chinook at some point in their range are known as spring salmon, king salmon, quinnat, blackmouth, jack salmon (for grilse) and tyee. The latter word is "chief" in the Siwash Indian tongue, and the Tyee Club of Campbell River, British Columbia, has, since its organization in 1924, defined a tyee as a chinook of more than 30 pounds. You get a bronze button for a 30- to 40-pounder. It takes 60 pounds or more to earn a diamond button. The Tyee Club has highly specific tackle requirements and limits its jurisdiction to the waters of Discovery Passage.

Coho

In 1972, while strolling up the Little Manistee River in Michigan, I clumsily frightened a 20-pound-plus salmon that darted out from the shadow of bankside alders, ran up through a shallow, pale-sand pool and sheltered under a bridge. Vouchsafed such an aquarium-clear view, I told my companion that it was a fine chinook for such a small river.

I was almost certainly wrong. Salmon in the Great Lakes are maintained by hatchery operations, and there is a weir on the Little Manistee where brood stock is trapped. One trapped coho weighed 39 pounds, 2 ounces, which is 8 pounds, 2 ounces more than the angling world record, a British Columbian fish caught in Cowichan Bay. A coho as big as a tyee would be a formidable fish! In fact, the Tyee Club gives its top coho award, a diamond button, for fish of 19 or more pounds.

As a practical matter, you could fish for decades without catching a diamond-size coho. Lake Michigan would no longer be a good place to try because its cohos are diminished in size (and its chinooks unremarkable, too; this is probably an hereditary contribution of the original brood stock). Most hook-and-line coho will run in the 6- to 12-pound range.

Coho and chinook are often part of a mixed-bag catch. Differentiating between them is usually simple for experienced anglers, but can be

Different stocks or races of chinook salmon follow widely varying migration patterns. An individual fish may wander many thousands of miles before returning to its natal river for the spawning ritual.

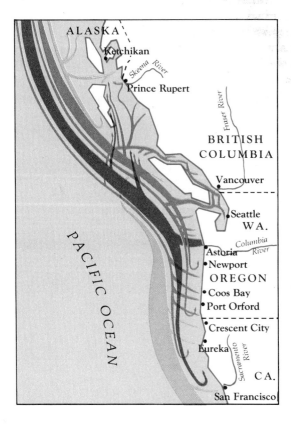

troublesome in some populations. One basic rule is that chinooks have a black gum line and coho gums are almost white. That works in salt water, but some coho populations in the Great Lakes have gray to black gum lines. The other rule is that coho have spots on the upper lobe of their caudal fin, chinook on both upper and lower lobes. Sheer size is as good a guide as any: your prospects of catching a 20-pound coho are exceedingly dim; that weight makes simply a typical chinook.

Coho have a distribution like chinook, from south of San Francisco (occasional strays to Baja California) to Hokkaido, although they are not nearly so much a high-seas rover as chinook. We tend to think of Pacific salmon as marvels of bioengineering, which return to their natal river, probably creek, and possibly pool, to spawn. Yet it is the strays who extend an anadromous species' range. The primeval history of migratory salmon would make an heroic saga, though we can at present only infer it.

Humanity has been busy attempting to extend the coho's range since the nineteenth century. Put-and-take angling for lacustrine coho has been attempted in Alaska, Washington, Oregon and California (which one would think already had a sufficient population of maritime coho), probably at the behest of biologists who wanted a glamourfish in their district to improve tourism. On the eastern seaboard, New Hampshire has a coho population, despite the argument of Lee Wulff that a state which once had Atlantic salmon really didn't need Pacific salmon, it needed the reintroduction of Atlantic salmon. In between coasts they can be fished in a growing number of states and provinces whose political leaders have been dazzled by the enormous economic success of the introduction of coho and chinook into the Great Lakes.

This was no easy task. It began in 1873 when Ohio, Michigan and Ontario devoted five years to freeing coho fry in Lake Erie and its tributaries, to utterly no avail. In the early 1930s, Ohio again stocked the fish, and cohos in the 3- to 5-pound range were caught, but no broodstock took hold. Michigan planted fish in tributaries to Lakes Huron, Superior and Michigan in 1966, after the collapse of that lake's commercial and angling fisheries for lake trout (due to overfishing and lamprey depredation). Drs. Howard Tanner and Wayne Tody of Michigan's department of natural resources, reasoned that the enormous Great Lakes' biomass of alewives and rainbow smelt needed a predator, and his department's hatchery

Alaska's Kenai River is renowned (and mobbed) for its enormous chinook salmon, such as this handsome specimen.

division was best equipped to produce salmonids. The coho stocking program produced a salmon craze that swept the Midwest, spread to every adjacent state and province, eventually embraced chinooks as well, and has generated hundreds of millions of dollars in tourism revenue. The fish were stocked as 4- to 6-inch smolts in May, and by September they were 17 inches long and as much as 2½ pounds. A year later, they entered rivers as mature fish averaging 11½ pounds. By 1970 sports fishermen out of U.S. Great Lakes' ports caught 700,000 pounds of coho in the first nine months of the year.

If there is a flaw in this inland salmon fishing, it is partial allowance on some rivers of snagging, or snatching. Even in runs that are wholly maintained by hatchery operation, encouraging or permitting snagging on the ground that the fish will otherwise be "wasted" is like encouraging hunters to jacklight deer or shoot sitting ducks. The tendency of fisheries biologists to practice

PACIFIC SALMON

The Spin-N-Glo cork drift bobber is popular with salmon drift fishermen and steelhead plunkers (essentially bait still-fishing in river current). Beneath it is a L'il Corky bait drifter. Both are customarily dressed with a mesh bag containing salmon eggs.

animal husbandry on public waters should be accompanied by strict control of the means of harvest. Traditional Mongol-American netting and spearing at specified sites is one thing, but a snagger boloing a No. 10/0 treble hook wrapped with half a pound of lead wire across a pool you are trying to fly-fish is not amusing.

Most of the fish stomachs I have examined have been empty, or contained more pulpy chyme than identifiable food forms, which was why the fish took my bait or lure in the first place—it was hungry. Biologists avoid this problem with electroshocking devices, nets and even shovels. The shovelers of redd gravel say the newly hatched coho alevins are negatively phototropic for two to three weeks, remaining in the comfortingly dark gravel and absorbing their yolk sac. Then they become positively phototropic, come out of the gravel and as fry (or parr) orient themselves with positive rheotaxis so they can watch the current bring them insects. Since they should be in quite shallow water if they don't want to be eaten alive by trout and senior parr, they have a diet largely composed of terrestrial insects that have tumbled into the shallows, plus the larger zooplankton. If you don't mind smudging your shirt front and getting your elbows wet, it is great fun to lie chin-at-the-edge of a salmon/steelhead river and watch parr feed.

As the young coho grows, it claims a stream territory, and eats insects precisely as trout. If it is

a lacustrine coho, it is going to have the company of a lot of young sockeye, almost all of whom spend one to two years in a lake before smolting. It is a hazardous association for the sockeye, because in one Alaskan lake young coho were found to consume seven times as many sockeye fry as did Dolly Vardens (once thought to be such passionate consumers of sockeye salmon that a bounty was put on them: Turn in a Dolly Varden tail and receive two cents; this nonsense continued until 1941).

In streams, coho largely confine themselves to pools. The gradient of riffles is evidently more than they care to endure. At the end of freshwater life they head seaward, where the diet becomes close-to-shore crustacea, even zooplankton. The universal wisdom of little fish is to remain in water too shallow for big brutes—at least until survival skills and confidence are acquired. As they grow, they become increasingly piscivorous, dining on brit, the young of herring, and sand lance in Alaska, for instance. But a curious specialization occurs in some schools or populations: So devoted are they to euphausiids, crab larvae, amphipods and the like, that they stay exclusively with Class Crustacea, and never achieve the size of coho, which take the usual 70 to 80 percent of finfish as their dietary mainstay.

When sea feeding, coho often associate with birds, though whether as symbionts or parasites remains to be determined. Commercial trollers

Pink Salmon

Pink salmon (Oncorhynchus gorbuscha) have the largest population of them all. The name comes from the color of the flesh, which has a lower oil content than the red myotomes of sockeye. They have an average life span of only two years. There are populations of even-numbered-year pinks principally in the northern part of their range, and of odd-numbered ones, mostly in the southern range. Total distribution is the same as the other oncorhynchids: California to Japan

Almost all pinks that are caught commercially are canned. The Canadian catch alone one year was almost 55,000,000 pounds. The United States, mostly Alaska, does more. One year the catch was 116,600,000 pounds. You can buy pink salmon up the Orinoco, up the Congo and across the street. Future enhancement will obsolete these figures.

The male pink undergoes the most grotesque spawning transformation of all Pacific salmon, sprouting a humped back and a greatly elongated kype. They spawn close to

Pink Salmon

the sea, sometimes even in tidal water. The young are unique in their lack of parr marks, but they are seldom seen, having an inclination to go quickly downstream to the sea or a waiting lake, sometimes without ever feeding in fresh water. You can fish The Egg and I streamer fly at the mouth of pink salmon rivers. They often go to sea with egg sac incompletely absorbed. Many must fall prey to bigger fish, or the Pacific Ocean would be stiff with pink salmon. A baby pink more than 2 inches long is out of the river. This precocity has proved to be extremely valuable to the species.

Southern races of pink salmon occupy an area of sea adjacent to the coast, but the

Alaskan fish are wanderers. They have been found in the Bering Sea halfway to the U.S.S.R. and as far south as the coast of California. The homing instinct is much less rigid than in the other Pacific salmon, too. This also is of value to the species.

Adult pinks have large, oval black spots on the tail, which has led them to be often mistaken for small chinooks. Now that identification pamphlets and books are widely available, people are becoming aware that they are catching pinks on occasion, even if they think they are trolling for coho and chinook.

Pinks school off river mouths, sometimes for weeks, before entering to spawn, and they continue eating the insects, copepods and who work out of the Columbia River keep a keen eye for shearwaters. If the birds are plummeting into the water and coming up with an anchovy or herring, salmon should be underneath; if the birds are afloat in their customary small flocks, it often signifies that they have fed too well to fly and must rest and digest. Salmon may or may not be in the vicinity. The underwater films of Charlie White depict murres balling herring underwater, and both salmon and gulls attacking the massed bait. In Canadian waters, the rhinocerous auklet herds herring and candlefish into bait swarms that salmon feed on. The small Bonaparte's gull, which wears a black cap in summer, is a good indicator of the presence of coho if it is diving. If it sits on the surface and dips its beak, it is taking plankton, and thereby becomes a good indicator of the *absence* of coho.

Fisheries biologists say the Great Lakes' cohos are eating alewives, rainbow smelt and even lampreys, though the stock of lampreys is now maintained at a reduced level by poisoning the young ammocoetes during their early years of life buried in river-bottom mud.

Since they are preeminently a top-of-the-water-column fish, coho often cause their prey to jump, but that does not mean most of the coho are on the surface. Sonar readings will generally show plenty of fish down 30 to 40 feet or so. These are likely coho waiting for some of the kill taking place overhead to trickle down to them. Markers

still another 50 feet below *those* should be chinooks.

The downtide side of an islet, promontory or abutment should be considered a coho-concentrating device. Small fish such as herring shelter from the current at such sites, and coho follow them. The salmon will also use any handy shoreline as an aid in balling baitfish, which are frequently seen leaping close to shore when harassed by cohos. Basically, coho prefer the top 30 feet of the water column. They are also a shoreline fish, with the proviso that they of course must follow their feed. Great Lakes coho are seldom found more than 10 miles off the beach. Much of their diet in both the Pacific and the Great Lakes is planktivorous baitfish, which must stay shallow where sunlight makes the plankton bloom.

The little pink salmon, such as this one from Resurrection Bay, Alaska, is named for the color of its flesh. They make a showy fight on light spinning or fly tackle.

miscellaneous small food forms they have always eaten. They do not like big, brawling current. Pick a river with a gentle gradient any time from late July through October, fly-fish with the tackle you would use for coastal cutthroat—most saltwater pinks are 2 to 7 pounds, with an average of 4—and have no hesitation at taking some fish to eat. The light flesh is probably better poached than broiled.

The Great Lakes Saga

Coho and chinook would probably disappear from the Great Lakes without hatchery support. They did in times past. Pink salmon, however, are there to stay. It is doubtful that they could be eliminated, if anyone wanted to. The stock came from the Skeena River in British Columbia. Ontario intended them for Hudson Bay tributaries. After the eggs were hatched, a few fingerlings escaped into Thunder Bay, which is contiguous with Lake Superior. Additional accidental and deliberate releases occurred, but the total was well under

22,000 fry of the 1955 year-class. Logically, they should simply have perished, but their 1959 grandchildren appeared in two Lake Superior streams and, by 1963, they were established in Lake Michigan. They are in all the Great Lakes now and constantly expanding their range.

In retrospect, it is very simple, even inevitable. Since pink salmon come out of the redd and immediately go downstream to their big-water destiny, they are not subject to months or years in Great Lakes tributaries that become lethally warm in summer. While chinook and coho parr are dying before they are old enough to smolt, pink salmon are already in the big lake straining zooplankton.

They mature at 14 to 19 inches and generally weigh less than 1½ pounds. Since the stock is mostly odd-year, every other August they school off river mouths, then make their spawning run in early September. Fish for them with small spinning lures and bright wet flies, presented repeatedly to male fish on the redd (or immediately before

pairing-off begins). Since this is a sport that can be practiced for approximately one week, every other year, it is not likely to produce a stampede of anglers. By the time they are at the river mouths or inside the rivers, their flesh has deteriorated to inedibility. As a food fish they logically should be taken in the lake before sexual maturation, but whether sport-caught or taken in some future commercial fishery, they will not be comparable to the ocean breed because of their inferior diet.

Some of these Skeena River odd-year fish have evidently survived a third year. Modest populations of even-year spawning has occurred in a few rivers. In the pink salmon, nature has produced a survivor.

PACIFIC SALMON

When smoltification takes place, coho revert to the negative phototropism of their alevin stage. By starlight small shoals of them travel downstream to the sea, skirting the shore to avoid intruding on the territories of trout and freshwater salmon. These latter are known as "residuals." A small percentage of coho linger more than two years in fresh water, and may sexually mature without going to sea. They are reported to never spawn, which is puzzling. If they did, they could have an evolutionary justification when salmon stocks suffer disaster at sea, such as the El Niño year of 1983. (Intrusions of warm water from the subtropics into the North Pacific altered the salmon habitat drastically. The spawning runs were only a fraction of normal volume and the fish were stunted.) Residuals are presently inexplicable.

If the smolts are wild stock, they have already imprinted on their natal river; if hatchery fish, they will imprint within forty-eight hours and remember that odor when they return from the sea (or lake) fourteen to eighteen months later. The lake, incidentally, must be sizable, and with large schools of pelagic baitfish if the coho are to prosper. Coho stocks of smallish inland lakes that stratify thermally are often forced into deep water containing little food during summer stratification. Such coho can complete their life cycle wholly as freshwater insect eaters, only inches long and ounces in weight.

Not that insects cannot remain an important part of the diet; even big Lake Michigan cohos, with a plethora of alewives available, continue to take insects, particularly mayfly nymphs, in which the lake abounds.

Downstream smolts do not tarry. Twenty miles within a week was reported in one study—a considerable distance for a fish less than 6 inches long. But when they reach salt water they seldom disappear over the horizon, unlike most of the other Pacific salmon (especially sockeye, whose oceanic voyaging is heroic). They skirt the shore both as outbound smolts and later as returning adults on their spawning run. This preference allows fishing from the beach at salient headlands in September, October and November when schools of inbound coho are passing.

Most cohos smolt after a year in fresh water, a few a bit earlier, at the end of their first summer. Residuals do not smolt at all and some fish may remain two to four years in fresh water, seemingly bent on the life of residuals, then suddenly turn silver and go off to sea. Despite this plasticity, the standard coho will spend approximately two and a half years reaching its weight of 1½ pounds, then in a mere six months time grow to its maximum size. This phenomenal growth is as remarkable as

Chum Salmon

The Mongol-Americans commonly referred to chum salmon (Oncorhynchus keta) as dog salmon, because dogs were the ultimate consumer of many of them. Nevertheless, chum smoke well and are a major subsistence food in the North. Their range is comparable to the other Pacific salmon, but in abundance they are skewed to the north, from the Columbia River to Kotzebue Sound north

of the Bering Straits.

Most chum spawn late in fall, but a few rivers have summer runs. They have been found as hybrids with pink salmon, although they grow considerably larger, up to a bit more than 30 pounds. The flesh is off-white, with the lowest fat content of all the salmons, but it is still completely edible and is taken in enormous numbers on the high seas, generally

by purse seines. The pale color and minimal oil make it inferior to sockeye and pinks as a revenue earner, but it is an important food fish worldwide.

They arrive at the river mouth already in a spawning condition, which is ugly. The males are dark with vertical green and red blotches that resemble nothing so much as running paint. Since angling for the season is normally over when they arrive, and the fish are already past their prime, they are virtually absent from the sport catch. They can be taken on lures and flies, but few bother to make the attempt.

Chum are for the most part confined to their natural range, but the U.S.S.R. managed to establish a stock in rivers debouching into the Barents Sea, some of which have strayed into Norway. It is curious to consider that this least sporting salmon is available in the nation that produces a magnificent race of large Atlantic salmon, the king of freshwater game fishes. Chum salmon belong to the history of nutrition rather than to that of sport.

Chum Salmon

Sockeye

Sockeye salmon (Oncorhynchus nerka) would be prized for their unique qualities if they were not so commonly available at the nearest grocery store. There is a freshwater version called kokanee, but some individuals of sea-run stock elect for a freshwater existence and kokanee have been known to go to sea. They spawn in huge swarms that literally tear the bottom of the river apart. They eat insects, plankton, amphipods and small fish, and they take the fly well. Really a very interesting fish, but that succulent red flesh with its high oil content withstands canning so well it is difficult to think of sockeye as a sporting species.

There are token populations as far south as California, but basically sockeye are a Pacific Northwest-to-Alaska fish in the eastern Pacific, and south-to-Japan on the other coast. In a good year, tens of millions of them will run to Alaska's Bristol Bay system of rivers, making the canneries hum. Pink and chum salmon outnumber sockeye, but superior flesh makes the latter more commercially important.

Sockeye spawn from late summer to fall in most rivers, and almost all populations need a lake to reach smolting size over the course of one or two years; then they go to sea for another two or three years. A few races spawn in rivers without lakes, and a few in lakes. Where the Babine River enters Nilkitkwa Lake in British Columbia, there is a weir to count returning fish to ensure that escapement from the river mouth nets is sufficient for the spawn (in addition to tributary streams, the spawning salmon have 6 miles of enhancement channels, increasing the lake's natural production of 30,000,000 to 35,000,000

Sockeye Salmon

smolts to 80,000,000-plus). When a run arrives, fisheries technicians man counting stations on the weathered Babine Fence until they are groggy. I have bottomed out an aluminum skiff following a channel that sockeye had turned into mountainous redds.

These fish, being far upriver, were deep into their mating colors, which for the males is a humpbacked scarlet with gangrenous-green head. Not a proper quarry for sportsmen. To fish them while they are still bright in rivers, stay close to the sea, or fish short coastal streams. When bright, they are a handsome, silvery fish of about 5 to 8 pounds and a leaper on the line.

When you have reduced one to capture, you will find it is immeasurably superior to the canned variety, tasty though that is.

Kokanee

The landlocked sockeye has a natural freshwater range comparable to the seagoing, but has been widely stocked. Populations exist in the Great Lakes, New York State and even New England. Most kokanee are 9- to 12-inch fish, although a rare giant of 8 pounds or so is occasionally reported.

Though largely planktivorous, their temperature preference of 50° to 59°F means

that during summer they will be in or near the thermocline in most lakes, where warm surface water suddenly cools (it is usually too oxygen-deficient below the thermocline to support fish life for long). Despite the plankton diet, they take small lures well. In large western lakes, such as Flaming Gorge Reservoir, Wyoming, and Lake Pend Oreille, Idaho, the tradition was to troll a small lure or bait, such as maggot, behind cowbell spinners—a series of four spinning blades mounted on a yard or more of flexible wire. Since the mouth is tender, a rubber snubber generally enters the tackle train somewhere.

With modern electronics to locate the large schools in which they customarily travel, deep jigging for them should be effective. When surface temperatures are sufficiently cool, they can sometimes be found on top and are susceptible to fly-fishing.

Kokanee are the fodder that produces some of the gross western trout that appear from time to time in the outdoor press. They are one of the few instances where man and trout are directly competitive for the same prey.

---

their universal death after spawning, but it occurs far from our eyes.

The return migration is accomplished by a combination of celestial and electromagnetic navigation. Canadian researchers working with Atlantic salmon in a tank surrounded by an electromagnet found they could confuse the fishes' sense of direction by altering the magnetic field, but only when they also denied them a view of the sky.

If daylight and iron-rich ethmoid sinuses guide the ocean wanderer's course, smell enables the fish to locate its home river. Blocking the salmon's nares thoroughly confuses it. It is likely that many salmon can discriminate so finely that they return to their natal pool. After all, some species of migrating birds return to the very nest from which they hatched. The whole point of a breeding migration is that it proved successful with the preceding generations, and a successful breeding policy is not to be tampered with. As much as 85 percent of spawning coho return to their home river, meaning 15 percent spawn elsewhere.

Spawning coho normally have empty stomachs—yet they take bait, lures and flies well. Since the fish do not have their nostrils connected

to the buccal cavity as we do, it is possible that taste for them is another means of confirming locale. The insects of a given creek could be specific for flavor.

In addition to natural hybrids with chinook, coho and pink salmon (*Oncorhynchus gorbuscha*) sometimes crossbreed. Ontario has reported a coho-steelhead hybrid, tentatively identified. A greater problem is that steelhead spawn after coho, and probably displace some coho redds.

U nlike chinooks, coho are not much given to multi-thousand-mile migrations up enormously long watersheds. A typical coho river is a short coastal stream.

It has been estimated that only 1 percent of the smolts that went to sea will survive to return, though optimistic hatchery operators have proclaimed 10 percent possible. In the Great Lakes, where the only predation on adult coho is by man and lamprey, returns as high as 25 percent have been noted. The profligacy of such a reproductive scenario would be mind boggling except that the numbers implicit are totally incomprehensible.

Confronted with a natural resource of such stupendous fecundity, humankind has done a respectable job of making it very difficult for some races of salmon to survive. Of the countless millions of fish that used to pour up the Columbia River, in recent years an escapement of only 600,000 salmon and steelhead is par. There are thirteen dams on the Columbia-Snake system now, and biologists estimate that 15 percent to 20 percent of a run is lost at each dam. The first fishway was built at the Bonneville Dam in 1930. It has been redone three times, most recently at a cost of almost $100,000,000. Between power companies and federal agencies, more than half a billion dollars has been spent in the past twenty years on fish passage programs. More appalling is that when Bonneville was first designed, there were no facilities for fish escapement whatsoever in the plans. That first ladder in 1930 was an afterthought. A great deal is now known on flow rates and light regimes to encourage different species of salmon to use the ladders, but keeping downstream smolts out of the turbines is a large and costly task involving major structural work on older dams. The loss of smolts going over spillways alone must be astronomical.

Coho can be taken in salt water by all the techniques and tackle used for chinooks, but they should be scaled down to a smaller size. Depending on locale, one would troll two-hook polar bear bucktail flies that represent a herring or candlefish (both with and without a spinner up front) in Cowichan Bay, British Columbia, or mooch a cut-plug herring in Puget Sound, or troll a sardine outside the Golden Gate. And there are some interesting recent variations.

Candlefish, it seems, spawn on a sand substrate and use sand as a refuge as adults. In the Pacific Northwest, coho and chinook anglers are using heavy, chromed, oblong spoons in an unusual jigging method. The spoon is dropped all the way to a sand bottom, then ripped free as if a panicky candlefish had seen the salmon approach and elected to run for his life. To minimize lure loss, a single Siwash hook mounted on a swivel is used.

When coho fishing, it should be borne in mind that though spawning runs can only be fished inshore in fall as they approach the river mouths, non-spawners and the year's prespawners can be fished whenever weather allows. In Puget Sound, anglers find concentrations of juvenile coho feed on little transparent shrimp-like euphausiids, which can be well imitated with flies fished on sinking or wet-tip lines and ordinary trout tackle. Euphausiids, of course, are not confined to Puget Sound. Though there are numerous species, they are basically black-eyed and often have luminous inner organs. A No. 6 bucktail with fluorescent wool body should do it. When surface fishing for cohos, either casting or trolling baitfish-imitating flies in the British Columbian fashion, try to fish dawn and dusk, for two reasons: There is generally a bite early and late, and there is often a calm. The latter is useful for spotting coho finning out (feeding very shallow so their dorsal fins break the surface). In calm water, also look for momentary swirling distortions of the surface. Coho often take their food by outpacing it and then doubling back.

Brackish-water fishing for anadromous salmonids is a study in itself. Regulars on the Smith River in northern California have a doctrine that their big chinooks in tidewater pools move to the top of the pool on the flood and return to the bottom of the pool on the ebb. On

Mooching

Unique to chinook and coho fishing is the practice curiously dubbed "mooching," which combines elements of trolling, deep jigging and soaking bait—and is elegantly suited to the peculiar requirements of the chinook. The nameless angler who invented mooching was a genius, but you must understand salmon a bit to appreciate his achievement.

Chinook are essentially a crepuscular fish that feed on top at low-light levels and are generally deep at midday unless there is overcast, wind or rain. Mooching is for balmy sunshine days. The bait is a herring, either whole, filleted or cut-plug (which means decapitated with a bias cut). A two-hook snell is used, and the bait rigged with some flexure so it will spin—for chinook you want a slow spin. The engines are shut down so you can enjoy the absence of that abominable racket that is the bane of trolling. Drifting with wind or tide you add enough sinker weight to let your line maintain an angle of 40 degrees to 60 degrees off the horizontal, depending on speed of drift. Fish on the windward side of the boat in water your electronics indicate is at least 100 feet deep, lower your herring to the bottom and start it coming up slowly. Washington State fisheries personnel, after extensive experiments, declared 60 to 70 feet the most productive depth for catching chinooks. Their counterparts in British Columbia prefer 90 feet. At any rate, when your herring is about halfway to the surface, drop it down again. Most interceptions will be on the drop.

This jigging with bait, or slow trolling with tide power—this mooching—is an extraordinarily soothing sport. There should be a few friends, plenty of iced bait, a cutting board, a generous picnic basket and rigged casting tackle in case overcast allows the salmon to come topside. With line as light as 15- or 20-pound-test, the herring will spiral seductively, and you will have memorably long fish fights with chinooks that are unencumbered by flashers and dodgers and all the impediments of trolling.

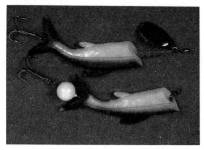

For moochers who prefer not to handle actual bait, Worden's Herring Plus III *(top)* and Herring Plus II are possibly unique instances of artificial lures designed to imitate cut bait.

the nearby Eel River, when fishing for steelhead in the early 1950s, we quickly learned that as high tide approached, flooding and extending a steelhead run into the next pool downstream, it was wise to move up into higher riffles to avoid salmon, who by the time steelhead are running well are red and inedible, and should be left to spawn unimpeded.

In rivers, anadromous salmonids should be fished for with flies, because fly-fishing tackle is more entertaining to use than any other gear. In practice, if a river is off-color, spoons will outfish the fly by dozens to one. After a heavy rain has swollen a river, bait will probably be your only hope.

Great Lakes chinooks begin their spawning runs in late August or early September, with cohos fast behind. October is the prime month to take them with casting tackle in running water, but there can be fresh-run coho as late as December. Fisheries biologists are working to extend the inshore availability of Great Lakes salmon through the development of early and late runs.

Because straying and stocking are steadily adding to the number of rivers with coho and chinook runs, a state-by-state list would be meaningless. Wherever salmon are found, information on their whereabouts is freely available, particularly on the Great Lakes.

The salmon, themselves, are probably overfishing. The alewife population deemed "infinite" when salmon stocking began on Lake Michigan is certainly not. There is no such thing as an infinite biomass. Proof, or rather evidence, is the decline in coho size on the lake. From the former average of 9 pounds, they are now down to about 5. However, this is a factor subject to control, because only 10 percent (or less) of Lake Michigan coho are of natural reproduction. The hatchery stock can be augmented or diminished according to estimates of its impact on the lake's baitfish supply. Hatchery economics indicate that coho production will be sacrificed to increased chinook production in the future. Coho need about eighteen months of hatchery holding (and feeding) before smoltification, chinooks less than a year, and some strains as little as four months.

But regardless of their size, coho whose flesh has not yet degenerated as the spawning process advances make such delicious eating that some of the Pacific Northwest fish make their way as air cargo to London, where they are smoked, then returned to the United States to be served as a delicacy. That seems much preferable to the "white salmon trout" the Lewis and Clark

expedition first encountered at Celilo Falls on the Columbia River. The fish was fried in bear oil (!), and William Clark said it was "the finest fish he had ever tasted."

Kenai River Chinook

The Kenai River lazily meanders through its delta in soft S curves, reaching out to the North Pacific. The broad, flat delta water, emerald green in color, is a stark contrast to its white-water

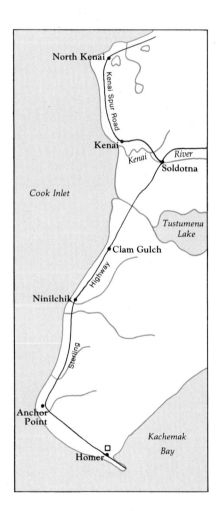

The proximity of the Kenai River to Homer, Alaska, means that fishing for its race of large chinooks is not going to be an experience in wilderness solitude.

beginnings. Fed and colored by glacial runoff and snowmelt, the delta is a delightful sight to Kenai River anglers who enjoy big chinook.

Anglers from around the world fish the Kenai River in its lower portion to find giant salmon. Between Soldotna and the river's mouth at Kenai, you will find outstanding trophy fishing. These salmon are Alaska's biggest. Ranging from 25 to 80 or more pounds, you are *likely* to catch a 50-pounder. The record is 93½ pounds.

The gravel bottom, devoid of snags, allows

PACIFIC SALMON

drifts of a mile or more in places. Generally, the most popular form of fishing is back drifting on the bottom. The boat is placed perpendicular to the bank and drifts with the current, using light motoring to maintain position. Line is weighted to carry the lure to the bottom. Preferred lures are Spin-N-Glos, Okie Drifters and Tadpollys off three-way swivels and a sinker.

Another successful method is to stabilize the boat over a deep hole with either an anchor or by back trolling. This allows access to areas where fish stack and rest. Lures are Spin-N-Glos, Tadpollys, Hot Shots or sliding sinkers with salmon eggs.

You will find greatest success close to the bottom behind gravel bars, islands or slack waters out of the river's main flow. The least successful method is bank fishing because of the lack of mobility. However, Centennial and Swift River campgrounds along with Morgan's Hole are good spots for bank fishing.

The rule of thumb on the Kenai is that darker waters and days take lighter, more attractive, lures. Bright days and clear waters take dark lures. Lures are generally the largest of a given design or style. Leaders for Spin-N-Glos use 18 to 24 inches of line. Tadpollys on a drift use 28 to 32 inches. Tadpollys are used in lower, clearer waters, especially when motoring upstream slowly.

The best explanation why the Kenai River consistently produces larger chinooks is time at sea. These salmon spend between four and seven years at sea before they spawn. Spawning begins early in May. The run peaks in late June and July, depending on natural conditions. Protective regulations have closed fishing for chinooks in August to secure a successful spawn.

In northern British Columbia, the mighty Skeena River is a migration route for Kitsumkalum-bound chinooks. Fishing the mouth of the Kitsumkalum is no undertaking for inexperienced boaters; the Skeena is an awesome river.

The best quality angling occurs in the lower river because the bright salmon are fresh from growth at sea. The salmon's long journey changes its body color from silver, as at sea and in the delta, to a reddish and ultimately a blackish tone in the headwaters.

For most anglers, fishing the Kenai River is a memorable adventure. Sex and age are no barriers. Guide services are excellent. While you should expect to be on the river in company with many other anglers, anticipate a unique experience and a great time. Experienced anglers set their own trophy requirements, then catch and release until their goals are met.

Contact Alaska Sportfishing Lodge Association for their current guide at 500 Wall Street, #401, Seattle, WA 98121; telephone (1-800) 352-2003.

Skeena River

On the Skeena watershed in northern British Columbia, a former world-record chinook in excess of 92 pounds has been caught, but fisheries personnel at one time weighed a spawned-out salmon carcass that scaled 107 pounds. The Skeena is a mighty river, more than 400 yards wide in places, and with a frighteningly powerful current at the best-known hot spot, the mouth of the Kitsumkalum River.

There is a variety of guide services available using both drift boats and jet-powered riverboats, but some of the local fishermen from the town of Terrace, at the confluence, have developed a curiously masochistic sport in which they are joined by guests from thousands of miles away. Fishing from the bank with stout casting tackle and two-handed rods, at the site of giant rip-rapping that prohibits running with the fish, they cast for these enormous salmon and then stand their ground like heroes. Trying to turn fish that frequently exceed 40 pounds with 30- to 45-pound-test line under such conditions is accepting handicaps most would consider insuperable.

Chinook are running up the Kalum, as it is locally known, as early as April 1st, but the giants arrive much later. The last two weeks in July are preferred. There are closures in June and August to protect spawning fish, so when booking a guide inquire where you will be fishing. The closures are limited areas on the Kalum and the Skeena, but they are excellent fishing sites.

The fish have a 90-mile run from the mouth of the Skeena at Prince Rupert, but their size makes that a three- or four-day affair at most. They are

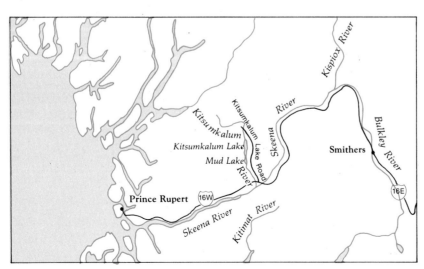

Kispiox River

River

Kitsumkalum River

Skeena River

Kitsumkalum Lake Road

Bulkley River

Kitsumkalum Lake

Mud Lake

Smithers

Kitsumkalum River

Prince Rupert   16W

16E

Skeena River

Kitimat River

bronzed, but still muscular.

The twirling lures named Spin-N-Glos are popular, mounted with a No. 5/0 single hook. When the hot spots are crowded, still-fishing with 8- to 10-ounce sinkers that break away on the strike is the practice. But really, the sensible way is to be out in a boat with a guide. I would not recommend bringing your own boat unless it is large and powerful and you are highly skilled in fast-water operations. I have seen whirlpools on the Skeena that would swallow a cartop skiff with one gulp.

Tributaries of the Skeena include famous steelhead streams, such as the Kispiox, Babine, Bulkley and Morice, but it should be borne in mind that these are also coho rivers. There is early coho in August on some rivers, particularly the Kitimat, but September and October are the main coho months.

Terrace has adequate lodging, which your guide can book for you, and there is plenty of opportunity for camping nearby. It is advisable not to stay on one river if the fishing fails or is slow. Moving to Smithers gives you better access to the Babine and Bulkley. If the Skeena is off color, remember the Kalum has produced an 83½-pound chinook itself. Someone claims to have lost a 6-foot chinook on the Kitimat. The Skeena watershed is one of the most fascinating for salmonids in the entire world. You can hear a taped, twenty-four-hour fishing report by phoning (604) 638-0557.

Rivers Inlet

Rivers Inlet, fed by five main rivers and several minor streams, is the home of a race of giant chinooks whose renown has brought sportsmen from across the continent.

There is no road to the 37-mile-long inlet, but Port Hardy, 60 air miles to the southeast, has a commercial airport, so charter aircraft is the customary means of access. Some Vancouver yachtsmen make Rivers Inlet a port of call on their summer cruise. They are at a disadvantage because big chinooks are not enamored of big boats. The professional guides who work out of the four or five fishing camps that open each summer prefer small outboard-powered skiffs for their maneuverability when mooching a cut-plug of herring, and as a drag to help tire big chinooks when being towed around the inlet for fights that have lasted as long as four hours. At Rivers Inlet, a chinook is considered big at 50 pounds or more. They have been taken in excess of 81 pounds. Many are lost.

Rivers Inlet, British Columbia, has produced a number of record-weight chinook salmon. Campbell River has been a favored coho fishery for more than half a century.

These tyee run from mid-July until the end of August, though the first few appear late in June. They were taken by commercial fishermen for local canneries, which began operation in 1882, continuing until the early 1950s. Two popular resorts, in fact, are based at old canneries.

Fisheries personnel carefully manage this trophy area, maintaining a weigh-in station and requiring a special chinook permit. The rock walls are clearly marked with yellow triangles defining trolling limits, and numbers displayed on both sides of the inlet allow anglers to report the location of their hookups.

Approximately half the catch has proven to be fish of five or six years, unusually long for chinooks, and their size can probably be attributed to extra feeding time at sea. Motor mooching, or very slow trolling, is the technique of choice. Tackle is usually a long mooching rod and 20- to 30-pound-test monofilament line. Terminal gear is a trio of No. 3/0 bait hooks mounted in tandem. The diagonally cut-plug herring is impaled at head and tail, slightly bent to make it rotate. With 40 to 60 feet of line out, the bait is held down by a keel sinker of 4 to 6 ounces. There are no regulations prohibiting fly-fishing or spinning with lures, but their comparative lack of efficacy means they are rarely tried. Anglers who come to Rivers Inlet are serious about acquiring a trophy. You should bring light tackle for the coho and pink salmon runs.

Despite careful management for more than three decades, the fishery seems to be declining. A week's trip to Rivers Inlet should produce a 50-pound-plus chinook, but that is half the rate of a few years ago. During the height of the season it is not unusual to count fifty boats trolling between The Dome and The Wall.

The Rivers Inlet resorts that are going to be open in a given year should be listed in the free annual publication *Travel Information & Accommodation Directory,* available from Tourism British Columbia, 1117 Wharf Street, Victoria, B.C. V8W 2Z2; telephone (604) 387-1642. This gives all pertinent information on each lodge, including rates.

You might also consider taking a deck of cards. The fishing tends to stop very suddenly if a pod of killer whales comes rolling up the inlet.

Fly-Fishing for Chinook

Even though fly-fishing for this largest member of the Pacific salmon family is typically less productive than angling with spinning or casting gear and flashy spoons, it is the challenge and potentially large size of the catch that attracts many dedicated fly-rodders. However, if the fish are present in suitable numbers, and if the angler understands the basic requirements that must be met to entice this exciting game fish to take a fly, long periods of time between strikes may not be the case.

Chinook salmon (also popularly known as king

Famed guide Bus Bergmann divides his year between Alaskan salmon and Florida Keys' flats fish. This is a Nugashik River chinook taken on a float trip.

salmon, especially in Alaska) enter a great many North American rivers during the late spring, summer and fall months. Heavy runs begin in most Alaskan rivers shortly after the ice is completely out of the lakes in early or mid-June, reaching a peak during mid-July. At the southern extent of its eastern Pacific range in northern California, the major runs typically begin in late September or early October.

Each individual fish begins to spawn approximately a week after it enters fresh water, except for those fish that enter Washington and Oregon rivers in the spring and still wait until fall to spawn. They first hold in deeper pools while they adjust to differences (such as salinity, temperature, etc.) between the ocean and the river. Then they move into shallower water, preferring clean gravel bottoms with a good flow of water for the spawning process.

When they first enter the rivers, their color is silvery with only a slightly darker back. Within the first two weeks, and usually about the time they settle down on a redd to spawn, they have already turned darker—from almost black or brown in some streams to bright red in others. Unlike other Pacific salmon, this transition to spawning colors does not signify a significant decrease in fighting ability (especially among the Alaskan kings). Only after a chinook has been actively spawning for several weeks, and its fins begin to show extensive white discoloration along their margins (a fungus), will it become less active when hooked.

Like all the other Pacific salmon, the chinook does not eat after it enters fresh water. In spite of this, it still is often willing to strike a fly, especially if that fly invades its holding or spawning territory. There is, however, one consideration that *must* be met in order to induce a chinook to strike any fly, no matter what the pattern: The fly must be presented to the fish at the same level it is holding, and regardless of water depth, that is usually close to the bottom. It's very rare for one of these fish to rise more than a few inches to take any fly.

Nevertheless, some patterns definitely work better than others. Weighted streamers are usually best, and may range from short, dark patterns similar to those used for steelhead to large, bright saltwater tarpon flies 6 inches long. Size and pattern are usually dictated by light and water conditions. The brighter the day and the clearer the water, the smaller the fly. On the other hand, when fishing a milky glacial river or one that is high and muddy because its watershed experiences considerable rain, large bright streamers often are the best (if not the only) producers.

During the past few years a growing number of anglers have begun to use streamers designed to imitate the flashy action of the spoons used so effectively on spinning or bait-casting tackle. The pattern is simple, consisting of bright artificial deerhair (i.e., Fishair) wings in such fluorescent colors as red, orange, yellow, pink, etc., surrounded by numerous strands of thin silvery Mylar. Length may vary from 2 to 5 inches, depending upon water conditions.

The jaws of a big chinook, especially the males, are very large and bony. This dictates flies tied on sharp hooks of sufficient size and strength to stay put. While a No. 1 or 1/0 hook might be suitable for a typical average 20-pounder, in some rivers these fish may average well over 30 (especially in Alaska), and patterns tied on No. 2/0 or 3/0 hooks are more likely to ensure a solid, reliable hookup.

While kings under 30 pounds can be taken from slower rivers on light fly gear, a larger fish can quickly become a serious problem, especially if the river is even moderately fast. At that point it becomes a matter of either following the hooked fish by boat or on foot, or losing it when you run out of backing. Even tarpon-size fly tackle may not be enough if a chinook of 40 pounds or more is hooked where there is a strong current.

Most fly-fishermen, especially if fishing Alaskan rivers where the fish tend to run stronger than those caught in the lower forty-eight states, prefer 11- to 13-weight rods and reels that hold at least 200 yards of 30-pound-test backing plus the necessary fly line.

Getting the fly down to the fish requires sinking lines. These may vary from moderate sinkers in shallow water with slow currents to the heaviest practical combination to cast in deeper and/or faster water. Fish holding in deep, very fast water often cannot be reached with any fly line, including leadcore shooting heads.

Leaders should be kept short, usually only 3 or 4 feet is needed. Shock tippets ahead of the fly aren't usually necessary, and, as a rule, you will get more strikes if the fly is tied directly to the class tippet, usually 12- to 15-pound-test for the larger fish.

NORTHERN PIKE

Esox lucius

AND
WHITEFISH

The First Biennial Report of the Fish Commissioners of Michigan (1875) described northern pike as "those Modocs of our waters who apparently mutilate and kill their more amiable, Quaker-like neighbors upon the total depravity principle." This purple prose was abandoned in the report of the following year, when the authors simply suggested that the pike be exterminated. Evidently, an ill-defined Lutuamian people of southeast Oregon, and far removed from pike country, met their match in one other ill-defined bit of allegory. Less than twenty years later, Tomlin, writing in *American Game Fishes,* was already recording a decline of the pike "through better fishing appliances, the pushing of railroads into unfrequented lake countries, and the ambition of lady anglers to join their husbands."

In terms of natural history, the pike is a survivor, with some 20,000,000 years of practice. Its now extinct fossilized forebear, *Esox lepidotus,* and the two are almost identical in appearance. The largest pike (50 pounds or more) are found in Europe, particularly in the temperate limestone lakes of Ireland and the subalpine waters of Germany and Switzerland, but for sheer numbers, the wilderness regions of the New World are incomparable. In North America, the pike is distributed from Alaska to Labrador and south to northern New England and from the Hudson River drainage of New York to eastern Nebraska, but it is the central provinces of Canada that are the prime areas for angling. Ontario, Manitoba and Saskatchewan have hundreds of lakes and rivers where pike seldom see an artificial lure. Saskatchewan has about 31,000 square miles of water area, Manitoba about 27,000 square miles and Ontario roughly 34,000 square miles (excluding its portions of the Great Lakes which would double the figure), so for the fisherman tourist the options are limitless.

The largest pike are not found in Arctic

Except for an occasional flick of its fins, a northern pike waits motionless to ambush its prey. The malevolent-eyed and evil-tempered waterwolf will attack fish one-third to one-half its length.

NORTHERN PIKE

latitudes, but from south of the United States border through the more temperate portions of Canada which provide an abundant food supply and a longer growing season. A one-year-old pike at the Arctic Circle in Great Bear Lake will average 3.9 inches in length, as compared to a 10.1-inch fish of the same year-class in Wisconsin; at age ten, a pike from Great Bear will average 27.6 inches in length, as compared to 42.6 inches in Wisconsin. For trophy pike, lakes such as McGavock, Sickle, Reed, Waskaiowaka, Kississing and Island Lake in Manitoba; Lloyd, Hatchet, Wallaston, Tazin, Tobin and Black lakes in Saskatchewan; Eagle Lake, Lake-of-the-Woods and Lake Nipigon in Ontario are particularly noteworthy, and in the Northwest Territories the Great Slave and Kasba lakes. To the east, Quebec produces some heavy fish in Lakes Camachigama, O'Sullivan and Whiskey, as well as the many rivers of that province.

The Cycle of the Season

Pike fishing is at its peak in the spring season, from as early as February to June, depending on the latitude. At this time, the fish move into shallow, weedy areas and are fairly easy to catch, especially in the morning and late afternoon. Light intensity has a great deal to do with both spawning and feeding activities. Generally speaking, noon or the period of direct overhead sun is the poorest from the standpoint of strikes obtained, and an experienced pike angler will relax at his lunch. The late afternoon hours after 3:00 P.M. are apt to be particularly good, but as the sunlight fades, the fishing again slows down and usually ceases at dusk. Unlike the muskellunge or the black bass, pike are not nocturnal. While it is hardly practical to fish by the clock, it is important to be on the water during the peak periods for best results. One study concluded that pike were most active between 8:00 and 11:00 A.M., then again at 2:00 to 4:00 P.M. There seemed to be a definite lull between shortly after 11:00 A.M. until 1:00 P.M. The peak activity came at about 3:00 P.M. and gradually declined toward evening (quite different from the muskellunge, which forages extensively in some waters at night). These feeding periods are not universal absolutes, but vary with the season and latitude. In the Far North, where summer days are long, the peak activity may occur as late as 6:00 P.M. South of this range in winter, where the days are short, the peak activity may be at noon. Among other factors, the wise pike angler learns to relate his successful hours to the sun's intensity.

Water temperature is another factor, in the sense that if it hits 65°F or above, the ratio of angling success falls sharply. This is of no importance in the northernmost part of the pike's range, where summer temperatures rarely rise out of the 50s, but throughout much of our lake country, the fishing goes into a summer slump. There are probably several factors at work when pike fishing declines.

Food consumed in warm water is not digested as rapidly as it would be at optimum temperatures. Despite the pikes' strong stomach acids, it is not unusual for them to swallow large fish and swim around for hours with their victim's tail portion protruding from the mouth while the other end is being digested. Assimilation is now a slow process. In a predation study on the Athabaska and Saskatchewan River deltas of Canada, investigators concluded that pike ate 10 percent of the local duck hatch, or 1,500,000 ducklings each year. The ducklings were available to the pike for a period of ninety days, and feeding experiments revealed that it required ten days for a pike to digest one duckling. It is also not unusual for a pike to swallow a 2- or 3-pound bass or sucker, so it takes only sporadic feeding during hot weather periods to satisfy its prodigious appetite. Pike are capable of ingesting other fish from one third to one half their own length. A 53-pound fish taken at Lough Conn, Ireland, in 1920 (considered to be a world record for many years) had a 30-inch long salmon in its stomach when caught. The pike measured 51 inches and was 36 inches in girth. The northern has teeth that can be depressed to allow the entry of a large object, and the long canines plus the formidable rows of teeth on the tongue and palate point backward to prevent any prey from escaping. A pike also has the unusually long stomach and short intestine of an essential carnivore, making the feat practical. Only the width of its victim is a discouraging dimension to the pike. Ideally, the food should be one third narrower than its closed mouth, but fish one third wider have been recovered in pike stomachs, and of course, the occasional northern is found choked to death on a fat bass or muskrat.

The migrations of salmon to their remote spawning grounds are television specials. The sight of great hordes of fish entering stream mouths, then leaping the falls, digging their redds, and finally, in most species, dying from their procreative effort, is one of the textbook triumphs of nature. By comparison, the northern pike is an introvert; the breeding male does not change color, because one of the functions of conspicuous

DISTRIBUTION

markings which appear in fishes at the beginning of a reproductive cycle is to announce the aggressive intentions of a territory owner. A crimson, bull-shouldered, hook-jawed, spawning sockeye salmon hardly resembles the streamlined silvery adolescent he was before reaching maturity. But pike claim no particular territory, nor do they dig redds, and their pugnacity is limited to a threatening posture which only the female assumes at the approach of courting males. At this time, with mouth menacingly agape, she may extend her fins, then arch her back and shove the male away with a sudden bending of the head. Or, with carnal whimsy, she may swim slowly forward to initiate a courtship. The chosen male is invariably smaller than the female, so the breeding pair becomes oriented in swimming side by side or, literally, "eyeball to eyeball." Just prior to spawning, the pike reduce their speed and parallel the shore, sometimes with their backs out of water. When the male is in juxtaposition with the female genital pore, he flips his tail under her body and mixes his sperm with her eggs as they are extruded. This may take place in such shallow water (from as little as 4 to 20 inches) that the resulting splash can be heard a hundred yards away.

A breeding ground is often far removed from the natural bailiwick of the pike. Their first choice is a sluggish inlet stream. If no inlet or outlet exists, then the fish will find a marsh. Apparently, a rise in water temperature is not the initial external stimulus, as pike congregate to spawn before any thermal change is noticeable. As our spring days grow longer and light intensities increase, the fish begin to move from deep water to shallow, weeded areas, seeking a place where the eggs will fall over dense vegetation. Because of this type of bottom and the constant movement of fish in their repetitive spawning acts, the eggs are broadcast over a wide area—perhaps a mile or more by one pair of pike. Although the female is bloated with thousands of eggs, she emits only half a dozen to sixty during each contact with the male, so the larger fish spawn during a period of several days, ceasing their activity at nightfall and resuming at daylight. Light has such a definitive effect on pike that according to researchers, most of the migration activity or movement to the spawning grounds takes place between 6:00 P.M. and 9:00 A.M., while the actual mating occurs during the reverse period, with the peak activity in the afternoon becoming most intense when the sun is brightest.

Fly-Fishing for Pike

The malevolent-eyed and evil-tempered waterwolf has long been identified with flashing spoons and wiggling plugs, and rightly so, but pike are at times among the easiest and more exciting fish to be taken on the fly rod. When northern pike are in the shallows, you can always count on plenty of action. No other freshwater species provides the beginner a more willing prize in equal weights.

The most exciting moment in taking pike on a fly is the strike. The nature of the game is such that invariably you are fishing very shallow, clear water—so you will often see fish churning the surface seconds before the strike. Pike don't merely "take" a fly; they charge at full speed and attack in a spine-tingling wake. Just short of its

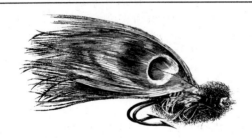

Fly-fishing for northern pike is a comparatively new sport in North America but it was in vogue in nineteenth-century England. The first known pike fly was as big as a feather duster and made from fragile peacock feathers.

(From *The Book of the Pike* by H. Cholmondeley-Pennel, 1865.)

target, the fish may come out of the water like a guided missile and explode on the lure with deadly accuracy. It is not uncommon to have northern pike race after a lure and nail it at boatside, literally under your rod tip. There are pike who almost seem to enjoy the game as much as their anglers.

Fly-fishing for pike with large streamers and poppers is not mechanically easy. Due to the wind resistance of these lures, it requires a modicum of skill. The angler who spends much of his time learning to cast instead of sighting targets will not catch many fish. Because most of the fishing is done in shallow, clear water, where fish tend to spook, more northern pike are taken at distances of 50 to 60 feet than at shorter ranges, so you must be able to cast reasonably well. The fisherman who can double-haul and toss a big fly 60 or 70 feet will boat many more pike than the neophyte.

Accuracy is also important. Fly-rod lures are fished near logs, fallen trees, stumps, weed beds and among lily pads where the first cast is most likely to draw a strike. Even a perfect second or third cast, after a bungled presentation, compounds the odds in hooking wary pike. These bulky artificials have a tendency to flop back on the leader, and you have to get a clean turnover so the lure begins "working" instantly.

A properly balanced outfit is essential to good casting and must be calibered for the job. Light fly rods used for stream trout fishing are a handicap on a pike bay. There is no tactical advantage in going light, nor does it add one iota to the sport. Graphite or graphite/boron rods of 8½ to 9 feet in length, that handle No. 8 or 9 floating lines are ideal because of the weight factor. These light, yet powerful, sticks make it possible to cast all day long without arm fatigue. A medium-size, single-action reel is adequate for any size pike you may encounter, as they seldom run very far into the backing; it should spool 100 yards of 20-pound-test Dacron under the fly line. A heavy fish will try to get back in the weeds or under timber; if the fish succeeds, it pays to slack off completely and not apply any rod pressure. Often, a pike will swim out of the entanglement and return to open water. Not all pike jump, but in the last moments at boatside, the fish usually does a lot of rolling—and this can be a leader snapper if you apply too much pressure.

The leader should be 8 to 9 feet in length. Use 30-pound-test for the butt section, followed by a strand of 25-pound, then shorter lengths of 20, 15, 12, and finally a 12-inch "shock" tippet of 30-pound hard nylon. Some anglers use wire tippets for pike. However, nylon is much the best because wire not only kinks, but the big fish often swallow the fly deep; if short metal leaders are employed—and they must be short to cast safely—a pike will often overbite the wire anyhow. In trophy-potential waters, where fish of 20 pounds or more are possible, I use 60- to 80-pound-test shock tippets; at these diameters, the lure should be attached with a Homer Rhode Loop so it can swing freely, as any knot that jams against the hook eye will hold it rigid and unlifelike in the water. Occasionally pike will chop through mono-filament, but this is seldom a problem. Their teeth are needlelike rather than razor-edged, as in its spiritual saltwater counterpart, the barracuda. When a northern pike cuts the leader, it doesn't bite through it, but frays the monofilament while it works back and forth.

Big pike want a big mouthful. Natural foods the

size of ducklings and muskrats hardly come within the scope of fly-rod imitations, although a mechanical duckling lure which was battery-operated, paddled about and did everything but quack was marketed in the United States some years ago. To our knowledge, it provided hours of entertainment for the angler and paralyzing skepticism among the pike.

The first pike fly, as conceived by British author H. Cholmondeley Pennel in 1865 (*The Book of the Pike*), was a veritable feather duster on a double hook. Undoubtedly it caught fish, but equally obvious by its peacock wing, it must have been torn to shreds after being mauled by the canines of a northern pike. As fly-rod tarpon anglers have discovered in recent years, "big" is a very relative term. Durability is really the keynote to selecting artificials for pike. Most saltwater streamer patterns are suitable and an assortment of bucktail and spayed-wing saddle hackle patterns tied on No. 2/0 and 3/0 hooks such as the Strawberry Blond, Jim Buck Fly and Phillips Bead Head Streamer should be in your box. And don't fail to include some dressed on weedless hooks; although weeds are not a problem in all pike waters, especially in the early season, it pays to have them on hand. One of the best dressings for pike is the Magnum, designed by American author Tom McNally (*Fly-Fishing*), who has specialized in this kind of angling for many years. His Magnum is a 6-inch-long, multi-wing streamer tied on a No. 3/0 hook. It is a simple dressing with a chunky chenille body, 6 or 8 saddle hackles tied in for the wing and several others palmer-style just ahead of the wing. It has a lively swimming action. McNally has taken pike up to 26 pounds on this fly.

For surface fishing, large bass bugs or their saltwater counterparts make excellent pike attractors. One lure, called the Skipping Bug, with a cedar body and bucktail cemented into its butt section, is a must. This lure, made by Bill Gallasch of Richmond, Virginia, comes in assorted colors and sizes. My favorites are yellow, red-and-yellow and red-and-white, in No. 1/0 to 3/0. The Skipping Bug has a 1½-inch-long body and with the bucktail tied in, it measures about 5 inches overall. My best luck has been with the red-and-white pattern on a No. 3/0 hook.

Tom Loving of Pasadena, Maryland, created an odd looking popper called the Gerbubble Bug, and it is made commercially by Jim Poulos of Wheeling, Illinois. This bug is flat on top and bottom, with hackles cemented in slits along its sides. These side hackles add to the bug's air

The Enigmatic Whitefish

Lake whitefish (Coregonus clupeaformis) are found throughout the North Country in the same waters as pike, lake trout and grayling. They provide excellent angling, especially when the larger fish are surface feeding. During calm weather with a good hatch of mayflies or caddis on the water, their repetitive feeding is unmistakable, yet often frustrating to experienced trout fishermen who cast to the rings of rising fish, or strike reflexively at the take. When you see a rise, the fish has already departed. Whitefish cruise as they feed, usually in a straight path, coming to the surface about every 6 feet (longer or shorter intervals depending on the abundance of insects). The trick is to determine the direction of the next rise of an individual fish and intercept it with your fly; but this is only half of the riddle.

Whitefish have extremely small mouths and, while the occasional big one will hook itself, the fish habitually "bump" the fly to drown it before taking it in their diminutive jaws. This requires a delayed strike—long enough to say aloud "lake whitefish" or better yet, Coregonus clupeaformis. An instant tightening of the line will merely pull the fly in the air. Without a proper pause you will miss fish after fish.

Lake whitefish can also be caught on light spinning tackle using very small jigs, spinners and spoons. As an escaping prey, these lures are taken without

hesitation, the only caution being the somewhat delicate membrane structure of the whitefish's mouth which is easily torn if too much rod pressure is applied.

Unlike the mountain whitefish (Prosopium williamsoni) common to western United States and Canadian

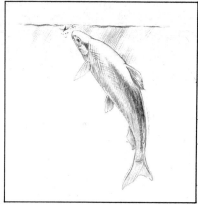

streams, the lake whitefish achieves substantial sizes. The present rod-and-reel record is 15 pounds, 5 ounces taken from Clear Lake (the Kawartha Chain), Ontario, in 1983. Specimens weighing 20 pounds have been netted by commercial fishermen in various Canadian waters.

This whitefish has few peers at the table and although usually marketed in smoked form, it is a gastronomic superlative in northern camps when gently poached and served with lemon butter.

153

NORTHERN PIKE

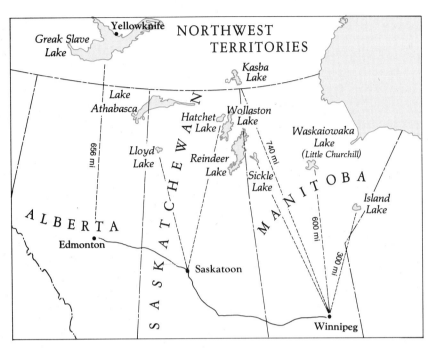

NORTHWEST TERRITORIES

Yellowknife

Great Slave Lake

Kasba Lake

Lake Athabasca

Hatchet Lake

Wollaston Lake

Waskaiowaka Lake (Little Churchill)

Lloyd Lake

Reindeer Lake

Sickle Lake

Island Lake

ALBERTA

Edmonton

SASKATCHEWAN

MANITOBA

Saskatoon

Winnipeg

656 mi

740 mi

600 mi

300 mi

There are countless productive pike lakes in central and northern Canada where trophy fish are abundant. Island, Little Churchill, Sickle, Wollaston, Kasba, Reindeer, Lloyd, Athabaska and Great Slave are popular locations. First-class camps are serviced by charter aircraft out of three major cities.

resistance, making it difficult to cast, but they give it a fluttering action on the water that few pike can resist. The bug looks alive even when sitting still. Another more orthodox popper is the White Bomber, which is also tied by Bill Gallasch. This saltwater lure is usually built on a large No. 5/0 hook, but with a short shank. It has long, white saddle hackles splaying outward in breather-style and measures 5½ inches overall. The Bomber is difficult to cast, but for really large pike, it's devastating.

Learning to work poppers and streamers for pike is easy. It may be necessary to experiment with different retrieves until you find an effective one for the water being fished, and even the mood of pike on a particular day, but usually any lure that looks alive will trigger a response. Always assume that a pike is watching the bug or fly from somewhere nearby, and concentrate on giving it a provocative swim—helpless or panicked. Generally, pike prefer poppers that are fished very slowly. Let the bug rest for eight or ten seconds after falling on the surface and after the rings settle, "pop" it just once. Gently—don't overdo it. Often a fish will swim up to a bug and hang motionless just below it, waiting for the lure to show another sign of life. The next "pop" can bring a slashing strike. There is a limit to how fast a hollow-faced lure can be worked, as the design will scoop up water and slow your retrieve by sheer resistance. A skipping-type bug, on the other hand, can be skidded and bounced along at all speeds due to its bullet-like body shape. A skipper

won't make that stimulating *kachug* sound that fish home on, but it kicks up enough fuss to draw hungry pike from a long distance. It is no different from the old "injured-minnow" bass bug of yesteryear (just bigger), and that's what you need.

Generally speaking, streamer flies are fished slowly by stripping the line with foot-long hauls, but don't become monotonous. Try to vary the return with a slow start, then gradually speed the fly along to get a darting, erratic motion, at times stopping it dead in the water to sink 2 or 3 feet before moving it again. Pike will take a streamer when it is moving, as well as when sinking toward bottom. After delivering a cast, quickly take the slack out of the fly line. Your rod tip must be held *low* as you strip, so when a fish strikes, you can raise the rod and hit him hard. Northern pike have tough mouths and it takes a solid yank to set the hook. (Hook points should always be touched with a file to make certain they are sharp.) No matter how you work a retrieve, if a pike should follow the streamer without taking, speed it along faster and faster; this "runaway" movement invariably provokes a solid hit. If your first cast was properly executed, yet the fish balked, by all means try again, but if the pike is still visible, on the next cast do *not* cast too close; try to place the lure 6 or 8 feet in front of, or even beyond the fish, and work it the same way. A fast return on its nose or tail will more often frighten than attract. Pike can be coaxed back. I've had northern pike follow a fly several times before finally taking, although this seldom happens if the retrieves have already been bungled by poor presentations.

Sickle Lake

It may well be that a significant fishing record was set on Manitoba's Sickle Lake in 1982. In the course of that season, which is a four-month period, 104 northern pike, each weighing 20 pounds or more, were boated by anglers on Sickle. The largest fish caught was a 28-pounder, and the present lake record is 31 pounds. Fortunately, nearly all pike taken at Sickle Lake are released unharmed.

There is only one camp here, Sickle Lake Lodge, and the management's policy is that each visiting angler may only kill one trophy pike per trip, presumably for taxidermy purposes. Other fish, such as walleyes and whitefish, can, of course, be kept for shore lunches. But the catch-and-release program of Sickle Lake has been so well received that many fishermen never kill a northern pike during their stay, which may be one reason why most guests catch more big pike during a week's fishing than they ever dreamed existed.

Sickle Lake is a "fly-in" location about 25 air miles from the northwestern Manitoba town of Lynn Lake. Visiting anglers primarily fish the 14-mile-long lake, but there are six others nearby that can be fished from the lodge. Portages are required to reach these adjoining waters.

All the lakes hold northern pike, but the biggest fish come from Sickle. The pike season runs from the last week of May through the third week of September. Big northern pike can be caught virtually any time, but the best shallow-water action is from late May through June. During this period, heavy pike ripe with spawn frequent weedy areas, shallow coves and the mouths of streams and creeks. They are readily taken on large streamer flies, popping bugs, spoons, spinnerbaits and a host of other artificial lures. Big pike go deep from July to September. Jigs, heavy spoons, diving plugs and weighted streamers with sinking lines are most productive. During the summer months, medium-action bait-casting and spinning tackle is most popular with lines testing 10 to 20 pounds. Be sure to bring single-strand wire leaders or ones made of heavy monofilament testing 50 to 80 pounds. Heavy-duty fly rods 8½ to 9 feet long calibered for 9- or 10-weight lines are best for casting large, air-resistant pike streamers and poppers in the all too frequent strong Canadian winds. Heavy-test monofilament leader tippets are a must. Wire is unnecessary for fly-fishing so long as anglers periodically check monofilament tippets for fraying. Some visitors include a light-action spinning outfit or a light fly rod in the 7- to 8-foot length for whitefish, which are remarkably game in Canadian waters.

Sickle Lake Lodge is one of the most comfortable wilderness fishing camps in Manitoba. It is owned by Canadian Brian McIntosh, a Princeton graduate. The lodge has many of the amenities one would expect an Ivy League graduate would incorporate into a home away from home. The camp's capacity is twenty anglers. There are three cabins that each accommodate six persons, one cabin that houses two anglers. Cabins have bedrooms and sitting areas. Each is completely paneled and carpeted, and there are electricity and a shower. There also is a main lodge, complete with dining room and lounge. Anglers fish from typical Canadian 16-foot-long, V-hull aluminum skiffs. The guides are Cree Indians.

Reservations can be made by writing Sickle Lake Lodge, Box 551, Dyersburg, TN 38024; telephone (901) 627-3228. Jim Chapralis of PanAngling travel service (Suite 730, 180 North Michigan Ave., Chicago, IL 60601; telephone [312] 263-0328) is the camp's official U.S. booking agent.

Great Slave Lake

Anglers can find excellent pike fishing beginning at Hay River, Northwest Territories, at the south end of Great Slave. Hay River may be reached by car via the McKenzie Highway, and also by air. From here a variety of excursions can be assembled to suit your needs, or you can boat or fly to Brabant Island (30 miles north) to stay at Brabant Lodge, the most famous big pike spot in this territory. From these waters and ancillary Beaver Lake, northern pike in the 20-pound range can be

expected. In peak years, 25-pound fish are taken in eye-opening numbers.

Further north throughout Great Slave, major lake trout lodges, such as Arctic Star, Plummers, Frontier and others, have excellent pike fishing only occasionally sampled by guests. Invariably, the northern pike will be found at river mouth deltas and in backwater arms and bays off the main lake. In some cases, small fishing boats can motor right into these spots. In others, boats must be dragged over narrow land necks or over bars to reach the fishing. Vegetation and shallow water are the attractors. These spots are not plentiful in an area of steep drops, boulders and vast depths, and when found will rarely lack numbers of good fish.

Pike on the fly rod is an ultimate angling experience in northern Canadian waters. Tom McNally, Outdoor Editor of the Chicago Tribune, *has taken fish to 26 pounds. Manitoba and Saskatchewan are his regular beat in the spring season.*

NORTHERN PIKE

A large landing net is ideal for boating and releasing northern pike. Many anglers do the job by hand, but the possibility of injury to both the fish and the angler is much greater. Sometimes the fish can be released while it is still in the water by twisting the hook free with a pair of pliers.

Anglers seeking quantities of fish (including large specimens) can work the drop-offs with action tail jigs. The lures should be hopped over the bottom, then left at rest so the tail dressing undulates. Standup-type jig heads are good for this. Standard spoons and jigs worked in the usual ways will take fish, but not so many as the former method.

The most exciting sport is surface fishing—especially to visible fish. Conventional casters and spinning enthusiasts will be hard put to improve on swimming plugs, darters and nodders like the Zara Spook. Some days color can make a difference. Include yellow, red-and-white and a selection of more subdued tones in your lure selection. Combine big fish and sight-fishing in ultra-clear water with a fly rod and you have the ultimate in sport with *Esox lucius.* If they are in the mood, pike will hit surface fly rod lures—hair bugs, popping and skipping bugs. Work the poppers quite slowly, swim the hair bugs steadily and bring the skipping attractors back smartly in brisk stop-and-go fashion. Though big bass-size bugs are effective, saltwater-size surface lures are even better.

However, a selection of long streamers should not be forgotten because northern pike of the Arctic will often take subsurface offerings only. In clear water, flashy Mylar is not a requisite, but you do want at least a few patterns that tail out and snake through the water. One of the more successful ties is the New Zealand Bunny fly made totally of fur. The fly is simply a strip of 1/8-inch-wide mink, rabbit or other fur on the hide. The strip is placed on the hook shank back, tied in near the bend, then palmer-wrapped forward to create a full body with the tail section extending back past the bend. It is important to have black Bunnies, but carry them in light contrasting colors as well. The 600 Series Aztec flies work well in red-and-yellow and black-and-yellow, with silver body on No. 3/0 hooks and 5-inch-long wings. Include some patterns with monofilament weed guards.

Waskaiowaka Lake

Located about 600 miles north of Winnipeg, Manitoba, 70,000-acre Waskaiowaka Lake is part of the Churchill River watershed. A fly-in camp,

156

Little Churchill Lake Lodge, serviced out of the town of Thompson, offers excellent cabin accommodations for anglers seeking large pike in quantity. The camp owner, Mike Dyste, dictates a trophy-only policy allowing just one fish to be killed per trip, which has resulted in quality sport with pike from 10 to 15 pounds common; in one recent season over 500 northerns exceeding 15 pounds (fish up to 30 pounds have been recorded) were caught, yet only 15 were killed for trophy mounts. Sound conservation practices coupled with the lake's remote location should maintain this fishery for years to come.

In addition to northern pike, walleyes are numerous in Waskaiowaka and are taken in its tributaries, especially in the spring season (June) when great shoals appear in the rivers for spawning. Lake whitefish are abundant in Little Churchill River and offer fine sport on light spinning, or fly tackle.

Reservations and information can be obtained by contacting Little Churchill Lodge, Route 1, Church's Ferry, North Dakota; telephone (701) 466-2850; or by contacting its United States agent.

WALLEYE

Stizostedion vitreum

In 1812, a Jesuit priest, ever mindful of his parishoners' Friday vows, stocked the Chemung River (a tributary to the north branch of the Susquehanna) with a wagonload of walleyes at Newtown (now Elmira), New York. History does not record how many fish the Good Father released, but their subsequent reproduction was so successful that the river system literally swarmed with "Susquehanna salmon." Among early European settlers several fish species of great table value were called salmon, but the popularity of the walleye has endured. On any weekend between mid-June and mid-July, 10,000 boats of all sizes invade the western basin of Lake Erie for an annual vendetta that will result in the capture of 3,000,000 walleyes. The exact dates and numbers of participants may vary, but this frenzied scene is duplicated in waters all over the American Midwest and north into Canada. This homely fish with eyes like moon marbles, and whose fighting style consists of occasional wiggles, is a classic food, the *doré* of French-speaking Canada, that ultimate ingredient in a *quenelle de brochet*, the "yellow pike" in a feathery light gefilte fish, and the traditional reason for lighting a fire at noon throughout the bush country. Although classed as a game fish, the walleye is preeminently a glorious panfish with a hungry audience counted in the millions.

The *Sitzostedion* genus has European as well as North American species and is the largest member of the perch family. There are three fish in North America. In addition to yellow walleye (*S. vitreum vitreum*), there is the subspecies blue walleye or blue pike (*Sitzostedion v. glaucum*), which is not related to the pike, and the smaller sauger (*S. canadense*). Blue pike were originally in Canada and Lake Erie and have that coloration. Walleye can usually be distinguished by a white or ivory tip to the lower fork of the tail fin, but sauger occasionally show it too.

The name walleye refers to the *tapetum lucidum*,

Walleyes are the North American equivalent of Europe's zander, *a generalized predator of small fish such as shiners. The glazed eye is due to a* tapetum lucidum, *which improves crepuscular and nighttime vision, just as it does in cats.*

WALLEYE

a layer on the retina that reflects light, so the rods that make for superior black-and-white vision in dim light will have a second opportunity to see whatever light has entered the lens. At night, their eyes glow like a cat's. The implications of this capability are two. One fishes for walleye with great expectations at dawn, dusk and night and, when daylight is bright on the water, walleye will take refuge in deep water or in shaded water. Stained or murky water is shaded, and so is windswept water and weedy water. Walleye guides tend to become nervous on clear, calm days.

Hook-and-line have taken walleye to 25 pounds (from Old Hickory Lake, Tennessee, in 1960; it was 41 inches long), and biologists have netted slightly larger fish, but anglers tend to take fish of 1 to 4 pounds. An 18-inch walleye is about a 2-pounder. A 14-pounder should be a yard long. That is a *lot* of perch.

DISTRIBUTION

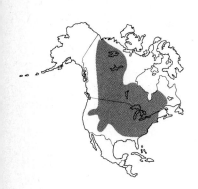

Before North America went berserk for impoundments, walleyes were considered deep-water fish of oligotrophic lakes (deep, cold, generally of glacial origin), but when bass fishermen began venturing into the woody or weedy shallows of impoundments intended primarily to generate electricity or store irrigation water, they often came out with walleyes. These anglers are on Lake Sharpe in South Dakota.

Walleyes are an early spring spawner, sometimes under the ice but usually shortly after ice-out. They spawn at night, schooled in clear and shallow water over gravel or rubble bottom. The female deposits 25,000 to 50,000 eggs per pound of weight. There is no parental care. The spawning site itself can be a stream or a lake. Hatching comes in a dozen or more days and, as soon as the egg sac is absorbed, the tiny fish seeks a deep-water sanctuary.

The yellow walleyes, though they often live in lakes, are a stream spawner and will migrate hundreds of miles to spawn. They are the giants of the genus. The little blue pike spawn in lakes. Sauger presumably spawn in both habitats. Now it gets a bit sticky: They all three will naturally hybridize.

Walleye glass minnows feed on cladocerans and other zooplankters, but graduate swiftly to minnows smaller than themselves. This is apt to be baby yellow perch, which normally hatch later than walleyes. These two perciformes are locked in a danse macabre. Over much of their natural range, walleyes would be unthinkable without yellow perch. Large walleyes, of course, are not interested in baby yellow perch. They are interested in big yellow perch, wherever they are available. Southern walleye populations make do with various shads and shiners, and Canadian walleyes wolf whitefish, mooneyes and the like. If it swims, walleyes will eat it, but oddly enough they are also dedicated entomophages. In spring

and summer, whole populations can be dependent on mayfly nymphs.

A scenario for walleye feeding in a typical lake would be mayflies in the spring, because they are actively moving about as nymphs before they hatch, and because most of the year-class of baitfish from last year became walleye fodder last year. This is why otherwise persnickety game fish are easiest to catch in spring. There is not a lot of baitfish available and predators must get a wiggle on if they are to satisfy their post-spawn appetite. A pair of mayfly nymphs impaled in a cruciform pattern on a small hook and fished under a bobber in fairly shallow water should do it for bait fishermen, but soaking bait is at a disadvantage when searching for an active predator. (Impaling hellgrammites, mayfly nymphs and caddis larvae in a cross allows them to be perceived as a double item, and allows both to wiggle independently. Mayfly nymphs are known as "wigglers" in the bait trade.) Fly-fishing large nymph patterns would be preferable, but just as southern largemouth bass fishermen are wedded to casting artificial lures, midwestern walleye fishermen are bait fanatics.

By summer the yellow perch young-of-the-year have grown large enough to be a fish rather than a glass minnow. They will be schooling in huge, dense formations and everything that eats meat will decimate them—walleyes, pike, muskellunge and the survivors of earlier yellow perch year-

classes. This widespread availability of food means poor fishing as a rule. With the summer sun overhead, clear-water walleyes will feed at twilight or at night.

By autumn the yellow perch are sharply reduced in numbers, but summer-spawning bait, such as shiners and shads, will be big enough to supplant them in the diet where available, which is likely to be in the walleye's southern range. In Canadian and midwestern waters, the end of the perch glut means hungry walleyes actively searching, and improved fishing.

Winter means ice fishing for walleyes up north, but in the southern range they will be active in big "bass" impoundments, which tend to have hodgepodge populations of black basses, muskellunge, striped bass, white bass/striped bass hybrids, rainbow and brown trout (often ignored by local anglers) and walleye (*usually* ignored by locals). Southern walleye in winter receive more attention from tourist anglers from the latitude of Minneapolis than from Dixie bass fishermen. The Yankee visitors would enjoy better sport shortly before the spring spawning runs, but at least in winter there is no glut of bait to make fishing exceptionally difficult.

In spring, if you find at day's end that few fishermen can report a caught walleye (in a lake of good reputation), you may have intercepted the spawn itself. The males spend approximately two weeks in the spawning area—or often in a number of them, traveling from one area to another looking for ripe females. The big females are thought to spawn swiftly, perhaps overnight. Eating goes on until the spawn and is avid shortly after it, but during those two weeks it is far better to seek another target species and leave walleyes alone with their seasonal lockjaw.

Color is the least reliable means of identifying fish species, and, of course, is the means we all use constantly. The stream-spawning yellow walleye is often olivaceous to olive-brown, but sometimes comes in a gray color resulting from a blue cast to its protective mucus. In Ontario, occasional orange mutants have been reported. The blue walleye is slate blue on the back, silvery on the flanks and has white pelvic fins. There is no differentiation (that we can perceive) between walleye sexes by color or morphology; but blue walleye have larger eyes than the yellow and they are mounted higher on the head.

One morphological characteristic that should be borne in mind is the presence on the opercle, the gill cover, of at least one sharp, short spine, a potential line and finger slasher. Since there are teeth everywhere in the head, from jaws to vomer,

WALLEYE

premaxillaries, palatines, even pharyngeal teeth and on the gill arches, just where you take hold of a walleye deserves consideration. A number of other fish in both fresh and salt water have a cutting edge or spine on the gill covers. I have long pondered the evolutionary import of this feature, and now believe some underwater photographs of smallmouth bass taken by William Roston perhaps account for it. When a bass takes a minnow or lure, one of its schoolmates will position next to its opercle in hope of capturing any bait that succeeds in wriggling out the gill opening. This is evidently a fairly frequent occurrence; many fishermen have reported catching two fish at a time, one strung through the gills and another on the hook.

Walleyes are a schooling fish, but the association is loose and also curious in that it is not necessarily confined to themselves: white suckers (*Catostomus commersoni*) have been observed participating in the school. Walleyes are not strongly migratory except during their spawning period (when they travel at night), and are seldom far from a major food form during the rest of the year. If your boat's electronics are indicating dense schools of yellow perch, tullibee, threadfin shad or whatever the predominant local baitfish, walleyes will be nearby.

Sexual maturity in male yellow walleyes is thought to be at two to four years, and in females at three to six years. The male will be 11 inches or more and the female will be 14 inches to 1½ feet. Killing immature walleyes for use as panfish is therefore damaging to the resource. These fish can last as long as twenty years in the northern range

and a dozen in the south. Spawning will take place at 42° to 52°F (most often at 44° to 48°F), and the act will involve from a single couple to a pair of big females and as many as six males. They have been observed swimming in circles, jostling, chasing each other and generally becoming quite frenzied prior to the spawn. During the act itself, walleyes will go into water so shallow that the female must roll on her side to disseminate eggs.

There are walleye populations from the Beaufort Sea near the Alaska border in Canada's Northwest Territories down to Gulf Coast states in the Old Confederacy. The Columbia River drainage in the Pacific Northwest has a large and growing fishery for introduced stock, and southcentral Arizona has walleyes an easy drive out of Phoenix, not far from the Mexican border. Nevertheless, our perception of them as a fish of the midwestern heartland is correct; the densest populations occur there.

That is the yellow walleye's distribution. The blue is an entirely different matter. It is considered as rare or even possibly extinct by some commentators, who evidently believe that hybridization with yellow walleye has submerged it into the yellow population. Nevertheless, James Little, a biologist for the Tennessee Wildlife Resources Agency, has for years monitored an introduced stock of blue walleyes at Dale Hollow Reservoir, that giant impoundment straddling the Tennessee-Kentucky border. They have hybridized with the local strain of yellow walleye where their ranges overlapped, so there are now three distinct populations—two pure and one hybrid. It would be a shame to lose the blue, though it is quite a small fish, often smaller than even sauger. At its maximum age of eleven, blue walleye will not quite reach 15 inches.

A piscine biomass of such enormous numbers and distribution was subject to commercial exploitation from the beginning of European man in North America. It is probably the most commercially valuable freshwater food fish. And, as invariably happens with a resource that can be converted into money, walleyes have been outrageously overexploited. In 1956, for instance, American and Canadian commercial fishermen took 24,000,000 pounds of walleye out of Lake Erie alone. That was the peak of production and the fishery promptly collapsed. The netters continued to remove ever-declining catches until they were banned from the lake in 1970. Without their ministrations, in just six years the population bounced back. Erie is at present as close to a guaranteed-catch walleye hot spot as sportsmen are ever likely to find.

Lake Erie, a refreshened reincarnation of its formerly polluted and commercially overfished self, is the No. 1 walleye producer in the U.S. On summer weekends, you can almost walk from boat to boat, all catching fish.

Tackle and Techniques

Angling for walleye was a small lake or close-to-shore affair under oars, and largely remained that way after the outboard motor became ubiquitous, although the muscle tone of walleye anglers deteriorated. But in approximately twenty-five years, the compact, portable sonar joined the outboard motor on board and it became easy to find offshore reefs previously hidden. Deep-water fishing with jigs and back trolling, sinker-bait combinations became popular. (Back trolling slows the progress of the skiff to a crawl; walleyes are largely disinterested in speeding bait.) Recent fuel shortages inspired the rediscovery of drifting with minnows, nightcrawlers or the newly popular leeches, and bass fishermen combing a shoreline with plugs and spinnerbaits have relearned the lesson of their grandfathers: there are walleyes in the shallow weed beds, especially at night. Any fish that will take a lure will take a fly, but walleye fishermen tend to be more interested in fillets than sport—it is, after all, a species desperately wanting in wiggle—so I doubt if walleye fly-fishing is an idea whose time is imminent.

Dakota Reservoirs

In the center of the North American continent lies a land reminiscent of gunfighters, prairie dogs, tumbleweeds and dusty prairies. Until a few years ago, "walleye" was a foreign word to most Dakotans, but the construction of new reservoirs changed the fishing scene dramatically. Today the Missouri River system produces an awesome amount of big walleyes. It is not rare to catch a two-man limit of ten fish that weigh upward of 60 pounds. Catches like this can be had within a few hours and because of the immense size of these reservoirs, there are areas that have yet to see a fishing boat.

A gourmet food base and prime habitat are the most prominent reasons why the river's walleye population has skyrocketed. Up until a few years ago, perch were about the only forage the walleyes had. Then the fish and game department started stocking spottail shiners and rainbow smelt, offering the walleyes a smorgasbord.

From western Montana down through North and South Dakota you will find five main river reservoirs that offer literally hundreds of miles of fishable water. All have excellent fishing. Getting on the lakes is no problem; there are launching ramps available and more are being built all the time. However, it is advisable to obtain a Corps of

The Dakota reservoir system is noted for excellent pike fishing, but there are also quantities of walleye that die of old age.

Engineers map showing the accesses.

Fishing seems to be good to excellent nearly anyplace and anytime but, of course, there are times of the year, areas, structures and presentations that are most productive. Early spring finds the walleyes congregating downstream from the dams. This is where they find prime spawning conditions. Since the water is cold and the fish lethargic, they will hold in slack water areas. The best spots are those with about 14 feet of water and just a little bit of current. You will find these pockets below wing dams, on the downstream side of islands, behind fallen trees, rock piles, etc. In some areas the walleyes spawn in tributaries, but not all reservoirs have inflowing tributaries so the fish make do with what they have.

As summer warms, the walleyes will move up in the shallows on points and flats. The best ones are those in the mid- to upper sections of the reservoir near spawning areas. The fish in these areas have eating in mind. This movement coincides with the spawning of many baitfish and the hungry walleyes quickly make up for their own spawning fast.

As summer progresses, walleyes gradually move to deeper structural elements. On Lake Sharp (the middle reservoir), walleyes are deep flat-orientated by mid-June. By mid-July, they usually head for still deeper water. There are some exceptions. On the reservoirs that do not have expansive flats, such as lower Oahe, parts of Lakes Francis, Case, Sakakawea and Fort Peck, the fish will use more typical summer walleye haunts such as drop-offs and breaklines.

Late fall finds walleyes moving back toward the dams and congregating in the tailwater sections.

WALLEYE

On their way upstream, the fish may stop to feed around deep cuts, steep drop-offs and flat edges. Don't be afraid to fish these spots; the Game and Fish Commission reports regularly taking fall walleyes at depths in excess of 40 feet.

Good fishing usually begins in mid-April and runs well into November or later. Early season anglers find their best success with a flathead minnow into the spawning areas. White is by far the most productive color, with yellow/chartreuse running a close second.

Remember, these shallow water walleyes are skittish, so be quiet. The ideal is to creep to within casting distance with an electric trolling motor and make long casts to the fish. With a little caution and skill you will take good numbers of fish from water as shallow as 2 to 3 feet.

Once the fish have moved deeper, a 'crawler harness (Lindy Rigs or Flikker Snells) tipped with 'crawlers or minnows reaps the best results. Since the fish are normally between 10 and 25 feet deep, you can either drift or troll to present the bait. If

This could be a yellow walleye, a blue walleye, a sauger or a hybrid of any of the above. In all cases, they are often lacking in wiggle, entertainingly moody and invariably delicious.

the fish are stacked up on top of an underwater point, try anchoring up higher on the point and casting to the depths, bringing your bait up to the fish.

In late summer, speed trolling is favored. Even though rock, gravel and sand points exist by the score, your best fishing is often found around shale points. The local favorites are the Hot'n'Tot and Snipe, although others take their fair share of fish, too.

In fall, the fish are less aggressive but run larger, so throw them something big. When the fish are

along steep breaks and drop-offs, use a Lindy Rig baited with a 5- or 6-inch minnow. In tailwater sections, use a three-eighths- to three-quarter-ounce jig tipped with a big minnow. Jigs with a stand-up head are easier to handle in moving water.

Greers Ferry Lake

Covering some 40,000 acres of the eastern foothills of the Ozark Mountains, Greers Ferry is the current favorite to overturn the world record 25-pound walleye. Specimens have already been taken on sporting tackle up to 22 pounds, 11 ounces, but even bigger fish have been documented by fisheries personnel while netting to gather eggs and milt for hatchery use. A national fishing contest, scheduled to coincide with the spring spawning runs, has become an annual event, putting sufficient interest in the walleye to make it likely that when the record falls it will happen here (worth a sizable cash reward for the angler who finally finds the big one).

Basically a mountain lake, Greers Ferry is deep and rocky. The upper portion is favored by spawning-period anglers under normal water conditions due to the three main tributaries that drain into the section. The Devil's Fork, Middle Fork and South Fork of the Little Red River all offer prime spawning grounds. Also located along the upper reaches are steep points and bluffs, submerged islands and deep coves. In essence, the upper end offers a wide divergence of water and fishing opportunity, which makes it a favorite with early season anglers. Later in the season there is less pleasure boating here as well.

The lower portion of the lake has broad expanses of relatively shallow water, substantial amounts of standing brush and timber, and numerous mud banks. Less affected by turbidity than the upper reaches, this sector is a favorite with fishermen in search of clear water. Due to the distance from the tributaries, temperatures fluctuate less and more slowly.

Most trophy hunters favor the forks of the Little Red and work them from February until early April with white or yellow jigs tipped with small minnows, deep running crankbaits or light jig-and-grub combinations. Running well upstream, often being forced to dodge rocky shoals, these fishermen concentrate on deeper pools and runs. Some favor the jigs, but a large portion use a plug like the long-billed 4½-inch Rebel in chrome and black for clear water and burnt orange for turbid conditions. These baits are worked deeply on a

164

slow retrieve (at least 10 to 12 feet).

Tactics change after the spawn. Nightcrawlers come into use. Whether fished from shore or by dropping the bait over the side of a boat, the crawler is weighted with only a small split shot and worked patiently along steep points and bluffs adjacent to the main body of the lake. Results are frequently substantial from a numbers standpoint, although few really large walleye are caught after the spawn. Most of the fish taken during the warm months range from 1 to 3 pounds.

When the fish move out of the 6- to 12-foot water and into the depths as temperatures rise, they generally hold just above the thermocline, which may extend as far as 35 feet below the surface. Jigging spoons and live bait will produce here, but trolling is the preferred method. This is also prime time for the lower reaches of the lake when pleasure boating allows the angler to work slowly over good locations. Electronic depthfinders can save hours of hunting under these conditions.

Possibly because walleye fishing is still fairly new in this part of the world, downriggers are not often employed on Greers Ferry. Those proficient in their use are among the most successful during the mid-summer period, frequently using the same type and color plugs used in the spring. The old standard Junebug-spinner-and-nightcrawler and other traditional walleye rigs are also good bets when teamed with downriggers.

With the present state record safely in hand, the regulars on Greers Ferry and fisheries biologists agree that not only does the lake have the potential to break the 25-pound mark, the fish is already there waiting for the right lure at the right place.

Dale Hollow Lake

Perched on the Tennessee-Kentucky border, this 61-mile-long lake with its 25,000 acres may be one of the best-kept secrets of walleye fishing. Long known as a waterway which produces oversized smallmouth bass, and more recently trophy muskellunge and even lake trout, Dale Hollow, in fact, has a double-barreled fishery for these deep-water dwellers. After impoundment, the runs of native walleye declined and stocking programs were initiated to hopefully offset the falling numbers, but a problem with water quality due to strip mines in the area hindered the reintroduction. When the pollution had been successfully controlled, these native stream-spawning yellow walleye returned under their own

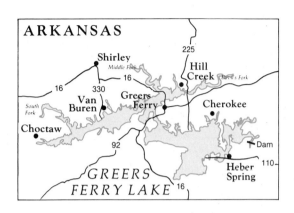

Biologists at Greers Ferry Lake have netted spawning-run walleyes that exceed the 25-pound world record.

power and it was found that shipments of fingerlings from New York and Wisconsin were lake spawners, or blue walleyes. These fish were successfully reproducing out in the main body of the lake before anyone fully realized their existence.

In the years immediately following impoundment, some huge fish were taken. During that first decade, the total of 20-pound and better fish was substantial but not well documented, and although few in this range are seen now, the number of 10-pound-plus fish is such that one will not impress a dock operator.

Top fishing is done during the spawning runs. The stream runners spawn from early March through early May and from mid-February through mid-April for the open water variety. For the former, the top spot is the East Fork of the Obey River, one of the two main tributaries of the lake where a combination of clean, moving water and proper bottom configuration draws huge numbers of gravid females and attendant males. Most other major arteries of Dale Hollow have similar, if smaller, runs. Out on the open water, lake spawners show up in greater numbers in the area from the Corps of Engineers' campground at Willow Grove downstream to the dam.

The yellow walleye prefer the deeper runs and pools of the incoming river and receive more attention than their lake-dwelling brethren, both due to a tradition of fishing here and lack of access and know-how for taking the newer variety. Along the East Fork, jigs are the first choice of most fishermen, followed closely by live bait. Deep-running plugs, spinner-and-worm combinations and other productive lures are seldom seen.

Lake spawners can be found around submerged islands, humps, bars and steep points on the big water and are taken on jigs when wind conditions allow. Many times, however, it is necessary to use crankbaits which can be worked down 10 to 15

165

WALLEYE

Dale Hollow contains both yellow and blue walleye strains and *hybrids of the two. Furthermore, the bass-oriented local anglers leave all three of these populations largely undisturbed.*

feet on light line, a method which may require either casting or trolling according to dictates of the weather.

During the warm-weather months the fish go deep, staying near the thermocline and making the angler probe depths of 40 feet or more. Trolling is the generally accepted method at such times with downriggers and electronic depthfinders giving a definite edge to the well-educated angler. Lures used at the extreme depths vary; some anglers prefer spinner/crawler combinations, while others opt for spoons or small, chrome-and-black plugs. Big jigging spoons account for a number of heavyweight fish on a year-'round basis for a handful of fishermen. Locating a general fishing area during the mid-year months is relatively simple since best results come from the area of open water near the dam.

Due to Dale Hollow's deep, cool water, there is generally decent fishing lakewide except during the heat of mid-summer and again during the spawn, as fish move up on gravel or rock points late in the day or after dark to forage on shad and alewives. This means they are in reach of even the casual caster.

Gouin Reservoir

When Quebec's provincial government built a dam across the La Loutre Rapids on the Upper St. Maurice River, it created a 500-square-mile reservoir holding some 1,750,000 gallons of water; at the same time, it also created an angling paradise.

Today, almost seven decades later, Gouin Reservoir, located in the heart of Quebec's hinterland, continues to provide some of the finest walleye and northern pike fishing to be found in North America. If that seems a strong statement to make, consider this: Until 1972 commercial

fishermen annually netted some 3,000 pounds of pike and walleye without making a dent in the stocks of fish. The few anglers who fish the inland sea these days don't even come close to the commercial harvest.

Walleye are exceptionally plentiful with average fish weighing between 3 and 4 pounds. Pike are considered a nuisance by walleye anglers. Pike of 15 to 20 pounds are caught regularly and fish of 30 to 35 pounds turn up every year. Prime time for walleye is early to mid-summer, while pike bite best in late summer. However, even in the second half of summer anglers can catch their limits easily; it just means they have to work a little harder at it.

From the opening of the season in the third week of May to about mid-June, the schools of walleye are still congregated in shallow bays where they spawned, but as summer progresses they move gradually toward the main body of the reservoir where they can be found around rocky islands and off points. Most anglers troll until they find a school of walleye, then anchor and cast to the spot.

One of the best rigs on the Gouin Reservoir is a nightcrawler on tandem hooks with a medium-sized, gold-and-silver hammer finish, Junebug spinner half a foot ahead of it and a small rubber-core sinker to get it down to the bottom where the fish are. Once a school has been located, almost any spinner salted with a bit of worm will catch fish.

Many corners of Gouin Reservoir are as yet unexplored, partially because anglers haven't yet found it necessary to strike out for the unknown and partially because only a few areas of this vast, island-studded maze are accessible. Vison, Markel and Déziel Bay near the La Loutre dam are heavily fished. A lumber road follows the northeast side for a few miles and the shoreline is administered by Hydro-Quebec which kindly turns a blind eye on anglers who camp there. Keep in mind that there are no facilities available.

On the southwest side, the Club de la Baie du Marmette has cabins, boats and motors available, but the area is accessible only by float plane. For details and reservations, write to Club de la Baie du Marmette, P.O. Box 317, Saint Sauveur des Monts, Quebec, Canada J0R 1R0.

There is no easy way to reach the Gouin Reservoir by road, but the least arduous is to drive to La Tuque and then approximately 60 miles by lumber road to the La Loutre dam site, a five-hour drive at the best of times. Alternately, anglers can drive to Parent and fly in in a chartered float plane.

Topographical maps 32B-6 through 32B-11 plus 32B-15 cover most of the Gouin Reservoir.

Siouxland Walleyes After Dark

For Sioux Indians, the whisper of migrating waterfowl signaled a time to pull summer camp and leave the lakes of northwest Iowa in search of fall jerky. Today those same V formations of ducks and geese are like a semaphore alerting fall anglers to the arrival of large walleyes.

All too often the weekend fishermen visiting this unique cluster of prairie lakes surrounding Okoboji, Iowa, return home convinced the legend of the giant Iowa walleye is just another Indian myth promoted by the local chamber of commerce. Seek out the tight-lipped natives. Ask to see their freezers stacked like cordwood with 5- to 10-pound walleye, and you realize there is truth in this legend.

The techniques passed down from father to son are treated with greater security than any government document stamped TOP SECRET. Next to method, the secrecy is extended to knowledge of the time and place of local walleye action. Information is shared in the privacy of the home. Discussion in local coffee shops is limited to a nod and a wink of the eye, but never an admission of numbers, sizes, location or time. Discovered and refined by the test of time, it is the uniqueness of their methods that sets these walleye specialists apart. A rundown of their tactics will produce walleye and other species, such as bass, muskellunge and northern pike. Here are the secrets to be applied.

Use insulated waders, not boats. Study the topography maps and work the rocky points that permit shoreline approaches. One of the most reliable clues to finding concentrations of fish will be the telltale "frog slicks" observed on the roads paralleling the water. As cold weather approaches, frogs leave the high ground and, as they cross the road in designated areas, the highway traffic strikes and kills a certain percentage. When you spot these frog slicks, rest assured that game fish will be lying just offshore waiting.

Aside from insulated underwear, now is the time to change equipment as well. The natives spool clear, colorless monos and never in a test heavier than 8-pound, with 4- to 6-pound preferred. Wire leaders are not used, although very small black wireform snaps are permissible and allow lure change without having to turn on a flashlight.

Artificial lights are used only in emergencies. Most anglers will wear a small light clipped on their caps to free both hands. When need forces them to turn on the lights they always turn and face away from the water first. Experience has shown that an errant flashlight broadcast across the water will destroy fishing action for the next hour.

Because these fish have excellent vibration detection as well as night vision, the shallow water angler must discipline himself not to betray his presence. As cruising walleye approach these shallows, they work their way in cautiously. The shuffle of a fisherman's boots on the sand/rock bottom is instantly telegraphed and a mass exodus follows. By the same token, weeds fouled on retrieved lures are not slapped off in the water. They are silently picked off.

Because the very best fishing is found after dark, and just before winter freeze-up, the angler must come mentally prepared. Patience is a virtue. Anglers will cast for hours without a strike only to limit out when a 15-minute feeding frenzy ignites the area. Weather fronts moving in accelerate the action.

Ice in the guides is a constant frustration. To minimize the problem, the locals have found that incorporating a blood knot or a very small black swivel several feet ahead of the lure will knock out the ice on the retrieve. It also serves as a handy reminder when fishing under these pitch-black conditions.

So long as the desire exists, trophy-size walleyes will continue to be caught in this fishing and hunting ground of the Sioux.

The walleye's eyeshine means it is a predator, specialized for night (at dusk it is already night under water). Move softly on a northern Iowa lake at sundown. It helps to have a spouse at home who believes fishing should be fruitful as well as recreational.

MUSKELLUNGE

Esox masquinongy

While it is a fact that Europe grows larger pike than North America in a specific sense, for *Esox lucius* is the pike of legend, only in the New World do we find its giant clone, the muskellunge. This whimsical king of the weed empire has been recorded to more than 100 pounds and a length of 6 feet. It would seem to be one of Nature's extravagances in the post-glacial age. But, if in fantasy we see an evil predator with a mouthful of recurved cardiform and canine teeth, in reality, *Esox masquinongy* is one of those unique North American game fish that requires stamina as well as study for angling success. On a rare day you may luck upon a muskellunge. However, you can also win a million dollar lottery with equal effort. The masters of this game often lapse into protracted maundering among themselves, yet muskellunge lore has an inexorability that is time-tested, if not always predictable.

Muskellunge are found in Alabama, Illinois, Indiana, Iowa, Kentucky, Michigan, Minnesota, Missouri, New Jersey, New York, North Carolina, North Dakota, Ohio, Pennsylvania, Tennessee, Vermont, Virginia, West Virginia and Wisconsin. In Canada, sizable populations occur in Quebec, Ontario and Manitoba. Their range is constantly being extended by fish and game departments which have come to recognize that (a) an enormous biomass of prey species annually dies of old age and (b) muskellunge are one of the fastest-growing fish in fresh water; at six months a muskellunge may be 8 inches in length, at age two it can reach 18 inches, and a five-year-old may be 30 inches long and weigh 7 pounds. Furthermore, a locale that offers productive muskellunge fishing inevitably has a healthy tourism industry. It is estimated that 25 percent of Wisconsin's tourists are muskellunge fishermen. In most states, 30 inches is the legal minimum for killing one, and possession limits are low. However, this is a trophy fish that graces more walls than tables. This was not always so as the "white salmon" of early

Eye sockets that are mounted dorsally have evolved on the skull, indicating that the muskellunge, the largest of the world's pike species, feeds upward. This puts floating life forms in peril and makes fishing with surface plugs advantageous—and thrilling.

MUSKELLUNGE

Midwest settlers was considered a prize food fish, which indeed it is.

One pioneer Midwesterner reported he had three quarters of a ton of muskellunge salted down, and considered one hundred 3- to 6-pounders a good day's catch. For 1890 alone Ontario figures show 651,406 pounds in the commercial catch, mostly from one lake. When this huge natural population of muskellunge had been reduced to where it was no longer economically worthwhile to net them, governments began yielding to angling interests and the new conservation ethic. They became a sport fish in Ontario in 1904, though Quebec didn't stop netting until 1936.

Hatcheries began in Wisconsin by the turn of the century and on New York's Chautauqua Lake in 1904. These pioneer pisciculturists learned that what had been so readily swept from the waters was going to be expensive to replace, for muskellunge will not take dead food. Whether in a hatchery or the wild, fry absorb their egg sac in about ten days and begin feeding on large, live zooplankton for one to three weeks, then they become piscivorous fish. The problems of a hatchery manager are to feed millions of water fleas to the young hatchlings and then provide them with millions of carp fry. Any failure in the food supply and they promptly eat each other. It takes about 6,000,000 food fish to produce 8,000 9-inch muskellunge. Juvenile cannibalism is common in the wild, too. Almost everything in their habitat with fins consumes baby muskellunge; survival rates are very low from the beginning.

They spawn in shallow water in spring, usually at night, when water temperature reaches 49° to 55°F. The spawning menage would typically be a large female accompanied by two males. There is no nest because they spawn on the move, dispersing the eggs over hundreds of yards of shore. Commonly only 30 to 35 percent of the eggs will even be successfully fertilized; but a 30-pound female might disperse four quarts of eggs. Those that manage to hatch find their environment is full of hungry northern pike fingerlings a few weeks older than they. The devastation that results is believed to contribute to the relative paucity of the species where it is dependent on natural reproduction.

The fixity with which muskellunge focus on their prey is a contributing factor in becoming prey themselves. While aligning their body for a whiplash dart at a victim they can be closely approached. Both as juvenile and adult, the muskellunge takes prey as the rest of their genus—amidships, pinning the catch in those canines and as a rule promptly returning to the concealment from which they launched the attack. This is never far because they are not physiologically prepared for long chases. The *Esox* are a sprint fish with literally blinding speed in sizes up to 18 inches. When concealment has been resumed, the muskellunge works his catch around until it is pointing down his throat. In this process some inevitable desquamation takes place, leading to an old tale that the pike family scale their dinner before eating it. Muskellunge who try to ingest spiny-rayed fish tail first would get their dinner caught in their throat, so everything is swallowed head first, including soft-rayed fish.

Muskellunge eat what swims in front of them when they are in a feeding mode, which seems to happen only after prior digestion is complete, for it is rare to clean a caught muskellunge with food in its stomach. They have no problem swallowing prey half their own size, so a 15-inch trussed sucker or lure would be an attractive angling possibility for 30-inch muskellunge. Observation of the fish in captivity indicates it will consistently refuse to take prey that seems wounded or sick. They will eat anything as long as it is healthy—and they are hungry. It requires 5 to 7 pounds of forage fish to put 1 pound of weight on a muskellunge, so a 40-pounder requires 280 pounds of dietary support.

Since the absence of a feeding mode will affect part of the population at the time you are on the water, and muskellunge population density on a superior lake will be only two fish per acre (less on typical lakes), there is a lot of water between catchable fish. Nevertheless, outstanding catches have occurred in modern times. On Leech Lake, Minnesota, in one week of July 1955, fishermen caught 140 muskellunge weighing up to 44 pounds (the expected ratio is two fish lost for every one boated). In two of those days, 55 muskellunge were caught. The rampage tapered off during the next week to finally total 163 muskellunge. This was after weeks of hot, humid, windless weather. One theory is that the weather brought whitefish and tullibee to the surface, triggering a muskellunge feeding spree.

DISTRIBUTION

Netted muskellunge from the Great Lakes have been reported to more than 100 pounds, but not authenticated. The *Lakeland Times* of Minocqua, Wisconsin, reported in its May 1, 1902, edition:

LARGEST MUSKALLONGE EVER CAPTURED!

Supt. Nevin of the State Fish Hatchery Commissioners, who has been taking muskallonge spawn at the Tomahawk and Minocqua lakes the past month, informes us that E. D. Kennedy and himself captured the two largest muskallonge ever taken in these waters. The largest one was caught in Minocqua Lake, and weighed 102 pounds, the other being taken in Tomahawk lake and weighed 80 pounds. After the spawn was taken from these monsters they were turned back into their native waters where they await the sportsman to try and get them. Mr. Nevin has taken muskallonge spawn at this place for the past four years, and says that in seining . . .

The largest rod-and-reel catch to date is 1 ounce short of 70 pounds, caught in 1957 on the St. Lawrence River. The tiger muskellunge, a largely sterile hybrid of muskellunge and northern pike that occurs naturally and is induced in hatcheries, has been caught to a bit more than 51 pounds in 1919 from Lac Vieux Desert on the Wisconsin-Michigan border. The tiger muskellunge, incidentally, is becoming a favorite of fisheries biologists because it can be reared easily in hatcheries and has a growth potential of 28 inches in just two years.

Muskellunge are a wholly freshwater fish at present, but the scenario for their presence and distribution in North America began with their entry into the Mississippi drainage from the sea. Fossilized muskellunge teeth have been found. They are absent from Europe now, which has only the pike, but southern European deposits dated to the Tertiary contain fossil Esocidae. Three subspecies of muskellunge have been identified in the past. Basically a Minnesota-Wisconsin-Michigan-Ontario-Manitoba fish (*Esox masquinongy immaculatus*), called the northern or tiger muskellunge (the latter name now preempted by the pike-muskellunge hybrid), a St. Lawrence River-Great Lakes basin fish (*Esox m. masquinongy*), and an Ohio River basin-Eastern Seaboard fish (*Esox m. ohioensis*). Supposedly they varied in the color pattern of their barring or spotting, but since then the Ohio River form has been introduced into Lake Erie and so many hatcheries are at work propagating muskellunge

that trying to maintain trinomial identification is probably hopeless. The fish can swiftly be differentiated in the field from other Esocidae. Its color markings are dark on a light background whereas pike's are light on a dark background, *usually*. It is more reliable to count the mandibular pores on each ventral surface of the lower jaw. Muskellunge will have six or more pores on each side of the jaw, pike five or less. It is untrustworthy to identify by the pattern of scalation on cheeks and gill covers; they vary too much. In the early 1930s, a so-called silver muskellunge was discovered in Lake Belletain near Nevis, Minnesota, and received hatchery propagation. The ground color was a uniform silver and each scale was flecked with gold. However, mandibular pores never exceeded five, cheeks were always entirely scaled and when crossed with other muskellunge the offspring were sterile. Therefore, we now have a pretty little silver *pike* mutant (*which see*).

The etymology of *masquinongy* and muskellunge

Most states with muskellunge fishing available have a 30-inch minimum length limit, and most dedicated muskellunge anglers would never kill one that small. Only giants are fit to mount. Many anglers release all their catches, seeking only the thrill of the fight.

MUSKELLUNGE

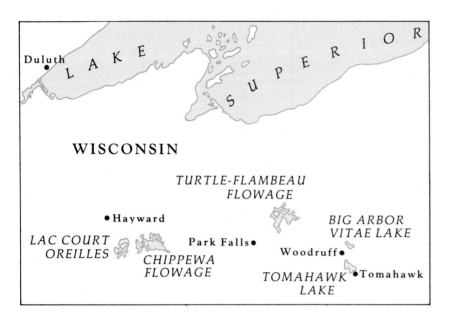

WISCONSIN

The airport at Hayward, Wisconsin, can be the jumping off place for excellent muskellunge sport for anglers who arrive from a distance.

has generated more heat than the subject merits. Filtered through the French-Canadian dialect, it is either from the Ojibway *mas,* meaning ugly and *kinononge* meaning fish, or from the Cree *mashk kinonge* meaning ugly or deformed pike, unless you are willing to settle for voyageur French *masque allongee* meaning long face. At any rate, it is muskellunge in the United States by decree of the Committee on Names of the American Fisheries Society, and the official Canadian designation is now maskinonge. Common fishermen of both nations invariably call it muskie.

Both Canadian and United States studies of muskellunge stomach contents have shown a highest percentage of yellow perch and a second choice of suckers of various species. This almost certainly indicates not a preferred food selection, but the taking of what is available of a suitable size. They also consume ducklings, muskrats and snakes and have been known to bite paddle blades and the leg of a fallen water skier. More than once computer studies of the catch reports made by members of Muskies, Inc., a Minneapolis-based conservation and propagation group whose members are passionate specialists in the fish, show a lure preference that would suggest a sucker (black bucktail weighted spinner) or a perch (green-and-yellow lures).

Though muskellunge and barracuda are near lookalikes in form, this is an example of convergent evolution. The two are completely unrelated but have a similar lifestyle and hunting technique. This in turn dictates that muskellunge are among the few freshwater fish that are best

angled in a saltwater fashion—that is, with lure speed *much* faster than is customary for the black basses, which are usually found in the same habitat. Whether trolling or reeling, the axiom is that if the muskellunge wants your lure or bait it is impossible to take it away from him. If there is an exception to this, it is in off-colored water, such as the often murky mountain streams of Kentucky and the Virginias, where a race of small muskellunge are fished with bass tackle and techniques. Fast fishing means trolling even as much as 8 miles per hour or reeling 5:1 gear ratio reels at the highest speed you can sustain.

Trolling Tackle

A stiff-action, 6- to 7-foot spinning or 5- to 6-foot bait-casting rod is suitable for trolling muskellunge. The reel should carry 200 yards of 20- to 30-pound-test monofilament or braided Dacron line and have a smoothly adjustable star drag. Arthur Lawton's world record fish, a thirty-year-old female who regurgitated a 2-pound pike at boatside, was taken on 30-pound-test with a braided steel leader and a 2-ounce drail ahead of his lure (the large Creek Chub Pikie Minnow trolling plug that is popular with striped bass fishermen in Atlantic waters). But Lawton was playing a specialist's game, trolling downstream to get his lure as deep as possible in the big St. Lawrence River, convinced that muskellunge of big-game dimensions were no longer shallow-water fish. Using his tackle along the shoreline of a Minnesota lake would be wretched excess, and probably futile. Nowadays, to fish 20 feet down as Lawton was doing, we simply drop a downrigger to that depth and continue to use the lighter tackle. Downrigger rods need to be long and springy so when a fish takes, it comes upright with enough authority to set the hook. Downriggers do limit trolling speed: Go too fast and even the 5- to 10-pound, streamlined lead weights will balloon toward the surface.

Deep trolling for muskellunge is effective twice a year: in the glare of mid-summer and again in early October, before the freeze but after weed beds have died and been deserted by baitfish. Bait will then be off deep points, sunken islands and other forms of underwater relief, and muskellunge in a feeding mode will be with them.

Finding lures that will remain stable at speed takes some searching. A few plugs won't broach at high rpm's, but spoons as a rule are more trust-worthy and Elwood "Buck" Perry's Spoonplug is a gem. This odd piece of metal comes in various

172

sizes, designed to track steadily at a predetermined depth (on metered line) regardless of trolling speed. Spoonpluggers are often mistaken for fishermen who have quit for the day and are running back to the dock.

Trolling big Pikie Minnow plugs deep and Spoonplugs knocking the bottom of the lake (both shallow and deep) isn't all of trolling by any means. Homer LeBlanc, the outstanding guide for decades on Michigan's Lake St. Clair, swears by spoons held down with a heavy drail and fished on a short line right in the wake of the boat. Running in water 10 to 18 feet deep at 5 knots or more he keeps his main lures no more than 4 feet off the corner of the stern and 2 feet deep, and another 15 feet astern and 5 feet deep. LeBlanc's thesis is that the propeller itself, and the boat's churning wake, are muskellunge attractants. In more than half a century of fishing for them he has caught in excess of 3,000 muskellunge.

Typically, trolling artificial lures or rigged baits is a matter of following lake margins (including shoreline weed-bed margins), but the use of depthfinders or even one's eyes to locate sunken mid-lake weed beds can be productive. The rule of thumb is that muskellunge will be scattered in weedy shallows during overcast weather, and in deep weed in sunshine. It is a generality to be observed just long enough to give your search for an uncommon species some point of departure. Many a big muskellunge has come out of a yard of water in summer sunshine.

Trolling a live sucker four or five boat lengths behind the boat at a dead-slow speed (or even a drift if the wind is advantageous) while casting a rigged sucker or an artificial lure into the shore is one of the most efficient angling techniques for muskellunge. If the fish, which is an inveterate follower, does not like the cast bait or lure, it may well take the one being trailed. This makes pleasant fishing for two friends, each alternating between the role of caster and helmsman/troller from time to time. A small casting bait and a large one for trolling make sense.

Casting

Muskellunge fishermen joke about lure casting, the apogee of the sport, probably to divert their attention from the chronic bursitis it induces. The giant plugs propelled by near-rigid rods sail out and *splash* down within a yard of each other—one! two! three!—for muskellunge are thought to need a target they are already aligned on or they won't bother striking. Then the reel hands begin their

frantic twisting at a speed that brings a grimace of fatigue or pain to their faces. When each retrieve is completed there is the ritual of the figure eight. This consists of immersing the rod (a little or a lot, depending on depth of water) with a dangle of 1 or 2 feet between rod tip and lure, and vigorously swinging the lure in a figure eight pattern. There should be no pause between the retrieve and the figure eight, just continuous motion. This performance is not limited to those occasions when a following muskellunge is seen, but concludes every retrieve. When a muskellunge strikes at boatside an unforgettable moment is experienced.

One elderly practitioner with a statistical bent calculated 600 casts a day would produce a muskellunge. An Ohio State study produced the

Large black bucktail spinners, such as these by Mepps, are consistently good producers on muskellunge among those who prefer not to troll, but casting often means hours of effort per fish.

figure of 100 hours per fish, and a Pennsylvania study concluded 75 to 100 hours per fish. The tiger muskellunge succumbs after a mere 20 hours of angling effort. At 100 hours of effort per muskellunge dispensed in eight-hour fishing days, we have twelve and a half days between catches, or more than six weekends. The pursuit of such a quarry calls for dedication far beyond the ordinary. It also calls for the consumption of much auto and boat fuel, restaurant meals and nights in local motels.

Thanks to muskellunge velleity, muskellunge fishermen have the peculiar need to communicate a frequently fishless experience, and they do so with a unique terminology:

"I had three follows last Saturday," means you were doing something right and, also, you were

MUSKELLUNGE

doing something wrong. When not in an active feeding mode, muskellunge will follow their curiosity almost like—as a matter of fact, like barracuda. The follower is the fish you hope you will catch via the figure eight. This works just often enough to make it a worthwhile addition to a lure caster's repertoire.

"I had a swirl this morning," means you experienced what can be one of angling's supreme thrills. One overcast afternoon on Minnesota's Cass Lake, I threw a black floating-diving plug alongside a vacant wooden pier that protruded into an utterly calm dark bay and, instead of pulling the plug under, I walked it in continuous quick wiggles across the surface. Suddenly yards behind my plug the lake raised up a great curl of glassy water and profiled momentarily in it was a huge green-barred muskellunge, as if he had been embedded in clear crystal. This is probably the fright reaction of a follower that realizes something is *wrong*.

Bucktail Spinners

Those little French spinners that are so popular for trout and panfish now come as much as 9 inches long and up to 1½ ounces in weight. You can buy them with single or double blades and single or double sets of treble hooks dressed with various shades of bucktail. Muskellunge, or at least muskellunge fishermen, prefer these in black. They cast well and don't resist fast reeling nearly as much as some other lures. Many fishermen who begin the day with a jerk bait are delighted to fish a bucktail in the afternoon. Computer analysis of catch statistics indicates bucktail spinners are to be preferred under any weather conditions, from clear through cloudy, to overcast and outright storm. They are the most taken lure from June through September but fall off badly in October, when deep-diving plugs and even jerk baits are superior.

Jerk Baits

These peculiar plugs are unique to muskellunge fishing and utterly contradict what fisheries workers think they know about the fish. Jerk baits are long, thin, bristle with two or three sets of treble hooks, float at rest and dive about 2 or 3 feet when jerked on a taut line. The drill is to immediately reel in the slack made by jerking, and before the plug surfaces, jerk it again. Allowing it to break the surface is fatal to success. Putatively, this arduous retrieve represents an injured or sick prey fish that can be easily taken, but you will recall young muskellunge are repelled by food that is not both alive and exhibiting normal conduct. Unfortunately, jerk baits are second only to bucktails in their acceptability to muskellunge most of the season, being surpassed a bit by deep divers in October. Jerk baits are usually factory finished in black, in sucker gray or in perch yellow-and-bars. This lure requires a poker-stiff rod to work properly and manufacturers have met the challenge. They are singularly unpleasant to fish. Muskellunge generally take them on the upfloat while the angler is reeling in slack. This leads to violent, backward-lunging strikes, and people have been known to go right out of the boat backward if they miss the hookup. Statistically jerk baits are at their worst in June, their best in July and steadily decline through the remainder of the season.

Diving Plugs

Oversized crankbaits, says the computer, are not bad in September and become the lure of preference in October. In September and October, most muskellunge are confronted with increasingly stormy weather and the computer reveals that is the weather of preference for fishing diving plugs. They are most effective in natural finishes. Almost every manufacturer of bass plugs makes some giant models for muskellunge (and often adds tinned or stainless steel hooks for the saltwater market). Magnum diving plugs that sink are my preference for muskellunge. Cranking down through 10 feet of unoccupied water to get to the fish's level is energy consuming when gravity will perform the task.

Spoons and Spinnerbaits

On those occasions when I have asked muskellunge fishermen why they invariably begin pike fishing with spoons but seldom use them for the greatest pike of all, I have encountered either blank stares or a song-and-dance about practicing proven techniques for each fish. Spoons take everything, granted equal time with other lures. The ease with which they cast and retrieve, the built-in action that makes them excellent lures for beginners, are probably why muskellunge fishermen abjure them.

Oddly, giant spinnerbaits are becoming more and more popular for muskellunge. They work very well on pike, too. I like the tandem-blade version. There is enough wire up front as an intrinsic component of spinnerbaits that eliminating the usual wire leader is possible, and it is always desirable to eliminate or at least minimize wire, even if it costs you a few fish.

Topwater Plugs

The computer says surface plugs are the worst way to fish muskellunge, and that the fish have no particular dinner hour (or breakfast, or lunch) except during the month of August when 7:00 to 9:00 P.M. is by far the best. During the evening quiet following a hot midsummer day, my first thought would be for a surface plug. Warm weather, a reasonably flat surface and the absence of sun almost dictate fishing the surface, and the computer analysis confirms this, adding that a slight breeze is better than dead calm.

Rods and Reels

Most muskellunge are fished for with 5½- to 6-foot plug-casting rods with two-handed grips, and the larger bass plugging reels filled with 12- to 30-pound-test monofilament line. Lure weights will be in the vicinity of 1 to 3 ounces, the weight of suckers sold at bait stations from 3 to 6 ounces. Rod tapers and wall scantlings reflect this duty.

Both rod and reel can be bettered and should be for two reasons. First, the problem of how best to cast from a boat for 10- to 70-pound fish that want a speedy retrieve has been thoroughly solved in the development of contemporary saltwater spinning tackle. With gear ratios comparable to the best plug-casting reels, plus the advantage of larger-diameter spools, spinning reels scaled for saltwater boat or light surf use can make a muskellunge understand that if it wants that sucker (or whatever it is) departing from its milieu with such extraordinary dispatch it had best get a wiggle on. Secondly, these reels are mated with two-handed spinning rods of 7 to 9 feet, and that extra length can be important for distance casting when the angler is seated.

Some years ago, before the development of telemetry equipment that enables fisheries biologists to implant radio tags in fish and monitor their movements, a clever study of muskellunge migration was done by a team that used balloons attached to the fish by a length of fine line pinned to their dorsal flesh. (They discovered that muskellunge, or at least their study fish, are great wanderers, that a muskellunge hole is unlikely to be long occupied by the same fish, that 25 miles per week of straight-line travel is not exceptional.)

Tom McNally, Outdoor Editor of the Chicago Tribune, *fly-fishing for muskellunge, a sport he often practices with a pattern of his own tying.*

When the biologists closed in to collect their balloons and free the subject muskellunge of those encumbrances, if they remained seated in the boat they could pick up the balloons, but if they approached standing, the muskellunge began to move off while the boat was still 30 feet away.

Terminal Tackle

Steel cable is the traditional leader material of most muskellunge fishermen because of its flexibility and resistance to kinking. Properly called "cable laid wire," it consists of ultrafine wire strands twisted in bundles, which are then twisted together. It is superior to solid wire, which is stiff and has a tendency to kink. The popular cable sizes are 45- and 60-pound-test; however, the saltwater practice of a heavy shock leader made of hard monofilament is becoming more acceptable to muskellunge fishermen. Tie a foot of 60- to 80-pound-test mono to your casting line with an Albright Special knot or, if you are fishing a bucktail spinner, join the shock leader and line with a sturdy black barrel swivel to minimize line twist. Few muskellunge can sever thick monofilament.

St. Lawrence River

From the outlet of Lake Ontario, whose mouth is 12 miles wide, to the towering skyline of Montreal, some 250 miles east, the St. Lawrence River is one of North America's most fertile muskellunge fisheries. Drop-offs, dense weed beds,

The St. Lawrence River yields muskellunge virtually in downtown Montreal, and it produced the world record. At the Lake Ontario end is another hot spot.

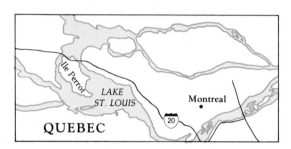

which include chara, potamogeton, elodea, majas and myriophyllum, and deep-water holes all help provide an ideal habitat for both prey and predator.

These big-river muskellunge grow large. The present all-tackle record of 69 pounds, 15 ounces was caught in the St. Lawrence in September of 1957. Even in this age of intensive fishing a "keeper" on the St. Lawrence is a muskellunge of over 20 pounds. Some in the 35- to 40-pound class are caught regularly.

The muskellunge season opens in mid-June, after their spawning period, and though a few fish are caught by pike and walleye anglers all summer long, prime time usually starts in the dog days of summer. Hot and muggy afternoons are best for day fishing, but more and more anglers are converting to angling at night. They find the muskellunge to be most active between 9:00 P.M. and midnight. However, this is probably a function of the constant daytime traffic of pleasure boats.

Muskellunge fishing is a specialized art and veteran St. Lawrence River anglers approach their sport with religious devotion. Changes in water quality or even the success of other fishermen in removing a muskellunge from a known holding area is important knowledge to the angler. One secret of success is to always have your lure in potentially productive water; if a fish has been displaced it could mean hours of fruitless trolling over barren acres because big predators are territorial in their feeding. Trolling with stiff 6-foot rods, large-capacity trolling reels and lead-core lines has become the most productive method. Though most fishing is done in 12 to 20 feet of water, the fast-sinking line is necessary to get a lure to the bottom in as short a distance as possible. Successful muskellunge fishing depends on precision trolling, following the contours of the weed-bed edges and/or "ambush points" without fouling the lure. Depthfinders are an important element in every muskellunge angler's bag of tricks. They allow the angler to troll with high accuracy, keeping his lure in the correct depth of water at all times.

Lures come in and out of fashion, but the 7-inch Swim Whiz in orange with black spots is extremely popular. In addition to an enticing action, the hollow Swim Whiz rises to the surface with a reduction in trolling speed which prevents fouling on tight turns and unforeseen stops. Though muskellunge have been known to fall for the proverbial bent pin, anglers on the St. Lawrence River take fish consistently using these refinements.

Prime time lasts from roughly mid-August until October, and occasionally a bit later. Several peaks do occur—one at the end of August and another in mid-September. Muskellunge are known to inhabit the better part of the St. Lawrence River system, but some of the best fishing is found between Kingston, Ontario, and Montreal, Quebec. The water surrounding Wolfe Island, near Kingston at the head of Lake Ontario, provides excellent muskellunge fishing and a few experienced guides operate out of the only village on the island, of the same name. Accommodations and meals are available at the hotel on Wolfe Island, but nearby Kingston (only half an hour away by ferry) has a wider choice in dining and lodging, including several big chain hotels.

The Thousand Island-Gananoque region also has some good muskellunge fishing, though for the most part undeveloped. Lake St. Francis, which is shared by Quebec, Ontario and New York, has extensive muskellunge populations, though its potential has yet to be realized. Several good fish have been taken as incidental catches by perch, walleye and pike fishermen, but consistently effective techniques have yet to be developed. Most muskellunge are taken with baited spinners. Guides and boats are available at Lancaster, Ontario, on the north shore of Lake St. Francis, and at St. Abicet, Quebec, on the south shore. The Lancaster Inn and other similar establishments are within walking distance of most boat liveries. Motels are available at St. Anicet.

Lake St. Louis, in the shadows of Montreal, has become known as a trophy muskellunge area, where trolling at night off Windmill Point on Ile Perrot produces the most fish. The gathering place for most Lake St. Louis muskellunge fishermen is the Lake St. Louis Anglers and Hunters Association clubhouse in Lachine and, by making inquiries, visiting anglers can usually find available guides. Equipment may be provided. Since Lachine is situated between cosmopolitan Montreal and Dorval International Airport, accommodations are plentiful and the dining outstanding. All the major hotel chains are located within a few minutes' drive of the fishing spot.

Wabigoon Lake

Immediately south of Dryden, Ontario, lies Wabigoon Lake, less well known than nearby Eagle Lake, but probably capable of producing the next world-record muskellunge. Wabigoon Lake has 20,000 acres of extremely silted water and more muskellunge over 50 pounds have come out of it in the past few years than any other lake in North America. Reports of the "Wabigoon monster," a fish reputedly in the 70- to 100-pound class, have been about for several years. Although the giant hasn't been caught, some impressive fish have been boated. In 1982 a 56-pound-plus fish took honors; in 1983 a 57-pounder was caught while walleye fishing.

Seeking this giant is no easy process. There are

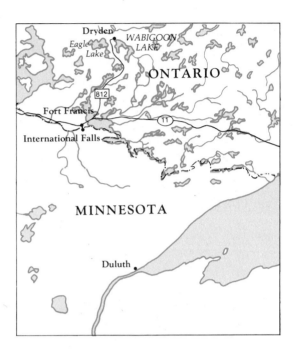

Wabigoon is quickly rivaling the popularity of Eagle Lake with muskellunge fishermen driving north from International Falls, Minnesota, into Ontario.

literally countless bays, points, rock piles, inlets, islands and weed beds to choose from in Wabigoon's sprawling acreage. With connecting lakes and waterways, there are over 50,000 acres to fish. Muskellunge are not the only game fish swimming in Wabigoon. Northern pike are caught everywhere, on almost anything. Walleyes to over 12 pounds are taken from the depths. Smallmouth fishing is excellent in some of the connecting lakes.

Until a few years ago, getting there was a long process, but the advent of Highway 812, which runs north from Highway 11, just west of Fort Francis, straight up to Dryden, made it simple. Now it is only a bit over a two-hour ride from the Minnesota-Ontario border.

Because of industrial plants, runoff water and other factors, Wabigoon's waters are dirty. In the words of one of the best U.S. muskellunge guides, Joe Bucher of Boulder Junction, Wisconsin, it's "the dirtiest water I've ever fished in." That definitely has a bearing on the whereabouts of the fish.

Although spawning should be long done by the time the season opens, a spring fisherman may be able to find some muskellunge near spawning streams and river mouths or, in some cases, in the marshy backwaters of the lake. Small bucktail spinners, normally dark ones, retrieved near shallow vegetation, are often the answer.

As summer begins, muskellunge scatter throughout the lake, but when they feed, it's normally in water from 2 to 6 feet deep. With the

MUSKELLUNGE

water off-color as it is, this shallow-water feeding is almost always the case (and that applies to all species of fish).

A favorite pattern would be fishing the shallow edge of cabbage weed beds that are scattered throughout the lake, but some years, because of cold, early-season weather, the weed beds don't develop properly. Then the fish seek out the lily pads, timber and other forms of shallow-water cover.

Black bucktails with fluorescent orange and chartreuse blades are the best choice. Baits such as Lindy's Hot Spot, the Butchertail, the Harasser and the Mepps Giant Killers are all popular. Try fishing these lures on the back and front faces of shallow weed beds, along the tips of rocky points, under the shade of overhanging trees and in the backs of bays, around stumps and lily pads. Use stout tackle built for this type of fishing and fish the baits fast near the surface.

On certain days, jerk baits, like the Teddie, Suick or Bobbie baits, produce strikes. Again the darker colors, such as the black sucker or natural cisco finishes, are better. Topwater lures with noise-making propellers are also productive.

Another excellent member of the bucktail family for searching out Wabigoon's muskellunge are buzz baits—any lure that can be moved quickly across the surface making lots of clatter. Lindy's Musky Buzz and the buzzing Butchertail are local favorites.

If there is one time of year when Wabigoon peaks for muskellunge, it is from mid-July to late August. Often the hottest, muggiest days will produce the most fish. Then they scatter over the structure and can become quite aggressive. Clear days will also produce fairly well; however, the fish will hold tighter to cover and you'll have to cover much more water to find an active fish.

Wabigoon Lake and the adjoined smaller lakes

Muskellunge and smallmouth bass are primary targets on Pennsylvania's Juniata River above its junction with the Susquehanna north of Harrisburg.

PENNSYLVANIA

KEY
1 Point Access
2 Newton-Hamilton
3 Granville
4 mifflintown
5 Walker
6 Muskrat Springs
7 Thompsontown
8 Greenwood
9 Amity Hall

offer central Canadian fishing at its finest. There are numerous resorts on the lake that offer everything from housekeeping plans to complete packages, or you can stay at a motel in Dryden and drive a few minutes each day to your fishing. For more information, contact the Chamber of Commerce in Dryden.

The Juniata River

Of all the rivers I have ever seen, the beautiful Juniata is set up best for fishing—not too big to be confounding, not too small to be restricting, it possesses great appeal to both the wading and floating fisherman. There are fishy-looking flats over submerged stones of all sizes and there is rushing water breaking between exposed ledges below which are deep holes. Then, too, there are inviting mouths of cooler feeder streams. The food supply for carnivorous bass, muskellunge and walleyes is not only producing, but holding up.

There is a great dividing line at the town of Ardenheim in Huntingdon County. Looking upstream to the right is excellent big water for big trout featuring good fly hatches and rises. Looking upstream to the left is a flood control impoundment, the pool of which has a 28-mile shoreline. The confluence is a famous muskellunge stretch called "The Point." Downriver are 90 miles of mainly floatable and wadeable water to the junction with the Susquehanna River at Duncannon, Perry County.

The river is accessible along most of its shoreline. Route 22 parallels it from Amity Hall upriver to Lewistown and this highway is not far removed from Lewistown to Huntingdon. In this great stretch of 90-mile river are nine Fish Commission Access spots at good pools where boats can be launched, a program initiated by the late Dr. Albert Hazzard, a renowned fisheries biologist. Thompsontown is very much in the middle of things. Cottages can be rented from Zook and Lyter, R.D. #2, Mifflintown, PA 17059.

Fly-Rod Muskellunge

Many fishermen feel fly-fishing for muskellunge is impossible or impractical; it is definitely possible and decidedly practical. Muskellunge in *shallow water* are as easy to take with standard fly-fishing tackle as with any other tackle or lure, and many times fly-fishing will account for more fish, including behemoths. Muskellunge of more than 40 pounds have been taken by fly-fishing in New

178

York's St. Lawrence River. In Wisconsin, muskellunge bettering 20 pounds have been landed by fly-fishermen.

The fall months, particularly October, are the best for muskellunge fly-fishing because the fish tend to visit the shallows more often then. This is not because the water is cooler than in summer, but because light penetration of the water is greatly decreased in the fall.

Despite the fact that quality sinking fly lines are being manufactured today, fly-fishing basically remains a shallow-water game, so muskellunge that are too deep are extremely difficult to catch by fly-fishing.

Standard fly-fishing tackle is used on muskellunge, but it should be a bit on the heavy side—that is, rods should be 8 to 9½ feet long, stout action and taking 8- to 11-weight lines. A 9-foot rod taking a 9-weight line is perfect. Reels should be quality, single-action types. The muskellunge is a strong-fighting fish, far superior to northern pike, but it is not tarpon, crevalle jack or amberjacks. The only real trouble a skilled fly-fisherman has in fighting a sizable muskellunge is snags. Usually a muskellunge is hooked near weeds, by stumps, around logs, sunken timber, etc., and unless the hooked fish is worked clear, the leader may foul and break.

Leaders can be as light as the angler dares, but the last 12 to 15 inches should be comprised of a shock tippet—hard nylon testing 20 to 60 pounds. Tippets heavier than that are rarely necessary.

Lures can be popping bugs or large streamer flies. Generally speaking, streamers are more effective. Both bugs and streamers should be tied on saltwater hooks, No. 1/0 to 3/0, and should be honed needle sharp.

Muskellunge are difficult to hook, so the angler should keep the fly rod tip low and close to the water during the retrieve, then lift the rod sharply upward and strike hard, *repeatedly*, when a fish hits.

Wisconsin has countless excellent muskellunge lakes, but a favorite for fly-fishing is famed Chippewa Flowage, near Hayward. Other good muskellunge fly-fishing lakes—all in northern Wisconsin—include Lac Court O'Reilles, Tomahawk Lake, the Turtle-Flambeau Flowage and Big Arbor Vitae Lake, to name only a few.

A muskellunge taken on the fly by Tom McNally. The large saltwater fly reel has a powerful drag designed to turn fish such as tarpon.

SMALLMOUTH BASS

Micropterus dolomieui

To me, autumn is a wonderful time of the year to be on a bass river. The mountains are aflame with color and the air is clear. A kingfisher will study my pool down the arrow of his beak, then *scree* in swift departure. I can hear grosbeaks and thrushes rustling among fallen leaves while whistling chipmunks gaily gather beechnuts for a winter's feast. Woodcock will be migrating down the valley and geese are trading cornfields across a cobalt sky, their raucous honking applauded by the laughter of the river's currents. But it's that magic pool shadowed by moss- and lichen-covered ledges that brings me back, year after year, where I once lost a big smallmouth bass that made three gill-flaring jumps before vanishing in its depths. I want to believe the same fish is still in its crepuscular lair waiting for my fly, but this brief encounter occurred a decade ago, and to materialize again, it would have to be over a hundred years old by human chronology. However, game fish are as compelling as the country they keep, and the rod-throbbing apparition of a bronzeback leaping over and shattering a mirrored surface turned scarlet and gold by maple and oak makes such sentimental hopes inevitable. Even a roll call of smallmouth rivers stirs up ghosts of seasons past— the Shenandoah, James, Potomac, Susquehanna, St. Lawrence, the Snake—indeed, the bronzeback haunts far more waters today than in the seventeenth century when Quebec's French settlers knew him by the Algonquin Indian name *achigan*, or "ferocious."[1]

The original distribution of smallmouth bass in North America extended from northern Minnesota to Quebec and down to the Allegheny Mountains, south to northern Alabama and

---

[1]*Achigan* is still the common name for bass in French-speaking Canada: *achigan à petite bouche* for smallmouth, and *achigan à grande bouche* for largemouth bass.

Cold, clear water and granite boulders are home to the smallmouth bass. Although the fish is widely stocked in various parts of the world, nowhere does the quality of its fishing compare to North America.

SMALLMOUTH BASS

DISTRIBUTION

eastern Oklahoma. This range has been greatly increased in Canada and the United States in areas adjacent to its native habitats and in widely dispersed watersheds elsewhere, being absent from Alaska, Louisiana and Florida. It is found in seven Canadian Provinces but the only notable fisheries occur in Ontario, Quebec and New Brunswick. In the nineteenth century, the smallmouth was considered a superior game fish to the largemouth bass, and transplants began in 1850 with a token twenty-seven fish delivered from Saratoga Lake, New York, to East Wareham, Massachusetts. Four years later, the by now legendary General William Shriver railroaded just twelve bass, a literal drop in a bucket which was hung on a locomotive water tender, from West Virginia to the Chesapeake and Ohio Canal. The canal drained into the Potomac River where they proliferated and became the seed for many subsequent plantings. By the 1880s, the smallmouth was widely distributed in the eastern half of the United States and the popularity of bass fishing exploded.

The controversy over which species is the gamest, the largemouth or the smallmouth, continued into the twentieth century with such exponents of the latter as author Zane Grey, who lived at Lackawaxen on the Delaware River. In an article published by *Field & Stream* in May 1912, he enigmatically challenged (after describing the capture of forty bass in one day, not one under 3 pounds and some over 4) his peers.

> I have caught a good many Delaware bass running over six pounds and I want to say that these long, black and bronze fellows, peculiar to the swift water of this river, are the most beautiful and gamy fish that swim. I never get tired of studying them and catching them. It took me years to learn how to catch them. Perhaps some day I shall tell you how to do it. But not until I have had the pleasure of seeing Dilg[2] and Davis, and other celebrated fishermen who have not yet honored me with a visit, breaking their arms and hearts trying to induce one of these grand fish to rise to an artificial fly. Because, gentlemen, they will not do it.

Delaware smallmouths were, of course, being caught on plugs, spinners, spoons and flies but Grey, a confirmed live-bait fisherman at the time, may well have scored heavily, although the weights he gave (none under 3 pounds) boggle the imagination for river bass, even in a pristine environment.

The smallmouth is a large member of the sunfish family (Centrarchidae) in a genus popularly known as the black basses. However,

Unlike an ordinary canoe, the square-stern Grand Laker has great stability and allows the angler to stand when casting even in a strong wind. This scene on Third Machias Lake is typical of southeast Maine's bouldery smallmouth bass waters.

adult black bass are not black. Newly hatched fry are nearly transparent but after the yolk sac is absorbed and the tiny fish are free swimming, they gradually turn black, hence the name. At a length of about a half inch, they become dark green, and with age the smallmouth turns to a patinaed bronze, which inspired the *nom de guerre* "bronzeback." Black bass have suffered many scientific names since that French naturalist Lacépède[3] first described both the smallmouth and largemouth in 1802. The single specimen of the smallmouth that he studied had a deformed dorsal, so the generic Latin, *Micropterus* (which means "small fin") is misleading. Yet the name was finally adopted based on historic precedence for all six black bass species.

The smallmouth bass encompasses two subspecies: the northern smallmouth *Micropterus dolomieui dolomieui* and the Neosho smallmouth, *Micropterus d. velox*. The Neosho smallmouth is found in the Neosho River and tributaries of the Arkansas River in Oklahoma, Arkansas and Missouri. The original habitat of this subspecies has been greatly reduced due to the construction

[2]Will F. Dilg, founder of the Izaak Walton League of America and early day exponent of fly-rod bass angling.

[3]Comte de la V. Lacépède, *Histoire Naturelle des Poissons*, (Plassan, Imprimeur-libraire, Paris, 1802).

of impoundments and subsequent environmental changes. The name *velox* means "swift" in reference to its characteristic as a game fish. The Neosho is more slender than the northern form and differs in that its lower jaw projects beyond the snout, and the upper mandible extends to, or nearly below, the posterior margin of the eye, as opposed to the anterior in the more common smallmouth.

The Cycle of the Season

In spring, smallmouth bass begin coming inshore when the water temperature reaches 55°F, and begin spawning as it approaches 60°F, which occurs from late April to early July, depending on latitude. The male bass constructs a circular nest on a gravel substrate in the shallows of a lake or stream by sweeping silt and debris from the bottom. These spawning areas are usually at depths of 2 to 10 feet on a gently sloping shore free of wave action (or away from strong currents in a stream). The female bass comes coyly from deep water where the male repetitively chases her to the

nest before pairing is accomplished. Eggs and milt are emitted at brief intervals of seconds in duration until the act is completed and the female departs. The male guards the eggs and subsequently may spawn with other females using the same nest, defensively remaining at the site to discourage predators until the schooled black fry are free swimming—usually a period of about one month. Nesting smallmouths are especially vulnerable to angling; however, because of a high reproductive potential there is no closed season in many states. Also, catch-and-release fishing is very popular in most camps today. In large bodies of water with minimal fishing pressure, smallmouth bass populations thrive with no apparent decline in the quality of the sport.

During the summer months, smallmouths abandon the lake shoreline and retreat to depths of 15 to 30 feet. This varies regionally and with prevailing weather conditions. The bass feed most actively in a water temperature range of 60° to 70°F, avoiding areas that exceed 73°F. However, they are often found for brief periods on mid-lake reefs and shoals at depths of 2 to 5 feet in the heat of August and will frequently return to forage along the shoreline during morning and evening hours. Extensive mayfly hatches or an abundance of wind-borne, terrestrial insects will also cause the fish to feed in warm surface water. But cooling temperatures in autumn bring smallmouths back into the shallows, which can be a peak time for trophy fish that fatten like black bears before hibernation. With the approach of winter, northern smallmouths move into deeper water. This school migration begins when water temperatures start to drop in the late fall, literally a mass exodus at 50°F, and the fish settle in currentless places devoid of light, squeezing between rock crevices, or settling in deep holes and even submerged logs. The bass become dormant as temperatures reach the lower 40s. Angling is, of course, possible in warmer southern waters, although the bass may be less active during severe or prolonged cold spells. However, some of the heaviest smallmouths ever taken nationally in recent years, fish from 8 pounds, 4 ounces to 9 pounds, 3 ounces, were caught during the November to February period in Alabama and Tennessee while northern bass were comatose.

Fly-Fishing for Smallmouths

In rivers and lake shallows, the smallmouth bass is a classic quarry of the fly-fisherman during the spring and fall seasons. Summer fishing is less

reliable when the bronzebacks usually retreat to deep water. The smallmouth can be taken on dry flies, wet flies, nymphs, streamers and, of course, bass bugs. Back in the days when James A. Henshall was codifying the tribal lore of black bass (*Book of the Black Bass*, Robert Clarke & Co., Cincinnati, 1881), he favored a split-bamboo rod weighing 8 ounces of not more than 11 feet in length. Add to this the hard rubber, German silver, or brass "click reel" popular in that era, which weighed from 10 to 12 ounces, and the angler was painfully swinging 1 to 1¼ pounds in repetitive casts. Since Henshall's observations were often sparsely purposive, his reference to the "general demoralization and used up condition of the flexors and extensors of my arms" was perhaps less a tribute to the sporting qualities of black bass, than the gameness of the angler.

Modern day bass fly rods and reels are, of course, much lighter; however, some distinction can be made between an all-purpose outfit capable of bucking winds that blow off the Beaufort scale (a condition common when fishing for Lake Okeechobee largemouths) while casting No. 1/0 and 2/0 plastic bugs, and smallmouth requirements. For bass fishing in general, a composite graphite/fiberglass or boron rod in an 8½- to 9-foot length, weighing 2⅞ to 3⅛ ounces, together with a large single action reel of aluminum or magnesium alloy of, say, 3½ ounces has a total weight of 6½ or 7 ounces. Such tackle is a sheer joy to cast with and has the backbone to throw large wind-resistant lures with an 8-weight forward line. However, the smallmouth specialist can use shorter and lighter rods, especially for river bass where lures on No. 4 to 10 hooks are generally more effective. I prefer a 1⅛-ounce, 8-foot graphite rod calibered for a 6-weight line in a double taper.

James River

For big smallmouths, few rivers in the East can compare with Virginia's James. And, unlike some rivers where the sport fishery is declining, catches of jumbo bronzebacks from the James are increasing. The Virginia Game Commission keeps a tally of the number of "citation-sized" (4 pounds or better) smallmouths caught in each fishery in the state. Twenty years ago the James produced fifteen such bass. For the next dozen years, the catch of big smallmouths rose and fell erratically, then began a sharp climb. From the mid-1970s through 1980, the catch of smallmouths weighing over 4 pounds increased from less than twenty to

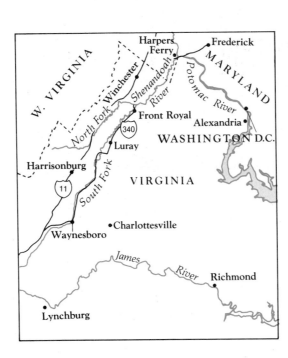

The James and Shenandoah are two of the best smallmouth rivers in the mid-Atlantic states. The North Fork and South Fork of the Shenandoah flow in a northeasterly direction, joining at Front Royal. Float fishing is popular in this river system, but there are miles of safe wading, especially in the shallower North Fork. There are also big bass in the Upper Potomac, particularly in the deep runs opposite Frederick, Maryland.

over seventy-five. In 1980, the top fish weighed 6 pounds, 7 ounces, second biggest in the state for that year. But the James doesn't just offer the potential for a bass, it also offers good *numbers* of fish. Catches of 50 to 100 bass per day are common during the prime April through October fishing period.

The James is the longest river lying wholly in Virginia. Rising in the Allegheny foothills, the river meanders southeastward for hundreds of miles, crossing the mountainous and piedmont sections of the state before it reaches the fall line at Richmond. This is the end of the bronzeback water, though there is good largemouth and shad fishing from the city on down, and prime saltwater sport where the James spills into Chesapeake Bay. The best smallmouth fishing occurs along the entire length of river from above Eagle Rock to Richmond. Places to *avoid* are areas near big towns, such as Lynchburg, where angling pressure is heavy, and also any long, slow stretches above the few dams found on the river. Especially popular areas include the sections around Eagle Rock, Buchanan, Glasgow, Big Island, Cartersville, Bremo Bluff and Scottsville.

Both float fishing and wading are popular on the James, and there are also many access areas where good shore fishing can be enjoyed. A copy of the "Freshwater Fishing and Hunting in Virginia" atlas put out by the Alexandria Drafting Company (6440 General Green Way, Alexandria, VA 22312; telephone [703] 750-0510) is an invaluable aid in planning float trips or picking out spots to wade or bank fish on the river. Before actually embarking on a float trip, first order a free Virginia index map from the U.S. Geological Survey, Distribution Section, 1200 S. Eads St., Arlington, VA 22202, and then order quadrangles for the sections you plan to cover. These detailed maps will allow you to accurately gauge the progress of your float and also show any potential hazards you might encounter, such as rapids or dams. There are a few tricky whitewater sections on the river. You should either portage these or lower the boat down along the shore on a rope. In any case, all your gear should be firmly lashed to the craft for retrieval in case of a spill. (For canoe rentals, transportation or guided outings, contact the James River Runners, RT 1, Box 106, Scottsville, VA 24590; telephone [804] 286-2338.)

While float fishing may be the most aesthetically appealing method for fishing the James, the largest smallmouths often come to the wading angler, since he can probe every promising piece of cover with repeated casts. Bait such as

Casting Lures for Smallmouths

Spinning and bait casting are the most popular methods of fishing for smallmouth bass. A variety of lures can be used, but the most effective weight range in both lakes and rivers runs from as little as one-sixteenth ounce to five-eighths ounce. The spinning rod angler has an advantage in the ability to cast very light baits (less than one-quarter ounce), which are sometimes more productive than the heavier sizes. However, the factors involved in a lure's success are myriad: size, shape, color, *action or vibration pattern, flash or its absence, and the operable depth of an individual bait. A complete assortment should include spoons, spinners, plastic worms, grubs, jigs, topwater plugs, floating-diving plugs, swimming or "count down" plugs, and deep diving plugs or "crankbaits." Those illustrated here are representative of the various types.*

hellgrammites, minnows and madtoms is popular on the James, but most anglers prefer spin fishing with artificials. Four- or 6-pound-test line works well, but the rod should have enough stiffness to set the hooks firmly. Grubs, jibs, floating diving plugs, topwater chuggers, plastic worms, spinnerbaits and crankbaits are favorite offerings. Plugs with natural scale finishes often produce the largest bass. For pure numbers of fish, it is hard to top a 3- to 5-inch floating Rapala or a one-sixteenth to one-eighth-ounce leadhead with a chartreuse yellow or white plastic twister tail. Bigger fish often fall for crankbaits and topwater chuggers such as the Lucky 13 or Whopper Stopper Throbber.

Fly-fishermen enjoy the James most from June through October, when the water warms into the 70s and high spring runoffs have receded. An 8- to 9-foot rod with 6- to 8-weight, forward floating line and 6- to 10-foot leader is a fine outfit for the river. Poppers, deer hair bugs, nymphs and streamers on No. 4 to 10 hooks are all used with good results on the James.

Shenandoah River

Unlike most eastern rivers, which flow in a southerly direction, the Shenandoah etches a northeasterly course as it winds through northern Virginia and the eastern tip of West Virginia. The North Fork of the river flows through the fertile Shenandoah Valley. The South Fork begins near Waynesboro and flows along the eastern slope of the steep Massanutten Range. Both forks join at Front Royal, where the main stem continues its winding course, entering West Virginia briefly before spilling into the Potomac at Harper's Ferry. As the crow flies, neither fork of the river covers more than 100 miles, the main stem barely 50. But

like most rivers, the Shenandoah snakes along so circuitously on its course that it offers many more miles of fishing potential than would seem likely. With its major feeders counted, the river system covers over 1,000 miles of smallmouth water, featuring easy accessibility, scenic beauty and safe boating and wading potential.

Smallmouth bass were introduced into mid-Atlantic rivers in 1854, when they were taken from the Ohio River drainage in West Virginia and dropped off of trestles. The Shenandoah soon became famous for its superb bronzeback sport. Though pollution, siltation, fertilizer runoff and dam building have taken their toll on this fabled river since then, the Shenandoah continues to provide quality smallmouth sport for spin, bait and fly-fishermen. Catches of 100 bass in a day are not uncommon. A skilled angler fishing a dawn-to-dusk day might easily take and release 200. Such an abundant bass population can be traced to an alkaline chemistry and a rich food supply. The Shenandoah flows over a geographic belt heavy with limestone beds. Populations of mayflies, caddis, stoneflies, damsel and dragonflies, dobsonflies and midges are high. Dace, shiners, chubs, suckers and madtoms also contribute to the bulging waistlines of Shenandoah bronzebacks.

Biologists have been at odds regarding the best management system for the Shenandoah. Some claim the river has too many bass, reducing the growth rate of the fish. Until recently, the river had a 12-inch minimum size limit. Currently, the North Fork and main stem of the river maintain this regulation. The South Fork above the power dam at Luray has no minimum size limit. The South Fork below this dam is now being managed with a slot limit. Bass between 11 and 13 inches must be returned to the water unharmed. Eight fish above or below these sizes may be kept (1983).

Since most Shenandoah bass average 8 to 14 inches, tackle should be scaled accordingly. A light or ultralight spinning outfit with 4- or 6-pound line is perfect. This rig will handle both bait and lures. Some of the heaviest fish caught in the Shenandoah come to live offerings. Madtoms (a small brown catfish) are the top bait for truly large fish, with 2- to 4-pounders turning up quite regularly on these morsels. Live shiners and hellgrammites vie for status as the second best bait. All three offerings should be fished on fine wire hooks with either one tiny split shot or no weight at all.

Lure fishing is the most popular angling method on the river, and thinking small is the key to

Jig and Pork Rind—A Most Versatile Lure

The leadhead jig with a pork rind trailer is one of the most versatile lures for catching smallmouths along steep, sloping shores. The lure can be cast in shallow water, left to sink to the bottom, then slowly retrieved in short hops by raising and lowering the rod, then reeling between each stroke to keep some tension on the line. The fluttering-tailed bait achieves a provocative swimming and diving action. This requires patience and practice, as it is important to "read" the lay of the line. Bass seldom hit a jig forcefully; just the slightest increase in line tension, a faint pull, a lateral movement of the line, or if the line suddenly goes slack while the lure sinks toward bottom will indicate a strike. Bass

often take a vertically sinking jig. Developing a feel for the lure's sinking coefficient is essential to success.

Popular smallmouth jigs weigh one-sixteenth to one-quarter ounce and are sensitively fished with a light rod on 4- to 6-pound-test line. Slow retrieves with frequent pauses are most rewarding. Jigs can also be fished directly below the boat in deep water and are especially effective in hot summer months if smallmouths venture below the 30-foot level. When deep fishing, let the jig sink until the line goes slack as it hits bottom. Crank up the slack and hop the lure slowly in a vertical plane. This is best accomplished from a drifting boat, keeping lure contact with the bottom structures.

success. Spinnerbaits, crankbaits, plastic-tailed grubs, spinners, marabou jigs, 4-inch plastic worms and topwater plugs all work well. Two standbys that old-timers rely on heavily are the Heddon Lucky 13 and the silver/black floating-diving Rapala. The Lucky 13 is especially good during high, stainy-water conditions. The Rapala draws action anytime, but is especially good in clear water. Bait and lure fishing are good from March through October, and even the hottest of summer days can produce excellent sport. With depths generally running from 2 to 8 feet, the Shenandoah offers superb fly-fishing potential. An 8- to 9-foot rod with 5- to 8-weight, forward floating line and 6- to 10-foot tapered leader fits the bill nicely. Hair bugs and poppers in No. 4 to 10 work well from late spring through fall. Streamers such as the Matuka, Muddler Marabou, Sculpin and Zonker in No. 4 to 8, and buggy-looking damsel, dragon and hellgrammite nymphs are productive all season, from April through October. Weighted versions of nymphs and streamers usually score best.

There is much good wading water on the Shenandoah, especially the shallow North Fork. Float fishing is very popular, with canoes, johnboats and even rubber rafts working well for this method. The best plan is to use two vehicles, dropping one at a takeout point 5 to 10 miles downstream while another transports boat, gear and fishermen upstream to the put-in point. For canoe rentals or transportation service on float trips, contact Shenandoah River Outfitters (RFD 3, Luray, VA 22835; telephone [703] 743-4159). For more information on the Shenandoah's fishing and a helpful map called "Boating Access to Virginia Waters," write Virginia Game Commission (Box 11104, Richmond, VA 23230).

Lake Champlain

Quite simply, one of the finest smallmouth fisheries in the United States exists throughout Lake Champlain's impressive 313,000 acres. The lake forms the border between northern New York, western Vermont and southern Quebec. As such, it is deep in traditional salmon-trout country where, until recently, bass have been treated as a sort of Cinderella fish. Contemporary anglers are beginning to change all that.

Those seeking remote country will not find it on Champlain. The lake shores are well settled, but the water is big and fishing is uncrowded. The draw for smallmouth anglers is a seemingly endless supply of 3½-pound fish and perhaps 10 percent of

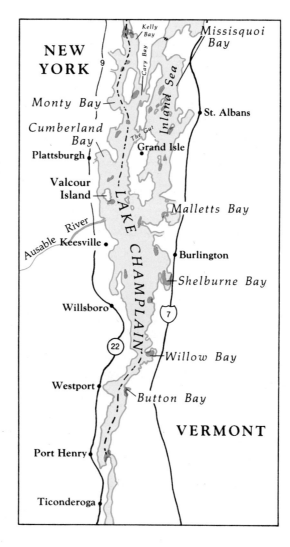

Some of the prime smallmouth spots in Lake Champlain are indicated in red. Marinas are located on both the Vermont and the New York shores. The broken line indicates state boundaries. It is important to know that state fishing licenses are not reciprocal in Champlain. You will need both to enjoy the great angling available on both sides of the lake.

Famed for its Atlantic salmon, New Brunswick also offers excellent smallmouth bass fishing. The Chiputneticook chain of lakes is particularly outstanding as is that stretch of the St. John River between Nackawic and Fredricton, above the Mactaquac Dam. Fish of 3 and 4 pounds are not uncommon in these waters.

SMALLMOUTH BASS

The meandering Shenandoah River, including all of its tributaries, offers an incredible 1,000 miles of smallmouth habitat. Fish like this one taken on ultralight spinning tackle are not uncommon. The river produces catches of a hundred or more fish in prime periods.

New York and June 15th in Quebec. Licenses are non-reciprocal. Fish and game departments do not necessarily condone catch-and-release fishing prior to these dates, but much of it is done.

Depending on the year, spawning may still be in progress at the start of the seasons. Smallmouths typically are located in 3 to 12 feet of water over gravel or egg-size rocks if they are guarding nests. Distinctive bottom formations, a boulder or downed tree in the vicinity makes the area all the more attractive. Rocky points and shallow edges of reefs that drop off into deeper water also produce early in the year. Fly-rod and spinning bugs as well as other surface lures provide the most enjoyable sport during the early season. Spinners and shallow running plugs also work quite well.

As the water warms, the smallmouths begin drifting from the shallows. They take up residence on some of the slightly deeper reefs and rocks, near sunken islands and weeds, off points and submerged ruins. Typical depth is about 15 feet. Surprisingly, some of the visible and underwater cover such as timber or weed beds that seem better suited to largemouths (of which the lake has ample share) will give up big smallmouth bass. Crayfish-simulating crankbaits, tight-vibrating plugs, jigs with hair or plastic action tails, Mepps No. 2 Spinner and Minnow, small plastic worms as well as a variety of leech-, crayfish- and minnow-imitating streamers on sinking fly lines are the ticket for summer fishing in deeper water.

Some of the best summer smallmouth action is enjoyed by those who push back the cocktail hour and work the charted shallow reefs and spoils near shore as sunset approaches. Smallmouths that held in deeper water by day regularly move in and up now, and anglers can catch them on fly-rod poppers or other small topwater lures as they work schools of forage minnows over these structures. The action can be wild for a short period as the sun is setting, then suddenly shut down or move to a different, though often nearby spot.

In September, Champlain smallmouths tend to roam the shallows more frequently. Many of the largest fish are taken during this month. Surface fishing may be had on those slick calm mornings and evenings, but breezes frequently keep the lake riffled, making subsurface lures a better choice. Fly-rod enthusiasts will want to use flashy streamers worked at mid-depths and just below the surface. Muddlers and similar patterns are effective when worked near the bottom over ledges and shallow reefs. Floater-diver Rapalas, spinners, small spoons and marabou jigs in white and yellow are good choices for those using spinning and

the population larger than that. Smallmouths from 5 to 6 pounds are taken.

The key to Champlain smallmouth fishing is immediately evident upon examining NOAA Lake Survey Charts 171 to 175 inclusive. From Rouses Point, New York, and East Alberg, Vermont, down to South Bay, New York, the number of plainly marked reefs, rocks, cribbings, ruins, snags and ledges is mind boggling. Most of them hold bronzebacks. Dozens of unmarked structures also hold the fish.

Bass season officially opens the second Saturday of June in Vermont, the third Saturday of June in conventional outfits. In a dry year, lake level will drop drastically, causing fish to move to further offshore holding spots.

Small cartoppers and rental skiffs are fine for morning and evening fishing, but anglers must keep a constant weather eye out. Wind normally builds toward noon. This is big water that can become dangerously rough quite suddenly. Happily, protected areas with good largemouth bass fishing offer an option when more exposed areas become choppy.

Lodging is available on both sides of the lake in key areas such as Bulwagga Bay, Button Bay, Kellog Bay, Porter Bay, Shelburne Bay, Mallet's Bay South and North Hero Islands, Isle La Motte and the Inland Sea.

Further fishing information is available from Information Division, Vermont Fish & Game Department (Montpelier, VT 05602; telephone [802] 828-3371) and New York Department of Environmental Conservation (Region 5 Headquarters, Ray Brook 12977; telephone [518] 891-1370).

Rainy Lake

Of all the waters in the Canadian North, some of the most wild, beautiful and yet relatively accessible are those of Rainy Lake, which stretches for over 100 miles on the Minnesota-Ontario border. The lake boasts a healthy population of northern pike, muskellunge, walleye and whitefish, but the prime target of most Rainy visitors is the smallmouth bass. Rainy is an angling classic. Its waters appear mahogany-hued from staining by shoreline tamarack roots. There are banks heavily wooded with spruce, fir, pine, birch and quaking aspen. There are sheltered bays, rocky shores, shallow reefs and sunken bars, scattered islands both big and small, cliffs and bluffs dropping straight to the water's edge, and sand and gravel shallows spotted with pencil reeds and lily pads. The air is crisp, clear and clean and wildlife abounds along its shores.

On any given day, an angler on Rainy can expect to catch fifteen to twenty-five bass. Most fish average about 1 pound and a number in the 2- to 2½-pound class will be caught. A 3-pounder is a nice smallmouth, and the lake record is a 6½-pound bass.

Big, buggy-looking nymphs, small streamers and popping bugs are effective on Rainy smallmouths when the fish are shallow, particularly during spring. Lightweight lures in the one-sixteenth-ounce to one-quarter-ounce range are most

Minnesota's boundary waters are popular among campers and canoeists. These are all productive bass waters, especially Lac La Croix and Rainy Lake. Rainy, with its 10,000-mile shoreline, is considered one of the best in Canada. Unique here are rental houseboats, which permit anglers to make extensive journeys in comfort.

Although famed for its salmon and trout fishing, the Columbia River system was first stocked with smallmouth bass in 1925 and they have since become established in a number of tributaries, notably the Snake. The fishing extends from below the Bliss Reservoir, near King Hill, to the mouth of the Columbia River. The Swan Falls area and Hells Canyon are especially popular for this species.

SMALLMOUTH BASS

appropriate. Anglers should have a wide assortment of small plastic-body "grub jigs," single-shaft spinners (such as the Mepps and Panther Martin), tiny spinnerbaits, and midget surface, shallow-running and deep-diving plugs.

Medium-action, fly-rod bass bugging tackle is in order for Rainy. Fly rods 7½- to 8½-feet long that will handle 7- or 8-weight lines are just right. Ultralight to light-action spinning tackle and lines testing 2 to 6 pounds are just the ticket for taking Rainy smallmouths. Though Rainy's water appears dark, it is actually quite clear and often fine-diameter lines are needed to fool even these wilderness fish. Also, light tackle is needed to toss small lures. And, of course, ultralight gear is most suitable in getting the most play from smallmouths.

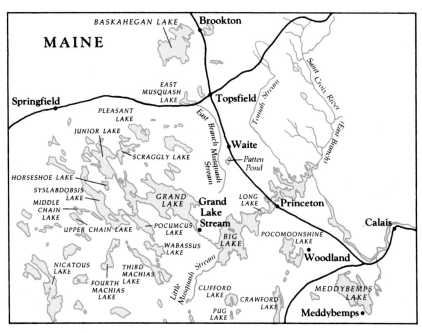

Southeast Maine is the smallmouth bass heartland. The pivotal town is Grand Lake Stream, which gives access to lakes in all directions. Bass fishing peaks in June and September, although deep-running lures and live baits produce fish during the summer period. In addition to bass, there are landlocked salmon in Big Lake, Grand Lake and Junior Lake.

Rainy Lake has good smallmouth fishing from May through October, but June and July are best. At such times the fish are in shallow water spawning on gravel and sand flats. Spawning smallmouths aggressively defend their bedding areas and the superb fly-rod bassing that can be had at such times will quicken the pulse of even the most jaded fishermen. The backs of coves, around sheltered flats, and on leeward sides of islands all are prime spots for spawning fish. Trophy-size smallmouths often bed in water 3 to 5 feet deep. If the bass are not in the shallows, top-water lures are obviously less effective. Use subsurface lures and concentrate on points at the mouths of bays, and also on slow-tapering

submerged rock bars of islands. Almost every point or bar is good for several smallmouths. The very best locations have rounded rocks no larger than a softball because such bottoms harbor large numbers of crayfish, leeches, minnows, hellgrammites and other prime smallmouth foods. You will seldom have to fish deeper than 15 feet, even during the heat of summer. Most of the time bass will be caught in water 3 to 10 feet deep.

Rainy is so large (a 10,000-mile irregular shoreline) that houseboating is the only practical method of working the vast, primitive bass-filled areas of the lake. It is also a most enjoyable way to spend a vacation. Anglers tow fishing skiffs behind the houseboat and so are completely self-sufficient. They can travel as far as they like, to fish as much and as varied water as they want. With a floating home on the water, anglers can spend all their time fishing and never work the same water twice. No long boat rides to distant spots are necessary since the craft can be anchored at whatever location the anglers choose. Most of the time the houseboat is moved to different spots (if desired) at night, usually by a guide, while the anglers sleep or lounge in the boat's spacious galley or on open-air decks. Being able to move your fishing camp at your own discretion, without losing fishing time, is much of the beauty of Rainy Lake houseboat trips.

There are several houseboat outfitters, such as Bill Fontana, who owns Canadian Wilderness Floating Lodges (Box 487, Fort Frances, Ontario, P9A 3M8; telephone [807] 274-6523). Fontana has been running houseboat fishing trips on Rainy for over twenty years and he does a completely professional job. He rents various size houseboats that you and friends and family can take out on Rainy by yourselves or with the aid of a skilled fishing guide or two. He arranges for all food, beverages, outboard motors, fishing skiffs, cooks and guides. Prices vary according to the size of the houseboat (they accommodate from two to twelve people, and range in size from 20- to 55-footers) and the services Fontana provides. This is a rare kind of angling experience. It's perfect for family-style fishing. There are no crowds. The water, the air and the surroundings are unspoiled and comparatively untouched by man. Yet the lake is easily accessible, and the houseboats offer all the comforts of home far from civilization. Even more remarkable is the fact that rentals are not expensive, particularly if several anglers split the cost.

Susquehanna River

Smallmouth bass were introduced into the Susquehanna in 1869 when a group of ardent local anglers delivered 200 fish from the Potomac River, where they had been planted in 1860. Prior to these dates, there were no bass, smallmouth or largemouth, in the eastern United States south of the St. Lawrence. Their subsequent spread into other rivers and lakes is possibly the greatest conservation achievement in the annals of American fisheries.

If one were to plan a water system for rectangular Pennsylvania, it would be difficult to surpass nature's design. Along the northern tier are wooded mountains with incredibly steep slopes that roll from county to county. Their peaks were leveled in the glacial age, forming flats which feature springs and hemlock swamps from which tumble miniature trout brooks. It is the habitat of black bear, deer and ruffed grouse. Some of these little streams angle westward to become a part of the Allegheny River watershed, others spill off to the east and ultimately enter the Delaware River, but the majority come down the midsection forming the mighty Susquehanna River, which feeds the food-rich Chesapeake Bay.

One great feeder, the North Branch, traverses the coal regions, which in the past caused pollution due to acid mine drainage and coal washings, but in this more modern ecological age is sufficiently clean to harbor game fish. Toward the setting sun is the West Branch, which flows out of New York State in the vicinity of Binghamton. The two large rivers come together at Northumberland, Pennsylvania, and some 20-odd miles downstream the Susquehanna is joined by the beautiful and productive Juniata.

The lower part of the river has the appearance of four connecting lakes. These are pools of dams above major power plants, the lowest of which is in Maryland and is crossed by US Route 1.

From the fishing standpoint, the Susquehanna has two pertinent elements going for it: vast quantities of crayfish, the finest bass food of all, and shallow water which lends itself to both wading and float trips. Where the current has battled its way between mountains, there are irregular limestone ledges creating foaming white-water spills above very deep pools. It is in these oxygenated areas where bass congregate in dog days when the river is low and hot. The river is so extensive that many a bass never sees a bait or lure and many die of old age.

Tradition was in the making shortly after the

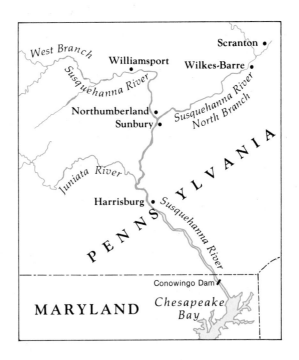

The best smallmouth bass (and muskellunge) fishing on the Susquehanna starts at its junction with the Juniata River and continues for about 45 miles downstream. The West Branch is also good, as is the North Branch above Scranton. In the Scranton-Wilkes Barre area, the river suffers from acidic pollution due to the coal mining industry. A big river throughout, the Susquehanna is most readily fished by boat.

turn of the century. It was inevitable that some trout fly-fishermen would apply their trade on this "new fish." A number of people in four sections of the Susquehanna River Valley had much to do with this bit of angling history. Tom Loving of Baltimore frequented the Maryland sector of the Susquehanna which encompassed the rock-studded 5 miles from the Conowingo Dam to Tidewater flats below the mouth of Deer Creek. He demonstrated how to catch bass and shad on his white bucktail flies, which he commercialized.

Ken Reid, the only well-known angler and writer to be appointed by a governor to the Board of the Pennsylvania Fish Commissioners, introduced the beautiful and then uniquely tied Messinger hair frog, a West Virginia import. Myron Shoemaker, an early commercial conservation educator from Lacyville along the upper Susquehanna, learned about Messinger's frog, and along with Ken Reid became a champion for fly-rod bass. Then, too, there were Calmac Bugs and Tuttle's Mouse and Devil Bug.

There were some local fly-casters who preferred to wade. The word spread among them that "the new fish" could be taken on the fly-and-spinner combination. Harry Dill, a fishing tackle salesman and purchaser, was the man who spread the word from behind the counter at the great old Harrisburg Hardware Store in the pre-World War I era.

Bass, being the obliging fish they are, were found to be susceptible to small lures called "plugs." Light-lure bait casting experienced its most severe growing pains in the New Cumberland sector of the Susquehanna with New Cumberland fishermen. This was before Bache Brown had introduced the spinning reel to American anglers. The American game of bait casting, although badly named, featured lures which weighed in at five-eighths ounce. It was

SMALLMOUTH BASS

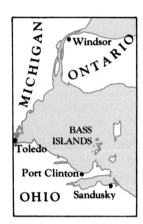

One of the most productive smallmouth fisheries in the midwest is the Bass Islands region of Lake Erie. Although close to large population centers and receiving heavy angling pressure, it continues to provide great numbers of bass. Port Clinton is the major fishing center.

discovered that river smallmouth bass reacted better to smaller lures. It was also discovered that bait-casting equipment could be refined to accommodate the quarter-ounce-size.

The first American-made lure in a small size was the creation of the national casting champion, Al Foss, and he named it after an erotic dance of the day, "Shimmy Wiggler." Along came Jim Heddon's mini-size Dowagiac with its high-grade front prop and low-grade finish which cracked and peeled. A little later Mack Magaro of San Antonio, Texas, sent along some of his beautiful, elaborate and effective Minno Bugs, a perfect weighted fly-and-spinner combination. The untimely death of its creator in a canoe accident terminated production of this lure which some regarded as the grandest for both lake largemouth and stream smallmouth ever made by the hand of man. It is over fifty years since the Shakespeare people placed on the market their superb river plug "The Midget Spinner." It gained fame on the

The Ten Thousand Islands region of Lake Ontario is a historic vacation spot for New Yorkers and Canadians alike and it is also one of our great eastern smallmouth fisheries. Prime bass water is found at Belleville and in the area from Henderson to Brockville.

Susquehanna; then its use spread to the Allegheny and Delaware rivers. Some "pluggers" carried nothing but these two lures.

Susquehanna bass do not achieve record size. Four-pound, 20½-inchers are not uncommon, but 5-pound, 22-inchers are rare. The grandest one known to this writer, which he saw and which was caught by a friend, weighed 7¼ pounds and was 23½ inches in length. It was caught below the broken-water ledge pockets downstream from the mouth of Sherman's Creek. However, this great river flows through angling history.

The Great Lakes

The smallmouth bass is native to the Great Lakes, entering the original basin during the late Pleistocene glaciation some 20,000 years ago. Today, introduced cold-water species, such as the rainbow trout, brown trout, coho and chinook salmon, play a dominant role in the Great Lakes angling scene, and as a result some of the bass fishing is comparatively untouched. However, due to a variety of habitats under 95,170 square miles of surface area in five lakes, the best bronzeback fishing occurs in widely scattered locations where gravelly islands and bays, shoals, rock piles, ledges and drop-offs provide the bottom structures, suitable water temperatures and food supply required by this species. For example, excellent angling can be found in Lake Michigan at the northern tip of the Lower Peninsula near Waugoshance Point, and offshore around Beaver Island during the spring season, or on the opposite side of the lake in waters bordering Door County, Wisconsin. The only large population of smallmouths in Lake Superior is in Chequamegon Bay. In Lake Huron, the channel islands near Hessel, Michigan, and famed Georgian Bay on the Ontario shore are stellar locations. The Stokes Bay area, also on the Canadian side of Huron, is another good spot. Yet the two really outstanding smallmouth fisheries in the Great Lakes are close to major U.S. cities and, despite heavy fishing pressure, remain incredibly productive year after year—the Bass Islands region of Lake Erie and the Thousand Islands of Lake Ontario.

The Bass Islands (about 12 miles north of Port Clinton, Ohio, extending to Isle St. George and east to Kellys Island) provide ideal habitat with rocky outcroppings and shoals where you can expect smallmouths of 1½ to 3 pounds, with the occasional 4-pounder, or rare 5-pounder. A viable rule here is that the best fishing occurs on the east

One of Virginia's best bass waters, the James, is a classic float stream for hundreds of miles from the Allegheny foothills to Richmond. To enjoy good fishing, avoid large population centers as well as the slow stretches above the few dams on this river.

side of these limestone islands in the spring, where the bottom substrate is more suitable for spawning, and on the west side in the fall due to prevailing winds. Boats can be launched at Catawba State Park near Port Clinton. There is also a ferry service to South Bass Island and Kellys Island where a limited number of boats and guides may be hired. By contrast, there are several hundred guides available at the four major marinas in the vicinity of Port Clinton. In addition to smallmouths, the Bass Islands are noted for their superlative walleye fishing, that most edible of freshwater species.

Lake Ontario maintains a significant bronzeback population in the Bay of Quinté on the Canadian side but it is the southeast corner of the lake on the New York shore from Henderson Bay to 28 miles below (downstream) Alexandria Bay, where the lake drains into the St. Lawrence River, that has long been a smallmouth mecca. In this beautiful Thousand Islands region there are so many hot spots—Galloo Shoal, Cherry Island, Chaumont Bay, Grenadier Island, Pigeon Island, Tibbet's Point, Wolfe Island, Featherbed Shoals, Grindstone Island—that it would take a lifetime to fish them all. Boats, guides and accommodations can be found at shore communities in and around Clayton, Watertown, Cape Vincent and Alexandria Bay. Bear in mind that the St. Lawrence is shared by the United States and Canada and a Canadian fishing license is required if you intend to angle across the border.

I have enjoyed wonderful smallmouth angling in the Great Lakes when bass are in the shallows, but in these inland seas they often fade into very deep water during the summer months, often dropping to 40 feet or more, and while readily taken by drifting live bait such as minnows,

crayfish and nightcrawlers near bottom, the action is not comparable to early (mid-June to mid-July) and late season (mid-September to late October) casting with artificials. Some of the popular lures are Arbogast's Sputterbug and Hula Popper, Heddon's Sonic and Lucky 13, Burkes Wig-Wag Worm, Mepps Black Fury, Cordell Spot, Rapala Count Down, and a one-quarter-ounce lead-head jig with black bucktail skirt and a black pork rind trailer.

LARGEMOUTH BASS

Micropterus salmoides

No species of game fish has been more inspirational in swelling the ranks of North American anglers than the largemouth bass. In 1968, an Alabama insurance salesman named Ray Scott decided that the world, or the United States, or at least the Deep South needed a professional bass fishing tournament circuit modeled on professional tennis and golf. As its Pied Piper, his Bass Anglers Sportsmen Society (B.A.S.S.), now boasting a membership of 400,000, was so successful that it instigated countless imitators until today hundreds of bass lakes host competitive fishing events. Organized on a catch-and-release basis, with points for returning live fish, they have brought technical advances in boat design, tackle design, and outdoor clothing design, and enormous publicity for the no-kill concept. In addition, they have created a cabalistic language that only another bass fisherman can comprehend. Over the years, these tournaments have developed into big-money events with heavy press and television coverage. Prior to B.A.S.S., fishing contests in the United States had been largely limited to local chamber of commerce promotional affairs, while American anglers marveled that European, and especially British and French, fishermen were so intensely organized for "match" fishing. Now everything has changed and the American national gift for excess has spawned an entirely new profession—the bass tournament angler. The competition is keen, and the top money-makers are formidable fishermen who follow the circuit the year-'round. Of course, the smallmouth bass is encompassed in tournaments, but the largemouth, with its greater geographical distribution, is the principal quarry. While there are those in the parish who frown on placing a price on Walton's gentle art, the game is firmly established in our national angling scene.

Largemouth bass are the giants of the Centrarchidae or sunfishes. This family is native only to North America and consists of thirty

Plug-casting surface lures, such as the Jitterbug, are an American tradition for largemouth bass, but the fish respond well to every conceivable form of bait and artificial. This is the fish that launched millions of boats and motors.

195

LARGEMOUTH BASS

species, the smallest of which, the Everglades pygmy sunfish (*Elassoma evergladei*), becomes a trophy at 1½ inches. The largemouth becomes a trophy at whatever size you deem it so, but any weight that would exceed the 22-pound, 4-ounce world record established in 1932 is the ultimate goal of serious bass anglers. Of the six black basses, the largemouth is unique by a jaw that extends past its eye, and a complete separation of the first and second dorsal fins. The name bass is from the Old English *baers*, meaning bristly, and that first dorsal can puncture your hand if the fish is grasped across the back, though experienced anglers are seldom wounded; the almost toothless mouth is fringed with brush-like cardiform teeth reminiscent of coarse sandpaper, and the fish can be grasped by its lower jaw. A "lipped" bass will become almost inert when lifted from the water.

These slab-sided, lacustrine fish with broad homocercal tails and extensive fin area have evolved for agility rather than speed, so angling for them is for the most part a leisurely sport. It lacks both the brute test of stamina that successful offshore saltwater fishing becomes and the arm-flailing, against-the-current physicality of stream trout fly-fishing. (It is in fact perverse to fish for largemouth bass in running water because they avoid it and will invariably locate in the stillest water to be found. You can selectively fish for them in a mixed population of river fish by seeking the bottom of the deepest pools, flotsam-bearing eddies or adjacent sloughs.)

Nevertheless, an agile predator that can grow to more than 20 pounds (in very few environments, which we will discuss later) is bound to be a popular quarry, because the necessary suddenness of its attacks will often make your gooseflesh prickle. A smallmouth bass can make a surface lure fall into a mute, momentary hole in the lake, and a trout will take an insect with the tiniest of dimples, but largemouth habitually kill at the top with vigor. The thrust of their feeding seems to be that anything on the surface is edible and might escape. Underwater they just inhale; evolution

DISTRIBUTION

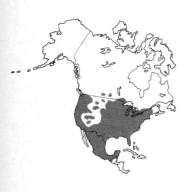

Early morning mist on Lake Fontana, Tennessee. Though such largemouth bass fishing is called "plugging a shoreline," the lures now are more apt to be plastic worms with bullet sinkers that dive for the bottom, rather than minnow-imitating traditional plugs.

does not design maws of such prodigious dimensions whimsically. However, they do have preferred food forms, as some fisheries biologists learned to their sorrow.

For decades the United States government, acting through the Hatchery Division of the Fish and Wildlife Service of the Department of the Interior, and the Soil Conservation Service of the Department of Agriculture, would subsidize a farmer who wanted to bulldoze a stock pond. Most state fish and game departments also contributed their advice or hatchery product. Everyone was certain that millions of ponds full of fish would be A Good Thing. And there was universal agreement that the warm-water pond fishery should be predicated on the piscine world's most inseparable predator-prey relationship: largemouth bass and bluegill sunfish. Millions of ponds now glitter across the face of North America as you overfly.[1] Just manufacturing the bulldozers kept an army of plebs employed, but the sport proved disappointing.

Biologists have since learned that though largemouth will, of course, eat bluegills, they would prefer not to. Being kin, the bluegill is bristly, too, and bass much prefer prey with soft-rayed fins. Shiners and minnows are lovely, and in two-tiered impoundments with warm shallows for bass and cool depths for trout, the bass will forage out of their temperature preferendum to gulp down trout with alacrity. Indeed, in certain southern California impoundments, where the Florida-strain largemouth reproduces naturally and plants of hatchery rainbows are regularly made to sustain a put-and-take trout fishery, largemouth bass consider the familiar rumble of an approaching hatchery truck to be tantamount to a farmhouse dinner gong.

It was also reported that in a bass-bluegill pond, the availability of bass to angling, combined with the reproductive efficiency of bluegills, soon reduced the bass population and allowed an enormous overpopulation of stunted bluegills. A superabundance of small bluegills will predate on both species, as both ova and juveniles, to the extent that reproduction is virtually prohibited. The afflicted farm ponds then achieved the next stage of degradation and became a biomass of thumb-sized bluegills and a few elderly bass who had only to inhale to be satiated.

Sadder and wiser, as the era of great impoundments began—the sort of superfluminae that would attract urban masses who lacked access to farm ponds—the fisheries scientists found a new prey hero: gizzard shad (*Dorosoma cepedianum*). This slab-sided herring is ubiquitous in eastern North America from Minnesota to Mexico. Rather than filter-feeding plankton as the other shads do, it grubs plant detritus out of the bottom mud, and grows spectacularly, which is a flaw from the viewpoint of largemouth. They must catch a gizzard shad young before it becomes too large to swallow (they top off at 3 pounds and 18 inches). Big bass love big gizzard shad, but few bass become *that* big. The fisheries biologists are now putting their trust in striped bass to crop the gizzard shad resource.

Two fish make perfect largemouth fodder: Another herring, the threadfin shad (*D. petenense*), seldom grows larger than 8 inches, has soft fins and is eminently acceptable to largemouth. It has been widely stocked in bass impoundments, as has been the golden shiner

[1]Construction estimate for the period 1936-1985 is 3,000,000 ponds averaging 1 acre each.

LARGEMOUTH BASS

who do not habitually fish on top of the water are simply sacrificing sport.

In a subjective sense, there are three largemouth bass: a northern strain of late spring spawners, a Florida strain that probably spawns year-'round but with a peak in February and March, and hybrids of the two. The latter occur both naturally and of recent years in hatcheries. The IGFA all-tackle world record of 22 pounds, 4 ounces was set in 1932 at Montgomery Lake, Georgia, and was almost certainly a natural intergrade. The outstanding underwater filmmaker Glen Lau, diving in Lake Miramar in southern California, saw a female largemouth that he estimated at 28 pounds. Lau's experience is such that he would be only ounces off scale weight. This fish would be either a stocked Florida strain or a natural hybrid. Florida largemouth differ morphologically from the northerns only in an elevated scale count, which makes excellent sense—their scales must encompass more bass than do those of northern fish.

(*Notemigonus crysoleucas*), a minnow that is enjoying a nationwide population explosion because it is a hardy baitfish and because its breeding season is very long, so for most of the year minnowettes are available to tiny bass, minnows to ordinary bass and 7- to 10-inchers to big bass. These two forage fishes have been the inspiration of many plastic-tailed jigs, countless commercial plugs and a few streamer fly patterns.

Crayfish and shrimp are preferred foods of largemouth. The fish must have cast-iron stomachs because they will gulp down hard-shelled, fully-clawed adult specimens with gusto. Crayfish are largely nocturnal, but when you see an individual occupying shallow water in daylight there is usually an explanation for such atypical behavior: It has just endured the fright of its life. With a clipped-deer-hair crayfish fly on a sinking line and short leader, cast to where the crayfish is *looking*.

The undershot jaw and quasi-dorsally mounted eyes of largemouth bass mean they have evolved for feeding upward. This makes them outstanding candidates for surface lures, a fact obscured for years by the popularity of plastic worms and jigs. These bottom-crawling artificials are unquestionably effective, but millions of insects, ducklings, voles and other surface-swimming creatures go down the gullets of bass, and anglers

Largemouth black bass spawn by nesting in shallow water beds formed by the little males fanning an area 1 or 2 feet in diameter with their tails to rid it of detritus. The males are a quite pugnacious fish all the time, but even more vigorously so when building and protecting their nest. The principal enemy of a brood once it is spawned will be bluegill sunfish, who are adept at making egg-stealing forays at lightning speed. A bedding male is not one to take lightly the invasion of his bed, and a streamer fly or popping bug is famously effective both before and after the spawn.

Our ancestors favored bass flies made with waterfowl breast feathers as wings, which when boldly dyed can have both the shape and colors of sunfish. The current fashion is for streamer flies. It should be borne in mind that our ancestors were country folk and we are not. Their opportunities for fish watching were in multiples of ours, but they had no biologists studying bass and making mass experiments in predator-prey relationships. We now know that slender, soft-rayed prey is the largemouth's preference and our flies and plugs reflect that progress. Fat lures still work well on bass conditioned to avoid thin ones. Many fish learn rapidly.

For his nesting site, the male bass prefers to put his back up against some sort of wall to keep his brood under his gaze and force danger to approach from ahead. He also wants water that is, and will remain, clean because if litter gets in with his brood, fanning to remove it may disturb the eggs. I was making a television film in southern Florida on a lake bearing a large population of the scoters universally called coots. The birds were feeding in their usual fashion by diving for bottom weed and surfacing to gulp what they had uprooted. They are not tidy feeders and a steady northeast wind had spread uneaten fragments over the lake. We had to fish plastic worms rigged in the weedless Texas style to avoid constant fouling, but had difficulty locating the beds until Virgil Ward reasoned that the only proper locale for nests was upwind of the coots, where a few yards of calm water were protected from the wind by a wall of

emergent vegetation. He was right. The beds were typically Florida calcareous soil, startlingly white against the surrounding dark bottom. We caught an enormous number of bass up to 10 pounds, a good weight even for the Florida strain. Other good walls for male bass to nest against are cypress, drowned timber, boulders and even just a close scattering of large rocks.

For a few days before spawning, the little males school in groups and the big females in their own aggregations. If trophy hunting, and you catch a 1- or 2-pound fish, it is probably best to move on. Females have been observed thumping their flanks against logs, undoubtedly to loosen the eggs. The invitation to spawn comes when the male leaves his nest, swims up to a bass and begins nipping

Lesser Basses

In addition to largemouth and smallmouth, the centrarchid basses come in four additional species and a number of subspecies. Their ranges are limited in comparison to the two most popular black basses, but in all cases they are capable of providing intriguing sport.

Spotted bass (Micropterus punctulatus) come in three subspecies, the northern spotted (M. punctulatus punctulatus), Wichita spotted (Micropterus p. wichitae) and Alabama spotted (Micropterus p. henshalli). The Wichitas are limited to West Cache Creek, Oklahoma. The Alabamas are the largest and have been taken from Lewis Smith Lake in Alabama to almost 9 pounds. They have been planted in California and are prospering in Lake Perris. Spotted bass can be identified by rows of horizontal spots below the lateral line and scales at the base of the second dorsal (largemouth have no scales there). They will go into deeper water than either largemouth or smallmouth. I have taken them by deep-jigging 60 feet down in Table Rock Lake, Missouri, and also when fly-fishing the Pedernales River in Texas below the LBJ ranch, where it is a clear, beautiful little stream. Natural hybridization with smallmouth bass has been reported, and that would be a difficult fish to identify.

Redeye bass (M. coosae) come in an Alabama River form and an Apalachicola River form. They will not spawn in lakes, and are very much fish of running water. Redeyes are similar to smallmouth and spotted bass, which also can have red-hued eyes, but the redeye bass also has red fins. They are found in Alabama, Georgia and southeastern Tennessee. Plantings

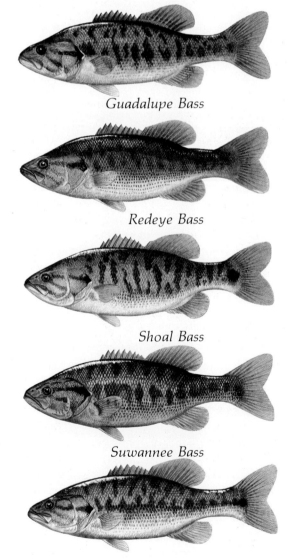

Guadalupe Bass

Redeye Bass

Shoal Bass

Suwannee Bass

Northern Spotted Bass

have been made in California and the Cumberland River system in Kentucky. Both forms have an opercular spot and the Apalachicolas carry a basicaudal spot as well. They have been taken to a bit more than 8 pounds, but are essentially a small, stream fish. Some biologists believe the Apalachicola redeyes deserve separate species status. They are popularly known as shoal bass throughout much of their limited range (mostly Georgia, but a few rivers in Florida and Alabama). The Alabama River form also has a thin white strip at the bottom of their lower caudal fin; this is lacking in Apalachicolas.

Suwannee bass (M. notius) are an even smaller stream fish that rarely top 10 inches. Their habitat is the acidic Suwannee River watershed in Florida, and their habit is to avoid streamside vegetation and position themselves in the thalweg, the main channel of the river— conduct highly unusual for a black bass! Suwannee bass can be identified by their blue chin and throat.

Guadalupe bass (M. treculi) are limited to a few streams in south-central Texas, which they occupy with largemouth and spotted bass. They are a small fish closely related to spotted bass, but can be differentiated from them because Guadalupes have rows of spots both below and above the lateral line, spotted bass below only. Look for them in fast water in Texas rivers, such as the Guadalupe, Pedernales and Llano. They will take the fly, small spinners and small jigs.

about its head. Since it is characteristic of all (or most) animals that the sexes have a distinctive bouquet, he has probably already determined her female nature, but they may be able to sex each other visually by size because males will sometimes swim a number of yards directly to a female. On the bed together the spawning can take hours in cool water, only minutes when it warms up.

Bedding bass have always been fished and the consensus of contemporary fisheries biologists is that even catch-and-release impairs the spawning success by weakening the breeding couple and destroying their resolve to defend the eggs until they hatch. However, many biologists also doubt the efficacy of hook-and-line to seriously affect a population larger than a farm pond. Even in a heavily fished pond the fish populations may have been skewed by angling, but the biomass remains essentially the same. Where human beings have

Monument to Largemouth

On March 15, 1984, almost 52 years after George Washington Perry caught the world-record largemouth bass, the state of Georgia unveiled a historic marker 2½ miles from Montgomery Lake

on Highway 117 to commemorate his catch. Few world records of any kind have survived for half a century and none has been more eagerly sought. Compared to the expensive bass boats equipped with space-age technology in use today, Perry's skiff was handmade from 75-cents worth of scrap lumber. He used a $1.33 bait-casting rod and a glass-eyed wooden plug—a Creek Chub Wiggle Fish—to subdue the 22-pound, 4-ounce monster. The bass measured 32 inches in length and 28½ inches in girth. Perry's luck ran out when he was killed in an air crash in 1974, but the farm boy from Rentz, Georgia, achieved a kind of immortality that has no modern counterpart.

frequently made deep incursions into bass populations, the means have been deterioration of water quality through pollution and habitat destruction. In largemouth bass waters, there is an enormous overproduction of eggs. They were intended from the beginning to feed bluegills and glass minnows. Of course, commercial fishing with seine and gillnets, with limbline, trotline, snatch hooks, grab hooks, slat basket, jug, spearing and other ingenious engines has been used at various times to reduce largemouth populations, but commercial traffic in the black basses became

illegal thanks to the efforts of United States Senator Harry B. Hawes (Dem., Missouri), whose book *My Friend the Black Bass* (New York, Stokes, 1930) reported his successful leadership of that particular conservation movement.

Most bass caught are small males. One radio-tagging experiment with sixteen tagged male bass reported fourteen of them succumbed to angling in a single spawning season. That sort of fish can be amusing on light fly or spinning tackle, but most anglers are equipped (and intent) on catching the big females, and here we get into theories of where and how to fish for largemouth that I believe are ultimately dependent on the sex of the fish. The big bass seem to be much more given to deep-water suspension, and that implies segregation by sexes. They also hunt in the warm shallows during summer nights, which we will discuss shortly.

Since largemouth can tolerate a wide variety of environmental conditions, they have been made ubiquitous throughout the United States, save for Alaska. It has been estimated that nearly half of all American anglers are primarily bass fishermen, which reflects not their superiority as a sporting quarry over, say, Atlantic salmon, but their overwhelming availability. It is only of recent years that a few fisheries biologists have entertained the concept that the enormous population of black basses might be subject to overharvest. Human population growth and future reductions in the workweek may bring widespread overharvest within credibility. An A. C. Nielsen survey of 1982 reported 14 percent of the U.S. population were bass fishermen. That would at the time total about 31,000,000 people, a very large number to ask any recreational resource to support.

If the present generous bag and possession regulations of most states are ultimately, under excessive angling pressure, to turn into catch-and-release, bass fishermen will learn there are better fish to fry.

Almost every one of the contiguous states is currently managing one or more bass lakes under special bag or length regulations to evaluate the effects of angling pressure. Within a decade or so there should be a data base from these experiments. In Texas, they estimate that large "bass" impoundments have a non-bass finfish component of 95 percent or more, but the popularity of bass fishing is crucial to the tourism

The largemouth bass is America's most popular game fish, found in every state except Alaska.

industry. Confronted with such a dilemma, everyone from investment bankers to gallus-snapping guides suddenly becomes a born-again conservationist.

The only states that have yielded largemouth bass of 15 pounds or more are California, Florida, Georgia and South Carolina. Glen Lau's 28-pounder may not represent the ultimate size attainable in a lightly harvested climax population of Florida. In 1773, the Pennsylvania naturalist William Bartram embarked on a four-year exploration of the American Southeast that took him far up the north-flowing St. Johns River in Florida. A party of traders he was traveling with showed him how they fished for "trout" with a lure made from the tail hair of a whitetail deer and some shreds from a red garter tied on three stout hooks, the famous "bob" or "jiggerbob" they had learned from the Indians they traded with. Bartram reported:

> *The unfortunate cheated trout instantly springs from under the weeds and seizes the supposed prey. They frequently weigh fifteen, twenty, and thirty pounds, and are delicious food.*

He is welcome to them as table fare, but I have never hooked a largemouth that would not jump at least once, and the prospect of a 30-pounder sailing through the air is awesome. Bartram ate his broiled bass slathered with a sauce of oil, oranges and salt and pepper, which no doubt contributed greatly to their palatability.

The biggest Florida-strain fish of recent years have been coming out of the impoundments maintained by San Diego's Water Utilities Department. These reservoirs were stocked with Florida largemouth in the late 1950s and by 1973 had produced a state record just 1 ounce shy of 21 pounds. A national craze for Florida broodstock developed and in many states the gene pool of well-adapted local strains is endangered by plantings of Florida fish, some of them made by fish and game departments that should be more concerned with the resource and less with the tourism industry, and some surreptitiously stocked by private interlopers. Largemouths themselves were originally found only from southeastern Canada down through the Great Lakes to Mexico and Florida, and no farther north on the eastern seaboard than Maryland. Nevertheless, the Florida-strain bass is not nearly as cold-resistant as northern largemouths and their genes circulating in a northern population are a potential source of massive winterkills.

For reliable big bass fishing, Florida's Lake Okeechobee, the nation's fourth largest natural lake, would be the destination of choice. Three convergent data lead to this conclusion. The gentleman who set the Okeechobee lake record of 17 pounds, 3 ounces, in 1971, lost another bass he reported as "much larger." Secondly, Roland Martin has chosen to live on the shores of Okeechobee. He is the most successful competitive bass fisherman in North America, with a casting arm as relentless as a metronome and a faultless knowledge of the quarry. He thinks Okeechobee is the best lake in the nation for limiting out with large bass, and the most reliable winter largemouth fishery in the United States (for weeks on end, during some winters, bass fishing in the United States is largely futile except from Lake Okeechobee south). And thirdly, a scan of largemouth bass record fish, state by state, shows a suspiciously large number taken during the

LARGEMOUTH BASS

months of December through March. Fishing a black jig-and-porkrind eel in the deepest holes to be found in Lake Okeechobee, on the sort of day when the orange grove ranchers have all their smudge pots burning, might produce something really gross.

If you would like to catch both more and larger bass without mounting an expedition to the far southern corners of the United States, then go angling in the nearest bass lake after dark during deep summer. This simply devastating strategy can

This stump fisherman is seeking largemouth on Lake Monstom, Alabama, but he could be on Toledo Bend in Texas or many older impoundments. Beware of drowned timber if the wind pipes up; it can collapse suddenly and with devastating effect.

be effective during both the dark and full of the moon. The proper technique for fishing bass on a summer night is from a boat because most snakes are nocturnal. A calm lake is desirable, which means staying off the big impoundments, because you want to surface fish and that practice is ineffective in a chop. For once the method of choice should not be fly-fishing, but plug casting with a reel that will not tangle or backlash, which means you may select from spinning, spin-casting or magnetically braked bait-casting reels.

Using such equipment, I have over the years fished, with popping plugs and wobbling-gurgling baits, such as the famous Arbogast Jitterbug, only to have more experienced friends outfish me two to one, or worse. Their lure is a floating, cigar-shaped plug with a little propeller at each end. Smithwick's Devil's Horse is a classic brand made

in Shreveport and sold throughout the South. They produce a whirring noise as you reel them steadily in. Do not try to be artful with twitches and pauses. Position the slowly moving boat a long cast from shore, cast the plug gently on the bankside water, then establish an unvarying track of sound across the surface. Give the bass a target to pursue. Try to fish where there is a plentitude of animal noises. Water too acidic or oxygen-deficient for frogs and insects is also inferior for bass. Talk becomes hushed at night because water carries sound so remarkably. After a time all you will hear are the little propellers, the frogs and crickets, and the irregularly recurrent *chugs* of taking bass.

Bait casting for largemouth has been an American tradition since early in the nineteenth century when a group of watchmakers in Kentucky began manufacturing the first bait-casting reels. In 1810, George Snyder reportedly made the original multiplying reel (geared down so the spool rotated many times for each turn of the handle). The best known builders of these turning-spool reels with jeweled bearings were Jonathon Meek and Benjamin Milam. The reels cost a fabulous $50.00 in those days, and were only affordable to the Gentry. Collectors now pay thousands for specimens in mint condition. Many were crafted of brass and nickel, silver, an alloy of nickel, and copper. Circa 1840 Meek made a solid silver reel for D. Vertner of Lexington, Kentucky.

These were called bait-casting reels because they cast bait, not lures. Minnows and frogs were popular for largemouth bass, but hellgrammites and juvenile crayfish were cherished when available. Bait fishing necessitates soft-tipped rods so as not to catapult the bait across the river and into the trees. Our great-grandfathers used supple, 10-foot, two-handed rods until James Heddon whittled his first plug at Dowagiac Creek in Michigan, initiating a craze for casting artificial lures that continues undiminished today.

Largemouth bass are most often found in very close proximity to weed and wood, and few of us have either the deadeye accuracy or steely nerves to fish ultralight lures on wispy lines in aquatic jungles. But with 30-pound-test you can slap down a half ounce plug on top of a lily pad, shred the pad and continue your retrieve. If some *elodea* gets in your way, uproot it.

Manufacturers of bass rods are going to extraordinary lengths of recent years to provide anglers with a more sensitive feel of what subtle lures such as jigs and plastic worms are doing as you nudge them along the bottom of the lake.

Firm handles fitted tightly to graphite or boron rod shafts are great aids to this type of fishing. We know from underwater photography that the slight *tap* we feel in our rod hand is the bass inhaling the lure.

Fly Tackle

Fly-fishing for bass has had a history of checkered popularity. Mary Orvis Marbury's *Favorite Flies and Their Histories*, a compilation that represents the national practice of the time (1892), lists forty-six bass patterns of the colorful, broad-winged type described earlier. Many of these were fished behind a small Indiana spinner blade. The spinner-and-fly combination fished on a fly rod is not acceptable fly-fishing for record-setting purposes, but it is marvelously effective.

It is to Ernest H. Peckinpaugh of Chattanooga, Tennessee, that we are indebted for the development of the cork-bodied bass bug. Shortly prior to 1910, he found bluegills would take his bucktail fly better if it was on the surface, and a small piece of cork kept it there. Then he found that bass liked it too. Nowadays they are more likely to be molded of compressed foam, and are widely used in salt water in addition to bass lakes, but I submit that fishing floating bugs is very close to the apogee of angling. It is not passive, as are dry-fly and nymph for stream trout (much of the time). You are constantly searching the water and working the bug to induce fish to take.

A good bass-bug rod should be as long as you can comfortably handle, for approximately an 8-weight line, and with a slow action. I have an elderly fiberglass bug rod that was produced to a design by the late Joe Brooks. It is almost as narrow in the butt as its thick tip, and has a leisurely casting cycle that drives high-windage bugs with ease. Unfortunately, they achieved this action through thick-wall construction and after an hour or so it becomes very tiring. Nowadays I favor a 9-foot boron rod overlined one size with a 9-weight line to slow it down.

Basically, three bugs will suffice: a cork popper, a cork slider and a clipped-deer-hair bug for the gentlest presentations in clear or very thin water. I always carry a McNally Frog as a sop to realism.

Bug fishing is essentially combing a shoreline, and a retrieve of much more than 4 feet is a waste of time. At that point, terminate with a pickup and present anew. The distance between presentations can be determined by lowering a bright *something* into the water until it disappears. That depth gives you the clarity of the water, as far

Bass bugs of clipped deer hair land softly on the water—until they waterlog. Cork or plastic foam bugs float all day— and tend to splat on delivery.

as a fish can be expected to see anything. Space your casts that far apart.

Bass-bugging is less than half as effective as fishing a streamer fly, and if the streamer has an Indiana spinner in front of it, probably less than 25 percent as effective. And, of course, fishing a streamer or other wet fly won't catch bass nearly as well as the plastic worm or a jig and pork rind.

Truman Reservoir

In October of 1979, Truman Reservoir began its existence. This new fishing destination is now living up to expectations as one of the finest bass fishing lakes in the Midwest. Many fisherman believe it will rival Bull Shoals, which was the superstar bass reservoir in the late 1950s and early 1960s.

Truman started out with a 15-inch limit on largemouth, which made it tough going for the first year, but now there are enough keepable fish to make any angler happy. Stocking began in rearing ponds before the lake was at normal pool. The stocked bass grew fast until the rising water finally covered these ponds, thus releasing thousands of 8- to 10-inch largemouth. These, plus native bass in the main rivers, provided

LARGEMOUTH BASS

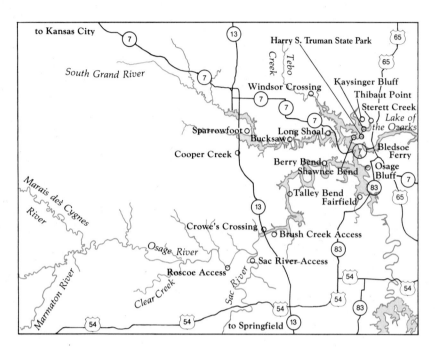

Formed by damming the Osage River, Missouri's 65,000-acre Truman Reservoir is best for largemouth bass in spring and fall. There are numerous resorts and guide services available.

anglers with a fishing bonanza. At this stage of the lake, there are enough bass in the 5- to 6-pound bracket to assure quality fishing.

Truman has almost 1,000 miles of shoreline when filled to normal pool. Much timber was cut down before flooding, but there are still 8,800 acres of standing timber, and veteran anglers who have fished Truman compare it to Toledo Bend in its heyday. Hundreds of coves and backwaters provide refuge during windy conditions. First-class marinas spread along the length are completely equipped to handle the thousands of anglers now testing the water.

Camping facilities, now numbering 821, are in operation. Truman is serviced by three towns: Osceola, Clinton and the dam site at Warsaw, Missouri. The shallow, rather dingy water makes this new impoundment a spinnerbait fisherman's Utopia. Seldom is it necessary to fish over 10 feet deep to have constant action. Many points and creek channels provide every conceivable type of structure for today's knowledgeable angler. One of the pluses to Truman is that the warmer it gets, the better the bass fishing. Due to its bottom makeup, most of the oxygen stays in the upper 10 feet of water, even in July and August when bass fishing is at its peak.

Being within reasonable driving distance of both St. Louis and Kansas City, Truman is drawing large numbers of fishermen. Not only does Truman have ample supplies of bass, it is perhaps the greatest crappie lake in the country. All types of fish are in Truman, including a striped

bass population, which has great potential, but largemouth fishing is the main attraction.

If you like casting topwater or spinnerbait lures, you will love Truman. It isn't unusual to hook thirty to forty bass on a good day. And you'll find enough over the 15-inch limit to fill your stringer with six largemouth.

Fishermen wishing further information may write to the Missouri Department of Conservation, P.O. Box 180, Jefferson City, MO 65102, or the Corps of Engineers, Project Office, Route 2, Box 29-A, Warsaw, MO 65355, which has lake maps available.

An excellent guide association has been formed consisting of licensed, insured and qualified members. Rates and information are available from Truman Lake Pro Guides Association, P.O. Box 1207, Warsaw, MO 65355.

Toledo Bend Lake

Toledo Bend Lake isn't as productive for bass as it once was. Age will do that. But even so, it still is better than most. One reason is size. When full, the reservoir built on the Sabine River separating Texas and Louisiana sprawls over 181,600 acres of pinewoods real estate. It is difficult to comprehend how much water that is until you actually get on the lake.

While the impoundment gets considerable fishing pressure, there is room for thousands of people on any given day. In addition, although a lot of the drowned standing timber has rotted and fallen, Toledo Bend nonetheless has retained an abundance of what bass fishermen call structure—downed timber, brushpiles, weed beds and other cover where black bass can take up housekeeping.

The relatively shallow lake also is fertile, growing largemouth bass in both numbers and size. In the Texas Parks and Wildlife Department's annual bass tournament survey in 1982, Toledo Bend was judged to be the state's number-one bass lake for the second year in a row.

Yet while the impoundment isn't rewarding fisherman with bass as it was a decade ago, age has its benefits. There are excellent facilities, cabins and campsites, on both sides of the lake in a picturesque setting of tall pines and moss-draped oaks. And if you are slightly overwhelmed by the vast sweep of water, wondering where to go and what to do, many competent fishing guides work Toledo Bend. Information on facilities and guides is available from the East Texas Chamber of Commerce, P.O. Box 1592, Longview, TX 75606 (Texas side), and the Sabine Parish Tourist

Commission, 920 Fisher Road, Many, LA 71449 (Louisiana). A guide is not a necessity, however. If you know anything about outfoxing a bass, you usually can find action.

While there are no hard-and-fast rules, bass being as unpredictable as they are, certain techniques for catching Toledo Bend bass have evolved through the years. How you fish depends in part on where you go. The reservoir might best be described as two lakes, split by the Pendleton Bridge, which connects the town of Many and Louisiana 6 with Texas 21 and Lufkin. The upper end is more forest, brush and vegetation; the lower half is deeper with more open water and large coves.

A typical cove south of the bridge is as large as some lakes. Local guides are pretty active in this area during the winter (January and February). Most of the bass will be in water about 20 feet deep or deeper, often hanging along the edge of an inundated creek bed. Deep-running plugs produce as does a lead-head jig with a pork eel and what locals call "spooning." A heavy chrome wobbling spoon is dropped straight beneath the boat, into structure-like brush, and jigged up and down, yo-yo fashion. You don't cast out because you will promptly hang up. With the yo-yo technique, if you do foul in the brush, you usually can jiggle the spoon and the weight of the lure will knock itself free.

In March, bass commence drifting toward shallow water to spawn. The spinnerbait is one of the most popular lures. During this time of year, there will be more angling activity above the bridge.

From April until June, fish off the points and back in the coves with crankbaits, spinnerbaits and plastic worms. At times, a minnow-shaped plug like the Rapala or Rogue will outfish all others.

May is the month for those who enjoy topwater action. Try just about any type of artificial which can be worked on the surface.

As the weather heats up, the bass head back to deeper water (anywhere from 10 to 18 feet deep). They also seem to concentrate, and where you catch one, you will likely take several. A plastic worm is the pet bait. Two of the more popular color combinations are grape with a fire tail and black with chartreuse.

On into the summer, bass fishing generally slows except for those who get out early and late in the day or at night, but there is one exception. This is the season when yearling-sized bass school in more open water to chase shad. A school of

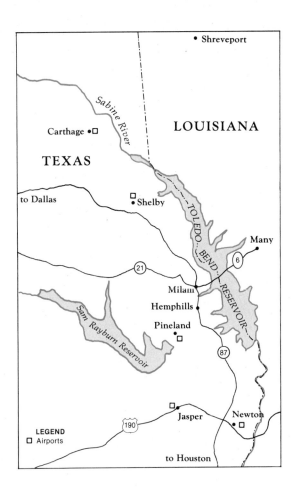

Toledo Bend Reservoir on the Texas-Louisiana border has long been the premier bass impoundment in North America—and still may be. Enormous acreages of drowned timber were left standing to provide shelter for bass; although much of it has rotted out in the intervening years, the stock of largemouth is still very large and has an excellent food base in threadfin shad.

black bass resembles a bunch of white bass attacking shad at the surface. Prowl about in your boat and watch for feeding fish. Once you sight activity, cut your motor quite a ways from the fish and drift close and toss a small topwater plug into the melee. Don't be surprised if you get a strike on virtually every cast.

Trolling with deep-running plugs also produces in the summertime. Look for drop-offs or underwater humps where bass might concentrate. If you catch a bass, make a wide swing and troll through the area again. That fish probably has company.

Texas and Louisiana have a reciprocal license agreement, which means that if you buy a license in either state, you can fish anywhere on the border lake.

Currituck Sound for Brackish Water Bass

A number of well-traveled fishermen have said North Carolina's Currituck Sound has the best topwater fishing for largemouth bass in America. It is shallow, weedy, large (120 square miles) and brackish. Several lodges along the western shore and up north at Knotts Island cater to fishermen, and guides may be engaged to pole you along a marsh shore. Its northern end is within minutes of a major airport. There is a healthy population of largemouth bass whose feeding habits are partly predictable. In short, it is an ideal location for

LARGEMOUTH BASS

traveling anglers who prefer to fish surface lures for largemouth bass.

Two factors influence Currituck Sound fishing most—wind and grass. Eurasian water milfoil dominates this shallow bay, fouling all but the largest outboard engines and the most weedless lures. Its filamentous tendrils cling tenaciously even to lures that work well through other vegetation. Anglers successfully fish artificials that are not weedless, however, such as the Jitterbug and Devil's Horse, by casting them carefully in clear water along weed beds and marsh banks. Weedless lures such as the Johnson Silver Minnow and plastic worms rigged to be weedless are highly successful. Bass bugs with wire or monofilament weed guards can be cast into grass beds with reasonable certainty that they will not hang up, at least most of the time. Bugs tied on keel hooks have proved to be practically weedless.

During the peak fishing months of spring and fall, winds in excess of 15 miles per hour are the rule on Currituck Sound. They are likely to be early and late in the day, and often you can find a lee shore, but high average wind velocity dictates your choice of fly-rod tackle. A 9-weight system is required most of the time. Experienced anglers carry lighter tackle for calm days, and for early and late on the windy days. However, highly air-resistant bugs and the omnipresent milfoil limit how light you may go. Seven-weight rods are the lower limit.

Six-foot casting rods calibrated to handle lures

Currituck Sound in North Carolina is the best-known brackish water fishery for largemouth bass. All saltwater coasts of the U.S. have some sodium-tolerant bass, however, and the delta of the Sacramento River in California is particularly well supplied.

weighing up to five-eighths ounce are in wide use on Currituck Sound. Reels should be light and comfortable to fish all day. Twelve-pound-test line is about as heavy as experienced anglers go, either on revolving-spool or spin reels. Ten-pound-test fly leaders are standard.

Largemouth bass in Currituck Sound, on the average, are smaller than those in southern farm ponds and freshwater impoundments. Fish typically will run from sub-keepers to 3 or 4 pounds, with the majority weighing over 2 pounds. There is a good chance of catching a 5-pounder any day, but 7-pound fish are uncommon. The northern sector of the sound, particularly Back Bay in Virginia, inexplicably produces more large fish. Ten-pounders are much more common there than south of Knotts Island.

It is numbers of fish you may catch that distinguishes Currituck Sound. On a good day, a skilled and persistent angler poled by an experienced guide may release several daily limits. Fifty-fish days are not uncommon. Then there are days when the bass do not cooperate at all.

In spring, a northeasterly wind regimen is changing to a southwesterly one. Southerly winds hold back the flow of water in Currituck, raising water levels along the marsh shores and generally improving fishing. Northerly winds blow water out of the sound and cause the fish to stop feeding and seek deeper water where they are hard to find.

The Currituck season is roughly April through October. Most fishing pressure comes in spring (May and June) but fishing can be excellent, particularly in early morning, even in July and August.

Several of Currituck Sound's fishing lodges are former farmhouses. Meals are served family-style at large tables, and there is fishing camaraderie in the high-ceilinged parlors after dinner. A stable of guides may serve a single lodge, or a fisherman may engage an independent guide and find a motel room or rental cottage along the beach at Kitty Hawk or Kill Devil Hills. It is only a short drive to the sound.

The North Carolina Travel and Tourism Division distributes a list of Currituck guides and lodges. Write to 430 N. Salisbury St., Raleigh, NC 27611; telephone (919) 733-4171.

Norfolk International Airport is just minutes from the northern end of Currituck Sound and the North Carolina beach resorts are no more than an hour and a half away by car. The Outer Banks Chamber of Commerce, telephone (919) 261-2626, has a directory of accommodations and listings of cottage rentals.

Lake Casitas

Until 1980, California's Lake Casitas was a quiet recreational retreat for folks from Los Angeles. On March 4th of that year a fireman/paramedic named Ray Easley caught a largemouth bass weighing 21 pounds, 3.2 ounces from the lake and neither Ray nor the twenty-plus-year-old reservoir has been the same since. That bass is the second largest largemouth on record.

Along with a handful of San Diego County lakes to the south, Casitas received plantings of Florida-strain largemouth in 1968 and 1970. The fish gleefully laid claim to erstwhile barren ecological niches and quickly grew into eye-popping, sausagelike creatures with stomachs that are blatantly obscene. The reason is soon evident.

As you fish this highland reservoir with its 7,000-acre water capacity (typically filled to 3,000 or 4,000 acres), it is likely that you will be entertained by the specter of a terrified 12-inch rainbow trout executing flying fish-like glides over the surface which will soon explode in the heaving wallow or clean break of a chasing bass whose size will make you gasp. The lake supports a multi-species fishery.

Casitas is no cover-rich lake filled with drowned timber, weeds and snags. Largemouths relate to bottom configurations, rock rubble and river currents. The slightest change in surrounding bottom composition can hold surprisingly large bass. Fishing is good for small-to-average largemouths, tough for the trophies.

Late February through March is prime time to catch big and small bass. The entire west shore with its small coves and backwaters holds good numbers of smaller bass. So do Wadleigh Arm, Canyon Station, Chismahoo Creek and Dead Horse Canyon. These spots are all marked on a free recreation map available from Lake Casitas Recreation Area, 11311 Santa Ana Road, Ventura, CA 93001. The spots also kick out larger fish. Unmarked super spots for big bass are all well known. A visitor will be given cheerful directions to The Rock Pile, Arrow Island (underwater), Deer Slope and the like. He can also locate the trophy grounds from concentrations of bass boats.

Expect no tranquility on Casitas; on any weekend a number of tournaments may be in progress. Add to that speedboats with wingback exhausts, the buzzing of radio-controlled model planes, bass boats cutting off trolling lines of big cruising boats, patrol boats equipped with megaphones for getting you off the lake at closing time (fishing is from sunrise to sunset), and you get the idea. But the lure of huge bass keeps bringing anglers, and always there is the dream of a new world record largemouth—a distinct possibility at Casitas.

The premier method for fishing average size fish here is with a small plastic worm rigged with a single split shot approximately 12 inches up your line. Because of clear water and the early exposure of bass to virtually every artificial and natural bait known to man, light lines are used. Eight-pound-test is the standard. Anglers go to 6-pound during especially clear-water periods. For the trophy fish, live crayfish and big waterdogs (aquatic salamanders) stand head and shoulders over all other baits, alive or fake. The only nearby source for quality baits of this type is a tackle shop in the town of Oak View. Many local anglers pick their own crayfish by night in streams. The crustaceans must be mainly green; the epicurean bass snub red crawdads.

The technique is to work the live bait over the underwater points, ridges and into pockets. Usually the bait is cast, left to its devices for a bit, then ever so slowly inched back to the boat. Depending on where you're fishing, you may drift using an electric motor or anchor. Sometimes split shot is used ahead of the bait.

Casitas Recreation Area is well supplied with boats, campground, snack bar and rental boats. Good motels are in the town of Ojai, and the manager of the El Camino Lodge will direct you to the better restaurants. There are some excellent dining spots in and just out of Ojai.

South around San Diego are a number of other lakes offering trophy bass fishing for the Florida-strain largemouths. Detailed information on them can be obtained from San Diego Recreation Department, Conference Building, Balboa Park, San Diego, CA 92010. Prime waters include: San Vicente, El Capitan, Lower Otay, Hodges, Miramar, Murray and Sutherland. These lakes have periods of total closure. Anglers planning a visit must check schedules. Opening days see large crowds and long lines of vehicles and boats, usually the night before.

BONEFISH

Albula vulpes

The world's greatest bonefishing can be found on sparkling sand shoals from the Florida Keys through the Bahamas, to the Yucatán coast of Mexico. Here, in the tropical western Atlantic, are thousands of square miles of island-dotted sea, where a light-tackle angler can hunt the gray ghost of the flats. A classic example of natural specialization, the bonefish feeds in mere inches of water, a visible but ever so wary quarry endowed with a demoniac swimming speed that is unstoppable against the banshee wail of a reel. Although there is no need to whisper in their presence, seldom is a voice raised in that fragile moment when a stalked fish comes within range. The very sight of a big bonefish easing slowly over the sun-dappled bottom, pausing here and there to switch its forked tail in the air, can start a grown man trembling. One wrong move on the angler's part, and the fish will bolt off the flat in a trail of bubbles, as though escaping a thousand unseen devils. This is a game of absolutes.

In a formal sense, the sport of bonefishing began under a cotton-ball sky in April of 1906, when a wiry young man by the name of Preston Pinder poled his skiff quietly across the flats near Upper Matecumbe Key in Florida. In the bow seat, with bait-casting rod in hand, was eighty-three-year-old Senator William Thompson Martin of Kentucky, the first guided bonefisherman known to angling history. Until that day, the customary methods were in forms of solo immobility—by casting a piece of crab from an anchored skiff or canoe, or from a folding chair while sitting on the beach. However, Pinder actively pursued his quarry and although the senator was soundly defeated (the tackle of that era was inadequate to the task), the concept of "hunting" bonefish was born. It took another half century to perfect the game in terms of tactics, tackle and the design of shallow draft skiffs, but the enthusiasm of its early practitioners was boundless.

The bonefish has no peer as a shallow-water forager. Its eyesight is legendary. Whether avoiding predators or playing cat and mouse with a snapping shrimp, it responds with incredible speed.

BONEFISH

Zane Grey, who was President of the Long Key Fishing Camp (which was built in 1906 and demolished in the hurricane of 1935), became so addicted to the sport that in his story *The Bonefish Brigade* that artful word vendor was at a loss: "I have never been able to tell why it seems the fullest, the most difficult, the strangest and most thrilling, the lonesomest and most all satisfying of all kinds of angling." After joining the Long Key Club, George LaBranche, author of those purist classics *The Dry Fly in Fast Water* (1914), and *The Salmon and the Dry Fly* (1924) became an iconoclast and abandoned his rivers to pursue the bonefish exclusively. President Herbert Hoover, humorist Irvin S. Cobb, and fishing experts Van Campen Heilner, John Alden Knight, and Joe Brooks found the bonefish an obsession, dictating a lifestyle that included buying second homes in the Florida Keys and Bahamas. Of course, anybody who has waded the flats until his toenails curled knows that the mystique lies in the fact that bonefishing is so predictably unpredictable, even when the quarry is feeding in plain sight. There are rare occasions when you can do no wrong: Tails and dorsals beckoned endlessly in that dimensionless glare of sky and water—a theater so hushed that you could hear a coconut drop on some distant island. But every good cast shattered the mirrored silence as your fly line went swishing away in a great curving spray with an audible *bump* at the backing. The bonefish accelerated faster and faster, running to infinity. By sundown, it had all been so easy. It was just a matter of how long your wrist held out. Yet on the very next day, at the perfect tide, bonefish swam over, under and around the fly, leaving it rocking in their wake.

To me, catching a record bonefish on the fly would be the ultimate angling experience. I had the chance once at Chub Cay and typically, the confrontation was anything but classic in a technical sense. My guide, Austin Pinder (a common surname in the Bahamas and the world of bonefish), was poling us across a mangrove-studded flat. I stood ready in the bow with shooting line coiled at my feet. After a futile morning without a target in sight, I turned to ask him about lunch, and there, not 30 feet behind our stern, was one of the biggest bonefish I've ever seen, following the puffs of marl made by his pushpole. Reflexively, I slapped my fly on the water. That fish took it in a gulp and kept right on swimming. I struck hard several times as the

chrome-plated specter slowly finned past our skiff. It was long seconds before the fish responded; then my line knifed through the water, singing like a cable in the wind, followed by 200 yards of backing. I was certain the fish would come to a halt, but it didn't, and when the spool was bare, my rod bucked in an agonizing arc. The fly popped out. We could still see that bonefish pushing water for another hundred yards or so, before it disappeared over the horizon. Austin said it would have gone 15 pounds—easily.

Why a fish with years of predator experience suddenly acts like the village idiot is no less explicable than the countless times a craftily worked fly is refused. You can make a perfect cast to an incoming tailer—the easiest shot in the book—and see the fish swim up to the fly, then turn away. You give the fly a few more inchy twitches and the fish circles back again, head down like a bull with his tail working jerkily as he gets ready to pounce. Pause and twitch. The bonefish follows, nose to feathers, as you ease the fly enticingly over the bottom. And there you crouch, shorts in the water, with sweaty armpits and steamed sunglasses, wondering what is wrong. Finally, the fish turns away, again uncertain, then bolts off the flat in sudden terror, as though he recognized a bomb with a burning fuse.

One of the more revealing physical features of the highly specialized bonefish, and perhaps the key to its behavior, is its adipose eyelid. It does not have a naked eyeball like a trout or bass. If you run your hand over the head of a bonefish, you will find that its eyes are protected behind a smoothly tough transparent sheath, a sort of face mask. There is a tiny pinprick opening centered over the pupil. A bonefish can literally bury its head in sand without being blinded, and when "mudding," its vision is not critically obscured by sediment. Some scientists have postulated that the same fatty tissue polarizes light, thus accounting for its keen eyesight. There are comparatively few other species having an adipose eyelid; it is modified in the mullet (another mudding fish) with a vertically elliptical opening at the pupil. It also appears on a few swift swimming species such as the wahoo and crevalle jack. Hydrodynamically, the sheath reduces water turbulence around the eyes when swimming at maximum speed. Bonefish may *tolerate* an angler's presence, even taking a fly almost at his feet, but its adipose eyelid suggests that sight is not an albulian problem.

There has been very little work done on imitative fly patterns for bonefish. True, effective dressings exist, but as in trout fishing, no single

pattern will produce day after day, in all seasons and all regions. Generally speaking, we know that bonefish feed actively in the brightest sun and calm water, at temperatures from 75° to 88°F. In the 69° to 74°F range, you will see a few too many fish with their number and activity progressively increasing as the water approaches 74°F. Below 68°F, (the temperature at which corals cease to grow, and within the definition of a tropical sea), bonefish disappear from the intertidal zone. Chilling water, strong winds and an overcast can produce good trout fishing from the Beaverkill to the Madison, but it is a negative condition on the flats.

Most bonefish foods are invisible to the angler. They are mainly discreet or burrowing animals hiding in the grass or substrate which the fish must flush or root out. School oriented, bonefish advance in a loose aggregate, poking, digging and blowing their food free. A bonefish "breathes" in normal fish fashion by drawing water into its mouth, then closing it while contracting the gill arches and raising the rear edge of its operculum, which forces water through slits between the oxygen-absorbing gill filaments. But when a bonefish suspects the presence of a crustacean, worm or mollusk, hiding just under the substrate, it instantly reverses the flow by a powerful adduction of its gill covers and jets a stream of water from its mouth and exposes the food. A foraging school leaves a telltale trail of excavated sand on the bottom where the bluish-gray marl has been disturbed. In a lush pasture, individual bonefish may spook a number of crustaceans simultaneously, which escape for a short distance

in panicked flight, and gradually the school scatters. Their feeding is a leisurely process, when compared to a bluefish or striped bass school, for example, so we must assume that shape, size, movement and color of various food forms are critical factors in angling success. All shallow water fishes have highly developed color vision; they can distinguish twenty-four different narrow spectral hues. The bonefish is a hunter when stalking the flats. In human terms, he is not unlike a reflexively conditioned bird shooter walking through a cornfield who responds to the sudden flight of an anticipated target. The man doesn't actually see his prey in detail, yet he instantly separates, by color, a hen from a cock pheasant or any other kind of bird that may be smaller, larger, faster or slower. The brain accepts or rejects the target before it is even in focus.

Bonefish Feeding Habits

For sheer gustatory enthusiasm, the bonefish is in a class by itself. Equipped with powerful clam-busting, pharyngeal teeth on its tongue and palate, it is an ultimate predator with a smorgasbord complex. In addition to bivalve and gastropod mollusks—such as venus clams, nut clams, ark clams, pectens, cockles, tellins, turbans, marginellas, cone shells, limpets, olive shells, snails and tulip conch—I have found squid, spiny lobster, mantis and snapping shrimp, swimming and grass shrimp, spider crabs, numerous swimming, walking and mud crabs, cusk and snake eels, sea horses, sea anemones, annelid worms, brittle stars, sea urchins and the remains of

The end of a perfect day at Deep Water Cay. Except for a summer hiatus beginning in mid-July to mid-September, bonefish can be caught at any time of the year throughout their range. Extremely hot weather or cold fronts, with their attendant winds, are the only conditions that will keep bonefish off the flats.

211

BONEFISH

Wading

The ultimate thrill for the fly-rod angler is stalking bonefish by wading and casting to tailers in shallow water. It is possible to approach the fish much more closely when on foot; however, it requires a firm bottom. Polarized glasses are essential in bright light, as the fish tend to disappear against the white sand background.

various fishes in bonefish stomachs. This is only a partial list. While bonefish appear to be opportunistic feeders, the fact is that the foods they consume vary according to the organisms available in different substrates (sand, marl, coral, silt, or combinations thereof, and the presence of marine vegetation). Food availability may change according to season, on a month-to-month or even weekly basis. I have found more than forty snapping shrimp in one bonefish stomach, with digested remains in the gut, which would indicate some degree of selectivity. A fly that resembles common food forms by color and size is often more effective than the large attractor-type patterns widely used. With the exception of the cusk eel, most bonefish foods are an inch to 2½ inches long, thus small flies (No. 4, 6 and 8) are generally more effective. Although the number of foods we can imitate with artificials is limited to about half a dozen forms, these occur with great frequency in stomach analyses.

A dominant forage among Florida and Bahamian bonefish is the snapping shrimp. This burrowing crustacean of the family Alpheidae looks like a tiny lobster with one large claw. Snapping shrimp live in coral crevices and in the hollow chambers of sponges; however, the young are dispersed over wide areas by water currents and appear abundantly at times on various substrates,

particularly in patches of turtle grass. When disturbed, the shrimp makes a sound like one of those "crickets" that kids used to bring to school. It's a metallic *click*, not loud, but puzzling if you happen to be wading where these crustaceans are abundant. For a moment, it may sound like you're standing in a bowl of Rice Krispies. The noise is made by the shrimp's wrist joint. Just the sound of water lapping against a skiff can send bonefish running off a flat, so the audible snapping shrimp must be an easy prey. These alpheids have a light brown or orange-brown body, banded in black, but some species are white, banded in greenish brown. Most of those I've found in bonefish stomachs are about 2 inches in length. Snapping shrimp dart rapidly in a few short bursts before hiding again, and I suspect that when bonefish tail in quick starts and stops, this is what they are feeding on.

Another favorite food of bonefish is the mantis shrimp. It doesn't resemble a shrimp at all, but looks like a freshwater hellgrammite with a fan-shaped tail. Mantis are members of the order Stomatopoda, encompassing about 200 species. In our waters, the false mantis, which are pea green to dark green in color, with seven thoracic segments, each edged in bright yellow, are most common. Those that I find in bonefish stomachs are usually 2 to 3 inches long. Some of the larger mantis or squillids may exceed a foot in length (if you handle any, beware, as they are armed with multi-toothed raptorial claws, and are painfully known as "thumb busters"). Mantis shrimp live in mud, sand or marl burrows, in grass beds and under dead coral rocks. However, they are active feeders, and bonefish not only dig them out, but find them crawling along the bottom.

The swimming shrimp family, Penaeidae, is the one most anglers are familiar with, when found on a leaf of iceburg lettuce, awash in cocktail sauce. There are three common penaeids in Florida and Mexican waters, the so-called pink shrimp, pink-spotted shrimp and the brown shrimp. While the traditional Pink Shrimp fly pattern is effective at times, especially in dim light over weedy bottoms, it is probably fished more than most dressings and wins an occasional hurrah by sheer popularity. It is a poor imitation at best. Color is a geographical characteristic among different shrimp populations. The pink species is most often light brown to reddish brown and may even be lemon yellow;

those in the Tortugas area achieve a "rosy" tone, with reddish-brown markings. Except for the sea bob, which turns black, shrimp only become pink after death. The pink-spotted shrimp differs in having a prominent reddish-brown spot on both sides of the tail, and the brown shrimp is reddish-brown suffused with blue or purple on the tail and legs. In living color then, penaeids are dominantly brown, and basic brown mixed with some other shade is, in my experience, most effective. These shrimp are not as common in the highly saline environments of the Bahamas where smaller "grass" shrimps of the families Palaemonidae and Hippolytidae are abundant. Grass shrimp are more

slender, usually 1 to 2 inches in length, and are a translucent brown, gray, green, blue or lavender with minute dark spots.

I have caught several large bonefish in years past while casting for barracuda with a top-water plug and in fact, the camp record at Deep Water Cay of 14 pounds was taken on a five-eighths-ounce Zaragasso. This lure could hardly suggest anything but a fish. Nevertheless, plugs are seldom attractive to bonefish. In stomach samples, vertebrate food forms rank low numerically, considering the large abundance of small fishes available on most flats. It appears that bonefish are piscivorous by chance or necessity, rather than

Bonefish Worldwide

Comparatively little is known about the bonefish, Albula (or white) vulpes (or fox). It is not certain that we are talking about the same fish on a worldwide basis. Due to morphological differences among various populations, there is reason to believe that three or more species with a "typical" dorsal fin are involved in our sport fishery. The longfin bonefish (Albula nemoptera), with its whiplike last dorsal ray similar to the tarpon's fin, and the so-called deep-water bonefishes (Pterothrissus belloci and P. gissu), with greatly elongated dorsals

comprising 58 to 60 percent of their total body length.

Although the deep-water forms have been collected only in West and South Africa and off the coast of Japan, the longfin is caught in various parts of the Caribbean south to Venezuela. It rarely occurs in the Bahamas or Florida Keys. The longfin is common enough in Jamaica to be sold as marlin bait. I have taken longfin bonefish on the flats west of Black River, the largest fish being only 13 inches in total length. It evidently does not attain a significant size.

Fossil albulids but not our familiar A. vulpes (which was first described by Linnaeus in 1758) have been found in many parts of the world dating back 125 million years to the Cretaceaus Period.

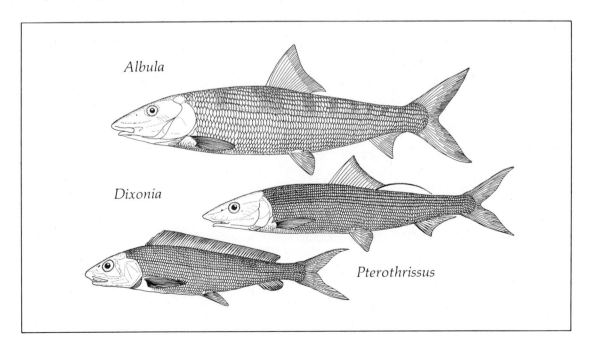

Albula

Dixonia

Pterothrissus

BONEFISH

Tips on Fly Fishing

● *You must be able to cast quickly and accurately to a distance of 60 feet even under adverse wind conditions. Bear in mind that both the boat and the fish are in motion and the presentation should be completed with no more than three back casts, placing the fly 4 to 6 feet in front of the bonefish. If the fly falls behind your target, the fish will spook instantly.*

● *You must learn to detect a strike without actually seeing the fly. Often you will be casting into a surface glare where visual contact is lost. Bonefish do not take a fly forcefully; usually they just mouth it. By keeping your rod tip down, touching the surface, and eliminating any slack in the line, you will feel the strike in your line hand. It will be a mere "bump" or tightening of the line as you retrieve. The posture of the fish is also an indicator: A taking bonefish will make a short dash forward, then stop in a head-down position.*

● *You will find that bonefish are usually an exception to the fast retrieve rule for most saltwater game fish. Often a stationary fly, or one that is sinking, will draw a strike. The most effective retrieve is slow, in very short pulls of 2 to 3*

inches, increasing its speed only if the fish turns away.

● *When bonefish are feeding over a firm bottom, you can get much closer to them by wading, especially on windy days. More bonefish are spooked by the sound of water slapping against the boat than by the flash of rod and line in the air. Even in a slight breeze, the steady slap-slap of water against the hull will trigger their mass departure before you can get within casting range.*

● *You will rarely find a trophy bonefish of 10 pounds or more in a big school. Their swimming speeds differ and the older fish show no desire to compete for food. Trophy bonefish usually appear as singles or pairs and occasionally in pods of three to six fish. Watch for their activity along channel edges.*

choice. One can discount the popular Cayman Island method of chumming with anchovies or sardines. Chumming with any food form simply creates an abnormal condition (effective though it may be) which doesn't reflect food habits. In both seine and rotenone collections that I made in small, isolated tide pools over a three-year period, the numerical abundance of vertebrates has always been high, but compared to stomach contents, low. The exceptions are the snake eel and cusk eel, which are minor in occurrence, the frillfin goby and juvenile schoolmaster snapper in the Florida Keys and islands of the northern Bahamas. The goby is well imitated by the Muddler Minnow fly pattern, and a dominantly orange fly the juvenile coloration of the schoolmaster.

Among the brightly colored bonefish foods are the segmented worms or annelids of the class Polychaeta. The polychates of flats importance are mainly burrowing forms found in sand, marl and coral crevices. Some species are blue or brown in color and others are iridescent red or orange. These worms emerge partially or wholly from their dens when searching for food. One polychate, known as the palolo worm, which is common to the Florida Keys, creates a feeding orgy even among tarpon during its brief breeding period when the worms swarm near the surface. Actually, the swarm does not consist of whole palolo worms, but individual segments from their posterior ends, called epitokes. This segment breaks off and swims to the surface where it literally explodes and releases its eggs or sperm. The mass epitoke phenomenon is triggered by warming water temperatures near the end of May and the beginning of June, usually when the moon reaches its third quarter. A "hatch" may occur as early as April and into July in the extremes of its western Atlantic range. It occurs in November and December in the South Pacific. The palolo epitoke is comparable to the trout angler's Green Drake in stirring fish to feed, and both bonefish and tarpon can become extremely selective as these hatches progress. Palolo worms attain a length of 2 feet or more, but the epitokes are only 2 to 4 inches in length.

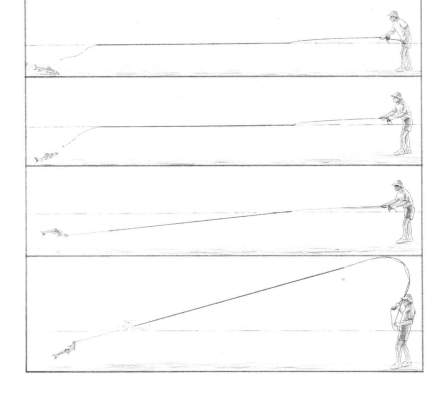

Florida Keys

The Florida Keys comprise a nearly 200-mile-long archipelago curving southwest from Miami. They begin where Sands, Elliot and Old Rhodes keys form the entrance to Biscayne Bay and extend to Key West. Except for the latter, there is no visible charm to the island chain. The narrow Overseas

Highway is a ketchup-smeared artery with plastic aromas of motels and new condominiums, and the wanging sound of stereos obscures flickering thunderheads on the Gulf horizon: Marinas and fish camps are squeezed between shopping plazas where acacia trees once stood; the road passes shacks and junked trailers and multi-million-dollar hotels with foundations sunk in the skeleton of a Pleistocene coral reef. In your headlight beam, you might see tiny Keys deer prodding a bag of roadside trash. Ever since 1912, when Henry Flagler completed his ill-fated railroad, which made the islands accessible by land transportation for the first time, tourists have flocked to the Keys. Flagler's dream was shattered by the 1935 hurricane, which dumped his tracks on the bay bottom.

Today, the Overseas Highway interconnects about twenty-five islands from the mainland to the southernmost community in the United States. Despite a carnival atmosphere, the highway is only marginally superimposed on the unspoiled "back country." There are approximately 400 mangrove-rooted islets scattered like a torn green tapestry on the northside of the chain, each varying from less than an acre to a few acres in size, which creates a shoal area of about 4,000 square miles. Seaward, the Keys face the deep indigo current of the Florida Straits, and while excellent fishing is found here, the vast flats on the opposite Florida Bay side provide some of the

greatest shallow water angling in the world for bonefish, permit and tarpon. The major fishing areas below Biscayne Bay are Key Largo, Islamorada, Marathon, Big Pine Key, Key West and the Marquesas. These are treated separately.

The Bahamas

The Bahama Islands are as far away from the rubbery smell of routine as the Arctic is from Zanzibar, yet in their periphery, no more than 48 miles from Florida. Flying from the explosive decibels of an American metropolis to the silence of the out islands can be unnerving. Over the rhythmic sucking sound of your guide's push pole, you may hear the *pop* popping of a donkey engine from some remote village, the flapping of a loose sail on an Abaco boat trading between cays punctuated by the *tap* tapping of its sole hungry occupant cracking a conch, or merely the sound of land crabs scuttling among the mangroves. There are said to be 700 qualifying islands and nearly 2,400 uninhabited islets in this 500-mile-long archipelago. While one of the deepest spots in the world's seas occurs in the Tongue-of-the-Ocean opposite Andros, the Bahamas have approximately 70,000 square miles of shoal water, which provide the most extensive bonefish flats in the world. Much of it can be sampled from established resorts, but many areas can only be reached by cruising yachtsmen, or charter boats

Although bonefishing is an exciting sport when a fish is hooked, the game is played in places of serene marine beauty where the horizon runs to infinity. Adrenaline-pumping runs of a powerful game fish merely underscore the nerve-calming silence of the remote cays, which have become an annual tonic for many anglers.

BONEFISH

out of Florida or Nassau. The following locations are accessible to the tourist angler where accommodations, guides and boats are available. With few exceptions, the quality of the floating equipment is generally well below the standards of guides in the Florida Keys, but on the other hand, there is infinitely more wadeable water and no heavy boat traffic; in some areas, you may fish for weeks and never see another angler.

Crooked Island

There are three islands encircling the shallow Bight of Acklins—Crooked, Fortune and Acklins. Columbus called this group "the fragrant islands" because of the aroma generated by the bark of cascarilla trees. In this heady atmosphere, you can boat and wade miles of virgin flats, where schools of 2½- to 5-pound bonefish often appear like dark clouds coming over the horizon. You will also find singles or pods of larger fish to 10 pounds or more. Rarely does a big bonefish occur in a big school *anywhere*. Their swimming speeds differ, and older fish have no desire to compete with a few hundred ravenous adolescents. For a trophy, wade along the channel edges after the school has scattered over the flat. The sight of forty or fifty tails in the air may send the adrenaline pumping, but if you can survive that, look for the big ones ghosting over the edge as the tide rises.

Although Acklins Island is the largest (150 square miles), Crooked Island offers the only

On the Flip Side

The value of the bonefish in the Bahamas far transcends a nickel per fish (you get two of them on a dime), but in 1966 the government sanctified Albula vulpes *in a way that people recognize best—on one of its coins. Various fish have achieved monetary immortality but none appears to be as antagonistic as the two on this ten-cent piece. A more familiar portrait could hardly have been etched of this "gray ghost" of the flats.*

Bonefish in the Bahamas

Bonefish are found throughout the Bahamas, but those areas with the most extensive flats or populations of large fish are of prime angling interest. The areas around Deep Water Cay, Chub Cay and Middle Bight off Andros offer countless miles of shallows with the possibility of trophy fish. Extensive flats where small fish are most abundant occur near Treasure Cay, the entire west coast of Andros, George Town and Long Island, and between Crooked and Acklins. Mini-flats exist from Walker Cay to Exuma.

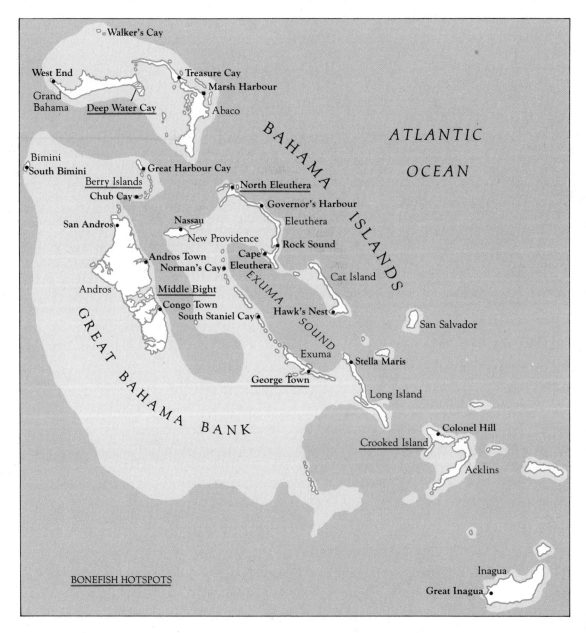

216

angling accommodation, with guides and skiffs located at Pittstown.

Long Island

Long Island abuts the Great Bahama Bank on its west shore. The east coast of the island is a dramatic headland (highest point 178 feet), where the hills drop suddenly to the sea. At present, the principal accommodation on this narrow, 60-mile-long island is at the north end in Stella Maris. Although the immediate flats areas are limited, huge schools of bonefish occur inshore over dominantly coral bottom at Bob Rock and on the hard sand banks out in the sound opposite Burnt Ground. The inside of the sound is composed of soft marl, which is constantly muddied (or "smoked" in the local patois), by feeding mullet and bonefish. Seaward, however, you can wade for miles in less than knee-deep crystalline water and stalk bonefish drifting with the ebb and flood, often with their dorsels out rather than tails out, turning in the current like trout on the mayfly.

The Cape Santa Maria area, at the northernmost tip of the island, has extensive flats, as well as creeks that can be fished at all tide levels. This is about a 20-mile drive from Stella Maris. Rental cars are available. Guides are available in Burnt Ground, but their equipment is generally poor. The accommodations at Stella Maris are first class.

Great Exuma

Great Exuma lies to the northwest of Long Island. Exuma straddles the Great Bahama Bank and offers a tremendous area of bonefish flats, running at least 25 miles, as the pelican flies, in one chain alone, encompassing a group of cays that extend roughly west of the Georgetown Airport as far out as Cokely Cay. These are intersected by a series of channels and creeks. Numerous banks also lie to the south. Bottom types vary from pure white sand to marl and sand, or sand and coral with patches of marl. You will also find both sparse and dense turtle grass beds. Wadeable flats are everywhere and provide hours of stalking. Exciting angling can be had at places like Bonefish Cay, where the schools work far back among the mangrove "ponds," then tail out in the current on an ebbing tide. It is very tricky casting in narrow streamlike openings, especially when 50 to 100 bonefish are all within range. The coral substrate harbors false mantis shrimp, as well as snapping shrimp. Here, the Green Mantis pattern is especially effective. Although the average bonefish is about 4 pounds,

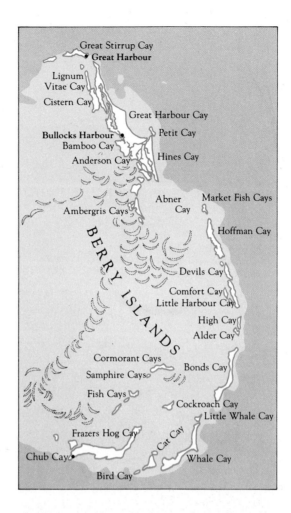

Sand bores indicate the 20-mile-long bank north of Chub Cay extending to Great Harbour Cay. This is an area that consistently attracts big bonefish in the 10-pound-plus class. The most productive location is the flats around Ambergris Cays, where wading is ideal on a hard sand bottom. Large permit also inhabit this area and at times appear in immense schools. The only viable resort accommodation at present is on Chub Cay, famed for its marlin fishing. A record bonefish is probable here.

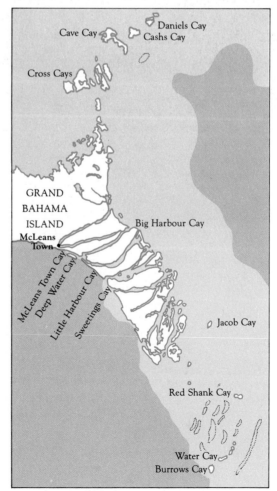

An Unspoiled Enclave

Except for two small native fishing settlements, the area at the east end of Grand Bahama is in a primordial state. There are over a hundred square miles of sand, marl and turtle grass flats intermittent from Daniel Cay to Burrows Cay, as well as many creeks that attract feeding bonefish. Permit also inhabit this area, with very large fish in the over-40-pound class occurring between Red Shank and Burrows Cay Barracuda and various snappers are abundant at numerous locations, providing fast sport for the light-tackle angler.

BONEFISH

large fish are fairly common, with the local record at 14¾ pounds, taken in 1980. This is the location for the Annual Bahamas Bonefish Tournament.

Georgetown is a bustling community geared for tourism. There are several first-class accommodations available, notably the Out Island Inn, which is unique in having its own skiffs and guides. The taxi drivers in Georgetown are reliable contacts for hiring bonefish guides, as they provide daily transportation between the hotels and the airport dock—a distance of 9 or 10 miles. However, one is well advised to make all arrangements for hotel rooms, transportation and guides well in advance of any Bahamian trip and have confirmation in letter form.

Eleuthera Island

On the map, 100-mile-long Eleuthera Island would appear to have extensive bonefish flats, but even its shoal west coast is deep inshore (10 to 20 feet) with many submerged reefs. There is limited fishing in the bays at Governor's Harbour, at Davis Harbour below Rock Sound and at Cape Eleuthera. The major Eleuthera flats are at the north end around St. George's Cay and Harbour Island.

St. George's Cay

St. George's Cay is a separate island at the northwestern tip of Eleuthera, reached by a short water-taxi ride to Spanish Wells. This village, first settled by the Puritans from Massachusetts Colony, is reminiscent of Cape Cod, with its gaily painted saltbox houses. Commercial lobster fishing by free diving from "smack" boats is the mainstay of the local economy.

The flats area around Spanish Wells is by no means extensive, but several miles of excellent wading bottom (principally sand over marl, with sparse patches of turtle grass) arc past the village out to Gun Point. These mini-flats are intersected by man-made channels. On a flood tide, schools of bonefish come out of the deep. The fish are spooky for 10 or 15 minutes, until they begin to tail. They continue to forage until late in the ebb, when the water is so thin that they are swimming with their backs out. I actually caught them in 4 inches of water. Evidently, the proximity of the channels makes their gourmet dinner hour a calculated risk. When hooked, they will also run off the flat into the deep, where a big fish can find numerous objects to wrap a leader around. Even village work boats roostertailing through the channels didn't disturb them when feeding. The average bonefish is probably 2½ to 5 pounds, but 7 to 9 pounds is a daily possibility. The local record is 14 pounds.

The author's ten fly patterns. Colors suggest common bonefish foods: (top) Pink Swimming Shrimp, Yellow Snapping Shrimp, Schoolmaster and Golden Mantis; (middle) Green Mantis, Brown Snapping Shrimp, Banded Snapping Shrimp and Brown Snapping Shrimp; (bottom) Bumblebee Shrimp and Grass Shrimp.

(Flies tied by Mary Beth Luscombe of Die-Werke International, Deland, Florida.)

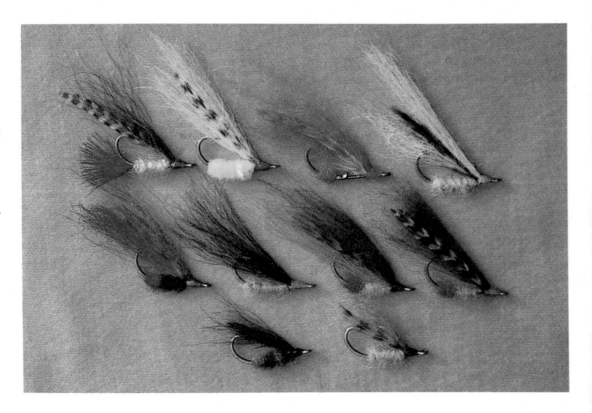

Nearby Curry Sound, on the Eleuthera mainland, about a 20-minute run to the southeast of Spanish Wells, with its picturesque "river" entrance, is worth investigating. Bonefish frequently invade the sound in vast numbers. A few small flats near the entrance are wadeable, but elsewhere the bottom is composed of soft, foot-sucking marl that will pop your topsiders off.

There are two comfortable resorts on Spanish Wells. Guides and boats can be reserved by the hotels; however, arrangements should be made well in advance.

Harbour Island

Harbour Island is a separate island at the northeastern tip of Eleuthera, reached by a short water-taxi ride to pretty Dunmore Town, the original capital of the Bahamas. There is a broad 3-mile-long pink sand beach on the east or ocean side of the island. Here, as at Spanish Wells, the flats area is not extensive, and your fishing hours are restricted to the tides. However, there is ample fishing from Nurse Creek to the Dixie Cays and some good wading bottom. On the flood and ebb tides, you may find fast action with tailers in the 3- to 5-pound class. Fish of 8 or 10 pounds make a polite appearance on occasion, but they meet a lot of anglers in the course of a season, and can be difficult.

Harbour Island has long been a popular family vacation resort, and several accommodations are excellent. Guides can be hired through the hotels.

Andros Island

Across the Tongue-of-the-Ocean is 2,300-square-mile Andros Island, the largest, yet comparatively unpopulated island in the Bahamas. The self-proclaimed "Bonefish Capital of the World," Andros has endless banks, particularly around its uninhabited west and south shores and at the north end, across Lowe Sound, in the Joulter Cays. The very best area for large fish is the North Bight, where 8 to 12 pounds is a daily possibility. The Bight, which bisects the island on a roughly northest to southeast axis, is a vast region of small cays and flats, which leads into the Middle Bight. There are miles of wadeable, firm, white sand bottom, as well as marl and turtle grass patches. This isolated area probably receives the least fishing pressure in the Bahamas, as there are relatively few accommodations.

Andros has a yo-yo resort history, beginning with Colonel Hank Thorne's old Bang Bang Club

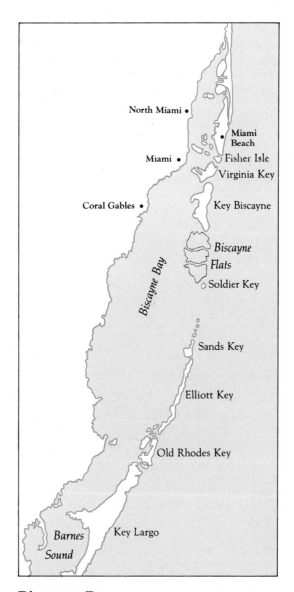

Biscayne Bay

Sparkling in the bright Florida sunshine, the vivid turquoise waters of Biscayne Bay not only add a unique beauty to Miami's skyline, but harbor one of the most impressive bonefish populations found anywhere. Starting from the Rickenbacker Causeway and Key Biscayne, a string of shallow flats stretches along the eastern perimeter of the bay down to Key Largo and beyond. The average size of the bonefish taken from this area is large, from 6 to 8 pounds, with a local record of 14 pounds. Trophy fish are spotted throughout the year, but April and May are the peak months.

Soldier Key is the first tiny island south of Key Biscayne, followed by the Ragged Keys, Boca Chica Key, Sands Key, Elliot Key, a tight group of small keys and then Key Largo. Bonefish and permit abound on both the ocean and bay side of these islands. In the middle of the bay just opposite Boca Chita Key, Featherbed Bank rises from the channel and offers excellent angling in spring, summer and fall. The other flats, however, remain good all year-'round. Some areas are better on an incoming tide, while others have more fish on a falling tide. Determining the best time to fish each flat is a matter of experience. However, the tourist angler will find competent guides and boats at the Key Biscayne marinas who make a specialty of bonefishing. The area is a mecca for boaters, swimmers and water skiers and numerous first-class accommodations are available.

BONEFISH

in the North Bight, and reaching seraphical heights in the 1950s, with the Lighthouse Club developed by Swedish industrialist Axel Wenner-Gren. Both went to death and taxes, and the only formal operation today is at Small Hope Bay, about 25 miles from the North Bight. Small Hope Bay itself has little to offer the angler; however, the resort can arrange trips with guides and boats to the North Bight.

Chub Cay

Opposite the north tip of Andros is a group of small cays collectively known as the Berry Islands. At present, the only operating facility here is at Chub Cay, which caters primarily to the big-game fisherman. The southernmost island, Chub, faces the Tongue-of-the-Ocean, where blue and white marlin, wahoo and dolphin are seasonally abundant. However, a 20-mile-long sand and marl bank extends from Chub Cay north to Great Stirrup that attracts some of the biggest bonefish in the Bahamas, particularly around Ambergris. Although small fish occur (most evident in cold weather), 6 to 8 pounds is common, and 10- to 12-pound fish are a daily possibility. On one four-day trip, my sampling of thirty bonefish, carefully weighed, averaged 7.1 pounds. Large schools of permit often occur on the same flats, especially along rocky (dead coral) shores, such as Cockroach Cay, and in the cuts between cays on flood and ebb tides.

Chub Cay provides excellent accommodations; however, the number of guides and boats is usually at a minimum, and it is advisable to make these arrangements well in advance.

Great Abaco

North from the Berry Islands is the second largest island in the Bahamas (649 square miles). Great Abaco is surrounded by countless small cays, creating an extensive flats area on the Little Bahama Bank. Some of the outer or oceanside cays, such as Munjack, produce bonefishing on isolated flats at the right tide, but most fishing is done on the west shore, or "inside," notably at Coopers Town and The Marls. The latter is an enigma to me. I have fished this endless warren of mangrove islands over a period of years, and never caught a bonefish exceeding 5 pounds. The Marls has an abundance of small fish, 1½ to 3 pounds, which at times can be taken to the point of boredom. The dominant silt and soft marl substrate doesn't allow much wading—in places, you'll sink out of sight. The Cooper Town area, on the other hand, has extensive hard sand banks with lush turtle grass pastures where 4- to 6-pounders are numerous. From here, the series of cays turning south toward Cave Cay, notably Smith Cay, Daniel's Cay and Cash's Cay, are all bordered by grass flats where large bonefish occur. This area is also within one hour boat range of Deep Water Cay.

There is only one resort on Deep Water Cay, which is a first-class operation devoted solely to bonefishing. The skill of the guides and the quality of skiffs and motors are excellent in all respects.

Mexico

Bonefishing in Mexico is limited to the east coast of Quintana Roo, one of the three states that comprises Mexico's Yucatán Peninsula. The fishing area extends from Cancun in the north and south to the tiny republic of Belize. There are many lagoons, flats and bocas (river mouths) that provide ideal habitat for bonefish. Although this coastline encompasses about 220 miles, the two

---

Bonefish in Mexico

Bonefish occur all around the Atlantic shores of Mexico but their chief distribution is along the east coast of the Yucatán Peninsula in the state of Quintana Roo. The major flats areas extend from north of Ascensión Bay and south to Belize; however, the only accommodations at present are located at
Boca Paila and Ascensión Bay. These are reached by air from Cozumel. Mexican bonefish are smaller than those found in Florida and the Bahamas, but they are more numerous, and well-run camps, plus a high percentage of calm days, make the area tremendously popular.

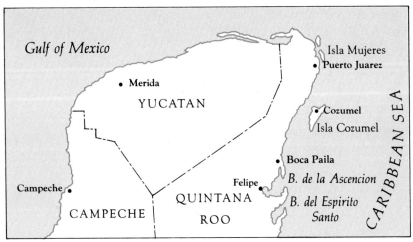

most productive areas for angling are at Boca Paila and Ascensión Bay.

Boca Paila

Boca Paila is about 90 miles south of Cancun and consists of a series of lagoons, mangrove islands, extensive flats and several rivers that drain into the Caribbean. The average bonefish found in this area is from 2½ to 3 pounds in size; although small compared to fish of the Bahamas and Florida, they come much more readily to a lure and provide hours of exciting sport, especially for the beginner. A 6-pound bonefish is an exceptionally good catch in these waters, and the largest recorded weighed slightly over 8 pounds. Nevertheless, it is an unspoiled shore offering more dependable winter weather than found in the North. As a bonus, fishing can be combined with fascinating side trips to the Mayan ruins at Chichén Itzá, Uxmal, Tulum and Cobá, on the Yucatán Peninsula. Archaeologists have identified more than 6,500 ancient buildings in this area, as well as one of the tallest pyramids in Central America. The Boca Paila camps arrange sightseeing tours to nearby Tulum and Cobá, which can be reached by auto in about 40 minutes. Other, more remote sites may be visited also. Tulum is unique in being the only Mayan ruin that overlooks the sea.

Boca Paila has two established first-class fishing resorts with competent guides and skiffs. The camps are similar in construction, offering comfortable cottages with high palm-thatched roofs in Mayan style. Both are located on the shores of the Caribbean with miles of white sand beaches. Boca Paila is only a 20-minute flight by small plane from Cozumel.

Ascensión Bay

Ascensión Bay is about 25 miles south of Boca Paila. This vast lagoon covers some 50 square miles, and provides some of the best bonefishing in Quintana Roo. The fish here average slightly larger than at Boca Paila. There are extensive hard sand flats for the wading angler. This area is so productive that guests staying at Boca Paila often elect to make the two- to three-hour boat trip necessary to reach the bay. Heretofore isolated, there is a new (1982) and comfortable camp located at Punta Pajaros, which can be reached by direct flights from Cozumel.

While the bonefishing is superb, the abundance of permit makes Ascensión a unique spot. Although the permit are uniformly small (6 to 8

pounds) when compared to those found in Florida and the Bahamas (18 to 40 pounds), they are much easier to take with an artificial lure. Before Boca Paila and Ascension were exploited, relatively few experts had boated permit on the fly—here the event is almost commonplace.

Bonefish are of minor food value and virtually all are released by sportsman anglers. When they are allowed a short period to recover before release, their survival rate is very high. Implanted with a sonic transmitter, one bonefish was tracked for three months after capture at Deep Water Cay. When possible, avoid releasing in the obvious presence of sharks or large barracuda: Both are capable of catching a "tired" bonefish. The fish should be grasped dorsally, behind the gills, to prevent injury in the ventral area.

TARPON

Megalops atlantica

Acentury ago, it was considered impossible to catch a giant tarpon on sporting tackle of any kind. Even with 200 feet of stout handline, S. C. Clarke, a contributor to Charles Hallock's *Camp Life in Florida* (1876), concluded that "No man is strong enough to hold a large tarpum [*sic*] unless he is provided with a drag or buoy in the shape of an empty keg attached to the line, which may retard or even stop the fish after awhile." However, in 1885, W. H. Wood of New York, an otherwise anonymous angler, caught a 93-pound tarpon on rod-and-reel, which falls short of the "giant" category of today, but it triggered frantic angling traffic to southern ports after a torrent of publicity in the weekly periodical *Forest and Stream.* Florida was still a mangrove and sawgrass wilderness, more remote than the Congo to European travelers, and even the staid *London Observer* was inspired to announce in 1886 that "Sportsmen may now go to Florida for the tarpon, as they now go to the Arctic Zone for the reindeer, walrus and musk-ox." But the giant tarpon remained an elusive trophy. One adventurer, Robert Grant, described a three-hour struggle using a heavy 8-foot trolling rod as "a hand-to-hand tussle with a wild beast." Reels of that era were without drags and applying pressure on the spool with a leather thumb was a heroic act. "The thumb and forefinger of my right hand, where, owing to the shortness of the handle, they came in contact with the screws and the side of the reel, were without skin and bleeding profusely. I had not realized the importance of gloves, having always fished for salmon with bare hands." Then, on April 30, 1898, Edward Vom Hofe, the skilled Brooklyn, New York, reel maker, boated a 210-pound tarpon in Captiva Pass. Since that day, the record has inched upward to a 283-pound tarpon, caught at Maracaibo, Venezuela, in 1956, but the maximum size of this species is known to be in excess of that figure; no synoptic history can ignore a possible

A school of tarpon invades a turtle grass flat in the Florida Keys.
Few sights are more compelling to the angler than the sudden appearance
in the shallows of fish that weigh in excess of 100 pounds.

TARPON

350-pound tarpon netted by commercial fishermen at Hillsboro Inlet, Florida, on August 6, 1912. Although the weight was only estimated, and perhaps liberally, the fish did tape 8 feet, 2 inches in length, which is measurably over the 300-pound mark (as a rule of thumb, 6 feet equates to 100 pounds, 7 feet to 200 pounds). Considering the passage of time, it may seem like nothing more than an exorcised hobgoblin, but during a low altitude aerial survey in 1981, a reliably estimated 300-pound tarpon was sighted on the banks near Homosassa—waiting like an armored Goliath for that ultimate contest.

The supreme adversary on light tackle is the repetitive jumper, most often a tarpon in the 40- to 90-pound class. One of the sea's great acrobats, the tarpon can leap 10 feet vertically and 20 feet horizontally. Fish have been known to jump over boats and, on rare occasions, into them, damaging both the craft and the angler.

DISTRIBUTION

Tarpon occur in all tropical, subtropical and warm temperate areas of the Atlantic. In North America, they range from the Gulf of Mexico to Virginia and appear as strays following the Gulf Stream as far north as Isaacs Harbor, Nova Scotia. They also inhabit the terminus of the Panama Canal near Balboa, but no population has ever become established in the Pacific. Although most abundant in Mexican and Florida waters, the fish seasonally appear off Texas, Louisiana, Georgia and the Carolinas. There are fishable populations of tarpon at a few islands in the Bahamas, chiefly around Andros, which has the requisite diluted salinities, due to its freshwater drainage; small migratory schools occur elsewhere in the Bahamas during the spring season, but essentially, the islands are not noted for this fishing.

There has been a decline in tarpon stocks in some Gulf areas which is largely attributed to the destruction of estuarine nursery grounds. The Texas coast, for example, was once an outstanding tarpon area, but beginning in the late 1950s the fishery went into a slump along the entire strand. Schools still appear in the summer months, but not in the numbers that made Texas ports famous. However, South Padre Island near the Mexican border, between Port Isabel and Port Mansfield, produced a 210-pound state record in 1973, and the West Delta of Grand Isle, Louisiana, posted a 222-pound, 12-ounce fish in 1979. Despite the fact that adults spawn offshore, the critical stage in their survival occurs after the metamorphosing larvae drift inshore where they remain as juveniles until 24 to 30 inches in length. Habitat destruction through pollution, dredging and filling has eliminated many former nursery areas. One of the few viable locations left today is the Everglades National Park. When they return to the sea,

tarpon have a life span of twelve to fifteen years. Small adults of 15 to 20 pounds are often caught far inland in rivers and canals, even in Lake Okeechobee. Tarpon can tolerate rapid changes from salt to brackish to fresh water; however, the freshwater environment must be calcium-rich (a deficiency in many coastal rivers) and not subject to prolonged cold weather. Their temperature tolerance is from 64° to 104°F, which makes them a fish in hot water and that's where the tarpon angler often finds himself.

Although small tarpon were taken on the fly before the turn of the century along the east and west coasts of Florida, there was no suitable tackle for slaying giants. Instead of our modern high-powered skiffs, tarpon anglers fished from rowboats and more often canoes, which a big tarpon could tow incredible distances, frequently swamping the craft. Unlike the space-age materials in use today, a 12-foot, 12-ounce ash and lancewood fly rod only provided ample leverage for the towing, but didn't exert enough pressure to stop a fish of over 40 pounds. By 1933,

fishing tackle had improved, and, while still inadequate to this particular sport, George Bonbright boated a 136-pound tarpon on a 9-foot bamboo fly rod near Long Key, Florida. Some of these early contests were titanic struggles—particularly with those occasional fish that vault over the surface horizontally and hit the water at Olympic speed, carrying the fight far away from the boat. Most tarpon will jump repeatedly in the same general area, and provided the tackle holds and the angler keeps a constant pressure on the fish, it can be expertly subdued within 30 to 50 minutes. However, the non-jumpers, usually big milt-laden males, can run the play into hours. Back in 1964, angler Bud Tepper of Plainfield, New Jersey, hooked one estimated at 160 to 180 pounds, while fishing with Captain Roy Lowe near Bahia Honda. The tarpon took that indefatigable pair on an unscheduled tour of eight keys before they were forced to break the fish off after dark. Tepper had the fish on for nine hours.

Fly-fishing for tarpon can range from sheer boredom to absolute chaos. Staked out on a heat-hazed sand bank, the angler may stand staring at the water hour after hour, until his brains turn to jelly and his legs begin to wobble. Fortunately, there are few dry runs in the season of the silver king. On a spring morning, when the tide is in flood, and giant specters appear over the white bottom, he is suddenly faced with something so awesome that it hits the gut like a shock wave—a file of 10, maybe 20, fish of 100 pounds or more, coming into focus, then vanishing in the sun's glare. All the dull moments evaporate instantly as the tarpon bunch up and turn straight for the boat. It is conceded that a hooked tarpon can leap 10 feet vertically and 20 feet horizontally. There is no reason to doubt this, since I have seen fish somersault over a skiff, clearing the angler's head by at least 2 feet, and even had one crash on deck in an explosion of scales that showered like silver dollars from a berserk slot machine. A big tarpon can absolutely wreck a boat. Both anglers and guides have suffered assorted broken bones and memorable bruises. This, however, is not a daily occurrence, and even if it were, no tarpon addict

TARPON

could be dissuaded from seeking immediate bodily repairs and venturing forth on the next tide. This is a *macho* sport, with a raw beauty and excitement all its own.

Ideally, the day begins about 8:00 A.M., when the sun is low in the sky, with your skiff staked out in about 3 feet of water on a slowly rising tide. Wearing Polaroids and a long billed cap, you stand rod in hand on the bow platform with 60 or 70 feet of fly line coiled at your feet. The sun isn't high enough yet to see clearly at any distance, and while watching the shimmering of light against turtle grass and sand you try to remember all the

The Clock System

*In all saltwater sight fishing, whether for tarpon, bonefish, permit, striped bass, red drum or any other shallow-water species, an experienced guide on his stern platform will often spot fish before the angler. Describing their position to the man holding the rod, who is standing at a lower angle and often looking into the sun's glare, is accomplished by a clock-face analogy. No matter in which direction the boat swings at any given moment, the bow is **always** pointed at 12 o'clock, while the stern represents*

6 o'clock. At an absolute right angle to the boat is 3 o'clock, and to the left 9 o'clock. In addition to giving direction, the guide will observe that fish are now at 100 feet coming straight for the boat or turning left or right. Whether you can see the fish or not, the chances of delivering an accurate intercepting cast are excellent as you already know the length of your fly line. Fortunately, it is better to cast short than over, as tarpon are spooked by a lure that falls behind them or by the falling line.

little things that can go wrong when you have to perform; your feet are clear of the shooting line with the belly portion trailed next to the boat (so all you have to do is drop the fly from your fingers and roll the head out straight into a long, fast cast), how to estimate the tarpon's swimming speed—which is ponderable as estimating quarterly income tax—their angle of approach, compensation for the rising breeze; check the reel's drag again (remember to back it off if you do get lucky and the fish makes a long run), don't forget to drop the tip of the rod to create slack in the line when the tarpon jumps. Above all, remember to keep pressure on the fish, always pressure with the full bend of the rod or the game will get out of hand with the tarpon running all over the ocean. There is a very slim margin between maximum pressure and breaking off. You can feel moths pounding in your stomach as vagrant shadows appear in the distance while you go over the checklist. Remember the guide is standing on the platform directly in back of you and for God's sake, don't snag *him* with your back cast. Guides are not expendable, and when hooked, they have no sense of humor. By the time he announces, almost casually, "One hundred feet at one o'clock," you are psyched into the violent world of the silver king.

With the sun still at a low angle, only the guide on his higher platform has an absolute fix on the approaching tarpon and while two o'clock is accurate, all you see is a movement in the water and you underestimate their speed. The fly lands in the middle of the school which causes them to spook and run a short distance, boiling at the surface and milling in circles. You must lead a tarpon the way you'd swing at a duck on the wing. But now, a second pod of fish is coming up the bank in the same direction and one monster rolls at one o'clock as you quickly strip the line back for another cast. This time the angle of light is right—dark shadows over white sand—and you shoot the fly about 10 feet in front of the lead fish. You retrieve the line slowly, imparting a slow jerking movement to the fly. The fish follows it but doesn't take, momentarily losing interest as he turns away. But like a giant cat eyeing a mouse, when you speed up the retrieve, he suddenly pivots and pounces, gulping the fly in a bucket-sized mouth. You wait for what seems like an eternity, and the guide shouts, "Hit 'em, hit 'em again, again," and the flat explodes as the tarpon twists into the air. For long minutes the experience will be out of focus while the slack line whipping off the deck scorches through your

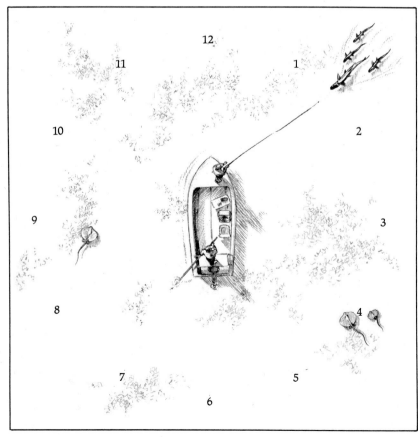

fingers as the fish sprints and madly flings himself skyward with his gills rattling like tribal drums. As the fish turns left, you arch the rod to the right; as he turns right, you arch it to the left, and as he runs straight away, you give him the full bend directly overhead. Pressure. At each jump, you "bow the rod down," dropping the tip to minimize the chance of a leader break. It is so easy to recite, yet so hard to remember these moves when over 100 pounds of furious tarpon decides to go over the horizon. As the backing line spins away, the diameter of the reel spool is decreasing, which increases the amount of drag, so you must back it off and "fine tune" by palming or fingering the line against the rod butt. Time and again you crank in backing and get the fly line on the reel only to lose what you gained. When the tarpon finally slows down and comes to the surface blowing tired bubbles, you may feel like jumping in the water and joining him. But at that moment of truth, the rod pressure must be unrelenting or the fish will get his second wind and start all over again—a phase where the odds are definitely not in your favor. As the fish swims slowly alongside the skiff, you must be careful to keep the leader away from that powerful tail. Your guide will have a long-handled killer gaff for a tarpon of this size, or simply cut the leader or snap the hook out to set it free as the game is finished. It's your option. Ego satisfaction at the dock, or 55 hallucinogenic minutes that you'll remember all your life.

Twice in my angling career I have hooked tarpon on the fly that would reach the ethereal 200-pound mark. One managed to snap the leader an instant before the gaff and the other made one jump and ran 6 miles from Big Pine Key out into the waters of the Gulf, where it sank like the iron-clad *Monitor* and defied salvage. After three painful hours, I had to break it off by pulling on the line. But win or lose, a fly-rod tarpon is an ultimate angling experience.

Tarpon Fly-Fishing Tackle

The potential size of tarpon found in a given area dictates the type and strength of tackle required. For example, fly-fishing in the brackish creeks and canals of south Florida, where baby tarpon abound, permits the use of relatively light rods, leaders and lines. A 9-foot fly rod matched to a WF8F line is perfectly adequate. One popular location for this kind of fishing is the Tamiami Trail Canal, between the towns of Ochopee and Marco along US Highway 41, and the connecting Everglades Canal along State Highway 29 and the

Marco Canal along State Highway 92. Tarpon in these waters run from a frantically jumping 2 to 10 pounds, as does the occasional snook. In many places, the canal is wide (80 to 100 feet) and the fish are shy, which often demands longer casts than you would need out on the Keys flats. Success here is dependent on quiet stalking to visibly feeding, rolling or cruising fish. There is always the possibility of hooking a snook of 15 pounds or more and for that reason, a shock tippet of 30- or 40-pound-test monofilament is recommended.

In the Florida Keys, or on the west coast grounds at Homosassa, where 100- to 150-pound fish are the norm, heavy tackle is essential: a 9- or 9½-foot graphite or boron rod suitable for WF11 to WF13 size lines. The WF12 floating line is most popular. This is matched with a heavy-duty saltwater reel, such as the Seamaster, Billy Pate or Fin-Nor with a multi-disc- or large-disc-type drag capable of maintaining a constant setting. The smoothness and reliability of the drag are absolutely critical to fighting giant tarpon. The reel must have a capacity to hold the fly line plus 250 yards of 30-pound-test Dacron or Micron backing. If your reel will not spool the full backing (which is true of some less expensive models), it is advisable to cut off 15 to 20 feet of the running portion of the fly line. The WF11 to WF13 sizes are milled at 33 meters, or 107 feet in length, which after cutting leaves 87 to 92 feet for the casting portion. It is most unlikely that you will ever have to reach this distance; it is more important to have an extra 30 or 40 yards of backing on the spool. Typically, a 100-pound tarpon will fight anywhere from 30 minutes to an hour, depending on the strength of the tackle, depth of the water and the pressure skillfully applied by the angler.

Leaders for this kind of angling are designed for durability rather than invisibility as tarpon are not shy. The key strand is the tippet, which may be 8-pound-, 12-pound- or 16-pound-test. This determines how the catch will qualify for record.

Tarpon Flies
Fly patterns for tarpon are non-imitative, but there are days when some color combinations work better than others and small sizes work better than large ones—and vice versa. Experienced anglers keep a good variety on hand in light and dark dressings. Some of the favorites are: (top row, left to right) Black and Orange Flapper, Die Werke Shrimp and Aqua Roach; (second row) Mid Nite, Apollo and Blue Sunset; (third row) Blue Flapper, Green Flapper and Tarpon Slider; (bottom row) Apollo I, Black Death and Cockroach. These are tied on carbon steel hooks.

(Flies tied by Mary Beth Luscombe of Die-Werke International, Deland, Florida.)

TARPON

The tarpon skiff, which evolved in the Florida Keys, is designed for high-speed running and maneuverability in shallow water. Essential to a good rig is the bow casting platform and a stern sighting platform for the guide. Outboard engines are often supplemented with electric motors for noiseless maneuvering in shallow water.

---

[1] Die-Werke International has designed a needle-sharp tarpon hook produced by Partridge of Redditch, England, made of high carbon steel that is four times stronger than those previously available. These hooks will not bend or break with a 16-pound-test tippet.

A 12-inch section of much heavier 60- to 100-pound shock tippet terminates the leader to prevent abrasion in the tarpon's mouth; this adds nothing to the actual breaking strain. Except for a few experts going for records, the 16-pound-test is obviously a better choice. A 9-foot-long leader is recommended and constructed as follows: the butt section, 6 feet of 30-pound-test-hard monofilament, followed by 2 feet of 16-pound-test, adding a 12-inch section of 80-pound-test shock tippet.

Tarpon prey on a variety of sea life, including

mullet, pinfish, needlefish, crabs and shrimp. Although fly patterns are considered non-imitative, the size and color combinations do affect results. A selection of subdued as well as bright flies is necessary. Fanciful pattern names, such as the Chinese Claw, Blue Death, Pink Fluff and Cockroach, don't suggest marine food forms, but they are undeniably effective. The basic tarpon streamer is tied on a No. 2/0 to 5/0 Monel or stainless steel hook,[1] with a simple saddle hackle and bucktail wing and a tinsel- or nylon-wrapped body. It differs from freshwater dressings in that the hackle is tied in just above the hook bend, leaving almost the entire shank exposed. This is an important non-fouling feature; on windy flats, a long 4- or 5-inch wing tends to wrap around the hook, inevitably at the most critical moment. Equally important is that the hook point be filed to needle sharpness. The sink-rate of the fly should not be too rapid, as tarpon will seldom take if it sinks beneath them.

Spinning and Bait-Casting Tackle

Tarpon are readily hooked on the flats and in channels on live baits, such as shrimp, crabs, pinfish or mullet. This is done with heavy-duty gear, by still fishing, drifting or casting to visible targets. Optionally, and to most of us more enjoyable, is sight fishing with artificial lures such as plugs, plastic worms or squids, lead-head bucktails and a topwater lure known as a slider or skimmer. In either method, both spinning and bait-casting tackle must be suitable for giant tarpon; many tourists coming to Florida for the first time arrive with freshwater rods and reels that are totally inadequate to the heavy stresses of even modest-sized 60- to 80-pound fish. For spinning you will need a stiff 7-foot rod and reel such as the Daiwa BG60 spooled with 15- to 20-pound-test monofilament; the latter test is preferred. For bait casting, use a stiff 7-foot rod and a reel such as the Daiwa 52H or 55H spooled with 15- to 20-pound-test. Customized rods are much superior to stock models; these are made from Fenwick or Shakespeare blanks (Ugly Stick) mounted with carbon silicone guides and Fuji reel seats.

Some experts out to set IGFA line-class records fish with 12- and even 8-pound-test; however, the average angler in big tarpon country is well advised to use a 15-pound-test minimum. This provides the best sport as you can pressure the fish, literally goading it into jumping, and terminate

A 9-Foot Fly Leader for Giant Tarpon

Tarpon are not leader shy and strong terminal tackle is absolutely essential. A heavy shock tippet protects the 15-pound-test monofilament from the tarpon's extremely abrasive mouth. The loop-to-loop connection formed with a Spider Hitch or Bimini Twist permits quick replacement of the fly by having premade tippets on hand. The Homer Rhode Loop

Knot allows the fly to swim freely in the water, despite otherwise rigid 80-pound-test material. This same leader design is suitable for many saltwater game fish—marlin, sailfish, yellowfin tuna, striped bass, large red drum, bluefish, etc.— when heavy No. 11- to 13-weight tackle is required.

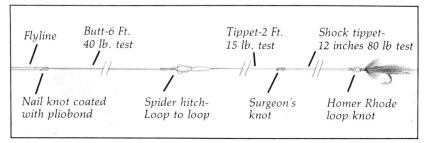

Flyline	Butt-6 Ft. 40 lb. test		Tippet-2 Ft. 15 lb. test		Shock tippet- 12 inches 80 lb test
Nail knot coated with pliobond	Spider hitch- Loop to loop		Surgeon's knot		Homer Rhode loop knot

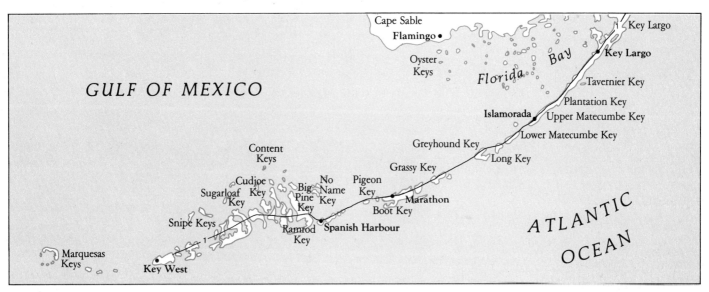

the play before your tarpon turns into shark bait. Old pros, like Gilbert Drake, Sr., who has enjoyed half a century on the flats, get as many jumps as possible before trying forcefully and purposely to pop the fish off when it settles down to a tired tug of war. Rare is the beginner who doesn't want to see his tarpon at boatside, if not on the dock, but diddling with a giant on cobweb line for hours on end is not sporting, as its recuperative powers and chance of survival are minimized. Florida flats are especially noted for hammerhead sharks which unerringly locate an exhausted fish.

There are various terminal rigs designed to protect the end of a casting line from abrasion against the tarpon's body, or prevent fraying in its mouth, which though toothless, has the texture of coarse sandpaper. Wire leaders are popular but the simplest, and to me safest, is to form about 3 feet of double line with a Bimini twist, then add a 2-foot length of 80- to 100-pound-test monofilament to the double line loop with an improved clinch knot. Tie on the lure with a Homer Rhode loop knot.

The Florida Keys

This intricate pattern of channels and banks is unique, covering some 4,000 square miles of shallows where tarpon can be sighted and caught on light tackle. Although the silver king is found throughout the Keys on both the Atlantic and Gulf sides, the popular tourist ports from the standpoint of amenities are Islamorada, Marathon and Key West; the town of Key West also provides access to the Marquesas Keys, an isolated group of islands that lie 28 miles to the west. The present tarpon record for Florida is a 243-pound fish taken in 1975 at Key West—a remarkable catch on 20-pound-test line.

All types of accommodations exist in the Keys, from basic fish camps to motels and first-class hotels. Although there are registered guides available, most of whom specialize in flats fishing,

during the peak season (from April through June) it is often difficult to get a charter without advance notice. Many regular anglers book their favorites from year to year. Guides can be hired through the more than one hundred marinas and tackle shops in the Keys, or at your hotel, or by contacting World Wide Sportsman, Inc. (P.O. Box 787, Islamorada, Florida 33036; telephone [305] 644-4615). Both the guide and his boat are critical elements to the sport. It requires local expertise to navigate the complex of islands and to arrive at productive locations on the right tide; some banks only hold fish at the incoming stage and others are better on the falling tide. Since the tide changes twice a day and advances approximately 50 minutes later every twenty-four hours, the guide must work with a set of familiar variables to determine where the fish will appear.

To meet the specialized requirements of the game, a 16- to 19-foot fiberglass or kevlar hull, powered with a 135-horsepower outboard motor, is typical. This rig can barrel along at 35 knots, which provides the capability of reaching widely separated locations in a minimum of time. The outboard is often supplemented with one or more electric motors for noiseless maneuvering. Tarpon are very sensitive to engine noises, and the guide will shut down a long distance from the area to be fished. When poling, most guides use a 14- to 18-

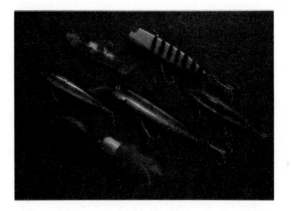

The entire length of the Florida Keys is tarpon country, encompassing some 4,000 square miles of shallow water. Most anglers who fish the upper Keys base in Islamorada. They use Marathon for the mid-section and Key West for the lower Keys and the Marquesas. However, accommodations can be found throughout the length of this island chain.

A great variety of spinning and bait-casting lures are used for tarpon but, essentially, jigs, plugs and topwater sliders are basic choices and reliable. The seven lures shown here are among the most popular: (top row, left to right) Mr. Twister and Creek Chub Wiggle Diver; (middle row) deep-running Mirro Lure, Rapala Magnum and shallow-running Mirro Lure; (bottom) two variations of the Worldwide Sportsmen Slider.

(Lures courtesy of Worldwide Sportsmen, Islamorada, Florida.)

229

*Even releasing a giant
tarpon is an awesome
experience. They were
once considered impossible
to catch on any kind of
tackle, but modern fly-
fishermen are approaching
the magic 200-pound
mark. A number of fish
equaling or exceeding this
weight have been hooked
in the Homosassa Bay
area.*

*The Homosassa Bay area
has become a Mecca for
record-seeking tarpon
anglers. Guides and boats
are at a premium during
the peak May period when
giant fish appear. Guides
from the Florida Keys
often charter for this area
if booked well in advance.*

foot fiberglass push pole, while the angler stands
on the bow-casting platform. For giant tarpon, a
needle point, 8-foot-long body or kill gaff is
essential if the fish is to be boated for record; even
with this stout instrument, many guides have been,
pulled overboard, some injured and nearly
drowned. A small lip, or release gaff, is also used
for fish under 60 pounds, but the tarpon must be
completely whipped before it can be employed.

Homosassa Springs

This west coast Florida port 75 miles north of
Tampa has become the Mecca for a coterie of
experts who sally forth each spring in search
of a 200-pound tarpon on the fly. A run of
exceptionally heavy fish arrives on the Gulf banks
in May, where tarpon of over 125 pounds are
commonplace. The current record for the fly rod
on 16-pound-test tippet is a 186-pound tarpon,
taken off Chassahowitzka Point in 1981 by
Thomas Evans, Jr., of Grifton, Vermont. A
number of fish that would make or exceed the 200-
pound mark have been hooked. Typically, these
Homosassa migrants are larger in girth than those
found in the Keys,[2] which may be due to their
maturation at this point, or lush feeding
conditions, or both. Schools are often sighted in

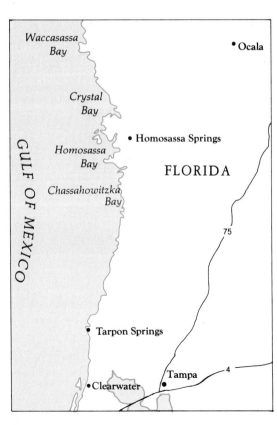

---

[2]Although 7 feet is the eyeball
rule for a 200-pound tarpon, it
is known that a 6-foot, 4-inch
Homosassa fish with a 46-inch
girth will provide the same
weight.

"daisy chain" formation, swimming in slow circles, one behind the other, suggesting a courtship act previous to spawning.

Tarpon fishing at Homosassa differs from the Keys in that it is accomplished in slightly deeper water. This, coupled with the wind and prevailing current, makes poling more difficult. In addition, the boat traffic has increased tremendously in recent seasons, making the fish skittish, thereby requiring longer casts upwind and down. Even the world's most experienced fly-rod anglers, experts like Billy Pate, Stu Apte, Al Pflueger, Flip Pallot, Carl Navarre and Steve Huff, find Homosassa a real challenge.

Constant rod pressure is the key to subduing tarpon of any size. Knowing exactly how much strain the tackle will tolerate is essential to success. A tarpon will quickly get its "second wind" if the angler tires, prolonging the fight and often ending with the fish breaking off.

231

PERMIT

Trachinotus falcatus

AND
OTHER JACKS

I have pursued the fabled permit, if not to the ends of the earth, at least to elephant trafficked Sri Lanka, which is hardly within the realm of a seven-day excursion fare, only to return and find that a new world record of 51 pounds, 8 ounces was caught 10 miles from my home in Mercedes-clogged Palm Beach, off the Lake Worth pier—a place no trophy hunter would expect to find *Trachinotus falcatus*. Permit are so unpredictable that baseball's angling superstar, Ted Williams, in his eminently practical volume, *Fishing the Big Three* (by John Underwood and Ted Williams, Simon and Schuster, New York, 1982), eliminated it as a contender for his ultimate triad of tarpon, bonefish and Atlantic salmon, simply because such a small number are caught on artificial lures that any discourse on the species produces a minor literary harvest. Indeed, like most flats anglers, I seldom plan a trip specifically to catch permit, with the exception of an occasional foray at Burroughs Cay in the Bahamas, where I am convinced a new world record is possible. I accept the fact that I will see permit from time to time when out for bonefish or tarpon and be frustrated once again. Even the sight of a permit school tailing over a sunlit flat is awesome, with their mirror-like forms shimmering in and out of focus as though contained in the crystal of a dream.

The permit is the rarest game fish in the world purely in terms of how few are caught, as opposed to how many anglers cast to them. Far from being scarce, professional Florida guides report seeing 1,000 permit in a single day on the Keys flats, and while this is far from common, sighting 100 fish is not unusual, yet the capture of even 1 is a notable achievement. I have caught 16 permit on the fly over a period of thirty years (this is one of few fish that anglers count and remember), after casting to hundreds (these we never count because you'd need a calculator). There are other anglers who have a better track record with the fly, but we can

*Coming on the flats with a rising tide, these giant permit are only
spectral forms when seen at a distance. Seemingly a foodless
environment, the bottom conceals an abundance of mollusks and crustaceans.*

PERMIT

all recite our scores over decades in low double-digit figures. Permit are not only difficult to deceive with a feathery fooler, but once hooked, a fish of 30 or 40 pounds may run 1 or 2 miles over an aquatic obstacle course that includes such traps as coral heads, sea fans, sponges and all sorts of vertical snags that a fish can wrap the fly line around. It will often contort its body, even bang its head on the bottom to get the hook loose, then take off again at speed. The game not only demands skill, but considerable luck.

Atlantic permit are found from Brazil to Massachusetts, through the West Indies and in the waters of Bermuda. However, in the sphere of this book, they only occur with frequency and great numbers in Florida, the Bahamas and eastern Mexico. The largest permit anywhere have been taken in Florida; the present world record (1983) and a dozen line class records were all caught between Stuart and Key West. There are three other closely related permit species in the Pacific Ocean, and one other species in the eastern Atlantic; however, the distinctions are chiefly skeletal, or in the relative length of fins and body depth. Few anglers ever catch one species, least of all the entire five. Young permit greatly resemble the generically related pompano and, indeed, are often marketed as pompano, and while body proportions are similar in fish up to 5 or 6 pounds in size, the fin ray counts will separate one from the other (see sidebar). Adult permit are usually bluish or grayish on the back, and the body is silvery, while the dusky tailfins and dorsal fin have a black anterior margin, which, at a distance, distinguishes a tailing permit from a tailing bonefish, as they feed similarly and often on the same flats.

DISTRIBUTION

The Deep Water Cay fishing resort at the east end of Grand Bahama offers access to hundreds of square miles of creeks and flats where the principal quarry are bonefish and permit. Although permit may be sighted throughout this area, the prime location for them is between Red Shank and Burroughs Cay, in a southerly direction from Deep Water. The camp record is for a 45-pound fish.

In the Florida Keys, it is generally believed that permit are most common on hard, rocky flats such as those near Key Biscayne and in the lower end of the island chain, especially south and west of Big Pine Key. However, two of the best spots that I know of for sighting large permit in the Bahamas are Burroughs Cay, which is surrounded by miles of white sand with patches of marl, and Ambergris Cay, another sand bank. Bonefish will come on the flats in mere inches of water, but the deep-bodied permit need more depth and arrive later in a flooding tide. They rarely create a "mud" with their feeding activity. The experienced angler looks for surface disturbances made by moving fish, or their waving tails and dorsals when rooting in the bottom. Always keep an eye open for feeding rays. Rays, with their powerful yard-wide wings, dig up large areas in search of mollusks and both permit and bonefish often follow close behind to share their bounty. Although a single fish will be seen occasionally, permit usually appear in a school of ten or more fish. I have never had any luck with the fly by casting to a group of fish. Those that I have caught were all singles, or doubles more or less isolated from the school. I somehow get the feeling that collectively, permit take a vote on what is edible, or artificial.

Floating Schools

Permit tailing on the flats is the classic situation whether the angler fishes with a fly or live bait. There is another feeding posture, however, which is less common, but when it occurs often results in

A permit hooked in deep water near one of the Key West wrecks is not as spectacular as one taken in shallow water, but the dogged play of a 20- or 30-pound fish is exciting at any depth, and to say that you have "caught one" is an angling distinction in itself.

fast action. This is known as a floating school, and is one of those rare times when the angler may hook one permit after another. Floating has its explanation in a tideborne abundance of crabs or shrimp. A school of fish may be seen holding or swimming very slowly just under the surface over deep water, oftentimes with their dorsals out. This usually occurs toward the peak of a tide when buoyant crustaceans are being swept along helplessly at the top. It is undoubtedly one of the most profitable times to cast for permit with artificials—if you're lucky enough to find a floating school. A choice place is in a deep cut between flats that permit are known to use. They will drop back with the ebb, and particularly where or when the current moves fast, as during a spring tide, a floating school might form. However, this does not guarantee fish in the boat. Captain Johnny Cass, a Florida permit specialist, once found a school near Content Cay milling around some drifting sargassum weed feeding on crabs. His two anglers hooked eight permit in a short period of time and landed none.

Tackle for Permit

The most popular permit tackle consists of a 6½-foot, medium-action spinning rod, a large capacity freshwater spinning reel with a reliable drag, and an 8- to 12-pound-test monofilament line. Some experts prefer bait-casting tackle with 12-pound-test, but this requires a bit more skill, particularly when working against the wind. At least 90 percent of all permit fishing is done with live bait

using a shrimp or small crab. These are mounted without a leader, the hook being attached at the end of 3 feet of double line made with a Bimini twist. A No. 2/0 Eagle Claw is an ideal size and pattern. However, permit will also strike leadhead

---

Permit Versus Pompano ID

The permit is a member of the pompano genus Trachinotus. *In juvenile sizes, the western Atlantic permit (T. falcatus) is often confused with the common pompano (T. carolinus), as they are identical in general appearance, and pompano of record sizes can easily be* mistaken for the much larger permit. However, they can be separated by the number of soft rays in the dorsal and anal fins, and the prominent rib bones (second, third and fourth) that can be felt through the sides of the permit.

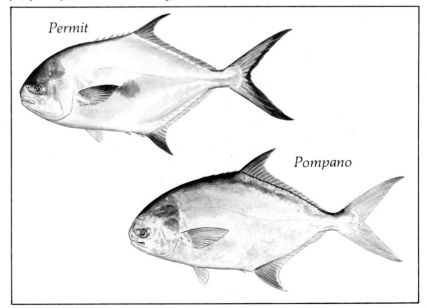

Permit

Pompano

PERMIT

At any size, the snub-nosed permit is a trophy game fish when taken on light tackle with an artificial lure. Fish of 30 to 40 pounds often require two hours to bring to boat when hooked in shallow water.

jigs in the one-quarter- to three-eighths-ounce sizes.

The fly-rod angler can use the same tackle recommended for bonefish (see page 214). Fly patterns should be dressed on larger hook sizes, however, with a No. 1/0 being most practical for these tough-mouthed fish. In recent seasons, permit specialists have been enjoying more success with slightly weighted flies such as the Puff, originated by Keys guide Nat Ragland. The weight is in the form of a pair of plastic eyes secured at the head of the fly, so that it sinks quickly and has an erratic jumping action when retrieved in fast pulls. The Puff has spawned a variety of eyed patterns in different colors, and although brown and black are favorites, most of my permit have been caught on white and yellow bucktail, winged flies. The majority of them took the fly almost instantly, before I could impart any action at all. My last permit taken at Grassy Key in the Bahamas snatched the fly on the surface before it could properly sink. But the Ragland concept is new to me, and may well be the answer to more consistent hookups.

North American Jacks

There are thirty-six species of jacks found in North American waters, ranging in size from the diminutive scads to the greater amberjack. In addition to the permit, at least five others are excellent light tackle game fish. All jacks are very strong swimmers, and some occur in shallow water where they can be caught on fly, spinning and bait-casting tackle. The trick in taking jacks on artificial lures is in using a fast retrieve. Jacks of one third the record weights listed are common. Powerful runs and plunges typify the jacks, but both the pompano and the bar jack will leap from the water when hooked.

Key West

Key West is one of the most productive locations in Florida for all types of saltwater fishing. This southernmost city in the United States mainland has become a trendy outpost with its street hawkers and dancers, restored mansions and tumbledown shacks. Nevertheless, this nineteenth century, deep-water port is a jump-off location for top-draw flats fishing. Local guides run to Mud Key, Barracuda Key, Content Key, Boca Chica Key, Newfound Harbor Key, Ramrod Key and islands too numerous to mention. One of the prettiest and most productive spots is the Marquesas Keys, a group of islands about 28 miles west from Key West. Permit and tarpon occur all around the Marquesas. As a dividend, there are many shipwrecks between Key West and the Marquesas and beyond (this area was a practice bombing range for Navy aircraft during World War II) which harbor huge populations of barracuda, cobia, snapper, grouper, crevalle jack, amberjack and permit. Fishing the wrecks is generally done with bait-casting or spinning gear by casting leadhead jigs with a piece of shrimp. However, for permit the usual technique is to chum an area, preferably with pieces of shrimp or crab and drift either crustacean in live form for bait. These chummed fish will also take a fly much more readily than those found on the flats. Key

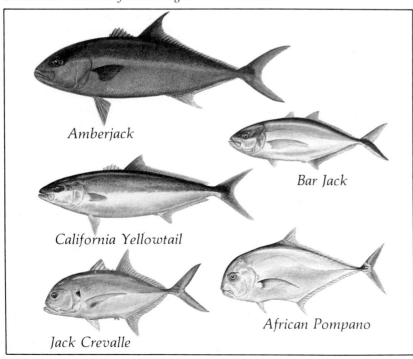

Amberjack

Bar Jack

California Yellowtail

Jack Crevalle

African Pompano

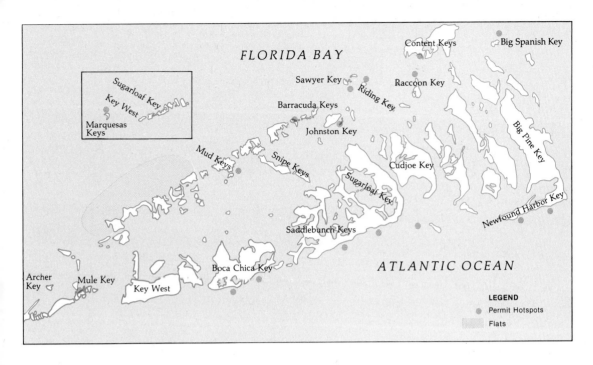

Permit are more numerous in the lower Florida Keys, especially in the Content Key to Key West area. However, they are well distributed throughout the entire chain, and hot spots, such as the ocean side of Long Key, Tea Table Key and Ocean Reef, produce many fish exceeding 20 pounds. The peak months on the flats are March to May and from late September to November.

West wrecks are probably the most productive permit grounds anywhere in terms of numbers of fish caught, although purist fly-fishermen, who view chumming in deep water as a less than sporting game, count these permit as "wreck fish," a separate category of achievement as opposed to fish stalked in shallow water. But with 20- to 30-pounders in evidence, especially from August through November, the experience justifies the means.

Burroughs Cay

This island, which lies 18 miles southeast of Deep Water Cay, has the potential for a new world record permit as fish exceeding 50 pounds have been sighted on numerous occasions. A run of giant fish occurred in the summer of 1982 (estimated as high as 70 pounds) but these might appear at any time.

Burroughs is uninhabited, although Bahamian conch boats sometimes lay in the lee between it and Little Burroughs. The extensive shallow bank consists of miles of pure white sand with only sparse patches of turtle grass extending in the direction of Red Shank Cay.

Burroughs is fished by anglers from the Deep Water Cay resort with a very high ratio of success (over 50 percent score one 20- to 40-pound fish per trip) with live bait. The resort record is 40 pounds, 8 ounces (1983). In view of this, and the fact that most visitors are neophytes seeking their first permit, very little fly-fishing is done at Burroughs. For some reason, bonefish are very rarely seen on these flats. It is strictly permit territory. The few permit stomachs I have autopsied revealed bits of crab, conch and sea urchins, but the great mass of food appears to be pea-sized snails common to this substrate. The angling is done by sight fishing from skiffs, but the

Snook

In North America, the snook (Centropomus undecimalis) occurs in Florida and Mexico, often feeding in the same areas with crevalle jack, red drum, seatrout or tarpon, especially where schools of mullet are plentiful. The snook is the only North American relative of the Nile perch of Africa (Centropomidae), which it surpasses as a game fish. It is strong, acrobatic and extremely wary. Snook are very sensitive to sudden cold snaps, becoming comatose at 60°F (15°C) and fishkills have occurred during severe winters. Ambient water temperatures account for their limited geographic distribution. In Florida, the snook is most

abundant in the southern portion of the state, and while the population has declined critically in the last decade due to loss of habitat and pollution, the species was given protected status in 1982 by establishing a legal size, bag limit and a closed season during its summer spawning period.

Considered a marine game fish, the snook is also found in brackish and freshwater rivers and even lakes with access to the sea such as Lake Okeechobee. The largest snook in Florida, exceeding 30 pounds, are caught chiefly in east coast bays and inlets from Vero Beach south to Miami, but numerically their population abundance is on the west coast from Boca Grande south through the Everglades region including Florida Bay. In Mexico, snook (known as robalo in Spanish) frequent all the major east coast river systems, notably in the Lagunas de Terminos of the Yucatán and along the shores of Quintana Roo. The common snook is also present on Mexico's west coast but another and larger species, the black snook (Centropomus nigrescens), which can exceed 60 pounds, is found in Baja California around Mulege and Loreto. However, black snook are seldom caught in great number.

All snook have razor-sharp gill covers. For this reason most anglers use wire leaders, whether fishing with plugs, spoons, jigs, flies or natural baits. At the very least, monofilament shock tippets of 60- to 80-pound-test are advised.

The Berry Islands of the Bahamas are noteworthy for big bonefish, but permit also appear regularly on the flats north of Chub Cay, especially in that area between Cockroach and Ambergris Cay. The average permit here is in the 20- to 30-pound class.

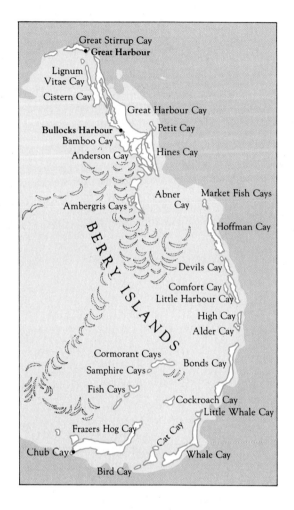

Permit Flies

Reliable fly patterns for the permit are not numerous. One innovation by professional guide Nat Ragland in the Florida Keys is the addition of plastic eyes in his Puff pattern to give the fly weight and create an erratic jumping action as it swims over the bottom. The following flies are recommended on the basis of having hooked more of these shy fish than others: (from the top) Sand Flea, Black Puff, Brown Puff, Moon Bug, T.W. Shrimp and, at the bottom, the Crab.

(Flies tied by Mary Beth Luscombe of Die-Werke International, Deland, Florida.)

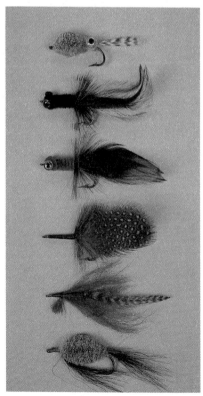

sand bottom is hard in most areas and easily waded.

Boca Paila

One of the most unique permit grounds is at Boca Paila in Mexico's Yucatán Peninsula. This east coast location has been popular for many years. There are several resorts on the water which offer all the amenities of civilization. Although bonefish are especially abundant on these flats, permit schools are often so numerous that you may cast to twenty or more fish in a morning session. These Yucatán permit are small, with the average fish at 6 to 10 pounds (22 pounds, 8 ounces is the only reliable record), but stalked fish come more readily to artificial lures than those found in Florida and the Bahamas.

In local Yucatán lore, which may be influential elsewhere, is the noontime phenomenon: From early morning until the sun reaches directly overhead, the Boca Paila permit can be stalked and hooked with some degree of certainty; but starting about noon, the fish become so spooky that it is almost impossible to get a shot at one, much less catch one. The Mexican guides relate this to the sun, believing that a permit can see the angler at much greater distances in an overhead light, probably more fact than fancy in this Mayan dogma.

The Other Jacks

Shortly after moving to Florida in 1952, I met a local angling expert who knew all the hot spots for snook. I had never caught a snook, so the first day we went fishing together, Ray Harmon showed me those little nuances in working a topwater plug with a whip retrieve. I was using a spinning rod that was vastly undercalibered for the job, but since I had no idea what I was supposed to catch, it really didn't matter. Properly instructed, I wandered down the beach until I saw a wake about 20 yards offshore, obviously made by a cruising fish. I cast my plug about 10 feet in front of it and before I could apply my newly acquired technique, the lure disappeared in a tremendous swirl. The fish charged and circled in all directions, and I set the drag tighter to slow it down. For 15 minutes I cranked and pumped, convinced that I had hooked a large snook. Finally, the fish relented, though stubbornly, and I led it back to the beach. I couldn't believe my eyes: a blunt-headed, slab-sided crevalle jack. I never realized that any fish so small could fight so hard. I doubt if it weighed 3

Map labels:

Great Stirrup Cay
Great Harbour
Lignum Vitae Cay
Cistern Cay
Great Harbour Cay
Petit Cay
Bullocks Harbour
Bamboo Cay
Hines Cay
Anderson Cay
Abner Cay
Market Fish Cays
Ambergris Cays
Hoffman Cay
BERRY ISLANDS
Devils Cay
Comfort Cay
Little Harbour Cay
High Cay
Alder Cay
Cormorant Cays
Bonds Cay
Samphire Cays
Fish Cays
Cockroach Cay
Little Whale Cay
Frazers Hog Cay
Cat Cay
Chub Cay
Whale Cay
Bird Cay

Usually taken over open water, the amberjack is a powerful bottom-plunging game fish. The largest of our jacks, it is most common on reefs and around wrecks and buoys, and is caught by various methods from surface trolling to deep jigging.

pounds. By 1966, I had taken countless jacks of all species, including a 40-pound, 10-ounce crevalle on the fly from the Loxahatchee estuary, which I would have to count as three of the most exhausting hours I ever spent with a rod. A fly reel, with its usual 1:1 gear ratio, is a punishing instrument when a non-jumping game fish runs off 200 yards of backing, again and again, as line recovery is a slow wrist-numbing process.

The jacks are members of a large family (Carangidae) of marine fishes found in all tropical and subtropical and some temperate waters of the world. Actually, there are eight genera of which sixty-seven species occur in the western Atlantic and eastern Pacific oceans. Many of these, such as the scads and leatherjackets, are too small to be of angling interest but others are powerful game fish; the Pacific yellowtail and roosterfish (see page 339), the greater amberjack, permit and crevalle of the Atlantic, and the giant trevally of the Indo-Pacific are all carangids. For sheer brawling power, jacks are giant killers. Locally, it has long been a standing ploy on days when sailfish are absent

from our Gulf Stream, and the captain has to produce some action to run to a reef off the Breakers Hotel where greater amberjack are usually in residence, and delighted to play with tourist anglers. Aside from trying to pull the anchor up with light tackle, the amberjack wins the comparison by animation alone. Our Palm Beach record is 108 pounds, well behind the 155-pound, 10-ounce world record taken on the Challenger Banks in Bermuda, but a formidable catch nevertheless. In general, jacks are indifferent foodfish, except for the related pompano, the bar jack and the prized Pacific yellowtail; however, in pioneer Florida days, hungry settlers used to shoot big crevalle for a "jack chowder" which merits no stars at table.

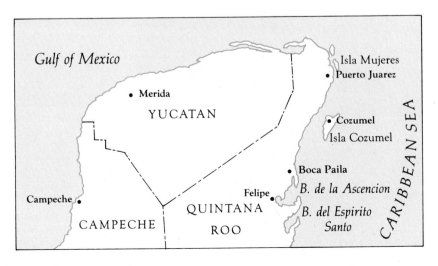

Permit occur throughout the Quintana Roo area from Cancun south; schools can appear almost anywhere. Although small permit of 6 to 10 pounds are common to bay waters, large fish are sometimes found on the "outside" or ocean beaches.

BARRACUDA

Sphyraena barracuda

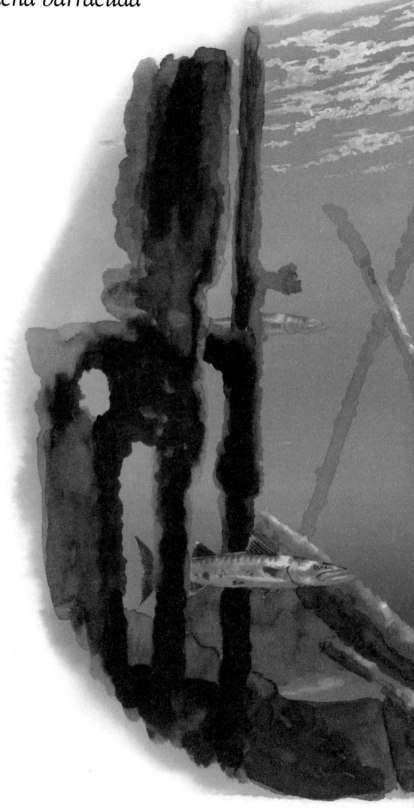

The great barracuda has an unpleasant body odor,[1] a mouthful of razor-sharp teeth and the disposition of a cornered wolf. It has been known to bite people, poison people and, on occasion, nearly induce cardiac arrest. The majority of barracuda are caught by tourists while trolling offshore for big-game species with comparatively heavy tackle. This is never interesting because in deep water the barracuda prudently dives for the bottom seeking the nearest coral head. Yet in shallow water, old razormouth has the speed of a rocket and will launch over the surface in a trail of wet sparks. One would imagine that so large a predator might strike any bait or lure but, actually, it becomes cagey on the flats, demanding skillful casting and a technique that transcends mere luck. The fact that barracuda habitually gape, wearing an almost permanent toothy grin, may well be an expression of disdain for clumsy angling efforts. And when eyed at boatside after a spirited play, the weight of a barracuda is consistently overestimated by all but veteran casters. If I had a dollar for every claimed 20-pound fish that actually scaled half that size, I would be a rich man indeed. Ego-inflated and innocent quotations aside, a barracuda not only *looks* bigger than other fish (in or out of the water), but its demonic fighting style in the shallows against light tackle defeats perspective at the moment of truth.

Broad jumping is the great barracuda's forte. In *McClane's New Standard Fishing Encyclopedia,* the late Joe Brooks attributes a 25-foot capability to them. On two occasions I have witnessed awesome horizontal leaps. Less known, because it

---

[1]The reason barracuda have such a distinctive smell is due to the copious amount of slime on adult fish, which aids in streamlining the body and in part accounts for its great swimming speed. This is not true of juvenile fish.

In the Florida Keys, great barracuda often situate themselves near bridges, lighthouses and other man-made structures, where they become public characters, virtually immune to angling. They are famous for broad jumping when hooked.

BARRACUDA

DISTRIBUTION

At Deep Water Cay Club on the eastern end of Grand Bahama Island, Burrows Cay is a hot spot for large barracuda. A rod, specially rigged for them, should be in the boat at all times when bonefishing. Barracuda are essentially a target of opportunity.

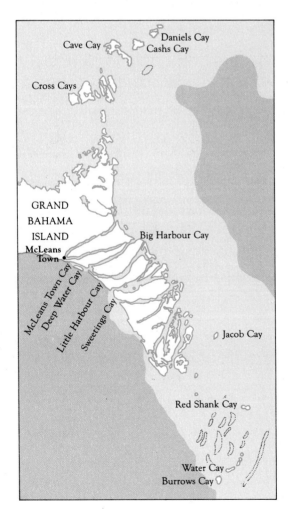

occurs less often, is the great barracuda's ability to *high* jump. I once hooked a fish that skyrocketed to a probable 15 feet above the water. I have seen free-jumping wahoo and hooked mako sharks reach similar heights, but in shallow water the sight is unforgettable.

This ability can pose problems. Captain John Eckard, one of the best light-tackle guides at Key West, has had hooked barracuda come aboard and land in his client's arms. One lady took a passing blow from an airborne barracuda that required nineteen stitches to close. For this reason, when casting for them, as the retrieve ends the pickup should be made to one side, rather than directly in front of oneself, on the ground that if a following barracuda jumps after a disappearing lure it would be prudent not to meet him head on.

Great barracuda grow to more than 80 pounds and a length of over 6 feet. In angling experience, a fish half that weight on light tackle would be the catch of two or three lifetimes. I took a 44-pound, 8-ounce barracuda while spinning a three-eighths-ounce Creek Chub Plunker surface plug on 8-pound-test line on the flats at Walker's Cay in the northernmost Bahamas in April of 1952. This fish was 5 feet, 5 inches long.

Barracuda become chunky at twelve to fourteen years of age, rather than adding weight in length. Their body coloration, a dull to bright silver with scattered inky black blotches, is no thing of beauty, although the crossbarred juveniles are delicate-looking, almost pearly in color. Historically, there have been numerous documented cases of barracuda attacking humans (their cleaver-like bite can be distinguished from that of a shark in consisting of two nearly parallel rows of tooth marks, as opposed to the jagged parabolic wound made by sharks) and what elicits an attack may be broadly summarized as surface splashing or erratic movements in the water, especially turbid water. However, considering the number of bathers, surfers, skin divers and wading anglers who daily enter barracuda habitat, such incidents are quite rare.

There are believed to be some twenty species of sphyraenids worldwide, and the great barracuda is one of the largest, second only to *S. jello*, an African species. Convergent evolution has shaped them like pikes, and early systematicists once classified them as *Esox*. The great barracuda is found in all tropical seas on both coasts of Africa, in the western Pacific, the Indian Ocean and Red Sea, indeed just about everywhere there is salt water warm enough for them (75° to 79°F optimum) except in the eastern Pacific. There are no great barracuda recorded for the Pacific coasts of North and South America, and the only eastern Pacific sphyraenids are comparatively small school fish. In Florida waters, adult barracuda migrate a short distance north in the spring and south in the fall following the 74°-plus isotherm. They also appear in the northern Gulf of Mexico during the summer months but vacate coastal waters with the advent of cold weather. The temperature preferendum of adult fish is a narrow one. Juveniles are evidently less mobile, or rather, have a broader range of acceptable temperature. In particular, they can withstand much warmer temperatures than adults, which allows them to get into very shallow, sundrenched water where adult barracuda cannot come to prey on them.

Juvenile barracuda have been observed as a schooling fish. One report of an estimated thousand 6-inchers in the Dry Tortugas (about 90 miles south of Key West) is credible because this site of Fort Jackson National Monument (where they incarcerated the doctor who set the leg broken by John Wilkes Booth during his assassination of Abraham Lincoln) is often stiff with adult barracuda as well. Adults do not school in the strict sense, but aggregations of large numbers occur at times until a length of just about a yard is reached. At sizes above that, they are either loners or travel in small groups. As barracuda grow, they change habitat. Foot-long juveniles favor sandy or weedy shorelines and mangroves. A bit longer and it is mangroves and reefs, and at 30-plus inches it is reefs and offshore waters. This means that many of the biggest barracuda become part of the catch by tuna and bill fishermen while trolling close to the reef line. However, with the first cool weather in the fall, barracuda of 10 pounds or more invade the shore areas behind reefs, in channel mouths and on the flats, providing excellent fishing through the winter season. A prolonged cold spell will send the fish back to deep and warmer water. Barracuda are territorial, cannibalistic and capable of killing very large prey. Nevertheless, they do congregate in loosely formed groups when feeding on schools of small fish such as mullet, herring, scads, mojarra, grunts, puffers or needlefish. In these foraging aggregations, the barracuda usually lie parallel to each other and at a distance on the flats their silhouettes often resemble cross ties in a railroad track. In the spring (May) the number of fish found in shallow water can be phenomenal in some areas of the Bahamas and Mexico. Despite their numbers these are often the most difficult barracuda to interest in a bait or lure.

Fishing the Flats

Sight fishing on the flats is the epitome of barracuda sport, yet despite being an aggressive forager, it is also one of the shyest of game fish when it comes to lure presentation. You can literally hit a shark on the nose with a well-aimed cast and it will strike a lure reflexively, but a barracuda is the very antithesis in predatory response—it will flash off to deep water and, like the proverbial toothless tiger, be thoroughly frightened. Once a barracuda is sighted (and preferably at a long distance), the game plan is to drop your lure 20 or 30 feet ahead of and beyond the fish and retrieve the bait across its line of sight. I have cast a plug more than 50 feet away from a big barracuda and triggered almost instant strikes. They are attracted to the far-off *plop* of a bait hitting the water and will come hungrily from incredible distances. Their eyesight is remarkable;

their hearing superb. It is almost impossible to reel fast enough to get the lure away from one, so the object is to draw the fish to the lure, rather than the logical practice of casting the lure to the fish. This must be accomplished at maximum range; short casts are not as effective as long ones of 100 feet or more. If the barracuda is suspicious, it will stalk the lure making false passes, and if the cast was short, the fish will quickly come in sight of the boat. Although barracuda are one of the most curious fish in the sea, and will examine your rod tip like a prospective buyer, almost invariably they lose their enthusiasm for a lure the instant a boat or angler is within view. It is the speed of the retrieve that provokes strikes, and with a short cast you will run out of water in a hurry. If the lure is retrieved slowly, one or more barracuda will follow the bait but make no attempt to hit it. If the lure is stopped, the barracuda will stop and turn away. If the lure is worked at a fast pace, and

Holding a fish with a grip inside *the gill cover can damage the gills irreparably. It would be better to hold it across the top of the head, pinning the gill covers flat under one hand if the barracuda is to be released.*

BARRACUDA

the barracuda pursues it without striking, a slight increase in its speed will generally bring a flashing hit. As a rule, that is not hard to do because the reaction of the individual barracuda is obvious.

There is no question that barracuda are attracted to flashing objects and one would assume that spoons are good lures. This is not true on the flats. Spoons have some success in deep-water trolling, but when casting in the shallows these subsurface baits are less effective and frequently snag in coral and grass. Actually, the number of lures suitable for barracuda is quite limited. The most popular bait is the tube lure (see below), which certainly accounts for over 50 percent of the barracuda caught today. However, it is not

Tube Lure

For many medical purposes, hospitals could not function without a rubber or plastic material called "surgical tubing." To skilled anglers operating on the flats, the same tubing is equally essential. It makes the greatest barracuda lure of all time.

Manufacturers of the material store and sell surgical tubing coiled on a drum. This gives the product a slight hemispherical set. You do not want to straighten that curve; therefore, store your surge-tube lures coiled in a circle. Since tube lures are not widely distributed, it may be necessary to make your own. Cut a 29-inch length of quarter-inch I.D. tubing with a square cut, double this and cut it in half with an acutely diagonal cut. You now have a pair of 14½-inch tubes with square-cut heads and tapering tails. Bend each tube in half to get the midpoint and make a hole there just large enough to accept the eye and shank of a No. 6/0 hook. Using a

#8 stainless steel single strand wire and the haywire twist, separately wire two hooks with sufficient length to go through a half-ounce egg sinker and fasten to a good quality swivel at the head. Chartreuse, fluorescent yellow, fluorescent red and natural are the preferred colors. At this point you have a standard tube lure to skitter across the surface like a fleeing needlefish. Captain John Eckard goes one step further. Working from the tail hookup to the center hook, but no further, he tightly wraps the lure around two fingers of one hand to make it take an acute set. The resulting shape is like the letter J and the lure is reeled to keep it submerged throughout the retrieve. Either way, skittering on top or rotating underwater, a tube lure produces the illusion of swimming needlefish with deadly effect.

infallible and an assortment of topwater plugs covers all occasions. Most modern plugs are made of hollow plastic which barracuda can easily puncture, but there are several good wooden plugs on the market that will take plenty of fish before being chewed to splinters. Floaters such as a chugger or stick bait are old reliables. A typical stick bait is the original Heddon Zaragossa, named after a street in the Pensacola, Florida, red-light district. This plug has been reincarnated as the Zara Spook. Stick baits float with their head out of the water and their tails submerged at a 45-degree angle. They are retrieved across the surface in rhythmic zig-zags called "walking the dog." This is done at a moderate pace with pauses when fishing for freshwater black bass, the method's original target species, but in salt water a more expeditious retrieve is recommended. You walk the dog by pointing your rod tip at the floating plug and reeling in while rotating the tip in 6- to 10-inch circles. The rotating tip pulls the lure from left to right in a herringbone pattern. My friend Chico Fernandez, the premier saltwater fly tier, hums a tune to establish a rhythm while walking the dog.

The way we fish for barracuda in the Bahamas and Mexico is to stalk them along mangrove shores by slow-poling parallel to the islands. Although the fish can be big, it's surprising how many you will spook in the course of a day. Unlike bonefish, which are almost constantly moving about, barracuda lie motionless and may appear as nothing more than a shadow on the bottom. This almost comatose state, whether for predation or protection, begins early in life. Postlarval barracuda, only inches long, have been observed standing head down and tail up amidst turtle grass, even swaying like grass in the current. During a high tide adult fish may lie right up among the mangrove roots and because of their ability to blend into any background, even a 3- or 4-footer is hard to see until you've had some experience. Small sharks, such as the lemon, shovelnose and nurse, are always common in the same areas, but these can easily be distinguished by the undulating movement of their tails. The flood and high water are the best fishing periods as a rule; as the water falls the barracuda retreat to nearby channels.

Barracuda are primarily a plug caster's quarry. They can be caught on large streamer flies and even topwater bugs, but two factors work against fly-fishing. You not only need to make very long casts, but the fly must be retrieved rapidly— which is faster than most people can strip line. A hundred curious barracuda will follow a fly for every one that actually strikes. This can make fly-

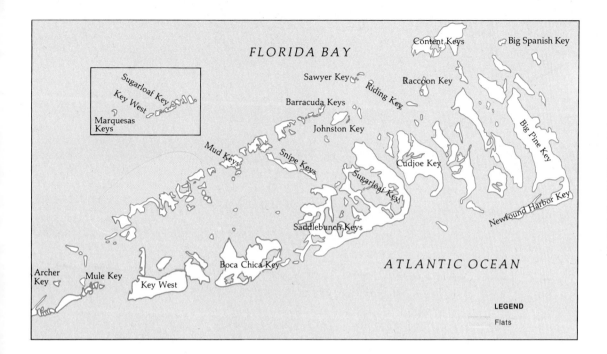

The Marquesas Keys, Key West and others of the Florida Keys have all produced record-book great barracuda. Sophisticated guides recognize that the publicity of record catches increases the demand for fishing on the flats.

fishing a tedious game for the beginner who might get a galloping case of bursitis before hooking the first big fish. Some anglers even tuck the rod between their legs after making a cast and yank the line back hand over hand. However, the normal method of retrieving works if accomplished at a swift pace. Fly-fishing for barracuda was seldom greatly successful until recent years, when a means of tying a needlefish representation was developed by Keys' fishermen Ray Donnersberger and George Cornish. A 9-inch length or longer of artificial hair, generally white underneath and blue or green on top, is whipped onto the hook. The tail end of this elongated streamer fly is then dipped into a rubber-based glue to maintain a needlefish profile (without flare) during the retrieve. Considering the barracuda's wicked dentition, either a heavy monofilament shock tippet or 6 to 12 inches of single-strand piano wire must be added to the leader.

The diet of a great barracuda is piscivorous, of course, but it contains one oddity. Large adults are often found to contain forage fish of approximately an inch long. This is one game fish (tarpon being another) where the big lure-big fish axiom is inapplicable.

Barracuda in the Florida Keys

Although barracuda occur on the flats throughout the entire year, they are most abundant during the cooler months (November to April). Even when water temperatures drop into the low 60s and bonefish, tarpon or permit are nowhere to be found, barracuda are usually plentiful. Of course, their appearance at specific shallow-water locations is unpredictable. They must be hunted over a wide area. Perhaps the premier spot for big

Ichthyosarcotoxism

This Graeco-English coinage means "fish flesh poisoning" and its most common manifestation in the Atlantic is known by the Spanish term ciguatera. *Ciguatera is a nerve poison acquired by eating various tropical marine fishes, and of the 300 species that have been implicated in transmitting the malady, the great barracuda ranks number one.*

Ciguatera kills 12 percent of its victims. This is most unfortunate on two bases: They are delicious, and they are sometimes sold or served in the guise of harmless fish. Florida prohibits their sale, but enforcing the prohibition is far beyond the state's capacity. A skinned fillet could be anything the seller wants to call it. The symptoms are bizarre. They begin as with gastroenteritis: nausea, stomach cramps, vomiting and diarrhea. Next follows joint and muscular pain similar to dengue fever, then prolonged lassitude, a profound weakness. Many victims suffer from inversion of temperature perception—hot coffee seems cold and a glass of ice water can seem scalding. Symptoms may persist or recur for weeks or months. And this comes from eating fresh fish without a trace of bacterial decomposition.

Ciguatera begins with certain dinoflagellates (plantlike microorganisms) that are found only in association with coral reefs. They secrete the toxin as part of their normal metabolism. It is ingested by small fish that graze on algae to which they are attached, and then is passed up the food chain. Top-of-the-chain predators such as great barracuda, certain groupers, amberjack, king mackerel and some snappers concentrate the toxin in their flesh as they grow. For this reason young fish, and fish not found in association

with coral reefs, are considered safe by people inured to the danger. Since only a small fraction of a local population of predatory fish will actually be carrying ciguatera, the odds are greatly against being poisoned, but they nevertheless exist.

Eastern Florida, the Bahamas and Caribbean have coral reefs and therefore a body of ciguatera folklore: A silver coin cooked with a fish will turn black if ciguatera is present, flies and ants will avoid toxic fish, barracudas with ciguatera have teeth that are dark or with dark bases. There is no factual basis for any of these. Only complicated laboratory tests can reveal its presence.

By eating young fish—say, no great barracuda of more than 3 pounds—you can minimize your prospects of ciguatera poisoning. Another safety precaution is to totally avoid eating species frequently implicated: barracuda, yellowfin grouper, black grouper, silk snapper, dog snapper, some of the "red snappers" (the great popularity of red snapper as a food fish means many other species are substituted to meet the demand) and hogfish.

Yellowtail snapper and vermilion snapper are considered safe fish, as are pelagic and estaurine species such as sailfish, swordfish, marlin, tunas, dolphin, wahoo, small kingfish, Spanish mackerel, seatrout, snook, grunts, red drum, flounder, croaker, sheepshead, whiting and mullet.

Ciguatera seems to become more frequent where the reef has been damaged, as by trawling, or mining for gem coral.

BARRACUDA

barracuda is the Dry Tortugas, especially in February and March. In addition, the Marquesas and the flats near Key West are noted for trophy fish. Generally speaking, barracuda in the Florida Keys concentrate around offshore structures such as shipwrecks, reef edges, lighthouse foundations and stilt-house pilings. Two of the most famous structures are Cosgrove Shoal Light and Smith Shoal Light, both a short distance from Key West. However, there are many similar hot spots as far north as the Miami Ship Channel. Schools of barracuda are usually visible near structures and they are less wary than fish found in very shallow water.

On the Keys flats, there are days when barracuda won't even strike a live bait, no matter how well it is rigged and presented. At other times they will flash out of nowhere and with razor-like teeth clip off any bait or lure that hits the water— especially those intended for some other species. However, a live bait such as a small blue runner, pinfish, grunt or silvery sardine usually gets quick results. These baits can be easily cast with light spinning or bait-casting equipment, and lines from 8- to 15-pound-test. Heavier lines can be used but tend to reduce casting distance and accuracy, and since flats fishing is a sight-fishing situation, those factors are important. Wire is necessary, extending at least a few inches ahead of the hook or lure. It should be as light as possible (20- to 30-pound-test) since these fish have excellent eyesight and tend to be leader shy in clear water. Use no swivels

The Other Barracuda

There are two barracuda in the eastern Atlantic with ranges that overlap the great barracuda. The northern sennet (Sphyraena borealis) is thought by many biologists to be either identical to or an intergrade with the southern sennet (S. picudilla), and at any rate it seldom tops a length of 15 inches. The range is from New England to Brazil, and it is a longshore schooling fish. The guaguanche (S. guachancho), an olivacious-silver fish, grows slightly larger, has a similar range, but rarely appears north of

Florida. It too schools inshore and is a prized food fish, as is the sennet. Neither guaguanche nor sennet are implicated in ciguatera poisoning.

In the eastern Pacific, there are the Pacific barracuda (S. argentea) from Baja to California with strays to Alaska, the Gulf barracuda (S. lucasana), a Baja fish insofar as is known, the Mexican barracuda (S. ensis) from Baja to Panama, and S. idiastes, sans common name and range unknown. The Pacific barracuda is both a sport and a

commercially available food fish that has been taken to a weight of 12 pounds and a length of almost 4 feet, though they average much smaller. None of these Pacific fish are known to carry the ciguatera toxin. Like guaguanche and sennet they make fine light-tackle sport, but are overshadowed throughout most of their range by species more numerous and prized, except for S. argentea, which receives such an intensive fishing effort it is believed to have suppressed the population.

Angling for Pacific barracuda generally begins about the turn of January/February in southern California and peaks during May/June. There are numerous local hot spots ranging from Santa Monica Bay (early) to Catalina Island. Techniques vary: chasing birds in a boat as school barracuda push bait to the top; establishing a chum line; jigging, either with an anchovy on a weighted line or with a variety of jigs and spoons. Anything the barracuda can interpret as an anchovy makes a suitable lure.

There is a culinary prize at the conclusion of successful Pacific barracuda fishing. Though the flesh is tasty, the large, saddle-shaped roes are delectable. It is also possible to cull males and return them alive. Male anal and pelvic fins have yellow or olive margins. The female's fins are edged with black.

Unlike the great barracuda, Pacific barracuda are not notably aerial. A long first run, followed by shorter subsequent runs, is more typical of their fight.

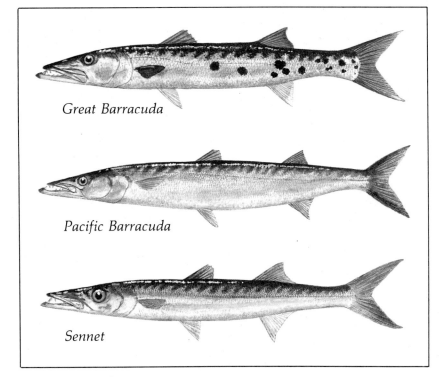

Great Barracuda

Pacific Barracuda

Sennet

if possible, but if you must, choose those finished in black. Shiny connecting hardware only encourages direct strikes on that piece of gear instead of the lure or bait itself.

When it comes to lures, slender floating and diving plugs, especially those with a bright silvery finish, are particularly effective. The most popular lure among South Florida anglers is the tube lure. The tube lure works best with spinning tackle because of the reel's greater retrieve ratio. Barracuda undeniably prefer an artificial that moves fast and in tubes, the faster the better. It is not uncommon for one of these predators to become so involved in chasing the lure that it follows to boatside before striking. The most popular colors are chartreuse, hot pink, bright yellow or orange. Long plastic worms of the type developed for bass fishing in those same colors will work very well, too; however, the first strike usually chops the worm to pieces whether you catch the fish or not. The best flies for flats barracuda are needlefish imitations. Tied on a No. 2/0 or 3/0 long-shank hook (i.e., Mustad 34007 pattern), they are usually 5 to 8 inches long. The most commonly used material is synthetic Fishair, which is available in much longer lengths than natural bucktail. The same colors as those mentioned above, plus translucent white, are effective for these flies, with perhaps some Mylar strands added for extra flash.

This small barracuda took a jig, presumably fished over a sand bottom rather than the turtle grass he is now inhabiting. Jigs tend to snag in turtle grass.

SHARKS

Elasmobranchii

In the great Age of Fishes, the Devonian (400-350,000,000 years ago) sharks were small fish with terminal mouths who suffered from the depredations of armored fish, the dominant vertebrate of the time. A large number of sharks are still small, but of the 350 or so species, most now have inferior mouths, which increase the bite pressure. Very large sharks, like the largest whales, tend to be plankton strainers, but scaled down only slightly from these are sizable pelagic sharks that actively prey on smaller teleosts and elasmobranchs (bony fishes and sharks and rays).

Few could be called "game" by any stretch of the term. As sporting quarry on the high seas, they are all inferior to the billfishes, but one of them, the shortfin mako, can simply leap higher than any other fish that swims in salt water or fresh. Another, the thresher family with their achingly long upper caudal lobes, takes a trolled bait well and leaps well. And three of them, the great white, tiger and the larger hammerhead species, grow to be big, even BIG. A great white that weighs a ton may be a lumbering creature, but it is going to lumber over an expanse of ocean for a few hours before you can exhaust him.

We shall examine these five species (and genera, in some cases) one by one, beginning with supershark, the magnificent mako, which is known to Chilean commercial harpooners as *albacora con dientes*—swordfish with teeth—although swordfish will never see the day that they can jump with mako.

Shortfin Mako (*Isurus oxyrinchus*)

There is nothing particularly short about this mackerel shark's fins, but the pectorals are shorter than the longfin mako (*I. paucus*). You tell them apart in various ways. The shortfin has a white

At top is the whitetip shark (Carcharhinus longimanus), which avidly bites people and can be found in great numbers beyond the 100-fathom line. Upper left is the great white; lower left is the mako; and lower right, the canard-snouted hammerhead.

SHARKS

mouth area, the longfin dusky or black. The longfin has large eyes, indicating that it goes deep and is active at night. If you are drifting offshore at night with deep baits and Cyalume lightsticks for swordfish and catch a mako, it is almost certainly a longfin. If you are trolling or chumming by day and hook a long, slender, pointy-nosed shark that jumps so high you can't believe it, that will be a shortfin mako. They both have teeth like bent fingers.

Makos are everywhere that salt water is not cold, which means quite far north in summer. A 1,080-pounder was caught off Montauk, New York, late in August. That is approaching top weight, which is thought to be about 1,250 pounds, probably a lady mako more than a dozen feet long. The swordfish with teeth fancies swordfish in its diet. Swordfish appreciate dozing on the surface after a night of deep feeding, and mako like to creep up behind them, bite off the tail to immobilize the fish and dine at leisure. Sometimes this works. Sometimes the swordfish wakes up in time and runs away. Sometimes it then comes back at extreme speed with its big sword in front of it. A prudent mako would then demonstrate its extraordinary leaping ability and depart. However, not all mako are prudent. In 1864, a badly punctured mako was taken with the remains of a swordfish in its stomach. The fish had earned his dinner dearly.

Blue water is the native habitat of makos, which means their food is the more rapid sort of fish—tuna, billfish and the like. To achieve the speed to outrun such prey, they also maintain elevated body temperatures. When a blackfin tuna runs away from a mako shark we have a bony teleost chased by a cartilaginous elasmobranch, and both these purportedly cold-blooded fishes will have body temperatures 7 to 10 degrees higher than the surrounding water.

They will come inshore, of course, if that is where the food goes. A large aggregation of bluefish coming inshore to eat sand lance will be pursued by mako, probably of the smaller sort. Setting up a shark chum line within sight of the beach is not apt to produce a giant, though it has happened. There are reports of California sea lions chasing and nipping at makos until the sharks fled. Presumedly these were juvenile makos, though a sea lion bull can be a highly belligerent and bellicose creature. Sea lions, incidentally, have been observed by divers feeding amidst blue sharks, which I would nominate for the shark beauty prize, probably with makos a close second. Blue sharks have an electric blue back, makos a

marine blue with a snow-white belly.

The common name is Maori for the species, and New Zealand is an excellent place to fish for them. Zane Grey's famous fishing trips there produced many makos, including his ninetieth, "and that should be enough," he said. Indeed. In North America the best populations, or at least the best organized fishing for them, is out of the port of Montauk. They are fished by chumming, but someone with a passion for a record mako should probably run out to the Gulf Stream in a large boat and chum.

Basically, one does not fish for mako, even if they are the nominal target species, even if you are entered in a mako tournament. Since they are a minority shark, one goes shark fishing and wades through lots of other species. A typical mako tournament produced 120 blue sharks, 110 sandbars and 50 makos.

All sharks can bite, even the sluggish, small-toothed nurse sharks that some fools in southern waters try to ride (and likely as not get bloodily mauled for their stupidity), but there is a great deal of difference in the aggressiveness of sharks, both between species and between individual fish. Absolutely no species goes for the boat, and even the angler, as often as mako. This speaks well for their intelligence, of course, but it also means handle with care. I have viewed a freshly gaffed mako at kissing distance as his teeth clicked while trying to take off my face. He knew he couldn't reach the gaffer and was willing to settle for me. The most experienced Long Island shark fishermen bring in a mako trussed like a Christmas turkey, absolutely immobilized, but still glaring and straining at the ropes.

Breeding has not been observed, but it produces litters of eight to ten pups, 27 to 28 inches long, whose intrauterine development is by ovoviviparity. After they hatch out of the egg they remain connected to a large yolk, sans placental connection with Mom. Longfin mako have two pups only, about 40 inches long, and probably consumed their siblings—oviphagy.

For anyone who thinks a leaping mako in the dark of the night sounds like grand fun, the Cuban commercials who fish for longfins report they take few at 10 to 50 fathoms, most at 60 to 120 fathoms.

Since measurement would probably be impossible, estimates of the height of those magnificent leaps vary. Zane Grey thought 15 feet was the best one of his fish managed; crazed guesses of 30 feet should *probably* be dismissed, and the number 20 is mentioned frequently. Let us just

DISTRIBUTION

say that no billfish can attain to such an altitude.

The caudal peduncle (the wrist before the tail) of mako bears the same horizontally flattened keels as many billfish and tuna, a beautiful example of convergent evolution. It most closely resembles the caudal peduncle of swordfish. *Albacora con dientes*, indeed.

White Shark
(*Carcharodon carcharias*)

White sharks are the largest predatory fish of carnivorous diet. Only sperm whales and killer whales are larger, and unlike white sharks they do not enter inshore shallow water to eat seals, sea lions and whatever else is silly enough to swim in shark-infested water. The largest game fish yet taken by fair angling methods was a 2,664-pound white shark caught in Australian waters by Alfred Dean on 130-pound-test line. Specimens in excess of 3,000 pounds have been harpooned off both the California and New York coasts. The very experienced charter captain Frank Mundus estimates his biggest harpooned white was 4,500 pounds. A 21-footer has been reported, but its weight of 7,302 is suspect. The 36½-footer whose jaws are in the British Museum has teeth about the same size as a measured set from a 16½-footer. That should not be. Trying to determine how large these creatures grow is difficult because of the inadequacy of our equipment. The open-sea longliners say there are things out there that simply destroy their heaviest equipment, snapping cable and chain and opening the largest hooks made.

And yet, even as with the California makos chased by sea lions, the famous Australian diving team of Ron and Valerie Taylor have seen a white shark so persistently harassed by a sea lion much smaller than itself the shark finally had to leave. Killer whales also attack white sharks, and their purpose is not just harassment.

Thanks to persistent publicity, there is unlikely to be even a farm boy in Iowa who could not identify a white shark on sight. Since they are a mackerel shark, in the Lamnidae family with makos and porbeagles, it is remotely possible to confuse a juvenile white shark with one of those, but juvenile whites carry a dark spot at the base of their pectorals. If you have to kill to make an identification, white sharks have triangular teeth with serrated edges, makos and porbeagles have teeth with smooth edges. The shark's teeth are necessary evidence when registering a world-

The glorious mako is one of the world's great game fish. It is also a delectable food. Probably no other fish can achieve as much elevation. Sometimes they try to come aboard and bite you with their big teeth.

record claim with the International Game Fish Association. They want a clear photograph of the front teeth. Tooth shape is unique to each species, and since the rest of a shark is tissue and cartilage that badly distorts out of water, teeth are how biologists identify them definitively.

This shark likes cooler water than most, but is not a creature of ice flows like the Greenland shark. Alaskan and Canadian sightings are rare and occur only in summer. Contrarily, sightings in the Gulf of Mexico occur only in winter. They seem to frequent coastlines that contain populations of marine mammals, especially those that breed ashore. The established sport fisheries for white sharks are southern Australia, South Africa and the easternmost end of Long Island, New York. So many attacks on divers and surfers have occurred in northern California waters that a white shark fishery could probably be based in San Francisco. The seal and sea lion herds are under protection there. The problem is that white sharks are seldom locally abundant. As with mako, you go fishing for common sharks such as blues rigged with light tackle for stand-up fishing. You hope to find mako, and in case the minor miracle of a white shark appears, you have one 130-pound-test rod and reel and the accoutrements of fighting chair, harness, heavy gloves and above all an able captain and quick boat. The heaviest sporting tackle made is actually ultralight when a typical

251

specimen of your quarry is a 15-footer that weighs 1,500 pounds.

I do not mean to exaggerate the difficulty of boating a white shark; they have been caught to more than half a ton on 20-pound-test line—by experts, and in times and places where local abundance made losses acceptable. But for the one white shark you may bait in a lifetime of fishing, tuna tackle is to be preferred. Besides, when fishing for large, strong fish the *feel* of their weight and strength cannot be experienced with a 5-pound drag on the reel. Light tackle deprives angling for brutes of its essence.

Fishing for whites is best practiced near a dead whale, near rocky islands crowded with bellowing pinnipeds or amidst a school of tuna, since large sharks often follow tuna schools to prey on the sick and the lame. Enormous amounts of chum are usually necessary to bring big pelagic sharks into your baits. Remember that IGFA regulations specify disqualification of any catch made by "Chumming with the flesh, blood, skin, or any part of mammals."

Whites reproduce their kind in a fashion and at times unreported in the scientific literature. Development of the pups is ovoviviparous. Birth is believed to take place at slightly under 50 inches, because the smallest catch on record was a 51-inch, 36-pounder. Beyond that nothing is known. Females are thought to reach sexual maturity at 11 to 14 feet, but "thought" in this context is probably a euphemism for "guessed."

White sharks, as the film series has made clear, are not white but gray, dun, brownish, black or blue, then dirty white on the ventral surface. The flesh is reported as red and oily like that of salmon, and delicious.

Tiger Shark (*Galeocerdo cuvieri*)

Tiger sharks will eat you dead or alive. This is the fish of those believe-it-or-not lists of stomach contents that include tin cans, a sack of coal, a wedding ring with finger attached and a collie dog. Tigers have even been known to swallow whole the huge horse conch. If they dissolve that shell they must have the digestive capabilities of a lime pit, but in all likelihood they probably evert their stomach periodically to cleanse it. A number of sharks and billfish have that ability, though swallowing it again undamaged would seem to be an easier task for a marlin than a shark.

Tigers are of the requiem family and occur wherever there is warm water. There seems to be a concentration in eastern North America, so you may fish for them from Mexico, through the Gulf, and as far north as New Jersey. They take to shallow water well in summer, but when it becomes too cold they move offshore into the Gulf Stream or migrate south. In the northern range, they are a boat-fishing quarry. By the time you get to South Carolina they are caught from the fishing piers that are endemic to that state (and have produced a cult of pier fishermen). The largest tiger shark ever caught, a 1,780-pounder, was taken on 130-pound-test line by a South Carolina pier fisherman! That is also the largest game fish that has come from North American waters. Do not attempt to emulate Walter Maxwell's remarkable 1964 catch from that North Myrtle Beach pier. Myrtle Beach accepted the recommendation of its Chamber of Commerce and banned shark fishing.

This is a prolific breeder among sharks, litters of thirty to eighty pups are thrown. They range in length from 2 feet to almost a yard at birth, have snow-white bellies, pale flanks and beautiful dark spots. As the tiger grows, his spots fuse into the stripes that give him his common name, generally of a brown tone on a gray ground color. They have a distinctively wedge-shaped snout; when seen from above it looks square cut.

There are reports of one measured to 30 feet long, and 18-footers weighing a ton are common in the literature, which remains speculative because of our ignorance of these fish. Adults of 10 to 14 feet are common.

Juveniles are often seen on top, but evidently they become photosensitive as they mature. Adults are largely night fish. Most sharks that can be considered game tend toward movements offshore by day and inshore at night, tigers particularly so. In shallow bays, establishing a chum slick at night, in summer, in water of 70°F or more, you should be in a sizable vessel; they have been known to attempt boarding the boat to get at the source of that delicious chum. At night, too, many seabirds rest afloat, and they figure frequently in tiger shark stomach examinations—which leads to an inevitable but foolish reverie of taking a tiger pup on an enormous dry fly. It shouldn't be difficult to catch them with noisy propeller plugs at night. Many of us have done that by day on other sharks. The trick is to establish a continuous, uninterrupted track of sound for them to follow.

The perfected technique for the giants is to load a Penn or Fin-Nor big game reel with 130-pound-test Dacron braid, attach that to 15 feet of stainless steel cable leader tipped with 5 feet of chain for it to chew on. The hooks should be a pair of No. 16/0 forged steel and the bait a big fillet to leach its nice scent into the water. It is best to use a fighting chair without a pedestal. Just set it flat on the pier or on the beach. A boat or paddleboard can take the bait out. When the tiger takes it, remember to dig your heels in hard. If you can catch one without a shoulder harness leading to the reel lugs you are probably ready for competition weight lifting.

Tiger sharks are consumed with gusto wherever they are caught. Follow the instructions in *The Encyclopedia of Fish Cookery* by A. J. McClane, which essentially involves getting the edible back meat out of the hide quickly, keeping it very cold, neutralizing the ammonia produced by the breakdown of urea in the flesh with a mild acidic marinade such as citrus, tomato juice, vinegar or milk (or leach it out in brine) and cook. When butchering you remove the fins, slice the length of the back, and girdle at head and tail. Your knife will dull less if you make punctures to break the hide, then cut from the inside out.

Thresher Sharks
(*Alopius spp.*)

The thresher, the smalltooth thresher and the bigeye thresher are the currently recognized variations on this unusual and evolutionarily dubious shape. Simply put, the tail is half as long as the body. Its use has been debated since antiquity by people with no experience of them, but most of them are hooked in the tail, which is evidence enough for their mode of attack.

All three feed on schooling fish such as menhaden, mackerel and bluefish. The mouth is small and small hooks are recommended for them, but since threshers are large sharks this seems questionable advice. The smalltooth is rare and reaches a maximum of 16½ feet, but 10 feet is closer to average. The bigeye will go to 18 feet. Its large, upward-looking eye and elevated body temperature are undoubtedly adaptations for deep-water existence. The common thresher is the family giant, with a 20-foot capability, weighing 1,000 pounds.

You identify the bigeye by its eye and by a groove atop the head. The smalltooth has a dorsal mounted far forward, so the free rear tip of the dorsal is ahead of the pelvic fins, which is not the case with the common thresher.

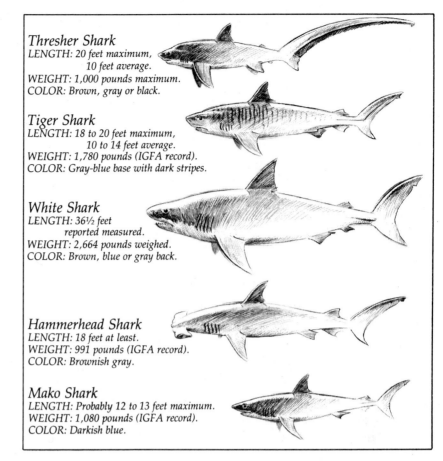

Thresher Shark
LENGTH: 20 feet maximum,
       10 feet average.
WEIGHT: 1,000 pounds maximum.
COLOR: Brown, gray or black.

Tiger Shark
LENGTH: 18 to 20 feet maximum,
       10 to 14 feet average.
WEIGHT: 1,780 pounds (IGFA record).
COLOR: Gray-blue base with dark stripes.

White Shark
LENGTH: 36½ feet
       reported measured.
WEIGHT: 2,664 pounds weighed.
COLOR: Brown, blue or gray back.

Hammerhead Shark
LENGTH: 18 feet at least.
WEIGHT: 991 pounds (IGFA record).
COLOR: Brownish gray.

Mako Shark
LENGTH: Probably 12 to 13 feet maximum.
WEIGHT: 1,080 pounds (IGFA record).
COLOR: Darkish blue.

They are cosmopolitan sharks of warm to temperate seas, but hot spots occur. In April, May and June the bigeye are common off Cape Hatteras. There is a summer thresher run off Santa Monica that takes marlin baits. The bigeye should be fished in the fashion of night swordfishing, with Cyalume lightsticks, and the bait at least 20 fathoms deep in much deeper water.

Threshers have four to six pups that are about 12 pounds and 5 feet long at birth. Bigeyes usually have two pups a bit more than a yard long, as do the smalltooth. A mount of one of those pups would make an ever-present reminder of the sheer *profligacy* of evolution.

Hammerheads
(*Sphyrna spp.*)

There are seven hammerheads in North American waters, a nice representation of the nine worldwide. Most of them are small, but all represent maximum utilization of the ampullae of Lorenzini present in sharks, skates and rays. The ampullae are subcutaneous electroreceptors of incredible sensitivity. In the smooth dogfish, for instance, voltage differences as minute as five thousandths of a microvolt can be detected. It is possible for a human diver, especially one bearing metallic objects such as air tanks, to be detected by the ampullae from at least a yard away. These direct current bioelectric fields are made more powerful when the skin is broken. Tests with blue

SHARKS

sharks have shown thirty-one bites on an electrically activated target versus seven on an unactivated one. It is possible with its ampullae for an elasmobranch to detect a flounder completely buried in the sand. The cartilaginous fishes have a greater sensitivity to electrical current than any other known creatures. The leading edge of the sphyrnid "hammer" is dense with ampullae of Lorenzini, and though their diet is catholic, they are known to have a taste for stingrays. One 12½-foot hammerhead contained fifty-four barbs in its mouth, head and jaws, another, the remarkable number of ninety-six embedded stingers. Hammerheads, incidentally, are one of the most recently evolved sharks.

To the five senses mammals possess of sight, hearing, touch, smell and taste, the fish add a sixth sense of lateral line perception of pressure waves (both those generated by other organisms, and reflections of those generated by themselves), and the cartilaginous fishes add a seventh sense of bioelectrical reception.

The small hammerheads are: S. corona, which has no popular name and ranges in the Pacific from southern Mexico south, and at 35 inches or so is the smallest of the genus; the scoophead (S. media), available from the Gulf of California south in sizes up to at least 5 feet; the bonnethead (S. tiburo), 1 to 1½ yards at maximum, commonly found inshore from New England south and southern California south (a schooling hammerhead, bonnets are great fun on light tackle; if you are getting bite-offs when fishing shrimp for spotted seatrout or weakfish, add a wire leader and catch a bonnet); and the smalleye hammerhead, a 5-footer at best that is found in the Gulf of Mexico.

The three serious hammerheads include the great hammerhead (S. mokarran), the giant of them all with a 20-foot capability. This circumtropical fish comes north in summer and gets into quite shallow water at times.

The smooth hammerhead (S. zygaena) is the most northerly: from the Gulf of California up to central California, and from Florida to the Canadian Maritimes. It commonly reaches 12 feet, and it migrates in large schools along the coastline. The scalloped hammerhead (S. lewini) is available at about the same size as the smooth, but its migrations don't carry it quite as far north in summer.

Hammerheads are dark on top, pale below and highly variable in tint. They can swim rapidly. They often school, sometimes in immense swarms numbering thousands of sharks. Divers who have swum amidst a school of scalloped hammerheads in the Gulf of California report they were neither mating nor feeding, but an occasional individual would perform an acrobatic maneuver that concluded with a violent collision with another hammerhead (perhaps establishing a social hierarchy, they speculate). Field investigations of large sharks by sharing their milieu is like the priesthood: It needs a true vocation.

Montauk

It would probably be no exaggeration to say that Montauk is the "cradle" of East Coast offshore sharking. Furthermore, the development of shark fishing into a major component of the offshore fisheries in the Northeast is largely due to the piscatorial and publicity efforts of one man—Captain Frank Mundus.

Mundus is, by any standard, a character—so much so that Peter Benchley quite obviously shaped his captain in Jaws to resemble Mundus. It was during the 1950s that Mundus built up his business of "monster fishing" at Montauk by appearing at the New York Sportsman Show with an exhibit of shark teeth and jaws, plus plenty of photos. Though other charter skippers were slow to react to the potential of this fishery, many private boatmen did get involved. Among the most prominent was a New York antiques dealer named John Walton, who sailed his Chief Joseph Brant all the way through Long Island Sound to fish weekends at Montauk—before finally moving the boat to the east.

It took a while to develop, but there's little question now that shark fishing is the major offshore money-maker for the large Montauk charter fleet, and many skippers specialize in the sport. The seasonal appearances of great white sharks off eastern Long Island invariably attract swarms of television photographers and national media to Montauk, while the two big annual tournaments (the Shark Tagging Tournament at Montauk Marine Basin and the Montauk Captains Association Charity Shark Tournament at Star Island Yacht Club) both draw huge crowds for the weigh-ins.

From Montauk, the sport of offshore shark fishing has spread north and south, but there's still probably no other port that can offer so many charter boats fishing for sharks, or such consistent results. From June well into the fall, there are sharks to be caught offshore of Montauk, and the boats rarely fail to produce before the day is out.

One of the nicest things about sharking at

Montauk is that the quarry is often fairly close to shore. A run of 10 to 12 miles south-southeast from the point brings you to Butterfish Hole with its 180- to 200-foot depths. Draggers work this area almost every day for yellowtail flounder, butterfish, ling and whiting—and sharks arrive in June to feed on the often abundant bottom fish. To be sure, Butterfish Hole doesn't produce nearly as well as it did up through the mid-1970s, but there are many other outstanding areas to the south, east and west.

The first shark to appear off Montauk in the spring is the porbeagle, a close relative of the mako and great white. Unfortunately, porbeagles were heavily fished by Norwegian longliners during the 1960s and have virtually disappeared from waters south of Cape Cod since then. Traditionally, they arrived with the schools of mackerel in the spring and could also be found in the cool waters of Coxes Ledge throughout the summer.

In terms of quantity, there is no question about the blue shark being number one among Montauk sharks. Blues prefer cool water and start arriving around late May. This early run consists primarily of immature blues running from approximately 30 to 100 pounds, though a few bigger blues will be found with them. Once located, the small blues often swarm around the boat in the chum slick and literally wait to be caught and released. This is the time to put away all the heavy gear and match the tackle to the size of the fish you throw the bait to.

It's not unusual, during the spring blue shark run off Montauk, for boats to tag forty or fifty in a day of nonstop action. If the fish are in Butterfish Hole, they also provide a great opportunity for small boat anglers to get to them on calm days, using the same tackle they normally employ on striped bass and bluefish. This migratory run varies considerably from year to year (possibly depending on water temperatures) but is almost always quite good sometime in June—though it rarely lasts beyond early July. Blues continue to form an important portion of the Montauk shark catch throughout the summer, though the fish are fewer and bigger. The average summer blue is in the 100- to 200-pound class, and even bigger specimens are encountered in September and October. This is the time for record seekers, as blues running in the 200- to 300-pound class are very common offshore.

Though the blue shark is recognized as a game fish by the IGFA, it really doesn't rank very high in that area. Blues are very easy to catch (making them ideal for beginners) and inordinately stupid.

It is quite common to catch a blue released the same day more than once, and I once caught the same blue three times in a two-hour period! Nevertheless, blues can provide fair sport on reasonably light tackle, and those big fall blues are real bruisers which seem to have found energy not available to the early season fish.

Blues may provide the quantity, but it's the mako that shark anglers really desire. Makos are almost never abundant, and catches of as much as five or six to a boat are considered exceptional— even if they're relatively small. Even one is prized (as a great game fish should be), and they grow large enough to interest the most jaded angler. Either shark fishermen have been getting better, or bigger makos have been swimming into our waters in recent years. As late as the mid-1970s, a 300-pound mako was considered to be an exceptional fish, and the initial New York State record, when that program was started in 1975, was a 405-pounder. Every year thereafter the record jumped by hundreds of pounds until the legendary Captain Frank Mundus put James Melanson on a 1,080-pound mako off Block Island on August 26, 1979, for a new all-tackle world record.

A long snout, very long pectorals and a startlingly vivid blue back and flanks mean blue shark. They are a numerically dominant population in many places, indicating high reproductive success, but they are absolute morons, one of the most easily caught fish in the sea.

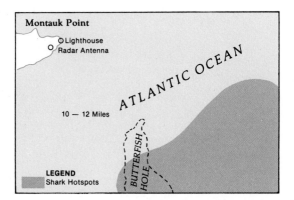

At the eastern tip of Long Island in the summer, a number of shark tournaments testify to a population of almost metropolitan concentration. Great whites, makos, blues, duskies and browns are available. This is the original home of Jaws.

SHARKS

While 300-pounders are no longer unusual, they are still trophy size as makos go. Indeed, any mako over 200 pounds can be considered to be a real prize. Makos are desirable not only because of their edibility (similar to swordfish), size and fierce appearance, but often as great game fish and the highest jumpers in fishdom. I say "often as great game fish," because every mako is quite different. Some get reeled to the boat with hardly a protest, while others fight their hearts out. The same applies to jumping. Some makos will provide three or four skyscraping leaps, while others won't jump at all.

Makos prefer warmer water than blues and don't usually show until late June or early July. July and August are the prime months off Montauk, though September would probably be just as good if there weren't so many other distractions at the time (such as giant tuna and the start of fall striper fishing). Indeed, I have seen makos brought into Montauk as late as early November.

Montauk shark fishermen also have a shot at several other species. Brown sharks (usually under 100 pounds) are common during the summer, and the very similar dusky provides an opportunity to slug it out with a bottom shark that often weighs 500 or 600 pounds. Small hammerheads are often encountered in Butterfish Hole during the summer. Surprisingly, these are among the fussiest of sharks—often refusing anything with a hook in it. They're also consistently good fighters on light tackle. Bigger hammerheads are frequently encountered farther offshore, particularly near the

canyon. A very desirable, but uncommon, summer visitor is the thresher. Like the mako and porbeagle, the thresher is highly desired as a food fish as well as for its sporting value. The few huge tiger sharks around are a real challenge even on heavy tackle.

The shark the general public most closely associates with Montauk is rarely caught on hook-and-line. Great whites are spotted off Montauk every summer, most commonly in early or mid-July. Almost invariably they are loners, though a number of whites were found feeding on a dead whale one summer. The whites that are spotted usually weigh from one to several thousand pounds, and though an occasional one is successfully harpooned, there have been no recent rod-and-reel catches of such fish. In the 1950s, the noted shark scientist, Jack Casey, caught a 1,000-pound white off Montauk on the *Chief Joseph Brant*. However, that wasn't an "official" catch, because his father fought the fish briefly before turning the rod over to Jack. A few much smaller whites are caught on rod-and-reel from time to time—some so small (around 50 pounds) that scientists believe the huge fish spawn in this area.

Montauk sharking can be as simple or as complicated as you want it to be. The easiest way to get involved is to charter one of the many boats operating out of that port. Those who want to try it on their own can get all the tackle and bait required at local marinas. Nothing heavier than No. 6/0 gear is required unless you're looking for one of those great whites. Almost any shark can be caught on a No. 4/0 rig with 30- to 50-pound line—provided you follow the big ones. Almost all Montauk sharking is done in less than 240 feet of water, and light tackle is quite appropriate. For instance, the 405-pound mako mentioned earlier was caught on a boat reel filled with about 200 yards of 30-pound mono.

Terminal tackle consists of wire leaders (usually #12), heavy-duty hooks (about No. 9/0 for most sharks), big game snap swivels and some flotation material to suspend your bait at specific levels. Bait can be almost anything, but bunker is the most readily available in port. Rather than fishing the whole bait, I prefer to fillet the bunker and put both sides on the hook. Sharks seem to hit the fillets as well and are much easier to hook in that fashion. Other popular baits include mackerel, squid, bluefish and fillets from any member of the tuna family. It is often possible to catch a ling or whiting off bottom while drifting, in which case you have as good a bait as you can find. Small bluefish are particularly effective because they

Along the leading edge of the hammerhead's hammer are electroreceptors that can perceive the presence of fish buried in sand. Hammerheads do a lot of damage to the skate and ray populations.

constitute the primary food of makos during the summer.

The key to shark fishing is chumming. Cans of ground bunker are purchased in port and can either be ladled over the side (after being cut with water) or placed frozen in a chum bag and hung over the side. Bunkers or other bait should also be sliced into pieces and "chunked" into the slick from time to time. Using the floats, baits are placed at varying intervals and distances from the boat.

Most sharks can be fought without moving the boat, enabling the other anglers aboard the opportunity to hook up at the same time. Unless the catch is desired for food or mounting, sharks should be released to fight another day. It's also wise to tag them before the release in cooperation with the National Marine Fisheries Service Shark Tagging Program which gathers data on migration and growth, primarily through the efforts of concerned sportsmen. In order to obtain free tags, write to Jack Casey, NMFS, Narragansett Lab, South Ferry Rd., Narragansett, RI 02882.

Though present-day shark fishing at Montauk may not be what it was twenty years ago, it still is the surest thing in big game fishing. With most shark anglers now firmly committed to conservation of the sharks, the outlook is bright for continued shark fishing from the "cradle" of the sport—Montauk.

Hammerhead Shark At Punta Pescadero

Hammerhead (*Sphyrna zygaena*) are abundant in the Sea of Cortez. Sport fishermen have ignored shark in the sea because of the great numbers of billfish, dolphin, yellowfin tuna, etc. However, commercial fishermen bring in thousands every year, most of them taken in nets. There is a ready market for them in Mexico. There are several areas where they seem to school: in a deep, 30 miles out of La Paz; the south end of Cerralvo island; 2 miles out from Punta Pescadero; 5 miles east of Cabo Pulmo, and several miles south of Cabo San Lucas. Hammerhead roam the waters in between these areas but, except for Punta Pescadero, never come close to the shore. The fin of a shark is infrequently spotted in the fishing waters of the sea, and very rarely is any type of shark seen around the shallow waters of the beaches.

All of these hammerhead-populated areas are worked only by commercial fishermen with the

Hammerheads seasonally swarm in the Sea of Cortez in non-spawning hordes, whose concentrations remain inexplicable to fisheries biologists. To pragmatic anglers, the answer is simply to go fishing for them.

exception of Punta Pescadero. Hotel Punta Pescadero has developed a clientele of hammerhead anglers who are making great sport out of hunting these big, tough battlers. They are nailing a lot of hammerhead.

They are found close in, one half to 1 mile from shore, directly in front of the hotel. The best bait is a bonito or dolphin head, freshly caught. Heavy tackle and a large hook are in order. The bait is lowered to the bottom then raised a few feet. The hook is set when the angler feels the bait moving away. The average hookup runs from 200 to 400 pounds, but they also come much larger. The world all-tackle record is 717 pounds, taken at Jacksonville, Florida on July 27, 1980.

The hammerhead fights deep and has incredible staying power. If not killed before boating, it could possibly remain alive for an hour or more. Don't bother to check this statement—just a slap from its tail could cause considerable pain.

Commercial fishermen take hammerhead all year with no apparent season. There is very little sport fishing experience to draw on at this writing and what there is would indicate spring as the most productive time of the year, but actually, that is the time that the hammerhead enthusiasts have been most active. We believe that the hammerhead are there year-'round for anyone who wants to take a shot at them.

257

RED DRUM

Sciaenops ocellata

One of the great pioneer saltwater anglers, Van Campen Heilner, wrote *The Call of the Surf* (New York, 1920) with artist Frank Stick, the first book devoted entirely to that subject. There was never any doubt in Van's mind that the red drum, the "coppery warrior of the tides," was the ultimate game fish. As a field representative for the American Museum of Natural History, with far-flung expeditions around the globe, Van was a free spirit. Soon after meeting him I stood in a booming Virginia surf at night, struggling to keep my footing in shifting sand while fighting a 40-pound red drum. The experience was unforgettable, not only for the dogged, mulelike, unrelenting pull that rocked my shoulders, but for that night itself. There was the threat of a sou'wester moaning in the dune grass and towering cumulus clouds were starkly silhouetted by bolts and thunderclaps, while the ocean glowed in the pulsing flashes of a distant lighthouse. My fish finally succumbed with the passive dignity of a spent champion, and when we gathered around the driftwood fire for rum-laced coffee, I felt that Van had compounded a brew of kindred souls.

The red drum has been a celebrated source of food and sport since our early day colonists followed the southerly wake of Captain John Smith. The fish was known in the Carolinas and Virginia as a channel bass and from Florida through the Gulf of Mexico as a redfish. Actually, the drum family (Sciaenidae) encompasses thirty-four different species in North America, which have in common a specialized drumming muscle that by rapid and repeated contraction against the gas bladder (acting as a resonator) produces an audible sound. The drumming of the males is louder than that of the females and is thought to attract the opposite sex during the breeding season.

In appearance, the red drum, *Sciaenops ocellata,* is a chunky fish, coppery red in color, and usually with a single haloed black spot, or ocellus,

A trio of red drum searches for blue crabs among the mangrove roots in Florida's Everglades. This shallow-water habitat is ideal for sight-fishing to cruising schools with the fly or spinning rod.

RED DRUM

at the base of its tail. Some populations are more silvery in color, and the rare fish will have two or more spots on its caudal peduncle. Joel Arrington, the modern Pied Piper of channel bass anglers, sent me a photo of a fish with sixteen ocelli, an extravagance of Nature but pertinent to any description. Its nearest counterpart is the black drum, *Poganias cromis*, a ponderous and spiritless relative that attains weights of over 100 pounds, and aside from being sooty black to silvery gray in color, it lacks even a single ocellus, and has whiskery barbels on its lower jaw. The red drum, like most sciaenids, is a euryhaline species being tolerant of both fresh and salt water, a virtue that is presently extending its range. Texas has enjoyed excellent success with hatchery-reared fingerlings which are now stocked in freshwater lakes as well as its coastal bays to supplement the commercially impacted sea populations.

The largest red drum, fish of 40 pounds or more, are caught from Chesapeake Bay southward to North Carolina. It has been postulated by researchers that these big fish represent an over-wintering population which migrates out into the Canyon when cold weather begins; the smaller "puppy drum" may drift north from southern nursery areas, and after feeding along the beaches, achieve some weight and remain in the area. The trophy red drums, taken in such locations as Assateague Island on the Maryland and Virginia border down the coast to Hog Island, Smith Island, Cape Charles and Hatteras in North Carolina, apparently follow an inshore to offshore migration route. By contrast, a "big" red drum in Florida waters is a 20-pounder on either the Atlantic or Gulf coasts.[1] The Gulf fishery from Florida to northern Mexico appears to be independent and doesn't contribute to the more easterly Atlantic populations. During the last century, there has been some change in the overall distribution of the redfish—at one time, for example, the fish was numerous around Long Island, New York, straying as far north as Cape Cod, Massachusetts, but their capture here is a rare event today.

Fly-fishing for red drum began well before the turn of the century. Dr. James A. Henshall, otherwise known as the patron saint of black bass fishing (*The Book of the Black Bass*, 1881), described the capture of redfish with a 12-foot, 12-ounce ash and lancewood "trout" rod in his subsequent book, *Camping and Cruising in Florida* (1884). In the doctor's gaudy era, big No. 5/0 and 6/0 wet flies, such as the Oriole, Yellow Sally, Red Ibis and other patterns made from the feathers of gay-plumaged birds, were prescribed for marine angling. That he frequently complained about the "general demoralization and used-up condition of the flexors and extensors of my arms" is less a tribute to the sporting qualities of the drum than the brute tackle of his day. It is worth noting, however, that Henshall also reported catching tarpon, bluefish, snook, ladyfish, crevalle jack and spotted seatrout—a whole spectrum of marine fly-fishing that is commonly believed to be of more recent origin.

Red drum are taken on the fly by sight fishing—visually spotting fish that are cruising, mudding or sometimes tailing in shallow water. Tailing fish are common to shoal areas such as Florida Bay, which extends between the mainland and the Keys, and on the grass flats and oyster bars of Louisiana and Texas. Usually, small pods or schools cruise slowly over the bottom in two or three feet of water, searching for crabs and shrimp, where their shadowy forms are easily recognized. The trick to catching redfish on the fly, or any artificial lure, is to first realize that sciaenids have poor eyesight, seemingly myopic, and the lure must be cast so that it passes as close as possible in front of an individual fish. However, in common with the bonefish, an on-the-nose cast will spook a red drum, so you must aim six or eight feet ahead of, and slightly beyond, your quarry, then retrieve at a speed that will intercept it. Much of my angling is done in the mangrove creeks of the Everglades, where fish cruise in and out of the root systems, a very frustrating spectacle with the reds appearing, then vanishing at the critical moment. Fly-fishing is a totally different experience from arcing a cast out in the open surf, but the game has many techniques, as we shall see.

Tackle for Red Drum

The kind of tackle to use for red drum, with the exception of surf casting, where conventional 10- to 12-foot rods equipped with standard multiplying or spinning reels are essential for long casts over the breakers, is for the most part any type of gear you prefer. On southeastern beaches, cut bait impaled on No. 5/0 and 6/0 hooks is pitched skyward with a 4-ounce pyramid sinker. Most casters prefer lines in the 30-pound-test class. On a day with a strong undertow, even this can seem light when 40- to 50-pound channel bass are cavorting beyond the farthest comber. But over the greater part of the redfish kingdom, where light tackle is much more effective, a standard 7-foot spinning rod with 10-pound-test line, or a

[1] Trophy red drum are taken in small numbers—a 51-pound fish at St. Petersburg in 1979, a 51-pound, 8-ounce drum from Sebastian Inlet in 1983 and a 54-pound fish taken from the Naples Pier in 1975—but these are exceptional catches.

comparable bait-casting outfit, or 9-foot fly rod with a 9- or 10-weight forward line is the common denominator. Local conditions may require adjustments, as in narrow mangrove creeks where even a small drum can burrow under oyster-covered roots on its first run; here a 15- or 20-pound-test monofilament line is more practical. It is also advisable to use a 12-inch wire leader with spinning or bait-casting outfits, and a 40-pound-test shock tippet on the fly rod. Red drum have very abrasive scales; in fact they are so tough skinned that even filleting one is a difficult job, and they have a talent for getting the line over their "shoulders" so a leaderless terminal rig invites losses.

The Ten Thousand Islands

Everglades National Park encompasses 1,400,533 acres in the southwest corner of Florida. This includes most of the Ten Thousand Island Region, a vast area of hammocks and creeks bordering the Gulf of Mexico on the west and Florida Bay on the south. It is one of the most unique marine habitats in North America. There is an ecological distinction between the sawgrass and palmetto "open" glades and the estuarine environment of the mangroves, but both are part of the park. To the casual observer, the entire watershed may look like nothing but an endless chain of shallow ponds connected by meandering creeks; however, the water level fluctuates not only through tide flow, but according to rainfall. The amount of rainfall (which affects the salinity), plus the water temperature, determines what kind of fish will be found where in any given period. Red drum and spotted seatrout are the most commonly sought species in these mangrove-bordered creeks, although tarpon, snook, ladyfish and crevalle jack occur sporadically, or abundantly at various locations.

The ascendency of the red drum as the principal game fish on the lower west coast of Florida is fairly recent. Historically, the snook was the most popular species in this area, but during the 1960s, their annual harvest diminished rapidly, and by the 1970s, the population reached a critical point. Researchers blame commercial netting, habitat destruction, pollution, cold-kills and insecticide spraying as the causative factors in their decline. In 1981, legislation was passed establishing the bag limit at two snook per day, with a controlled season during the spawning period from June 1st to July 31st, at which time the only legal snook are 18 to 26 inches in length

Fly-fishing for trophy red drum off Oregon Inlet in the spring and fall seasons is a new sport. After boating this 28-pounder, Miami angler Chico Fernandez took a 42-pound, 5-ounce red, the largest caught on a fly to date.

(3½ to 7 pounds). Fishing for snook, which occur in the same habitat as the red drum, and are caught on similar lures, is again a major fishery.

The Ten Thousand Islands is eminently a light tackle area, as the redfish average 4 to 8 pounds in size, with only the unusual catch exceeding 20 pounds. The most popular lures are leadhead jigs, any of the flashy silver and gold slow-sinking plugs, and that legion of plastic baits in worm, shrimp and grubtail designs. For stalking fish with the fly rod, breather-type streamers in yellow-and-red and yellow-and-white on No. 1/0 and 2/0 hooks are local favorites.

Generally speaking, spring and fall are the best periods for fishing in the Everglades. Heavy summer rains normally begin at the end of June and continue through September. Aside from the storms themselves, which invariably culminate in

RED DRUM

Although larger red drum frequent Florida east coast waters, the Ten Thousand Islands region and Florida Bay produce fish in quantity. In addition to reds, this area is noted for spotted seatrout and snook, which are caught by the same fishing methods.

lightning bolts, prolonged rains create freshwater conditions and most game species remain in the higher salinities of the Gulf. The winter season can be uncertain also; high winds will muddy the creeks and estuaries, and as the water temperature drops below 60°F, angling success declines rapidly.

Fly-Fishing for Trophy Red Drum

Sight fishing to schools of large red drum in deep water with the fly rod is a totally new sport. Chico Fernandez's record catches on the fly at Oregon Inlet in May of 1981 promise to attract a great many anglers to the Outer Banks of North Carolina. Fernandez, a Miami angler, caught a 28-pound, 8-ounce red drum on 15-pound-test leader, followed by a 42-pound, 5-ounce fish taken on 12-pound-test. The latter is the largest red drum ever taken on the fly.

As a procedure, sight fishing for red drum is not novel on the Outer Banks. As far back as the late 1920s, spring and fall trollers often spotted schools of fish weighing upward to 60 pounds and maneuvered their spoons ahead of them with telling effect. Later, innovators began to cast spoons and metal squids to them with spectacular results. This type of fishing occurs with regularity at Oregon, Hatteras and Ocracoke inlets, and sometimes westward to Pamlico Sound. However, fly-fishing requires a closer approach to our quarry, despite the fact that veteran sight casters experience those days when drum appear boldly under the boat. When a school has been located, it is possible to approach within 50 feet, provided

there are no nearby craft to interfere. The fish are difficult to see in poor light. With experience, they may be spotted in several ways: by emerging tails and dorsal fins, by oil slicks created in their feeding and by silhouette color if the water is clear. A large (4- to 6-inch wing) fast-sinking streamer fly is required. Fernandez's fish were caught on a 6-inch-long sailfish fly tied on a No. 4/0 hook. A sinking tip or full sinking line is essential because red drum are bottom oriented in their feeding. The fly must drop 6 to 10 feet quickly, into and under the school.

For this kind of fishing, a 12-weight system fly rod is necessary as the weather is invariably windy, and the fish weight factor is considerable. These mulish drum run from 20 to over 50 pounds. Large "choppermouth" bluefish are usually among the drum schools, so flies are often lost when blues are inadvertently hooked. Although heavy monofilament shock tippets are essential, bluefish will frequently cut these, requiring a hasty lure change before the redfish disappear.

The trophy red drum fly season begins in April, but weather conditions are not reliable until May. The opportunities for sight fishing diminish in June when the fish move farther into the sounds. The fall season begins in September, but October is prime, and even November can bring good angling. Outboard powered skiffs in the 17- to 20-foot class are appropriate in these sheltered waters.

North Carolina's Outer Banks

North Carolina's Outer Banks have long been known as one of the top locations for trophy red drum in the surf. These thin barrier islands extend from Virginia due south to Cape Hatteras, where they bend back to the southwest and run to Cape Lookout, then bend westward and run back to the mainland at Morehead City, enclosing an enormous estuary. Red drum migrate through inlets which intersect the barrier islands and along the beaches in spring and fall. These fish winter off the Virginia capes and Outer Banks, then begin to move along the beaches and into the inlets in late March. By June, almost all the drum are in the sounds, where they remain until late summer when the smaller fish, locally called puppy drum, first exit the sounds, followed by the older red drum in September and October. November is the peak fall month for surf fishing for these larger drum.

The consistency with which trophy red drums,

that is, fish over 40 pounds, can be found in the surf has diminished over the past twenty years. Catching them never was a certainty, but it is speculated that beach traffic or lights along the beach at night have caused the fish, and particularly the large ones, to change their migratory patterns and eschew waters close inshore more so than in the past. Nevertheless, huge drum do appear sporadically in the surf during the spring and fall. There is the occasional stray fish that chances on a hook baited for jumbo bluefish, and there are times when schools of old drum appear, often at night, remaining for hours or a few days—just long enough for word to spread and for local anglers to arrive and catch a modest number. The most productive spot for giant drum is the tip of Cape Hatteras: The Point. This is the hub of Outer Banks surf fishing for many species, the site of congregations of surf anglers and their vehicles in sometimes awesome numbers, and, not coincidentally, where many a trophy red drum has been hauled up on the beach.

The red drum specialist is a breed apart from the normal run of beach fisherman. His quarry is large to begin with, and frequently appears at night. A red drum is not put off by dirty water that accompanies high winds. Consequently, the drum fisherman is a persistent, hardy angler, strong enough to handle the magnum tackle necessary to cast 8 ounces of lead and a hefty chunk of bait in strong tides and winds a long distance from the beach. Trophy drum in a high surf require a heavy-action rod of 10 to 12 feet in length. Conventional reels should be spooled with 30-pound-test line; only the largest spinning reels can be employed, and they should be spooled with 20- to 25-pound-test monofilament. Pyramid sinkers, which hold the chunks of mullet or other oily baitfish to the bottom, must weigh from 4 to over 8 ounces depending on the current. From time to time, one or more shoal islands will form off The Point due to the dynamic interplay of tide and wind in this high-energy environment. When these occur, they invariably attract an abundance of red drum. Often, these islands are a long cast from where a fisherman dare wade out into the breakers. Only anglers with sufficient casting skill will score.

A four-wheel-drive vehicle is necessary to drive from the paved road at Hatteras Lighthouse down the beach about 3 miles to The Point. If you had no weighty equipment to carry, you could walk, but the surf man without his icebox of bait and his tackle and food is in for a long day, or night. Fishermen who do not have their own beach

vehicles and specialized tackle may hire guide service from one of several locations on Hatteras Island, at Nags Head to the north and at Ocracoke. These guides provide the vehicle, all tackle and bait, and the most important ingredient of all—local knowledge. Neophyte drivers on the beach are well advised to exercise caution to avoid getting stuck. A four-wheel drive does not guarantee easy passage, as there are numerous soft spots where unskilled drivers may encounter trouble. A current list of guides is free on request from the North Carolina Travel and Tourism Division; telephone (919) 733-4171.

Most of Hatteras Island is within the Cape Hatteras National Seashore, which regulates beach driving, but beach fishermen are permitted

Red drum are abundant in Florida's Everglades region and, while the average fish is smaller than those in the northeast, the thrill of sight fishing for schools along the mangroves is a reward in itself. Specialist guides, such as Tony Reckert (above), are equipped for running and poling these shallow rivers.

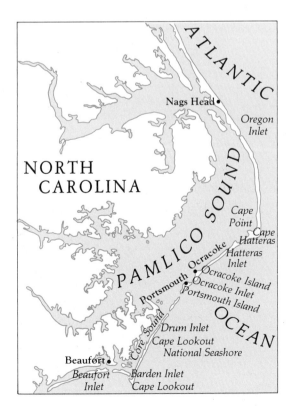

North Carolina's red drum migrate through all the inlets that intersect the barrier islands in spring and fall. These runs begin in late March. By June, most of the fish are in Pamlico Sound. They begin to exit in September and are found in the surf along the outer beaches.

263

access during the prime fishing months of fall and spring (April and May, and October and November). Current driving regulations may be obtained from park headquarters in Manteo, or by calling (919) 473-2113.

Motels and rental cottages abound on Hatteras Island. For an accommodations directory and a list of cottages, phone the Outer Banks Chamber of Commerce at (919) 261-2626. Motels are likely to be booked to capacity during peak fall and spring months, so advance reservations are recommended.

Virginia's Eastern Shore

This area offers the same potential for trophy red drum as North Carolina's Outer Banks. While the present world record is a 90-pound fish from North Carolina, Cape Charles, Virginia, is marginally not far behind with an 83-pound channel bass. Furthermore, the lower Eastern Shore has been producing more drum than ever before due largely to a tactical change in angling methods. Where this sport was once locally pursued almost exclusively by dedicated surf fishermen, most red drum are now being caught from boats rather than the beach.

The two popular techniques today are sight fishing from a slowly cruising boat during daylight hours and anchoring offshore at dark to still-fish with live bait. Sight fishing is accomplished by casting artificial lures to "mudding" schools in shallow water. Still-fishing is simply a matter of finding the feeding lanes and intercepting the drum with a hooked peeler crab, cut mullet or live spot (a croaker).

Obviously, the more exciting method is hunting the fish with artificials. This is at its peak beginning in late March along the Outer Banks, or late April in Virginia. Any small, shallow draft boat is suitable provided it has a bow platform for the angler to sight fish. The inshore areas are normally murky, so there is little chance of seeing individual targets; the presence of a school is revealed by a contrasting discoloration of the water. The most effective lures are active swimmers worked close to the bottom. Most red drum are hooked in water of less than five feet in depth, so floating plugs with diving lips are popular, as are jigs with lively plastic tails, or the single hook Hopkins Spoon. Treble hooks (plus) are not in great favor. Since most big red drum are returned to the water (only the small "puppy" drum, fish of no more than 10 pounds, are worthy at table), a single hook lure allows a quick release with no injury to the fish.

Surf fishing is popular on Virginia's barrier islands, but since they can only be reached by boat, most fishermen stay aboard and cast from an anchored, or drifting, position. If the weather is

The Outer Banks of North Carolina have long been famous for trophy red drum. Our fall season finds the surf crowded at Cape Hatteras when the big fish are in the breakers. Despite cold winds in the peak period of November, dedicated surfers will still be on the beach.

brisk, however, the boats head around the lee side of the islands and the anglers carry their gear ashore. Given the vagaries of weather, there is always the likelihood of using the beach, so it is prudent to request permission beforehand from The Nature Conservancy, Brownsville, Nassawadox, Virginia 23413; telephone (804) 442-3049. This conservation organization owns the islands and permits surf fishermen to use them; the only restriction is no fires and no overnight camping.

The fall run of red drum begins in early September off the town of Cape Charles on the lower Eastern Shore. Almost every evening, a small flotilla of boats will anchor in 30 to 40 feet of water a couple of miles offshore to live-bait fish. Some evenings, more sandbar sharks are caught than drum, but this shark species accompanies the channel bass so it is not a bad omen. By October, the action moves from the bay to the barrier islands again, although the fish are not as densely schooled as they were in the spring spawning season. Autumn offers some classic beach fishing when northwesterly breezes suppress the nearshore swells and big drum pick up baits cast into a flooding slough beyond the first breakers. Like all trophy experiences, you only need one 60-pounder pulling line inexorably from a revolving spool while you brace yourself against the surging surf and sucking sands to feel part of a tradition dating back to the dawn of saltwater angling history.

Port Mansfield

Port Mansfield is located in the middle of some of the most unspoiled country left along the Gulf of Mexico. It is situated on a spit of land jutting into the lower Laguna Madre and is completely isolated on three sides by the vast and privately owned King Ranch. Few of the thousands of tourists who flock to the Rio Grande Valley each winter ever see the port. This small community is at the end of the road (State Highway 186) about 26 miles from Raymondville, Texas. For the angler seeking red drum or spotted seatrout, it is well worth a detour.

The lower Laguna Madre is a vast, shallow bay. Its maximum depth is about 8 feet and most areas are 2 feet or less; when the tide is out, long stretches of flats are exposed. The technique here is very similar to bonefishing, in which a wading angler can search for his quarry in very clear water, on a firm, grassy bottom. There are countless miles of productive water; however, it is necessary to search the flats by boat until feeding fish can be located. For this reason, morning hours are

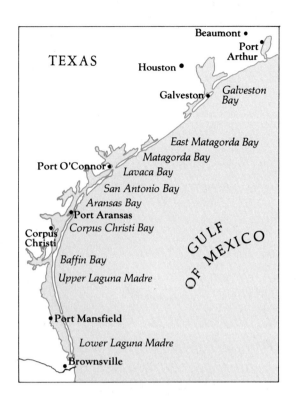

Red drum are found all along the Texas coast and are especially numerous from Matagorda Bay south to Brownsville. An outstanding location is Lower Laguna Madre, which can be fished from Port Mansfield. This vast shallow bay is a paradise for the light-tackle angler.

most successful because of the calm. Afternoon invariably brings winds that make sighting difficult. Polarized glasses are essential.

Since the red drum on the flats only run from 2 to 6 pounds, there is no need for heavy tackle. Spinning or bait-casting gear with 8-pound-test line is eminently suitable. Fly rod tackle calibered for long casts (8- to 9-weight forward line) is recommended, as these fish are spooky in thin water. Spoons, particularly the gold Johnson Sprite, and leadhead jigs with bright plastic tails are effective lures. The fly-rod angler should stock some weedless bucktail or streamer patterns.

A deep-dredged ship channel connects Port Mansfield with the Gulf of Mexico, forming a pass through Padre Island (the southern extreme of the Padre Island National Seashore dead-ends at the channel). When fish are not on the flats, they drift back into deep water. You can wade along the edge of the ship channel and work these deeper spots with good results.

A boat is essential on Laguna Madre as some of the best flats areas are 20 miles north of Port Mansfield. Anglers who do not trailer their own craft can rent locally or hire a guide (which is recommended for tourists unfamiliar with the area). Information on guides and facilities is available from the Port Mansfield Chamber of Commerce, Box O, Port Mansfield, Texas 78598; telephone (512) 944-2354. A Texas saltwater angling license is required.

BLUEFISH

Pomatomus saltatrix

On several occasions in recent years, unstable weather coincided with a tremendous run of bluefish pursuing dense, block-long schools of mullet down Florida's east coast. In each incident, an offshore storm had generated a heavy sea discoloring the inshore waters. Tourists from the chill climates of Europe, Canada and the northern states, happily paddling in the warm subtropical sea, were suddenly surrounded by hordes of frantically leaping mullet but made no effort to retreat to the sand. To a knowledgeable angler, the "feeding frenzy" would have been a warning more apparent than the dorsal fin of Peter Benchley's fabled white shark. Victims were rushed to Miami's emergency wards with a variety of wounds rarely seen in the bikini littoral.

The destructive agent is a fish of remarkable ferocity. Indeed, we can be thankful they do not grow larger in Florida; further north it might exceed 20 pounds. The biggest caught so far by angling weighed 31 pounds, 12 ounces, taken off the coast of North Carolina in January 1972. Professor Spencer F. Baird, first U.S. Fish Commissioner and an enthusiastic angler, described them in his *Report to the United Fish Commission* in 1874:

> *The Bluefish has been well likened to an animated chopping-machine, the business of which is to cut to pieces and otherwise destroy as many fish as possible in a given space of time. Going in large schools, in pursuit of fish not much inferior to themselves in size, they move along like a pack of hungry wolves, destroying everything before them. Their trail is marked by fragments of fish and by the stain of blood in the sea, as, where the fish is too large to be swallowed entire, the hinder portion will be bitten off and the anterior part allowed to float away or sink. It is even maintained, with great earnestness, that such is a gluttony of the fish, that when the stomach becomes full the contents are disgorged and then again filled. It is certain that it kills more fish than it requires for its own support.*

Bluefish will eat delicious fare, such as mullet, or anything else that swims, with the same abandon. This is one of the most common game fish in coastal Atlantic waters, but it is subject to mysterious population fluctuations.

BLUEFISH

Professor Baird wasn't far off the mark. An exhaustive study of bluefish feeding conducted at the Sandy Hook Marine Laboratory indicated that bluefish eat until full and then lose interest in their quarry, though they can be promptly restimulated by larger prey. As for disgorging, this is common with many fish in the throes of resisting hook and line, or when netted. It is true that bluefish often do not clean their plate: Flounder are sometimes caught with a wholly or partially healed bite, evidence of snacking on the part of a passing bluefish that had to keep up with its school.

Professor Baird's accusation of tail-biting has not been substantiated. Bluefish bite at the head of prey fish up to about 6 inches long, then they bite at the midsection, which takes a sandwich bite out of flatfish and separates slender fish into a discarded head and tail plus the part that is swallowed.

As with shark and cubera snapper, this is a fish to handle with care. (Your digits are just the right length to be severed.) A bluefish out of water will watch an approaching hand with his near-side eye and *lunge* when he thinks he can reach it. If you are wearing waders, sea boots or foul-weather gear it is simplest to pin the fish between your knees or feet and disengage the hook with long-nose pliers before stowing your bluefish in the ice chest.

This animated chopping machine is the most popular saltwater game fish extant: A 1979 survey of United States Atlantic coastal anglers produced the figure of 25,428,000 bluefish taken on hook-and-line. The catch weighed 96,661,000 pounds. Bluefish constituted 31.2 percent of the marine recreational catch, excluding tuna and sharks, and was the target fish for 26 percent of mid-Atlantic recreational anglers. By comparison the commercial catch is insignificant: 0.53 percent of landings from Maine to Virginia in 1978.

Bluefish are seasonally found from Massachusetts to Florida, in the southern Gulf of Mexico and the Caribbean (off Cuba) and off the East Coast of South America. On the other side of the Atlantic they appear from the Azores and Portugal, down the coast of Africa and around the Cape of Good Hope. They are in the Mediterranean and the Black Sea, and there is a good population around Australia. Throughout their range they are migratory and appear to find temperatures from the mid-40s to mid-80s acceptable, with the late 60s optimal. Really cold

or hot water blocks the migration even if favored prey species are continuing into it. Some biologists have developed elaborate schemata for annual north-south migrations stimulated by seasonal temperatures and perhaps photoperiod; other biologists favor inshore-offshore migrations. Within the seasonal migration pattern bluefish follow prey migrations. Some of their favorite prey, including mullet in the south range and menhaden in the north, are planktonic, and therein lies a curiosity.

It is axiomatic among oceanic fishers that along with squalling seabirds the most likely sign of underwater predation is a "slick" (an oily upwelling generally a few dozen yards in circumference). Slicks have a fresh-vegetable bouquet often compared with cucumbers. A variety of predatory fish have been taken from the vicinity of slicks, but as a rule bluefish are there in quantity. I believe slicks to be the stomach contents of plankton-filtering prey released by bluefish rending the creatures. Some observers think slicks are diatom blooms that attract menhaden and mullet that in turn attract bluefish. One of us is wrong. At either rate the angler's drill is the same: Cast or troll through the edge of the slick, not the center. Bluefish are ferocious but they can be disturbed, frightened and displaced from even a favored environment by too rude an evidence that something large and animate is at hand. The quickest way to get to the bottom of a slick is with a diamond jig or one of those squids (saltwater terminology for heavy-metal spoons) that resemble a chrome-plated diagonally sliced cut of salami.

The lore of birds and bluefish includes the opinion of one experienced captain that royal terns (orange bill, black cap, usually white forehead) specialize in following bluefish and sandwich terns (black bill with yellow tip, black cap) prefer tuna. Terns are generally more excitable and less trustworthy than gulls, but if storm petrels are pecking at an oily slick you *know* bluefish are down there.

There appear to be at least two separate breeding populations of United States bluefish. The southern spring spawners mate offshore and the northern summer spawners inshore. In western Long Island Sound, Captain Bill Herold has developed a charter fishery for finning-out spawners during the month of June. He finds the fish take surface lures well when fished over depths of 40 to 80 feet. Other observers have testified that spawning bluefish will *not* take, though they become ravenous after the spawn. Patently we have a great deal to learn about this fish.

We do know that they have been commercially taken to 45 pounds off North Africa and to 40 pounds off North America. The present age-growth chart stops at fourteen years and a bit more than 17 pounds, with a fork length of 35 inches. Oversized fish are often sexless and of no greater age than the majority population.

The fertilized egg needs forty-eight hours to develop at 32.5 parts per thousand salinity and 68°F. At 2 inches they begin schooling and at 3 inches will attack bait. By September, young-of-the-year bluefish will reach 7 inches. Approximately one year is required to take a half-pound, 8-incher to a 2-pound, 14-incher. (They are commonly known as snappers when less than a pound and can be caught inshore on light fly and spinning tackle. They constitute a separate fishery in their own right.) This fish, which begins schooling so tiny, is thought to stay with its year-class throughout life. These school populations decrease with age and size until only a handful, or even a lone fish, remains.

There are reports of anomalous schooling behavior. I have found schools of large Florida bluefish that either were all male or only males were eating. Since no one can imagine a dieting bluefish, segregation of adults by sex should be investigated. Lyman (1974) reports that Hatteras sport and commercial fishermen take injured and scarred specimens for approximately two weeks each year before the main populations arrive. This observation, if accurate, indicates "hospital" schools.

Most known schooling fish species have no leader. The front rank fish become the left flank when the school turns right. Bluefish schools are evidently packs organized like wolves or human hunters. There is a pecking order and fighting between individuals to maintain it, and the leader will harry laggard fish by nipping at their tails. Biologically the function of a school is protection and the function of a pack is increased hunting efficiency (both facilitate breeding). We may be using misleading nomenclature in discussing the social organization of bluefish.

The species goes through unexplained population fluctuations (similar to striped bass and weakfish) that cannot be called cycles because there is no sequence or rhythm to them. That 'twas ever thus can be seen from the publication in

Hooked up to a Hatteras bluefish on a sultry September afternoon, this angler will need to be wary of his bare feet when he beaches his fish.

1794 of the Collections of the Massachusetts Historical Society containing Zaccheus Macy's *Short Journal of the First Settlement of the Island of Nantucket, With Some of the Most Remarkable Things That Had Happened Since, to the Present Time:*

> . . . from the first coming of the English to Nantucket, a large fat fish called the Bluefish, thirty of which would fill a barrel, was caught in great plenty all around the island, from the first of the sixth month to the middle of the ninth month. But it is remarkable, that in the year 1764 . . . they all disappeared and that none have ever been taken since. This has been a great loss to us.

But at the same time Nantucket was deprived the Chesapeake could have been surfeited. Water temperature variations are most often cited as the cause of these nonperiodical population swings. The closer fisheries biologists look at what is an

BLUEFISH

acceptable temperature niche for a species the more complicated the matter becomes. At different ages a fish may occupy different niches (see Chapter 25, Striped Bass), and the temperature preferendum of major prey species may be the determinant. An exploding population of the American sand lance (*Ammodytes americanus*), popularly called the sand eel, has been the principal prey for Atlantic inshore predatory fish the last few years and no one has the faintest idea why this is so, although the sand lance's beach-loving conduct (it can burrow out of sight before your eyes) may make surf fishing more productive when it is in a population upswing.

The dentition of bluefish makes metallic lures advisable, except that metal lures don't float, and fish taken on topwater lures are superior entertainment. Our forefathers used lead drails that they polished with beach sand and twirled overhead like a gaucho's *bolas* before letting fly, and retrieved the tarred cotton line hand over hand. They also favored trolling under sail, in centerboard catboats, often with an artificial squid or a bone lure (a short section of hollow chicken bone strung on a wire leader and seated around a long-shanked hook). Some of the more expensive squids were made of mother-of-pearl or ivory. The first edition of *Fishing with Hook and Line: A Manual for Amateur Anglers, Containing also Descriptions of Popular Fishes, and Their Habits, Preparation of Baits, etc.*, by Frank Forester (H. W. Herbert), published circa 1850, refers to Down East fishermen taking bluefish with "common" pewter spoons. Since Julio T. Buel received the first U.S. patent for a metal spoon in 1834 and didn't begin manufacturing them until 1848 (with some publicity from Forester), the bluefish spoon became common with remarkable rapidity. Actually, spoons are of prehistoric origin, but Buel's were painted and feathered, definitely not "common" or homemade.

Another popular trolling lure a century and a half ago was the cedar jig: a lead head up front, a hook at the rear and a round cedar body between. Like the drail-derived squid, this had little or no intrinsic action, but attracted bluefish by the boat's progress and vigorous pumping on the line to make it dart.

All of these have modern counterparts. The squid went from lead drail to tin squid and is now chromed brass or hammered stainless steel. The hollow chicken bone is now rubber or plastic

surgical tubing bent into a curve to make it rotate, which provides the illusion of undulation. The cedar jig became first wooden and now plastic plugs, and in a divergent development the lead head acquired a tail of bucktail hair, and latterly of soft plastic in a piscine shape, that hydraulic pressure artfully wags from side to side. Bluefish adore jigs and leave the bucktail a stubble and the plastic tail in shreds.

The world of commercial fishing has donated diamond jigs to the sport of bluefishing. This ancient European cod and mackerel lure has removed cod in tonnage beyond computation from the Grand Banks. When adapted to bluefishing the traditional rigid treble hook at the rear resulted in too many cases of the fish wrenching or twisting itself off. A single hook mounted to the diamond with a swivel between them solved that. This lure is bounced off bottom and then reeled as fast as you can turn the handle until halfway to the surface—as high in the water column as bluefish are likely to suspend—then dropped again. Properly performed, the intervening fish fights will be welcome relief from the fatigue of retrieving.

These permutations of primitive saltwater lures into their contemporary lightweight descendants were made possible by the development of mechanically sound freshwater bait-casting reels (by nineteenth-century Kentucky watchmakers) and their adaptation to saltwater rod casting, which finally allowed the retirement of tarred cotton handline.

The star drag mechanism for braking powerful fish was patented in 1902 but not widely distributed until years later. Prior to that, braking a fish was done by pressing with one's thumbs on a leather pad riveted to one of the reel's pillars so the leather bore hard against the diminishing spool of line. Alternately, thumbstalls made of leather, rubber or finally elastic cloth with a leather thumb pad were popular. When Abercrombie & Fitch succumbed to bankruptcy in 1977 (reborn in 1979 under new ownership) they still had the elastic cloth type in stock.

"I'm afraid we were oversupplied with that item when the star drag was introduced," said a salesman. That is odd, because the drag was reportedly developed by William Boschen and George Farnsworth, angler and guide of the Catalina Tuna Club, and "someone at Abercrombie & Fitch." (George Reiger, *Profiles in Saltwater Angling*, Prentice-Hall, viii plus 470. 1973.)

Current tackle suitable for bluefish runs the gamut from ultralight spinning and midge fly rods (for snappers) up to 20-pound-test casting or trolling tackle. Charter captains, accustomed as they are to rank novices, may use 50-pound line, a wretched excess the experienced avoid by taking their own tackle aboard charter craft. If doing so, make clear when booking what type of tackle you use.

Bluefish are customarily taken in the northern states while fishing for striped bass, bluefish or weakfish and in the south while fishing for red drum, spotted seatrout or bluefish. In its mid-range, the Carolinas, the fish is angled for in combination with big red and black drum, and striped bass. There are techniques for avoiding bluefish that are more certain than those for specializing in them. Bluefish find freshwater distasteful, so if the water you are fishing tastes sweet you are a striped bass fisherman. Bluefish avoid really murky water, but the drums will tolerate it. Bluefish are highly piscivorous, so fishing a shrimp or shrimp-like lure in a rush-lined bay is a weakfish or spotted seatrout undertaking.

A technique for *locating* bluefish is to fish with a light monofilament line tied directly to a small lure. The consequent bite-offs establish you have found them. Nevertheless, wire leaders are not mandatory; a 60-pound-test hard monofilament shock leader 12 inches long will catch quite a few bluefish before it becomes too nicked to trust. Experienced spinning and fly-fishermen increasingly tie lures directly to light line and are willing to accept bite-offs as the price of more action. A tube lure 8 or more inches long with a single-strand wire inside the tube (that has been haywire twisted to a swivel eye snug against the sinker at its head) doesn't need a wire leader; it is quite literally built in. The ubiquitous saltwater streamer fly called *Lefty's Deceiver*, the one that has long saddle hackles or artificial hair tied as an elongated tail, topped by a streamlined collar of hair, can be tied just at the rear of a long-shanked hook whose bare shank will offer considerable protection. The freshwater bass fisherman's spinnerbait, a jig with a spinner mounted overhead atop a vertical V of bent wire, is another likely candidate for bluefish. It works very well in 1- or 2-ounce sizes on pike and muskellunge, and I have taken barracuda on it. Fish duck their upper lip under the spinning blade to bite the jig, and the V of bent wire prevents access to the line.

Technological advance and affluence are continuing to mold our bluefishing. For a quarter of a century after World War II the lone surf-caster roaming the beaches, afoot or in a beach buggy, was the prototype bluefisherman. Mass production of small craft and trustworthy outboard engines has put many of these anglers afloat, where their long-butted, 10½-foot high-surf rods would be an encumbrance. The jetty rod of 7½ to 8½ feet with a shorter two-handed butt has become a popular boat casting rod. Single-handed spinning and fly tackle are also appearing.

It is a precept among bluefishermen that when a surface lure hits the water or a countdown lure reaches its depth, you begin rapid reeling and pause naught until possession is regained. Big-spooled spinning reels with high-speed gear ratios do this very well, plug-casting reels with their

Gerri Roadarmel with one of an identical trio of 12-pound bluefish she caught while trolling an umbrella rig near the Midway Buoy off Montauk, Long Island, in November.

smaller-diameter spools almost as well, and fly tackle does it miserably. Never say die. A popping bug can be kept in continuous-if-not-rapid motion, and its noise level often will substitute for speed. A streamer can be given a sizzling haul with the line hand yanking from stripping guide to full extension behind the back, and then the rod can rip the fly through another 6 feet of water before it

BLUEFISH

becomes aerial. This 12 feet of lightning retrieve, executed repetitively to a seen or suspected bluefish, should be enough to determine if it is eating or digesting. A nice use of fly tackle is to have it ready to cast to bluefish that are following a lure or following a hooked fish as it is brought to boat.

In a sense bluefish are always digesting, because their almost insatiable appetite is the consequence of powerful stomach acids that rapidly process food. The acids of a dead bluefish promptly begin to dissolve their container, so this is one fish that should be cleaned and iced immediately. It should also be promptly eaten. Frank Forester had the right recipe for them:[1]

> There is not pleasanter summer day's amusement than a merry cruise after the Blue-fish, no pleasanter close to it than the clam-bake, the chowder, and the broiled Blue-fish, lubricated with champagne, learnedly frappe, and temperately taken, no unpleasant medicine.

And Robert Barnwell Roosevelt, writing in his *Gamefish of the Northern States of America* (1862), advised the successful trolling bluefisherman to land at Fire Island (on the southern shore of Long Island, New York) and:

> Either cook his fish by a fire built from the wraiths of the sea, or get a fashionable dinner from Dominy or t'other man that keeps a hotel there.

Fillet and broil your fresh bluefish. The extremely fine grain of the myotomes simply dissolves into mush when cooked wet.

Some biologists have speculated on the basis of similarity of jaw structure and musculature that bluefish are related to piranhas, but surely that is an example of the same convergent evolution that has made barracuda and pikes so similar. Others have posited a distant relationship to the jack family, and there *does* seem to be a facial resemblance to jacks, but it remains unproven.

The pursuit of bluefish leads you to the sea's edge and end. The pursuit of sand eels and mullet leads bluefish there, too. You meet in a sizzling froth of salt wash thrashing and grappling at each other. Take care that you are the one who takes hold. If the fish is in excess of your food requirements you can release it unmaimed. It cannot.

Montauk

Because of the variety of areas available, New York's Montauk sportfishing fleet probably enjoys the most consistent bluefishing on the entire coast. They arrive within range of the boats by late May and are continuously available to them until mid- or late November. (Catches of 300 to 500 pounds or more are common, even on half-day trips.) However, unlike the striped bass fishing (where almost all the catch is made within a few miles of harbor), successful bluefishing often calls for long boat runs. The need for these long runs has become more apparent in recent years since bluefish appear only sporadically on local grounds, but provide consistent action off Block Island.

The first spring bluefish at Montauk are often encountered a good distance to the east. Charter boats trolling for pollock in late May and early June start catching bluefish around Sharks Ledge, which is southeast of Block Island. At that time these fish are usually found close to the surface in relatively warm water and can be trolled on umbrella rigs fished on approximately 100 feet of wire line. As the season advances bluefish will go deeper in response to warming temperatures. Thus, by early July it may be necessary to fish 250 to 300 feet of wire in order to reach them.

Some bluefish are also caught in the rips off Montauk Point in June, though they rarely

A Montauk mate prepares bluefish chum while leaving harbor. The chum is menhaden, colloquially mossbunker or bunker, a prolific clupeoid of the western Atlantic, widely used for fertilizer, for the oil in house paint, and as chicken feed.

[1]Herbert, Henry William. *Frank Forester's Fish and Fishing of the United States and the British Provinces of North America.* London. Third Edition. 1849.

provide any consistent action until July. Schools are constantly working their way inshore during June. Frequently they'll settle in for several weeks about 8 to 10 miles south of the Point in approximately 120 feet of water. As with the early Block Island migration, these bluefish are found close to the surface. Fish them from mid-June to mid-July.

By mid-July, inshore bluefishing is usually consistent enough to eliminate those long runs. Every year there are sporadic local concentrations of bluefish. These may occur as close as the Pocketbook area (about 4 miles north of the inlet) or at Cerebus Shoal (a couple of miles farther north). Small bluefish, along with weakfish, often pour onto Shagwong Reef, just a couple of miles to the east. The rips off the Point can also be very productive. However, the most consistent action occurs at a series of deep-water rips starting at Midway Buoy—5 miles east of the Point.

The Sub Buoy, another 3 miles to the east, may be even more productive. There are depths of over 100 feet on both sides of this buoy, which marks the channel used by submarines going into New London, Connecticut. Two miles southeast of the Sub Buoy is Southwest Ledge, another bluefish hot spot—though it's hard to work around all the lobster pots, which are drawn under when the tide is running. If all these spots fail to produce a full box, the angler can run northeast to the Southeast Light corner of Block Island (approximately 6 miles) or southeast toward Shark's Ledge. During the summer there's usually a massive body of 6- to 12-pound fish located in 80- to 100-foot depths south and southeast of Block Island.

Another broad area that has been productive some years is the so-called Triangle. Draw a line from Midway Buoy south to the MC Buoy (approximately 5 miles offshore) and then back northeast to the Sub Buoy. That last line actually drops into very deep waters, but just west of it you will find the 60-foot curve and most of the bluefish. At other times the blues will be scattered over the broad plateau of 40- to 50-foot depths extending back toward Midway. Weakfish are frequently mixed in with the bluefish here, and at all the other sites mentioned, except in the deep-water areas south and southeast of Block Island.

Around mid-August the most consistent fishing for 10- to 15-pound bluefish develops at the Cartwright Grounds, between 6 and 8 miles south of Montauk Point, and continues well into October. Only the arrival of spiny dogfish in October and a lack of interest in bluefish when stripers start hitting inshore puts an end to this fishing. There are probably still large bluefish to be

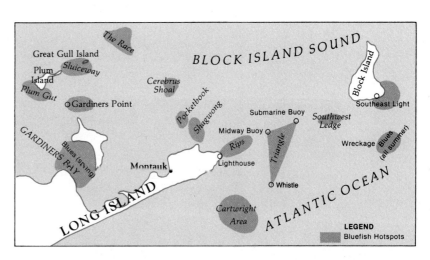

caught in November if anyone would bother with them. Nowhere else does the angler have a better opportunity for 20-pound bluefish, particularly if he fishes at night.

The Montauk charter and private boat fleets concentrate on these 100-foot depths. The Viking and Marlin fleets send at least one party boat each to Cartwright every night, and the anglers aboard invariably return with huge catches. Although trolling and jigging work well at Cartwright, the majority of bluefish are caught on whole or half baits, fished on drail rigs just off the bottom. Herring and butterfish are the most common baits, but bunkers, whiting, eels and numerous others will work. Best of all is a live bergall (cunner) or conger eel caught on the spot.

During the fall great numbers of 2- to 4-pound bluefish pour out of Long Island Sound and round the Point before heading south. This migration often produces wild action from Shagwong Reef to the Point, and along the South Shore. Surface plugs (particularly poppers) are effective during this period.

The bluefish season ends in mid-November closer to Block Island at the Hooter Buoy or Southwest Ledge. They have been caught at the latter as late as Thanksgiving Day, but are usually chased by northeast storms a week or two before then.

Montauk boaters also have a large choice of bluefishing areas to the west, though they rarely take advantage of them. Cherry Harbor, on the west side of Gardiner's Island, is noted for its early run of blues, while the north side produces good fishing in the summer and fall. The waters are relatively shallow and are best fished with popping plugs. To the northwest you'll find the Ruins, Plum Gut, Pigeon Rip, the Sluiceway and The Race—all famous bluefish areas.

Between the eastern end of Long Island, otherwise known as Montauk Point, and Block Island, lie some of the finest bluefish trolling and jigging grounds yet discovered.

273

BLUEFISH

The majority of bluefish caught in this area are trolled on umbrella rigs. These are armed with tube lures, which closely imitate the sand eels that infest the region and provide the basic diet for most predators. Bluefish usually strike readily at almost any tube. Eighty- and 100-pound-test leaders are often employed and don't seem to have a negative effect. Of course, the umbrella rigs (which are always fished on wire line) also offer the possibility of multiple catches. Bluefish will also hit a wide variety of trolled lures, but many of them are quickly ruined by their sharp teeth.

Fly-fishing is short casting and needs concentrations of fish to be effective.

Perhaps the most enjoyable and consistent method of catching bluefish in this area is jigging them with diamond jigs. This method can be used anywhere there are bluefish, but is particularly effective in deeper waters. It doesn't work well when the fish first arrive and are in the warm upper waters. Though bluefish don't hit lures too well at night, party boats (which are all well lit) often do well with diamond jigs in the dark—particularly with luminescent lures.

Whereas a slow retrieve of the diamond jig is recommended for weakfish and stripers, the jig can hardly be moved fast enough for bluefish. Double-headers are a possibility by adding a tube on a dropper loop 1 or 2 feet above the jig. Be sure to use heavy leader material when doing this or you'll suffer a great many bite-offs.

The third major method of catching bluefish around Montauk involves the use of bait on a drail rig. Party boats do well with this rigging off Block

Island in the summer and throughout the season at The Race. In shallow areas especially, it's possible to catch bluefish on light tackle with lead-head jigs and other lures. However, there has been less surface action since sand eels became so dominant in the ecosystem and most predators have turned to feeding on them in the depths.

Surf casters at Montauk probably get more action from bluefish than from any other species found in the area. There's always the hope of a charge of bluefish. In September and October the fishing is often quite good for days at a time, and it's spread over a much greater area than the stripers normally populate. For instance, the sandy beach along the South Shore from Ditch Plains to Hither Hills State Park frequently produces concentrated action in the fall. Metal lures (Hopkins and Kastmasters) and popping plugs are most popular. Those without beach buggies will do best by concentrating on the rocky areas under the Lighthouse, which can be reached easily from the parking lot at the Point.

Provided you have a full day in which to fish, Montauk can guarantee you a bluefish from June to early November—even at times when there are scarcities to the west. Historically, bluefish have been cyclical in nature. However, as long as the cycle of abundance continues, Montauk Point will be one of the finest sport fisheries in the world!

Giant Bluefish on Fly

Jumbo bluefish winter off the North Carolina capes. In spring and fall they forage along the beaches and in the roily shoal water that extends off the capes. Surfmen and boaters may encounter single bluefish or, more often, schools of them, anywhere along the coast, but perhaps the most dependable location for fly-fishing is Cape Lookout.

Three capes extend off the North Carolina coast—Hatteras, Lookout and Fear. Lookout, in the middle, has less extensive shoals and usually calmer water off the point and more protected water in the bight, and is easier for boat access. Barden's Inlet is navigable by small boat in all but the worst weather.

You need calm weather for fly-fishing. Unfortunately, such conditions are only partly predictable on North Carolina's Outer Banks. Prevailing winds reverse themselves in spring and fall so that weather systems frequently change at the times that bluefish are present. Four months offer the best prospects for fly-fishing—April and

May, November and December. May and November have the best weather. Being at Cape Lookout during calm weather is mostly a matter of luck, though your chances are improved by studying weather maps and marine weather reports. Experienced anglers go there prepared for other forms of fishing also, including plug and spin casting and trolling.

In spring, big bluefish are thin. Average weight is probably around 12 pounds, although you see fish weighing from 6 to approximately 16 pounds. In the fall, bluefish weigh from 12 to 18 pounds or more; only a few reach 20 pounds.

Spring bluefish may or may not feed readily. A shallow sandbar west of the Cape Lookout jetty sometimes holds bluefish in the early morning while boat traffic is light. These fish can be teased into striking by repeatedly casting large popping bugs near them and picking them up noisily. A hook-up appears to stimulate feeding.

Fall bluefish are not so reticent. They are actively feeding to store up energy for winter and usually take a popping bug without hesitation. Streamers are consistent only during a feeding frenzy.

In spring and fall, bluefish are frequently found on the shoals that extend for several miles off the tip of Cape Lookout. When the weather is calm for several days the water clears, sometimes enough to spot cruising bluefish among the shoal humps. Sight fishing then becomes possible. Otherwise, it is necessary to cast blindly to breaking seas on the bars and to deeper water under diving seabirds. Sometimes the air is full of gulls, terns, pelicans and gannets that may signal massive invasions of giant bluefish. Fishing is usually best early in the morning, but bluefish can show up on the shoals at any time.

No. 11 fly-rod systems are appropriate in the windy conditions that are common at Cape Lookout. On calm days, a No. 10 system is entirely adequate for bluefish, since there are no obstacles on which they may break your leader. Veterans recommend floating lines. Large white poppers with concave faces about the size of a dime are consistent producers. Flashy 3/0 streamers serve well for hooking following fish, but are inefficient at enticing first strikes. Wire shock leaders are absolutely necessary.

Outboard boats above 17 feet in length are recommended for these waters. In especially calm weather, smaller boats may be employed close to the inlet.

Harkers Island is the logical starting point for fishing Cape Lookout. A list of restaurants, motels and marinas can be obtained from the Carteret County Chamber of Commerce, 3401 Arendel Street, P.O. Box 1198, Morehead City, N. C. 28557; telephone (919) 726-6831. A list of charter boats out of both Morehead City and Harkers Island may be obtained from the same source. Some skippers will not permit fly-fishing, so it is advisable to inquire before booking.

From Raleigh, four commuter flights a day serve New Bern, which is approximately an hour's drive from either Morehead City or Harkers Island. Rental cars are available.

Bluefishing's most interesting moment is often unhooking the fish without losing any of your own blood. Not everyone survives this test successfully!

BLUEFISH

Outer Banks for Surf Blues

Giant bluefish have not always populated the Outer Banks surf. There were reports of them in the fall of 1935 at Hatteras, then they disappeared entirely from the Outer Banks (and from the western Atlantic Ocean, as far as fishermen could tell) for 30 years.

Only a few bluefish returned in 1965, then again in subsequent falls in trace numbers until they showed up at Nags Head in November 1972. Hundreds of thousands of fish populated the Outer Banks beaches that fall and winter and their numbers have held up ever since. Although there are fewer now than in the early 1970s, there is still a good population of bluefish in the western Atlantic. How long they will remain is anyone's guess. Experts say the species is subject to sudden die-offs when their numbers reach a certain density. Going back to the nineteenth century, there were periodic surges in population, followed by long periods of absence.

Small bluefish are year-'round residents of the Outer Banks. Fish weighing over 6 pounds are migratory. By June, North Carolina waters are empty because of migration to New England. In October the first fish return, but November has been the best month for surf fishing. By late December, the bluefish are in dense schools off the capes. The best known area is off Cape Fear in the vicinity of Frying Pan Shoals Navigation Tower. The fish that winter off the capes may make forays into the Outer Banks surf during winter months, but these trips are brief and unpredictable. By April, the bluefish begin to move inshore, feeding in preparation for their spring migration. At this time they are thin. Outer Banks bluefish average about 12 pounds in spring. In fall, they average 15 pounds.

There are two surf fishing seasons on the Outer Banks—spring and fall. The peak months are May and November. Sometimes, to the dismay of surf fishermen, bluefish do not come into the surf sloughs in great numbers even though there is a concentrated population offshore. But when the right combination of wind and current entice baitfish into the surf, bluefish are likely to be right behind them. Thousands of birds dive and squall, bluefish slash the surface running bait up on the sand, beaching themselves in the process, and are carried out again by the next wave. Excited anglers stand waist deep in the breaking seas slinging heavy metal lures or topwater plugs into the melee. Such a concentration is a memorable fishing phenomenon and can occur anywhere on the Outer Banks. But certain sites are more likely to be besieged by big bluefish. The tip of Cape Hatteras is one, as are both the north and south sides of Oregon Inlet and the north side of Hatteras Inlet.

The all-around rod for bluefish in the surf would be a 9-foot, heavy-action model for casting lures up to 6 ounces. You could lob bait on days when action is slow, and still have fun with 12-pound fish on artificials. Large spin reels should be spooled with 15- to 20-pound-test monofilament.

Successful surf fishing requires mobility. Schools are here today, gone tomorrow. A four-wheel-drive vehicle makes life easier, although there are sites where a lucky pedestrian might happen on a school close to a paved road. Most of the Outer Banks are within the Cape Hatteras National Seashore, which regulates beach driving. During the bluefish seasons, most of the beach is open for driving. Beach driving regulations may be obtained from the seashore office in Manteo, telephone (919) 473-2117, and at ranger stations throughout the seashore.

Anglers lacking a proper beach vehicle may hire a guide. There are several on the Outer Banks from Nags Head to Ocracoke. They provide the vehicle, tackle and bait or lures. A current list may be obtained from the North Carolina Travel and Tourism Division, 430 North Salisbury St., Raleigh, NC 27609.

The nearest commercial airport is at Norfolk, where rental cars are available. Cape Hatteras is a two-and-one-half-hour drive. The Outer Banks Chamber of Commerce provides an accommodations list; telephone (919) 261-2626.

SPOTTED SEATROUT

Cynoscion nebulosus

AND

WEAKFISH

To a European angler, the name sea trout (two words) refers to the anadromous brown trout, and while that noble game fish occurs in some fresh waters of North America also, the name seatrout (one word) refers to a totally unrelated marine species which haunts the bays, surf and brackish rivers of the southern United States. Formally known as the spotted seatrout *(Cynoscion nebulosus)*, it lacks the endurance, wild speed and acrobatic bent of its salmonid namesake, yet it is the most popular game fish in its geographic range because it occurs in abundance throughout a long season and comes readily to all types of lures. Few seafood can match this delectable member of the drum family at the table.

Spotted seatrout belong to the same genus as our northern weakfish or "gray trout," the silver seatrout, sand seatrout, the California white seabass and corvinas of the Pacific.[1] The range of seatrout and weakfish overlaps to some extent, but they are easy to identify; both are marked with black or bronze spots, but on weakfish, these are small and appear as undulating streaks that run downward and forward along its back, while the spots on a seatrout are large and distinct, providing its most common name, "speckled trout." These spots become less prominent with age and almost disappear on fish of 10 pounds or more. Both species take artificial lures as well as live baits, and they can be rated on a par as game fish. The real difference lies in their respective habitats, as our southern trout is essentially a very shallow-water form compared with the northern tide runner, with some of the best fishing often occurring at knee depth. I have caught trout in the

---

[1] Seatrout and weakfish comprise a subfamily of the drums (Otolithinae), characterized by large terminal mouths and two prominent canine teeth in the upper jaw.

*Oyster bars are favorite foraging areas for the spotted seatrout
and weakfish (middle distance). The range of these related
species overlaps north to Chesapeake Bay and south to Cape Canaveral.*

SPOTTED SEATROUT

10-pound class in little more than a foot of water over an oyster bar that was just wet enough to float the fish. Stalking these spotted monsters can be a kind of excitement in itself, especially on a dead calm morning when the tide is sucking out and finger mullet gather in the holes, which become seething cauldrons of food for needle-toothed predators.

Seatrout are sensitive to temperature extremes. They prefer water in the mid-60s to mid-70s, which probably explains why the best angling occurs in late spring and fall throughout much of the fish's range. During severely cold weather, they will move offshore to warmer depths, but on rare occasions, a sharp temperature drop can cause a cold-kill among populations that lingered inshore, leaving thousands of dead fish floating on the surface. Normally, as the water temperature drops, trout in the mid-Atlantic region, for example, will congregate in "holes" and continue to feed. Some of the best fishing along the Core Banks in North Carolina occurs in the winter months from November into February, when big schools crowd in deep pockets along the beach. It is not unusual for a late season angler to take thirty or forty trout with spin gear and small lures from a very small area. Hot summer temperatures have a similiar effect in more southerly regions, although the schools will move inshore at night to feed. Much of this fishing is done from causeways and bridges by drifting a live shrimp, needlefish or small mullet with the tide. Ordinarily, night fishing is best during a flowing tide. It doesn't seem to matter whether it is flooding or ebbing, so long as it is moving. However, in my experience, the very best time for big trout is from first light until about 8 A.M., and on a falling tide from two hours before the change to one hour after. Ideally, this should be in a period from the new to full moon.

Trout can be highly selective at times, especially when the schools concentrate to feed on shrimp. These crustaceans drift with the tide just under the surface, and the fish make a distinctive splash and "popping" sound as they gobble the shrimp. In calm water, this activity is accompanied by rapid wavy movements on the surface, and there is seldom any mistaking the situation, as trout will boil behind a plug again and again without touching it. They are obviously attracted by the sound of the lure, which probably suggests another feeding fish. This response is so well known that commercial fishermen sometimes use a "splash pole" or long cane pole rigged with a noisemaking bobber just over a shrimp bait with

deadly effect. There are many rough-bottomed banks where stop nets or haul seines cannot be used by market fishermen, so the practice is an ancient art. However, don't be misled. There are two schools of thought about catching *big* trout with artificials, and it is important to understand both.

Spotted seatrout are found along the Gulf Coast states, in Florida and up the Eastern Seaboard to Chesapeake Bay, sometimes straying as far north as New York. There is excellent fishing to be had along the coasts of Alabama, Mississippi, Louisiana and Texas. The Chandeleur Islands, located about 30 miles off Louisiana's southeast coast, are well known for their extraordinary seatrout fishing, particularly for fly-rodders. The Texas coast has many miles of prime spotted seatrout shallows. San Luis Pass, at the lower end of Galveston Island, is a top spot for wading anglers, as is the 100-mile-long bay-like Laguna Madre. Other fine seatrout areas include Georgia's Cumberland, St. Andrews, Altamaha and Ossabaw sounds; St. Helena Sound and Murrells Inlet in South Carolina; North Carolina's Pamlico and Core sounds, the tidal marsh areas of the Cape Fear and Newport rivers; and the eastern backwater areas of the Chesapeake Bay in Virginia and Maryland. Despite a dwindling habitat, large seatrout are still caught on the east coast of Florida, particularly around Cocoa, Melbourne, Vero Beach and south to Fort Pierce. Here, fish of 5 pounds are common from April to June, 8- to 10-pounders are possible, and two fish weighing 14 pounds were taken in the 1982 season. Over on the west coast, 800-square-mile Florida Bay produces in quantity, but the fish are much smaller. Actually, there is far more angling along the Gulf shore in a miles-available sense; however, a 4-pound trout is above average here. Tagging studies indicate that seatrout populations do not make extensive migrations, so areas where large fish occur are likely to produce quality catches with regularity. In a three-year period at Pine Island, Florida, where 2,538 fish were tagged and 271 recovered, only one trout had moved more than 30 miles. In a subsequent study, 5,409 were tagged in two weeks and the recoveries during the next four months totaled 1,349 trout, or almost 25 percent—a very high return.

Tackle for Seatrout

Spinning tackle is by far the most popular gear for seatrout. Bait casting is just as effective, and indeed, for calloused thumbs the multiplier has no

DISTRIBUTION

peer, but in either case, you have to be able to make *long* casts. Do not underestimate the virtue of distance on the flats. Big trout will often follow a plug all the way back to your rod tip before striking. They are notorious "window-shoppers," and the longer they have to boil and make passes behind a bait, the more fish you will catch. A standard 5½-foot bait-casting rod or a 6½-foot spinning rod designed for one-quarter to five-eighths-ounce baits is ideal. A freshwater-size reel spooled with 8-pound-test monofilament on the spinning rod and 10-pound-test with the multiplier is most efficient. For lures, you should stock small spoons in the quarter-ounce size, plastic shrimp, bucktail jigs, darter and popping plugs. But, for big trout, you need a quiet swimmer. The eight-, nine-, and ten-year-old trout, or those in trophy sizes, do not feed in schools for the obvious reason that there aren't many survivors in an old age group, and they not only become more wary, but shy away from the company of smaller trout in the search for food. According to local lore, the heaviest fish are more or less solitary hunters, and my experience indicates that it is true. Noise seems to make these trout suspicious rather than arousing their interest. When the big ones are feeding, you can take a fair number by covering a wide area, but these are individual targets and far more cautious. I once scored three 6-, an 8-, a 10- and an 11-pounder during one tide in the Banana River on an actionless plug—one that comes straight back in the water without wiggling—by stalking surface cruising singles. The most popular pattern is a needlefish design in green and silver, a slow sinker that can be teased along in spasmodic jerks, or left to swim deeper over lush pastures. Another old reliable is a fatter bait that resembles a mullet, but the only action permissible is a bobbing motion imparted by smooth strokes of the rod tip. It doesn't make a sound. Many old-timers who fancy the shape of a new plug's body even remove the metal or plastic lips which the manufacturer artfully designed.

Seatrout are usually caught from small boats, by wading and, in some areas, just by walking along a riverbank or beach. There are many places where you only have to drive your car to the waterside and start wading. Of course, fishing from a skiff covers more area, and the usual procedure is to drift with the wind, making blind casts until you locate trout. Then you can anchor and work the spot thoroughly—or, if the bottom is firm, get out and wade. During cold weather, especially in the Gulf, trout move farther offshore and may be found at 10- to 20-foot depths, but here again, the fish are usually first pinpointed by drifting and casting before dropping the anchor. In creeks, there are certain shell beds, points, grass patches and mangrove islands that produce trout season after season, and these may be widely scattered over 8 or 10 miles.

Oyster bars and grass beds are ideal habitats for spotted seatrout and weakfish. Crabs, shrimp and other crustaceans thrive in this kind of water and, undisturbed by siltation or pollution, the productivity of sciaenids can be phenomenal. This bay at Cape Lookout, North Carolina, is typical of "trout" country.

281

SPOTTED SEATROUT

Seatrout fishing does not require specialized fly tackle. Any standard medium-weight outfit will serve nicely. An 8½- to 9-foot fiberglass or graphite rod calibered for a WF8F or WF9F line is perfect. An inexpensive, single-action reel with interchangeable spool is sufficient; although a floating weight-forward line will cover most situations, there are times, especially in winter, when you will have to swim a fly deeper, and a sinking line or sinking-tip line should be available on that extra spool. Tapered leaders with 12- or 15-pound-test tippets are suggested, as trout have

Both seatrout and weakfish are caught in the surf. Unlike red drum or striped bass, they are usually found in quieter water around deep holes. These fish tend to avoid a heavy or shallow surf. Fast-sinking lead-head jigs are ideal lures for this kind of fishing.

small canine teeth, not sharp enough to warrant a heavy shock tippet, but sufficiently abrasive to cut lighter diameters. These fish aren't skittish, so the leader need not be any longer than the rod.

Fly-fishing for seatrout is not only fun, but sometimes more effective than other methods, especially when the fish are selectively feeding on small natural baits like shrimp, silversides and anchovies (so-called glass minnows). Generally speaking, the simplest patterns are effective. Even the most amateur flytier can turn out a basic trout bucktail. All you need is a No. 1/0 hook, some white and dyed-green bucktail, plus a few strips of Mylar. Use the white bucktail for an underwing

and fasten it so that the hairs extend about 1 inch beyond the hook bend. Tie a bunch of green bucktail over the white and add a half dozen strips of Mylar for topping. It's not necessary to make a body. This same fly tied with a red-and-white wing, or all pink or all yellow, and the Mylar strips, provides an effective color range. Any of the "breather"-type streamer flies with splayed hackle wings are also standard and need be no more complicated than a busy hackle at the hook eye and a long divided wing. The real problem is taking trout when they are feeding on the bottom in grass beds. For this, you will need streamers tied on a keel hook with the bend and barb turned up.

Naturally, popping bugs are often deadly on school trout, and any of the saltwater models marketed will take fish. I prefer bugs with an elongated, slender body and a bucktail or saddle hackle tail. This design casts easily in a wind, which is really how these lures should be evaluated. Highly air-resistant bugs with wings or beer barrel bodies are next to useless on the flats. Bear in mind, the same virtue of distance applies in fly-fishing, with the longest casts scoring more trout. The angler who can reach 60 feet or more has a better chance of success. All yellow, red-and-white and blue-and-white bugs dressed on No. 2 and 1/0 hooks are effective everywhere.

Cape Lookout

North Carolina has three capes jutting into the Atlantic—Hatteras, Lookout and Fear. Lookout, in the middle, boasts a bight so beautiful and so protected from wind from every quarter that during World War II, it was designated a harbor of refuge. Still, commercial boats stream to it when storm flags are raised and holiday boaters of every stripe gambol in its tranquil waters when the weather is fair. Cape Lookout has all the features that seatrout specialists look for in a fishing location—an inlet between the sound and the ocean, a maze of marsh islands and channels, a jetty to hold bait and lee shores in any wind.

Barden's Inlet pierces North Carolina'a sandy barrier islands at Cape Lookout, draining Core Sound to the north and Pamlico Sound beyond, both nursery and feeding grounds for speckled trout. Extensive marshes along the Outer Banks are laced with channels that are feeding locations and migratory routes for trout on the way to the inlet and the Atlantic Ocean beyond in late summer or on the way back in spring. Part of North Carolina's seatrout never leave the sounds where they are born and mature. Others migrate along the beaches and are also targets of surf fishermen in fall.

Two specific locations at Cape Lookout bear investigation on any trip. The Short Turn is a deep marsh creek on the eastern end of Shackelford Island, just a short distance off the Barden's Inlet channel. A crowd of boats on fall weekends usually marks the location for novices. Lead-head jigs weighing up to 2 ounces are favored here because of the depth and current. When weather permits boating outside the inlet, Cape Lookout jetty should not be overlooked. This 200-yard-long line of rocks frequently harbors seatrout late in the season—from November until Christmas. From September through October, fish are more likely to be found inside the inlet. In any season, lead-head jigs and MirrOlures are the choice of experienced fishermen.

Seaworthy craft of 19 feet and over are recommended for ocean fishing here, except in the calmest weather. Smaller skiffs are not only adequate, but recommended for fishing shoal waters inside the inlet. Some of the best marsh locations require careful navigation, and anglers are subject to being left high and dry on low tide.

The Carteret County Chamber of Commerce (telephone [919] 726-6831) can provide a list of motels on Harker's Island, which is the usual starting point for fishing Cape Lookout. There are no trout-fishing guides in the area, although charters for inshore and offshore trolling for other species are available there and at Moreland City. Anglers in their own boats are advised to use marine charts, both for navigation until they become familiar with the area, and to find likely fishing locations. Channels through the marshes are good bets on falling tides.

Large bluefish inhabit the area, wreaking havoc on anglers' lure supplies. Wire leaders practically guarantee zero scores on trout, so there is no choice but to lay in a good supply of lures and expect to lose them when the bluefish are numerous. Seatrout begin to appear at Cape Lookout in September. Fishing may remain good into January on mild days when boats can get out, but fishable weather is very unpredictable after Thanksgiving. When it occurs, the trout are likely to cooperate.

Chesapeake Bay

Chesapeake Bay is the most reliable angling area anywhere for large weakfish between the months of May and September. Although other bays along the coast have spring runs of weakfish, the

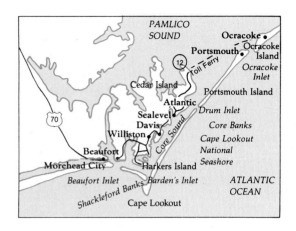

Chesapeake's is many times larger, because the bay itself is so much larger than any other estuary in the lower forty-eight states, and because its 8,100 miles of estuarine shoreline harbors abundant foods for adult weakfish and creates ideal nursery conditions for juveniles. However, size alone does not account for the Chesapeake's ability to produce trophy-sized weakfish (locally called gray trout), through the dog days of July and August. Depth is the key to consistent catches of big trout, and the lower Chesapeake has many drowned river channels to which the fish retreat during the heat of the day and from which they forage into crab-abundant shallows when the sun sinks below the horizon. Although the average depth of the Chesapeake is only 21.2 feet, there are many spots in the bay in excess of 75 feet, and one fabulous hole off Bloody Point on the south end of Kent Island that plunges down nearly 175 feet.

When weakfish first enter the bay in April, they rest in some of the deeper channels off the lower Eastern Shore of Virginia. Water temperatures are still too cold for active feeding, and anglers have little luck with bait at this time. Some fish are caught on artificials bounced on the bottom, but many of these are snagged rather than hooked in the mouth. This is the time of greatest harvest for the gill-netters, and in recent years countless tons of somnambulant weakfish have been taken from the lower Chesapeake in April and even into May if the warming spring is late.

Ocean water varies in salinity, and off the Virginia capes it averages 32 ppt (32 parts of salt per thousand of water). Yet the proximate lower Chesapeake rarely has such a high percentage of salt in its tidal waters except at the end of an extremely dry summer. In the spring, as weakfish move in from the sea, they find surface-water salinities in the lower bay to be 20 ppt even as close to the sea as a line drawn between the

Barden's Inlet at Cape Lookout is one of the top seatrout locations in North Carolina. A maze of marsh islands and channels with a lee shore in any wind, it provides vast feeding areas between the ocean and the sound.

Indian River, between Titusville and Fort Pierce, produces the largest seatrout in Florida. Trophy fish are most numerous from April into July. Seatrout of 4 pounds are common and the local record (IGFA) is 15 pounds, 6 ounces.

283

Eastern Shore town of Cape Charles and Norfolk. West of this line, salinities decrease until mid-bay surface waters in April are only 10 ppt and as low as 3 to 4 ppt above the Chesapeake Bay Bridge. Therefore, weakfish probably move into the deep holes of the lower bay because the heavier, saltier waters found near bottom more nearly approximate the oceanic environment they just left.

Since the bay's largest tributaries, other than the Susquehanna whose drowned lower flood plain is the Chesapeake, flow from the western shore, the greatest volume of fresh water which enters

channel of the Pocomoke River and its steep sides at Crammy Hack and Stone Rock—where the bottom plunges from a few feet below the surface to 90 feet, all within less than 100 horizontal yards—are popular hot spots in June, and the 110-foot depths of the Tangier Channel represent the most popular fishing hole in July. A city of lights seems to rest on the water each weekend as hundreds of anglers seek recreation and relief from sultry evenings ashore. By mid-summer, bait (usually bits of peeler crab on high-low bottom rigs) come into their own as the most popular way to take trout. Smart fishermen vary this offering with live mummichogs, squid strips and, most productive of all, small live spot or snapper bluefish when they are available.

In the spring and again in the fall, when large fish frequent the pilings of the Chesapeake Bay Bridge-Tunnel, bait-tipped, swimming-tail jigs with a tube-covered hook are preferred lures, and the fish are located with a depth recorder. Drifting with a recorder and jigs is not only a more active way to pursue fish than anchoring with bait, jigging enables you to catch more fish, even when the weakfish are reluctant to take bait. If you are after trophy fish, the best time to fish the Chesapeake is May and probably the best area is the vicinity of Old Plantation Light off the town of Cape Charles. Although weakfish spawn from April to August, the bigger fish spawn first, and their pre-spawning weights are what provide those extra trophy pounds.

Mason's Beach, on the Chesapeake Bay in Virginia, represents about the northern limit for the spotted seatrout. Yet, as with a good many game fish—especially Sciaenidae like seatrout and drum—trophies, meaning pre-spawned females, migrate farther north than their young. For that reason, some huge spotted seatrout are caught every spring in the Chesapeake, and the all-tackle International Game Fish Association world record of 16 pounds was caught one May evening in 1977 by a surf caster on Mason's Beach. Unless spring is delayed, the spawning run of spotted seatrout begins in the lower reaches of the Chesapeake in late April and early May. As the water warms and, equally important, as salinity levels increase due to the waning winter runoff from the Chesapeake's tributaries, the seatrout move up the Eastern Shore to spawn and to forage, especially at night, in shallow bays and creeks. The best way to take these large fish is with small live spot fished close to bottom on light tackle. Pieces of peeler crab are also used on high-low bottom rigs, but they are definitely less tempting to older and wiser

To Cook Seatrout

Seatrout and weakfish are gourmet caliber foods. However, both species are delicately fleshed and quickly lose flavor if not iced soon after capture. The simplest preparations are best; a butter-broiled fillet with fresh herbs such as chervil, tarragon, dill, basil or mint leaves and sprinkled with lemon is reason enough to go "trout" fishing. A dividend often overlooked by anglers is the roe, which compares with that of the shad. Although

smaller than shad roe, seatrout and weakfish of 5 pounds or more produce substantial portions in the spring to summer season. Before cooking the roe, wash gently, being careful not to break the connecting membrane enclosing the two pouches known as a "set." Pat dry with a paper towel. You will need the following ingredients for each set (averaging 6 to 8 ounces) which are delicious when butter-sautéed.

AL McCLANE'S SEATROUT ROE RECIPE

2 tablespoons flour	2 slices bacon, crosscut in threadlike fingers
¼ teaspoon salt	
⅛ teaspoon pepper	2 toast points, buttered
2 tablespoons clarified butter	1 tablespoon minced parsley
1 tablespoon finely snipped chives	lemon wedges

1 tablespoon butter

Combine the flour with the salt and pepper. Dust the roe lightly with this mixture. Warm the clarified butter on low heat in a small sauté pan and add the roe. Rotate the roe in the butter, then sprinkle with the chives. Add the bacon bits. Cook over medium heat until the roe is browned on both sides (the interior of the roe will become opaque) and the bacon crisp. Mount the set on toast points. Quickly brown the additional butter in pan remainings, scrape and pour over the

roe. Sprinkle with parsley and serve with lemon wedges.

This recipe is suitable for all edible roes, such as mullet, shad, bluefish, mackerel, whitefish, smelt, dolphin, herring, flounder, etc., provided quantities of ingredients are adjusted to the size of the sets, or in the case of small roes to their number; it would require 12 to 18 sets of herring or smelt roe to make one portion.

the bay comes from the Potomac, James, York and Rappahannock rivers and forces the weakfish and other oceanic migrants east along the Virginia peninsula where higher salinities and warming temperatures encourage the fish to move to new staging depths in June and July. The drowned seatrout. Some anglers drift at sunset on a rising tide over bars and flats and work the shallows with plastic-tail jigs, such as the Stingray Grub, and swimming plugs, such as the MirrOlure. Few of the fish taken on artificials will be of record size; however, some of them will be less than 3 pounds, but 5- to 6-pound fish are not uncommon.

Mason's Beach offers an unusual experience in that it is one of the last places along the Atlantic Coast where with traditional surf-casting techniques, an angler has a chance of catching a record-class fish. Most of the fishing is done at night with dedicated regulars very concerned lest newcomers and visitors shine lights on the water, splash or make other unnecessary commotion along the shore. The bay is often calm on spring evenings with very little surf, and noise readily spooks big seatrout cruising the shallows. If you don't catch a seatrout, you are likely to take home a huge bluefish or a citation-sized (in excess of 40 pounds) channel bass as a consolation prize.

Great South Bay

Great South Bay is one of the most productive waters on the East Coast. Depending on water temperatures, weakfish arrive in Great South Bay sometime between the end of April and May 10th. Peak fishing occurs until mid-June, with the very best usually around the last two weeks in May. Great South Bay weakfish are big, averaging 8 to 14 pounds during the spring spawning run. They aren't as abundant as the weakfish in nearby Peconic Bay, but they do run bigger—with 12-pounders fairly common. Being so close to large population centers, there is always lots of boating activity in Great South Bay, and the shallow-water fishing seems to suffer considerably during the day. During the spring weakfish season, many of the boats in the fleet sail between 2 and 5 P.M. and fish until sunset or just a bit later. The weakfish usually bite best at that time, and fishermen get a chance to enjoy some fine light tackle sport.

Whether fishing from private, party or charter boats in the spring, the basic Great South Bay weakfish technique normally involves drifting. Some anglers prefer live bait, while others stick with a variety of lures. All manner of lead-head jigs will work, and those rigged with plastic grub or shrimp tails. However, in recent years, the most popular lure has been a quarter-ounce jig head to which is attached a 9-inch plastic worm. Favored colors are purple, red, white and black. A variation on this is to drift a jig head and

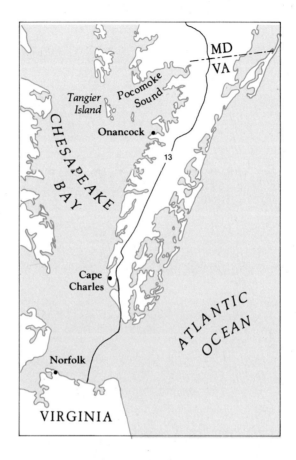

Chesapeake Bay is the northernmost limit of the range of spotted seatrout, which occur here from May into September. Trophy fish are most evident early in the season, particularly off the town of Cape Charles near Old Plantation Light.

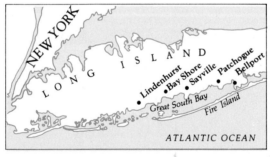

Great South Bay is one of the most productive weakfish locations on the East Coast, with fish of 8 to 12 pounds common in the spring season. Numerous marinas exist between Lindenhurst and Bellport, where skiffs and party boats are available.

sandworm combination, while other anglers have had success by drifting a plastic worm and sandworm combination weighted down with a split-shot. Regardless of the bait or lure used, it is important to use very light tackle and to vary split-shot and jig head sizes in accordance with the strength of wind and tide. The lighter the line you use, the more fish you will catch. Light spinning tackle is preferred and nothing heavier than 12-pound-test mono should be spooled.

The favored spots in the spring are the flats and channels around islands such as the West Channel, the Heckscher Flats and the channel from the Coast Guard Station on Fire Island to Ocean Beach. It isn't difficult to locate those spots in the spring as you will have plenty of company

SPOTTED SEATROUT

from dawn to dusk. Sometimes the private boats manage to do fairly well throughout the day in the channels by drifting sandworms. The biggest weakfish are usually found in the holes, with somewhat smaller fish on the flats. By mid-June the spawning run is over and the nature of the fishery changes completely. There are fewer weakfish spread over vast portions of the bay. Significant numbers of smaller weakfish may enter the bay, and they are ideal candidates for the few specialists that chum with grass shrimp during the night and at dawn. That was the traditional method of weakfishing in Great South Bay until the fish virtually disappeared in the 1960s. Relatively few anglers have returned to that delightful method of fishing simply because the grass shrimp are harder to locate than the weakfish. They are not normally available for sale, which means that the angler must seine them himself in the drains on the many marsh islands in the bay. Unfortunately, grass shrimp have also declined over the years—perhaps due to the filling in of wetlands and a lowering of water quality.

Another specialized summer fishery is directed toward the biggest weakfish—and that is something which Great South Bay is noted for. This involves fishing with small live baits in August and September. Best of all, if they can be found, are juvenile menhaden or "moss bunkers." The next choice is a small live juvenile or "snapper" bluefish. This fishing for tide runner weakfish is popular around the Coast Guard Station and Lighthouse areas and is usually best in late August and early September, though it can last into mid-October. While the quantities involved in summer fishing aren't usually

impressive, the quality is exceptional. Fish of 12 to 14 pounds are the norm, and a local expert, Joe Giallanzo, set an IGFA record for 6-pound-test line with a 17½-pounder taken on August 25, 1976—one of the biggest weakfish ever caught in the United States.

While most of the emphasis is on the bigger weakfish, which seem to prefer areas toward the Fire Island side of the bay, there is quite a fishery for smaller weakfish well inside the bay during the summer. These weakfish average about 3 to 3½ pounds (with a few to 5 or 6 pounds) and are caught on the "mainland" side at such areas as Nicoll's Point, Bayport and Blue Point. Most are taken in water 10 to 12 feet deep on drifted squid strips. East of the lighthouse and just west of Kismet lies Kismet Reef, an area which has proven to be a reliable producer of big weakfish in the summer and fall. Live-lining is the best bet, but bucktail jigs and umbrella rigs also score on the reef. Another productive area throughout the season is along the Fire Island shore from the bridge to the lighthouse. Weaks are scattered throughout that range and can be caught on umbrella rigs trolled on wire line. The fishing is best on ebb tide, but weed pouring out of the bay makes it impossible to troll or even cast. Therefore, the best bet is to try this on the first of the ebb—before the weed problem becomes too severe. Fire Island Inlet itself is a very good bet in the summer and fall. Trolled umbrella rigs will work, and diamond jigging is often effective between the Sore Thumb and Democrat Point. A new reef located close to shore off Oak Beach is already becoming a hot spot for weakfish. Shore anglers can locate the area by the presence of several groins along the beach.

One of the joys of fishing Great South Bay is the convenience involved. The mainland offers skiff rentals at Babylon, as well as party and charter boats at Lindenhurst, Babylon and Bayshore. One of the biggest party boat and large charter boat fleets in the country is located at Captree Boat Basin, at the east end of the barrier island that stretches from Jones Inlet on the west to Fire Island Inlet. From the basin, boats are only minutes away from the inlet and most of the favored weakfishing areas mentioned.

It is also possible to catch weakfish from shore in this area. There are two public piers at Captree and shoreline fishing is available there in both the State Boat Channel and in Fire Island Inlet. The channel seldom produces weakfish except during the night and dawn hours, but surf casters are sometimes successful under the sun from Captree

Trout Tout

Seatrout expert Ed Wagner of Jensen Beach, Florida, favors a double lure rig for the spinning rod. Although the Trout Tout is a popular and effective lure in itself, Wagner greatly increases the

number of strikes from big fish with the addition of a trailing streamer fly. Fully 60 percent of Wagner's trophy fish are taken on the fly.

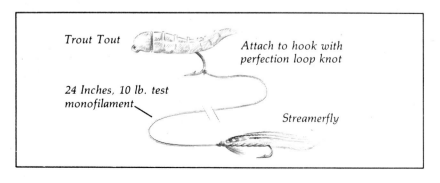

Trout Tout

Attach to hook with perfection loop knot

24 Inches, 10 lb. test monofilament

Streamerfly

to the west. The west end of Fire Island also offers fishing opportunities in Robert Moses State Park. There is a pier in Fire Island Inlet and often fine surf casting on both sides of the barrier beach. It should also be noted that area boats do very well with weakfish in ocean areas outside the inlet throughout the summer and fall. These fish are often found in dense schools and can be trolled with umbrella rigs on wire line, diamond jigged or hooked on squid baits drifted near bottom.

Port O'Connor

Port O'Connor is nothing more than a dot on the map of Texas located on a peninsula where two bays meet, due south of Victoria. State Highway 185 provides the only access. The so-called Back Bay is Espiritu Santo and the Front Bay is Matagorda, and together these provide countless miles of angling for spotted seatrout and red drum. Tourists will find little else to do in Port O'Connor except to go fishing, but the quality of the sport is among the best on the entire Gulf of Mexico.

The Port O'Connor area is ideal for the light tackle angler. Both bays, and especially Espiritu Santo, are very shallow, so wading with spinning or bait-casting gear is possible. However, a boat is required to reach the hot spots; some guides use airboats and jetboats to traverse the thin water. Spoons and jigs are the most effective lures here. After prolonged winds, floating sea grass can be a problem in getting weed-free retrieves; under these conditions local experts rig a one-eighth-ounce lead-head jig with a red or orange plastic tail and tie it behind a clear bubble float for additional weight.

The better wading areas are Pringle Lake and Lighthouse Cove along the backside of Matagorda Island, and around the many small islands, especially Grass Island in Espiritu Santo Bay. The backside of Matagorda Peninsula, about 12 miles southeast of Port O'Connor, is another choice location. For boating anglers, the so-called big jetties which protect the man-made ship channel through Matagorda Peninsula are very productive. Large seatrout and redfish are taken along these granite boulder projections from spring into late fall, mainly on live shrimp and finger mullet. The best fishing occurs during a tide change, incoming or outgoing.

For large spotted seatrout, local residents fish around the wells in Matagorda Bay. There are many gas wells scattered throughout this large body of water. The wells are fish attractors due to the oyster shell pads built around the pilings to

Spinning tackle is the most popular gear for surf fishing because it prevents backlashes, especially in strong winds, and because the reels have a high rate of retrieve. The length of the rod (8½ to 14 feet) and its action, from limber to stiff, must be calibered to the weight of the lures used and the distances you have to cast.

keep the platforms stable. Wells that consistently pay off in fish are the Goldstein Field, a cluster of wells along the Matagorda ship channel off the little town of Indianola north of Port O'Connor, and the Palacios Field, a series of wells along the Palacios channel which angles off the Intracoastal Waterway.

Boats and guides are available in Port O'Connor. Information can be obtained at the Port O'Connor Fishing Center; telephone (512) 983-2930. A Texas saltwater fishing license is required.

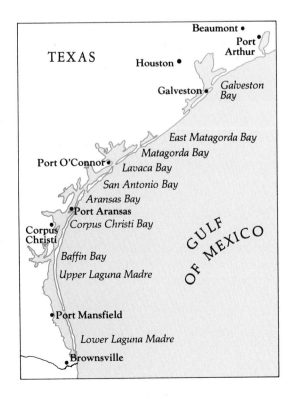

The Texas coast is famous for its seatrout and red drum fishing, particularly in the vicinity of Port O'Connor and Port Mansfield. The "trout" do not run as large as more northerly populations, but they are abundant in shallow bays, where light-tackle fishing excels.

287

STRIPED BASS

Morone saxatilis

I n the summer of 1623, some fortunate netting of striped bass by their single boat fed the *Mayflower* colonists for three months. The fish was so admired at table that the first conservation measure in the New World was decreed on its behalf, in the Massachusetts Bay Colony in 1639:

> And it is forbidden to all men, after the 20th of next month to imploy any codd or basse fish for manuring the ground, upon paine that every pson, being a fisherman, that shall sell or imploy any fish for that end, shall loose the said priviledge of exemption from public charges, & that both fisherman, or others who shall use any kind of said fish for that purpose, shall forfet for every hundred or such fish so imployed for manuring ground twenty shillings & portionally for a less or greater number; pvided, that it shall be lawful to use the heads and offal of such fish for corne, this notwithstanding.

In 1670 the Plymouth Colony funded the first public school in the New World (at Cape Cod) on the income accruing from the bass, mackerel and herring fisheries. Earlier, at Jamestown in the Virginia Colony, Captain John Smith noted: "The Basse is an excellent Fish, bothe fresh and salte . . . . They are so large, the head of one will give a good eater a dinner, and for daintinesse of diet they excell the Marybones of Beefe."

Captain Smith was correct. They grow large. There is a commercial catch record of *several* bass landed at Edenton, North Carolina, from the Roanoke River in April 1891, that weighed 125 pounds each. Rod-and-reel catches nowadays top off at 78 pounds in salt water, the most recent all tackle world record. Typical bass in the saltwater sport catch run 6 to 10 pounds, which make a fine light tackle fish and a delicious dining experience. In fresh water, the environment in which striped bass are now advancing due to state stocking programs, the fish grows faster but dies younger. The International Game Fish Association's

A weight potential to more than 100 pounds helps make striped bass a prized catch for sportsmen, but the fish are normally harvested at 2 feet or less. The commercial catch is favored by East Coast restaurants and their patrons.

STRIPED BASS

landlocked bass record is 4 ounces shy of 60 pounds.

This fish naturally ranged from the St. Lawrence River to northern Florida, with a small population from western Florida to Louisiana. The southern and Canadian populations are essentially riverine, but the mid-Atlantic bass migrate each spring and fall along the coast, feeding heavily in the sea and returning to the vicinity of their natal rivers to overwinter.

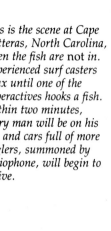

DISTRIBUTION

There is a sizable Hudson River race of striped bass that in summer populates the western half of Long Island Sound, northern New Jersey waters and along the south shore of Long Island. These fish may make a larger contribution to the northern stock than was previously thought.

These latter fish were the population that provided stock, which, in 1879 and again in 1881, were shipped on the new transcontinental railroad to San Francisco Bay for planting in the Pacific. Only a total of 432 fish in both stockings went into the Bay. Commercial landing records for the offspring of this planting came to 1,200,000 pounds in 1899. Since 1935 the fish has been restricted to sportsmen in the Pacific. It has established itself as far north as the Columbia River on the Oregon-Washington border. It is interesting that this Pacific adaptation is a slow process. Bass are relatively recent in the northern bays and do not make coastal movements to speak of. The Coos Bay population evidently stays put. The likely answer is that cold Pacific waters are below the preferred temperature of the adults (near 68°F) and young (near 77°F).

Bass spawn from February through summer from the bottom to the top of their geographic range at an optimum temperature of about 65°F. At about 70°F their eggs won't hatch, so soaring temperatures stop the spawn. The water must be fresh and flowing or only minimally brackish. The eggs hatch in two or three days depending on temperature. Hatching must be complete before they reach salt water, and river turbulence is necessary to prevent eggs and larvae from sinking, which is why many reservoirs do not have natural reproduction. Females will be at least four years old, but more likely five. Precocious one-year-old males can spawn, but most start at age three. A spawning scenario normally features a menage of one female and a number of males. Since female striped bass far outlive and outgrow males, an

elderly cow may spawn with a dozen, or even dozens, of males. The hectic affair is accompanied by much thrashing and splashing. They bump her, evidently to loosen her eggs, and as the males exhaust their milt they are replaced with fresh suitors. At about age ten, male striped bass begin to disappear from the population. Perhaps they die off, but speculations that a few may change sex are supported by fish taken that contained both milt and ova in spawning condition. In some Pacific coast populations as much as 4 percent may be hermaphroditic.

Striped bass are a school fish all their lives. It is believed that only quite elderly females who have outlived their year-class travel and feed alone. Fish school by size, because within a species, swimming speed is correlative to size. Big fish eat little fish because they can swim them down. Big striped bass chasing bait have been clocked at 20 miles per hour.

Theodore Gordon, the father of American dry-fly-fishing and progenitor of the Catskill school of delicate flies for finical trout, wrote in one of his *billets-doux* to the British angling press: "Large

striped bass were at one time fished for at the Falls of the Potomac with large flies. I have killed them with Bumble-puppy flies." The Bumblepuppy was a Gordon streamer pattern that he varied at whim.

Bass fishing became a suitable sport for the Gentry, and as the post-Civil War era developed into the Gilded Age, striped bass were pursued with style. For sport one did what one did for lunch: one formed a club of gentlemen. West Island, Narragansett, Point Judith, Gay Head, Bar Harbor, Pasque Island, Squibnocket and Cuttyhunk acquired clubs of well-born bass fishermen. The first was on West Island in 1862, but Cuttyhunk, of course, became the most famous. The Cuttyhunk Striped Bass Club was founded in New York City in 1865.

The rocky islands and promontories of Massachusetts and Rhode Island were readily reached from centers of industry such as Boston, Philadelphia and New York City, so when a comfortable clubhouse had been constructed, it was only necessary to have the bass stands built and manned. Bass stands were constructed by drilling holes in the rocks for wrought iron pipes, surmounting the ironwork with a wooden catwalk, and often concluding the catwalk with a platform that could hold the crew. The crew consisted of local lads who would arise early and begin chumming. Put enough chopped clams, crabs, menhaden or lobster into a running tide on a sunny summer morning in the Elizabeth Islands and you are quite likely going to have a striped bass arrive so close underfoot that you can throw an utterly weightless bait out (as indeed you should whenever fishing a chum line). After a sound breakfast at a decent hour the sports would draw lots for stands and march off to engage giant striped fish in desperate struggles over the possession of a few hundred yards of the new twisted linen Ashaway line that Captain Lester Crandall was supplying the clubs,[1] such an improvement over the tarred cotton hand lines still used by the plebes. At the conclusion of a bully battle the chummer became a gaffer.

The equation had a fatal flaw: The mills of New

[1] Mounted on brass reels that were the coastal equivalent of Kentucky bait casters, the linen lines were being advertised by John Conroy in the New York sporting press in 1837, and Arrmah Tiffaney patented one in 1838. The reels were 2:1 retrieve ratios for the most part. Rather than plebian brass, the Gentry preferred theirs silver-plated, until the vom Hofe family began making superior specimens from German silver, an alloy of copper, zinc and nickel that is still used for ferrules on expensive split-bamboo fly rods.

STRIPED BASS

England were driven by dams that blocked the bass's spawning runs. The quality of the angling declined in a few decades, and by 1907, the Cuttyhunk Club had disbanded, though you can still see the old clubhouse, now in private hands, and find holes in the rocks where the iron pipes were.

It is also possible that the bass decline was simply a natural megacycle induced by causes we have not yet fathomed (there is a well-documented minor cycle every six years). In the 1930s and 1940s they came back. Weakfish, bluefish and striped bass have thus far in this century gone through major population declines and resurgences that still tax our understanding despite a host of theories.

It is not true that striped bass will eat anything. They have teeth only on the maxillary and tongue, which means they cannot take a bite out of something too big to swallow, but their mouth is very big (the head constitutes about 25 percent

of the entire body), so in their near-shore environment there is comparatively little they cannot gulp. They do have preferences, though. The common synonym for striped bass in the South is "rockfish," and this indicates a preferred habitat. rockpiles are favored dwelling places of crabs and lobsters. Another preferred food is the American eel.

North of San Francisco Bay there is quite a bit of anti-striped bass sentiment among the local anglers who themselves fish overwhelmingly for salmon, steelhead and trout. Studies to determine if bass prey, to any measurable extent, on salmonids have thus far been mixed. An Umpqua River, Oregon, study that went on for nine months in 1972 indicated shrimp was 63 percent of the striped bass diet, smelt totaled 17 percent, and the remainder was herring, perch, anchovies, crabs, sculpins, lampreys, salmonids and shad. The proportion of salmonids was only 0.3 percent. A Coos Bay study brought salmonids in at 7

Hybrid Bass

After biologists discovered that striped bass could be a stockable, wholly freshwater game fish, they began considering how to use its voracity in smaller lakes with tributary streams inadequately long for natural spawning (the two- or three-day egg-to-larva maturity period must be spent constantly floating downstream; if the fertilized egg settles to the bottom in slack water such as a lake it dies). The answer was to cross Morone saxatilis *with its small freshwater relative the white bass (*Morone chrysops*). This interesting creature has been named "whiterock bass" by officialdom but is universally known simply as the "hybrid." They have been reported to exceed 20 pounds, but nothing that size is in the International Game Fish Association's records.*

Hybrids have many virtues from the viewpoint of watershed management. They are probably sterile, so overpopulation through

natural reproduction isn't a worry. They tolerate warm water better than striped bass, so their range can be extended farther south. They are hardy, exhibiting the typical vigor that usually accompanies hybridization. They are more voracious than striped bass and, therefore, more easily caught (the feeling is widespread among fisheries biologists that a fish uncaught is a fish wasted). Their growth rate is incredible: They can reach 8 pounds in only 2½ years!

Hybrids can be identified in the field by broken stripes. They work even closer to shore than striped bass. I have seen them chasing shad in Georgia's Clark Hill Reservoir while our outboard motor's lower unit was dragging sand. They will love you for showing them anything that can be mistaken for a gizzard or threadfin shad. This is a schooling fish and can be taken in

quantity once located. Weirdly, runaway hybrids have on two occasions found their way into

Chesapeake Bay, the last great producer of Atlantic striped bass, leaving both sport and commercial

fishermen puzzled at what they had in hand—a bass with broken stripes.

Striped Bass

Hybrid Bass

White Bass

percent of the spring diet. That would be bass consuming smolts en route to the sea. Adult bass will consume large numbers of trout in cool freshwater reservoirs where other food is scarce, and fisheries managers should take care to manage for one species or the other, not both.

Striped bass are both diurnal and nocturnal, with a strong bias toward late evening and early morning feeding in school fish. Large (old) cows eat by sunlight, moonlight or any light; a 50-pound fish has to keep at it pretty much around the clock. Interval netting and stomach analysis by biologists have shown the prime feeding time for school fish begins at nightfall and continues for long enough to fill up, with a second feeding period shortly before sunrise. By day, striped bass may feed exclusively on a single food form and demand that you match that. At night they go to bottom and evidently take whatever opportunity comes along. Their dorsally mounted eyes and bias-cut mouth angle indicate they feed upward by preference, which makes sense in a fish with nocturnal inclinations because even starlight alone on a moonless night is enough to silhouette overhead food to a creature whose eyes have a *tapetum* (the cat's source of eye shine) on the retina. This reflects light so the rods which give good black-and-white night vision can see a photon a second time, intensifying the image. Bait or lures worked two or three feet above the bottom at night are in the real target zone.

Stout spinning tackle took this bass from the New York Bight. It would be a toss of a coin to decide whether the fish is of the Hudson River or Chesapeake Bay race.

Summerkill

Charles C. Coutant, the senior research ecologist at Oak Ridge National Laboratory's Environmental Sciences Division, has for years made a study of fish thermal preferences. Coutant was asked to investigate a die-off of mature striped bass that first occurred on Tennessee's Cherokee Lake in 1972, six years after stocking. Under a canopy of buzzards drawn to dead bass washed ashore, Coutant and his assistant captured bass and implanted temperature-sensitive ultrasonic and radio transmitters.

"As we would tag a fish and release him into the water, he would immediately dive for deep water, then surface and dive again. This continued for about two hours until the fish finally died. We suddenly realized that since we were tagging in the summer months, the fish we captured were in a cool thermal refuge. But in the course of our tagging our boat would drift away from the spot. A released fish would dive to find cooler water, but instead would encounter a region of low oxygen.

When he came to the surface for air, the water was too hot. Thermal refuges, we have since learned, can be quite small."

Coutant's group once captured forty striped bass from a locale the size of an office conference table.

The problem is that juvenile striped bass select a thermal niche about 85°F, the temperature at which they grow best. But as they mature, their thermal niche gradually decreases toward the 68°F of adult bass, and adult bass are relatively inflexible on acceptable temperatures: A few degrees of variance is all they will tolerate. If the impoundment has stratified in summer and acceptable temperatures are below the thermocline (a narrow stratum of rapidly declining temperature), the fish will suffocate in the oxygen-poor water of the hypolimnion, the cooler bottom stratum. Warm water is so biologically unacceptable to adult striped bass that gizzard and threadfin shad in the warm surface waters of the epilimnion will remain untouched by starving bass.

STRIPED BASS

Coutant studied more than 200 adult tagged bass, one of which made a 72-mile journey in four weeks to locate a thermal refuge.

"This difference in thermal preference apparently is an evolutionary adaptation that prevents the adults from feeding on their young in their native large saltwater estuaries," Coutant says. "The summer die-offs can be avoided if striped bass are stocked in reservoirs where they have plenty of cool, oxygenated water in the summer. Our work also means that oxygen-depleting pollution sources can be particularly hazardous for adult striped bass."

His discoveries may account for the increased nocturnality of Atlantic saltwater striped bass in summer, and the extremely limited areas of dense, deep-water bass concentration found then. If six years proves to be the age of temperature maturity in the fish, we are talking about 6-pound males and 10-pound females, the males about 24 inches fork length and the females 26 inches.

When the late Henri Soulé closed Le Restaurant du Pavillon de France at the 1939 World's Fair in New York and opened Le Pavillon in Manhattan, he inaugurated a vast emigration of French chefs who found that satisfying the new-found American taste for haute cuisine was an extremely lucrative business. Some of them passed through the kitchen of M. Soulé and some directly opened their own restaurants without that formality, but after a few weeks amid the alien corn, all of these *toque*-proud Pierres and Andrés would give the culinary press almost identical interviews. They desperately missed their beloved *poulet de Bresse* and considered our chickens scarcely edible, they conceded our Black Angus beef the equal of their white Charolais but, *mon Dieu*, what a glorious fish we had in the striped *loup*. They all created lovely striped bass dishes that you can enjoy to this day (for a pretty penny) in elegant surroundings on Manhattan's chic East Side. I have savored many of them, but whenever I am satiated with the saucier's art I remember that mother knows best and simply slide a fillet of striped bass under the broiler for no longer than it takes to toss a salad and pull the cork on a bottle of *auslese* hock, then sit down to one of life's happiest experiences. There is more to fishing than catching fish.

Striped Bass Hot Spots

There may be joy to be found taking 5-inch striped bass on dry flies in spring, but perhaps you would rather consider where a 50-pounder might best be encountered? These hot spots have withstood the test of time.

ATLANTIC SALT WATER

**Shagwong Reef,
Montauk, New York.**
On form, a live eel or a big plug held down by wire line and fished at night on an ebb tide in October or November should be best. A 76-pound former world record fish fulfilled all those specifications (eel, not plug), but was caught in July.

**Sow and Pigs Reef,
Cuttyhunk, Massachusetts.**
An eel at night on a perigee tide in October.

**South Shore,
Block Island, Rhode Island.**
Surf casting a big popping plug from the beach in August through October.

**Outer Cape,
Cape Cod, Massachusetts.**
Live-lining a fresh mackerel from a drifting boat from late July to September.

Sandy Hook, New Jersey.
Try a live Atlantic menhaden on a moving tide in September to November.

PACIFIC SALT WATER

Russian River, California.
A live anchovy or surfperch fished deep on a slack tide in spring or summer, or a big diving plug.

Umpqua River, Oregon.
As above with wiggling bait or big plugs. Alternately, try fly-fishing. The river yielded a 40-pound, 4-ounce fish in July 1970, that set a 12-pound tippet record.

FRESH WATER

Colorado River, Arizona.
An anchovy is the ticket, in May or June.

Norris, Percy Priest and Cherokee reservoirs, Tennessee.
Lead-head jigs ("doll flies" in the southern vernacular) or shad jigged above the crests of submerged islands in spring as the fish feed ravenously just after dark or just before dawn, or in summer when big, hungry bass are concentrated in available water near 68°F (about 35 to 45 feet down in Norris, which has the biggest fish, some exceeding 50 pounds).

This boat is working the famed Sow and Pigs reef at Cuttyhunk Island, part of the Elizabeth Islands archipelago near Martha's Vineyard, Massachusetts. They can legitimately hope to catch large bass.

Montauk

Montauk is located right on the route for the great schools of stripers migrating along the northeast coast from the Chesapeake spawning grounds to summering areas in cooler climes. In times of greater abundance, there were substantial summering populations of striped bass from New Jersey north. However, in recent years there have been relatively few summering stripers south of Montauk. Even more so than in the past, peak striper fishing occurs during the migratory runs in the spring and fall.

It was at Montauk that the famous (or

infamous, depending on your point of view) umbrella rig was created. The umbrella rig works well on stripers of all sizes in the rips off the Point, both spring and fall, and particularly when the dominant bait is sand eels. It must be fished on wire line close to the bottom in depths of 20 to 40 feet, and the choice of tube size, color and arrangement can be critical to success under varying conditions. The bucktail or feather jig tipped with pork rind isn't used as often as was the case in the 1950s, but it is still the most effective way to troll when the bass are on larger baits such as baby weakfish. The bucktail and pork rind is fished on wire line as close to bottom as possible (it should bump bottom at times) and must be jigged vigorously.

Most of the large charterboat fleet working out of Montauk concentrates on wire line trolling, but there are other ways to catch striped bass in that area. A few specialists, such as Captain John DeMaio, have been very successful in catching stripers with diamond jigs. DeMaio takes four-man parties in a 30-foot skiff (with stern controls) which he runs himself without a mate. He uses diamond jigs of 3, 4 and 6 ounces with single hooks on a swivel, and ties directly to his 30-pound mono. The *Vivienne* stems the tide over various bottom lumps off the Point (which are located by ranges, graph recorder and Loran C numbers) while the anglers drop their jigs to bottom. As soon as the jig hits bottom, the angler reels up a few turns very slowly, pauses and then drops the jig back again. After two or three drops the jig is far astern in the tide and the angler must reel in and start over. This power jigging technique requires a great deal of effort but, as practiced by experts like DeMaio, it can be very effective, because the jig is worked only over the likeliest bass haunts.

It is also possible to catch stripers off the Point by diamond jigging on the drift, and that technique is effective when large schools are present. Just as in power jigging, it is important to get a good bounce off bottom and to then reel very slowly for a few turns before pausing and dropping back. A faster retrieve will catch bluefish, but few stripers.

The most consistent bass action at Montauk occurs at night. There are two primary methods: wire-line trolling and drifting with live eels. Though big stripers are often caught in the same rips they frequent during the day, it is also possible to catch them in very shallow waters where they are rarely encountered in daylight. Depths of 10 to 20 feet on Shagwong Reef and off North Bar can

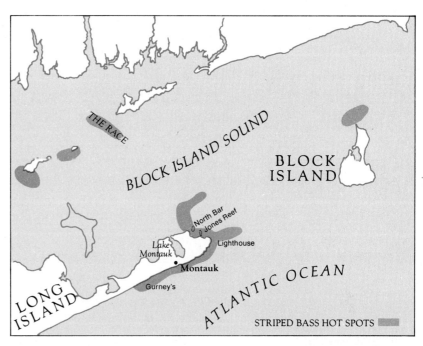

be particularly productive in the fall.

The lures favored for night wire-line trolling are large plugs, feather jigs tipped with pork rind, rigged eels, eelskins and artificial eels. Among the favored swimming plugs are the Danny, Stan Gibbs, Goo-Goo Eyes, Creek Chub Pikie and Luhr Jensen J-Plug. All lures must be trolled slowly just off bottom into the strong tide (ebb preferred, especially in the fall). It doesn't seem to help if the jigs are jigged—in direct contrast to fishing such lures during the day.

Live eels have long been used at Montauk for live-line fishing close to shore. However, it wasn't until 1978 that a few private anglers figured out a method of fishing them just off bottom in the deep rips. Working around the Great Eastern Buoy area during the full moon period in August, a few boats returned every night with over 1,000 pounds of big bass before the word got out. Though there has never been a blitz to match that one, there is very good live eel fishing at times every season.

The basic technique is quite simple. The terminal rigging revolves around a three-way swivel. The main line (usually 30- to 50-pound-test) goes to one eye of the swivel, a 6-foot leader (50- to 80-pound-test) to the single No. 5/0 to 7/0 hook is tied to another eye, and less than a foot of heavy mono is tied into the remaining eye for the sinker. The eel is lowered to bottom and then raised a turn. As the boat drifts, the angler must continually adjust his line so the eel rides just over bottom without getting snagged on the mussel beds. In deeper water the bass tend to gather

From the marinas of Montauk at the eastern tip of Long Island, striped bass fishermen launch their boats for a variety of seasonally active destinations.

where plateaus drop into deeper water, therefore, the anglers look for such ledges in perhaps 40 feet of water, which drops off to 50 feet quite rapidly.

Montauk is a surf caster's paradise in that its rocky shores attract a wide variety of game fish and access is possible without a beach buggy. While you are much better off with a buggy, it's no problem to park at the field just behind the lighthouse and walk down to the rocks just under the light or to Jones Reef just north of there. A little farther to the north is another hot spot, North Bar. Shagwong Point can be good in the fall, but most of the other good striper areas are along the rocky portion of the south shore from the Point to Ditch Plains. Access to those spots is difficult. The sandy beaches to the west are usually stripped clean by the haul seiners, but the bar at Gurney's Inn can be productive at times.

Relatively few stripers have been caught from the surf during the day in recent years except for periods when storms roll through in fall. Most of the bass, and almost all of the big ones, are caught at night. Favored lures for daytime sport are poppers and metal (Hopkins and Kastmasters). At night, swimming plugs steal the spotlight. Montauk standards include the Stan Gibbs Darter and "bottle plug" (wooden-lipped swimmer), Rebel and Cordell Redfin. Teasers are often rigged ahead of these lures when the fish are feeding on small baits. The most successful surf casters at Montauk don wet suits and wade or swim out to offshore boulders from which they can cast farther out and avoid most competition.

Few rod-and-reel fish are taken before mid-May. Charter boats usually start looking for the first fish in the rips by the third week in May. The spring migratory run is over by late June, though night fishing may be good into early July if there is a full moon at that time. The summer is usually pretty quiet except for the possibility of a few good nights around the full moon periods. September used to produce the first of the fall run, but in recent years it has been little better than summer. October always produces spurts of good day and night bass fishing, with the last two weeks generally the most dependable. Early November is also very good, unless severe storms kill the fishing early. After mid-November, bass fishing at Montauk is a gamble, though there have been years when Thanksgiving produced the best fishing of the fall—and when the fishing ran into almost mid-December!

Santee-Cooper's Freshwater Striped Bass

Santee-Cooper is the birthplace of landlocked striped bass, created when bass became entrapped by the impoundment of the Santee-Cooper lakes, Marion and Moultrie. Fishing techniques here vary with the seasons. Spring brings many catches on cut bait (any baitfish cut into the particular shape the angler believes most successful for him). Cut bait is normally fished right on the lake bottom just as one would fish for any bottom feeder. Live shiners may also be used for spring stripers and are fished approximately 12 inches off bottom.

For summer stripers, bait yields to trolling. The striper schools appear to be on the move during this time of year, therefore an angler must move to find them. A depthfinder is recommended during this time. Don't overlook the use of live shiners once you have located the school.

During fall, and/or winter, surface schooling of

The development of modern freshwater striped bass fishing began on the famous Santee-Cooper lakes Marion and Moultrie.

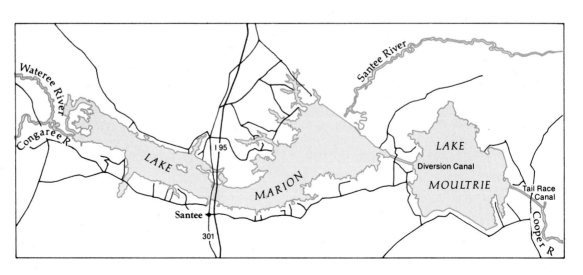

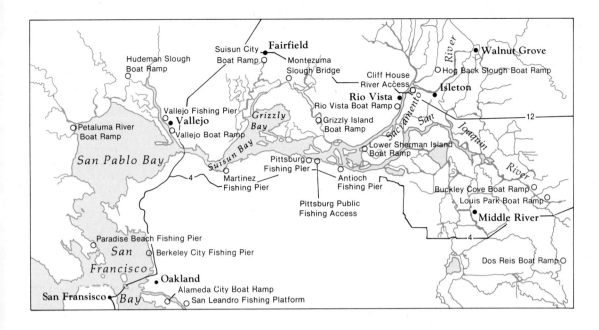

Striped bass migration routes through San Francisco Bay, San Pablo Bay and the delta of the Sacramento River are complicated.

landlocked striped bass is common. Usually the anglers, when observing this, become as frenzied as the fish. A live shiner works well during this time. One may locate the bass by watching for gulls which attack the schools of shad from above, when schooling stripers attack the shad from beneath. Fishermen race to the area in high-powered boats for their share of the action.

When a school of stripers is spotted surface feeding, have a top-water lure ready and maneuver to the *windward* side of the school so you can drift through the activity, or you may fish shiners from 10 to 20 feet down on one rod while having the topwater lure ready to cast toward the swirls.

Lakes Moultrie and Marion have 170,400 acres of water in which fish may hide, so the problem is finding the fish—where you find them depends on the calendar. With so much water, the stripers do move around according to the time of year. During the cold winter months, fishing is slow. Stripers are caught by those brave souls who don't mind cold weather and long hours spent fishing deep. Generally, striper schools can be located with depthfinders. The best methods are to drift fish or troll. Remember, during the cold season stripers are seldom found in shallow water. Most are caught in Lake Moultrie or the canal linking the two Santee-Cooper lakes together. The canal is especially good for bottom fishing.

During spring—March, April and May—fishing shifts to the Congaree, Wateree and Santee rivers, which the stripers use for their annual spawning ritual. Seasoned striper fishermen concentrate on the rivers and upper Lake Marion, where the best fishing is along the old Santee River channel.

Late in May the stripers return to the lakes, and during the summer months of June, July and August, the stripers are found in both lakes.

Come fall—September, October and November—the stripers are usually scattered, with water temperature influencing where they roam.

There are some fifty to sixty landings scattered around the area. Want to spend two days or more? You may utilize the Santee State Park, which has modern rental cabins (some of which have docking facilities at your doorstep), a restaurant, tackle shop, campground and fuel pumps. You may wish to check in at one of the many motels that cater to fishermen.

It is best to have a guide on your first trip. There are plenty around. Just ask at any landing or tackle shop for recommendations. Of course, you will need a South Carolina fishing license, also available at most tackle shops.

Fishing information may be attained from Santee-Cooper Promotional Commission, P.O. Box 12, Santee, SC 29142; South Carolina Department of Parks, E.A. Brown Building, 1205 Pendleton Street, Columbia, SC 29202; or South Carolina Wildlife and Marine Resources, P.O. Box 167, Columbia, SC 29202.

Western Striped Bass Migrations

The majority of western striped bass movements occur in one spawning habitat located in the inland deltas of central California. The disadvantage of this circumstance is that the future of striped bass fishing on the Pacific seaboard is dependent upon this one population and environment. A good or bad spawning season will affect the fishery for the following three years.

We have already seen the populations of Western bass plunge from an estimated 10,000,000 adult spawn-capable stripers in the mid-1960s to less than 750,000 in recent years. A series of low-water years, pesticide chemicals, petroleum products, delta water deportation and the California-based Pacific Gas and Electric Company's slaughtering of an estimated 500,000,000 fingerling stripers *annually* at their

STRIPED BASS

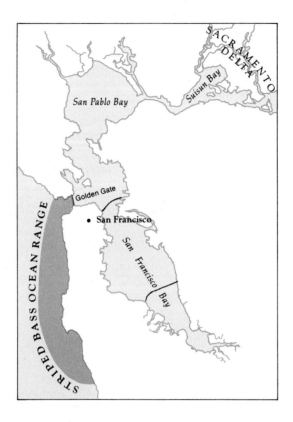

Unlike the Atlantic populations, the California striped bass makes very limited migrations.

A San Francisco surf caster brings his bass ashore. The bass population has declined dramatically in recent years due to human degradation of its environment.

Pittsburg, California, power plant have all contributed to the stripers' sharp decline.

On the positive side, California still produces enough striped bass fishing to encourage new generations of fishermen who enjoy catching striped bass in fresh, brackish and salt water twelve months of every year.

The key to productive year-'round bass fishing in California is knowing where the bulk of the fish are at any given time. Though there are always a few schools of stray and straggler bass spread out through the entire range of habitats, it is mass migrations moving within these habitats on a regular cycle that account for the greatest catch.

The western striper population cycles annually throughout several hundred miles of freshwater rivers, some 1,800 miles of delta, another 100 or so miles of brackish water bays, and finally another 30 miles of open ocean. Despite its scope, the pattern is amazingly simple.

Stripers spawn in the spring months, which really means that the bulk of the spawn-capable fish are schooled in the eastern end of the delta where rivers like the Yuba, Feather, Lower Sacramento and San Joaquin flow into it.

Following the spring spawning months, post-spawned stripers resume their westward migration towards the sea. By late May to early June the fishery moves down out of the rivers, through the deltas and into the brackish bays. The first bay adjoining the delta is Suisun Bay, the next westward bay is San Pablo and then, finally, San Francisco Bay. Striper anglers armed with bait, lures and fly intercept the migratory bass in these three bays from late May through the middle of July.

By the end of July, the majority of adult bass have pushed beneath the Golden Gate where they encounter the saltier waters of the Pacific Ocean. Odd as it may sound, the entire ocean range of our western bass population is less than 30 miles, extending from Point Bonita just outside and north of the Golden Gate to about Martin's Beach, south some 30 miles on the coast.

The biggest stripers within the mass of the migration will stay at sea feeding on anchovies, herring and occasionally pompano until late September, then the migration of well-fattened bass heads east again, back inside the bay. During their ocean feeding sprees, surf casters and live bait drift boats take a toll of the fishery.

Once back inside the bay, the stripers' mood changes considerably. Big schools break up into smaller groups that spread out all over both San Francisco and San Pablo bays. The stripers will rest within these bay waters from September to approximately mid-December.

From mid-December through March, the bulk of the fishery is making its way up out of the brackish water bays, through some 1,800 twisted miles of deltas and into the major tributary rivers where they will actually spawn, commencing about mid-April and continuing through the end of May. Some spawn as late as June, depending on water conditions.

The key to year-'round success is to keep yourself positioned over the thickest concentrations of bass. You've got to be willing to pick up and move when the bass do, and to change your technique and methods as the fish's moods change with new environments.

Oregon

I should mention another West Coast striper population that has turned from a great (but untapped) fishery to an almost extinct fishery, and is now making a comeback . . . again.

The Umpqua River is Oregon's only estuary where stripers are known to reproduce. Once nearly wiped out by commercial shad netters, striped bass are now making a strong comeback in Oregon with the mouth of the Umpqua River supporting the majority of the action. This is principally a spring fishery for lure and plug fishermen, although bait anglers can do well.

Race Point for Cape Cod Striped Bass

Few of the other classic hot spots can offer the consistent opportunities for striped bass that Race Point does. Guarding the opening of Cape Cod Bay, "The Race's" currents provide a perfect gathering place for feeding game fish, which gorge themselves upon sand eels (*Ammodytes americanus*), squid and mackerel. Moreover, this area faces the southwest (source of the prevailing winds), which provides a healthy onshore surf, a condition which, when combined with the currents of the Race, frequently presents game fish to the rod.

From early June to mid-October, the night-roving surf caster will find his best fishing two hours either side of low tide. During this period he may opt to baitfish fresh sand eels on the bottom or cast with swimming plugs. Many regulars use popping plugs during sunrise and sunset. The Race itself is marked geographically by Race Point

Streamer flies and bucktails, now often tied with long synthetic hair, are used for striped bass fly fishing. Skipping bugs (center row) should be used more. They bring exciting surface strikes by slicing across the top.

Light, and the above conditions occur directly in the fore of the light, but it is possible to prolong fishing by moving east through a host of hot spots where ebbing currents form.

The Traps, a spot named late in the last century for a place where commercial fishermen hauled their laden nets, is the first deep-water casting station. Here, many use rigged eels to probe the deeper water. Moving east, one can cast from any number of points that are formed by the currents for several miles, never leaving the influence of the Race. But to the caster who is interested in the finest four hours of the night, the flats in front of Race Light itself present the greatest opportunities when the combined influences of wind and tide come together. Earlier in the season, stripers will predominate, and it will not be until July that the

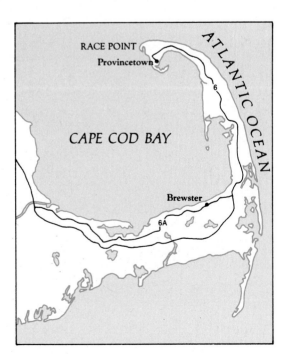

Race Point near P'town is the Cape's most heralded hot spot for surf casting and trolling. The Brewster flats are fine for fly-fishing, but they can be dangerous if the tide catches you too far from shore.

STRIPED BASS

first bluefish are available, these building in numbers and size that can stagger the imagination. Whatever influences in the Race appeal to one species, these unaccountably do the same with the other. It is thus not at all unusual for surf casters to be indulging themselves in a great number of both bass and blues at one time in a foam-swept maelstrom blown white by a welcome wind. And while the distance of casts is reduced considerably by the sou'wester, this is more than made up for by the close proximity of these species, which seem to delight in hammering at targets scant yards from the dry beach where baitfish clamber for momentary safety. This is beach buggy country, a way of saying that four-wheel drive is needed to

each angler on board in the event of surfacing game fish, which are pinpointed by working birds. When night trolling, best done with the aid of a moon, the wire line tows a large swimming plug. For the boatman, hours are less critical because fish are within range at any tide and easily evident by their markings on the graph recorder. But the wind for them remains a curse.

Brewster Flats

Those with a penchant for high adventure, and without four-wheel drive, might test the Brewster Flats. Here the bottom contour of Cape Cod Bay falls off so slightly that it is possible to walk the flats at low tide for over a mile before reaching water that is deep enough to support stripers. One hardly notices the seemingly unimportant dips, which are only ankle deep. Any time the bass are willing to chance these shallows for feeding, they are quite susceptible to fishing. Evidence of this can be heard as they "womp" and slosh at bait. Their prime target is the sand eel, which is best imitated with a small, floating, Finnish balsa swimming plug.

Flats are comfortably wadeable 4½ hours down in the tide, but of overwhelming importance is the utilization of compass, tide chart and watch. Fog can come without warning, causing landmarks to disappear, often forcing the angler to navigate his way back no later than an hour after low tide. With such a shallow gradient, a rising tide comes deadly quick and survival is dependent upon getting out in the right direction on time. This calls for a measure of discipline when stripers are hunting the flats, their activity seeming to accelerate with the rise in water. Unless one has tasted the fear of walking through the "unimportant" dips that were hardly noticed on the way out, one might find it difficult to leave the action—and scant minutes later, impossible.

Fan Clubs

The widespread popularity of striped bass with coastal anglers should have prepared us for the rampant enthusiasm occasioned by its introduction into fresh water. The fish has become a cult object with southern and southwestern freshwater bass fishermen who struck into what they thought was a largemouth and discovered they had hold of a piscine freight train. Enthusiasm needs company, and modern striped bass enthusiasts have organized themselves on the pattern of the largemouth-oriented Bass Anglers Sportsman Society (which see).

Striper is the straightforward name of one such organization, founded "to preserve and manage the striped bass fishery both fresh- and saltwater" as well as to educate in both management and harvesting techniques. They publish a bimonthly magazine aptly titled Striper, and conduct twenty-seven annual tournaments for members only. One tournament pits qualifying contestants to fish for cash awards that will be donated to their state fish and game department. Another tournament organization is the American Striped Bass Society, "dedicated to the wise conservation, management, education and promotion of the American striped bass and hybrid and to promoting the success of state stocking and research programs." The ASBS bimonthly is Striped Bass Magazine.

Non-tournament striped bass conservation groups include Stripers Unlimited and Save Our Stripers. The presence of so many passionate advocates of striped bass amongst humanity would seem to indicate that the fish has manipulated its major predator into mitigating that predation and even vastly extending its own natural range— the hallmark of a successful species!

move about on the beach. Moreover, your vehicle's drive train must be augmented with low tire pressures—never over 15 psi.

Boats that ply the Race rips come either from Provincetown or other Cape Cod Bay fishing villages like Wellfleet. There is also a small contingent of highly specialized surf-launched boats that are pushed off with four-wheel-drive vehicles. These vessels troll jigs with wire line deep enough to raise puffs of sand on the bottom. All keep a casting rod with popping plug ready for

London Bridge Striped Bass in Arizona

Stripers are frequently the topic of conversation in Lake Havasu, which was formed by the construction of Parker Dam near the town of Parker, Arizona. The surface of the lake is 450 feet above sea level. When it is full it contains nearly 40 square miles of fishing. The lake has a total capacity of over 600,000 acre-feet. What this means is the lake level never drops more than 10 feet. During the summer months the level is kept

300

high, and during the winter it is lowered to make room for runoff. This makes it very difficult to run the river during the winter months, but the danger is mostly sandbars that will not destroy lower units or boats, just a little pride. However, there are a few rock piles out there, so navigate with care.

Below Davis Dam, at the uppermost part of Lake Havasu, the water level raises and lowers approximately 4 to 6 feet overnight. It is possible to become stranded out there while night fishing. At the opposite end of the lake, approximately 80 miles downriver by Parker Dam, the lake is 90 feet deep. The main depth of the lake is approximately 50 feet. A good depthfinder is handy on this lake for more than one reason.

In 1968, McColloch Oil Corporation announced they had purchased the legendary London Bridge. It was numbered and disassembled, transported and reconstructed block by block for a mere $7,000,000 and three years of hard work. It now stands in Lake Havasu, creating a channel for monster stripers to swim through each year. That transported bridge is working very well as one of the major tourist attractions in Arizona.

Another transplant is the Lake Havasu striper. In 1962, a combined effort of California Fish and Game and Arizona Fish and Game brought 83,000 fingerlings and 950 yearling stripers to Lake Havasu. Could these fish possibly spawn and develop a self-sustaining population? In 1966, 10- to 15-pound stripers began appearing on

fishermen's stringers. Since then many 50-pound stripers have been caught over the years, the first in 1976.

Please don't let me mislead you, these fish are few and far between. But it does happen, and with luck it can be done. There were years when you had to work hard to catch just one fish. There were excellent guides working on the lake who gave up guiding for stripers because of the lack of fish. But that is no longer true. Two tremendous spawns have occurred and the next few years should be the best ever.

If you would like to catch one of those giant Havasu stripers, first learn the movements of the fish. Most of them stay in the lake during the cool months. As the water warms up in April to about 65° or 70°F, they move upriver to spawn. They gather in large schools and feed heavily on shad. This is when you will see them breaking water. You may already have heard the term *jump fishing;* this is when it is used. Fishermen sit and wait for the fish to break water during feeding, then they run their boats up close to the school of fish and cast lures into the melee. A Cordell Spot 2300 series works well for this because it is a one-ounce lure and casts a long distance. One word of caution: If you run your boat right into the school you will spook them.

When schools of stripers are smashing shad, they are mostly swimming through, killing and injuring them, and eating what they can. Then they drop down and return to the feeding area and feed on dead and injured shad that have drifted to the bottom. The larger bass stay below the smaller ones and feed on what comes their way. So to catch a large striper you should get your lure down through the smaller fish. This is done by using a small white jig. Jigs are a good way to catch stripers all year long.

Colorado River striped bass follow their prey and their spawning needs in and out of Lake Havasu.

Striped bass move into swift current to spawn. They will use the upper half of the river, about the first 50 miles from Davis Dam and downriver. They do not spawn all at once. It takes place over a period of almost three months.

The diet is a broad one. They eat mostly threadfin shad, supplemented with crawdads, bluegills, minnows and trout. Trout for bait is forbidden.

As summer passes on, the fish slowly return to the lake, and the cycle repeats itself in January.

The best technique for fishing the river is to use surface lures like pencil poppers and floating-diving plugs, while jigs and baitfishing also work.

Then moving back into the lake, where there is no current, stripers can be caught just about any way you prefer to fish. Vertical jigging is popular in the deeper parts of the lake using a Hopkins Shorty 75. There are many areas on the lake where you can catch stripers off the bank with regularity. One very important point is that stripers are active at night. Many of the larger fish are caught at night using bait.

You may fish twenty-four hours a day on Lake Havasu. It is possible to catch stripers in the lake and river year-'round; however, river fishing is best when the fish are spawning, and fishing in the lake is best in winter.

There are several fishing licenses and stamps required to fish on the Colorado River. Check at local tackle shops before fishing. The lake is patrolled by the Arizona Game and Fish, California Game and Fish, and Nevada Game and Fish, and they all do their job well.

Keith Gardner unhooks a small bass that was taken on Lake Mead, Nevada, during a blazingly hot July morning.

302

SHAD

Alosa sapidissima

The Gregorian calendar has been our measure of time since the year 1582 (not a very old system when compared with the reckonings of more ancient cultures), but to early New England settlers, the spiritual (and gastronomical) beginning of each year was in April, when the shadbush blossomed in great clusters of white flowers and the mottled brown caddis, or "shadfly," emerged in clouds to dance in the warming sun. After a long winter's diet of salty pickled meats, these harbingers of the shad runs to come promised a bounty that measured in countless tons of good eating. Although the migrating shad were joyously captured with nets, spears and traps in Colonial times, by 1849, Henry William Herbert, who wrote under the pseudonym Frank Forester, was already praising fly-fishing for American shad with his trout rod. Subsequently lauded as the "poor man's salmon," shad not only achieved game fish status, but was transplanted more than a century ago from the Atlantic to the Pacific, where it prospered in western coastal waters. It even migrated north into rivers on the Kamchatka Peninsula of the Soviet Union, which somewhat belies the name American shad.

Shad are members of the herring family (Clupeidae). They are anadromous, like salmon, maturing in salt water and spawning in fresh water. There are three North American species in the genus *Alosa:* the American or white shad, the hickory shad and the Alabama shad. Related species occur elsewhere in the world, such as the Allis shad of Europe (which seldom exceeds 2 pounds and is of minor angling value) and the hilsa shad of southeast Asia, but the only sport fishery of any consequence exists in North America.

The American shad (*Alosa sapidissima*) is the largest member of its genus and the most widely distributed on our continent. This shad will average 3 to 5 pounds, and though fish of 13

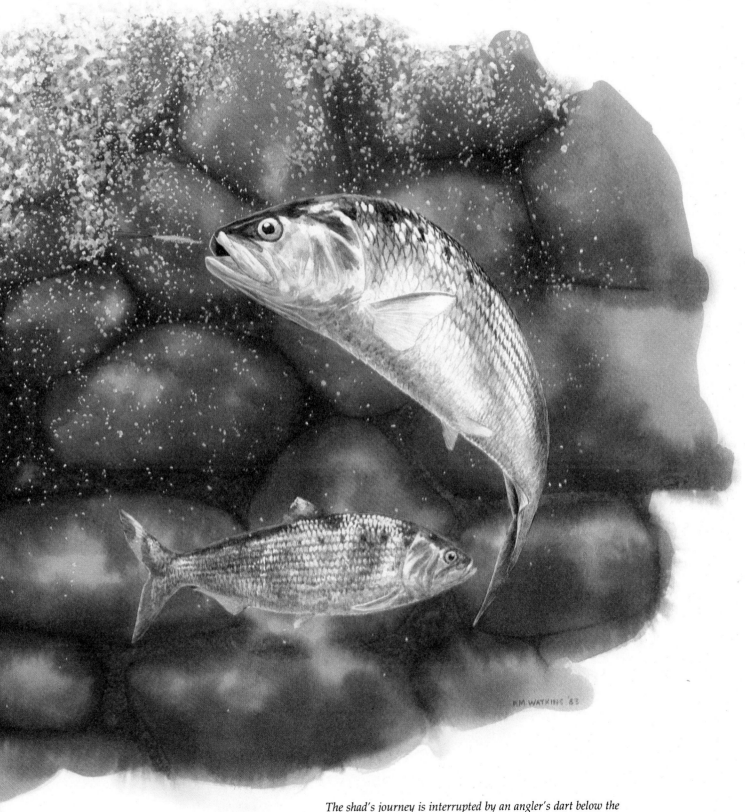

The shad's journey is interrupted by an angler's dart below the
remains of an old Connecticut River dam. Shad do not feed in
fresh water before spawning, yet will strike a variety of flies and lures.

305

SHAD

pounds have been netted, the rod-and-reel record is 9 pounds, 4 ounces from the Delaware River in Pennsylvania (1979). In the southern portion of its range, the shad rarely attains 6 pounds in size, an environmental limitation predicated on ambient water temperatures.

American shad mature and make their first spawning run at four to five years of age. Among northern populations about 30 percent will survive and become repeat spawners. The second-time migrants, and a much smaller percentage of third and fourth time spawners, are the oldest shad (eight to nine years) and the largest—weighing 8 pounds or more. These repeat spawners are found from Chesapeake Bay, north to the Palmer River in Massachusetts. Post-spawning survival is rare south of Cape Hatteras, and the mortality rate is total at the latitude of the St. Johns River in Florida. The shad's survival is correlated with energy demands at higher stream temperatures; adult shad, like the Atlantic salmon, do not feed in fresh water until their post-spawning period. After a long migration (American shad tagged in Canada's Bay of Fundy were recovered five months later in Florida's St. Johns River, a straight line distance of 1,375 miles) and a tremendous loss in body weight, often as much as 40 percent, the fish simply lack the fat reserves to return to the ocean. In the colder northeastern rivers and those of the Pacific coast, a substantial number of shad are able to make the return journey.

American shad are found from the Sand Hill River in Labrador to the St. Johns River in Florida, and on the Pacific coast from southern Alaska to Bahia de Todos Santos in Baja California. The most productive Western shad waters are the Columbia River in Oregon and Washington; the Umpqua and Rogue rivers in Oregon; and California's Klamath, Trinity, Russian, Sacramento, Yuba, Feather, American and San Joaquin rivers. On our East Coast, the popular shad streams are the Merrimack in Massachusetts; the Salmon, Scantic, Eight Mile and East rivers in Connecticut; the Connecticut River in Connecticut, Massachusetts and Vermont; the tri-state Delaware; and the Susquehanna River, which has seriously declined; at present (1984) the mainstream and its tributaries in Pennsylvania and Maryland are closed to shad fishing as part of a restoration program. However, the Potomac, Winter's Run, Gunpowder, Patuxent, Middle River and Octoraro and Deer Creeks have shad runs; in Virginia the Pamunkey, Mattaponi, York, James, Chickahominy and Rappahannock rivers are

DISTRIBUTION

popular locations; North Carolina's Cape Fear River and South Carolina's Edisto River are the top spots; in Georgia, the Altamaha, Savannah and Ogeechee provide some shad fishing in the winter and spring months. The Atlantic distribution of American shad terminates in the St. Mary's and St. Johns of Florida.

Shad are very rarely caught in salt water. In 1981, a freak current caused schools of silvery fishes to blitz the beaches around Martha's Vineyard, Massachusetts. Even the local graybeards—on an island where fishing is a way of life—could not identify their mysterious bounty without the help of an icthyologist. While at sea, shad normally remain offshore in deep water, following the isotherms at a temperature range of 55° to 60°F, which sends the schools in a northerly direction in spring, where they summer in the Gulf of Maine and the Bay of Fundy, then in a southerly direction in the fall. American shad have been caught by trawlers at depths below 400 feet and over 100 miles from shore, so these migrations occur over a vast area. While at sea, the fish fatten on plankton and krill. As spawning time approaches and the colder coastal rivers begin to warm, the mature shad return to their natal streams oriented by tidal flow, light intensity and an olfactory ability to taste/smell the familiar chemical substances of individual rivers.

In their extreme southerly range, water temperature is a reverse phenomenon, as rivers there normally run over 65°F throughout most of the year. Shad begin entering Florida's St. Johns, for example, when the river becomes "cool" after the first chill winds of late November. Thus, the farther north the shad stream, the later its run begins. The peak migrations, when shad are most abundant, occur in the 62°- to 67°F-temperature range. Broadly speaking, the best fishing is in January at the latitude of the St. Johns, during May in Chesapeake tributaries north to Massachusetts, and in late June around the Gulf of the St. Lawrence. This has a parallel on the Pacific coast where California's Feather River peaks in late May, while the Columbia River far to the north is shad-filled during the first week in July. Small "buck" shad dominate the earliest catches with the percentage of roe, or female, shad increasing as the season continues to progress.

Hickory Shad

The other important shad is the hickory, *Alosa mediocris*, which is considerably smaller than the American shad, and not as widely distributed.

Hickories up to 5 pounds have been recorded, but they generally run from 1 to 2 pounds, and a 3-pound fish is bragging size. Nevertheless, the hickory is a high-jumping acrobat when taken on light tackle. While this species is found along the Atlantic coast from Florida to the Bay of Fundy, it is common only in the southern part of its range. The most productive waters would include the Potomac (even in downtown Washington, D.C.); Maryland's Deer and Octoraro creeks, the Choptank, Northeast, Patuxent, Pocomoke, and both the East and West Wicomico rivers; the Rappahannock in Virginia; and the Pitchkettle and Grindle creeks in North Carolina. The Rappahannock draws a tremendous concentration of hickories in a short stream mileage around Fredericksburg, and according to Boyd Pfeiffer, author of *Shad Fishing* (Crown, New York, 1976), this is the premier river for that species today.

In the thermal cycle of a season, hickories migrate into fresh water when the river temperature is 50° to 52°F, usually preceding the run of white shad by about two weeks. And unlike the larger species, which remains to spawn in the main stream, hickory shad prefer small tributaries. The migrations of the hickory are not wholly understood; those entering the streams that drain into Pamlico Sound, for example, are known to be spawning fish, whereas the stocks coming into Chesapeake tributaries evidently reproduce in brackish water even though they densely school in what appears to be a spawning run. Nevertheless, the hickory shad invades much shallower water than does the white and provides excellent fly-fishing. Invariably, you will get three or four jumps out of even a small hickory, and, inch for inch, it is more spectacular than many freshwater game

fish. A 2-pound, 18-inch hickory is dynamite. In those rivers where the hickory occurs with the white shad, the two species are easily separated; the hickory has a long projecting lower jaw, while the American shad's lower lip is entirely enclosed in the upper jaw when the fish's mouth is closed.

Alabama Shad

The third shad species (but of little angling consequence) is the Alabama shad (*Alosa alabamae*). This fish is smaller than the hickory, averaging ¾ to 1½ pounds. The Alabama shad is not widely distributed, being limited to the Suwannee, Apalachicola and Alabama river systems. There is no major sport fishery for this shad, and, in fact, it is so similar in appearance to the "skipjack," or river herring (*Alosa chrysochloris*), which is abundant in these same waters, that most anglers assume that they have caught a large skipjack. The Alabama shad is taken mainly in the tailwaters of big impoundments. However, as a game fish, it is not comparable to the white and hickory.

Fishing Technique

Shad are notoriously susceptible to changes in water level and temperature, and sometimes the best angling is had when comparatively few fish are in the river, and conversely, bank-to-bank schools can be totally disinterested in a well-cast lure. The water may warm to just the right range for taking fish, then a sudden cold snap knocks the game dead, or a late spring rain puts the river in flood, and that wild action of yesterday becomes a muddied memory. The angler works on a critical

SHAD

balance—measured in Fahrenheit and cubic feet per second, a combination that only the shad understands; but at least we can grope for the principle. In northern rivers, shad fishing is most productive early in the morning and again in the evening, rather than during bright daylight hours. The fish seem to be inspired by dank weather, and a light spring drizzle will often provide a full day of taking shad. This is particularly true of the hickory, which is inclined to quit when light intensity reaches the sunglass stage. But for whatever this rule is worth to a Yankee fisherman, the southern shad strikes freely in bright light. Slightly turbid water is a plus, as opposed to clear or muddy water.

Fly-fishing is most effective in shallow rivers. It is possible to take fish in the deeper parts of the Connecticut, the Delaware or the Sacramento, but you need normal water levels and the ability to handle long casts with a fast-sinking line as shad may hold bottom at 10- to 15-foot depths. As a rule, fresh-run shad will not come readily to the fly. They require repetitive casting and great patience on the part of the angler. However, after the ripe fish have been in the river for a few weeks the ratio of strikes to casts will increase. This is strictly a wet-fly game until late in the season. After spawning, shad move out of the deep pools and begin feeding again before making their downstream journey to the ocean. Dry-fly-fishing can be very effective in this post-spawning period when mayfly hatches appear on the water.

The fly rod for shad should be 8½- or 9-feet long. It must be powerful enough to handle a 7- or 8-weight sinking tip or high-density sinking line on long casts. Remember, also, that American shad are relatively large fish and extremely strong. Because the fly must be worked deep, the standard approach is to cast quartering upstream. The fly, ticking the pebbles, drifts down with the current. Occasionally, short twitches or jerks should be imparted to the fly, especially when it swings wide in the current at the end of a drift. It is important to keep a taut line. With any appreciable amount of slack, it is difficult to detect a strike, which is usually nothing more than a light tap and sometimes repetitive taps. If the current isn't running too fast, you may be able to work a school from the upstream side by making a short cast, then paying out line to ease the fly back among the fish. When it drifts near the shad, raise and lower your rod tip to impart an enticing action in the fly. Hickory shad are especially prone to a snappy jigging movement, which often excites strikes when less animated retrieves fail.

Shad can be fussy about fly patterns at times, preferring one color to another, but generally a white or yellow wing is reliable in sparsely tied marabou or calftail, with a fluorescent chenille or Mylar body to add some flash. The best hook sizes for American shad are No. 6 and 8 (3x or 4x long) and slightly weighted with lead wire for fast sinking. Hickories respond more readily to No. 8 and 10. The important thing is how the fly is fished; it must swim at shad level, not 3 or 4 feet over their heads. I am a long leader exponent for most kinds of fly-fishing, but a 7½-foot leader should be maximum, as the fly will sink more quickly. This should be tapered to a 4-pound-test tippet for hickory shad and 6-pound-test for the larger American.

Spinning tackle is by all odds the most popular gear for shad fishing. A 6½-foot rod, calibered for 6- or 8-pound-test monofilament line, is the standard bearer, although more and more anglers have been flirting with lighter equipment in recent years, using 4-pound-test line; this refinement is not only sporting, but the wispy line helps to sink tiny baits fast, an advantage when seeking bottom-hugging fish. When cast across and upstream, the lure swings down over gravel, and despite the occasional hang-up, it puts the bait where white shad hold. These fish follow the channels, so deep fishing is the name of the game. However, light tackle is not practical everywhere; in the swift waters of the Connecticut River, for example, where large shad are always a possibility, success with a 4-pound-test line belongs to the expert with a sensitive hand.

Two basic lures are widely used: a small spoon and the "shad dart." The best spoons are 1- to 1½-inches long in silver or nickel finish with gold an alternate choice. Favorite designs nationally are the Cather, Drone, Hopkins, Pet, Chum, Kastmaster, Nungesser and Dardevle. The shad dart is a tapered, lead-bodied offspring of the venerable Quilby Minnow. More shad are caught on darts than any other lure; a one-eighth-ounce size is most popular, but these range down to one-thirty-second ounce. Shad show a definite preference for very small lures at times, and to compensate for their light weight they are commonly rigged in tandem, either two darts, or a dart and a spoon for quick sinking in strong currents. The technique of fishing these baits is to cast across stream, allowing the lure to swing down while giving it a gentle jigging motion in a slow retrieve. When fishing from an anchored boat, the simplest method is to cast quartering downstream, then let the lure hang in the current while working the rod tip to give the spoon or dart some hopping action.

Regardless of the tackle used, shad should be played with a delicate hand and not rushed to the net. Shad have a fragile mouth structure, and a hook will tear free if you apply too much pressure. Individual fish can be quite spectacular aerially, particularly when taken early in a run either rocketing skyward or even greyhounding across the surface. Hanging broadside in running water, even a 3-pounder can give the illusion of weighing twice its size.

Delaware River

Each spring in early March, shad by the thousands gather in the Delaware Bay. Here they pause, waiting for the river's water temperatures to warm, triggering what may be the longest spawning migration in the country.

The more precocious males will head the run, eager to reach the spawning grounds after spending three or more years at sea. The larger, heavier females will follow closely, and both will travel the full length of the Delaware, even entering its east and west branches above Hancock, more than 350 miles upriver. They are large fish, males or "bucks" averaging between 2 and 3 pounds, and females or "roes" between 3 and 4 pounds.

The number of shad that run up the Delaware river each season varies, but fisheries biologists today estimate the population to be between 100,000 and 200,000 fish. The majority of the bucks that enter the river to spawn are four years old and rarely are taken over 4½ pounds. Most roes are a year older with weights generally less than 8 pounds. In 1982, the official New York State record for shad was broken twice by fish caught in the Delaware, the largest being caught May 9th, weighing 7 pounds, 6 ounces.

The main problem facing Delaware shad populations is the water pollution near Philadelphia. Industrial as well as municipal sewage causes the oxygen in the river at times to be less than 2.0 ppm, even down to no oxygen in a significant stretch of the water. High flows caused by autumn rains are very beneficial in flushing the newly spawned baby shad through this polluted barrier. Obviously, in the years when this occurs, more juvenile shad as well as spent, spawned shad make it to the sea and ensure a greater return in future years. This pollution of the lower river long ago destroyed much of the shad's previous spawning grounds. Today the most important

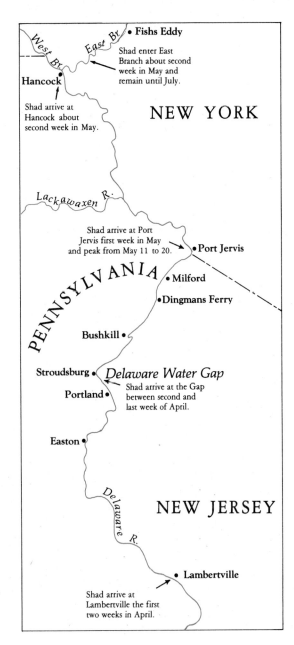

Shared by three heavily populated states, the Delaware River draws a tremendous number of shad anglers. There are many good fishing locations; the most famous are at Lambertville, with its annual Shad Festival, and the Zane Grey Pool, where the Lackawaxen enters the Delaware. Hot spots are always jammed with boat trailers on weekends.

nursery areas are located in the vicinity of Tusten and Lordville, 295 and 325 miles from Delaware Bay.

Shad are a unique fish with remarkable stamina and ability. They enter fresh water from salt water, swim through stretches of heavily polluted water, through shallow rapids and deep pools to reach the cold, clean spawning waters hundreds of miles from the sea. Studies show that sonic-tagged shad averaged 6.6 miles a day in their migration up the river, with individual fish reaching 20 miles in a single day.

The spawning run begins when the river's water temperature reaches 50° to 55°F, usually in mid-April, and runs through June, peaking in May. Shad are caught at Lambertville, New Jersey, in the first two weeks of April and at the Delaware Water Gap between the second and last week, arriving in the Port Jervis, New York, area in the first week of May. The best catches in this part of the Delaware often occur during the period between May 11th and 20th, especially when

SHAD

water temperatures are between 51° and 64°F. In the upper river sections, around Hancock, New York, and in the East Branch of the Delaware, the run arrives a little later, about the first week of May, and continues into July. Shad are available to Delaware anglers for almost four months of the year. They are a favorite food fish of many anglers; their flesh is white, flaky and tasty. Those fortunate to catch a roe are doubly rewarded, since their eggs, or roe, are considered a delicacy.

Darts are the most popular lure on the river and are especially effective when trolling the larger, deeper pools of the middle and lower river sections. The most popular colors are red-and-white or red-and-yellow, with tails of bucktail or calftail. Good combinations are red head, white body and yellow tail; or red head, yellow body and red tail. Some have painted eyes, and the most productive sizes are one-eighth ounce and less. Shad have rather small, delicate mouths, therefore spoons and spinners should also be on the small side.

Fly-fishing for shad is mostly done on the upper Delaware and its East Branch. Wading and getting close to a school of fish greatly aid the fly-rodder and enable him to get the fly down to the shad's level, somewhere near the bottom. A sinking line

Angling author Art Lee pursues the shad runs every spring on the Delaware River. Fishing here usually begins in mid-April and continues into July in the upper river. Morning and evening are peak times, but overcast days are often productive.

works best and backing is a must, as Delaware shad are strong, vigorous fighters and can easily take all the line from the reel. The more popular flies are wet-fly patterns especially tied for shad. Many use hair from deertails and calftails for wings, tinsel for bodies and fluorescent red or pink wool, or chenille for butts or heads. Most patterns used on the Delaware are local and brightly colored with various dyed materials. Some fishermen tie their flies on gold hooks and add weight to the fly, others prefer to add weight to the leader to get the fly down.

Shad are also taken on the surface with dry flies. Many are caught each season by trout fishermen fishing from Callicoon upriver. Toward evening, particularly in the last half hour before dark, they will rise in and among the trout. This seems to be related to water temperature or the number of flies on the water. Perhaps it is that they get caught up in the feeding activity of the trout and follow suit. Their rises are distinguishable from trout in that they make a distinct sipping noise when they take a surface fly. They constantly move about the pool seeming never to take a fly in the same place twice. The trick is to keep casting the fly ahead of the shad as it moves past, guessing where it will rise next. If the fly and the fish come together, the fish will take. They are not very selective.

The best time to fish for shad is morning and evening. Midday is considered poor; however, overcast days can be productive. The fish can be located by just looking in pools from a boat or canoe, or even by wading. Their silver, large-scaled bodies appear bluish in the water, and when they are present in good numbers, they are not too difficult to see, especially with polarized glasses. It is difficult to describe what good shad water looks like or where the fish lie in a particular type of water, but time-honored places can be learned by watching where others fish for them. On the Delaware River some of these hot spots are in or around Trenton Falls, New Hope, Frenchtown, Easton, Belvidere and Dingman's Ferry, between New Jersey and Pennsylvania; and Port Jervis, Lackawaxen, Ten Mile River, Barryville, Narrowsburg and Equinunk, in that part of the river between New York and Pennsylvania.

Connecticut River

In 1614, when Dutch navigator Adriaen Block discovered the mouth of the Great River that the Indians called *Quoneh-ta-cut,* he had no concept of its 407-mile length, nor sailing before the wind could he envision what was to become one of the most completely developed rivers in the eastern United States in terms of hydroelectric power. The Connecticut River rises in a small pond at 2,551 feet elevation below Mt. Prospect in New Hampshire. It is a mere brook as it bubbles into Third Lake, but it flows through precipitous walls of rock in a series of wild cascades below Second Lake to become the major river in New England. It attracts the largest American shad run in the East. Due to improved water quality and the installation of new fish ways, the number of migrating shad has increased drastically in the last census decade from 53,000 in 1971, to 380,000 in 1981, recorded at the Holyoke fish station. Once called "the best landscaped sewer in America," the Connecticut has experienced a renaissance indicated by the modern return of Atlantic salmon, which stopped migrating in 1814.

American shad enter the Connecticut River about mid-April, penetrating Massachusetts in mid-May, and arrive in Vermont and New Hampshire waters in late May or early June. Enfield Dam, the most popular fishing location in Connecticut, is synonymous with the name "shad." However, from the river's mouth in Long Island Sound upstream to the dam, the better angling is found in its tributaries, notably the Salmon, Eight Mile, Hammonassett and East rivers. There are many accessible spots above Enfield, and outstanding here is the mouth of the Farmington River and the Windsor Locks area. In the Massachusetts portion of the Connecticut River, excellent fishing is found at Holyoke, Sunderland and Turners Falls. In Vermont, the top spots are at Vernon, Brattleboro and Bellows Falls. Public ramps and boat rental facilities are available at various points along the river.

Columbia River

This largest North American river entering the Pacific Ocean, together with its myriad tributaries, is the most important trout and salmon drainage in the world. It flows 1,214 miles from its source in Columbia Lake to Astoria, Oregon. Tens of millions of chinook and coho salmon, steelhead and cutthroat trout, sturgeon, smelt and American shad invade its vast estuary at various times during nine months of the year. An estimated 2,000,000 American shad enter the Columbia in May with the runs peaking in June and July, during which period catches of twenty-five fish are commonplace. These shad average 4 pounds for the bucks and 6 pounds for the roes.

Due to its heavy flow and swift currents, shad

The artificial flies for shad are sparsely tied and are not meant to be imitative. Bright colors are the rule, usually with tinsel bodies and fluorescent butts or heads. Dark colors are successful at times, so it pays to stock both. Most shad fly patterns are local rather than standard dressings.

angling in the lower Columbia is essentially limited to casting from the bank or a boat. Wading is dangerous in nearly all areas. Some of the most popular locations are below Bonneville Dam near Bradford Island, at the Dalles, below the John Day Dam and at the mouth of the Washougal River. Spinning with darts and spoons is the most successful method, although fly-fishermen can score when using lead-core or high density sinking lines.

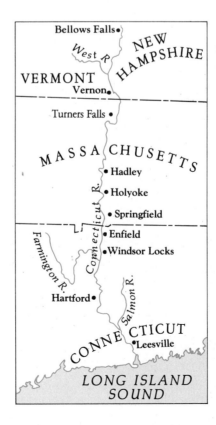

Connecticut River shad begin appearing in early April at Leesville and reach Massachusetts in mid-May. They arrive in Bellows Falls, Vermont, and New Hampshire in late May or early June. The comparatively new fish ladder at Turners Falls makes it possible for both shad and salmon to reach Vermont and New Hampshire for the first time since 1798, when the river was blocked by a dam.

311

SHAD

St. Johns River

In 1777, that peripatetic naturalist William Bartram described the "St. Juan" as a river full of roaring crocodiles "sic," and while it is not without its share of alligators today, there are wilder landscapes in nearby Disneyland. One of the few rivers in the United States that flows northward, the 273-mile-long St. Johns in Florida rises in a marsh norm of Blue Cypress Lake and enters the Atlantic at Mayport, just above Jacksonville. This southernmost shad river attracts the earliest run of fish, usually beginning in late November with the peak in February and continuing to late April. Best known for its largemouth bass, the character of the water is totally different from the swift rocky rivers of the North. The St. Johns has barely perceptible currents (for the most part) with a sand and muck bottom. There is very limited shore fishing from sod banks in the Puzzle Lake area. The sport is pursued almost exclusively by boat, however, and there are many public ramps and boat rental facilities.

The most popular shad fishing locations are in the headwater section of the St. Johns from east of Sanford to west of Cocoa, a distance of approximately 65 miles. The river between Lake Monroe and Lake Harney, and between Lake Harney and Puzzle Lake, is especially productive. American shad in the St. Johns run smaller than northern or western U.S. populations; the bucks average about 1½ pounds and the roes 2½ pounds. Because it is a terminal population composed of onetime migrants, a 5-pound fish is exceptional here.

Sacramento River

The first introduction of American shad to Pacific waters was made in the Sacramento River of California in 1871. Together with its major tributaries, the American, Yuba and Feather rivers, it is the most important fishery in the West. An estimated 2,000,000 shad enter the Sacramento and limit catches (presently twenty-five per day per angler) are the rule rather than the exception during peak periods. In a steelhead-oriented society, it is endemic that fully 50 percent of the anglers are fly-fishermen. Boat fishing is practiced on the lower Sacramento; however, most of the river can be fished from the bank, and a large portion of the upper river is eminently suitable for wading. Though the river is usually crowded, especially in the month of May, a holiday atmosphere prevails and even beginners score handily.

Shad enter the Sacramento from San Francisco Bay in March but do not begin hitting lures aggressively until the water temperature reaches 66° to 68°F, which is usually in April. The peak runs are in May and June, at which time the fish are spread throughout the river as far as the Red Bluff Diversion Dam, which is the upstream limit of the shad. There are many popular locations beginning at the city of Sacramento up to Red Bluff, but the most celebrated is Woodson's Bridge Pool at Woodson's Bridge State Park near Corning. In the Sacramento's tributary streams, the lower 20 miles of the American River are productive, with the top spots at Sailor's Bar and below Nimbus Dam near Rancho Cordova. The lower 10 miles of the Yuba River have excellent fishing, particularly in the Walnut Avenue Pool and below the Daguerra Point Dam. On the Feather River shad occur up to Oroville Reservoir. Its most famous location is Shanghai Bend.

The Sacramento River watershed is one of the most popular shad locations in the West. Fish usually enter the first week in April, reaching Woodson Bridge State Park in May. The peak period throughout the river as far north as Red Bluff occurs in May and June. Shanghai Bend, on the Feather River, and Nimbus Dam, on the American, are also productive and often crowded spots.

BLUE MARLIN

Makaira nigricans

AND
SWORDFISH & WHITE MARLIN

When I first went to work as
fishing editor at *Field and Stream*
in 1947, the old office looked
like a taxidermist's shop. I suppose it was what
visitors expected. Screwed to the walls like
ancestral portraits were various animal heads,
notably a moose with its tongue hanging out, and
a number of fish including the front quarter of a
glassy-eyed, 600-pound blue marlin that looked as
if it had gone berserk and charged madly across
Madison Avenue, rammed our publisher's wall
and got its head fatally stuck. Actually, mounting
part of a giant billfish makes sense if it must be
included as decor. My departed friend Lou
Marron, who caught the world's record swordfish
in 1953, had his prize mounted in its entirety by
Al Pflueger—all 16 feet of an 1,182-pound
monster which was shipped from Miami to his
New York apartment in a 24-foot reinforced crate
by railroad flatcar. Uncle Lou discovered that his
broadbill, which now represented a considerable
five-figure investment, wouldn't fit through the
doorway, hallway or windows of his apartment,
and short of blasting a hole in the building, the
swordfish was about to become a permanent
fixture on the sidewalk of 57th Street.
Fortunately, a Manhattan fishing tackle
emporium, seeing the publicity value, was willing
to have its storefront removed to provide a
temporary home for the old gladiator, who was
ignominiously dismissed to the basement of the
Museum of Natural History. Personally, I've never
been fond of stuffed fish, as I hate to take my work
home with me, but David vs. Goliath is more than
a myth—in big game angling it's a way of life.

In Swahili the word "safari" means "a walking
up," and I always think of blue marlin or
swordfishing as an aquatic safari because both
games are a laborious process of stalking vast areas
of ocean. Statistically, on blue marlin you will
average one fish boated for every eighteen days on
the water. Nobody has computed that ratio on

Nature contrives for a bounty of balao or "ballyhoo" to drift north in
summer when blue marlin follow the same path. When hooked, the blue
marlin seems inexhaustible, running deep and leaping high in the air.

BLUE MARLIN

swordfish. Some masochistic anglers have chased broadbill for a lifetime and never boated the first one. I have baited at least 100 and caught six, and all of these were foul-hooked, an inherent problem with the swordfish. My old mentor, Captain Walter Drobecker of Montauk, a master of the sport, believed that fully 90 percent of all broadbills boated are snagged somewhere other than the mouth, a peculiarity we will explain later. The blue marlin, however, is another story, a kind of "when it rains it pours" saga with days of plenty and an element of chance that has escaped owl-eyed historians.

I recall five near record catches boated by unsalted anglers on a one-day charter who just wanted to see what it was all about (two), wanted to enjoy a beer drinking day on the ocean (two), and to kill time between canceled airline reservations (one). A sixth angler, Jack Herrington of Allison Falls, Pennsylvania, who had never caught a billfish of any kind before, spent one day off Nags Head, North Carolina, and *did* boat a former record Atlantic blue marlin weighing 1,142 pounds. But the climactic catch occurred in Hawaiian waters in 1972, when three California vacationists went out for a day and hooked an 1,805-pound blue marlin that soon exhausted the trio and ultimately the mate and finally the skipper after hours of struggle. Under the inviolate rules of the International Game Fish Association, to qualify for record, nobody is allowed to touch the rod except the angler, and this monster required five men to bring it to boat. So despite the one in eighteen statistic, there is a tremendous element of luck involved. I recall one day under a cobalt sky at Chub Cay in the Bahamas when I invited along wife, daughter, brother-in-law and sister-in-law. We ran about 6 miles into the Tongue of the Ocean before dropping a bait and were instantly surrounded by tailing blue marlin. All hands tied into at least one fish, and we put a dart tag in three of 400 to 500 pounds. The fact that so many blue marlin *are* caught by innocents who wouldn't know a fighting chair from a barber's chair should be inspirational to the casual tourist who enjoys good health.

No sound is more stirring than the cold cough of a 45-foot Hatteras just before dawn. The water is black as ebony, but it will soon turn to molten gold, then orange when the sun gets an edge on the world, and the lime-colored shallows before the dropoff will suddenly dissolve in an inky blue deep that is the home of *Makaira nigricans*. If there is one word for a hooked marlin it is "awesome." Catch, or simply witness, its capture just once and you will understand why some people get so emotionally involved that a half-million dollar investment in a boat (without options) becomes a passion. The unremitting blast of a blue marlin, hammering the water flat as it jumps, twists, and greyhounds with unbridled power, is a scene of such primitive beauty that you will exhaust all adjectives in the telling after. Any fish that weighs more than a quarter of a ton yet miraculously stays in the air seemingly defying gravity in a contest of mutual skills is no less explicable than the words of Plotinus, who is reputed to have explained the Mystic Vision. The blue marlin will then plunge deep and test your willpower as it bulldogs a hundred fathoms below the boat. You must now use rod pressure to prod it back to the surface. This sounds impossible when you are hooked to something the size of a baby elephant, but it is the "white knuckled" beginner who fights a big fish with his arms and shoulders who becomes exhausted. All the leverage applied in pumping must come from your legs, and with feet planted firmly against the footrest of the fighting chair, you can raise your harnessed body from the seat and lean back while you apply pressure and slowly gain line in repeated strokes. This is the painful part that tests your muscles. It could go on for hours. Eventually the line will rise horizontally toward the surface, and once again the marlin is airborne, rocketing across the sea. If you succeed and the mate finally grabs the leader, remember this is not necessarily a blood sport; your choice is a flying-gaff for the kill, or the tagging pole for a release that will embed a small identifying harpoonlike dart that the marlin will wear for years to come. Almost all of our present-day knowledge on the migrations, growth and abundance of big game species has been derived from tag recoveries.

Both the swordfish and the blue marlin are of worldwide distribution in warm and temperate seas. In the western Atlantic, the swordfish occurs from Mexico to Newfoundland, while the blue marlin doesn't often wander north of Cape Cod, although it may occur as a stray in the Gulf of Maine. In the eastern Pacific portion of North America, swordfish are distributed from Mexico to Point Conception near Santa Barbara, California, but when the ocean is warm they wander as far north as Oregon. Pacific blue marlin seldom occur north of Acapulco, Mexico. This marlin appears to make regular north-to-south migrations, moving away from the equator in warm seasons and back again in the cooler months in both the Atlantic and Pacific oceans. In general, there is much overlapping of distribution between the two species and a similarity in their feeding. Both forage extensively on smaller fishes, squid and octopuses and almost anything edible that they can capture; even young swordfish have been found in blue marlin stomachs. The broadbill, however, often venture into very deep water to feed (they have been photographed by submersile vehicles at over 2,000 feet, where one attacked the Woods Hole Oceanographic Institute's submarine the *Alvin,* getting its sword inextricably wedged in a seam). When taking a single food item, the swordfish simply opens its mouth and swallows, but when feeding on compact masses of fish or attacking large prey, it uses its bill to slash and maim. The scientific name *Xiphias gladius* refers to that short broad sword once carried by the Roman legions. The swordfish has a long and ancient history of ramming ships and other floating objects, and as Oppian of Corycus (A.D. 161-180) observed:

> *Nature her bounty to his mouth confined*
> *Gave him a sword, but left unarmed his mind.*

The two pivotal developments in big game fishing other than the fast-planing hull of a modern sport fisherman were the innovation of outriggers and the creation of the tuna tower. In writing of his adventures with Pacific marlin, Zane Grey described the agony of sitting in a chair while holding the rod and a 5-pound bait astern. The drag of that weight created by friction in the water wore the angler to a nub long before a marlin compounded the felony. For a brief period California anglers tried using short bamboo outriggers of 5 to 10 feet in length to tow their baits, then in the 1930s they began using kites. However, this was a fickle method as there has to be enough wind to keep the kite flying and the direction of the boat is confined to a beam wind or going to windward, and it requires something short of a gale to hold a big bait on the surface. In 1934, the legendary Captain Tommy Gifford built the first pair of duraluminum outriggers, which angled off both sides of his boat like a pair of radio antennas. They were 45 feet long, and while not as sophisticated in construction as modern outriggers, he did solve the problem. With today's solidly braced anodized aluminum outriggers it is possible to troll any bait from a small ballyhoo for sailfish to an 8- or 10-pound bonito or dolphin for marlin. Nearly thirty years passed before the sec-

The white marlin is the premier light-tackle billfish in western Atlantic waters. Whites greyhound and jump, often twenty or more times, making them a spectacular quarry. Expert anglers take these fish on 12-pound-test line.

ond development made it possible to direct the easily trolled baits on an elusive target.

The ability to see surfacing billfish at a great distance is, obviously, a tremendous advantage. Swordfish are seldom hooked by blind trolling, and while blue marlin are commonly taken in that manner, spotting fish visually can make the difference between a good or bad day. A person of average height, say between 5 feet, 6 inches and 6 feet tall, standing on the seashore at water level, is viewing between 3 and 3.2 statute miles when looking at the horizon. The idea of putting a man above the water on a platform to see greater distances is as ancient as the crow's nest, but it was never applied to sport fishing boats in a practical manner until the Cat Cay Tuna Tournament of 1952, when the first tubular aluminum tower was installed on a boat by the Rybovitch Boat Works in West Palm Beach, Florida. At 20 feet above the water, which is the modern-day average of the platform, from what has come to be known as the tuna tower, an observer can see 6 miles to the horizon. Not only is the horizontal distance doubled, with minimal surface glare the vertical distance is vastly increased, making the sighting of big fish swimming underwater much easier. Today the tower is no longer a simple lookout platform, but a complete control station with electronics from which the boat can be steered with precision. For example, when a swordfish is sighted, the mate can take the line by hand from the rod tip to the tower while the skipper maneuvers the boat into a viable position to present the bait, then drop the line free at exactly the right moment. From the tower's vantage point this can be done even when a fish isn't visible on the surface.

Until the 1950s, billfishing of any kind was limited to anglers who had the money to charter expensive sport fishermen in the 40-foot class. With the advent of self-bailing, fast-planing fiberglass hulls and modern trailers capable of transporting and launching boats up to 26 feet in length, these center-console outboards made the game financially feasible for the man of modest pockets. Today, there are thousands of anglers fishing offshore from Cape Cod to Mexico in 19- to 26-foot boats that are capable of subduing most big game fish. Furthermore, the advances in electronics have made navigation simple and safe with Loran C and a VHF radio. A good depth-finder, preferably a graph recorder, may not be essential, but it definitely offers an advantage in locating fish. My own boat, a Mako 21 powered by a 175 horsepower Evinrude, is comfortable in all but the foulest weather, and while not as glamorous or versatile as a big Hatteras, Rybovitch, Bertram or other six-figure fishing machines (in some cases seven figures), it has been a reliable workhorse between Florida and the Bahamas.

Billfish Geography

Despite their widespread distribution, the ports that see major blue marlin runs each season are comparatively limited. I would put Cozumel, Mexico; Chub Cay, Walker's Cay and Bimini in the Bahamas; Key West, Panama City and Destin in Florida; Cape Hatteras, North Carolina; and Montauk, New York, high on the list for the

western Atlantic, and Cabo San Lucas as the best bet on the Pacific side of Mexico. Big swordfish are likely to appear anywhere but my vote would be out of Nantucket, Massachusetts, again Montauk, New York, and in Mexico at either Pamilla or Cabo San Lucas. Bear in mind that all these locations offer a variety of angling, not only for billfish but other species as well: We have in one August day taken 200- to 300-pound bigeye tuna, yellowfin tuna, mako and albacore at Montauk—after baiting a broadbill that spooked, and boating a tripleheader on white marlin. All of the ports mentioned are productive areas for other game fish, so reluctant broadbills or the absence of blue marlin may go almost unnoticed. There is considerable fishing done over the submarine canyons off the coast of New Jersey, which range from 70 to 90 miles offshore beyond the 30-fathom curve. The most popular areas here are the Hudson, Wilmington, Washington and Baltimore canyons. However, the target species is primarily tuna (yellowfin and albacore), which comprise over 80 percent of the fish boated. The number of blue marlin and swordfish caught over these canyons is very low in comparison to the Long Island grounds a short distance to the north.

Blue Marlin at Cape Hatteras

It is the proximity of the Gulf Stream to Cape Hatteras that accounts for the remarkable success offshore anglers have had on blue marlin out of Hatteras Village, North Carolina, and Oregon Inlet to the north. The stream approaches the tip of the cape closer—12 nautical miles—than at any point north of Cape Kennedy, Florida. The run to the Gulf Stream out of Hatteras Inlet, which is set back to the southwest from the cape point, is usually about 18 to 20 miles, depending on the location of that wandering ocean current on any given day. The much larger fleet that works out of Oregon Inlet also is in reach of blue water off Cape Hatteras and frequently runs southeasterly 40 miles to fish alongside boats out of Hatteras Inlet.

The first blue marlin caught off Cape Hatteras was taken in 1938 by a New Jersey angler, Hugo Rutherford. That fish, a 439-pounder, was followed the next year by a 594-pounder caught by Marshall Dana of Ohio, fishing with Rutherford. Dana's fish stood for almost twenty-five years as the largest blue marlin caught north of Florida, but there were sightings of much larger fish, and bigger Hatteras blue marlin were lost over the years.

Then, in the mid-seventies, two "granders" were taken within a year. In 1974, Jack Herrington, fishing with Captain Harry Baum 39 miles south-southeast of Oregon Inlet, caught a blue weighing 1,142 pounds. Eleven months later, Dr. Fulton Katz, fishing with 80-pound line on a private boat out of Hatteras Inlet, caught a blue weighing 1,128 pounds. This latter fish still stands as the 80-pound-line-test IGFA record, although Herrington's fish, caught on 130, has been eclipsed by a blue marlin landed in the Virgin Islands off St. Thomas in 1977 and weighing 1,282 pounds. The average size of blue marlin off Cape Hatteras is determined by the relative mix of larger females and smaller males. In years when females are more plentiful, the average is over 300 pounds. When males predominate, the average weight is under 300 pounds. In recent years, several blues weighing over 700 pounds have been caught off Cape Hatteras.

The odds of catching a blue marlin on any given trip offshore are small anywhere. Studies have shown that in good years off Cape Hatteras anglers caught one blue in about ten trips. However, on many of these trips, if not most of them, the party was after other species as well and, therefore, did not concentrate strictly on blue marlin fishing. Boats that target blue marlin specifically and fish exclusively for them day after day exceed the average catch per unit of effort by a substantial margin.

Charter fleets based at Hatteras and Oregon Inlet primarily troll natural baits for billfish. Some are rigged to swim, some to skip. Only a few have recently begun to troll artificial lures, but the results have been encouraging. The fleets are a mixture of older craft whose skippers pioneered blue-water fishing off North Carolina's Outer Banks, and larger, newer and faster sport fishermen. Most of these are wooden boats made locally by master boatwrights, and all are fitted with modern electronics for navigation and communication. Offshore trips begin at dawn and return to the dock between 4:00 and 5:00 P.M.

In Hatteras Village, there are perhaps fifteen boats available for blue-water charters. An hour's drive north at Oregon Inlet Fishing Center, there are about twenty-five. These boats book parties far in advance, some a year or more ahead, so it is well to call for reservations at the earliest opportunity.

Three marinas at Hatteras berth sport fishing boats that are available for charter. They are:
Foster's Quay
    telephone (919) 986-2515.

Hatteras Fishing Center
    telephone (919) 986-2532.
Hatteras Harbor Marina
    telephone (919) 986-2305.
The fleet at Oregon Inlet operates out of Oregon Fleet Fishing Center, a facility of the Cape Hatteras National Seashore. Boats may be booked directly through their skippers at their home phones, but the number for the fishing center reservations desk is (919) 441-6301.

The nearest commercial airport to this area is at Norfolk, Virginia, where there are rental cars for the one-and-one-half-hour drive to Nags Head

Western Atlantic Billfishes

Female blue marlin are the giants of the billfish family (males never exceed 300 pounds) in the western Atlantic. Taxonomists are not in complete agreement as to whether they are the same species as those found in the Pacific; some consider them a subspecies. There is a considerable difference in their lateral line structures, for example; on Pacific fish it is formed in simple chain-like loops and on Atlantic blue marlin in a more intricate series of reticulations.

In addition to the blue marlin and sailfish, three other species of billfish can be found in the western Atlantic, and these are easily recognized. The white marlin is readily identified by its long pectoral fins, which are rounded rather than pointed at their tips. The swordfish has, in addition to its flat bill, a high sickle-shaped dorsal fin and no posterior portion characteristic of related istiophorids. The longbill spearfish is elongate and slender, its sides flattened rather than rounded. Its bill is actually short in comparison to other istiophorids, being only twice as long as its lower jaw. This spearfish is nowhere abundant and is rather prized for its scarcity.

There is a possible sixth species of billfish in the western Atlantic, the so-called hatchet or axe marlin, which is presently considered a variation of the white marlin. The hatchet differs notably in having two spots at the base of each dorsal membrane. Anglers catching "white marlin" that fit this description could contribute to their study by sending specimens to Dr. Donald de Sylva at the University of Miami Marine Laboratory.

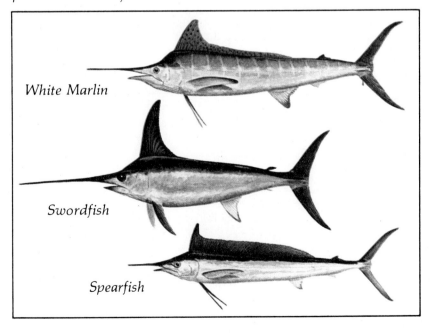

White Marlin

Swordfish

Spearfish

(which is the beach community convenient to Oregon Inlet), or two and one half hours down the Outer Banks to Hatteras Village.

Detailed information on offshore fishing is available from the North Carolina Travel and Tourism Division, 430 N. Salisbury St., Raleigh, NC 27611; telephone (919) 733-4171.

Long Island Swordfish

In every phase of fishing, techniques come and go. However, there is practically no other fishery where the basic techniques have changed so completely as in Long Island swordfishing. Until recent years, this involved the daytime spotting of surfacing fish; now almost all the catches are made by blind fishing in great depths at night. Swordfish are quite different from other billfish in that they cover great ranges of depths, often in a single day. The same fish spotted finning on the surface at high noon may have been feeding 200 or 300

The swordfish season on Long Island begins in mid-June at Shinnecock, with the fish gradually moving east to the Montauk area. The Cartwright grounds have been productive in years past, but today most fish are sighted beyond that, over the 40-fathom line.

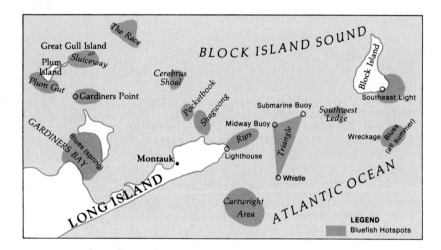

fathoms during the night. Until the late 1970s, swordfish were taken on rod-and-reel off the Long Island coast only by surface fishing. Since swordfish forage primarily in the depths, those fish spotted on the surface are seldom interested in feeding. Consequently, swordfishing was an expensive sport. It was necessary to spend countless hours on the water in order to find the fish and then, only about one out of ten could be expected to hit the bait. As if those odds weren't bad enough, veteran anglers expected to lose most of the swordfish they did succeed in hooking due to their soft mouths. Two-hook rigs (No. 12/0 to 16/0) were used, and the basic technique involved keeping the fish headed away from the boat so that when the hooks pulled they might snag the

swordfish on the outside of its body. Montauk Captain Carl Darenberg insisted that the vast majority of surface-baited swordfish that were brought to dock were snagged—even though originally hooked in the mouth.

Surface swordfishing off Long Island is strictly an East End proposition. The prime areas are from Shinnecock east, with the fish coming in from offshore waters around mid-June and then moving steadily eastward. The prime time is from mid-June to mid-July. Depending on water temperatures, the fish will move in quite close to the beach. Carl Darenberg remembers sighting swordfish back in the 1950s that were so close to shore that he could see Gurney's Resort in Hither Hills, and he could almost always spot a swordfish either early in the morning or late in the day at the first rip on the Cartwright Grounds just 6 miles south of Montauk Point. In those days, a run of 20 or 30 miles offshore was exceptional, and the boats never even checked the areas beyond the 40-fathom line, which is where most sightings are made today. Spotting the swordfish was the first and most important aspect of this fishing. The serious fishermen added tuna towers or similar structures above their flying bridges in order to expand their field of vision. Sharp-eyed mates were hired to stay aloft and do nothing but spot fish. Once sighted, the swordfish was baited by carefully swinging the bait in front of the surfaced fish and then allowing it to sink on a slack line. This was usually done by the captain from the bridge. A long drop-back is necessary in order to let the broadbill swallow the bait as deeply as possible, rather than being hooked in its soft mouth. Although this basic technique has worked for years, and will continue to produce in the future, it is very inefficient. Not only are few of the fish tempted to strike, but the vast majority are swimming just under the surface where they are rarely spotted from a boat. Carl Darenberg solved that problem by copying the harpooners and using aerial spotting. Three or four boats would share the cost and hire a plane, which would then cover the area to be fished and radio the nearest craft when a fish was sighted. The submerged fish could be blindly baited by following the instructions of the pilot. Swordfishing success picked up considerably with this technique because more fish could be baited, and the bait could be presented much farther from the boat to broadbill that just weren't sunning themselves. According to Darenberg, virtually every broadbill they spotted would at least look at the bait.

There is still some surface swordfishing done off

the east end of Long Island, but very few fish are caught in that fashion. Probably due to intensive commercial fishing, the population is way down, and it is rare to sight one inside 40 fathoms now. On the other hand, unheard of numbers of swordfish have been boated since the late 1970s by fishing in the depths of the canyons at night. This sport was developed in Florida and, when brought north, instantly produced exceptional swordfish catches. Whereas most of the daytime canyon trolling is done along the edges of the drop-off, night swordfishing is usually practiced in hundreds of fathoms well out in the canyons. Baits (usually large squid) are drifted at various depths, and "light sticks" are tied to the leaders or bait in order to help attract the scattered swords. As with the surface fishing, 80-pound tackle is considered standard for this fishing, though broadbill of under 100 pounds are probably more common than the larger fish at night. The surfacing swordfish are usually in the 200- to 400-pound class. Unfortunately, night fishing has declined considerably since its initial success and the pressure of commercial longlining will probably tend to keep the inshore population of swordfish low in the future. Nevertheless, quite a few swords are still caught in this fashion, and it represents the best opportunity off Long Island for those anglers committed to the pursuit of our most elusive billfish. All Long Island south shore ports provide access to the night fishery, with west end boats concentrating on Hudson Canyon, while those east of Fire Island work the Fish Tail. There's a good chance of a canyon swordfish any night during the summer, and most catches are made in August.

Cabo San Lucas

Broadbill are found in the Sea of Cortez between La Paz and Cabo San Lucas. Most are taken at Cabo San Lucas with an occasional report north. The average weight is around 150 pounds, but females over 500 pounds have been boated. At Cabo, broadbill are found mostly in two areas, outside Gorda Banks and in front of the lighthouse at Cabo Falso. Gorda Banks are 27 miles north of Cabo and are the most productive. They are directly out from Punta Gorda. They are made up of the inner bank, 5½ miles from shore, and the outer bank, 8½ miles from shore. Broadbill are usually found on the outside edge of the outer bank. The best shot is drifting squid, at night, 100 feet deep. The depth should be varied; if no action results, go down to 500 feet in increments of 100 feet.

Although fishing at night undoubtedly produces more strikes, a great number of broadbill are taken in Baja by daylight during the months of March and April—the peak months. This fishing is

BLUE MARLIN

conducted in the same area at Gorda Banks. At the lighthouse at Cabo Falso most broadbill are found 4 to 8 miles directly out, and on the edge of Jaime Banks, 17 miles from shore. While the concentrations are at Gorda and the lighthouse, broadbill are sometimes sighted and hooked in between, especially in front of Puerto Chileno. Once sighted, they must be approached with caution (without radical changes in engine speed or direction, especially toward the fish). They can be spooked very easily. The boat should be eased into a position where the bait can be tossed, then gently pull away about 50 yards and slowly ease off on the throttle. The best bait is a live *caballito*, a small mackerel with a yellow tail. The leader should be very heavy, braided steel because of the broadbill's violent use of its bill. A large hook, No. 12/0, should be embedded an inch behind the head of the bait.

It is advisable to notify the fleet operator or the boat captain the day before going out if broadbill are the quarry. This will give them time to arrange for whatever live bait is available. Also, the captain will then head immediately for the broadbill feeding grounds. In this same area will be striped marlin, dolphin, and perhaps wahoo, so normal trolling procedures will apply. However, a couple of rods, rigged for broadbill, can be set aside, and an alert surveillance maintained by both anglers and crew.

There are nine hotels in the vicinity of Cabo San Lucas, four in town and the other five stretched out to San Jose del Cabo. It is always advisable to make reservations for hotel, boat and airline. Cabo has one trailer park, and there is one at San Jose del Cabo. The marina at Cabo San Lucas has a launching ramp for trailered boats. The 1,000-mile transpeninsular highway from Tijuana to Cabo San Lucas should be driven with extra caution. Baja California is pretty much open range, and cattle are a hazard. Speed should be kept under 55 miles an hour, and night driving is definitely not recommended.

White Marlin

In the summer of 1938 everyone (and his brother) went fishing for white marlin out of Ocean City. They went to the shoal about 22 miles southeast by south from the Maryland port that Paul Townsend called "Jack's spot" after his brother, who used to troll it from a *schooner* before their sport fisherman was delivered in 1932. The few people who had money for *la vie sportif* had the limited number of Ocean City charter captains booked solid, and maneuvering room on the Jackspot was scarce. Into this melee in 1938 steamed the traitor to his class aboard the presidential yacht *Potomac*, big as a bloody battleship. The Gentry cursed his passage, but an insouciant Franklin Roosevelt, projecting his cigarette holder like a marlin's rostrum, had chosen his mount well. The *Potomac* proved to be one of those hulls that charter boat captains dream of finding, a vessel whose resonances lured fish as the Lorelei's aria enchanted *die Rheinslusslotsen*. The presidential party caught marlin as if they owned the ocean. Roosevelt probably got the idea to try billfishing from Hemingway, who dined with him at the White House on July 8, 1937, and found the food insipid.

At Ocean City they began keeping white marlin catch records two years before FDR's outing:

1936—175
1937—200
1938—781
1939—1,343

That is a steep climb, but it has happened more than once and presents a puzzle. Look at seventeen years of roller-coasting:

1965—654	1974—855
1966—544	1975—687
1967—1,146	1976—335
1968—1,735	1977—363
1969—2,507	1978—768
1970—2,098	1979—941
1971—2,206	1980—1,476
1972—837	1981—933
1973—600	1982—246

White marlin are an inescapable by-catch of the longline fishermen, and Japanese records insist that 1965, a miserable year at Ocean City, was absolutely the peak of abundance in their catch. The plot will thicken.

This marlin is the most migratory of them all if our present understanding is valid, and considering how many of them have been tagged and the tags recovered, it probably is (that 1980 catch of 1,476, for instance, represents 434 boated and 1,042 released, many with a tag in their shoulder).

In short, there are discrete populations: a South Atlantic one that provides admirable fishing for Brazilians, and the North Atlantic population that we fish. This latter group winters off the northern coast of South America and is fished by Venezuela. Some of it provides the summer run to United States mid-Atlantic fisheries (basically from Cape Hatteras to Cape Cod, with concentrations off the drowned continental shelf canyons that were cut by Pleistocene rivers when much of the world's water was locked in ice sheets and sea levels were hundreds of feet lower than today), and some of the North Atlantic white marlin enter the Gulf of Mexico fishery.

Just as the Townsend brothers were instrumental in locating and defining the mid-Atlantic run, the Gulf of Mexico group was discovered by the research vessel *Oregon* of the United States Fish and Wildlife Service in 1955. The *Oregon* made longline sets off South Pass at the mouth of the Mississippi River and picked up both white and blue marlin. These marlin are primarily fished now by New Orleans big game anglers. Other stocks are found in the northeastern Gulf, where boats reach them out of the Florida ports of Pensacola, Destin and Panama City.

Tagging recaptures indicate that *some* of the Venezuelan fish become New Orleans fish, then Florida fish and eventually mid-Atlantic Bight fish, looping the Caribbean before passing through the Yucatán Channel between Cuba and Mexico and then north to the United States.[1] In fall, the mid-Atlantic Bight fish, many with barbed tags in their dorsal meat, head offshore and then south. But in addition to this vast annual migration, there must be local populations as well, because the biggest white marlin (over 100 pounds) are almost all Bahamian and Florida fish in the North Atlantic.[2]

Two of the dozens of recaptured tags had been at large more than nine years, and in 1982 a tag planted almost twelve years before was recaptured from a rather haggard 6-foot, 65-pounder. So we are dealing with a species that has a longevity potential of thirteen or more years.

The possibility exists that the Cape Hatteras-to-Cape Cod summer migratory population is largely juvenile, else why not more giants? But that twelve-year-old tag from a 65-pound fish may indicate subspecies or races. We have a single summer stock with two feeding concentrations, one in the Gulf and one in the mid-Atlantic Bight. I am haunted by the fear that intense marlin fishing at the base of the Statue of Liberty would disclose a new local population. Every year a few of these creatures are caught from the fishing *piers* so popular in the Carolinas!

What does an epipelagic predator with the speed to run down tuna want with chunk bait being soaked off a pier? They have, in fact, a catholicity of diet that even other billfish would

These modern sport-fishermen, fully equipped from tuna tower to sophisticated electronics, represent millions of dollars afloat as a marlin tournament gets under-way. The tower and outriggers were key developments in the evolution of big game angling technique.

envy. In addition to the usual mix of locally available squid and finfish disclosed by stomach analysis, white marlin have also yielded (on more than one occasion) crabs and octopods. I assume those octopods are the large female of the paper nautilus (the male is minuscule), which is frequently found at the surface, and the crabs swimming species such as blue crab. Juvenile broadbill swordfish and hamerhead sharks have also appeared in the diet.

Spawning seems to be a spring phenomenon. A monthly gonosomatic index of Florida Straits white marlin (186 specimens) indicated April and May spawning. In 1935 Ernest Hemingway reported: "White marlins breed off Cuba in May. They breed in the same way that a grouper does, except that as they are a fish of the current, they breed in the current while the male heads in the opposite direction, and while they are side by side the female expels the eggs and the male the milt; the male then catches the eggs in the basket-like opening of his gill covers and lets them pass out through his mouth."

The latter operation sounds as if Papa Hemingway may have been getting into the daiquiris a bit early that day, but the basic idea of broadcasting eggs and milt into the water column is no doubt accurate. They enter the breeding population at an eye-fork length of about 4 feet and a weight of approximately 45 pounds, age unknown.

A National Marine Fisheries Service poll once disclosed that white marlin require 17.8 days of trolling per caught fish. That must include fishing some singularly inauspicious water, because in late

[1] John Rybovich, who built the most beautiful, effective, admired and expensive big-game fishing yachts prior to his retirement, tagged a white marlin at Cozumel, Mexico, in 1980 that was recaptured at South Pass, Louisiana, in 1981.

[2] The Brazilian fish are bigger than anything Yankees see, and they are thought to conduct annual transatlantic migrations between South America and Africa.

BLUE MARLIN

summer a boat with a through-hull thermometer fishing on top of one of the mid-Atlantic canyons *should* be into marlin. You want 70° to 80°F water. In addition to the Gulf Stream, warm core eddies 45 to 120 miles in diameter can also be fished and, as important, cold core eddies avoided. At sea temperatures of 65°F and colder, you are not marlin fishing. You may still be fishing for bluefin or yellowfin tuna, but the marlin are gone.

And this is the answer to the Ocean City catch records. When the Gulf Stream pulls too far offshore to be readily reached, catching declines sharply and some allied phenomena also occur. One is a reduction in the charterboat fleet as unemployed crews go into other lines of work, another is a sharp increase in the mosquito fleet of high-speed vessels under 30 feet long, and a third is the overnight tournament, whose contestants sleep during a night run to the canyons, then fish the next day.

The impact of this sport fishery on the resource is formidable. In 1936, there were a dozen charter

boats out of Ocean City. The number swelled to thirty-nine in 1939 and after the WWII hiatus rose to about seventy by the early 1970s. But those were the principal access to the marlin, whereas now there are thousands of trailerable center-console craft that spend the summer weekends as far as 50 or 60 miles offshore. John Jolley, a biologist and billfisherman formerly with the Florida Department of Natural Resources, estimates that the total billfish catch per year in the western North Atlantic is 80,000 to 100,000 fish, and 80 percent of those are caught by recreational angling, with half the fish released and half killed. If we accept the 80,000 figure that means 32,000 billfish per year are killed, and all the taxidermists in the land couldn't be stuffing that many fish. Some of them are eaten, of course, but most are weighed, photographed and trashed. A case can be made that getting Americans to release half their catch is a great improvement: the Ocean City 1939 catch of 1,343 fish was made up of 84 released and 1,259 killed. Now that charter

Long pectoral fins and spectacular leaps are typical of the white marlin. Both pelagic and migratory, the white is usually found in tropical and warm temperate waters, wandering as far north as southern Massachusetts during the summer months.

boat captains are a minority form of access to marlin, tournament organizers have a responsibility to promote releasing fish.

High-speed trolling with artificial,lures is the modern rage for this fish, because the Japanese longliners report it is the least numerous and most widely dispersed in their catches, but surely this is a function of its intensely migratory lifestyle. When local accumulations are really intense, and with modern electronics to pinpoint them, white marlin can be fished almost as if they were Florida sailfish balling bait in winter: that is, run out to where you *know* they are and get live bait over for slow trolling. High-speed trolling is essentially a technique for fish that have a lot of water between them (and it has provided a revelation in the distribution of game fish), but when you know where they are, when your Loran C has found the place and your sonar has established their presence, nothing catches fish as certainly as live bait, not even fly-fishing.

Fly-Fishing for White Marlin

White marlin by fair fly-fishing dates back to 1972, when Dave Chermanski became the first with a Florida fish. Billy Pate took a Venezuelan white marlin in 1975, and my friend Chico Fernandez, the professional tier of saltwater flies, caught and released one on September 12, 1979, fishing out of Nags Head, North Carolina. The Chermanski and Pate catches are a part of International Game Fish Association record-fish history.

Why would anyone *want* to take a lure intended for catching trout in streams and offer it to oceanic game fish? The opposite, in fact, seems to be the case. Before Aelian's remarks on Macedonian dry-fly-fishing for stream trout, so often quoted by fly-fishermen as the earliest reference to their sport, Martial, who was fifty years Aelian's senior, wrote: *Avidum vorata decipa scarum musca?* Which the great British classicist A. J. Butler (1850-1936) has translated as "All know how the greedy wrasse swallows the fly and is fooled" (in *Sport in Classic Times*, E. Benn, London, 1930). Dr. Butler, an Oxford don and Eton fellow, also paraphrases Aelian on trolling flies (we are late in the first or early in the second century of the Christian era):

> Ten young fellows, he says, in the very flower of their age, embark on a boat which must be very light and therefore very fast, and, after ranging themselves on either side and after eating a very hearty meal, they take to the oars and pull. . . . One man seated at the stern lets out a couple of lines, one at either side of the boat, and from each of these lines others are suspended, all fitted with hooks. Every hook carries a bait made with Laconian purple wound about with white wool, and every hook has also a sea-mew's feather attached, so that it flutters gently as the water heaves against it. The pelamyds rise keenly at the sight. . . .

"Pelamyds" should be our old oceanic friend of worldwide distribution in warm seas, the skipjack tuna (*Euthynnus pelamis*). I have cast to skipjack and had followers but no eaters, probably because my retrieve lacked the speed that can be achieved by a ten-man scull. However you hook your white marlin, trolling or casting with bait, lure or fly, you have had predecessors that go beyond antiquity into the Mute Epoch, probably into the Lithic Ages. You share with all of them, even those now fossil, an experience utterly unlike trout

BLUE MARLIN

A big game angling resort, Walker Cay faces one of the most productive billfish grounds in the Bahamas. In addition to blue and white marlin and sailfish, there is an abundance of dolphin, yellowfin tuna, mako and tiger sharks, wahoo and a variety of reef species, such as giant groupers, barracuda and amberjack. Walker is extremely popular among American and Canadian anglers.

stream angling. I marvel when practicing either that both are subsumed under the single portmanteau term "fishing."

Oregon Inlet for White Marlin

Experts say it is wind direction that accounts for so many white marlin off Oregon Inlet on North Carolina's Outer Banks. Because of the orientation of the coastline, prevailing summer winds are onshore south of Cape Hatteras, offshore north of the cape. Offshore winds cause upwelling of cooler, nutritious water from the depths, creating conditions favored by plankton, cigar minnows and other bait species, and finally white marlin as you go up the food chain. Oregon Inlet is the first inlet north of Cape Hatteras and the door to probably the best white marlin fishing in North America.

Whites summer from Cape Cod to Cape Hatteras in the western Atlantic, and off Oregon Inlet, they are present in fishable numbers from June until mid-October. The prime time is mid-August to early October. Prevailing summer winds are southwesterly. The wind regimen changes to northeasterly before fall, so that in August and September it blows hot from the southwest most of the time, then cool from the northeast for a few days. These northeasters concentrate billfish off

Oregon Inlet. Some days marlin are schooled and "balling" bait. Anywhere from one to several whites will circle tight schools of cigar minnows, occasionally slashing into them to feed. Daily catches of half a dozen whites per boat are routine at this time and as many as seventeen have been caught on one boat in a day off Oregon Inlet.

Oregon Inlet Fishing Center is a facility of the Cape Hatteras National Seashore. About thirty boats there charter for offshore fishing, and there is room in the marina for a few private craft. Charter rates are based on a party of six or less. They are still lower than or competitive with rates for offshore trips elsewhere on the Atlantic coast.

White marlin average 40 to 65 pounds off the North Carolina coast. For experienced anglers, they are about right on 20-pound-test line. On 30-pound-test, they give a good accounting of themselves, but are boring on 50-pound. Unfortunately, the fish occur in waters frequented by blue marlin, which average about 300 pounds and reach over 1,000. Blue marlin like the small ballyhoo baits skipped for white marlin, and whites like the bigger baits streamed for blues. Consequently you get occasional mismatches, with blues stripping 30-pound rigs and whites giving ho-hum fights on 80.

Charter boats have heavy tackle suited for the average inexperienced angler rather than the fish. For maximum enjoyment of white marlin, veterans of offshore fishing will bring their own light tackle down to 20-pound-test. You should clear personal tackle with your skipper in advance, however, and then be prepared for breakoffs or cleaned reels from blue marlin and the yellowfin tuna that have been common off Oregon Inlet in recent years.

A restaurant at the fishing center serves early breakfast, or you can pick up coffee and sweet rolls at all-night convenience stores at Nags Head. Food and drinks are not provided by the boat, but bait and ice are. Most days, marlin fishermen unavoidably catch such delicious species as tuna, wahoo and dolphin. It is well to bring an insulated box for transporting these home for the freezer.

White marlin are edible, too, and they are at their best smoked. But few anglers have facilities for handling such large fish, so, unless the fish is wanted for a mount, they are customarily released off Oregon Inlet. The North Carolina Salt Water Fishing Tournament gives citations for released white marlin and for those you kill, provided they weigh 50 pounds or over.

There is heavy demand for charters during the white marlin season, so it is well to make reservations in advance. The fishing center opens and begins booking in March, but individual skippers will take reservations before that. A few boats are booked for the entire season a year in advance. For charter information and reservations, call the center at (919) 441-6301.

Since the white marlin season occurs during a period of changeable weather, many days are too windy for offshore fishing. Disappointed anglers may prowl the Outer Banks beaches and enjoy the Indian summer weather. A list of surf fishing guides is available from the North Carolina Travel and Tourism Division, telephone (919) 733-4171. Fishing for channel bass can be good at this time.

The nearest commercial airport to Oregon Inlet and the resort community of Nags Head is Norfolk, Virginia, about 1½ hours by car to the north.

The Outer Banks Chamber of Commerce, telephone (919) 261-2626, has a listing of accommodations.

Ocean City Marlin

It is not often that a writer has a chance to correct an old error in research, but I do and will because the true story is so much more entertaining than the one I published in *Profiles in Saltwater Angling* ten years ago, and because the true story is integral to the history of Ocean City, Maryland, in its claim to being the white marlin capital of the United States Atlantic coast.

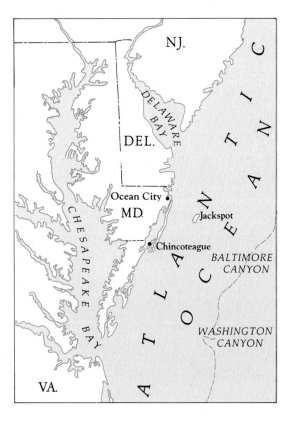

Ocean City, Maryland, is still one of the principal white marlin areas in the eastern U.S. A drowned barrier island known as the "Jackspot" made the city famous in years past, but, today, the productive grounds are 50 miles out at the edge of the continental shelf.

In a footnote on page 332 of *Profiles*, I wrote that the origin of the name "Jackspot"—Ocean City's most famous marlin ground—dated back to when it was "called the Jack's Pot after an old Maryland market fisherman." I was told that story by a waterman whose grizzled appearance gave the anecdote all the authenticity it seemed to need! However, after publication I met a more reliable source who said I had the crucial details right without knowing it when the rest of my footnote stated that the ground had been "pioneered by Paul and Jack Townsend in 1935, with Captain Bill Hatch as their guide." According to Ted Harvey—who was a personal friend of the Townsend brothers, who himself helped pioneer angling in the Florida Keys in the 1920s, and who founded one of the most important land acquisition and conservation groups in the mid-Atlantic, Delaware Wildlands—the Jackspot got its name when one of the bevy of outdoor writers from eastern seaboard newspapers who had come to Ocean City to photograph and write about the many marlin the Townsends were catching asked Paul Townsend where exactly he and his brother were catching the fish. Paul nodded toward his brother and said enigmatically, "At Jack's spot." In the column it came out as "the Jackspot," and so it has been ever since.

Ironically, this fabled Maryland hot spot

BLUE MARLIN

THE BAIT-RIGGER'S HANDY GUIDE

SPECIES	WEIGHT	BAIT	LINE	HOOK	LEADER MATERIAL	SPEED
	100-300 lb.	Strip bait, ballyhoo or mullet	6 lb.	3/0	15' #3 wire or 30 lb. monofil	
			12 lb.	4/0	15' #4 wire or 40 lb. monofil	3-5 knots
			20 lb.	5/0	15' #6 wire or 50 lb. monofil	
	300-600 lb.	Mullet or mackerel	30 lb.	6/0	15' #8 wire or 80 lb. monofil	3-5 knots
			50 lb.	8/0	15' #10 wire or 120 lb. monofil	
	600-900 lb.	Mackerel or bonito	80 lb.	10/0	30' #12 wire or 200 lb. monofil	3-6 knots
			130 lb.	12/0 +	30' #15 wire or 300 lb. monofil	
	500-1,500 lb.	Artificial plastic lures	50 lb.	2-12/0	15' #12 wire or 200 lb. monofil	8 knots
			80 lb.	2-14/00	30' #15 wire or 300 lb. monofil	
			130 lb.	2-16/0	30' 2 × #15 wire or 500 lb. mono	
	500-1,000 lb.	Live bonito or runner	50 lb.	10/0	15' #10 wire or 120 lb. monofil	3 knots
			80 lb.	12/0	30' #12 wire or 200 lb. monofil	
			130 lb.	14/0	30' #15 wire or 300 lb. monofil	
STRIPED MARLIN	100-300 lb.	Strip bait, ballyhoo or mullet	6 lb.	3/0	15' #3 wire or 30 lb. monofil	3-5 knots
			12 lb.	4/0	15' #6 wire or 40 lb. monofil	
			20 lb.	5/0	15' #6 wire or 60 lb. monofil	
			30 lb.	6/0	15' #8 wire or 80 lb. monofil	
			50 lb.	8/0	15' #10 wire or 120 lb. monofil	
ATLANTIC SAILFISH	30-140 lb.	Strip bait, ballyhoo or mullet	6 lb.	3/0	2' #3 wire + 12' 30 lb. monofil	3-5 knots
			12 lb.	4/0	2' #4 wire + 12' 40 lb. monofil	
WHITE MARLIN	40-160 lb.		20 lb.	5/0	2' #6 wire + 12' 60 lb. monofil	
			30 lb.	6/0	2' #8 wire + 12' 80 lb. monofil	
PACIFIC SAILFISH	40-220 lb.		50 lb.	8/0	2' #9 wire + 12' 90 lb. monofil	
BROADBILL SWORDFISH	40-100 lb.	Live bait, squid or mullet	6 lb.	4/0	15' #3 wire or 30 lb. monofil	Drift or 3-4 knots
			12 lb.	5/0	15' #5 wire or 50 lb. monofil	
			20 lb.	6/0	15' #7 wire or 70 lb. monofil	
	100-300 lb.	Squid or mackerel	30 lb.	6/0	15' #9 wire or 90 lb. monofil	Drift or 3-4 knots
			50 lb.	8/0	15' #10 wire or 120 lb. monofil	
	300-1,000 lb.	Squid or mackerel	80 lb.	10/0	30' #12 wire or 200 lb. monofil	Drift or 3-4 knots
			130 lb.	12/0	30' #15 wire or 300 lb. monofil	
BLUEFIN TUNA	50-175 lb.	Mullet	30 lb.	5/0	15' #9 wire or 90 lb. monofil	Chum or 3-8 knots
	100-400 lb.	Squid	50 lb.	6/0	15' #10 wire or 120 lb. monofil	
	300-700 lb.	Mackerel	80 lb.	8/0	30' #12 wire or 200 lb. monofil	
	500-1,000 lb.	Herring	130 lb.	10/0	30' #15 wire or 300 lb. monofil	
GAME SHARKS	50-150 lb.	Squid	30 lb.	5/0	15' #8 wire or 80 lb. monofil	Chum or 3-4 knots
	100-300 lb.	Mackerel	50 lb.	6/0	15' #10 wire or 120 lb. monofil	
	300-500 lb.	Herring	80 lb.	8/0	30' #12 wire or 200 lb. monofil	
	500-1,000 lb.	Whiting	130 lb.	10/0	30' #15 wire or 300 lb. monofil	

Chart supplied by Penn Reel Company.

328

straddles the Maryland-Virginia border—if such a border were to continue offshore for 21 miles. In other words, the Jackspot is as close to Chincoteague, Virginia, as Ocean City. In 1939, charter guide Johnny Cass was hired by Virginia to publicize the billfishing to be had off the Commonwealth, and on July 4th, Johnny and his crew brought into Chincoteague eleven white marlin, which were photographed and shipped to Richmond for display as "Virginia-caught fish." But by 1939, it was already too late: Atlantic anglers had come to look on Ocean City as their mecca for summer marlin.

A more melancholy irony associated with the Jackspot and the other drowned barrier islands 20 to 30 miles off the mid-Atlantic coast where the best billfishing was found from the 1930s through the 1950s is that these banks or "hills" rarely produce white marlin at all today. No one has yet come up with a reasonable explanation as to why these former glory grounds have faded. Some say increased fishing pressure has pushed the billfish back to the edge of the continental shelf, which was always their principal summer staging area but which has only been "discovered" during the past two decades by sportsmen in faster, far-ranging boats. Others speculate that changing water temperatures and/or chemistry have affected all inshore fishing and in the process forced the marlin back to the continental edge. Whatever the cause, unless the angler wants bluefish or bluefin tuna, he runs right over the Jackspot on his way to deeper water.

The nature of billfishing off Ocean City has changed in other ways. First, while the only way to catch a marlin in the 1950s was aboard a charter boat, today far more fish are taken from private boats, some of them larger and better equipped than a charterman ever dreams of owning. Although on a summer weekend as many as one hundred boats run out of Ocean City to the Baltimore Canyon, 52 miles from the jetties, or the Washington Canyon, about the same distance but farther south, only about thirty of these are charter boats. With daily charter rates rising, increasing numbers of marine anglers rationalize the acquisition of their own boats and equipment. Whether or not this is the most cost-effective way to go marlin fishing (and I know it is not!), every year dozens of new boat owners trailer their hulls to Ocean City, because this many-faceted recreational city is still the most logical and productive port north of Oregon Inlet from which to pursue marlin. Indeed, during the prime holiday months of July and August, Maryland is better than North Carolina for white marlin, because this billfish species generally ranges farther north along the continental edge than either blue marlin or sailfish. And while wahoo may not be as abundant off Ocean City as off Cape Hatteras, school-sized yellowfin tuna are.

Furthermore, over the past ten years, private and charter skippers fishing out of Ocean City have shown themselves to be among the most innovative blue-water fishermen anywhere. They were among the first to experiment with high-speed trolling lures for billfish. And if one month, rigged eel daisy chains seem to be the ticket to successful marlin fishing, almost every boat off Ocean City will be trolling one or two of these rigs. Elsewhere along the coast, you will hear that it is "too much trouble" as fishermen continue dragging more conventional ballyhoo and mullet.

Finally, Ocean City regulars have become largely a catch-tag-and-release crowd. They don't buy the fantasy parroted elsewhere that tagging data is used by Japanese long-liners to find marlin concentration zones—as though the Japanese don't have charts, satellite photography, Loran, depth recorders, water temperature gauges and common sense of their own to locate marlin concentrations. Ocean City fishermen understand that tagging information will do more to enhance their own long-term recreational interests than it will ever do for foreign fishermen.

The state of Maryland publishes and updates annually a handy *Tidewater Sportfishing Guide,* which can be obtained by writing the Department of Natural Resources, Tidewater Administration, Tawes State Office Building, Annapolis 21401; and the Ocean City Chamber of Commerce (zip code: 21842) responds readily to requests concerning accommodations and other activities in the area. The local Chamber of Commerce has nearly half a century of experience in catering to blue water anglers, and that is another good reason to consider fishing from Ocean City for the Atlantic's most spectacular billfish.

Chub Cay White Marlin

The word "Bahamas" is derived from *baja mar*—low or shallow sea, and many a Spanish galleon went aground learning that deep water is scarce in the archipelago's 100,000 square miles of subtropical Atlantic. But 35 miles north of the capital of Nassau are the Berry Islands, whose southwesternmost cay was known for a certain Madam Frazer, who ran hogs there. Considerably after its piggy period, Frazer's Hog Cay became the site of a

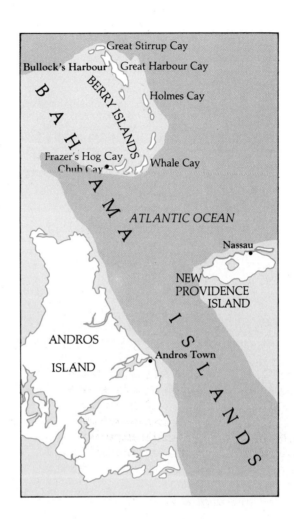

supremely comfortable, plush, private club, with stiff dues and a marina that can berth seventy-six yachts at one time. Why would seventy-six millionaires want to park their playthings at the Chub Cay Club? Because it is just a few hundred yards from the mile-deep waters of Tongue of the Ocean, a protrusion of blue water into the seemingly endless shallows of the Great Bahama Bank. Tongue of the Ocean is a superlative fish trap for large pelagic creatures such as white marlin, blue marlin, sailfish, wahoo, bluefin tuna, blackfin tuna, dolphin and bonito.

The Chub Cay Club still has private members, but now it also accepts non-member anglers, providing full accommodations as well as charters for both blue-water and flats fishing. The bonefish are enormous, but so are the white marlin, that special Bahamian breed that seems more akin to the monsters from Brazil than to the little American whites. World records have been set at Chub Cay, and doubtless will again, but the fishery is noted for the volume of its billfish as well as for their avoirdupois. In a 1983 members

BLUE MARLIN

tournament, thirteen anglers on a dozen boats fished for five days and caught twenty-seven white marlin, sixteen sailfish and seven blue marlin.

If you are not bringing your own boat to Chub Cay, you will want to charter. If no charter boat is currently in harbor, they will order one to run over from Nassau for you, so it is essential to book your fishing when making reservations. There is a 5,000-foot air strip that receives scheduled Bahamas Air service from Nassau as well as charter flights from Florida.

The best billfishing is often in an extension into the Great Bahama Bank of the Northwest Channel, rather than Tongue of the Ocean proper. This pocket of the Tongue fishes best when south and southeasterly breezes blow (the right weather is most trustworthy in spring and summer). However, the coast of Andros is often fished by anglers out of Chub, as is the Tongue itself.

Facilities ashore include comfortable air-conditioned rooms, restaurant and bar, pool, tennis, an outstanding scuba operation, dispensary, liquor store and gift shop, etc.

Actually, it is the adjacent flats, the bait playing back and forth off the shallow Banks, that make the Chub Cay pocket so productive. This means the marlin are certainly eating some of the largest bonefish known to man. It makes sense to also book a flats skiff and guide for some light-tackle variety when planning a marlin hunt.

For information contact Chub Cay Club, Chub Cay, Berry Islands, Bahamas; telephone (809) 325-1490. The club checks twice daily with its Miami booking office; telephone (305) 445-7830.

Destin, Florida, is the new star in a galaxy of marlin ports. The billfishing requires a long run offshore, but an excellent charter fleet is berthed here. From April through September both blue and white marlin appear in abundance.

Destin

Destin has changed in many drastic ways, but in fishing it has not. It offers some of the best offshore fishing in the United States. This Florida port was, at the turn of the century, a quiet little village on the Gulf of Mexico. But, like so many old fishing towns, it has now become a large resort community where visitors from Georgia, Alabama, Mississippi, Louisiana and northern Florida congregate to enjoy the beauty, the snow-white sand, the sun and, of course, the fishing. Where once beautiful beaches were only disturbed by fishermen and beachcombers, now rows of large condominiums line the shores, but Destin has protected much beach area that can still be enjoyed by all. The sea along the jetty and where the Choctawhatchee River empties into the Gulf will remind one of Bahamian waters with the blues, whites and turquoises blending into breathtaking beauty in the form of sandbars and channels. This is where red drum and sea trout abound. Destin is located between Pensacola and Panama City in the Panhandle of Florida, not far from the Alabama line.

With this growth came new, modern sport fishing facilities. The local charter fleet is excellent. There are draft boats for inshore reef fishing, small bay boats and, of course, the large, high-speed fishing machines to run to the billfish grounds 60 to 90 miles offshore. If you are in Destin and need fishing information, a good place to start is at the tackle shop, The Destin Fishing Hole. Anglers traveling to this area will find numerous motels with efficiencies at reasonable prices. The local restaurants specialize in native seafood. All the amenities and Panhandle atmosphere make Destin a delightful place to visit and fish. It may become the blue marlin capital of the United States, with white marlin a close contender. The billfishing requires a long run offshore, but from April through September marlin is the only game in town.

Offshore areas known as "The Elbow" and "The Nipple" are generally alive with fish. There are always weed lines off the Loop Current and birds hovering over schools of bait, while flying fish take to the air in numbers too vast to count. Here one can find blue marlin, often in excess of 500 pounds, white marlin, sailfish, wahoo, big yellowfin tuna, dolphin and blackfin tuna. Artificial lures (konaheads) are most popular today for all species, and they are trolled at high speeds, from 8 to 16 knots. As many if not more 22- to 28-foot center-console boats fish this area as

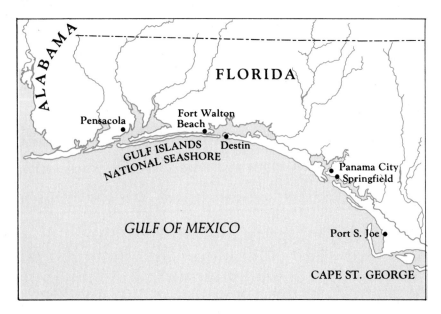

FLORIDA

Pensacola

Fort Walton Beach

Destin

GULF ISLANDS NATIONAL SEASHORE

Panama City
Springfield

GULF OF MEXICO

Port S. Joe

CAPE ST. GEORGE

do 40-foot cruisers, but the Gulf is subject to heavy winds at times, and small boaters should make a careful weather check before making a long run.

Destin also has tremendous inshore fishing with great variety. Starting in late March, cobia begin showing up off those same beautiful white beaches, swimming with rays and turtles. The fish average 20 pounds but reach well over 50 pounds. Cobia offer anglers a great battle on light tackle. They will take live bait or artificials equally well. King mackerel appear during the summer with school fish running between 10 to 15 pounds, but big kings to 50 pounds are common. Late summer and into the fall will provide good red drum action along with trout. Last August we saw a local angler bring in a catch of redfish averaging 14 pounds caught at the jetty by drifting live bait. Amberjack are year-'round residents. Bluefish, pompano and flounder are late summer and fall species. Large grouper and snapper can be found off structures and wrecks throughout the winter months. So, the options and incidental catches on non-marlin days cover the whole panoply of Gulf fishing.

Most visiting anglers headquarter at the Harbor View Inn; telephone (904) 837-6171, which has its own marina. There is an annual Billfish Release Tournament in the latter part of August.

STRIPED MARLIN

Tetrapturus audax

AND
BLACK MARLIN

No other fish will leap so often as striped marlin. Of the 25,000-odd species of fish in the Earth's waters, they are unique in their determination to aerialize. Mako shark will jump higher (when they choose to jump at all) and great barracuda will broad jump 20 to 30 feet of water on occasion, but striped marlin are incomparable in their willingness to leap repetitively, tirelessly, endlessly.

It is sometimes possible to specify why fish leap. Wahoo and king mackerel become loftily airborne when they swim at speed up from deep water and miss their target. Mako, tarpon and great barracuda have all been known to intentionally board a boat seeking retaliation for being hooked. In the throes of the fight-flight syndrome, they chose to fight.

Free-jumping fish are hypothesized as trying to rid themselves of unwanted commensals, such as remoras or the small parasitic isopods called sea lice. That a limbless creature should occasionally try to scratch by impact seems both reasonable and unprovable.

Why do hooked fish jump when they are not attacking the angler? Surely the most common reason for leaping is the negative taxis instinctive to animals under restraint. They leap contrary to the drag of the sunken line, out of the same powerful urge that leads dogs to strain at their leashes and convicts to escape. Indeed, the most common time for a fish to sound is when close aboard with the pull upward. There is also an argument from hydrodynamics. The particular form of leaping called greyhounding has been found to be a more energy-efficient means of propulsion than sustained swimming for marlin-sized creatures when a "cross-over" speed of approximately 10 knots is reached.[1]

---

[1] The experiments of D. Au and D. Weihs reported in *Nature, 284* (5756): 548-550 (April 1980) were with dolphins. The crossover speed increases with body size.

Schooling squid are a favorite food of striped marlin, whose great speed allows them to chase down whatever target of opportunity strikes their fancy. They are a Pacific and Indian ocean fish, esteemed by gourmets.

333

STRIPED MARLIN

But whatever the reason they do it, offshore fishing for many of us would be unacceptable without it. I will not pay for a blue-water charter on a day that promises tuna alone. To be charged an outrageous sum, and to be bored for hours before the thrilling moment, there must be in compensation at least the prospect of something long and glorious flying through the sky while we all cheer.

DISTRIBUTION

Catch records of the Japanese longline fleet make it clear that this fish is the most abundant of the marlins. It is widely distributed in the Pacific Ocean between latitudes 50°N and 50°S, and there are Indian Ocean populations, but none in the Atlantic. Within North American waters, there are two sport fisheries, a modest one of about 40 metric tons per annum off southern California (a historical average of 812 fish per season, but double that has been recorded), and a much larger one in the Sea of Cortez, as its Spanish discoverers dubbed what U.S. maps call the Gulf of California

Two rod lines lead to the outrigger clips and a teaser plows in the wake as this vessel trolls for striped marlin.

(that part of the San Andreas Fault thus far invaded by water; and more will follow). The southern California fish are largely Mexican stock following bait north for the summer. They arrive in July and are gone by November; September is the peak of the run. What they want is warm water, and records show that a few degrees make an extraordinary difference. A sea surface reading in the 66° to 68°F range will be only half as productive as one of 70°. The great 1981 southern California hook-and-line catch was accompanied by widespread 70° water, and, even as far north as Oregon, offshore anglers on the albacore grounds reported 68° readings. In August, a salmon charter boat 2 miles up Oregon's Umpqua River caught a 123½-pound striped marlin, the first time the species had ever been reported north of California's Point Conception, and the first time in fresh water.

Within their usual geographic range they are normally found further offshore than sailfish and closer inshore than blue and black marlin. Why this should be with epipelagic predators capable of migrating thousands of miles is a mystery, but it is both proclaimed by authority and confirmed by experience. I have taken most of my sailfish within sight of the beach, most striped marlin within 5 miles, and endured some tedious long boat rides after blue marlin. It is difficult to avoid the suspicion that major predatory fish distribute themselves to escape undue competition, and to associate with their own kind, their natural broodmates.

The Sea of Cortez fish are there all year-'round in some volume, with seasonal high points. Between LaPaz and Cabo San Lucas I have never failed to find them.

Biologists hypothesize a single Pacific Basin stock of striped marlin, or two stocks: northern and southern. Those we fish in North American waters are slightly smaller than the Ecuadoran striped marlin, markedly less prepossessing than the Chilean giants the old Cabo Blanco mob used to take in the early 1950s as light-tackle relief after battling half-ton-plus black marlin and *much* littler than the New Zealand monsters that crowd the record book. Striped marlin in the eastern North Pacific weigh just about what their antagonists do—100 to 200 pounds soaking wet. They are a splendid game fish. The New Zealand heavyweights top out at more than 400 pounds.

Striped marlin, blue marlin, black marlin, white marlin and sailfish can all exhibit vertical blue stripes. If there is any doubt whether you have a blue marlin or a striped one, look at the

dorsal fin. Striped marlin have a first dorsal as high as the body depth, especially the first five rays, and profusely spotted. Blue marlin have a stubbier dorsal, with few or no spots. I once spent more than an hour on a marlin that crashed the bait, jumped once at a distance and sounded. The very experienced captain and mate and my very experienced fishing partner agreed that it was surely a blue, but, when I finally derricked him to the boat, he proved to be a highly atypical striped. In retrospect we should have killed that fish instead of tagging him, to keep his dour bloodline out of the gene pool. The number of vertical stripes will vary from 14 to 20, and the purplish-blue color of them is glowingly intense. This has been attributed to excitement, as a mating display comparable to the bright plumage of birds and to stimulation by warm water.

North American striped marlin spawn southwest of Cabo San Lucas (the tip of Baja California Sur) in the vicinity of the Socorro and Revillagigedo islands in mid-summer. There may be other sites. Japanese longliners report marlin there run in pairs and a hooked fish will be accompanied by another until it is boated. (Mexico now prohibits this fishery.) The fish broadcasts 10,000,000 to 30,000,000 eggs each (survival to maturity is estimated at less than 10 fish per million, a logical impossibility since the ocean would be stiff with marlin if that many got through). The San Diego blitz of striped marlin in August and September consists of hungry post-spawners.

The force that can direct fish wandering over an

Fly-Fishing for Marlin

If your passion for light tackle extends to the fly rod, you are indebted to Key West ex-captain Lefty Reagan, now retired, and especially to the late Dr. Webster Robinson, who developed something that superficially seems impossible—a practical means of fair fly-fishing for billfish. Dr. Robinson and Captain Reagan were plagued by sailfish robbing them of marlin trolling baits early in the 1960s and decided to keep a rod rigged with a strip bait on a light-wire hook ready to be deployed. When a sailfish entered their marlin array, the strip bait was flipped in front of him and promptly taken, then as he began his run the drag was tightened down and the light hook straightened. A stung sailfish will seldom return. Robinson reasoned that the strip bait could be replaced by a large fly-rod popping bug. In 1962, he made the first billfish fly-fishing catch, taking a Pacific sailfish in Panama. He went on to take the first fly-fishing marlin, a Baja striped fish, aided by his wife on the teaser and Captain Reagan, and eventually totaled five fly-caught striped marlin before his death.

The drill is to troll a hookless teaser, and, when the billfish takes it, pull it immediately out of the fish's mouth. Sometimes this must be done repetitively with a lethargic fish, or merely once if it is obviously enthusiastic and flashing its bioluminescent stripes. Then the hookless teaser bait is yanked out of the water and into the boat and the fly slapped down (after the teaser or angler calls, "Out of gear!").

Dr. Robinson fashioned his poppers

hook up on a No. 7/0 hook to go into the soft tissue at the base of a marlin's bill, and fished a floating fly line and used a Panama bait for a teaser (a sort of thick, meaty, heavily stitched strip bait that will withstand much battering). Any successful innovation is bound to be modified in time, and nowadays my friend Bob Stearns, who has run his fly-fishing take of both Pacific and Atlantic sailfish to fifty, and has lost both striped and blue marlin, uses a hook-down popper on a 4/0 hook with a sinking line, which drops under the fish and avoids tail-wrapping (and casts better in the wind). Stearns has a hook-up ratio of 80 percent, and 100 percent of his fish are stuck in the meaty base of the bill, since that is concave and the long, thin tongue convex. Stearns uses plastic squids for teasers—as Dr. Robinson doubtless would if he were alive today.

Striped marlin on the fly have to date succumbed to Dr. Robinson, Billy Pate, Winston Moore and Harry Kime, all using the original teasing technique, but the renowned and redoubtable Lee Wulff took his 148-pound record fish out of Salinas, Ecuador, by simply motoring out in a skiff to within casting distance of a finning-out marlin—and casting to it!

enormity of ocean to a specific geographical place at a specific time is probably magnetic. The earth's geomagnetic field can provide direction, time and location of local landmarks, and laboratory work in Hawaii has already demonstrated that tropical tuna have enough of a highly magnetic iron oxide in their ethmoid sinuses to respond to magnetic conditioning experiments. The material, magnetite, is also in marlin, dolphin and green sea turtles. Also, the ocean depths are sometimes illuminated by linear flashes of phosphorescence that point toward land. How they are induced is unknown, but all successful species by definition use their milieu well. If the marlin, incidentally, is over 200 pounds it is almost certainly a damsel and she may be accompanied by as many as five males.

Larval striped marlin are sans bill, have huge, toothy maws and large eyes. They are not found below 72°F. At about three quarters of an inch the little monster begins sprouting its rostrum, or bill. At 5 inches it looks like a sailfish, with an enormous dorsal, which it maintains until the fish reaches about 60 pounds, at which time one can say this is definitely a marlin. Sexual maturity is believed to occur at a length of 5 feet, which is believed to be a 3-year-old, but there is a great deal of hypothesis in aging marlin. Their scales do not deposit annual accretions in the tidy fashion of salmonids, and attempts at aging by ear otoliths and the like remain highly speculative. At least 15,000 metric tons of striped marlin are taken annually by Japan, Korea, Taiwan and the United States, largely as a bycatch of tuna fishing, yet biologists know next to nothing about them. It is very difficult to study a large wild animal that inhabits an ocean larger than all the world's land masses combined, has a speed potential estimated in excess of 50 miles per hour, feeds on just about anything it pleases, is subject to predation only from man and, possibly, killer whales and mako sharks, and is unlikely to loll around an aquarium while you take notes.

Black Marlin

Of the istiophorid billfish, the giants are the two species of the **Makaira** *genus:* **nigricans** *or blue marlin and* **indica** *or black marlin, each with a one-ton-plus potential. Both are available in the waters of our study area, but black marlin are limited to el Mar de Cortes. Their density is very low according to the longliners, and their reputation among sport fishing crews is that of loners, despite the pronouncement of science that they are a schooling fish (as contrasted to blue marlin, for instance). Nonetheless, Leon Tack caught a 1,029-pounder that was on the record books for a time while fishing out of the Hotel Bahia Las Palmas south of La Paz, so you don't absolutely* **have** *to fly to Australia to catch a grander.*

The usual black marlin encounter in Baja is that something resembling the pup of a nuclear submarine rises behind the bait on your 30-pound rig, snaps the line instantly and is gone. Black marlin won't fin out as well as striped marlin and broadbill swordfish, so their visitations tend to be brief. In the unlikely event you spot one before your boat crew, immediately yell like a banshee for the swordfish rod which all boats carry. Hooked up to a big black marlin on 130-pound-class line, you are still fishing light tackle. Some day a Baja angler fishing 20- or 30-pound is going to hook a grander that commits suicide. It has already happened in Australian waters.

All you need is one dumb enough to jump itself to exhaustion and fail to sound before the crew can run it down and set the flying **gancho** *in its back.*

The Japanese call this brute **shirokajiki***, or white marlin, because it occasionally crops up as an albino. This is presumed to be the origin of reports by pioneer big game anglers of "silver" marlin.*

Though the high forehead, short, thick rostrum and small dorsal make large specimens unmistakable, smaller blacks can be confused with blue marlin. The classic test is that black marlin pectorals do not fold back against the body. Evidently that huge head-and-shoulder weight needs the constant support of two hydrofoils. Unfortunately this does not hold true of small fish whose pectorals don't become rigid until they have gone morte.

There are demonstrably distinct populations of this fish, but Mead Johnson tagged one off the Australian Great Barrier Reef in September 1972, and it was recaptured in April 1975, off the New Zealand coast, 2,000 miles away.

The largest black marlin caught so far have been about three-quarters of a ton, 15 feet long and 6 feet in circumference! They have come from Peru or Australia, but monsters have been lost in Baja waters . . .

Wherever they occur, striped marlin eat the local delicacies. Saury, sardines, jack mackerel and anchovies are frequent in southern California stomachs. More than thirty-eight species of fish were taken from them in one Mexican study. This must have included squid, because in May, Pacific squid (*Loligo opalescens*[2]) spawns in the Sea of Cortez and the marlin gorge until they resemble large striped sausages with a cocktail pick at one end. Under such conditions, fish watching is often more profitable than fishing, but persistence will generally produce an eater. Whatever they eat it doesn't always rest well on their stomachs. Striped marlin, like other billfish, frequently suffer from gastric ulcers. These have been variously attributed to nematode infestation and even spawning stress(!) but in all likelihood are mechanically induced by the pricklier parts of their prey. A diet that includes whole skipjack and similar fish with formidable dorsal spines must be occasionally lacerating.

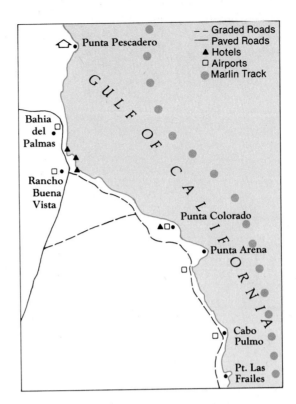

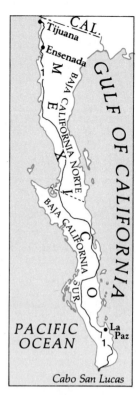

New hotels and expanded existing hotels are almost constantly under construction in Baja's East Cape area to accommodate gringo *striped marlin anglers.*

Baja California Sur, particularly from its capital of La Paz south to Cabo San Lucas, has one of the world's finest concentrations of striped marlin.

The Japanese call black marlin white, blue marlin black and striped marlin red—*makajiki.* In the latter case they are referring to flesh color, which is pink to dark red, probably varying with diet. I have enjoyed it in the form of marlin salad, prepared exactly as one would a tunafish salad, but my appreciation is modest compared with the cash-on-the-line esteem of Japanese gourmets, though this is of recent development.

Tuna, particularly bluefin and southern bluefin, are cherished by Japanese for *sashimi* and *sushi* and historically brought highest prices on the Tokyo Fish Market, but in 1954 the Bikini Atoll hydrogen bomb test by the United States caused fallout contamination of tuna that made them less acceptable to Japanese housewives. Under the name of *kajiki-maguro* or "billfish tuna" the marlins, sailfish and swordfish gained consumer ascendency, ironically, because of course they were contaminated, too. Striped marlin acquired a market position as the best of the billfish tuna, and consumption of them now is almost wholly as *sashimi*—like those late-season pen-fattened bluefins the Canadians sell to Japanese buyers for enviable prices. To my palate the flavor of cooked striped marlin is superior to and more delicate than albacore, and much better than yellowfin tuna. It must make marvelous *sashimi* if it truly

At the mouth of the Gulf of California, marlin trolling ranges are often within sight of land.

[2]Not a fish, of course, but a cephalopod of the phylum Mollusca.

337

STRIPED MARLIN

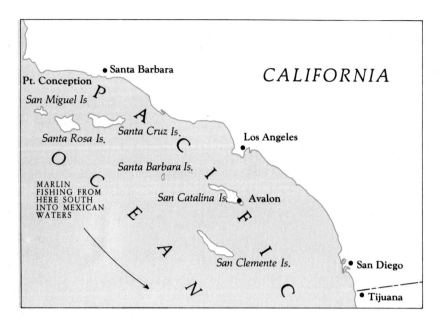

Pt. Conception
San Miguel Is
• Santa Barbara
CALIFORNIA

Santa Rosa Is.
Santa Cruz Is.
Los Angeles •

Santa Barbara Is.

MARLIN
FISHING FROM
HERE SOUTH
INTO MEXICAN
WATERS

San Catalina Is. • Avalon

San Clemente Is.
• San Diego

• Tijuana

Southern California fishing for striped marlin peaks in September. The first sport-caught marlin was taken off Catalina Island.

approaches the flavor and texture of bluefin tuna, which I try to save until last, as a special treat, when eating *sashimi*, but I seldom have the willpower to hold out.

Thousands of these fish have been caught, photographed on the dock and carted off to rot because American culinary traditions exclude them. Marlin were included in the swordfish commercial catch during the period 1925 to 1937. Their sale is now prohibited in the United States, a futile conservation gesture in view of the enormous current stocks of billfish—despite severe longline pressure—and discriminatory against swordfish, too.

At the end of the peninsula bordering Tokyo Bay there is a cave where archaeological excavations have produced spears and bones from striped marlin (and other billfish) that have been dated to the Jomon Era, 3,000 to 4,000 years BP.[3] Whether this was a harpoon, net or hook-and-line fishery is unknown. In addition to their passion for fish, the Japanese tend to be catholic about techniques. However, it is worth noting that a harpoon fishery exists today for swordfish and striped marlin in this vicinity (Izu Island), which may well be of prehistoric origin. The fish are iced and delivered fresh to market rather than frozen, as has been the case since about 1967 with the world-ranging fleet of longline tuna-*maru* vessels.

The earliest rod-and-reel catch of striped marlin would seem to have been that of Edward T. Llewellyn in 1903, while fishing Catalina waters. That makes the fish second to bluefin tuna at the dawn of big game fishing: Dr. Charles F. Holder, founder of the Catalina Tuna Club, took the first

tuna on sporting tackle in 1898. It was 1913 before W. C. Boschen managed to hang onto the first swordfish. There were giants on the water in those days—or perhaps madmen. To fight tuna and billfish with direct-drive reel handles that spun like work in a runaway lathe, your only drag a smoking leather thumb stall, is mind boggling. The Catalina Tuna Club keeps meticulous records and, in the first half century after Llewellyn's fish, a total of 4,618 striped marlin had succumbed to club members. Thanks in part to thorough records, this marginal fishery is now so rationally exploited that the catch rate per annum approaches 500 fish most summers—and that is basically a three-month season that invariably peaks in September.

But even if marlin fishing began in the Catalina Channel, that fishery is peripheral to the outstanding sport to be had virtually year-'round at the southern end of Baja California Sur. The catch records from Baja escalate on an annual basis as more hotels are built to accommodate more fishermen, and the charter fleets expand. Catch per unit of effort slid for a while under heavy longline pressure, but Baja is now off limits to longliners. The National Marine Fisheries Service annual Pacific billfish angler survey for 1978/1979/1980 indicates Baja striped marlin catches of 1,212/1,399/2,432. Many unreported fish are caught, of course, and nowadays most of them are released. If this fishery has a flaw, it is popularity. Sometimes it seems as if every saltwater fisherman west of the Mississippi wants to spend Easter, Christmas and one of the spring months fishing Baja.

In 1969, I began the practice of carrying fresh-from-Hawaii konahead lures with me on blue-water charters. (To say that was premature understates the case.) From Baja to Cozumel to St. Thomas I was told in vociferous intonations that those crimes against nature were never again to be seen aboard this vessel, running fast enough to bring out their action would attract only tuna, billfish need to smell real meat, etc. In defense of these reactionary captains, I must admit doing it their way often put fish in the boat. In fact, I have come to the conclusion a marlin not already gorged will eat whatever you put in front of it on the grounds that, even if the fish doesn't recognize it, it is probably edible. Nowadays the artificial lure revolution is almost won, but bait perversely

---

[3]Not even close for an antiquity record. A coastal Greek cave excavation yielded steer-sized tuna bones dated to the Mesolithic, 7,000 to 10,000 BP. Our troglodyte ancestors must have been formidable boat builders to fashion sea-going vessels with stone tools.

maintains its popularity. Plenty of southern California boats will pull a quintet of artificials past a marlin and, if it refuses, *cast* a live bait to the fish. This practice is catching on in Baja, too.

The eclectic captains of Baja will probably never desert their beloved San Diego frozen flyingfish. The fact that these are foreign to the Sea of Cortez is irrelevant: The marlin eat them. But Baja skippers also carry an assortment of lures now, and fast trolling (10 to 15 knots) is practiced. Your basic Mexican commercial marlin charterman thinks he is ill-equipped without flyingfish, lures and some live-in-the-baitwell grunts, mullet, sierra or the like. Belt *and* braces is

---

Roosterfish

Every angler should have a bête noire, a fish to temper the arrogance bred by his successes. I have failed to take roosterfish at La Paz in the Sea of Cortez, which has showered record catches over others, at Punta Pescadero, at Punta Colorada, at Punta Arena—which is customarily the actual fishing spot for those world records listed as caught at Buena Vista—at Cabo San Lucas and at Isla Coiba in the Republic of Panama. I have helped roosterfishing neophytes boat their fish and, most insufferable of all, have been required to listen to their advice. In 1974, I had a world-record roosterfish following my streamer fly at Punta Pescadero in such shallow water it was like bonefishing, but before he could swallow it, a brown pelican crashed on top of him in one of their typical, falling-out-of-the-sky, clumsy, stupid dives. The rooster certainly disappeared like a bonefish. The pelican peered about in gawky bewilderment, wondering what happened to the little fish he had tried to steal from

pez gallo. What happened to it was that I had it in the air, futilely attempting to present it again. The wake of that rooster's departing dorsal left a trail of bubbles. Later that day I lost the all-tackle world record . . .

The name derives from that dorsal, of course. Gringos *assume it is supposed to be reminiscent of a comb, but since the fish inhabits a Spanish-speaking coast (Baja to Peru) it was more likely named for the plume-like tails of fighting cocks. The first dorsal of eight spines has seven elongated, the longest about half of body length. This fish is a jack in every respect except that it is not, so instead of Carangidae it gets a family and genus as well as a species all to itself—* Nematistius pectoralis *of the* Nematistidae. *One cannot complain because roosterfish jump beautifully— and jacks never.*

Roosterfish have a warm water niche remarkably similar to striped bass in northern climes. They roam beaches, especially those with dark green weed and kelp beds, and haunt rockpiles. Since there is no dentition, you can interest big roosters in small bait and lures. Big with this species means larger than 100 pounds, though not much larger. Spoons or biggish swimming plugs are probably best among artificials, but they will take popping plugs, jigs and streamer flies. Live bait makes hookups come much more easily. That makes bait popular with light-tackle anglers who need a lot of hookups to compensate for their many breakoffs.

Tagged roosterfish indicate populations are localized. They seldom move more than a few hundred miles at most. They must do some wandering because a sighting in the Coronado Islands was made years ago, which is practically San Diego, and recently one was actually caught north of Ensenada. These would be individuals or loose groups[4] following a warm isotherm, because the Baja roosterfishing season peaks from June through September. This is definitely a warm water fish.

Every year since 1967 the Los Angeles

Billfish Club has sponsored an International Roosterfish Tournament, fishing out of the Hotel Punta Colorado south of La Paz. Contestants are limited to a total of 30 anglers and there is a long waiting list. In the fashion of southern California fishermen, they vie with each other in such irrelevancies as light tackle and even barbless hooks. It is likely only a

question of time before that waiting list begins another tournament. The use of live bait for easy hookups and light tackle for long fish fights makes roosterfish a fine tournament quarry. Socializing is much a part of the traditional saltwater tournament scene, and when evening comes and you have glass in hand, it is also necessary to have something to talk about. And, after all, everyone can catch roosterfish in Baja in summer—except me.

[4]Juveniles school closely and are prized trophies. In southern California saltwater angling circles, a baby roosterfish mount sitting on one's desk or cocktail table is ultimate chic. Frederick H. Berry, reporting in *McClane's New Standard Fishing Encyclopedia* (1974), says the smallest specimen known was three-eighths of an inch. The giants exceed 5 feet.

Hotel Punta Pescadero
□ **Punta Pescadero**

Bahia de Palmas

SEA OF CORTEZ

▲ Hotel Palmas de Cortez
□ ▲ Rancho Buena Vista
□ ▲ Spa Buena Vista

La Rivera
Punta Colorada □ ▲
Punta Arena
El Rincon □

BAJA CALIFORNIA

Cabo Pulmo □

Punta Las Fraíles

□ AIRPORTS
▲ RESORT HOTELS
■ ROOSTERFISH HOTSPOTS

STRIPED MARLIN

Billfish Tournament

Mexico, in recent years, has been staging about 360 fishing tournaments per annum, including some of the world's most prestigious. The Classic Billfish Tournament at Cabo San Lucas is a light-tackle event with rules that make it not for the neophyte. The International Light Tackle Tournament, a wandering event, is often staged at Cabo. The Charity Tournament at Hotel Cabo San Lucas is a highly social undertaking whose proceeds support local orphans. All three of the above are likely to bring out the Hollywood fishermen. In times past, both Bing Crosby and John Wayne were Baja habitués. They have many successors. For the past few years, David Halliburton, owner of the top-ranked Hotel Twin Dolphin at Cabo, has been staging the Baja "Release" Deep Sea Fishing Tournament and donating the proceeds to the National Coalition for Marine Conservation. Typical of the Baja-Southern California stress on light tackle, the "Release" is limited to 12- and 20-pound-class line. Points are earned on the species of fish hooked, line strength, length of the fight, tagging and world record potential. Then the line is cut. Billfishing tournaments everywhere are changing rapidly. Big jackpots and enormous calcuttas have stimulated the arrival of boat teams drilled like SWAT teams, but the age of blacktie victory dinners and a few pieces of silverware to stand on an étagère shelf is still with us.

their attitude, and I am no longer willing to gainsay men who process marlin in the sheer volume they do from La Paz south to the Cape. The Spanish-speaking, walnut-stained, Mongol-American captains and mates of the five big Baja charter boat fleets are the most experienced marlin fishermen alive. Innovators they are not, but they will produce fish as long as you are capable of turning the little handle on the pulley that makes the string wind in.

The trend in lures is toward a resilient but firm plastic capable of high-speed trolling and able to resist barracuda, wahoo and dolphin bites. My old hard konaheads are virtually museum pieces, as is the intervening generation of soft vinyl squids and skirts that shredded easily when bitten. The theory of soft-headed lures is that they have a squid-baitfish texture that lead marlin to hold them long enough for striking, even for dropping back to let them swallow as we do when trolling bait.

Some highly successful marlin bums are of the opinion that color matters. A few years ago a rage for hot pink came out of Hawaii and swept the world. I know one experienced billfisherman whose passion for fluorescent green squid verges on the unnatural. Unfortunately, investigations by the Japanese Society of Scientific Fisheries and the Woods Hole Institute of Marine Biology disagree. Experimenting with anesthetized fish, they implanted microelectrodes on their optic nerves and exposed the eyes to the spectrum, one color at a time. They got no response to red, green or yellow, but a positive response to blue. Dissection confirmed the finding: *Everything* looks blue-gray to striped marlin, blue marlin, black marlin, yellowfin tuna, bigeye tuna, skipjack tuna, dolphin and wahoo. Doubtless that list will be extended. One skipper with a remarkable string of big game tournament victories allows his anglers to fish any color they please. He claims he changes colors only when he is bored.

There remain two legitimate bases for colorful marlin lures. If one color is consistently attacked, then that is the shade of blue-gray they want at the time even if it is hot pink to you. The other is angler convenience: A lure or bait you can clearly see is necessary to the incessant scanning for weed, for a foul-hooked line and, above all, for a bill in the baits. That is why you are out there.

Proper tackle for striped marlin fishing is my

business for me and yours for you. There is no question that light tackle demands superior skills. There are 200-poundish-IGFA-record striped marlin taken on 8-pound-class line. These are technical athletic accomplishments of Olympic virtuosity. My taste is for brief, extremely violent fish fights, and I find 50-pound-class tackle used to the limit of my strength (as aided by a shoulder harness) is just right for fish of my own size (160 pounds). If the running sea permits standing and using a rod belt, so much the better. As I age, I will probably prefer lighter tackle. The *violence* of a marlin overpowered by tackle that forces it to fight close to the boat is one of the greatest excitements angling offers. A distant marlin jumping on the far horizon thrills me not, and the prospect of putting all that line back on the reel is dismaying. There is much tedium inevitable in offshore fishing; I prefer tackle that does not contribute to it.

At dinner one night under the stars, a dinner in the courtyard of the Hotel Los Arcos in La Paz, the late Ray Cannon, author of the bestselling *Sea of Cortez*, discoursed on myriad subjects, including his theory of rhythm pumping. Ray was then in his eighties. Ordinary pumping is to pull the rod upright, then reel down to spool the line gained. Short pumping is to pull the rod up just a few inches, perhaps only an inch, then reel down to spool the line. Rhythm pumping is a short pump, and another, and another until the rod is upright. *Then* you reel down. The idea is not to spool line, but to interrupt the fish's breathing sequence. If you continually pull his mouth open, you are simultaneously closing his gill covers, since they work in a toggle sequence. You have to find the right rhythm, and, according to Ray, the fish will become violent if you find it and are suffocating it.

The next day I gave an amateurish performance with a small marlin for half an hour, and just when double line was lifting off the water and inching toward the rod tip, the fish sounded like a giant tuna, like a ton of bricks. Under a blazing midday sun I long pumped, short pumped and rhythm pumped that infernal animal back to the surface from many hundreds of yards deep. Nothing I could do would gain more than a few inches at a time. They poured buckets of ocean over me. Finally I peered over the transom and through incredibly clear sea water saw a tiny marlin far below. He was bill-wrapped, nothing could interfere with his breathing cycle, and he was holding himself 90 degrees to the line of pull, exactly as a bluegill sunfish does when a child reels it in. Why a member of a hyperactive species

should suddenly succumb to passive resistance I haven't the foggiest, but the mate soon had wire in hand and I collapsed into a fighting chair.

"You wan' heem, senor?" he asked.

"No, go ahead and tag him."

Try to do that, so we may learn more about this aquatic unicorn, which is so important as a food fish and as a sport fish, but of whom we know shamefully little. I still don't have a picture on the wall of me standing beside a dead striped marlin, and I don't think the quality of my life suffers at all from that lacuna.

SAILFISH

Istiophorus platypterus

AND
DOLPHIN

They say that we have no seasons in Florida—no time when forests color or snow falls or the Pump Room puts shad roe on its menu or New Yorkers dash to the Hamptons. I admit that our changing times must be abstractions in the eyes of an unsalted urbanite, yet almost every month brings a subtle and beautiful transition when you live on the edge of the ocean, as I do. That first northeaster in November will deliver silvery pompano and sennet in the bays and after the wind blows around the card to our prevailing southwesterly, then swings into the northwest quadrant as a cold front forms, legions of bluefish and Spanish mackerel parade south along the Florida Peninsula. Just before Christmas, a series of cold spells will form a moving barrier in the ocean, a well-defined zone of 68° to 70°F water, classically known to oceanographers as the 20° isotherm. Schooled, always at the margin of this isotherm, will be that most peculiar fish with a sail on its back, an extravagance of fin that according to fossil records evolved in the Upper Eocene age some 10,000,000 years ago. When the winds are brisk you can, from a rolling deck over the 50-fathom line, see sailfish coasting on the downwind face of the waves with the upper lobe of their tails in the air as though dancing in some stylized quadrille. This ancient ritual coincides with the flight of the snowbirds—the millions of tourists who annually migrate to Florida—of which uncountable thousands become "instant" big game fishermen. Among billfish, which includes the swordfish, marlin and spearfish, the sailfish is an anomaly as it is of a size and disposition to pleasure the most inexperienced angler, while testing the mettle of experts who seek their quarry with incredibly light tackle.

When West Indies explorer Charles de Rochefort wrote his *Histoire naturelle et morale des îles Antilles de l'Amérique* (1658) he named the sailfish "sea woodcock" or *bécasse de mer* in

In an underwater ballet, sailfish erect their dorsal fins, creating a fence as they "ball the bait." Circling a school of pilchards until they become a dense balloon-like mass, the sails attack their prey.

343

SAILFISH

deference to its long bill. Evidently, de Rochefort was a gourmet sailor. Subsequent authors called it needlefish, flying-needle, spike-fish, beaked-fish and a host of other pointed names until science adopted the generic *Istiophorous* meaning sail-bearer, which is its most unique feature. The enormous dorsal fin of the sailfish, particularly when manufactured of fiberglass by a generous taxidermist, creates the impression of great size; however, the average weight of the Atlantic form is only 30 to 60 pounds, while those in the Pacific run 80 to 110 pounds. Actually, the body of any istiophorpid is very slender over a 6- to 10-foot length, and the height of the dorsal is twice that of the body depth. The sail, which is normally retracted in a groove along the midline of its back when swimming at speed, can be purposely erected creating a huge silhouette underwater. When a group of sailfish are feeding on schools of sardines or pilchards, their upright dorsals literally form a fence as they circle the frantic bait concentrically, herding them into a dense ball until one sailfish darts in and attacks the now compacted mass. This circling, popularly known as "balling the bait," is repeated again and again until that school is decimated; then the pod of sailfish hunts another hapless school. When sailfish are feeding in this fashion, just below or at the surface, experienced skippers swing their bow into the wind and back down on the circling fish. One can literally throw a live bait to them. This results in some of the wildest action imaginable when our charter boat fleet is in full force and a hungry percentage of the estimated population of 800,000 sailfish on any favorable winter day along Florida's Gold Coast is balling the bait. Boats return to dock with their outriggers flying 30 to 40 release pennants. However, the times of plenty are not too frequent and, in my experience, during recent mild weather winters raising half a dozen sailfish (often augmented by dolphin, wahoo and king mackerel) is a very good day indeed. Florida sailfishing is at its best when the weather is at its worst.

In the western Atlantic, sailfish undertake regular seasonal movements. There appears to be a center of abundance off the coast of Florida where some fish remain the year-'round. But in the spring, large numbers of them tend to move northward from this area, possibly following the northward movement of their food as the water warms. But as soon as the cold north winds start to blow in the fall, the sailfish school up and swim southward again. The Rosenstiel School of Marine and Atmospheric Sciences (formerly Institute of Marine Science and Marine Laboratory) of the

An Atlantic sailfish shatters the bait and the sea off Palm Beach, Florida. It is generally agreed that the sail does not have the stamina of the marlins but its aerial displays are no less exciting. Often two fish are hooked simultaneously, a stirring sight even to veteran anglers.

University of Miami marked and released 1,259 sailfish between 1950 and 1958 and nine tags were returned. Members of the Port Aransas (Texas) Rod and Reel Club marked and released 515 sailfish between 1954 and 1962 and obtained three returns. The Cooperative Game Fish Tagging Program of the Woods Hole Oceanographic Institution has marked and released 12,525 sailfish between 1954 and May 1972, with 97 tags being returned.

The majority of the returns showed limited movements; most were between localities along the southeast coast of Florida and the Florida Keys. The longer migrations did not follow a distinct pattern, but many of them showed a tendency toward movements between tropical waters (northeast coast of South America, the Lesser Antilles and the Straits of Florida) in the cold season and temperate waters (the Gulf of Mexico and the United States coast between Jacksonville, Florida, and Cape Hatteras, North Carolina) in the warm season.

Sailfish Tackle and Procedure

Although western Atlantic charter boats will routinely supply 30-pound-test tackle for the inexperienced angler, the popular gear among old salts is 20-pound-test Dacron or monofilament line with a regulation 5½-foot S-glass or graphite rod (total length including the butt). Many experts fish as light as 8 pound-test, and super-stars like Stephen Sloan and Nicolas Deren knock off records with cobweb lines. Sloan boated a 58-pound, 12-ounce Atlantic sailfish at Cozumel, Mexico, in 1982, while Deren shipped a Pacific sailfish of 76 pounds at Pinas Bay, Panama, that same year—both on 2-pound-test. The popular reel size is 2/0 for the 20-pound outfit. Leaders are usually 2 feet of 6- or 8-weight wire, plus 12 feet of 60- to 80-pound-test monofilament with No. 4/0 to 6/0 hooks. Pacific sailfish are generally fished with heavier tackle, either 30- or 50-pound-test

with the popular reel size at 4/0. The leaders are usually 2 feet of 8- or 9-weight wire with 12 feet of 80- to 90-pound test monofilament. The popular Penn International series of reels uses a numerical system for designating sizes instead of the "0" (which means ocean reel) so the Internationals run by pound test such as Penn International #20, #30, #50, #80.

As in most big game fishing, the standard procedure is to troll four baits. Two lines are clipped to the outriggers on each side of the craft and these are fished farther astern than the flat lines so the baits swim clear of the boat's wake. The two flat lines are fished over the transom and these baits skip or swim in the wake. Some anglers use outrigger pins tied to the stern cleats so they can keep the reels on the flat lines in free spool, thereby achieving the same "drop back" effect when a fish strikes as they do with outriggers. The rods are generally left in the rod holders until a fish is sighted or a strike occurs. It is always prudent to assign one or two rods to each angler before the

SAILFISH

fishing begins. When the action does take place you will know which rod to grab, otherwise a double hookup will be as confusing as a fire drill on a Chinese riverboat. There are no viable rules on how far the baits should be trolled astern; it depends on wind, the height of the sea and the speed of the boat. A good skipper will vary the distance until the baits are swimming properly. Flat lines are usually fished from 40 to 75 feet astern and the outrigger lines from 75 to 125 feet astern. Typically, one flat line may be fished at 45 feet while the other is 60 feet out; one out-rigger line may be fished at 90 feet and the other 120 feet. This provides a good spread of water coverage.

Most experienced sailfishermen fight their fish from a standing position in the cockpit. They use a rod belt with a small gimbal mounted on it or use only a leather fighting belt with a round receiver for the butt. Actually, standing up is the most efficient way to battle a game fish of the size of a sailfish. An angler has greater mobility and control over the rod. However, fighting chairs are standard equipment on all charter boats and a great asset to the beginner. Fighting chairs have gimbals mounted in the forward edge of the seat in the center. A pin running through the gimbal fits inside a slot in the butt of a trolling rod. An angler sitting in the swivel chair with the butt resting in the gimbal finds that he can move the rod tip up and down and sideways with ease. The pin in the slot of the butt also prevents the reel from moving from side to side.

Fly-Fishing for Sailfish

By the mid 1970s, less than a dozen anglers had taken Atlantic or Pacific sailfish on fly tackle, yet in less than ten years those numbers have grown into several hundred or more. Moderately priced fishing camps with boats and guides suitable for this activity, such as Club Pacifico or Tropic Star in Panama, and Bahia Pez Vela in Costa Rica, have brought the potential for this form of fishing out of the millionaire sportsman class to within reach of many less affluent anglers.

More and more anglers who have caught many sails on more conventional tackle are turning to fly-fishing for them because they feel it is the most exciting way of catching these grand game fish. This is perhaps more understandable when the techniques involved are considered.

The fish is "located" via standard trolling techniques, except that in this case there are no hooks in the baits. Once the sail attacks the hookless bait/teaser, someone on board other than the angler (i.e., the mate) slowly reels that bait closer to the boat, allowing the excited fish to catch and grab it now and then. The procedure is much like teasing a cat with a ball of yarn. Once the fish is within comfortable casting range, the boat is taken out of gear and the teaser simultaneously yanked from the water. The angler casts a large streamer or popper to the sail, and if everything goes as planned, the fly is immediately taken.

The average Pacific sailfish is close to 100 pounds. The average Atlantic is about half that weight. Both are strong fighters when hooked on fly-tackle. Anglers usually choose rods designed for 11- to 13-weight lines, such as those typically used for big tarpon. Any reel used should have a smooth drag and the capacity for at least 200 yards of 30-pound Dacron backing. Many anglers have now started using some of the superbig fly reels, such as the SeaMaster Mark III Wide or Mark IV,

The so-called Sailfish Sector on Florida's Gold Coast extends from Stuart to Miami. Although there are fluctuations in catch rate on a daily basis at various locations, with the fish moving southward during northerly winds and north when the wind is southerly during the peak winter season, there has been no decline in angling success. Most productive is that stretch of Gulf Stream from Jupiter to Stuart in the month of January, when the prestigious Gold Cup and Master's Tournaments take place.

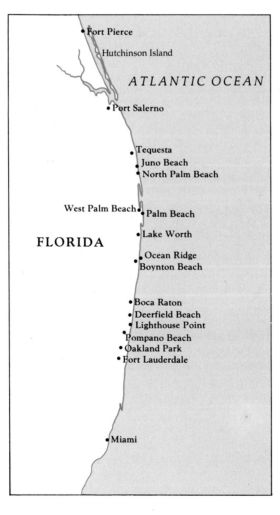

Fort Pierce
Hutchinson Island

ATLANTIC OCEAN

Port Salerno

Tequesta
Juno Beach
North Palm Beach

West Palm Beach
Palm Beach

Lake Worth

FLORIDA

Ocean Ridge
Boynton Beach

Boca Raton
Deerfield Beach
Lighthouse Point
Pompano Beach
Oakland Park
Fort Lauderdale

Miami

or the No. 4 Fin Nor. These reels are especially helpful for the larger Pacific sails because they will hold 350 to 500 yards of backing.

Floating lines can be used for this fishing; however, they tend to get wrapped up in the fish's large tail fins much more readily than sinking lines. Also, sinking lines will get the streamer down below the surface a lot faster, which makes the fly more quickly visible to the fish. A good compromise line that works well with both popper and streamer is the slow sinker, such as the Scientific Anglers Wet Cel II. It doesn't sink fast enough to pull the popper under the surface, and in fact seems to improve hookup potential because it helps "anchor" the popper in the surface film well enough that the wave created by the striking fish cannot as easily push it away.

The most effective fly patterns for either sailfish aren't complicated, but they must be large enough to be easily seen. Five to 6 inches long are ideal for Atlantic sails, and 6 to 8 inches for the Pacific fish. They should be very full, not at all sparse. These fish are accustomed to eating large baitfish, and if the fly is too small it might be simply overlooked.

There are a number of materials that work well on sailfish flies, including long saddle hackle feathers and bucktail. More recently the most popular material has been an artificial bucktail called Fishair because it is available in lengths up to 12 or more inches. The 70 denier hair is best.

Colors that have proven particularly effective as of this writing are all-white, white with a blue and/or green back, all-yellow, yellow with a green back, and chartreuse with a dark green back. Very likely, color isn't nearly as important as size.

Although sailfish streamers have been tied on hooks as large as No. 7/0 or 8/0, and even these have had their gaps enlarged with the idea that the hook would go around the sail's lower jawbone if this were done, more experienced anglers have found that a short shank No. 3/0 or 4/0, such as the Eagle Claw 254 SS, is all that is needed. Those smaller sizes are a lot easier to cast, and become even more effective if their gaps are opened up very slightly.

The leader should be constructed in the same manner as it is for big tarpon. Twelve inches of 80- to 100-pound-test monofilament is best, followed by at least 15 inches of class tippet if you want to conform to IGFA regulations. A leader butt is not only unnecessary, it makes casting the big streamer more difficult. Most anglers experienced in this type of fishing make a small loop in the end of the fly line and a loop large enough to pass

Although Pacific and Atlantic sailfish are the same species, the former attains a larger size. Fish of almost 200 pounds (they average about half this size) have been taken at Baja California and La Paz, Mexico. Marlin are the most sought billfish in the Sea of Cortez, but the sail makes a spectacular trophy.

through on the butt end of the class tippet (i.e., using a surgeon's knot, make a loop in the double line formed by the Bimini twist). This facilitates a quick change of leaders and flies.

It is particularly important not to strike the fish too quickly when it takes the fly. Give it time enough to completely close its mouth; then swing the rod sideways until the line is as tight as the tippet will tolerate. Hold steady pressure and wait for the sail to react. Once the billfish is hooked, try to avoid the temptation to watch those first few spectacular jumps and concentrate on clearing any loose fly line until you are safely on the reel. You will have plenty of time to watch it jump throughout the fight, which just might turn out to be a bit longer and tougher than you expected.

Cozumel

To the veteran Florida billfisherman, Cozumel, Mexico, is the place to relive the good old times when catches of twenty sailfish a day were not uncommon. The quality of the angling can best be measured by the number of strikes rather than the number of fish caught; fifty strikes a day is not unusual here.

The first-time visitor will find Cozumel's reputation for sailfishing well justified. Cozumel is a topographically unattractive low island covered by thick scrub. The town of San Miguel, as well as its many hotels, are located on the west shore of the island. There are two marinas, one at the Hotel El Presidente, which is south of town; the

SAILFISH

Gulf of Mexico

Merida

YUCATAN

Isla Mujeres
Puerto Juarez

Cozumel
Isla Cozumel

Boca Paila

Felipe
B. de la Ascencion

Campeche

QUINTANA
ROO

CAMPECHE

B. del Espirito
Santo

CARIBBEAN SEA

The prime sailfish grounds in Mexico extend from Cozumel to Cancun and Isla Mujeres. In the peak period (April into June), the catch rate is extremely high, especially at Cancun and Isla Mujeres, often reaching 20 to 26 sailfish per boat trip. Cozumel boats favor the sector from Puerto Morelos to Tulum. White and blue marlin, swordfish and bluefin tuna occur in this same area.

other, Club Nautico, is north of town and is the one favored by the American boats. San Miguel offers a variety of shops, markets and some good restaurants. There is also a ferry to the mainland docking here. Several airlines provide service to the island both from the United States and Mexico. Around town, taxis are plentiful but expensive. Cozumel's excellent accommodations are almost totally geared to scuba diving as the area is an underwater paradise. Even at the height of the spring billfish season, divers outnumber fishermen by a hundred to one. Located as it is along the westerly edge of the Yucatán Channel,

Cozumel is far enough offshore so that the vagaries of continental weather have no influence on the clear visibility of the warm Caribbean waters flowing over the magnificent reefs that surround the island.

By default, Cozumel holds title to outstanding billfishing that rightly belongs to the Yucatán since there are no other marinas or acceptable shore accommodations south of the new resort of Cancun, which is 60 miles farther north. The Cozumel boats troll the area from Porto Marelos south to Tulam, a distance of about 45 miles. This fishing is often within a couple of hundred yards of the beach, rarely more than half a mile offshore. The peak sailfishing at Cozumel occurs in April, May and June. It is also the season for white marlin, blue marlin, broadbill swordfish and even giant bluefin tuna, but on 20-pound-test there is little chance of boating the latter. In 1982, an angler caught all four of the billfish species in one day for a super grand slam. This is probably the only place in the western Atlantic where this can be accomplished.

Sailfish and white marlin here often appear intermingled as they are in Venezuela in September and October. Many anglers believe it is the same group of fish. The sailfish average good size for Atlantic populations—fish of over 50 pounds are quite common. Yet, anglers who have

The survival rate among released sailfish is excellent if the fish is hooked and played quickly (within 20 minutes) and the leader cut as close to the hook as possible. Sailfish were long believed to have a brief life span, but tagging and releasing has demonstrated that some sailfish live to ten years.

visited both places find Cozumel sailfish more challenging, more aggressive at the bait, difficult to hook—frustrating better describes this basic fishing effort but then this only heightens the satisfaction of coming tight on the fish. Even the most experienced angler will find a Cozumel sailfish a real challenge on 8- or 10-pound-test line. The strength, stamina and acrobatic abilities of these fish are always impressive. Few are landed without some assistance from the boat and a split double with fish running in opposite directions demands expert maneuvering by the man at the wheel.

As in most ports, the fishing at Cozumel is influenced by the weather. The angler who is fortunate enough to have the wind fresh out of the northeast blowing against the current will see action comparable to the Palm Beach and Stuart areas of Florida during our winter northwesters. The sailfish appear in schools coming to the flatline and outrigger baits in "cover ups" and it's the fortunate angler who can boat one when four hit simultaneously. The preferred bait among Cozumel skippers is the easy-to-rig and durable ballyhoo, which can be taken by a variety of species. At the end of a day the fishbox will often contain dolphin, wahoo, king mackerel, cero mackerel, bonito, blackfin tuna, an occasional juvenile bluefin tuna, large snappers (mainly yellowtail and mutton) and some grouper if the baits settle deep on the turn. The Mexicans utilize any species landed including the billfish; for the boat crew it can be something to barter for some dockside service.

Another Cozumel dividend is night sword-fishing. The angler will see enough broadbill during the day to assure himself he is in the right place to give it a try, as conditions here are ideal (drifting in a very tight current, on the west side of the island a mile or two offshore, in calm water with no stray ships to worry about). Indeed, if you see another boat it is probably another sword-fisherman. Broadbill as large as 500 pounds have been taken here, and the catch rate is quite good.

For the vacationing angler who is reluctant to leave the hotel before dawn, Cozumel is the place to be. There is ample time for a late breakfast, checking tackle or even a little shopping. The time to be at dockside is 10:00 A.M.; seldom are baits in the water before 11:00 and it will still be a long day, since it is usually dark when the skipper returns to the marina. Mornings are invariably calm and the fishing really starts with the midday breeze. It gets better as the afternoon wears on with the best of it at sundown.

An owner who has a boat capable of making the 455-mile run from Key West to Cozumel without a fuel stop will find it well worthwhile. For the angler who isn't an owner, there are Mexican charter boats available at the Club Nautico Marina which are well crewed and equipped, but he should take his tackle with him since what is on board is always on the heavy side.

The Golden Dividend

Wherever sailfish are caught in the Atlantic or Pacific oceans, the dolphin is not far behind. Indeed, it comes as a golden dividend. Imagine a fish cross-sectioned like a cleaver that swims so swiftly under aerodonetic flyingfish that when they terminate their sparkling long *grand jeté* the dolphin is there to reward them with a chomp, a chew and a pharyngeal spasm. The density of water exceeds air by a factor of more than 800, but from a tuna tower, I have watched a school of flyingfish become an escadrille, while underwater a bar of blue-freckled gold lightning effortlessly paced the covey as if impatient for a foregone conclusion. One July day in 1969, in the Sea of Cortez, we were running out to the marlin grounds near Isla del Espiritu Santo north of La Paz at what the captain said was 17 knots, and I judged from the wake was closer to 12, when a big bull dolphin began greyhounding up our port quarter from a distance of 200 yards. We had a pair of Jap feathers on the troll and I reached for one rod to reel it in while watching its high forehead and golden body broach and descend with startlingly sudden magnifications. I managed to get out of the fighting chair and lay one hand on the rod when the fish had both feathers in its mouth and was jumping, color flushes racing down its flanks, head tossing like a tarpon obviously outraged to discover the pair of little fish it had spotted in our foaming wake from 200 yards away were fakes, mere metal and feathers. The fish died in the fishbox, thundering its rage with tail beats that made the mate bounce as he sat on the lid to hold it down. That night around the pool we ate fish fingers dipped in fiery sauces and soothing guacamole, washed down with tequila.

Most high-speed fish are fusiform, shaped like a torpedo (to put the relationship precisely backward), but dolphin have taken another road down the aeons from the silurian. Their form allows great speed but also maneuverability, which is essential to their survival.

The habitat for juveniles is weedy jungles of a brown marine algae belonging to the genus

SAILFISH

Sargassum, ubiquitous in warm oceans. Also known as gulfweed, it is the habitat of many unique fauna evolved solely for life within it—a maze of green and brown plants buoyed up by nodules that are air sacs, spotted with white incrustations of small marine creatures. Here is found the sargassumfish (*Histrio histrio*), which resembled a plant with fins, seahorses (*Hippocampus* spp.) and filefish. Here, in a green world banded with golden sunshine and shot with blue, the dolphin earned its gorgeous coloring.

Its compressed form is the hallmark of fish that must maneuver with agility in a confined environment, just as do the freshwater centrarchid sunfishes such as bluegill. But his length and falcate tail profile are like the jacks, fish noted for

Saltwater expert Roy Donnersberger took this big bull dolphin on the fly. Dolphin are usually found around floating debris or windrows of sargassum weed. Their swift strike is no less spectacular than their leaping and greyhounding when hooked.

great strength when they get a line over their shoulder and run out of sight.

Dolphin begin as part of the sargassum-dwelling zooplankton, grow with incredible rapidity into an active predator on anything animal that can be swallowed in one piece and continue as a gulfweed dweller until they outgrow the available prey species. Then (if they live long enough), they develop into a pelagic wanderer with the speed to run down flyingfish, to escape (sometimes) the enormous marlin and tuna that prey on them, yet retain a life-long willingness to snuggle up to sargassum weed, or anything else that floats, any object that provides some visual stimulus in the optical void of the sea. Transoceanic yachtsmen have reported that the recognizably individual dolphin have kept pace with them for thousands of miles. Thor Heyerdahl on one of his rafting

expeditions found they like to rub against floating objects (probably scratching) and at least one biologist believes their fascination with buoyant objects is part of their schooling mechanism, which obviously is a *powerful* instinct in dolphin.

Schooling in combination with fearlessness makes them not a relatively easy fish to catch. When a mob of dolphin arrive in the wake of an offshore vessel intent on a display of your marlin baits, it is possible for fish hogs to take every one if they take care not to lose a fish. A runaway will take all or part of the school with him.

There are two species in this one-genus family (*Coryphaenidae*), the common dolphin and the pompano dolphin. The latter resembles, in both sexes, a small, stocky female of the former. Their relationship is unclear. One observer noted a mixed school, but a Russian research vessel that was accompanied by a large school of pompano dolphin was promptly deserted when a few common dolphin approached.

Cannibalism is common with dolphins. Common and pompano dolphin have been successfully interbred in confinement and the hybrids are apparently fertile, a rarity.

There are some curious anomalies in the schooling process. As a rule, fish school by year-class because of swimming energetics; a little fish simply cannot keep pace with larger ones. I have seen many dolphin schooled under sargassum windrows with great variation in size, perhaps they were all schooling with the sargassum rather than each other. Stock samplings have disclosed high percentages of females in juvenile schools under weed, but more equitable sex distribution in open ocean fish. This accords with the secondary sexual characteristic of dimorphism. The big bulls with their high foreheads are immediately distinguishable from females and juveniles, something that is true of no other pelagic fish. You cannot sex other marine game fish without examining their gonads, but if at some early stage the sexes are going to segregate, in the dolphins' case by males going offshore in mixed-age schools of pelagic wanderers, then when reunion of breeders is achieved they should be able to identify gender without a gynecological examination.

Dolphin are the most beautiful fish that swim and they have inspired great art. The doyen of Abstract Expressionism, Jackson Pollock, produced his drip-and-scatter technique of paint application obviously pursuing the example of dolphin. Their chameleon-like ability to shift bionic color display in response to both positive and negative tropism[1] has inspired minor art as well. The color of dolphin, photographers, is best when the animal is unstressed and wholesome. It degenerates before one's eyes in a captured, gaffed and dying fish.

Dolphin are most beautiful at their first gasp, not their last. Unlike sundown, they live more beautifully than they die. Free dolphin you cannot devour on the day of their capture. The remarkable virtue of the flesh withstands freezing as well as most fish, but since it is one of the tastiest that swim, why subject it to deterioration? If you insist on eating only fresh fish, you have a perfect excuse to go fishing more often. I have eaten much mediocre dolphin because charter boat mates are unwilling to engage in a battle royal with a freshly gaffed specimen capable of tearing the cockpit apart. The customary practice of swinging the writhing creature into a fishbox and letting it suffocate out of harm's way is wasteful of palatability. It should be slain quickly, then deprived of its tail to encourage thorough bleeding (and gutted and gilled and chilled immediately, the colder the better). If you can tell the difference between grass-finished and grain-finished beef you can tell the difference between the bled and un-bled dolphin.

It is still possible to find charter boat captains and mates convinced the catch is theirs save, perhaps, for a steak or two that you may take home. Because dolphin are the major constituent of the offshore sport fishing catch in places such as south Florida, there is a veritable industry engaged at dockside in selling off dolphin. If you are accustomed to employees selling your personal possessions for their own profit, by all means allow this. When I pay for an offshore charter the disposition of the fish is accomplished to my satisfaction before my checkbook comes out of my pocket. These questions should be resolved before the charter is even made.

Dolphin are among the largest finned components of the tropic and subtropic oceanic epipelagic biomass because of their incredible fecundity and growth. Can you believe 1 pound to 36 pounds in eight months?[2] Will your credulity accept 5 pounds growth per month? Almost all dolphin you catch will be young-of-the-year. A 2-year-old will average 27½ pounds. A dolphin with one annulus on its scales, that is a fish who has celebrated its first birthday but not yet its second, will be about 13 pounds. The record-book monsters that fill the IGFA listings, fish in their 70s and 80s, are 4-year-old males, the last of their year-class. For one to reach 6 years would be as incredible as a 125-year-old man.

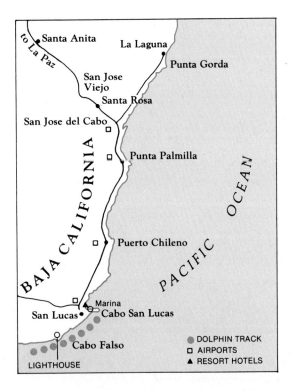

Dolphin are plentiful at Cabo San Lucas from November through January, with December the peak month. Schools usually occur close to shore (about 1 mile out) and for 2 to 3 miles in either direction from the lighthouse.

The most productive dolphin grounds in Baja California are on the East Cape in the Punta Colorada region. Fish are present the year 'round, but the peak period is from May through September. Generally found about 5 miles offshore, dolphin congregate off Pescadero, Colorada and Arena points and the north end of the live coral Pulmo reef.

[1]Tropism is reaction to external stimuli. Juvenile dolphin in the sargassum jungle are strongly barred, a passive camouflage. Adults are more variegated and have an instantaneous color-flux, as befits a stalking predator.

[2]In a captive fish. Length/weight studies of wild fish are slightly, but only slightly, less amazing. Dolphin aquaria must be tightly capped or they will leap out, accurately exiting even through a quite modest hole in a covering net.

SAILFISH

Dolphin evidently spawn either year-'round or virtually so, and multiple spawning of both sexes is presumed. The lumina of mature females' ovaries (sexual maturity begins before they are six months old) have yielded three separate development stages of ova, categorized by fisheries scientists as *ready, willing* and *eager*. Between three categories of dolphin—immature, maturing and mature—eleven modalities of egg development have been discerned. Dolphin are a dolphin factory. Egg production is thought to vary (with size of fish) between 250,000 and 3,000,000 per annum, and males with milt may be as small as 16 inches and only weeks old.

Flotsam on a sun-soaked sea is the first place to look for dolphin, and anything that lives in association with floating objects has been found in their stomachs. This may be the least selective fish that swims. Stomach contents contained sargassum weed in 28 percent of one analysis; many of the fish were juvenile females, and this is thought to be ingested incidentally to fish, crustaceans and other zoological residents of the algal environment. Dolphin have been found to contain nocturnal prey species with the volume increasing during the full moon, so keeping that ferocious digestive system from grumbling is evidently a full-time occupation. Negatively phototropic creatures that migrate toward the surface at night also appear in dolphin stomachs.

L arval dolphin feed on copepods for the most part, but they begin preying on little slivers of fish while they themselves are only three quarters of an inch long! Flyingfish have figured as a major diet component in some studies (25 percent of total food weight in an analysis of 373 adult common dolphin taken off the coast of North Carolina; a recent study of pompano dolphin indicated flyingfish were their *major* food). I am confident further research on these two dolphin will disclose that diet shifts with age and size from the residents of the sargassum community to epipelagic school fish. A 20- to 90-pound carnivorous animal cannot support itself with the modest food forms that dwell in floating weed.

Anything that wants to can eat dolphin, but they are not without defenses. The young are heavily barred, as is the pattern of light and shade in their gulfweed environment, and the genera's extreme lateral compression makes them hard to see when facing directly away or toward you.

Lateral compression is a fairly recent development of piscine evolution. Skates and rays tried horizontal compression early on, the tubular or fusiform shape is most common, but lateral compression makes most efficient use of a fish's swimming muscles, and allows both superior maneuverability and camouflage.

Nevertheless, the physical laws governing wave propagation by solid bodies dictate that big fish are faster than small, so dolphin have gone down the gullets of bluefin tuna, yellowfin tuna, all the billfishes, etc. I once watched a 500-pound black marlin strung up by its tail on the scales suddenly become a 470-pounder when 30 pounds of bull dolphin fell out of its untrussed mouth. Since this was during a tournament the failure to tie that mouth shut was costly. Larval dolphin are reported as a significant food form of larval broadbill swordfish in the Pacific and Indian oceans. That must be an accident of sampling; senior dolphin larvae would surely feed on junior swordfish given the opportunity.

Not many dolphin have been tagged and recaptured, but one that was covered 60 miles in its two days at large. The little ones will follow their home patch of sargassum long distances in the Gulf Stream. They have been caught as far north as Prince Edward Island on the Atlantic Coast, but this can be interpreted as a fish simply following the surface isotherm it found most comfortable, a Gulf Stream meander. South African researchers report maximum dolphin concentrations when the surface reaches about 85°F, which explains why after a good day's dolphin fishing you look like a negative image of a raccoon—pale around the eyes, where your sunglasses were, and dark elsewhere.

That fondness for floating structures has produced a clever commercial technique for dolphin fishing. In Japan it is called *shiira-zuke*; in the Balerics it is *matas*; and off Malta it is *kannizzati*. Basically, it is to put out rafts of bamboo or cork planks and, when a school of dolphin have settled in the shade, make a purse-seine set around the whole kaboodle.

As a rule, sport fishermen take dolphin with marlin or sailfish trolling gear, and this is to be deplored. They respond marvelously to casting tackle and are great fun on it. I have learned to never go offshore without both fly-fishing and plug casting or spinning tackle. Even if the nominal target species is big tuna or marlin, the cost of blue-water fishing is such that one should be prepared for every opportunity. It helps to have more than one type of casting tackle rigged and ready to use because, voracious as they often are, dolphin are quickly educable. I have seen them become bored with the surface plug that took three in swift succession and then *race* to be the first to take a large streamer fly cast on a lead-core shooting head. A fish with such physical speed must necessarily have accompanying mental processes. If you have chum aboard, that will hold a school well for casters, but chum is not normally part of a billfishing day.

Dolphin are a leaping rather than a running fish and I have never worried much about adequate backing for them, but people who throw lures and flies at dolphin are sometimes appalled to see them gulped down by great long fish with spiked noses. For *those* you will need all the backing you can muster. I have a fearsomely expensive fly reel that holds a fly line plus 600 yards of 30-pound-test braided polyester backing. I know perfectly well that some day I am going to be spooled of every last inch of it, yet the excitement of offshore casting is such to make that prospect just another thrill in the most thrilling aspect of the sport. Trolling is admittedly the sensible way to fish when there is a great deal of water between fishes, but to stay with troll when fish can be cast to is wasteful of sport.

A school of racing, leaping dolphin seem to me the very spirit of the ocean personified, so I am saddened to report that mariculture of them is increasingly practiced. They can be harvested after three or four months in penstocks, offer no particular difficulty to the farmer and will even accept commercial pellet feed.

Even if dolphin are destined to become supermarket freezer fare, they will be so for someone other than me. I will take mine from under a windrow of sargassum or from under a sheet of newspaper, dealt overboard from the Sunday newspapers as from a giant deck of cards only half an hour before as we were running out to blue water. I will even take mine on marlin tackle that is too stout for them if they come so fast there is a hookup before you can get lighter gear deployed. Any day with dolphin in it is a good day to be alive and on the ocean, the sea, the last completely wild place.

TUNA

Thunnus thynnus

AND
MACKEREL

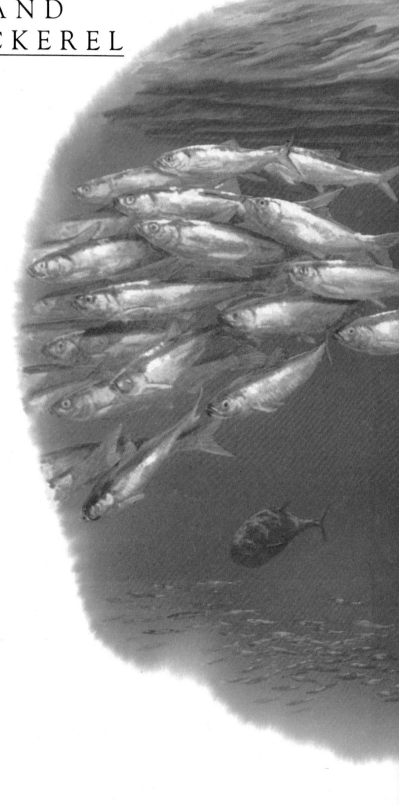

In his *Universal History*, Polybius of Megalopolis (205 to 125 B.C.) wrote that tuna wander deep in the sea to a place where an oak tree grows and there they feed on its acorns becoming so fat that they finally explode. The ancient fishermen of the Mediterranean believed that in years when few *cordili* or juvenile tuna appeared most of the adults had consumed too many acorns before mating. Aristotle (384 to 322 B.C.) observed in his *Historia Animalium* that the "sea pig" lives but two years and having survived the dangers of overeating will grow to a weight of 15 talents (1,200 pounds). Although exploding tuna were mentioned by naturalists well into the Middle Ages as an explanation for their years of abundance and scarcity, in these modern times, even with a now voluminous knowledge of their life history, periodically it would appear that whole populations do indeed meet some mythological fate. Ever since the 1930s, the bluefin tuna has been changing its migration path, leaving anglers mumbling in a void. Until the 1950s, Wedgeport, Nova Scotia, was considered the giant tuna capital of the world. Then, the fishery collapsed and giant tuna began appearing in the waters around Newfoundland in the 1960s. A decade later, the scene shifted to Prince Edward Island—and other concentrations were located off New Brunswick and at the Canso Causeway, which links Nova Scotia and Cape Breton Island.

Juvenile bluefin tuna do not migrate as far north as Canada, and even tuna in the 100- to 300- pound class have been virtually unknown there for decades. Yet, in the early days of Nova Scotia tuna fishing (in the 1930s and 1940s) many of the fish caught were mediums—though they were considered giants at the time. For instance, a number of tuna caught in the 1949 international Sharp Cup competition at Wedgeport ranged from 110 to 200-pounds. Later, during the great runs off Newfoundland, most of the tuna were in the 500- pound class. It wasn't until 1970 that the

354

A school of giant bluefin tuna feeding on herring off the coast of New Brunswick. The retractable first dorsal fin may be extended when the fish is excited or feeding (see the fish in the foreground), but it is usually folded back when the fish are swimming at speed.

355

TUNA

supergiants started to show. Nine-hundred-pounders were caught off Prince Edward Island, but the first "grander" was a 1,065-pound bluefin boated by Glen Gibson of River Bourgeois, Nova Scotia, near Canso Causeway on November 16, 1970. Since then, there have been hundreds of 1,000-pounders boated off both Prince Edward Island during late summer and early fall and at Canso Causeway in October and November. The world record has approached 1,500 pounds and nobody is prepared to say just how much bigger Canadian tuna might grow or where they will appear. Though giant tuna are found in St. Margaret's Bay, Nova Scotia, as early as May, the rod-and-reel fishery has not been starting until July. The best fishing begins in August, and the average size increases steadily as the fall season advances. The major port on Prince Edward Island is North Lake, where dozens of charter boats are available. The Canadian government has restricted tuna fishing to the commercials who fish for lobster or net cod during the early portion of the year. Thus, the boats are not the sophisticated craft that one associates with American tuna fishing, but rather lobster boats with makeshift fighting chairs installed for the season. Though large tuna are caught, the hookup ratio is quite low as a general rule. The charter rates are also low, as any tuna boated belongs to the crew and is worth thousands of dollars when shipped to Japan. Unlike the lean tuna of the Bahamas, these are the fat *Matsu hamu* dear to the heart of the Tokyo market.

There are 23 species of the tuna and mackerel family (*Scombridae*) found in North American waters, ranging from the little chub mackerel (*Scomber japonicus*), which is seldom more than a foot in length, to the giant bluefin tuna (*Thunnus thynnus*), known to reach 14 feet in length and a weight of 1,600 pounds. Bluefin tuna are worldwide in distribution, but the largest are caught in the western Atlantic. The bluefin has a robust body tapering to a pointed snout. It has shorter pectoral fins than other American tuna and two dorsal fins; the rear one is fixed but the forward dorsal is retractable in deference to its swimming speed that can exceed 50 miles per hour. It has such thick muscles that the body temperature can be as much as 37.4°F greater than that of sea water as the internal heat cannot be dissipated rapidly when the tuna is actively feeding. Tuna live 30 years or more and feed on a tremendous variety of fish, squid and crustaceans, at times foraging very deep as luminous benthic fishes are found in their stomachs. The tuna are

brute game fish which often take hours rather than minutes to subdue.

If the sport had a pivotal beginning, Charles Frederick Holder caught the first large bluefin tuna on rod and reel off Catalina Island, California, in June of 1898. This is a rather ephemeral record as tuna were boated by other anglers before that time, which Holder freely admitted, but nobody recorded their sizes so his 183-pound fish holds title by default. Pacific bluefins are nowhere nearly as large as the Atlantic population; in fact, the current record of 363 pounds, 8 ounces out of Avalon in 1983 supersedes a 250-pound record caught in 1899. By definition, the term "giant" is a tuna with the minimum weight of 310 pounds, so the Avalon catch boated by Jim Salter of Newport Beach is the first *giant* tuna ever taken in the Pacific. In 1924, Zane Grey caught a 758-pound bluefin off Yarmouth, Nova Scotia, and from that year on, the sport of big game fishing boomed. Like other pioneers, Michael Lerner, Van Campen Heilner and S. Kip Farrington, these stalwarts fought their fish from an open dory. Novelist Ernest Hemingway is often identified with feats of derring-do in big game circles, and indeed he brought the first tuna to gaff at Bimini, Bahamas, in 1935, but the legendary angler is soft-spoken William Carpenter of Wilmington, Delaware, with a lifetime record of 642 giant bluefins, and a one-day record of 16 which surpasses Hemingway's all-time total. Standing in Carpenter's shadow is Elwood K. Harry, president of the International Game Fish Association with 612 tuna, and a one-day record of 14. On the distaff side, no woman has matched Ann Kunkel of Palm Beach, Florida, with a lifetime record of 110 giant bluefins, of which 106 were tagged and released. One of Kunkel's tuna taken at Cat Cay was recaptured four years later off the coast of Uruguay, which added one more clue to the mysteries of their migrations.

The Migration of Bluefin Tuna

The development of a successful method of tagging giant bluefins in 1954 provided the first positive information on its migrations. Significant tagging of giant northwestern Atlantic bluefins has been carried out in two areas, the coastal waters off southern New England and eastern Canada in summer and early fall, and the Cat Cay-Bimini area of the northwestern Bahamas in May and June. The most numerous tag returns

DISTRIBUTION

356

have been from releases off New England and Canada. All of these were recaptured in the western North Atlantic in the general tagging area in the same or subsequent summers or early autumns, and in the Gulf of Mexico or adjacent parts of the northwestern Caribbean in spring or late winter. These returns are consistent with migrations between a summer and early fall feeding area off New England and parts of Canada, and a spring spawning concentration in or near the Gulf of Mexico. They provide little or no information on the winter habitat of the giant tuna. Tags from two bluefins were recovered in the south Atlantic, one off Argentina in February and another off Brazil in March. These returns probably indicate the southern extremes of the wintering area of the western Atlantic giants. Although these returns are surprising, they do not negate the proposed migratory cycle.

The most puzzling returns from giant bluefins tagged in the western Atlantic were nine from fish released in the Bimini-Cat Cay area in May-June and captured off the western coast of Norway in August-October. Four of these fish had completed the 4,200-nautical-mile journey in periods of from 51 to 121 days. These migrations are dramatically opposed to the concept of a fixed migratory pattern and can be explained in two ways:

(1) Large contingents of bluefin tuna which have left the Straits of Florida traveling northward may, in some years, follow the ocean currents directly to the Norwegian coast instead of departing from them to reach their usual American feeding grounds. Rodewald (1967) showed a possible relationship between the recorded transatlantic migrations and years when the eastward currents were strengthened by unusually strong westerly winds. Tiews (1964), assuming that unusually thin tuna noted in the late-season Norwegian commercial catches were individuals which had recently arrived from the western Atlantic, estimated the numbers recruited to these catches. His estimates indicated little or no recruitment in most years, but up to 39 percent of the catches in two separate periods.

(2) Giant bluefins from the eastern Atlantic, as well as those of the western Atlantic, spawn in the Gulf of Mexico. This startling concept was proposed by Rodriguez-Roda on the basis of distinctive scars caused on giant bluefins by a small shark (*Isistius brasilensis*) whose distribution is thought to be limited.

With a long history of appearing and disappearing in different geographical areas, the pelagic and migratory tuna has drawn anglers to New Brunswick during the last decade. Lee Wulff took this 895-pound bluefin at Caraquet, off the northeastern tip of that province.

The former explanation seems more probable than the latter for the following reasons: The studies of Rodewald and Tiews indicate maximum transatlantic migration in the same years in which transatlantic tag returns were most numerous and in addition, the regular migration of giant bluefins across the ocean in summer would conflict with their normal feeding habits and physiological development. Giant bluefins on both sides of the Atlantic spend the summer and early fall feeding heavily in rich coastal waters and grossly increasing their weight and fat content. These reserves are necessary for the fish to survive the long periods of meager feeding in winter and spring, and the demands of spawning. The cycle proposed by Rodriguez-Roda would require the giants to spend much of this feeding period in food-poor oceanic waters while they expended an enormous amount of energy in swimming across the Atlantic. It seems more likely that these mass transatlantic migrations are occasional rather than annual.

357

TUNA

Although bluefin tuna periodically disappear from former areas of great concentration, the general pattern of their migrations established by 30 years of tagging is shown here. These migrations are dramatically opposed to the concept of a fixed migratory pattern, which is explained in the text. (Map compiled by Frank Mather, Woods Hole Oceanographic Institution.)

Tagging has provided positive evidence of migrations of giant bluefin from summer/early fall feeding grounds off New England and Canada to spring spawning areas in or near the Gulf of Mexico, and some evidence of a return migration through the Straits of Florida to the northern feeding area. Winter returns are so few, however, that it is necessary to resort to deductions from catch data, chiefly of the Japanese longline fishery, to find this winter distribution and complete the proposed migratory cycle. The Japanese catch records show that bluefin, presumed to be giants, are widely distributed over the Atlantic from Bermuda and Cape Hatteras southward through the late fall, winter and early spring. Thus, it is probable that, when the giants leave their relatively small coastal feeding area off

northwestern North America, they disperse very widely over the warm waters of the Atlantic as far as the Equatorial Current system and, as indicated by tag returns, sometimes even farther south. The monthly progression of the Japanese catches suggests an early spring movement along the northeast coast of South America and a spring migration northward between the Bahamas and Bermuda, somewhat analogous to the northward May-June migration through the Straits of Florida.

Thus, as of 1984, a three-part migratory cycle is emerging:

(1) A movement of concentration in late winter and early spring from very extensive wintering areas to spawning areas in or near the Gulf of Mexico. It is possible, however, that the breeding grounds are much more extensive than is now believed.

(2) A late spring migration concentrated in the eastern Straits of Florida, but dispersed between the Bahamas and Bermuda, from the spawning areas to the summer/early fall coastal feeding area between northern New Jersey and Newfoundland.

(3) A fall dispersion from this feeding area to the warm waters of the south Atlantic.

A complete knowledge of this cycle requires a very difficult and costly tagging effort, particularly during winter and spring, and more tag returns from recaptured fish.

The warm season distribution of giant tuna, during which most of the recreational catches of these fish are taken, includes our coastal waters and offshore banks from northern New Jersey to Newfoundland, including the outer part of the Bay of Fundy and southern part of the Gulf of St. Lawrence. Schools of giants appear in limited areas, however, and numerically these concentrations have varied greatly, and often unpredictably, with the passage of time. Some of the first recreational efforts occurred in the "Mud Hole" off New York harbor, however, giant bluefin have been taken here only occasionally in recent years.

The next area of interest, working eastward and northward along the coast, is around Block Island and off the western coast of Rhode Island. Fishing in this region has fluctuated greatly, but has been very productive in recent seasons (1981 to 1983). Continuing northward, the bays of Massachusetts—Cape Cod, Massachusetts and Ipswich bays—have all provided great fishing. Historically celebrated Ipswich Bay, the first to be

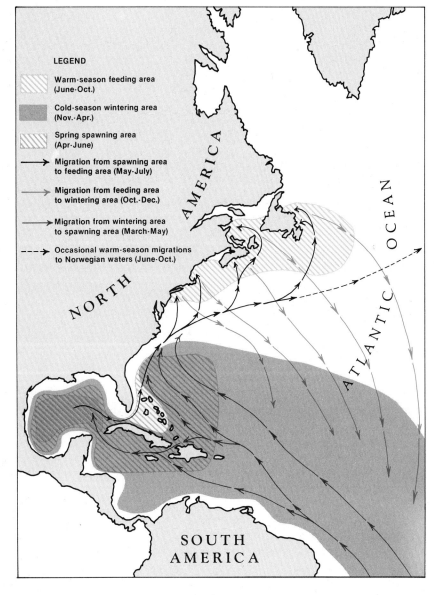

LEGEND

Warm-season feeding area (June-Oct.)

Cold-season wintering area (Nov.-Apr.)

Spring spawning area (Apr-June)

→ Migration from spawning area to feeding area (May-July)

→ Migration from feeding area to wintering area (Oct.-Dec.)

→ Migration from wintering area to spawning area (March-May)

--→ Occasional warm-season migrations to Norwegian waters (June-Oct.)

NORTH AMERICA

ATLANTIC OCEAN

SOUTH AMERICA

Lee Wulff (left) *and skipper Larry Cronin form a veteran tuna team. Big game angling is not a solo sport but demands boating skills coordinated with the movements of the fish and the efforts of the angler.*

exploited, has become the least important while Massachusetts and Cape Cod bays are generating the bulk of the United States rod-and-reel catches. Perversely, the fishing usually begins in July in Massachusetts waters, in August off Rhode Island, and in September or even October off northern New Jersey. The Caso Bay area of Maine was also among the first to be developed in the United States, but now only occasionally provides any angling. In Nova Scotian waters, the fabled Soldiers Rip near Wedgeport attained major importance in 1937 and was the scene of the International Sharp Cup Matches. As the fishery there declined, the tournament was briefly moved to Cape St. Marys, north of Yarmouth, then was abandoned due to the lack of fish. Conception and Notre Dame bays, on the east coast of Newfoundland, provided remarkable giant tuna fishing in the 1960s. One of the last and most important areas to be developed was the southern Gulf of St. Lawrence. This sport fishery began off the north coast of Prince Edward Island in 1970 and is still the most important. Since then, Chaleur Bay in New Brunswick and the Canso Causeway in Nova Scotia have become productive. This region is notable for producing extremely large bluefin, including the present world record of 1,496 pounds.

Cat Cay and Bimini

Beginning in 1931, Cat Cay was perhaps the most exclusive and expensive angling club in the world, frequented by captains of industry, titled Europeans, much of Hollywood and just plain millionaires. This lush island on the western edge of the Grand Bahamas Bank is little more than two miles long and half a mile wide, but

strategically located at "Tuna Alley." From early May until the second week in June, bluefin have poured across the banks hard by the Gulf Stream drop-off. At this point in their migration, these fish are lean 400- to 500-pound brutes heading north for a summer banquet of herring, whiting and butterfish from New Jersey to Nova Scotia. Three of the most prestigious tournaments on the tuna circuit originated at Cat Cay: The International, The Individual and The Team Tournament.

The most glamorous of these was The International. This was a team effort with countries from all over the world sending their best anglers to represent them. Some twenty teams from Australia, New Zealand, South Africa, Spain and Argentina would participate in the five-day event. The flags of all nations were flown during the tournament and the Governor of the Bahamas attended the festivities. An International night ashore was an experience not to be forgotten.

The Individual Tournament was considered to be the ultimate test of angler and boat. Undeniably, the crew plays a vital role in giant tuna fishing. The angler only feels the pain. The boats are ideally small, stripped down fishing machines designed for speed and maneuverability. The crews are all skilled tuna men with fantastic eyesight and strong, tireless legs to sustain them in the tower for hours on end in all kinds of weather. There was only one angler assigned to each boat for all five days of the tournament. Weather was no factor as they would go out under any conditions short of a hurricane, but always praying for a south wind to nudge the fish up through "Tuna Alley" as the drop-off west of Cat Cay is known. The Team Tournament was composed of teams representing various fishing clubs and

TUNA

organizations and was predominantly American as only one American team could fish in The International. Even women were accepted in this tournament and did have a team fishing in it several times.

Due to death and taxes, the club closed in 1964. The Bimini Big Game Fishing Club had by this time built a hotel and docks and so the tournaments were relocated at that island, which is only an extra half-hour run to Tuna Alley. In 1971, Cat Cay reopened, having been bought by Al Rockwell, president of Rockwell International, and the tournaments returned to the original site.

The yellowfin tuna provides a real challenge for the light-tackle angler. Fish exceeding 100 pounds are often sought on 12- to 20-pound-test, such as this 138-pounder taken on 20 with spinning tackle. Pound for pound, the yellowfin is considered by many veterans to be the strongest of all tuna.

However, by this time the tuna runs were diminishing and The International was canceled, while The Individual and Team competitions became release tournaments. This was a big break from tradition, but the unpredictable tuna probably went off to the mythical oak tree. The 1983 Individual Tournament at Cat Cay, with 23 boats and 23 anglers aboard, caught and released *two* bluefin tuna in five days of fishing. This doesn't mean the giants have abandoned Tuna Alley as the Bahamian cycle could start again.

Cat Cay is a private club and is not open to the public except for tuna entries. The Bimini Big Game Fishing Club is open to the public and has rooms, cottages, bar and restaurant, dockage and gas. The Bimini Blue Water Marina is smaller and quieter, but excellently equipped for dockage and has a limited number of rooms. The service, bar and restaurant are tops. You should bring your own boat over as the charter boats there are not well equipped for tuna fishing. There are many boats for tuna charter on the Florida east coast that have all the necessary equipment and will bring bait and essentials over with them.

Montauk Tuna

Until 1970, the Montauk area was the best bet for giant tuna in the United States, but at that time the world record was less than 1,000 pounds. That summer, Dr. Richard Hausknecht fished a good run at Butterfish Hole aboard his *Galetea* and hooked into an exceptionally large fish. His boat broke down and he had to carry the rod across to another boat before defeating the huge tuna. That bluefin edged the record a little closer to the "grander" mark and made Montauk the very temporary giant tuna capital of the world. The honor only lasted a couple of weeks before the first 1,000-pounder was taken at Prince Edward Island. After that there was an explosion of 1,000-pound catches at Prince Edward and, in 1971, the finest giant tuna run in United States history started in Massachusetts Bay. Since then Montauk has had its ups and downs, though the 1980s started off with the best giant tuna fishing in a decade. The first 1,000-pounder was boated by Captain Larry Thompson on Bob Aplanalp's *Sea Lion* out of Montauk Yacht Club in 1977, and a few others have been caught on the Block Island grounds since then. However, the average size of the giants found north of Cape Cod has been much greater— and it was the appearance of the 1973-year-class (the only "super" year-class since the early 1960s) as "mini-giants" in 1980 which really revived tuna fishing fortunes off Block Island.

To prove the fickleness of the giant tuna, Montauk skippers have over the years headed in three different directions to find the best fishing. There have always been giant tuna around Block Island, but the biggest boost to Montauk tuna fishing occurred in 1949 when they were discovered off Watch Hill, Rhode Island—a convenient run to the north across Block Island Sound. Within a few years, the fame of Rosie's Ledge (off Watch Hill) and Nebraska Shoal (off Charlestown) spread up and down the coast, and the United States Atlantic Tuna Tournament moved its headquarters to Rhode Island. When that fishing died out during the 1960s, attention turned to Butterfish Hole, about 12 miles south-southeast of Montauk Point. There were some very good runs in that area, though it wasn't consistent from year to year. The most unusual tuna run out of Montauk (and one that will probably never be repeated) occurred in 1969, when the tuna schooled behind the huge Russian trawlers working about 30 miles south-southwest of the point. Just as they often do in Butterfish Hole behind the much smaller American trawlers, those tuna would follow the huge bags of whiting, ling and butterfish being drawn to the surface and feed on the groundfish falling out of holes in the nets. There was a large concentration of giant tuna in that area for a couple of weeks, and the Montauk tuna catches were the best since the heyday of Rosie's Ledge—though these giants were bigger.

Since the 1970s, the trend has been back to Block Island. Though giants are often sighted around Southwest Ledge and south of the island, most of this fishing occurs to the east. The smaller tuna (315 to 500 pounds) seem to favor areas southeast of Block, while the largest fish are usually found in the Mud Hole (not to be confused with the Mud Hole off the North Jersey coast), about 10 miles east of Southeast Light. That latter area is worked hard by Rhode Island draggers for ling and whiting, a factor that seems to add to the attraction for giant tuna. Naturally, these areas are fished by Rhode Island and eastern Connecticut boats as well as those from Montauk—and it is not unusual to see 100 or more working a spot on a decent weekend late in the season.

By and large, giant tuna fishing out of Montauk is a late summer proposition. Giants swim by the area in June and early July, but don't often hit at that time. On the Fourth of July weekend in 1981, Captain Walter Haab boated two on his charter boat *Seacon* from among a bluefish trolling fleet working south of the Cartwright Grounds—but those schools only stayed around a few days and rarely hit a bait. There have been July runs in Butterfish Hole, but real giant tuna action normally breaks open in mid-August. The best of the fishing will usually occur between then and mid-September, rarely lasting any longer than that.

The basic method of catching giant tuna at Montauk hasn't changed a great deal over the years. In most cases, the boats will anchor up and chum with chunks of bunker, herring, ling or

Popular North American Scombrids

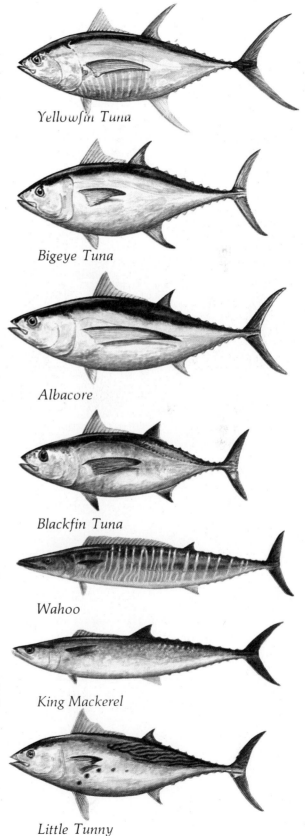

YELLOWFIN TUNA
Thunnus albacares
Commonly found from Mexico to New Jersey, the colorful yellowfin attains a size of over 300 pounds but most weigh 20 to 120 pounds.

Yellowfin Tuna

BIGEYE TUNA
Thunnus obesus
Found in the warm temperate waters of the Atlantic and Pacific, the bigeye attains a size of over 300 pounds but averages about 150.

Bigeye Tuna

ALBACORE
Thunnus alalunga
Recorded to 71 pounds on both coasts, the warm-water albacore makes seasonal migrations into colder zones of the Pacific and Atlantic.

Albacore

BLACKFIN TUNA
Thunnus atlanticus
Found in the western Atlantic from Brazil to Cape Cod, the blackfin usually runs 10 to 20 pounds but has been recorded to 42 pounds.

Blackfin Tuna

WAHOO
Acanthocybium solandri
Seasonally migratory, the wahoo occurs on both coasts of Mexico to North Carolina. It averages 15 to 30 pounds but has been recorded to 149 pounds.

Wahoo

KING MACKEREL
Scomberomorous cavalla
Found in the western Atlantic from Brazil to Cape Cod, king mackerel is common in the southern U.S. Usually smaller than wahoo, it has a record of 90 pounds.

King Mackerel

LITTLE TUNNY
Euthynnus alletteratus
This migratory tuna occurs in the western Atlantic from Brazil to Cape Cod. Recorded to 27 pounds, it appears at the surface in dense schools.

Little Tunny

361

TUNA

whiting. The same species may be used for bait, though large butterfish are also favored. The best bait is normally a live whiting or ling. It is also possible to chum with chunks on the drift, provided that there aren't too many boats in the area. Draggers pulling their nets are always worth a look, and sport fishing boats will often drift and chum in their spills. Some giant tuna are also caught by trolling, and that is probably the best method to try in July before they have settled down. A large mullet is a popular bait, but mackerel and squid are also good. It is quite likely that the high-speed trolling lures favored for canyon trolling will also prove effective on giant bluefins at various times.

While giant bluefins may be the most glamorous

The wahoo is one of the swiftest fish in the sea, with a probable speed of 50 miles per hour. Wahoo often make a wild jump when taking a bait but otherwise are notorious for their incredibly fast runs. The firm white flesh is a gourmet treat.

of the tuna caught off Montauk, it is the school bluefins that fill the boxes. To be sure, school tuna fishing is nothing like it used to be and probably never will be again. Prior to 1960, anglers were fishing a virgin resource, virtually untapped by commercial interests. Then a few East Coast seiners started after the vast schools, and they attracted the West Coast superseiners. Within a few years most of the schools were wiped out, and the appearance of Japanese longliners in the 1970s put even more pressure on a stressed population. Hopefully, a new quota system imposed on the bluefin tuna fishery in 1982 (through the International Commission for the Conservation of Atlantic Tunas) will lead to a recovery of the species and fishing similar to that enjoyed until the mid-1960s. Even with coastal school tuna

fishing in a bad slump throughout most of the 1970s, Montauk always provided some fishing. Unlike the giants, the young bluefins do not enter Block Island Sound, but they do frequent ocean waters reasonably close to shore. At Montauk they are often found only a few miles offshore to the southwest, though Butterfish Hole and 120-foot depths south and southeast of Block Island are better bets. In late August it is not unusual for bluefish jiggers to hook school tuna while fishing in 80 to 90 feet of water south of Block Island. Most Montauk school tuna are taken by trolling. The popular lures are feather jigs, cedar jigs and the various high-speed, offshore trolling lures. In the heyday of Montauk school tuna fishing (during the 1950s that was the primary summer fishery for the charter and private boat fleet), huge catches were often made by keeping a hooked tuna in the water at all times. That tuna would hold the attention of the rest of the school which would be caught on butterfish jigs dropped to them. School bluefins (which can be of any size between 10 and 100 pounds or more, depending on the year-class represented) start arriving in July, but in recent years the best fishing has been in August and early September. Since these are schooling fish, the action can be wild in a given area for several days at a time and then suddenly drop off to nothing when the school moves.

Far more abundant in recent times have been the "offshore" tuna. Yellowfin tuna are regularly encountered along the edge of the continental shelf throughout the summer, but they also work much closer to Montauk as the season progresses. By early September, it is not unusual for them to be caught as close as 25 to 30 miles offshore. These yellowfins average about 40 to 80 pounds, though much larger specimens are taken on occasion. Where there are yellowfins, there are usually albacore. Small albacore (20 to 30 pounds) may be found in great abundance all summer from 40 miles out right to canyon waters. From late August into the fall, much bigger albacore are encountered—some being in the 60- to 70-pound class. The prize tuna for the canyon fisherman, however, is the bigeye, a species which averages 150 to 250 pounds and sometimes exceeds 300. Bigeyes are rarely hooked from canyon waters. They present quite a challenge to the angler in 600- to 1,200-foot depths, and those seeking them use 80-pound-test outfits. All three "offshore" tuna are normally taken on high-speed lures trolled at 8 to 10 knots. The bigeyes prefer lures running underwater and are much harder to fool than the plentiful yellowfins and albacore. The target area is the "Fish Tail," an indentation of the 100-fathom line in Block Canyon about 70 miles south of the point. The long run can be easily justified by the catches which frequently run well over 1,000 pounds per boat.

Skipjack tuna can be encountered from about the 120-foot curve all the way off to the canyon, though they are most frequently encountered at areas in between. Though often abundant, these 6- to 15-pound average tuna don't get much attention from Montauk sport fishermen as they are rather small for the tackle usually employed and aren't considered to be in the same class with the other tuna as a food. To compound the problem, they have soft mouths and regularly tear off after being hooked. This has earned them the local name "mushmouth." However, seiners seek out the skipjack schools for the canneries, and they are sought by sport fishermen for use as strip baits.

The "other tuna" in Montauk waters is the little tunny which frequents the shorelines and isn't normally encountered very far to sea. The first schools arrive around late August and they are most abundant in September and early October. Most of the time they feed on schools of very small bait and are, consequently, quite difficult to hook. Some are taken on umbrella rigs trolled on wire line, and an occasional one will hit almost any type of lure. However, most little tunny will take only small lures (primarily lead-head jigs) cast in front of them while they are actively feeding and retrieved as fast as possible. This is perfect light-tackle sport and there is virtually no competition for the fish, which are looked down on by local anglers due to their poor eating qualities. Yet, the little tunny (which averages 8 to 12 pounds) is certainly one of the fastest and gamest fish to be found anywhere in the world—and a real challenge to both hook and hold on light spinning tackle.

Mexican Yellowfin Tuna

Mexico consistently produces the largest yellowfin tuna from North American waters. The current world record of 388 pounds, 12 ounces was caught at San Benedicto Island in 1977, on 80-pound-test line. These tuna are plentiful in the Punta Colorada Region of Baja California between Mulege and Cabo San Lucas. They are taken at Mulege, Loreto, La Paz, Las Arenas, San Jose del Cabo and Cabo San Lucas. However, except for two "Tuna Holes," running into a school of migrating tuna is more good luck than good

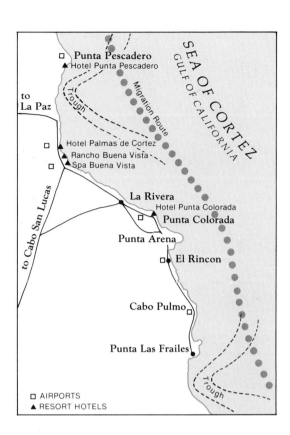

Two unusual troughs, running close to the beach near Punta Pescadero and Punta Las Frailes, provide consistent yellowfin tuna fishing in Baja California. Migrating tuna find an inshore abundance of baitfish known as sardinas in these "holes" and feed here for prolonged periods. Mexico produces the largest yellowfins in North America.

management; therefore, we will discuss the Punta Colorada region between Punta Pescadero and Los Frailes Bay which encompasses the "Tuna Holes," and makes tuna fishing less dependent on luck.

The "holes" are actually deep troughs that run in to within 75 yards of the beach. This allows the tuna to invade areas where the baitfish are feeding inshore. Substantial numbers of these yellowfins do not leave with the traveling school. This accounts for two spots where an angler can go to fish specifically for tuna and not depend on the luck necessary to find a migrating school. One of the troughs cuts in near shore about 3 miles south of Punta Pescadero. In many cases, fish are hooked so close to shore that careless boat operation could mean getting trapped in the breaking surf. The other trough is in Los Frailes Bay, 18 miles south of Punta Colorada. This trough runs even closer to the beach than at Punta Pescadero. This is the result of a breakoff of a large section of the underwater shelf a few years ago. This underwater cliff comes closest to shore about 2 miles south of Punta Los Frailes. Los Frailes, a large, beautiful bay with miles of white, sandy beaches, is unoccupied except for a couple of small ranch houses. A real estate development is projected for the area but may be some time materializing. Most of the fishing in this region is accomplished out of the fishing resorts indicated on the map. All of the resort's boats can fish the trough near Punta Pescadero, but Hotel Punta Colorada has the advantage of being able to fish either one.

A big influence on the tuna catch is the availability of live sardinas, unquestionably the most effective bait. (Sardinas does not necessarily mean "sardines" as this is Mexican colloquial for all small silvery fishes; in Baja it specifically refers to a clupeid, the Pacific herring.) *Sardinas* move with the warm water and so are in abundance during the hot months, June through September. Dead *sardinas* will attract tuna, but they will strike with less frequency. If neither of these are to be had, a fast trolled albacore feather will work well.

While tuna have been taken on a variety of trolled spoons, feathers and Rapala type plugs, the white albacore feather obtains the best results as far as artificials go. Recommending tackle is a problem. Usually, if the first tuna hooked is a 35-pounder, all the rest will be about equal in size. The same applies to an 85-pounder. This, of course, is a generality—there are times when one fish will weigh 25 pounds and the next over 100. However, if an angler boats a 100-pounder on light tackle, it would be advisable to shift to heavy if he intends to boat many fish.

Locating tuna at either of the troughs is fairly simple and the technique is the same. At Punta Pescadero run to within 300 yards of shore about 3 miles south of the point. Parallel the shore at a slow speed, tossing out a handful of *sardinas* every 100 feet, at the same time keep an eye out for boils. When a boil is sighted, move offshore of the boil, cut the engine—normally the boat will drift toward shore. Scatter a couple of handfuls of *sardinas* in the direction of the drift. Using a No. 4/0 Mustad-Viking hook, toss the *sardina* bait out and let it drift. Set the hook as soon as the bait is taken—the tuna will swallow it in a gulp. Once hooked, the tuna will dive as deep as possible. Pound for pound, yellowfin tuna are one of the most powerful fish in the sea and they have tremendous stamina. This, to the angler, means work. They do not leap nor use tricky maneuvers—just power! It is a pumping action from start to finish.

Every angler knows that a gathering of birds should be investigated. If the birds are working over porpoise it is quite possible that the porpoise are in front of a school of tuna. At times, the tuna will be breaking the surface but more often they will be running below. The boat should be angled to approach the porpoise from the rear while trolling a feather 150 feet behind the stern. If the porpoise are swimming erratically when sighted, constantly changing direction, they may be feeding *with* the school of tuna. Again, fast troll a feather, weaving through the area of action. When feeding, the school may work the area for hours and a pair of anglers could keep fish hooked through the entire time. These schools are sometimes huge, containing hundreds of tons of fish.

The crews of the charter boats are experienced and knowledgeable concerning the waters of the region. But, marlin being the glamour fish, they will head out to the marlin grounds unless otherwise instructed. If an angler wishes to fish for tuna, the resort owner should be contacted the day before going out so that he can, if possible, have a boat crew out early in the morning to net *sardinas*. Yellowfin are a prize foodfish. They are the quarry of the great San Diego tuna fleet along with fleets from Mexico and many nations around the globe including Russia and Japan. Broiled, barbecued or canned, yellowfin are delicious. Campers who trailer skiffs often bring canning equipment and put up their own surplus.

The weather in the summer months is hot, but most hotel rooms are air-conditioned and there is usually a cooling breeze out on the water. A real compensating factor for the heat is calm waters—there are very few windy days in the summer which would keep the boats from going out.

King Mackerel in the Carolinas

Thanks to the development of new techniques and the overkill of king mackerel by commercial fishermen in Florida, North Carolina has become the state to visit if you want to catch a trophy king. Big mackerel to 50 pounds move up the Atlantic coast from both sides of the Florida peninsula as the sea warms in the spring, and local experts employ just two methods to catch these fish from May through September.

Trolley-rig fishing was developed for piers and involves two complete angling outfits. A hefty surf rod is used to throw a large mushroom-type sinker well away from the pilings of the pier. The sinker bites securely into the bottom, and the surf rod is secured to the pier rail. The second, actual angling rod is then fished with a live bait suspended from a release clip attached to the trolley line.

As in kite fishing, a trolley-rig enables an angler to keep his bait at the surface so that large, hook-and-leader-shy king mackerel see a minimum of terminal gear. Kite fishing, however, is impractical on a crowded and stationary platform like a pier. Even with trolley-rigs, fishermen take up a lot of pier space. However, they are dependable customers and because they are after the kind of big fish that make the sports pages of coastal newspapers, many pier operators reserve the T-shaped ends of their piers exclusively for trolley-riggers.

Baby bluefish seem to make the best bait, but live spot and mullet catch their share of the kings. The average pier-caught fish is larger than his 8- to 12-pound brethren found farther offshore and which are most frequently seen in large schools in the fall. Semi-commercial rod-and-reelers—meaning recreational fishermen who wink at both ethics and the law—catch and sell many thousands of these smaller fish each October by trolling spoons and feathers on wire lines, planners, heavy sinkers and a few down-riggers.

However, the large, near-shore kings hunt alone or in small pods, and since they are survivors of the autumn slaughters, they are rarely fooled by an artificial lure and will frequently bite off the unhooked portions of live bait. King mackerel have fabulously sharp teeth, and wire leaders are a necessity, which only adds to the difficulty of fooling a trophy fish. Some anglers use thin, single-strand copper wire stained brown or black. (Shiny stainless steel wire is passé.) Others use coated wire, but only the lightest pound-test available. Coated wire can be tied without tools, knots down well, and the plastic coating can be melted for extra purchase. Its popularity is based on the angler's faith that even a small crimped sleeve on uncoated wire is too easily perceived by wary mackerel.

The wariness of big kings has inspired a refinement of the trolley-rig for small-boat fishermen. Again, although kites would do the same job, it is awkward to try to fish more than one kite at a time, while by slow-trolling live baits, anglers can fish up to five or six rods at a time, thereby creating the impression that a small school of menhaden is passing through.

J. R. Thompson, of Wrightsville Beach, and several other guides in the area pioneered the slow-trolling technique with live baits. The concept caught on like wildfire in the Carolinas after Thompson and his friends began winning every king mackerel tournament they entered. The secret, J. R. insists, lies in the freshness of his live menhaden baits. The fish are caught in a cast net the morning of the outing, not the evening before. Menhaden are not a hardy species in captivity, so J. R. uses not only a powerful pump to circulate the water in his live well, he has a complete back-up system as well. Furthermore, unless the fishing is so fast he is likely to use all the baits he has caught, J. R. tosses over any menhaden beginning to show stress or weakness.

Most anglers use treble hooks with their live baits, although this is not allowed by rules of the International Game Fish Association. However,

Skyrocketing

A unique feeding habit of the mackerel is "skyrocketing," a phenomenon most often seen when schools of cero (shown here) or king mackerel attack migrating baitfish, such as the Spanish sardine. The swift swimming mackerel literally follow a vertical path in jumping and diving to capture their food in sharp-toothed jaws while leaping and descending. Cero average somewhat larger than the common Spanish mackerel, often weighing 10 to 14 pounds, and are strong game fish on light tackle.

state contests don't care how you hook the fish, and neither do most fishermen. J. R. Thompson uses two No. 2 or 4 bronze treble hooks, plus a short-shank No. 1/0 to secure the menhaden through the nostrils and to keep it swimming near the surface. Free-swinging hooks that ride alongside the menhaden, but which are not embedded in the bait, produce more and larger mackerel. Single hooks embedded in the bait (IGFA style) will catch kings; you must simply expect a good many more hits than hookups.

The beauty of the slow-trolling technique is that it allows you to use lighter tackle than you usually associate with catching "smoker" kings. Twelve-pound line is about ideal, even though you may have trouble keeping the occasional amberjack from breaking you off in the rubble of one of the many artificial reefs built by the state of North Carolina and where some of the best near-shore king mackerel fishing is found.

For detailed information about angling opportunities and conditions, as well as about places to stay, write the Chamber(s) of Commerce in the coastal town(s) you are planning to visit. Pier fishing for king mackerel is increasingly a limited-entry proposition, and you may have to become a non-resident member of a local angling club to gain access to the end of the pier.

ACKNOWLEDGMENTS & CREDITS

We are particularly grateful to the following authors, who provided their angling expertise for various chapters:

Gerald Almy for the James River and Shenandoah River sections in Smallmouth Bass; **Joel Arrington** for the Currituck Sound for Brackish Water Bass section in Largemouth Bass, for the Fly-Fishing for Trophy Red Drum and North Carolina's Outer Banks sections in Red Drum, for the Giant Bluefish on Fly and Outer Banks for Surf Blues sections in Bluefish, for the Cape Lookout section in Spotted Seatrout, and for the Blue Marlin at Cape Hatteras and Oregon Inlet for White Marlin sections in Blue Marlin.

Bill Baab for the Monument to Largemouth section in Largemouth Bass; **Robert J. Behnke** for the Subspecies of Cutthroat Trout (including sidebar) section in Cutthroat Trout.

Jim Chapralis for the Boca Paila and Ascensión Bay sections in Bonefish; **Trey Combs** for the Olympic Peninsula Steelhead section in Steelhead; **Bill Cullerton, Jr.,** for the Kazan River section in Arctic Grayling; **William Curtis** for the Pyramid Lake section in Cutthroat Trout.

Frank Daignault for the Race Point for Cape Cod Striped Bass and the Brewster Flats sections in Striped Bass.

Charles K. Fox for the Letort River and the Cumberland Valley section in Brown Trout, for the Juniata River section in Muskellunge, and for the Susquehanna River section in Smallmouth Bass; **Jim Freeman** for the Klamath River section in Steelhead.

Jerry Gibbs for the Lake Memphremagog section in Landlocked Salmon, for the Great Slave Lake section in Northern Pike, for the Lake Champlain section in Smallmouth Bass, and for the Lake Casitas section in Largemouth Bass; **John Gleason** for the Lake Taneycomo Trout section in Rainbow Trout and for the Truman Reservoir section in Largemouth Bass; **Larry Green** for the Western Striped Bass Migrations and Oregon Bass sections in Striped Bass and for the Sacramento River section in Shad; **George Gruenfeld** for the Restigouche River, Matapedia River, Moise River, York River, George River, and Grand Cascapedia sections in Atlantic Salmon, for the Kaniapiskau River and Lac-St-Jean sections in Landlocked Salmon, for the Eagle Lake and Mistassini Watershed sections in Brook Trout, for the Quebec Red Trout section in Arctic Char, for the Goudin Reservoir section in Walleye, and for the St. Lawrence River section in Muskellunge.

Hal Janssen for the Ugashik Lakes section in Arctic Grayling; **Paul C. Johnson** for the Siouxland Walleyes After Dark section in Walleye.

Jerry Klink for the Hammerhead Sharks at Punta Pescadero section in Sharks, for the Cabo San Lucas section in Blue Marlin, and for the Mexican Yellowfin Tuna section in Tuna; **Lefty Kreh** for the Rainbow Fishing in Alaska section in Rainbow Trout; **Bob Kulwin** (with **Steve Rajeff**) for the Kenai River Chinook section in Pacific Salmon; **Ann Kunkel** for the Cat Cay and Bimini section in Tuna.

Glen Lambert for the Santee-Cooper Freshwater Striped Bass section in Striped Bass.

Frank Mather for the Migration of Bluefin Tuna section in Tuna; **Bill McMillan** for the Washougal River section in Steelhead; **Bob McNally** for the Madison River section in Brown Trout, for the Sickle Lake section in Northern Pike, and for the Rainy Lake section in Smallmouth Bass; **Tom McNally** for the Great Lakes Saga and the Great Lakes Salmon Migration sections in Pacific Salmon and for the Fly-Rod Muskies section in Muskellunge; **John Merwin** for the Baxter State Park section in Brook Trout and for the Battenkill River section in Brown Trout; **Bill Munro** for the Destin section in Blue Marlin.

Bob Nauheim for the Babine River and the Dean River sections in Steelhead.

Eric Peper for the Namekagon River and Henry's Fork of the Snake River sections in Rainbow Trout; **C. Boyd Pfeiffer** for the Connecticut River section in Shad.

Steve Rajeff (with **Bob Kulwin**) for the Kenai River Chinook section in Pacific Salmon; **George Reiger** for the Robertson River section in Arctic Char, for the Virginia's Eastern Shore section in Red Drum, for the Chesapeake Bay section in Spotted Seatrout, for the Ocean City Marlin section in Blue Marlin, and for the King Mackerel in North Carolina section in Tuna; **Al Ristori** for the Montauk Sharks section in Sharks, for the Montauk Bluefish section in Bluefish, for the Great South Bay section in Spotted Seatrout, for the Montauk Striped Bass section in Striped Bass, for the Long Island Swordfish section in Blue Marlin, and for the Montauk Tuna section in Tuna; **John Rybovich** for the Cozumel section in Sailfish.

Marty Sherman for the Oregon's Deschutes River section in Steelhead; **S. R. Slaymaker II** for the Brodheads Creek section in Brown Trout; **Mark Sosin** for the Biscayne Bay section in Bonefish; **Bob Stearns** for the Fly-Fishing for Chinook section in Pacific Salmon, for the Barracuda in the Florida Keys section in Barracuda, for the Fly-Fishing for White Marlin in Blue Marlin, and for the Fly-Fishing section in Sailfish; **Dick Swan** for the Michigan's "Big Three" section in Steelhead.

Russell Thornberry for the Bow River section in Rainbow Trout; **Russell Tinsley** for the Toledo Bend Lake section in Largemouth Bass, for the Port Mansfield section in Red Drum, and for the Port O'Connor section in Spotted Seatrout.

Rich Uhley for the London Bridge Bass in Arizona section in Striped Bass.

Ed Van Put for the Beaverkill River section in Brown Trout and for the Delaware River section in Shad.

Stan Warren for the Greer's Ferry Lake and Dale Hollow Lake sections in Walleye; **Dwight Webster** for the Strains of Brook Trout and Their Management section in Brook Trout; **Babe Winkelman** for the Dakota Reservoirs section in Walleye and for the Wabigoon Lake section in Muskellunge; **Lee Wulff** for the Minipi River section in Brook Trout.

A number of other people were of great help in providing information that was not readily available. We would like to acknowledge their kind cooperation.

Elwood Harry, president, International Game Fish Association; **John Marsman,** president, James Heddon's Sons; **Richard Kotis,** president, Fred Arbogast Company; **Bing McClellan,** president, Burke Fishing Lures; **Peter Foley,** Boone Bait Company; **Bill Gerlach,** president, Ande Line Company; **Bud Leavit,** *Bangor Daily News;* **Edwin Andresen,** *Saltwater Sportsman;* **George Hommel,** *World Wide Sportsman;* **Leigh Perkins,** president, Orvis Company; **Tom Paugh,** editor, *Sports Afield;* **Clare Conley,** editor, *Outdoor Life;* **Vic Dunaway,** editor, *Florida Sportsman.*

Our special thanks also go to **Mary Beth Luscombe,** of Die-Werke International, for tying the bonefish, tarpon and permit flies that appear in the color plates.

CONTRIBUTING PHOTOGRAPHERS

In writing this book we searched far and wide for the best possible pertinent photographs available. Our thanks go to the following photographers, who helped us to this end:

Pierre Afree, 230; **Gerald Almy,** 91, 103, 188, 193, 307; **Ande Inc.,** 322; **Joel Arrington,** 203, 212, 239, 243, 261, 264, 275, 281, 282, 287, 291, 317, 324, 362; **Bill Baab,** 200; **Peter Barrett,** 251, 255; **Christopher Batten,** 139; **Dick Blume,** 27; **Silvio Calabi,** 34; **Ari DeZanger,** 30; **Gil Drake,** 225, 231, 321, 348; **Larry Green,** 298; **Gary Gretter,** 7, 23, 28, 80, 81, 138, 142, 161, 164, 173, 185, 196, 216, 218, 227, 229, 238, 272, 294, 299; **George Gruenfeld,** 11; **Hal Janssen,** 117; **Paul Johnson,** 167; **Lefty Kreh,** 237; **Bob Kulwin,** 137; **Kris Lee,** 5, 310; **Tom McNally,** 153, 155, 175, 179; **Ed Mendus,** 156; **Tom Montgomery,** 38, 39, 41, 57, 59, 63, 97, 108, 113, 132, 146; **Tim O'Keefe,** 201, 244, 247; **Ed Park,** 79, 87, 92; **Tom Paugh,** 228; **C. Boyd Pfeiffer,** 107, 198, 202, 311, 334, 347; **Dave Richey,** 86, 151; **Kay Richey,** 171; **Al Ristori,** 256, 271, 293, 301, 302, 336; **Marty Sherman,** 84; **Mark Sosin,** 341, 345; **Bob Stearns,** 236, 360; **Charles Waterman,** 350; **Dennis W. Williams,** 235; **Joan Wulff,** 357, 359.

Cartography   Whitman Studios

Pencil Drawings by John Rice

BIBLIOGRAPHY

Anderson, Robert D. "Feeding and Spawning of Bluefish," *Sea Frontiers*, November-December 1978, pp. 335-338.

Baglin, R. E., Jr. *Sex Composition, Length-Weight Relationship, and Reproduction of the White Marlin, Tertrapturus albidus, in the Western North Atlantic Ocean.* National Oceanic and Atmospheric Administration, National Marine Fisheries Service, Southeast Fisheries Center Miami Laboratory, Contribution No. 78-44M, Fishery Bulletin, Vol. 76, No. 4, 1979, pp. 919-925.

Bailey, Reeve M., chairman, and the Committee on Names of Fishes. *A List of Common and Scientific Names of Fishes from the United States and Canada.* Special Publication No. 6 Washington, D.C.: American Fisheries Society, 1970.

Balon, Eugene K., ed. *Charrs: Salmonid Fishes of the Genus Salvelinus.* The Netherlands: W. Junk, Publishers, The Hague, 1980.

Bartram, J. *Diary of a Journey Through the Carolinas, Georgia and Florida from July 1, 1765 to April 1, 1766.* (Annotated by Francis Harper.) Am. Philos. Soc., *Transactions*, Vol. 33, 1943.

Behnke, Robert J. "The McCloud River Rainbow Trout," *Trout*, Spring 1983, pp. 35-38.

Bender, Reese, "Behemoth Bass: A Look at the Striped Bass in Oregon," *Oregon Wildlife*, Vol. 38, No. 6, 1983, pp. 3-7.

Benson, Norman G. "The Freshwater-Inflow-to-Estuaries Issue," *Fisheries*, Vol. 6, No. 5, 1981, pp. 8-10.

Castro, Jose I. *The Sharks of North American Waters.* College Station, Texas: Texas A. & M. University Press, 1983.

Cavender, Ted M. "Taxonomy and Distribution of the Bull Trout, *Salvelinus confluentus* (Suckley), from the American Northwest," *California Fish and Game*, Vol. 64, No. 3, 1978, pp. 139-174.

Clark, Eugenie. "Sharks, Magnificent and Misunderstood," *National Geographic*, Vol. 160, No. 2, 1981, pp. 138-186.

Corkum, L. D., and P. J. McCart. *A Review of the Fisheries of the Mackenzie Delta and Nearshore Beaufort Sea.* Western Region, Department of Fisheries and Oceans, Winnipeg, Manitoba, Canadian Manuscript Report of Fisheries and Aquatic Sciences No. 1613, 1981.

Dahlke, L. W., and M. R. Falk. *Data on Arctic Char from the Jayco River, Northwest Territories, 1975.* Western Region, Fisheries and Marine Services Department of Fisheries and the Environment, Winnipeg, Manitoba, Fisheries and Marine Service Data Report No. 156, 1979.

Davies, W. D., W. L. Shelton and S. P. Malvestuto. "Prey-Dependent Recruitment of Largemouth Bass: A Conceptual Model," *Fisheries*, Vol. 7, No. 6, 1982, pp. 12-15.

deLaundonniere, R. G. *A Notable Histoire Containing Foure Voyages Made by Certain French Captaines into Florida*, trans. M. Richard Hakluyt. London: R. H. Evans, 1810.

deRochefort, Charles. *Histoire Naturelle et Morale des Îles Antilles de l'Amérique.* Rotterdam, 1658.

deSylva, Donald P. *Systematics and Life History of the Great Barracuda.* Studies in Tropical Oceanography, Vol. 1. Miami, Fla.: Institute of Marine Science, 1963.

Donaldson, Lauren R., and Timothy Joyner. "The Salmonid Fishes as a Natural Livestock," *Scientific American*, Vol. 249, No. 1, 1982, pp. 51-58.

Fabrizio, Mary C. "Determining the Origin of Striped Bass in Rhode Island Waters," University of Rhode Island Graduate School of Oceanography, *Maritimes*, Vol. 27, No. 4, 1983, pp. 13-14.

Fabrricus, E., and K. J. Gustafson. *Some New Observations on the Spawning Behavior of the Pike Esox lucius.* Report No. 39. Drottingholm, Sweden: Institute of Freshwater Research, 1957.

Falk, M. R., and D. V. Gillman. *Impact of a Sport Fishery on Arctic Grayling in the Brabant Island Area, Northwest Territories.* Environment Canada, Fisheries and Marine Service, Freshwater Institute, Winnipeg, Manitoba, Technical Report Series No. CEN/T-74-7, 1974.

————, and L.W. Dahlke. *Data on the Arctic Char Sport Fishery at Tree River, Northwest Territories, 1978.* Western Region, Fisheries and Marine Service, Department of Environment, Winnipeg, Manitoba, Fisheries and Marine Service Data Report No. 153, 1979.

————, and D. V. Gillman. *Mortality Data for Angled Arctic Grayling and Northern Pike from the Great Slave Lake Area, Northwest Territories.* Environment Canada, Fisheries and Marine Service, Freshwater Institute, Winnipeg, Manitoba, Data Report Series No. CEN/D-75-1, 1975.

————, and D. V. Gillman. *Status of the Arctic Grayling and Northern Pike Sport Fisheries in the Brabant Island-Beaver Lake Area of the Mackenzie River, Northwest Territories.* Fisheries and Oceans, Freshwater Institute, Winnipeg, Manitoba, Canadian Manuscript Report of Fisheries and Aquatic Sciences No. 1553, 1980.

————, D. V. Gillman and L. W. Dahlke. *The 1972 Sports Fisheries of Great Bear and Great Slave Lakes, Northwest Territories.* Environment Canada, Fisheries and Marine Service, Freshwater Institute, Winnipeg, Manitoba, Technical Report Series No. CEN/T-73-8, 1973.

————, D. V. Gillman and L. W. Dahlke. *1973 Creel Census Data from Sport Fishing Lodges on Great Bear and Great Slave Lakes, Northwest Territories.* Environment Canada, Fisheries and Marine Service, Freshwater Institute, Winnipeg, Manitoba, Data Report Series No. CEN/D-74-5, 1974.

————, D. V. Gillman and L. W. Dahlke. *1974 Creel Census Data from Sport Fishing Lodges on Great Bear and Great Slave Lakes, Northwest Territories.* Environment Canada, Fisheries and Marine Service, Freshwater Institute, Winnipeg, Manitoba, Data Report Series No. CEN/D-75-3, 1975.

————, D. V. Gillman and L. W. Dahlke. *Comparison of Mortality Between Barbed and Barb-less Hooked Lake Trout.* Environment Canada, Fisheries and Marine Service, Freshwater Institute, Winnipeg, Manitoba, Technical Report Series No. CEN/T-74-1, 1974.

Ferguson, R. G. "The Preferred Temperature of Fish and Their Midsummer Distribution in Temperate Lakes and Streams," *Journal of the Fisheries Research Board of Canada*, Vol. 15, No. 4, 1958.

Foster, N. W., and C. G. Atkins. *Sebago Salmon.* First Report of the Maine Fish Commission, 1867.

Fraser, J. M. "The Smallmouth Bass Fishery of South Bay, Lake Huron," *Journal of the Fisheries Research Board of Canada*, Vol. 12, No. 1, 1955.

Gillman, D. V., and L. W. Dahlke. *Sport Fisheries in the Brabant Lake and Hay River Areas of the Northwest Territories, 1972.* Department of the Environment, Fisheries and Marine Service, Fisheries Operations Directorate, Central Region, Winnipeg, Manitoba, Data Report Series No. CEN/D-73-2, 1973.

Goode, G. B. *American Fishes: A Popular Treatise upon the Game and Food Fishes of North America.* Boston: Estes and Lauriat, 1887.

Harry, Elwood, and M. B. McCracken. *1983 World Record Game Fishes.* Fort Lauderdale, Fla.: The International Game Fish Association, 1983.

Henshall, J. A. *Book of the Black Bass.* Cincinnati: Robert Clarke and Company, 1889.

Horning, W. B., and R. E. Pearson. "Growth Temperature Requirements and Lower Lethal Temperatures for Juvenile Smallmouth Bass," *Journal of the Fisheries Research Board of Canada*, Vol. 30, No. 8, 1973.

Iverson, E. S., and D. C. Tabb. "Subpopulations Based on Growth and Tagging Studies of Spotted Seatrout, *Cynoscion nebulosus*, in Florida," *Copeia*, 1962.

Kaffka, Jay. "Walleye, the Heavyweight Dud," *Arkansas Game & Fish*, Vol. 13, No. 4, 1982, pp. 6-8.

Kristofferson, A. H., and G. W. Carder. *Data from the Commercial Fishery for Arctic Char, Salvelinus alpinus (Linnaeus), in the Cambridge Bay Area, Northwest Territories, 1971-78.* Western Region, Department of Fisheries and Oceans, Winnipeg, Manitoba, Canadian Data

Report of Fisheries and Aquatic Sciences No. 184, 1980.

———, and D. K. McGowan. *Data on Arctic Char*, Salvelinus alpinus (*Linnaeus*), *Collected from Test Fisheries in the Baffin Region, Northwest Territories, 1975-79*. Western Region, Department of Fisheries and Oceans, Winnipeg, Manitoba, Canadian Data Report of Fisheries and Aquatic Sciences No. 255, 1981.

MacLeish, Wm. H., ed. "Sharks," Woods Hole Oceanographic Institution, *Oceanus*, Vol. 24, No. 4, Winter 1981/82.

Marshall, K. E. *A Bibliography of the Arctic Char*, Salvelinus alpinus (*Linnaeus*), *Complex to 1980*. Western Region, Department of Fisheries and Oceans, Winnipeg, Manitoba, Canadian Data Report of Fisheries and Aquatic Sciences No. 1004, 1981.

———, *A Bibliography of the Lake Trout*, Salvelinus namaycush (*Walbaum*), *1970-77*. Western Region, Fisheries and Marine Service, Department of Fisheries and the Environment, Winnipeg, Manitoba, Fisheries and Marine Service Technical Report 799, 1978.

———, and J. J. Keleher. *A Bibliography of the Lake Trout* Cristovomer namaycush (*Walbaum*), *1929-69*. Environment Canada, Fisheries and Marine Service, Freshwater Institute, Winnipeg, Manitoba, Technical Report No. 176, 1970.

Mather, F. J., III. "Recaptures of Tuna, Marlin and Sailfish Tagged in the Western Atlantic," *Copeia*, 1960.

———, A. C. Jones and G. L. Beardsley, Jr. *Migration and Distribution of White Marlin and Blue Marlin in the Atlantic Ocean*. Contribution No. 169, National Marine Fisheries Service, Southeast Fisheries Center, Miami, Fla., 1972 (Also Contribution No. 2512, Woods Hole Oceanographic Institution, *Fishery Bulletin*, Vol. 70, No. 2, 1972, pp. 283-298.)

McCart, P. J. *A Review of the Systematics and Ecology of Arctic Char*, Salvelinus alpinus, *in the Western Arctic*. Canadian Technical Report of Fisheries and Aquatic Sciences 935, 1980.

McClane, A. J., ed. *McClane's New Standard Fishing Encyclopedia and International Angling Guide*. New York: Holt, Rinehart and Winston, 1974.

———, and Arie deZanger. *The Encyclopedia of Fish Cookery*. New York: Holt, Rinehart and Winston, 1977.

Miles, D. W. *The Life Histories of the Spotted Seatrout*, Cynoscion nebulosus, *and the Redfish*, Sciaenops ocellatus. Annual Report, 1949-50, Marine Laboratory, Texas Game, Fish and Oyster Commission.

Mostofsky, David I., ed. *The Behaviour of Fish and Other Aquatic Animals*. New York: Academic Press, 1978.

Morrow, James E. *The Freshwater Fishes of Alaska*. Anchorage, Alaska: Alaska Northwest Publishing Co., 1980.

Moshenko, R. W. *A Preliminary Assessment of the Arctic Charr Sport Fishery on the Robertson River (Koluktoo Bay), Northwest Territories, 1979*. Canadian Data Report of Fisheries and Aquatic Sciences No. 306, Winnipeg, Manitoba, 1981.

———, and D. V. Gillman. *Data on the Biology of Lake Trout*, Salvelinus namaycush (*Walbaum*), *from Great Bear and Great Slave Lakes, Northwest Territories 1974*. Environment Canada, Fisheries and Marine Service, Freshwater Institute, Winnipeg, Manitoba, Fisheries and Marine Service Data Report No. 103, 1978.

———, and D. V. Gillman. *Creel Census and Biological Investigation on Lake Trout*, Salvelinus namaycush (*Walbaum*), *from Great Bear and Great Slave Lakes, Northwest Territories, 1975-76*. Western Region, Fisheries and Marine Service, Department of Fisheries and the Environment, Winnipeg, Manitoba, Manuscript Report 1440, 1978.

Mraz, D. *Observations on Large and Smallmouth Bass Nesting and Early Life History*. Wisconsin Conservation Department Research Report No. 11, 1964.

Nakamura, E. L. *An Analysis of the Catches and Biology of Big Game Fishes Caught by the New Orleans Big Game Fishing Club, 1966-1970*. East Gulf Sport Fishing Marine Laboratory Report, 1971.

Netboy, Anthony. *The Atlantic Salmon: A Vanishing Resource?* Boston: Houghton Mifflin, 1968.

1982 Billfish Newsletter. U. S. Department of Commerce, National Oceanic & Atmospheric Administration, National Marine Fisheries Service, Cooperative Marine Game Fish Tagging Program & Pacific Billfish Angler Survey, 1983.

Porterfield, Byron, "Innovative New York Fish Farm Cultures, Markets Striped Bass," *Aquaculture*, Nov.-Dec. 1981, pp. 20-22.

Power, G. "The Evolution of Freshwater Races of the Atlantic Salmon (*Salmo salar* L.), *Arctic*, 1958.

Rawson, D. S. *The Pike of Waskesiu Lake, Saskatchewan, A Preliminary Report*. American Fisheries Society, *Transactions*, Vol. 62, 1932.

———. *Estimating the Fish Population of Great Slave Lake*. American Fisheries Society, *Transactions*, Vol. 77, 1974.

Russell, Ken. "Fishing Pressure and Its Effect on the Catch," *Farm Pond Harvest*, Spring 1983, p. 17.

Scott, W. B., and E. J. Crossman. *Freshwater Fishes of Canada*. Department of the Environment, Fisheries Research Board of Canada, Ottawa, Ontario, Bulletin 184, 1973.

Shimizu, Uzuru. "Unexpected Developments in Red Tide Research," *Maritimes*, Vol. 27, No. 1, 1983, pp. 4-6.

Shomura, Richard S., and Francis Williams, eds. *Proceedings of the International Billfish Symposium, Kailua-Kona, Hawaii, 9-12 August 1972*. National Oceanic and Atmospheric Administration Technical Report NMFS SSRF-675. Washington, D.C.: National Marine Fisheries Service, 1975.

Solman, V. E. F. "The Ecological Relations of Pike, Esox lucius L., and Waterfowl," *Ecology*, Vol. 26, 1945.

Strasburg, Donald W. "A Report on the Billfishes of the Central Pacific Ocean," *Bulletin of Marine Science*, Vol. 20, No. 3, September 1970, pp. 575-604.

Stroud, Richard H., and Henry Clepper. *Black Bass Biology and Management*. Compiled from the National Symposium on the Biology and Management of the Centrachid Basses at Tulsa, Oklahoma (1975). Washington, D.C.: Sport Fishing Institute, 1975.

Thorson, Thomas B. "The Impact of Commercial Exploitation on Sawfish and Shark Populations in Lake Nicaragua," *Fisheries*, Vol. 7, No. 2, 1982, pp. 2-10.

Tinsley, Jim Bob. *The Sailfish, Swashbuckler of the Open Seas*. Gainesville, Fla.: University of Florida Press, 1964.

Warner, K., and O. C. Fenderson. *The Salmon and Trout Fishery of the Fish River Lakes, Maine*. American Fisheries Society, *Transactions*, Vol. 92, No. 3, 1963.

Webb, Paul W. *Hydrodynamics and Energetics of Fish Propulsion*. Fisheries Research Board of Canada, Ottawa, Ontario, Bulletin No. 190, 1975.

Webster, D. A. *Smallmouth Bass*, Micropterus dolomieui, *in Cayuga Lake*. Ithaca, N.Y.: Agriculture Experimental Station, Cornell University, 1954.

Wilk, Stuart J. *Biological and Fisheries Data on Weakfish*, Cynoscion regalis (*Bloch and Schneider*). National Oceanic and Atmospheric Administration, National Marine Fisheries Service, Northeast Fisheries Center, Sandy Hook Laboratory, Highlands, New Jersey, Technical Series Report No. 21, 1979.

———. *Biology and Ecology of the Weakfish*, Cynoscion regalis (*Bloch and Schneider*). Proceedings of the Red Drum and Seatrout Colloquium, October 19-20, 1978, pp. 19-31.

———, W. W. Morse and D. E. Ralph. "Length-Weight Relationships of Fishes Collected in the New York Bight," *Bulletin of the New Jersey Academy of Science*, Vol. 23, No. 2, 1978, pp. 58-64.

World Record Game Fishes. Fort Lauderdale, Fla.: International Game Fish Association, 1983.

Achigan, 180
African pompano, 236
Alabama shad, 304, 307
Alabama spotted bass, 199
Albacore tuna, 318, 361, 362
Albee, Bob, 30
Amberjack, 116, 236, 239, 245, 326, 331
American Fisheries Society, 18
  Committee on Names of Fishes of, 125, 172
American Museum of Fly Fishing, 48
American shad, 304-306
  accessibility of fishing waters for, 311, 312
  distribution of, 306, 311, 312
  flies, fly-fishing for, 311
  identification of, 307
  regulations and restrictions on, 306, 312
  seasons for catching, 306, 310, 311, 312
  spinning for, 311
  techniique used for, 307-309, 310
  water conditions for, 306, 310
  weight and length of, 304-306, 311, 312
American Striped Bass Society, 300
Andros Island, bonefish fishing at, 219-220
Arctic char, 114-121
  accessibility of fishing waters for, 114, 120, 121
  accommodations for anglers, 120, 121
  backing for, 119
  bait casting for, 121
  baits and lures for, 116, 118, 119, 121
  behavior of, 116, 118, 119
  best sites for, 120-121
  breeding and management of, 120
  clubs for, 120
  distribution of, 12, 111, 116, 117, 118, 119, 120, 124
  Dolly Varden vs., 119
  flies, fly-fishing for, 116, 117, 118, 119, 120, 121
  as food fish, 115, 117
  hooks for, 117, 119
  identification of, 118, 119, 120
  Inuit fishermen of, 115, 116, 117, 121
  leaders for, 119
  lines for, 116, 117, 119, 121
  migrations of, 116
  natural prey of, 115, 116-117
  reels for, 119
  regulations and restrictions on, 120
  relicts of, 120
  rods for, 119
  season for catching, 116, 120, 121
  shooting heads for, 118, 119
  spawning habits of, 116, 118, 120
  spinning for, 118, 119
  technique used for, 116, 117-118, 119, 120, 121
  tippets for, 119
  varieties of, 118, 119, 120, 124
  water conditions for, 116, 118-119
  weight and length of, 116, 119, 121
  weighting of tackle for, 118, 119, 121
Arctic grayling, 52, 104-113
  accessibility of fishing waters for, 109, 111, 112
  accommodations for anglers, 112
  backing for, 110
  baits and lures for, 105, 108, 109, 110-111, 112, 113
  behavior of, 105, 106-107, 108-109
  best sites for, 110, 111-113
  breeding and management of, 106, 113

cooking of, 106
distribution of, 106, 107, 108, 109, 110
European species vs., 108, 109, 111
flies, fly-fishing for, 108-110, 111, 112, 113
hooks for, 109, 112, 113
identification of, 106
information sources on, 112, 113
leaders for, 113
lines for, 109, 110, 112, 113
migrations of, 111
natural prey of, 107-108, 110, 111
nocturnal fishing for, 110
reels for, 110, 113
regulations and restrictions on, 113
release method for, 109
rods for, 111-112, 113
schooling of, 107, 110
seasons for catching, 108, 110, 111, 112, 113
spawning habits of, 105, 106-107
spinning for, 109, 110, 111, 112, 113
taste of, 106
technique used for, 107, 108, 109-111, 112-113
tippets for, 108, 112
trophy, 108, 109, 110, 111, 112, 113
varieties of, 106, 108, 110
vision of, 104-106, 110
water conditions for, 106, 108
watercraft in fishing for, 110, 111, 113
weight and length of, 106, 108, 109, 110, 111, 112, 113
weighting of tackle for, 109-110, 112
Aristotle, 354
Arrington, Joel, 260
Ascensión Bay, bonefish fishing in, 221
Assinica trout, 26-27, 29
Atherton, John, 42
Atlantic salmon, 2-15
  accessibility of fishing waters for, 8, 10, 11, 12, 14
  accommodations for anglers, 8, 9, 11, 12, 13-14, 15
  backing for, 10, 13, 14
  baits and lures for, 4, 12
  behavior of, 4, 6-7, 9, 116
  best sites for, 8-15
  black (spent; kelts), 4, 15
  breeding and management of, 2, 4, 7, 8, 45
  clubs for, 4, 8, 10, 11, 12, 13
  costs in, 4, 8, 9, 11, 12
  distribution of, 3, 4, 5, 7-8, 311
  "estuarine," 18
  flies, fly-fishing for, 4-6, 7, 8, 9, 10, 11, 12, 13, 14, 15
  hand tailing in, 11
  hooks for, 5, 9, 11, 12, 13, 14
  identification of, 18, 44
  information sources on, 8, 10, 13, 14
  leaders for, 9, 10, 11, 13, 14
  lines for, 8, 9, 13, 14
  migrations of, 2, 7
  in North America vs. Europe, 4
  pools (lies; holding waters) of, 6-7, 9, 10, 11, 12, 13, 14
  progressive casting for, 6
  regulations and restrictions on, 4, 8, 9-10, 12, 13, 15
  in reserved waters, 8, 10, 11, 12, 13-14
  rods for, 4, 5, 8, 10, 13, 14
  seasons for catching, 2, 5, 9, 10, 11, 12, 14, 15
  sea trout vs., 44
  spawning habits of, 9, 12, 118
  spinning for, 12

steelhead vs., 79
technique used for, 4-7, 9, 10-11, 12
tippets for, 13
transplants of, 7, 8
trophy, 2, 10
water conditions for, 2-4, 5-7, 9, 10, 11, 12, 13, 14-15
watercraft in fishing for, 8, 9, 10, 11, 12, 13
weight and length of, 2, 4, 9, 10, 11, 12, 13, 14, 15
Atlantic Salmon Association, 8
Axe marlin, 319

Babine River, steelhead fishing in, 90-91
Bachman, Robert, 38-40, 56
Backing, *see specific fish*
Bahamas, bonefish fishing at, 215-216
Baird, Spencer F., 266-267
Bar jack, 236, 239
Barracuda, 240-247
  bait casting for, 243-244, 246
  baits and lures for, 242, 243-244, 245, 246, 247
  behavior of, 240, 241, 242-244, 246, 247, 332
  best sites for, 245-247
  ciguatera poisoning due to, 245
  distribution of, 217, 236, 242-243, 326
  flies, fly-fishing for, 244-245, 246-247
  as food fish, 245
  hooks for, 247
  identification of, 242, 244
  jumping by, 240-242
  leaders for, 245, 246
  lines for, 242, 246
  migrations of, 242
  muskellunge vs., 172, 174
  natural prey of, 243, 245
  odor of, 240
  reels for, 247
  regulations and restrictions on, 245
  release method for, 243
  seasons for catching, 243, 245, 246
  spinning for, 242, 246, 247
  as target of opportunity, 242
  technique used for, 240, 242, 243-245, 246
  tippets for, 245
  trophy, 245, 246
  varieties of, 242, 246
  water conditions for, 241, 242, 243, 244, 245, 246
  weight and length of, 240, 242, 243, 245, 246
Bartram, William, 201, 312
Bass, 72, 167, 178, 288-290
  impoundments, 160, 161
  varieties of, 292
  see also specific bass
Bass Anglers Sportsmen Society (B.A.S.S.), 194, 300
Battenkill, brown trout fishing at, 47-48
Baxter State Park, brook trout fishing at, 32-35
Beaverkill, brown trout fishing at, 42, 44, 45-47
Behnke, Robert J., 56n, 96, 119
Benchley, Peter, 79
Bergmann, Bus, 146
Berry, Frederick H., 339n
Bigeye tuna, 340, 361, 362-363
Big Manistee River, steelhead fishing in, 85, 86-87
Billfish
  contamination in Pacific waters of, 337
  species of, 319, 336
  see also specific billfish
Billfish tuna, 337

Bimini, bluefin tuna fishing at, 360
Biscayne Bay, bonefish fishing in, 219
Black bass, 172, 182, 196
  subspecies of, 199
Black drum, 260
Blackfin tuna, 329, 330, 349, 361
Black grouper, 245
Black marlin, 336-338
  accessibility of fishing waters for, 337
  baits and lures for, 338-340
  behavior of, 336
  distribution of, 336
  as food fish, 337
  identification of, 336, 337
  lines for, 336
  regulations and restrictions on, 337
  technique used for, 339-340
  trophy, 336
  water conditions for, 334
  weight and length of, 336
Blackmouth, 136
Black salmon (spent; kelts), 4, 15
Black snook, 237
Block Island, South Shore, striped bass fishing at, 294
Blueback trout, 34, 120
Bluefin tuna, 354-363
  accommodations for anglers, 360
  baits and lures for, 362
  behavior of, 355
  best sites for, 359-363
  distribution of, 324, 328, 329, 348, 349, 354, 355, 356-357
  fishing tournaments for, 359-360, 361
  as food fish, 338
  giant, 360-362
  identification of, 355, 356
  migrations of, 354, 356-359
  natural prey of, 355, 356
  seasons for catching, 356, 358, 359, 361, 362
  school, 362
  technique used for, 361-362
  trophy, 356, 359, 360
  water conditions for, 362
  watercraft in fishing for, 356, 359, 360
  weight and length of, 354-356, 359, 360, 361, 362
Bluefish, 266-276
  accessibility of fishing water for, 272-273, 274, 275, 276
  accommodations for anglers, 275, 276
  bait casting for, 270, 276
  baits and lures for, 268, 270, 271, 272, 273-274, 275, 276
  behavior of, 266-267, 269, 275
  best sites for, 272-276
  distribution of, 260, 262, 266, 267, 300, 331, 338, 342
  ferocity of, 266, 267
  flies, fly-fishing for, 268, 271, 272, 273, 274-275
  as food fish, 272
  giant, 274-275, 276
  hooks for, 270, 275
  information sources for, 275, 276
  leaders for, 270, 274, 275
  lines for, 271, 274, 276
  migrations of, 268, 273, 276
  as most popular saltwater game fish, 268
  natural prey of, 266, 267, 268, 270, 274
  population fluctuations of, 269, 276
  reels for, 276
  regulations and restrictions for, 275
  release method for, 268, 275
  rods for, 270-271, 275, 276
  seasons for catching, 268, 272-273, 274-275, 276
  slick associated with, 268

spawning habits of, 268-269
spinning for, 269, 271, 275, 276
technique used for, 268, 269, 270, 271-272, 273-274, 275, 276
trophy, 266
water conditions for, 268, 269-270, 271, 272, 273, 274, 275
watercraft in fishing for, 270, 271, 272, 273, 274, 275
weather conditions and, 266, 274-275
weight and length of, 266, 269, 273, 275-276
Blue marlin, 314-320
accessibility of fishing waters for, 319-320, 337
baits and lures for, 319, 326, 330, 338-340
behavior of, 315, 317, 334, 335, 336
best sites for, 318-320
depthfinders for, 318
distribution of, 316-317, 318, 323, 326, 327, 329, 330, 348
flies, fly-fishing for, 335
identification of, 319, 334-335, 336
information sources on, 319, 320
lines for, 319
migrations of, 317
natural prey of, 315, 317
outriggers for, 317, 323
regulations and restrictions on, 316
seasons for catching, 330
technique for, 316, 317-318, 339-340
trophy, 316, 318, 319
tuna tower for, 317, 318, 323
varieties of, 317
water conditions for, 316
watercraft in fishing for, 316, 317-318, 319
weight and length of, 316, 318, 319, 330
Blue pike, 158, 160
Blue shark, 250
distribution of, 255
identification of, 255
weight and length of, 255
Blue walleye, 158, 161, 162, 164, 165, 166
Boca Paila
bonefish fishing at, 221
permit fishing at, 238
Bonbright, George, 225
Bonefish, 208-221
accessibility of fishing waters for, 215-216, 218, 219, 221
accommodations for anglers, 215-216, 217, 218, 219, 220, 221
bait casting for, 213
baits and lures for, 213, 214
behavior of, 208, 209, 210-214, 218
best sites for, 214-221
distribution of, 208, 210, 213, 235, 238, 239
fishing tournaments for, 218
flies, fly-fishing for, 210-211, 212, 214, 217, 218
as food fish, 221
identification of, 213
natural prey of, 211-214
release method for, 221
seasons for catching, 211, 219
speed of, 209, 210
technique used for, 208, 210, 212, 213, 214
trophy, 214, 216, 219
varieties of, 213
vision of, 209, 210, 211
water conditions for, 208, 209, 211, 216, 217, 218, 219, 220, 221
watercraft in fishing for, 208, 216,

218, 219, 220, 221
weight and length of, 210, 213, 214, 216, 217-218, 219, 220, 221
Bonito, 329, 349
Bonneville cutthroat trout, 98, 99
Boschen, W. C., 338
Boschen, William, 270
Bow River, rainbow trout fishing in, 68-71
Brewster Flats, striped bass fishing at, 300
Broadbill, see Swordfish
Brodheads Creek, brown trout fishing in, 50-52
Bronzeback, see Smallmouth bass
Brooks, Joe, 50, 203, 210, 240
Brook trout, 24-35
accessibility of fishing waters for, 29, 30, 32-33, 34
accommodations for anglers, 29, 31, 32, 33, 34
baits and lures for, 28, 31, 32, 35
behavior of, 26, 28, 30, 40
best sites for, 29-35
breeding and management of, 24, 26-27, 28, 29, 30, 32, 46, 120
distribution of, 12, 22, 24-26, 27, 28, 46, 48, 51, 65, 97, 98, 101, 120
favorite flies for, 28
flies, fly-fishing for, 28, 29, 31, 32, 33, 34, 35
gullibility of, 27
hooks for, 28, 31, 32
identification of, 26
information sources on, 30, 31, 32, 33
lines for, 31, 35
migrations of, 26-27
natural prey of, 25, 27, 28, 29, 30, 34
recipe for, 32
regulations and restrictions on, 30, 31, 34, 35
rods for, 35
sea-run (salters), 26-27
seasons for catching, 28, 31, 35
"sea trout" as misnomer of, 26
spinning for, 31, 32, 35
as "squaretails," 26
strains of, 26-27
technique used for, 27, 29, 32, 34, 38
transplants of, 24, 26-27, 46
trophy, 28, 30, 31, 34
water conditions for, 24, 26-27, 30, 32
watercraft in fishing for, 31, 33, 34, 35
weight and length of, 24, 27, 28, 29, 30, 31, 33, 34
Brown shark, 255, 256
Brown trout, 36-53
accessibility of fishing waters for, 46, 47, 51, 52
accommodations for anglers, 48, 52
anadromous (sea trout), 44-45
baits and lures for, 38, 41, 42, 43, 47
behavior of, 38, 39-40, 41, 100, 109
best sites for, 45-53
breeding and management of, 36-38, 40, 41-43, 45, 46, 48, 49, 51, 53
clubs for, 46
cooking of, 43
distribution of, 20, 26, 27-28, 38, 42, 61, 62, 69, 71, 98, 103
electronic temperature gauge for, 43
European breeding stock in New World of, 36-38
flies, fly-fishing for, 38, 43-44, 45,

47, 48, 49-50, 51-52, 53
as formidable game, 38, 40
hooks for, 42, 43, 49, 50
identification of, 19, 41, 48
information sources on, 47, 48, 52
natural prey of, 40-41, 43, 47, 48, 49, 50, 51-52, 53
nocturnal fishing for, 43, 45, 46
regulations and restrictions on, 42-43, 47, 48, 51
in reserved waters, 46, 50-51
rods for, 38
seasons for catching, 40, 41, 43, 45, 46, 47, 49, 50, 51, 53
as "sea trout," 26
spawning habits of, 41
stream improvement projects for, 42
technique used for, 38, 41, 43-44, 45, 48, 49-50, 53
transplants of, 27-28, 36-38, 42, 46, 48, 51
varieties of, 37, 44-45
vision and smelling power of, 40, 41
water conditions for, 38-39, 41, 42, 43, 45, 46, 47, 48, 49, 51, 52-53
watercraft in fishing for, 52, 53
weight and length of, 40, 41, 45, 47, 48, 52
wild vs. domesticated, 40
Bucher, Joe, 177
Buel, Julio T., 270
Bull trout, 119, 124
Burroughs Cay, permit fishing at, 237-238
Butler, A. J., 325

Cabo San Lucas, swordfish fishing at, 321-322
California yellowtail, 236
Cannon, Ray, 340
Cape Cod, Outer Cape, striped bass fishing at, 294
Cape Hatteras, blue marlin fishing at, 318-320
Cape Lookout
bluefish fishing at, 274-275
spotted seatrout fishing at, 282-283
Carolinas, king mackerel fishing at, 364-365
Carpenter, William, 356
Casey, Jack, 256, 257
Cass, Johnny, 235
Cassaway, Zep, 126
Cat Cay, bluefin tuna fishing at, 359-360
Catfish, 57-58
Cavender, Ted, 119
Cayley, Sir George, 36, 38
Cederholm, Jeff, 78
Cero mackerel, 349, 365
Chandler, Leon, 112
Channel bass, 285, 327
Char, relicts of, 119
Chatham, Russell, 82
Chermanski, Dave, 325
Chesapeake Bay
spotted seatrout fishing in, 284-285
weakfish fishing in, 283-284
Chinook salmon, 130-136
abundance of, 135
accessibility of, 143, 145
accommodations for anglers, 145, 146
back drifting for, 144
backing for, 147
bait casting for, 135
baits and lures for, 135, 136, 142, 144, 145
behavior of, 133, 135, 142, 146
best sites for, 143-147
breeding and management of, 130-132, 134, 135, 137, 139,

143, 145
clubs for, 136
color of flesh, 132-133
depthfinder for, 135, 142
distribution of, 45, 85, 86, 92, 112, 130-132, 134, 137
flies, fly-fishing for, 45, 135, 145, 146-147
hooks for, 136, 145, 147
identification of, 130, 136-137, 146
information sources on, 144, 146
leaders for, 136, 144
lines for, 81, 135, 142, 143, 145, 147
mooching for, 142, 145
natural prey of, 132-134
reels for, 147
regulations and restrictions for, 144, 145
rods for, 81, 135, 143, 145, 147
seasons for catching, 85, 134, 143, 144, 145, 146
shooting heads for, 147
spawning habits of, 133, 134, 136, 143, 144, 146
spinning for, 145
synonymous names for, 136
technique used for, 135-136, 142-147
tippets for, 147
tourism and, 132, 137
transplants of, 130-132
trophy, 130, 136, 143, 144, 145
varieties of, 134, 136, 141
water conditions for, 85, 134
watercraft in fishing for, 85, 144, 145
weight and length of, 122, 130, 136, 137, 143, 144, 145
weighting of tackle for, 145, 147
Chub Cay
bonefish fishing at, 220
white marlin fishing at, 329-330
Chub mackerel, 356
Chum salmon, 140
distribution of, 140
identification of, 140
weight of, 140
Cobb, Gary, 28
Cobb, Irvin S., 210
Cobia, 236, 331
Coho (silver) salmon, 136-143
baits and lures for, 138, 141, 142, 143
behavior of, 138-140, 142-143
birds associated with, 138-139
breeding and management of, 134, 136, 137-138, 139, 140, 141, 143
depthfinder for, 142
distribution of, 86, 90, 111, 132, 134, 137, 145
flies, fly-fishing for, 90, 136, 138, 141, 142, 143
identification of, 132, 134, 136-137
migrations of, 134, 140-141
mooching for, 142
natural prey of, 138-139, 140, 142
regulations and restrictions on, 137
as residuals, 140
seasons for catching, 134, 140, 142, 143, 145
spawning habits of, 132, 134, 140, 141, 143
tackle for, 142, 145
technique used for, 136, 138, 142-143
tourism and, 132, 137
transplants of, 134
trophy, 136
varieties of, 130, 134, 141
water conditions for, 134, 138-139, 142-143
weight and length of, 134, 136, 137, 140, 143

Colorado River, striped bass fishing
  in, 294
Colorado River cutthroat trout, 99
Columbia River, shad fishing in, 311
Connecticut River, shad fishing in,
  310-311
Cook, William J., 30
Cooper, Ray, 30
Cornish, George, 245
Coutant, Charles C., 293-294
Cozumel, sailfish fishing at, 347-349
Crandall, Lester, 291
Crevalle jack, 236, 238-239, 261
Cronin, Larry, 359
Crooked Island, bonefish fishing at,
  216-217
Crosby, Bing, 340
Cubera snapper, 268
Cumberland Valley, brown trout
  fishing at, 48-50
Currituck Sound, largemouth bass
  fishing in, 205-206
Cutthroat trout, 94-103
  accessiblity of fishing waters for, 96,
    98, 101, 102, 103
  accommodations for anglers, 100,
    103
  baits, natural and live, illegal for
    non-Indians, 102
  baits and lures for, 102,
  behavior of, 40, 96, 99-100
  best sites for, 100-103
  breeding and management of, 96,
    97, 98, 100-101, 103
  brown trout vs., 97, 98, 100
  distribution of, 24-26, 68, 94, 96,
    97, 98, 99
  flies, fly-fishing for, 96, 102
  identification of, 96, 99
  information sources on, 101, 103
  leaders for, 102
  lines for, 102
  migrations of, 99
  natural prey of, 99, 102
  rainbow trout vs., 54, 73, 96, 97,
    99
  regulations and restrictions on, 96,
    98, 100, 101, 102, 103
  rods for, 102
  seasons for catching, 94-96, 101,
    102
  shooting heads for, 102
  spawning habits of, 74n, 98
  steelheads vs., 99
  susceptibility to angling of, 96,
    99-100, 103
  technique used for, 96, 102
  transplants of, 98, 101
  trophy, 100, 101
  varieties of, 95, 96-98, 99, 100,
    101, 102
  water conditions for, 96, 97, 98-99,
    101, 102
  weight and length of, 99, 100, 101,
    102

Dakota reservoirs, walleye fishing in,
  163-164
Dale Hollow Lake, walleye fishing in,
  165-166
Dana, Marshall, 318
Darbee, Elsie, 44
Darenberg, Carl, 320
Dawson, Gus, 18
Dean, Alfred, 251
Dean River, steelhead fishing in,
  91-93
Deep-water bonefish, 213
Delaware River, shad fishing in,
  309-310
DeMaio, John, 295
Deren, Nicolas, 345
Deschutes River, steelhead fishing in,
  87-88
Destin, white marlin fishing at,

330-331
de Sylva, Donald, 319
Dilg, Will F., 182
Dill, Harvey, 191
Dog snapper, 245
Dolly Varden, 68, 111, 124, 138
  Arctic char vs., 119
  classified as bull trout, 119-120
Dolphin, 349-353
  backing for, 353
  bait casting for, 352, 353
  baits and lures for, 340, 353
  behavior of, 332n, 336, 349, 350
  breeding and management of, 353
  distribution of, 220, 322, 326, 327,
    329, 330, 351, 352
  flies, fly-fishing for, 352
  as food fish, 351
  identification of, 350-351, 352
  magnetite in, 336
  natural prey of, 350, 352
  reels for, 353
  sailfish associated with, 349
  schooling practices of, 350
  seasons for catching, 351
  spawning habits of, 352
  speed of, 349, 350
  technique used for, 352, 353
  varieties of, 350
  water conditions for, 350, 352
  weight and length of, 351
Donaldson, Lauren R., 56, 61
Donnersberger, Ray, 245, 350
Drake, Gilbert, Sr., 229
Drobecker, Walter, 316
Dusky sharks, 255, 256

Easley, Ray, 207
Eckard, John, 242, 244
Eleuthera Island, bonefish fishing at,
  218
Encyclopedia of Fish Cookery, The
  (McClane), 253
Endangered Species Act, 100
European grayling, 108, 109, 111

Farnsworth, George, 270
Farrington, S. Kip., 356
Fernandez, Chico, 244, 261, 262, 325
Field and Stream, 314
Fisheries and Oceans Canada, 116
Florida Keys
  barracuda fishing at, 245-247
  bonefish fishing at, 214-215
  tarpon fishing at, 229-230
Flounder, 331
Fontana, Bill, 190
Forester, Frank (Henry William
  Herbert), 270, 272, 304
Foss, Al, 192

Gallasch, Bill, 153, 154
Gapen, Don, 28
Gardner, Keith, 46, 65, 302
George River, salmon fishing in, 13,
  14-15
Giallanzo, Joe, 286
Gifford, Tommy, 317
Gordon, Theodore, 290-291
Gouin Reservoir, walleye fishing in,
  166-167
Grand Cascapedia River, salmon
  fishing in, 9, 10-11
Grand River, steelhead fishing in, 85,
  86
Gray char, 125
Gray Eagle, Billy, 122
Gray trout (lake trout), 124
Gray trout (weakfish), 283
Great Abaco, bonefish fishing at, 220
Great barracuda, see Barracuda
Greater amberjack, 236, 239
Great Exuma, bonefish fishing at,
  217-218
Great Lakes, smallmouth bass fishing

in, 192-193
Great Slave Lake, northern pike
  fishing in, 155-156
Great South Bay, weakfish fishing in,
  285-287
Great white shark, see White shark
Green, Seth, 28, 126
Greenback cutthroat trout, 99
Greers Ferry Lake, walleye fishing in,
  164-165
Grey, Zane, 79, 182, 210, 250, 317,
  356
Grilse, see Salmon
Grouper, 236, 245, 326, 331, 349
Guadalupe bass, 199
Guaguanche, 246
Gulf barracuda, 246
Gullspang salmon, 18-19

Haab, Walter, 361
Haig-Brown, Roderick L., 61, 74, 82
Haldane, J. B. S., 133
Halliburton, David, 340
Hammerhead shark, 248, 249,
  253-254
  baits and lures for, 257
  behavior of, 254
  distribution of, 254, 256, 257
  identification of, 253, 254
  seasons for catching, 257
  special sense detection by, 253-254,
    256
  varieties of, 254
  weight and length of, 254, 257
Harbour Island, bonefish fishing at,
  219
Harmon, Ray, 238
Harry, Elwood K., 356
Harvey, George, 44
Harvey, Ted, 327
Hatchet marlin, 319
Hausknecht, Richard, 360
Hayeur, Gaétan, 18
Hazzard, Albert, 178
Heddon, James, 192, 202
Heilner, Van Campen, 210, 258, 356
Hemingway, Ernest, 322, 323, 356
Henry's (North) Fork of the Snake
  River, rainbow trout fishing in,
  60, 64-68
Henshall, James A., 184, 260
Herold, Bill, 268
Herrington, Jack, 316, 319
Hewitt, Edward Ringwood, 42, 43, 44
Heyerdahl, Thor, 350
Hickory shad, 304, 306-307
  distribution of, 307
  identification of, 307
  technique used for, 307-309, 310
  weight and length of, 307
Hill, Doug, 112, 113
Hogfish, 245
Holder, Charles F., 338, 356
Homosassa Springs, tarpon fishing in,
  230-231
Hooks, see specific fish
Hoover, Herbert, 210
Huff, Steve, 231
Humper, 124
Hybrid bass, 292

International Game Fish Association,
  18, 116, 120, 251, 255, 288-290,
  292, 316, 325, 351, 365
Izaak Walton League of America,
  182n

Jack salmon, 136
Jackspot, white marlin fishing at, 322,
  327-328
James River, smallmouth bass fishing
  in, 184-186
Janssen, Hal, 117
Johnson, Mead, 336
Jolley, John, 324

Juniata River, muskellunge fishing in,
  178

Kamloops rainbow trout, 56, 58,
  59-60, 90
Kaniapiskau River, landlocked salmon
  fishing in, 22-23
Katz, Fulton, 319
Kazan River, Arctic grayling fishing
  in, 112-113
Kenai River, chinook fishing in,
  143-144
Key West, permit fishing at, 236-237
King mackerel, 364-365
  accessibility to fishing waters for,
    365
  accommodations for anglers, 365
  bait and lures for, 365
  behavior of, 332, 365
  distribution of, 245, 331, 349, 361,
    365
  fishing tournaments for, 365
  hooks for, 364, 365
  information sources on, 365
  leaders for, 364, 365
  lines for, 365
  rods for, 364, 365
  seasons for catching, 364
  technique used for, 364-365
  weight and length of, 361, 364,
    365
King salmon, 136, 146
Kipling, Rudyard, 79n
Kite, Oliver, 44
Klamath River, steelhead fishing in,
  83-85
Knight, John Alden, 210
Kokanee salmon, 141
  distribution of, 141
  technique for catching, 141
  weight and length of, 141
Kristofferson, A. H., 116n
Kunkel, Ann, 356

Lacépède, Comte de la V., 182n
Lac-St-Jean, landlocked salmon
  fishing in, 22, 23
Ladyfish, 261
Lahontan cutthroat trout, 96, 98, 99,
  100-101
Lake Casitas, largemouth bass fishing
  in, 207
Lake Champlain, smallmouth bass
  fishing in, 187-189
Lake char, 125
Lake Havasu, striped bass fishing in,
  300-302
Lake Memphremagog, landlocked
  salmon fishing in, 20-22
Lake Taneycomo, rainbow trout
  fishing in, 71-72
Lake trout, 122-129
  Arctic grayling vs., 109, 110
  bait casting for, 110
  baits and lures for, 124, 128
  behavior of, 123, 124, 125, 127,
    129
  breeding and management of, 122,
    124, 126, 128, 129, 137
  as char, 122
  distribution of, 29, 111, 122, 124,
    126, 127, 128, 129, 165
  flies, fly-fishing for, 127, 128
  as food fish, 126
  identification of, 124, 125
  lines for, 128
  migrations of, 124, 128
  natural prey of, 113, 124, 127, 128
  regulations and restrictions for,
    127, 129
  seasons for catching, 124, 128, 129
  spawning habits of, 124, 125, 127
  splake as hybrid of, 126
  synonymous names for, 124-125
  taste of, 124

372

technique for, 124, 127, 128, 129
transplants of, 126, 128
trophy, 122, 125-126, 129
varieties of, 124, 126
vision of, 124
water conditions for, 122, 124, 126, 127-128
weight and length of, 122, 125-126, 127, 128, 129
Lake whitefish, 153
distribution of, 153, 157
flies, fly-fishing for, 153
weight of, 153
Landlocked salmon, 16-23
accessibility of fishing waters for, 21, 22, 23
accommodations for anglers, 23
Atlantic salmon vs., 17, 18
bait casting for, 20, 22
baits and lures for, 20, 21, 22-23
behavior of, 20
best sites for, 20-23
breeding and management of, 18, 19, 20
brown trout vs., 19
distribution of, 17, 18-19, 190
flies, fly-fishing for, 19, 20, 21, 22, 23
hooks for, 21, 23
identification of, 18, 19
information sources on, 22, 23
lines for, 19, 20, 23
migrations of, 16-18, 21-22, 23
natural prey of, 18, 19, 20, 22, 23
regulations and restrictions on, 21, 23, 35
rods for, 20
seasons for catching, 20, 21, 22-23
spawning habits of, 18, 20
spinning for, 21
technique used for, 19, 20-23
transplants of, 18, 19, 20
trophy, 19
varieties of, 18
water conditions for, 16-18, 20, 21-23
watercraft in fishing for, 20, 21, 22, 23, 33, 35
weight and length of, 18, 19, 20-21, 22, 23
weighting of tackle for, 20, 23
Largemouth bass, 194-207
accessibility of fishing waters for, 204, 205, 206
accommodations for anglers, 204, 205, 206
bait casting for, 202-203, 207
baits and lures for, 160, 195, 196, 198, 199, 202, 203, 204, 205, 206, 207
behavior of, 196-197, 198, 200
best sites for, 203-207
breeding and management of, 197, 198, 200-201, 203, 207
distribution of, 188, 189, 194, 196, 200, 201, 312
fishing tournaments for, 194, 207
flies, fly-fishing for, 203
identification of, 196
information sources on, 204-205, 206, 207
leaders for, 206
lines for, 203, 206, 207
natural prey of, 197-198, 202, 207
nocturnal fishing for, 202
reels for, 202, 206
regulations and restrictions on, 194, 200, 203, 205
rods for, 202-203, 206
seasons for catching, 201-202, 204, 205, 206, 207
smallmouth vs., 182
spawning habits of, 198-200
technique used for, 198, 200, 202-203, 204-206, 207

tourism and, 200-201
transplants of, 197, 201, 203, 207
trophy, 196, 198, 200, 207
varieties of, 194-196, 198, 199
water conditions for, 196, 199, 202, 204, 205-206, 207
watercraft in fishing for, 195, 198, 202, 205, 206, 207
weight and length of, 196, 198, 199, 200, 201, 204, 206, 207
Lau, Glen, 198
Lawton, Arthur, 172
Leaders, see specific fish
LeBlanc, Homer, 173
Lee, Art, 5, 310
Lemon shark, 244
Lerner, Michael, 356
LeTort, brown trout fishing at, 38, 48-50
Lines, see specific fish
Little, James, 162
Little tunny, 361, 363
Llewellyn, Edward T., 338
Loch Leven trout, 38, 45
Longfin bonefish, 213
Longfin shark, 248-250
Long Island (Bahamas), bonefish fishing at, 217
Long Island (New York), swordfish fishing at, 320-321
Loving, Tom, 153, 191

McCart, P. J., 116
McClane, A. J., 69, 253
McClane, Susan, 43
McClane, William, 28
McClane's New Standard Fishing Encyclopedia, 240
McClellan, Bing, 43
MacDonough, A. R., 28
McIntosh, Brian, 155
Mackerel, varieties of, 356
Mackinaw, 124
McMillan, Bill, 82
McNally, Tom, 96, 153, 175, 179
Madison River, brown trout fishing in, 43, 51, 52-53, 69
Magaro, Mack, 192
Mako, see Shortfin mako
Marinaro, Vincent, 49
Marlin, 335, 338-340
fishing tournaments for, 340
magnetite in, 336
rhythm pumping for, 340
tackle for, 335
see also specific marlin
Marron, Lou, 314
Marston trout, 120
Martial, 325
Martin, Roland, 201
Martin, William Thompson, 208
Matapedia River, salmon fishing in, 3, 5, 11-12
Mather, Frank, 42
Mather, Fred, 38
Mausser, Karl, 76
Maxwell, Walter, 252
Meek, Jonathan, 202
Melanson, James, 255
Mexican barracuda, 246
Meyers, Jim, 112
Minipi River, brook trout fishing in, 29-30, 34
Miramichi River, salmon fishing in, 9, 15
Mistassini Watershed, brook trout fishing in, 31-32
Moisie River, salmon fishing in, 12-13
Montana grayling, 106
Montauk
bluefin tuna fishing at, 360-363
bluefish fishing at, 272
shark fishing at, 254-257
striped bass fishing at, 294-296
Moore, Winston, 335

Mottley, Charles M., 60-61
Mountain whitefish, 52, 153
Mundus, Frank, 251, 254, 255
Muskellunge, 168-179
accessibility of fishing waters for, 172, 176, 177, 178
accommodations for anglers, 177, 178
bait casting for, 172, 173, 175
baits and lures for, 170, 172-175, 176, 177, 178, 179
behavior of, 170, 172, 174, 175, 176, 177-178
best sites for, 176-179
breeding and management of, 168, 170, 171
catches vs. angling hours for, 173
depthfinders for, 173, 176
distribution of, 61, 62, 63, 64, 165, 167, 168, 169, 189, 191
flies, fly-fishing for, 175, 178-179
hooks for, 174, 179
identification of, 169, 171
information sources on, 177, 178
leaders for, 172, 175-176, 179
lines for, 172, 173, 175, 176, 179
migrations of, 171, 175
natural prey of, 170, 172
nocturnal fishing of, 150, 176, 177
officially designated names of, 172
reels for, 172, 175, 176, 179
regulations and restrictions on, 168, 171
rods for, 172, 175, 176, 179
seasons for catching, 172, 174, 176, 177, 178, 179
spawning habits of, 170
spinning for, 172, 175
technique used for, 169, 172-176, 177, 178, 179
tippets for, 179
tourism and, 168
trophy, 168, 171, 172, 176, 177
varieties of, 171
water conditions for, 172, 176, 177, 178, 179
watercraft in fishing for, 172
weather conditions for, 172, 174, 175, 176, 178, 179
weight and length of, 168, 170, 171, 172, 176, 177, 178, 179
weighting of tackle for, 172, 175
Muskies, Inc., 172
Mutton snapper, 349

Namekagon River, rainbow trout fishing in, 61-64
National Coalition for Marine Conservation, 340
National Marine Fisheries Service, 135, 323, 338
Shark Tagging Program, 257
Needham, Paul, 40
Norris, Percy Priest and Cherokee reservoirs, striped bass fishing at, 294
North Carolina Outer Banks
bluefish fishing at, 276
red drum fishing in, 262
Northern muskellunge, 171
Northern pike, 148-157
accessibility of fishing waters for, 154, 155, 156
accommodations for anglers, 154, 157
backing for, 152
bait casting for, 156
baits and lures for, 152-154, 155, 156
behavior of, 148, 152
best sites for, 154-157
as carnivore, 150
distribution of, 29, 62, 63, 64, 148-150, 154, 166, 167, 177, 189

European vs. New World, 148
flies, fly-fishing for, 152-154, 155, 156
hooks for, 153, 154, 156
information sources on, 155, 157
leaders for, 152, 155
light intensity and, 150, 152
lines for, 152, 155
migrations of, 152
natural prey of, 150
reels for, 152
regulations and restrictions on, 151, 154-155, 156, 157
release method for, 156
rods for, 152, 155
seasons for catching, 150-152, 154, 155
spawning habits of, 150-152, 155
spinning for, 155, 156
technique used for, 152-154, 156
tippets for, 152, 155
trophy, 150, 151, 154, 157
varieties of, 171
water conditions for, 150, 155
watercraft in fishing for, 155
weight and length of, 148, 150, 151, 154, 155, 157, 166
Northern spotted bass, 199
Nurse shark, 244

Ocean City, white marlin fishing at, 327-329
Okoboji lakes, walleye fishing in, 167
Olympic Peninsula, steelhead fishing at, 82-83
Oregon Inlet, white marlin fishing in, 326-327

Pacific barracuda, 246
Pacific salmon, 130-147
abundance of, 135, 138, 141
distribution of, 85, 86, 90, 92, 111, 112, 130-132, 134, 137, 138, 139, 140, 141, 145
migrations of, 134, 136, 137, 140-141
tourism and, 132, 137
varieties of, 134, 136, 140, 141
see also specific salmon
Pacific yellowtail, 239
Pate, Billy, 231, 325, 335
Peckinpaugh, Ernest H., 203
Peper, Eric, 60
Perch, hybrids of, 160, 162
Permit, 232-238
accessibility of fishing waters for, 236
accommodations for anglers, 238
bait casting for, 236
baits and lures for, 221, 232, 234, 235, 236, 237, 238
behavior of, 234-235, 238
best sites for, 236-238
distribution of, 215, 217, 219, 220, 221, 234, 239
flies, fly-fishing for, 232, 234, 236-237, 238
in floating schools, 234-235
hooks for, 236
identification of, 234, 235
natural prey of, 234, 235, 237
pompano vs., 234, 235
as rarest game fish, 232
seasons for catching, 237
spinning for, 236
technique used for, 236, 237, 238
trophy, 232, 234, 236
varieties of, 234, 235, 236
water conditions for, 233, 234, 235
watercraft in fishing for, 237
weight and length of, 232, 234, 235, 236, 237, 238, 239
Perry, George Washington, 200
Pflueger, Al, 231, 314

Pike, 111, 112, 124, 163, 171, 174
  European, 148, 168
  see also specific pike
Pinchot, Gifford, 43
Pinder, Austin, 210
Pinder, Preston, 208
Pink salmon, 138-139
  behavior of, 139
  breeding and management of, 139
  distribution of, 138, 139
  flies, fly-fishing for, 138, 139
  identification of, 138
  migrations of, 138
  seasons for catching, 139
  spawning habits of, 138
  tackle for, 139
  technique used for, 139
  transplants of, 139
  varieties of, 140, 141
  water conditions for, 139
  weight and length of, 139
Pollock, 272
Polybius, 354
Pompano, 234, 235, 236, 239, 331, 342
Pompano dolphin, 350, 352
Porbeagle shark, 255
Porpoise, 364
Port Mansfield, red drum fishing at, 265
Port O'Connor, spotted seatrout fishing at, 287
Poulos, Jim, 153
Pray, C. Jim, 81
Punta Colorado, yellowfin tuna fishing at, 363-364
Punta Pescadero, hammerhead shark fishing at, 257
Pyramid Lake, cutthroat trout fishing in, 99, 100-102

Quebec red trout, 120
Quinnat, 136
Quintana Roo, bonefish fishing at, 220-221

Race Point, striped bass fishing at, 299-300
Racers, 34
Ragland, Nat, 236, 238
Rainbow cutthroat hybrid, 96, 100, 101
Rainbow trout, 54-73
  accessibility of fishing waters for, 63, 64, 65, 71, 72
  accommodation for anglers, 61, 64, 68
  anadromous form of, see Steelhead
  backing for, 60, 66
  bait casting for, 60, 73
  baits and lures for, 58, 60, 62-63, 65, 66-67, 70, 71, 73
  behavior of, 55, 58, 60, 61, 70, 72
  best sites for, 61-73
  breeding and management of, 54-61, 62, 63, 68, 72, 197
  cutthroat vs., 54, 73, 96, 97, 99
  distribution of, 20, 26, 29, 41, 46, 49, 51, 52, 53, 54-55, 60, 79, 90, 91, 98, 101, 103
  flies, fly-fishing for, 57, 58, 60, 62-63, 64, 65-67, 69-71, 72-73, 90
  genetic diversity of, 56-57
  hooks for, 66, 70, 72, 73
  ice fishing for, 59
  identification of, 57
  information sources on, 52, 71, 72, 73
  learning experiments with, 61
  lines for, 60, 66, 69, 73
  natural prey of, 55, 56-57, 58, 60, 62, 66-67, 69-71, 72
  nocturnal fishing for, 62, 63, 71
  pure strains of, 57

reels for, 66, 73
regulations and restrictions on, 56, 62, 65, 66, 72
rods for, 60, 66, 73
seasons for catching, 60, 62, 66-67, 70, 71, 72, 73
spawning habits of, 56, 57, 60
spinning for, 60, 73
technique used for, 58, 60, 62-63, 65-68, 69-71, 72-73
tippets for, 66
transplants of, 54-61, 71
trophy, 59, 62, 65, 72, 73
varieties of, 54, 60-61, 73
water conditions for, 56, 57, 58-59, 60, 61, 62, 65-66, 68, 69, 71
watercraft in fishing for, 61, 62, 64, 68, 71
weight and length of, 56, 58, 59, 60, 62, 65, 70, 71, 72
weighting of tackle for, 66, 72, 73
Rainy Lake, smallmouth bass fishing in, 189-190
Rawner trout, 122
Reagan, Lefty, 335
Reckert, Tony, 263
Redband trout, 56n, 59, 61
Red drum, 258-265
  accessibility of fishing waters for, 263, 265
  accommodations for anglers, 264
  bait casting for, 261, 265
  baits and lures for, 260, 261, 262, 263, 264, 265
  behavior of, 258
  best sites for, 261-265
  breeding and management of, 260
  distribution of, 258, 260, 287, 330, 331
  flies, fly-fishing for, 259, 260, 261, 262
  as food fish, 258, 264
  hooks for, 260, 261, 262, 263
  identification of, 258-260
  information sources on, 263, 264, 265
  leaders for, 261, 262
  lines for, 260-261, 263, 265
  migrations of, 260, 262, 263
  natural prey of, 259, 260
  nocturnal fishing for, 258, 263
  reels for, 260, 263
  regulations and restrictions on, 261, 265
  rods for, 259, 260-261, 262, 263, 265
  seasons for catching, 261-262, 263, 264, 265
  spawning habits of, 261
  spinning for, 259, 261, 263, 265
  technique used for, 259, 260, 262, 263, 264-265
  tippets for, 262
  trophy, 260, 261, 262-263, 264, 265
  varieties of, 258
  water conditions for, 259, 260, 261-262, 263, 264, 265
  watercraft in fishing for, 262, 264, 265
  weight and length of, 260, 261, 262-263, 264, 265, 331
  weighting of tackle for, 263
Redeye bass, 199
Redfish, see Red drum
Red snapper, 245
Red-spotted brook trout, 33
Red trout, 120
Reels, see specific fish
Reid, Ken, 191
Reiger, George, 114-116
Reindeer trout, 128
Restigouche River, salmon fishing in, 8-13
River herring, 307

Rivers Inlet, chinook fishing in, 145-146
Roadarmel, Gerri, 271
Robertson River, Arctic char fishing in, 120
Robinson, Webster, 335
Rochefort, Charles de, 342-343
Rockfish, 292
Rockwell, Al, 360
Rocky Mountain whitefish, 68, 69
Rods, see specific fish
Roosevelt, Franklin, 322
Roosterfish, 339
  distribution of, 339
  fishing tournaments for, 339
  weight and length of, 339
Roston, William, 162
Runbacks, see Steelhead
Russian River, striped bass fishing in, 294
Rybovich, John, 323n

Sabre-tooth salmon, 130
Sacramento River, shad fishing in, 312
Sailfish, 342-349
  accessibility to waters for, 348, 349
  accommodations for, 348
  baits and lures for, 344, 346, 349
  behavior of, 335, 343, 344, 349
  best sites for, 347-349
  distribution of, 319, 326, 329, 330, 344, 345, 346
  fishing tournaments for, 346
  flies, fly-fishing for, 346-347
  as food fish, 337
  hooks for, 346, 347
  identification of, 334, 344
  leaders for, 345, 347
  lines for, 345, 347, 349
  migrations of, 344
  natural prey of, 343, 344
  reels for, 345-347
  release method for, 348
  rods for, 345, 346
  seasons for catching, 344, 346, 348
  technique used for, 344, 345-346, 347, 349
  tippets for, 347
  trophy, 347
  water conditions for, 342, 344
  watercraft in fishing for, 344, 346, 349
  weather conditions and, 344, 349
  weight and length of, 344, 345, 346, 347, 348
Saimma salmon, 18-19
St. George's Cay, bonefish fishing at, 218-219
St. Joe River, steelhead fishing in, 85-86
St. Johns River, shad fishing in, 312
St. Lawrence River, muskellunge fishing in, 176-177
Salmon, 26, 76, 78, 79, 80, 89, 134
  breeding and management of, 142, 143
  see also specific salmon
Salmonids, 26, 36, 41, 45
  Arctic char as strongest of, 114
  bass as predators of, 292-293
  diet-weight ratios in, 107
  egg care by, 41
  giant, 130
  paleontologists' discovery of, 130
  species, races, and strains of, 26-27, 54, 78
  transportation of eggs to New World habitats, 36-38
Salter, Jim, 356
Salters, see brook trout
Sandy Hook, striped bass fishing at, 294
Santee-Cooper, striped bass fishing at,

296-297
Sauger, 158, 160, 162, 164
Save Our Stripers, 300
School tuna, 362
Schwab, Peter J., 81
Schweibert, Ernest, 50
Scombrids, North American, 361
Scott, Ray, 194
"Sea Trout," 26, 44, 45, 278, 330
  as anadromous brown trout, 44-45
  Atlantic salmon vs., 44
  distribution of, 44
  weight and length of, 45
Sennet, 246, 342
Shad, 304-312
  bait casting for, 308
  baits and lures for, 305, 308, 310
  behavior of, 309, 310
  breeding and management of, 304
  dart fishing for, 305, 308, 310
  distribution of, 304, 306, 307, 311, 312
  flies, fly-fishing for, 191, 304, 308, 310, 311
  as food fish, 310
  hooks for, 308
  identification of, 310
  leaders for, 308
  lines for, 308
  migrations of, 304, 309
  rods for, 308
  roe of, 310
  seasons for catching, 309-310, 312
  spawning habits of, 309
  spinning for, 307, 308
  tackle for, 308
  technique used for, 307-309, 310
  tippets for, 308
  trophy, 309
  trout behavior vs., 310
  varieties of, 304
  water conditions for, 307-308, 309, 310, 312
  watercraft in fishing for, 312
  weight and length of, 307, 309, 312
Shapwong Reef, Montauk, striped bass fishing at, 294
Sharks, 248-257
  accessibility of fishing waters for, 255
  aggressive attacks by, 249, 250, 251
  baits and lures for, 256-257
  barracuda vs., 244
  best sites for, 254-257
  chumming for, 250, 252, 257
  distribution of, 250, 251, 252, 253
  fishing tournaments for, 250, 254, 255
  hooks for, 256
  identification of, 248-250, 251, 253
  leaders for, 256
  lines for, 256
  reels for, 256
  regulations and restrictions on, 251, 252, 257
  tagging of, 257
  tooth shape of, 250, 251
  tourism and, 254
  trophy, 250, 251, 252, 255-256, 257
  varieties of, 244, 248, 253, 254, 255
  watercraft in fishing for, 256
Shenandoah River, smallmouth bass fishing in, 186-187, 188
Shenk, Eddie, 50
Shoal bass, 199
Shoemaker, Myron, 191
Shooner, Gilles, 18
Shortfin mako, 248-251
  behavior of, 250, 255, 332
  distribution of, 250, 255, 326
  fishing tournaments for, 250
  as food fish, 251, 256

identification of, 248-250, 253
jumping by, 250, 251, 255
natural prey of, 250
seasons for catching, 256
water conditions for, 250, 255
weight and length of, 250, 255-256
Shovelnose shark, 244
Shriver, William, 182
Sickle Lake, northern pike fishing in, 154-155
Silk snapper, 245
Silver marlin, 336
Silver muskellunge, 171
Silver pike, 171
Siscowet, 124
Skeena River, chinook fishing in, 144-145
Skipjack, 307, 325, 340, 363
Sloan, Stephen, 345
Smallmouth bass, 180-193
  accessibility of fishing waters for, 185, 186, 187, 190, 192, 193
  accommodations for anglers, 189, 190, 193
  bait casting for, 185, 192
  baits and lures for, 182, 184, 185-187, 188, 189-190, 191-192, 193
  behavior of, 183-184, 186, 188
  best sites for, 184-193
  breeding and management of, 181, 182, 184, 186, 189, 190, 191
  distribution of, 20, 62, 63, 64, 162, 165, 178, 180-182, 184, 194
  flies, fly-fishing for, 184, 186, 188, 190, 191
  hooks for, 184, 186
  identification of, 182
  information sources on, 185, 187, 189, 190
  largemouth vs., 182
  leaders for, 186, 187
  lines for, 184, 185, 186, 187, 190
  migrations of, 184
  natural prey of, 184, 186, 190, 191
  reels for, 184
  regulations and restrictions on, 183, 186, 187, 188, 191
  rods for, 184, 185, 186, 187, 190
  seasons for catching, 183, 185, 187, 188, 190, 192, 193
  spawning habits of, 183-184, 188, 190
  spinning for, 185, 186, 187, 188, 189, 191
  technique used for, 184, 185, 186, 187, 188, 190
  transplants of, 182, 186, 189, 190
  trophy, 184, 190
  varieties of, 182-183, 199
  water conditions for, 183-184, 188, 189, 190, 192
  watercraft in fishing for, 182, 185, 186, 187, 189, 190, 191, 193
  weight and length of, 182, 184-185, 186, 187-188, 189, 190, 192
  weighting of tackle for, 185, 187
Snapper, 236, 245, 331
Snapper, bluefish, 269
Snook, 227, 237, 238
  distribution of, 237, 261
  weight of, 239
Sockeye salmon, 140-141
  breeding and management of, 56, 141
  distribution of, 111, 141
  identification of, 141
  pink salmon vs., 138
  spawning habits of, 141, 151
Soulé, Henri, 294
Sow and Pigs Reef, Cuttyhunk, striped bass fishing at, 294
Spanish mackerel, 342
Spearfish, 319

Speckled trout, 278
Splake, 126, 127
Spotted bass, 199
Spotted seatrout, 278-287
  accessibility of fishing waters for, 281, 283, 287
  accommodations for anglers, 283
  bait casting for, 280-282, 287
  baits and lures for, 278, 280, 281, 282, 283, 285, 286, 287
  behavior of, 280, 281
  best sites for, 282-283, 287
  depthfinders for, 284
  distribution of, 261, 278, 279, 280
  flies, fly-fishing for, 280, 282, 286
  as food fish, 278
  hooks for, 282
  identification of, 278
  information sources on, 283, 287
  leaders for, 282, 283
  lines for, 281-282, 286
  migrations of, 282-283, 284
  natural prey of, 280, 281, 282
  nocturnal fishing for, 280, 285
  recipe for, 284
  reels for, 281-282, 286
  regulations and restrictions on, 287
  rods for, 281-282, 286
  seasons for catching, 280, 282-283, 284
  spawning habits of, 284
  spinning for, 280-281, 286, 287
  technique used for, 280-282, 284-285
  tippets for, 282
  trophy, 281, 283, 284, 285, 286
  varieties of, 278
  water conditions for, 278, 280, 281, 282, 284, 287
  watercraft in fishing for, 281, 283, 287
  weight and length of, 280, 281, 283, 284, 285, 286
Spring salmon, 136
Squaretail, 26
Stearns, Bob, 335
Steelhead, 74-93
  accessibility of fishing waters for, 82, 83, 84, 86, 87, 90, 91, 92
  accommodations for anglers, 87, 88, 91, 92
  as anadromous form of rainbow trout, 74-76
  Atlantic salmon vs., 79
  backing for, 83, 91, 92
  bait casting for, 79, 83, 90, 92
  baits and lures for, 76, 79, 80, 82, 83, 84-87, 88, 90, 91
  behavior of, 74, 76, 78-79, 82, 85, 92, 116, 143
  best sites for, 82-93
  breeding and management of, 56, 57, 75, 76-79, 82, 85, 86, 87, 88, 89, 90, 91
  distribution of, 74, 75, 76, 79, 145
  drop-back method of, 86
  flies, fly-fishing for, 79, 80-82, 83, 84-85, 88, 89, 90, 91-92
  floating bobber for, 80-81, 83, 87
  as food fish, 79
  half-pounders (jacks), 76, 83, 84
  hooks for, 74, 81, 87, 88, 90, 92
  hot-shottin method in, 86, 87
  identification of, 77, 78, 79, 91
  Indian rights and, 78, 82, 85
  information sources on, 85, 87-88, 90, 91, 93
  leaders for, 81, 82, 87, 91
  lines for, 80, 81, 83, 84, 87, 88, 90, 91, 92
  migrations of, 76, 78, 86
  natural prey of, 76, 79, 80
  noodle rod method of fishing for, 81, 86, 87

rainbow vs., 99
reels for, 79, 80, 81, 83, 87, 90, 91, 92
regulations and restrictions on, 82, 87, 88, 89, 90, 91, 93
rods for, 79, 80, 81, 82, 83, 84, 87, 88, 90, 91, 92
as "runbacks," 77
salmon eggs in diet of, 76, 79, 80, 86
seasons for catching, 76, 79, 82-84, 85, 88, 89-91, 92
shooting heads for, 84, 87, 91, 92
spawning habits of, 74n, 76-77, 82, 91
spinning for, 79, 80, 83, 84, 87, 90
technique used for, 80-93
tippets for, 88
transplants of, 74n, 75, 78, 85, 86, 87, 89
trophy, 74, 76, 78, 83, 88, 90, 92
varieties of, 60, 74n, 87, 141
water conditions for, 78, 79, 82, 83, 85, 86, 89, 90, 92
watercraft in fishing for, 76, 80-81, 84, 85-86, 87, 92
weight and length of, 56, 74, 75, 76, 78, 83, 84, 86, 88, 90, 92
weighting of tackle for, 79, 80, 81-82, 87, 91
Stenton, J. E., 126
Stick, Frank, 258
Striped bass, 288-302
  accessibility of fishing waters for, 291, 296, 300
  accommodations for anglers, 297
  bait casting for, 295-297, 298, 299, 300, 301, 302
  baits and lures for, 291, 294, 295, 296, 297, 298, 299, 302
  behavior of, 290, 293, 298-299, 301-302
  best sites for, 294-302
  birds associated with, 297, 300, 301
  breeding and management of, 288, 290, 292, 301, 302
  chumming for, 291
  clubs, 291-292, 300
  cooking of, 294
  depthfinders for, 296, 297, 301
  distribution of, 197, 204, 290
  fishing tournaments for, 300
  flies, fly-fishing for, 290-291, 298, 299
  hooks for, 295
  identification of, 292
  information sources on, 297
  leaders for, 295
  lines for, 291, 295
  migrations of, 290, 294, 296, 297-299
  natural prey of, 292-293, 298, 299, 301, 302
  nocturnal fishing for, 294, 295, 296, 299, 302
  population swings of, 269, 292, 297-298, 299
  reels for, 291n
  regulations and restrictions on, 288, 290, 297, 302
  rods for, 293
  seasons for catching, 294, 295, 296, 297, 298-299, 301, 302
  spawning habits of, 290, 297, 298, 299, 301, 302
  spinning for, 293
  technique used for, 293, 294, 295-297, 298, 299-302
  transplants of, 290, 301
  trophy, 290, 294
  varieties of, 292
  water conditions for, 270, 288, 290, 293-294, 297, 299
  watercraft in fishing for, 295, 296, 297, 300

weight and length of, 288, 289, 290, 292, 294, 301
Striped marlin, 332-337
  accessibility of fishing waters for, 337
  accommodations for anglers, 337, 338
  baits and lures for, 335, 338-340
  behavior of, 332, 335
  distribution of, 333, 334, 335, 337, 338
  flies, fly-fishing for, 335
  as food fish, 333, 337-338
  greyhounding by, 332
  hookless teasers for, 335
  hooks for, 335
  identification of, 334-335, 336
  leaping by, 332, 335
  lines for, 335, 340
  migrations of, 334
  natural prey of, 333, 337
  regulations and restrictions on, 335, 338
  seasons for catching, 334, 335, 338
  spawning habits of, 335-336
  speed of, 333, 336
  technique used for, 334, 335, 339-340, 341
  varieties of, 334
  water conditions for, 334, 336
  watercraft in fishing for, 334
  weight and length of, 334, 336, 340
Stripers Unlimited, 300
Sunapee trout, 120
Susquehanna River, smallmouth bass fishing in, 191-192
Suwanee bass, 199
Swan, Dick, 81, 86
Swordfish, 314-318
  accessibility of fishing waters for, 321
  accommodations for anglers, 322
  baits and lures for, 321, 322
  behavior of, 317
  best sites for, 320-322
  distribution of, 250, 316, 318, 348
  hooks for, 320, 322
  identification of, 319
  leaders for, 322
  lines for, 321
  locating of, 320
  natural prey of, 317
  nocturnal fishing for, 320, 321, 349
  regulations and restrictions on, 338
  rods for, 322
  seasons for catching, 320, 321
  tackle for, 317, 320, 321, 322
  technique used for, 317-318, 320-322
  trophy, 314
  tuna towers for, 317, 318, 320
  watercraft in fishing for, 318, 322
  weight and length of, 314, 321, 349

Tack, Leon, 336
Taimen, 122, 130
Tanner, Howard, 137
Tarpon, 223-231
  accessibility of fishing waters for, 229
  accommodations for anglers, 229
  backing for, 227
  bait casting for, 228-229
  baits and lures for, 228, 229, 245
  behavior of, 224, 225, 226-227, 231, 332
  best sites for, 229-231
  distribution of, 215, 222, 223, 227, 236, 261
  flies, fly-fishing for, 224, 225-228
  hooks for, 228
  information sources on, 229
  leaders for, 227-228, 229

Tarpon (cont'd)
  lines for, 227, 228, 229
  migrations of, 224
  natural prey of, 214, 228
  reels for, 227, 228
  release method for, 230
  rods for, 222, 224, 227, 228
  seasons for catching, 225, 229, 230
  spawning habits of, 224
  spinning for, 228-229
  technique used for, 222, 226, 231
  tippets for, 227-228
  trophy, 222-223, 229, 230
  water conditions for, 224, 229, 231
  watercraft in fishing for, 224, 228, 229, 230
  weight and length of, 222, 223-224, 225, 227, 229, 230
Taylor, Ron and Valerie, 251
Temiscamie trout, 26-27, 31
Ten Thousand Islands, red drum fishing at, 261-262
Tepper, Bud, 225
Thompson, J. R., 365
Thompson, Larry, 360
Thoreau, Henry David, 26
Thresher shark, 253
  distribution of, 253
  as food fish, 256
  identification of, 253
  weight and length of, 253
Tiffaney, Arrmah, 291n
Tiger muskellunge, 171
Tiger shark, 252-253
  diet and digestive system of, 252
  distribution of, 252, 326
  as food fish, 253
  identification of, 252
  tackle for, 252-253
  water conditions for, 252
  watercraft in fishing for, 252, 253
  weight and length of, 252
Tillmans, Carl, 8
Tippets, see specific fish
Tody, Wayne, 137
Togue, 124
Toledo Bend Lake, largemouth bass fishing in, 204-205
Touladi, 124
Townsend, Paul, 322, 327
Trout, 178, 191, 331
  ecology of, 38-40, 54-61
  see also specific trout
Truman Reservoir, largemouth bass fishing in, 203-204
Tuna, 354-364
  distribution of, 268, 318, 354, 356, 361-363
  fishing tournaments for, 354, 359-360
  "offshore," 362
  population fluctuations of, 354, 358
  regulations and restrictions on, 356, 362
  varieties of, 356, 361

weight and length of, 254, 361, 362, 363
Tyee, 136, 145

Ugashik Lakes, Arctic grayling fishing in, 111-112
Umpqua River, striped bass fishing in, 294, 299
United States Fish and Wildlife Service, 323

Van Put, Ed, 44, 65
Vermilion snapper, 245
Virginia, Eastern shore, red drum fishing at, 264-265
Vom Hofe, Edward, 222, 291n
von Behr, Baron Lucius, 38

Wabigoon Lake, muskellunge fishing in, 177-178
Wagner, Ed, 286
Wahoo, 332
  distribution of, 220, 322, 326, 327, 329, 330, 361
  as food fish, 362
Walleye, 158-167
  accessibility of fishing waters for, 162, 163, 165, 166
  accommodations for anglers, 166
  baits and lures for, 160, 161, 163, 164-165, 166, 167
  behavior of, 161, 162, 163-164, 166, 167
  best sites for, 163-167
  birds associated with, 167
  breeding and management of, 162, 163, 165
  depthfinder for, 166
  distribution of, 20, 158, 160, 161, 162, 177, 178, 189, 193
  flies, fly-fishing for, 160, 163, 166
  as food fish, 158
  frog slicks as indicator of, 167
  hooks for, 160, 166
  ice fishing for, 161
  identification of, 158, 161
  information sources on, 166
  lines for, 166, 167
  migrations of, 160, 162
  natural prey of, 160-161, 163
  nocturnal fishing for, 160, 163, 167
  regulations and restrictions on, 162
  seasons for catching, 160, 163-164, 166, 167
  spawning habits of, 160, 161, 162, 163, 165
  technique used for, 80, 163, 164-166, 167
  transplants of, 158, 162
  trophy, 160, 164, 165, 167
  varieties of, 158, 160, 162, 164, 166
  vision of, 159, 160, 167
  water conditions for, 160, 163-164, 165, 166

watercraft in fishing for, 163
  weight and length of, 160, 162, 163, 164, 165, 166, 167
  weighting of tackle for, 165, 166
Walleyed pike, 63, 157
Walton, Izaak, 43, 109
Walton, John, 254
Ward, Virgil, 199
Washougal River, steelhead fishing in, 88-90
Waskaiowaka Lake, northern pike fishing in, 156-157
Waterman, Charles F., 108
Wayne, John, 340
Weakfish
  accessibility of fishing waters for, 286-287
  baits and lures for, 278, 283, 284, 285, 286
  best sites for, 283-284, 285-287
  chumming for, 286
  distribution of, 273, 278, 279, 280
  identification of, 278
  lines for, 285, 286
  population swings of, 269
  reels for, 287
  rods for, 287
  seasons for catching, 283, 284, 285, 286
  technique used for, 284, 285-287
  trophy, 284, 286
  water conditions for, 278, 280, 282, 283-284, 285, 286
  watercraft in fishing for, 285, 286, 287
  weight and length of, 280, 284, 285, 286
  weighting of tackle for, 285
Webster, Daniel, 30
Weighting of tackle, see specific fish
Wenner-Gren, Axel, 220
Westslope cutthroat trout, 97, 98, 99
White, Charlie, 135, 139
White bass, 292
Whitefish, 29, 111, 128, 153
  distribution of, 153, 155, 189
  as food fish, 153
  grayling vs., 106
  tackle for, 153
  see also specific whitefish
White marlin, 322-331
  accessibility of fishing waters for, 324, 325, 327, 328, 329, 330, 337
  accommodations for anglers, 327, 329, 330, 331
  baits and lures for, 325, 329, 330, 338-340
  behavior of, 326
  best sites for, 326-331
  catch-tag-release policy for, 323, 325, 329
  distribution of, 318, 322-323, 324, 326, 348
  fishing tournaments for, 323, 324,

330, 331
  flies, fly-fishing for, 325-326, 335
  as food fish, 326
  identification of, 319, 324, 334-335
  information sources on, 327, 328, 330, 331
  lines for, 317, 326-327
  migrations of, 322-323
  natural prey of, 323, 326
  seasons for catching, 326, 327, 330
  spawning habits of, 323
  technique used for, 325, 329, 339-340
  trophy, 329
  water conditions for, 324
  watercraft in fishing for, 322, 324, 325, 326, 328, 329, 330-331
  weight and length of, 323, 326, 327, 329
  wind direction in fishing for, 326, 330
Whiterock bass, 292
White shad, 304
White shark, 249, 251-252
  distribution of, 251, 255, 256
  identification of, 251, 252, 253
  regulations and restrictions on, 251, 252
  seasons for catching, 256
  tackle for, 251
  water conditions for, 251
  weight and length of, 251, 252, 256
Wichita spotted bass, 199
Wild and Scenic River Act, 63
Willers, William B., 54
Wolff, Dick, 30
Wulff, Lee, 4, 29-30, 43, 60, 137, 335, 357, 359

Yellowfin grouper, 245
Yellowfin tuna, 363-364
  accommodations for anglers, 364
  baits and lures for, 340, 363-364
  birds associated with, 364
  distribution of, 318, 324, 326, 327, 329, 330, 362, 363
  as food fish, 364
  hooks for, 364
  seasons for catching, 362, 364
  technique used for, 364
  water conditions for, 363-364
  weight and length of, 361, 362, 363, 364
Yellowstone cutthroat trout, 97, 98, 99, 100, 102-103
Yellowstone River, cutthroat trout fishing in, 96, 97, 99, 100, 102-103
Yellowtail snapper, 245, 349
Yellow walleye, 158, 160, 161, 162, 164, 165, 166
York River, salmon fishing in, 13-14
Yucatán Peninsula, bonefish fishing at, 220-221